CIBSE Concise Handbook

CIBSE

Registered charity number 278104

ISBN 978-1-903287-94-1

Typeset by CIBSE Publications Department

Printed in Great Britain by Page Bros (Norwich) Ltd., Norwich, Norfolk NR6 6SA

Foreword

This third edition of CIBSE's best-selling Concise Handbook provides members with an up-to-date source of reference to help them to locate fundamental information quickly, and find out where the comprehensive information is located in the full CIBSE Guides. This Handbook, which includes selected information from the 2007 edition of Guide C and the newly published Guide M, has been produced to help members to give quick responses to enquiries and to provide easy access to the detailed information available in other CIBSE publications. In only a fraction of the space taken up by the full CIBSE Guides, the Concise Handbook offers a quick snapshot of the salient information — enabling you to understand the main issues and to do some outline calculations prior to producing a fully worked-out plan.

The Concise Handbook will be of value both to practicing building services engineers and to those who have recently entered the building services field. Based on the CIBSE Student Data Book, the Concise Handbook provides a summary of key areas, including the more commonly used information and tables. The information it contains is fully revised and is consistent with the information in the most recently updated Guides.

It should be emphasised that this publication cannot and does not replace the full Guides, but is intended to be a ready point of reference. The full Guides will always remain as the most detailed information source.

We very much hope that you will find this publication, and those that follow it, useful for giving you a head start in preparing quick general answers to questions raised by the construction team at the start of projects and to point you in the direction of the detailed guidance when you need it.

Jacqueline Balian
CIBSE Director of Information and Policy

Acknowledgement

The material in this Concise Handbook comes from the CIBSE Guides and the Society of Light and Lighting's *Code for lighting*, many of which received funding from Government research funds, and all of which could only be produced thanks to the generous contributions of time and effort by CIBSE and SLL members.

Author and co-ordinating editor

John Armstrong

Editor

Ken Butcher

CIBSE Director of Information and Policy

Jacqueline Balian

Note from the publisher

This publication is primarily intended to provide guidance to those responsible for the design, installation, commissioning, operation and maintenance of building services. It is not intended to be exhaustive or definitive and it will be necessary for users of the guidance given to exercise their own professional judgement when deciding whether to abide by or depart from it.

Contents

Guide G: *Public health engineering*

Code for lighting

CIBSE Concise Handbook

Introduction

This Handbook is made up of selected extracts from the following CIBSE/SLL publications:

— CIBSE Guide A: *Environmental design* (2006) (prefix 'A')

— CIBSE Guide B: *Heating, ventilating, air conditioning and refrigeration* (2001–2) (prefix 'B')

— CIBSE Guide M: *Maintenance engineering and management* (2008) (prefix 'M')

— CIBSE Guide C: *Reference data* (2007) (prefix 'C')

— CIBSE Guide F: *Energy efficiency in buildings* (2004) (prefix 'F')

— CIBSE Guide G: *Public health engineering* (1999) (prefix 'G')

— SLL *Code for lighting* (2002) (prefix 'L')

Section numbers, table numbers and figure numbers correspond to those in the source publication from which the information has been abstracted. To avoid confusion, these numbers are prefixed by a letter, e.g. 'A', 'B' etc., to identify the source publication.

An indication of the information contained in the source publications but omitted from this Handbook is provided at the end of the section appropriate to the source publication.

CIBSE technical publications are subject to continual review, and should always be referred to for the most up-to-date information. This Handbook is a selection of charts, graphs and tables (many of which have been abridged) to provide an insight into the quality and quantity of information available.

It has been produced to provide the frequently used tables and reference information as well as demonstrating the wide and detailed range of reference data available in CIBSE publications However, for detailed data, the full publication must always be referred to.

Guide A: Environmental design

A1 Environmental criteria for design

A1.1 Introduction

A1.1.1 Comfort

Comfort has been defined as that condition of mind that expresses satisfaction with the environment. The indoor environment should be designed and controlled so that occupant's comfort and health are assured. There are individual differences in perception and subjective evaluation, resulting in a base level of dissatisfaction within the population. The aim should be to minimise this dissatisfaction as far as reasonably practicable.

A1.1.2 Health aspects

Good health can be defined as 'a state of complete physical, mental and social well-being, not merely the absence of disease and infirmity'. It indicates that the indoor environment should be managed to promote health, not avoid illness. If environmental conditions are within the comfort limits set out in the full CIBSE Guides then the risk of occupant dissatisfaction and sick building syndrome is reduced, though not eliminated.

A1.2.2 Thermal comfort: annotated definitions

Operative and dry resultant temperatures

The operative temperature (θ_c) (previously identified as 'dry resultant temperature') combines air temperature and mean radiant temperature into a single value to express their joint effect. It is the weighted average of the two depending on the heat transfer coefficients by convection (h_c) and radiation (h_r).

Operative temperature can be measured using a globe thermometer, typically with a globe diameter of 40 mm, placed away from direct sun. Temperatures can vary within a space, so readings should be taken in several places.

A1.3 Thermal environment

A1.3.1 Factors affecting thermal comfort

A person's sensation of warmth is influenced by the following main physical parameters, which constitute the thermal environment: air temperature, mean radiant temperature, relative air speed, humidity.

Besides these environmental factors there are personal factors that affect thermal comfort: metabolic heat production, clothing.

It is also required that there be no local discomfort (either warm or cold) at any part of the human body due to, for example, asymmetric thermal radiation, draughts, warm or cold floors, or vertical air temperature differences.

Further information in relation to temperature, air movement, draughts, humidity, clothing and metabolic heat production is given in Guide A, section 1.3.

A1.3.1.1   Temperature

The room air temperature and radiant temperature may be combined as the operative temperature. Temperature is usually the most important environmental variable affecting thermal comfort. A change of three degrees will change the response on the scale of subjective warmth (Table A1.1) by about one scale unit for sedentary persons. More active persons are less sensitive to changes in room temperature. Guidance on temperatures suitable for various indoor spaces in heated or air conditioned buildings is given in Table A1.5 and, for unheated spaces in buildings in warm weather, in Table A1.7.

Table A1.1 Thermal sensation scale

Index value	Thermal sensation
+3	Hot
+2	Warm
+1	Slightly warm
0	Neutral
−1	Slightly cool
−2	Cool
−3	Cold

A1.3.1.2   Air movement and draughts

Where air speeds in a room are greater than 0.15 m·s⁻¹ the operative temperature should be increased from its 'still air' value to compensate for the cooling effect of the air movement. Suitable corrections are given in Figure A1.1. The figure applies to sedentary or lightly active people. Alternatively, the influence of mean relative air speed can be calculated using the PMV index, as described in Guide A section 1.3.2. Note that air speeds greater than about 0.3 m·s⁻¹ are probably unacceptable except in naturally ventilated buildings in summer when higher air speeds may be desirable for their cooling effect.

A1.3.1.3   Humidity

Humidity has little effect on feelings of warmth unless the skin is damp with sweat. For sedentary, lightly clothed people moisture may become apparent as operative temperatures rise above 26–28 °C. Thus, for most practical purposes, the influence of humidity on warmth in moderate thermal environments may be ignored and humidity in the range 40–70 % RH is generally acceptable. However, humidity may be important in the context of microbiological growth, the preservation of artefacts and the reduction of static electricity, see Guide A section 8.3.3.

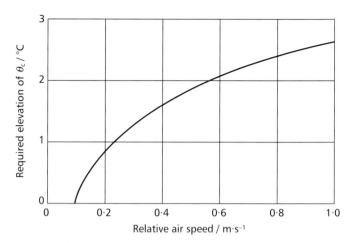

Figure A1.1 Correction to operative temperature (θ_c) to take account of air movement

A1.3.1.4   Clothing

Clothing insulation values for typical clothing ensembles are given in Guide A Table 1.2. The insulation provided by other clothing ensembles may be estimated by summing the insulation values for individual garments, see Guide A Table 1.3.

A1.3.1.5   Metabolic heat production

Metabolic heat production is largely dependent on activity. Table A1.4 gives metabolic rates for specific activities. .

Table A1.4 Typical metabolic rate and heat generation per unit area of body surface for various activities

Activity	Metabolic rate / met	Heat generation / W·m⁻²
Resting:		
— sleeping	0.7	41
— reclining	0.8	46
— seated, quiet	1.0	58
— standing, relaxed	1.2	70
Walking (on level):		
— 0.9 m·s⁻¹	2.0	116
— 1.3 m·s⁻¹	2.6	151
— 1.8 m·s⁻¹	3.8	221
Office work:		
— reading, seated	1.0	58
— writing	1.0	58
— typing	1.1	64
— filing, seated	1.2	70
— filing, standing	1.4	81
— lifting/packing	2.1	122
Occupational:		
— cooking	1.4–2.3	81–134
— house cleaning	1.7–3.4	99–198
— seated, heavy limb movement	2.2	128
— machine sawing	1.8	105
— light machine work	1.6–2.0	93–116
— heavy machine work	3.0	175
— handling 50 kg bags	4.0	233
Leisure:		
— dancing (social)	1.4–4.4	82–256
— callisthenics/exercise	3.0–4.0	175–233
— tennis (singles)	3.6–4.0	210–233
— basketball	5.0–7.6	291–442
— wrestling (competitive)	7.0–8.7	407–506

Note: average surface area of an adult human body is about 1.8 m²

A1.4 Design criteria

A1.4.1 General

Table A1.5 gives general guidance and recommendations on suitable winter and summer temperature ranges (together with outdoor air supply rates, filtration grades, maintained illuminances and noise ratings) for a range of room and building types. The operative temperature ranges (which are based on the indicated clothing insulation (clo) and metabolic rates (met)) correspond to a predicted mean vote (PMV) of ±0.25 (see Guide A section 1.3.2). These give a base level from which corrections may be made for non-standard situations.

The met and clo are defined as follows:

— clo: the unit for thermal insulation of clothing where 1 clo = 0.155 $m^2 \cdot K \cdot W^{-1}$. A clothing ensemble that approximates to 1 clo consists of underwear, blouse/shirt, slacks/trousers, jacket, socks and shoes

— met: the unit used to express the physical activity of humans, where 1 met = 58.2 $W \cdot m^{-2}$. One met is approximately the metabolic rate of a person seated at rest. The average body surface area for adults is about 1.8 m^2, therefore 1 met is equivalent to approximately 100 W of total heat emission.

Table A1.5 provides guidance for indoor temperatures for buildings with full year-round temperature control. However the guidance is not always applicable to buildings without cooling or air conditioning systems under summertime operation. For free-running modes, such as non-air conditioned buildings operating in summer, higher internal temperatures may be generally acceptable.

Table A1.5 Recommended comfort criteria for specific applications

Building/room type	Winter operative temp. range for stated activity and clothing levels*			Summer operative temp. range (air conditioned buildings†) for stated activity and clothing levels*			Suggested air supply rate / (L.s⁻¹ per person) unless stated otherwise	Filtration grade‡	Maintained illuminance¶ / lux	Noise rating§ (NR)
	Temp. /°C	Activity / met	Clothing / clo	Temp. /°C	Activity / met	Clothing / clo				
Airport terminals:										
— baggage reclaim	12–19[1]	1.8	1.15	21–25[1]	1.8	0.65	10[2]	F6–F7	200	45
— check–in areas[3]	18–20	1.4	1.15	21–23	1.4	0.65	10[2]	F6–F7	500[4]	45
— concourse (no seats)	19–24[1]	1.8	1.15	21–25[1]	1.8	0.65	10[2]	F6–F7	200	45
— customs area	18–20	1.4	1.15	21–23	1.4	0.65	10[2]	F6–F7	500	45
— departure lounge	19–21	1.3	1.15	22–24	1.3	0.65	10[2]	F6–F7	200	40
Art galleries — see *Museums and art galleries*										
Banks, building societies, post offices:										
— counters	19–21	1.4	1.0	21–23	1.4	0.65	10[2]	F6–F7	500	35–40
— public areas	19–21	1.4	1.0	21–23	1.4	0.65	10[2]	F5–F7	300	35–45
Bars/lounges	20–22	1.3	1.0	22–24	1.3	0.65	10[2]	F5–F7	100–200[5]	30–40
Bus/coach stations — see *Railway/coach stations*										
Churches	19–21	1.3	1.15	22–24	1.3	0.65	10[2]	G4–F6	100–200	25–30
Computer rooms[6]	19–21	1.4	1.0	21–23	1.4	0.65	10[2]	F7–F9	300	35–45
Conference/board rooms	22–23	1.1	1.0	23–25	1.1	0.65	10[2]	F6–F7	300/500[7]	25–30
Drawing offices	19–21	1.4	1.0	21–23	1.4	0.65	10[2]	F7	750	35–45
Dwellings:										
— bathrooms	20–22	1.2	0.25	23–25	1.2	0.25	15 L·s⁻¹	G2–G4 (extract)[8]	150[4]	—
— bedrooms	17–19	0.9	2.5	23–25	0.9	1.2	0.4–1 ACH to control moisture[8]	G2–G4	100[4]	25
— hall/stairs/landings	19–24[1]	1.8	0.75	21–25[1]	1.8	0.65	—	—	100	—
— kitchen	17–19	1.6	1.0	21–23	1.6	0.65	60 L·s⁻¹	G2–G4 (extract)[8]	150–300	40–45
— living rooms	22–23	1.1	1.0	23–25	1.1	0.65	0.4–1 ACH to control moisture[8]	G2–G4	50–300	30
— toilets	19–21	1.4	1.0	21–23	1.4	0.65	>5 ACH	G2–G4	100[4]	—
Educational buildings:										
— lecture halls[9]	19–21	1.4	1.0	21–23	1.4	0.65	10[2]	G4–G5	500[10]	25–35
— seminar rooms	19–21	1.4	1.0	21–23	1.4	0.65	10[2]	G4–G5	300[10]	25–35
— teaching spaces[9]	19–21	1.4	1.0	21–23	1.4	0.65	10[2]	G4–G5	300[10]	25–35
Exhibition halls	19-21	1.4	1.0	21–23	1.4	0.65	10[2]	G3–G4	300	40

Table continues

Table A1.5 Recommended comfort criteria for specific applications — *continued*

Building/room type	Winter operative temp. range for stated activity and clothing levels*			Summer operative temp. range (air conditioned buildings†) for stated activity and clothing levels⋆			Suggested air supply rate / (L.s⁻¹ per person) unless stated otherwise	Filtration grade‡	Maintained illuminance¶ / lux	Noise rating§ (NR)
	Temp. /°C	Activity / met	Clothing / clo	Temp. /°C	Activity / met	Clothing / clo				
Factories:										
— heavy work	11–14[11]	2.5	0.85	—[12]	—	—	—[13]	Depends on use	—[14,15]	50–65
— light work	16–19	1.8	0.85	—[12]	—	—	—[13]	Depends on use	—[14,15]	45–55
— sedentary work	19–21	1.4	1.0	21–23	1.4	0.65	—[13]	Depends on use	—[14,15]	45
Fire/ambulance stations:										
— recreation rooms	20–22	1.3	1.0	22–24	1.3	0.65	10[2]	F5	300	35–40
— watchroom	22–23	1.1	1.0	24–26	1.1	0.65	10[2]	F5	200	35–40
Garages:										
— parking	—	—	—	—	—	—	6 ACH (extract)	—	75/300	55
— servicing	16–19	1.8	0.85	—	—	—	—	G2–G3	300/500	45–50
General building areas:										
— corridors	19–21	1.4	1.0	21–23	1.4	0.65	10[2]	—[16]	100	40
— entrance halls/lobbies	19–21	1.4	1.0	21–23	1.4	0.65	10[2]	—[16]	100/200[4]	35–40
— kitchens (commercial)	15–18	1.8	1.0	18–21	1.8	0.65	—[17]	G2–G4	500	40–45
— toilets	19–21	1.4	1.0	21–23	1.4	0.65	>5 ACH	G4–G5	200	35–45
— waiting areas/rooms	19–21	1.4	1.0	21–23	1.4	0.65	10[2]	—[16]	200	30–35
Hospitals and health care buildings:										
— bedheads/wards	22–24	0.9	1.4	23–25	0.9	1.2	10[2]	F7–F9	—[18]	30
— circulation spaces (wards)[19]	19–24[1]	1.8	0.75	21–25[1]	1.8	0.65	10[2]	F7–F9	—[18]	35
— consulting/treatment rooms	22–24	1.4	0.55	23–25	1.4	0.45	10[2]	F7–F9	300/500[18]	30
— nurses' station[19]	19–22	1.4	0.9	21–23	1.4	0.65	10[2]	F7–F9	—[18]	35
— operating theatres	17–19	1.8	0.8	17–19	1.8	0.8	0.65–1.0 m³·s⁻¹	F9	—[18]	30–35
Hotels:										
— bathrooms	20–22	1.2	0.25	23–25	1.2	0.25	12[2]	F5–F7	150	40
— bedrooms	19–21	1.0	1.0	21–23	1.0	1.2	10[2]	F5–F7	50/100	20–30
Ice rinks	12	—	—	—	—	—	3 ACH	G3	—[20]	40–50
Laundries:										
— commercial	16–19	1.8	0.85	—[12]	—	—	—[21]	G3–G4	300/500	45
— launderettes	16–18	1.6	1.15	20–22	1.6	0.65	—[21]	G2–G3	300	45–50
Law courts	19–21	1.4	1.0	21–23	1.4	0.65	10[2]	F5–F7	300	25–30
Libraries:										
— lending/reference areas[22]	19–21	1.4	1.0	21–23	1.4	0.65	10[2]	F5–F7	200	30–35
— reading rooms	22–23	1.1	1.0	24–25	1.1	0.65	10[2]	F5–F7	500[23]	30–35
— store rooms	15	—	—	—	—	—	—	F6–F8	200	—
Museums and art galleries:										
— display[24]	19–21	1.4	1.0	21–23	1.4	0.65	10[2]	F7–F8	200[25]	30–35
— storage[24]	19–21	1.4	1.0	21–23	1.4	0.65	10[2]	F7–F8	50[25]	30–35
Offices:										
— executive	21–23	1.2	0.85	22–24	1.2	0.7	10[2]	F7	300–500[7]	30
— general	21–23	1.2	0.85	22–24	1.2	0.7	10[2]	F6–F7	300–500[7]	35
— open–plan	21–23	1.2	0.85	22–24	1.2	0.7	10[2]	F6–F7	300–500[7]	35
Places of public assembly:										
— auditoria[26]	22–23[1]	1.0	1.0	24–25	1.1	0.65	10[2]	F5–F7	100–150[5]	20–30
— changing/dressing rooms	23–24	1.4	0.5	23–25	1.4	0.4	10[2]	F5–F7	300	35
— circulation spaces	13–20[1]	1.8	1.0	21–25[1]	1.8	0.65	10[2]	G4–G5	200	40
— foyers[27]	13–20[1]	1.8	1.0	21–25[1]	1.8	0.65	10[2]	F5–F7	200	40
— multi-purpose halls[28]	—	—	—	—	—	—	10[2]	G4–G5	300	—
Prison cells	19–21	1.0	1.7	21–23	1.0	1.2	10[2]	F5	100[4]	25–30

Table continues

Table A1.5 Recommended comfort criteria for specific applications — *continued*

Building/room type	Winter operative temp. range for stated activity and clothing levels*			Summer operative temp. range (air conditioned buildings†) for stated activity and clothing levels*			Suggested air supply rate / (L.s^{-1} per person) unless stated otherwise	Filtration grade‡	Maintained illuminance¶ / lux	Noise rating§ (NR)
	Temp. / °C	Activity / met	Clothing / clo	Temp. / °C	Activity / met	Clothing / clo				
Railway/coach stations:										
— concourse (no seats)	12–19[1]	1.8	1.15	21–25[1]	1.8	0.65	10[2]	G4–G5	200	45
— ticket office	18–20	1.4	1.15	21–23	1.4	0.65	10[2]	G4–G5	300	40
— waiting room	21–22	1.1	1.15	24–25	1.1	0.65	10[2]	G4–G5	200	40
Restaurants/ dining rooms	21–23	1.1	1.0	24–25	1.1	0.65	10[2]	F5–F7	50–200[5]	35–40
Retailing:										
— shopping malls	12–19[1]	1.8	1.15	21–25[1]	1.8	0.65	10[2]	G4–G5	50–300	40–50
— small shops, department stores[22]	19–21	1.4	1.0	21–23	1.4	0.65	10[2]	F5–F7	500	35–40
— supermarkets[29]	19–21	1.4	1.0	21–23	1.4	0.65	10[2]	F5–F7	750/1000	40–45
Sports halls[30]:										
— changing rooms	22–24	1.4	0.55	24–25	1.4	0.35	6–10 ACH	G3	100[20]	35–45
— hall	13–16	3.0	0.4	14–16	3.0	0.35	10[2]	G3–F5	300[20]	40–50
Squash courts[30]	10–12	4.0	0.25	—	—	—	4 ACH	G3	—[20]	50
Swimming pools:										
— changing rooms	23–24	1.4	0.5	24–25	1.4	0.35	10 ACH	G3	100[20]	35–45
— pool halls	23–26[31]	1.6	< 0.1	23–26[31]	1.6	< 0.1	0–15 L·s^{-1}·m^{-2} (of wet area)	G3	—[20]	40–50
Television studios[26]	19–21	1.4	1.0	21–23	1.4	0.65	10[2]	F5–F7	—[32]	25

Notes: Except where indicated[1], temperature ranges based on stated values of met and clo and a PMV of ±0.25. Upper temperature of stated range may be increased and lower temperature decreased by approximately 1 °C if PMV of ±0.5 (i.e. 90 PPD) is acceptable (see section 1.3.2). Calculation assumes RH = 50% and v_r = 0.15 m·s^{-1}. Insulation value of chair assumed to be 0.15 clo for all applications except dwellings, for which 0.3 has been assumed.

* See section 1.4.3. for additional data and variations due to different activities and levels of clothing.

† Higher temperatures may be acceptable if air conditioning is not present, see section 1.3.1.

‡ See also chapter 8, Table 8.2, which gives requirements for specific pollutants.

§ Illumination levels given thus: 200–500 indicate that the required level varies through the space depending on function and/or task. Illumination levels given thus: 300/500, indicate that one or the other level is appropriate depending on exact function. Illumination levels in this table give only a general indication of requirements. Reference must be made to the table of recommended illuminances in the SLL *Code for lighting* and CIBSE/SLL Lighting Guides for design guidance on specific applications (see notes to individual entries).

[1] Based on PMV of ±0.5

[2] Assumes no smoking. For spaces where smoking is permitted, see section 1.7.2.

[3] Based on comfort requirements for check-in staff

[4] Local illumination may be required for specific tasks

[5] Dimming normally required

[6] Follow computer manufacturers' recommendations if necessary, otherwise design for occupant comfort

[7] Refer to Lighting Guide 7: *Office lighting*

[8] Refer to The Building Regulations: Part F1: Means of ventilation

[9] Podium may require special consideration to cater for higher activity level

[10] Refer to Lighting Guide 5: *The visual environment in lecture, conference and teaching spaces*

[11] The Workplace (Health, Safety and Welfare) Regulations 1992 require 13 °C where there is severe physical effort

[12] In the UK, air conditioning is not normally appropriate for this application. Cooling may be provided by local air jets. Some applications (e.g. steel mills, foundries) require special attention to reduce risk of heat stress

[13] As required for industrial process, if any, otherwise based on occupants' requirements

[14] Depends on difficulty of task

[15] Refer to Lighting Guide 1: *The industrial environment*

[16] Filtration should be suitable for the areas to which these spaces are connected

[17] See CIBSE Guide B, section 2.3.6.

[18] Refer to SLL *Code for lighting*

[19] Design for clothing and activity levels appropriate to nurses

[20] Refer to SLL Lighting Guide 4: *Sports lighting*

[21] As required for removal of heat and moisture

[22] Based on comfort requirements of staff

[23] Study tables and carrels require 500 lux

[24] Conditions required for preservation/conservation of exhibits may override criteria for human comfort; abrupt changes in temperature and humidity should be avoided.

[25] Critical conservation levels may apply, refer to Lighting Guide 8: *Lighting in museums and art galleries*

[26] Performers may have wider range of met and clo values than audience, along with higher radiant component, necessitating special provision

[27] Dependent on use

[28] Design for most critical requirement for each parameter

[29] Special provision required for check-out staff to provide conditions as for small shops

[30] Audience may require special consideration depending on likely clothing levels

[31] 2 °C above pool water temperature, to a maximum of 30 °C

[32] Depends on production requirements

Table A1.7 General summer indoor comfort temperatures for non-air conditioned buildings

Building type	Operative temp. for indoor comfort in summer / °C	Notes
Offices	25	Assuming warm summer conditions in UK
Schools	25	Assuming warm summer conditions in UK
Dwellings:		
— living areas	25	Assuming warm summer conditions in UK
— bedrooms	23	Sleep may be impaired above 24 °C
Retail	25	Assuming warm summer conditions in UK

A1.7 Determination of required outdoor air supply rate

A1.7.1 General

Ventilation requirements for a wide range of building types are summarised in Table A1.5. Detailed information on specific applications is given in chapter 2 of CIBSE Guide B.

For consideration of indoor air quality, see Guide A chapter 8.

A1.7.4 Ventilation effectiveness

Guidance on the ventilation effectiveness for the ventilation arrangements shown in Figure A1.12 is given in Table A1.10. In each case, the space is considered as divided into two zones:

— the zone into which air is supplied/exhausted

— the remainder of the space, i.e. the 'breathing zone'.

In mixing ventilation (cases (a) and (b) in Figure A1.12), the outside air supply rates given in Table 1.10 assume that the supply zone is usually above the breathing zone. The best conditions are achieved when mixing is sufficiently effective that the two zones merge to form a single zone. In displacement ventilation (Figure A1.12(c)), the supply zone is usually at low level and occupied with people, and the exhaust zone is at a higher level. The best conditions are achieved when there is minimal mixing between the two zones. The values given in Table A1.10 consider the effects of air distribution and supply temperature but not the location of the pollutants, which are assumed to be evenly distributed throughout the ventilated space. For other types of displacement system, the ventilation effectiveness (E_v) may be assumed to be 1.0.

A1.9 Acoustic environment

Noise affects people in different ways depending on its level and may cause annoyance, interference to speech intelligibility or hearing damage. The acoustic environment must be designed, as far as possible, to avoid such detrimental effects (see CIBSE Guide B chapter 5 for detailed information).

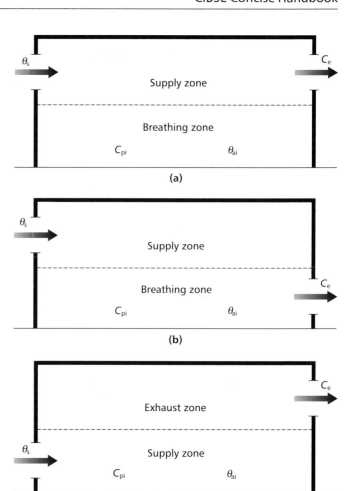

Figure A1.12 Supply/extract arrangements for ventilation; (a) mixing, supply and exhaust at high level, (b) mixing, supply at high level, exhaust at low level, (c) displacement

Table A1.10 Ventilation effectiveness for ventilation arrangements shown in Figure A1.12

Ventilation arrangement	Temp. difference (/ K) between supply air and room air, $(\theta_s - \theta_{ai})$	Ventilation effectiveness, E_v
Mixing; high-level supply and exhaust (Figure A1.12(a))	< 0	0.9 – 1.0
	0 – 2	0.9
	2 – 5	0.8
	> 5	0.4 – 0.7
Mixing; high-level supply, low-level exhaust (Figure A1.12(b))	< –5	0.9
	(–5) – 0	0.9 – 1.0
	> 0	1.0
Displacement (Figure A1.12(c))	< 0	1.2 – 1.4
	0 – 2	0.7 – 0.9
	> 2	0.2 – 0.7

A1.9.2 Human hearing response

When sound levels are measured, the variation in the sensitivity of the ear can be taken into account by incorporating frequency-weighting networks in the measuring instrument. The most widely used of these is the A-weighting network, which rises gradually to 1000 Hz, thus discriminating against lower frequencies. The reason for these differences arises from the different equal loudness responses of the human ear over a range of sound pressure levels, see Figure A1.15.

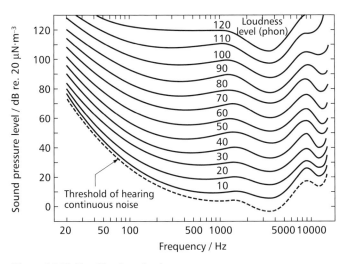

Figure A1.15 Equal loudness level contours

A1.9.4 Noise due to building services and other sources

The acceptability of noise from building services does not depend only upon its absolute level and frequency content, but also on its relationship with noise from other sources.

Reasonable design limits to minimise annoyance from broadband continuous noise from building services installations are given in Table A1.15. If the noise contains recognisable tones or is intermittent or impulsive it will be more annoying and the appropriate NR value from Table A1.15 should be corrected using the factors given in Table A1.16.

A1.9.5 Speech intelligibility

Speech intelligibility is dependent upon the ambient noise and the distance between listener and speaker. Table A1.17 gives an indication of the distance at which normal speech will be intelligible for various ambient noise levels.

Table A1.17 Maximum steady noise levels for reliable speech communication BS 8233 by permission of the British Standards Institution)

Distance between talker and listener (m)	Noise level, L_{Aeq} (dB)	
	Normal voice	Raised voice
1	57	62
2	51	56
4	45	50
8	39	44

A1.9.6 Hearing damage

Exposure to high noise levels, such as may occur in a plant room, can cause temporary or permanent hearing damage. Where workers are exposed to high levels of noise, the noise levels must be assessed by a qualified person. The Noise at Work Regulations 2005 identify two levels of 'daily personal noise exposure' (measured in a manner similar to $L_{Aeq,T}$) at which actions become necessary. These levels are 80 dBA for the lower level and 85 dBA for the higher level, corresponding to advisory and compulsory requirements. In addition, for impulse noise, there is a lower peak level

Table A1.15 Suggested maximum permissible background noise levels generated by building services installations

Situation	Noise rating (NR)
Studios and auditoria:	
— sound broadcasting (drama)	15
— sound broadcasting (general), television (general), sound recording	20
— television (audience studio)	25
— concert hall, theatre	20–25
— lecture theatre, cinema	25–30
Hospitals:	
— audiometric room	20–25
— operating theatre, single bed ward	30–35
— multi–bed ward, waiting room	35
— corridor, laboratory	35–40
— wash room, toilet, kitchen	35–40
— staff room, recreation room	30–40
Hotels:	
— individual room, suite	20–30
— ballroom, banquet room	30–35
— corridor, lobby	35–40
— kitchen, laundry	40–45
Restaurants, shops and stores:	
— restaurant, department store (upper floors)	35–40
— night club, public house, cafeteria, canteen, department store (main floors)	40–45
Offices:	
— boardroom, large conference room	25–30
— small conference room, executive office, reception room	30–35
— open plan office	35
— drawing office, computer suite	35–45
Public buildings:	
— law court	25–30
— assembly hall	25–35
— library, bank, museum	30–35
— washroom, toilet	35–45
— swimming pool, sports arena	40–50
— garage, car park	55
Ecclesiastical and academic buildings:	
— church	25–30
— classroom, lecture theatre	25–35
— laboratory, workshop	35–40
— corridor, gymnasium	35–45
Industrial:	
— warehouse, garage	45–50
— light engineering workshop	45–55
— heavy engineering workshop	50–65
Dwellings (urban):	
— bedroom	25
— living room	30

Note: dBA ≈ NR + 6

Table A1.16 Corrections to noise rating for certain types of noise

Type of noise	NR correction
Pure tone easily perceptible	+5
Impulsive and/or intermittent noise	+3

limit of 112 Pa and a higher peak level limit of 140 Pa. These peak action levels control exposure to impulse noise. Suppliers of machinery must provide noise data for machines likely to cause exposure to noise above the action levels.

A2   External design data

A2.1   Introduction

CIBSE Guide A chapter 2 provides basic weather and solar data required for manual calculation of heating and cooling loads in the UK and Europe.

In this Handbook, some data are provided for London (Heathrow) only by way of example. CIBSE Guide A and the associated CD-ROM provide similar data for other UK locations and design data for worldwide locations.

A2.3   UK cold weather data

A2.3.1   Winter design temperatures

Outside design temperatures are near-extreme values of dry bulb temperature used to determine the sizes of central plant, distribution systems and room terminals for heating in winter. Design temperature has a large influence on the capital cost of building services systems, and some influence on running costs. No single design temperature is given for a particular location; rather, a range from which the designer can select an appropriate design temperature in consultation with the client (bearing in mind the previous sentence).

The selection method reflects the thermal response of the building by defining two different averaging times. For most buildings, a 24-hour mean temperature is appropriate. However, a 48-hour mean temperature is more suitable for buildings with high thermal inertia (i.e. high thermal mass,

low heat losses), with a response factor $f_r \geq 6$. Response factor is defined in Guide A chapter 5.

Figure A2.6 shows the average number of times per year that 24-hour and 48-hour mean temperatures for London (Heathrow) fall below a given value.

An alternative approach, useful for an air heating system, is to determine the temperature that is not exceeded for a given frequency of occurrence. Table A2.4 provides, for eight sites, the winter dry bulb temperatures equal to or exceeded by specified percentage of hours in the year with coincident wet bulb temperatures.

A2.3.2   Warm front condensation

In addition to the condensation that may occur due to moisture generated within buildings, see Guide A chapter 7, condensation may also occur when the weather changes at the end of a cold spell, if a cold air-mass is replaced within a few hours by a warm, moist air-mass. For heavy-weight structures, the atmospheric dew-point may rise more quickly than the surface temperature, producing temporary condensation on such surfaces exposed to outside air. This is most likely to happen internally on surfaces in poorly heated or unheated buildings such as warehouses and storage buildings.

Table A2.5 shows the frequency of such conditions for eight UK locations. These values are based on positive differences between the dew-point temperature in the middle of the day (mean of values at 09, 12 and 15 GMT) and the mean dry bulb temperature of the previous day (mean of hourly values from 01 to 24 GMT). Note that Table A2.5 is not a cumulative distribution. Therefore, the 0.0 to 0.9 bin represents only those values that lay between 0.0 and 0.9.

A2.4   UK warm weather data

A2.4.1   Coincidence of wet and dry bulb temperatures

For use in air conditioning plant design, Table 2.6 gives hourly dry bulb temperatures equal to or exceeded by specified percentages of hours in the year with coincident hourly wet bulb temperatures.

The frequency of coincidence of wet and dry bulb temperatures is important for air conditioning and natural venti-

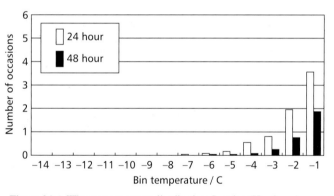

Figure A2.6 Winter temperature distribution: London (Heathrow) (1982–2002)

Table A2.4 Wintertime dry bulb temperatures and coincident wet bulb temperatures equal to or exceeded for given percentages of hours in the year (approx. 1982–2002)

Location	Hourly temperature (/ °C) equal to or exceeded for stated percentage of hours in the year							
	99.6%		99%		98%		95%	
	Dry-bulb	Wet-bulb	Dry-bulb	Wet-bulb	Dry-bulb	Wet-bulb	Dry-bulb	Wet-bulb
Belfast	−2.6	−3.1	−1.2	−1.8	−0.2	−0.8	1.3	0.5
Birmingham	−5.4	−5.6	−3.4	−3.8	−2.0	−2.4	0.3	−0.4
Cardiff	−3.2	−4.0	−1.6	−2.4	−0.4	−1.2	1.5	0.6
Edinburgh	−5.4	−5.6	−3.4	−3.7	−1.9	−2.3	0.3	−0.5
Glasgow	−5.9	−6.0	−3.9	−4.1	−2.1	−2.6	0.2	−0.5
London	−3.3	−4.0	−1.8	−2.5	−0.6	−1.3	1.4	0.5
Manchester	−3.6	−4.0	−2.2	−2.7	−0.9	−1.7	0.9	0.0
Plymouth	−1.6	−2.6	−0.2	−1.2	0.9	−0.1	2.9	1.9

Table A2.5 Average number of occasions per year when the mean of the dew-point temperature at 09:00, 12:00 and 15:00 exceeds the preceding day's dry bulb temperature by the amount indicated (approx. 1982–2002)

Amount by which dry bulb temperature is exceeded / K	Average number of occasions per year for stated location*							
	Belfast	Birmingham	Cardiff	Edinburgh	Glasgow	London	Manchester	Plymouth
0.0–0.9	21.7	18.8	21.9	17.4	18.8	14.7	16.1	21.5
1.0–1.9	10.7	10.3	10.9	11.2	11.3	8.1	8.9	10.6
2.0–2.9	6	5.9	6	5.4	5.6	4.4	4.2	5.4
3.0–3.9	3.4	2.4	2.7	3.1	3.2	3	2.7	2.3
4.0–4.9	2.1	1.9	1.5	1.5	2.3	1.2	1.2	0.9
5.0–5.9	0.4	0.9	0.4	0.75	1.3	0.9	0.4	0.7
6.0–6.9	0.3	0.3	0.3	0.2	0.4	0.3	0.2	0.2
7.0–7.9	0.05	0.3	0.05	0.2	0.3	0.1	0.05	0.05
8.0–8.9	0	0.1	0.05	0.1	0.3	0.2	0.05	0
9.0–9.9	0	0.05	0	0.05	0.05	0	0	0
10.0–10.9	0	0.05	0	0	0	0	0	0
11.0–11.9	0	0	0	0	0.05	0	0	0
>12	0	0	0	0	0	0	0	0

Notes: single zero indicates no occurrences; calculated using 24-hour average daily dry and wet bulb temperatures and standard pressure.

Table 2.6 Summertime dry bulb temperatures and coincident wet bulb temperatures equal to or exceeded for given percentages of hours in the year (approx. 1982–2002; see Table 2.1)

Location	Hourly temperature (/ °C) equal to or exceeded for stated percentage of hours in the year							
	0.4%		1%		2%		5%	
	Dry bulb	Wet bulb	Dry bulb	Wet bulb	Dry bulb	Wet bulb	Dry bulb	Wet bulb
Belfast	22.6	18.0	20.8	17.1	19.3	16.3	17.3	14.9
Birmingham	26.1	19.2	24.1	18.2	22.4	17.3	19.6	15.9
Cardiff	24.6	19.0	22.6	18.0	21.0	17.2	18.6	16.0
Edinburgh	22.2	17.8	20.6	16.8	19.2	15.9	17.2	14.6
Glasgow	23.5	18.2	21.3	17.1	19.7	16.2	17.4	14.7
London	28.0	20.0	26.0	19.1	24.3	18.2	21.5	16.9
Manchester	25.5	18.8	23.4	17.9	21.7	17.0	19.0	15.6
Plymouth	23.5	18.7	21.8	17.9	20.4	17.2	18.5	16.1

lation design for warm weather. Table A2.12 gives these data for London (Heathrow), over 24 hours, for the four months from June to September. These data may be used to plot the percentage frequencies of combinations of hourly dry bulb and wet bulb temperatures on a psychrometric chart. This enables the frequency with which the specific enthalpy exceeds given values to be determined, from which summer design conditions may be established.

Table A2.12 Percentage frequency of combinations of hourly dry bulb and wet bulb temperatures for June to September: London (Heathrow) (1982–2002)

Dry bulb temp. / °C	Wet bulb temperature / °C													Total
	−2 to 0	0 to 2	2 to 4	4 to 6	6 to 8	8 to 10	10 to 12	12 to 14	14 to 16	16 to 18	18 to 20	20 to 22	22 to 24	
−2 to 0	0	0	0	0	0	0	0	0	0	0	0	0	0	0
0 to 2	0	0	0	0	0	0	0	0	0	0	0	0	0	0
2 to 4	0	0	0.01	0	0	0	0	0	0	0	0	0	0	0.01
4 to 6	0	0	0.01	0.14	0	0	0	0	0	0	0	0	0	0.15
6 to 8	0	0	0	0.20	0.57	0	0	0	0	0	0	0	0	0.77
8 to 10	0	0	0	0.01	1.08	1.67	0	0	0	0	0	0	0	2.75
10 to 12	0	0	0	0	0.21	3.87	3.65	0	0	0	0	0	0	7.73
12 to 14	0	0	0	0	0.03	1.33	8.32	5.33	0	0	0	0	0	15.02
14 to 16	0	0	0	0	0	0.39	3.87	10.68	4.88	0	0	0	0	19.82
16 to 18	0	0	0	0	0	0.03	1.77	6.16	9.26	2.06	0	0	0	19.28
18 to 20	0	0	0	0	0	0	0.23	3.35	5.60	4.54	0.30	0	0	14.01
20 to 22	0	0	0	0	0	0	0	0.91	3.48	3.54	0.95	0.01	0	8.89
22 to 24	0	0	0	0	0	0	0	0.05	1.20	2.79	1.38	0.08	0	5.50
24 to 26	0	0	0	0	0	0	0	0	0.24	1.43	1.37	0.24	0	3.27
26 to 28	0	0	0	0	0	0	0	0	0.04	0.42	0.87	0.35	0	1.69
28 to 30	0	0	0	0	0	0	0	0	0.01	0.09	0.38	0.26	0.01	0.74
30 to 32	0	0	0	0	0	0	0	0	0	0.01	0.11	0.15	0.03	0.29
Total	0	0	0.01	0.35	1.89	7.29	17.84	26.49	24.72	14.88	5.34	1.08	0.04	

A2.4.2   Design temperatures — approximate method

Where wet and dry bulb temperature data for the required locality are not sufficiently comprehensive to enable the above analysis, Guide A section 2.4.2 gives an approximate method for establishing design temperatures using only general information available from the UK Met Office or other sources.

A2.5   Accumulated temperature difference (degree-days and degree-hours)

Accumulated temperature differences are relatively simple forms of climatic data, useful as an index of climatic severity as it affects energy use for space heating or cooling. Accumulated temperature differences are calculated as the difference between the prevailing external, dry bulb temperature and a 'base temperature'. This is the external temperature at which, in theory, no artificial heating (or cooling) is required to maintain an acceptable internal temperature.

Two types of degree-day are used in building services engineering. Heating degree-days (K·day) indicate the severity of the heating season and therefore heating energy requirements. Cooling degree-days (K·day), or cooling degree-hours (K·h), indicate the warmth of the summer and hence cooling requirements. The most widely used form of accumulated temperature difference is heating degree-days, which have proved particularly useful in monitoring heating energy consumption in buildings from year to year.

Table A2.17 gives 20-year averages of monthly and annual heating degree-day totals for all 18 degree-day regions, referred to the traditional standard base temperature of 15.5 °C. These data are standard degree-day totals, calculated from daily maximum and minimum temperature.

Table A2.23 gives heating degree-day and cooling degree-hour totals for a range of base temperatures for London (Heathrow). Cooling degree-hours are calculated when the external dry bulb temperature exceeds the stated base temperature. Degree-day data may be obtained from (http://vesma.com).

Table A2.17 Mean monthly and annual heating degree-day totals (base temperature 15.5°C) for 18 UK degree-day regions (1976–1995)

Degree-day region		Mean total degree-days (K·day)												
		Jan	Feb	Mar	Apr	May	Jun	Jul	Aug	Sep	Oct	Nov	Dec	Year
1	Thames Valley (Heathrow)	340	309	261	197	111	49	20	23	53	128	234	308	2033
2	South-eastern (Gatwick)	351	327	283	218	135	68	32	38	75	158	254	324	2255
3	Southern (Hurn)	338	312	279	222	135	70	37	42	77	157	246	311	2224
4	South-western (Plymouth)	286	270	249	198	120	58	23	26	52	123	200	253	1858
5	Severn Valley (Filton)	312	286	253	189	110	46	17	20	48	129	217	285	1835
6	Midland (Elmdon)	365	338	291	232	153	77	39	45	85	186	271	344	2425
7	W Pennines (Ringway)	360	328	292	220	136	73	34	42	81	170	259	331	2228
8	North-western (Carlisle)	370	329	309	237	159	89	45	54	101	182	271	342	2388
9	Borders (Boulmer)	364	328	312	259	197	112	58	60	102	186	270	335	2483
10	North-eastern (Leeming)	379	339	304	235	159	83	40	46	87	182	272	345	2370
11	E Pennines (Finningley)	371	339	294	228	150	79	39	45	82	174	266	342	2307
12	E Anglia (Honington)	371	338	294	228	143	74	35	37	70	158	264	342	2254
13	W Scotland (Abbotsinch)	380	336	317	240	159	93	54	64	107	206	286	358	2494
14	E Scotland (Leuchars)	390	339	320	253	185	104	57	65	113	204	290	362	2577
15	NE Scotland (Dyce)	394	345	331	264	194	116	62	72	122	216	295	365	2668
16	Wales (Aberporth)	328	310	289	231	156	89	44	44	77	156	234	294	2161
17	N Ireland (Aldergrove)	362	321	304	234	158	88	47	56	102	189	269	330	2360
18	NW Scotland (Stornoway)	336	296	332	260	207	124	85	88	135	214	254	330	2671

Table A2.23 Monthly heating degree-day and cooling degree-hour totals to various base temperatures: London (Heathrow) (1982–2002)

Base temp. / °C	Monthly heating degree-days (/ K·day) for stated base temperature											
	Jan	Feb	Mar	Apr	May	Jun	Jul	Aug	Sep	Oct	Nov	Dec
10	150	140	99	61	16	2	0	0	4	22	84	132
12	207	192	151	101	37	8	1	2	11	46	130	187
14	267	247	208	150	72	24	6	8	28	86	184	246
15.5	314	290	255	192	105	45	16	18	51	124	228	293
16	329	304	269	206	117	52	20	23	59	135	243	307
18	391	360	331	264	168	91	45	50	100	192	302	369
18.5	406	373	345	277	182	102	55	58	113	207	317	384
20	453	417	393	323	224	138	82	87	152	253	362	431
Base temp. / °C	Monthly cooling degree-hours (/ K·h) for stated base temperature											
	Jan	Feb	Mar	Apr	May	Jun	Jul	Aug	Sep	Oct	Nov	Dec
5	1347	1216	2166	3236	5935	7820	9965	9630	7232	5101	2507	1622
12	8	20	109	443	1626	2972	4787	4467	2454	962	158	43
18	0	0	2	32	274	635	1388	1158	308	33	0	0

A2.6   World-wide weather data

The CD-ROM that accompanies Guide A provides climatic design information for some 250 locations world-wide. These have been selected from the 4422 locations for which such data are given on the CD-ROM that accompanies the 2005 ASHRAE Handbook: *Fundamentals*.

A2.7   Solar and illuminance data

A2.7.1   Solar geometry

Two angles are used to define the angular position of the sun as seen from a given point on the surface of the earth, see Figure A2.11. These are:

—   *Solar altitude*, γ_s: the angular elevation of the centre of the solar disk above the horizontal plane.

—   *Solar azimuth*, α_s: the horizontal angle between the vertical plane containing the centre of the solar disk and the vertical plane running in a true N–S direction. Solar azimuth is measured clockwise from due south in the northern hemisphere and anti-clockwise measured from due north in the southern hemisphere. Values are negative before solar noon and positive after solar noon.

Other important angles for solar geometry are:

—   *Wall azimuth*, α: the orientation of the wall, measured clockwise from due south in the northern hemisphere and anti-clockwise measured from due north in the southern hemisphere.

—   *Wall–solar azimuth angle*, sometimes called the *horizontal shadow angle*, α_f: the angle between the vertical plane containing the normal to the surface and the vertical plane passing through the centre of the solar disk, i.e. the resolved angle on the horizontal plane between the direction of the sun and the direction of the normal to the surface.

Numerical values of altitude angle and bearing to the nearest degree are given in CIBSE Guide J Appendix A6.

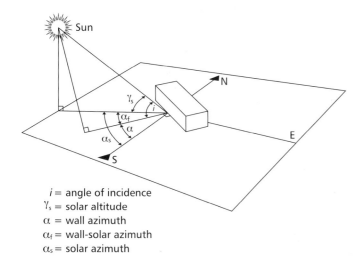

i = angle of incidence
γ_s = solar altitude
α = wall azimuth
α_f = wall-solar azimuth
α_s = solar azimuth

Figure A2.11 Solar geometry

A2.7.3   Solar irradiation

A2.7.3.1   Monthly mean daily irradiation on inclined planes (UK)

Table A2.27 provides values of monthly mean daily irradiation on a range of inclined planes for the London area (Bracknell). These are based on measured data for the period 1983–2002. A ground albedo of 0.2 was assumed.

A2.7.3.2   Near-extreme global irradiation with associated diffuse irradiation (UK)

Tables 2.30 to 2.32 in Guide A provide values of near-extreme hourly irradiation (formerly termed 'design maxima') for London area (Bracknell), Manchester (Aughton) and Edinburgh (Mylnefield), respectively. The tables provide mean hourly irradiation values associated with a known exceedence of daily global irradiation and are intended for use in risk-based design applications. They provide the basis for the tables of solar cooling load provided in Guide A chapter 5.

A2.7.4   Sol-air temperatures for the UK

The procedure for estimating long-wave radiation loss and the calculation of sol-air temperatures are given in CIBSE Guide J: *Weather, solar and illuminance data*. Guide A Tables 2.34 to 2.36 provide and hourly air and sol-air temperatures for the London area, Manchester and Edinburgh.

These tables were derived from the 97.5 percentile daily global irradiation exceedence data given in Guide A Tables 2.30 to 2.32, in combination with the associated month by month mean hour ending synoptic data. The associated hourly means of the synoptic data were extracted for the same days used to determine the 97.5 percentile irradiation data sets. It was assumed that synoptic time and LAT were identical.

Standardised values for the various parameters were assumed, as follows:

—   *short-wave surface absorptance*: α_{rad} = 0.9 (dark coloured surface), 0.5 (light coloured surface)

—   *long-wave surface absorptance/emittance*: $\alpha_1 = \varepsilon_1 = 0.9$

The long-wave radiation was calculated using sunshine data when the solar altitude was above 6° and cloud data when the solar altitude was 6° or less. The solar radiation was set to zero when the solar altitude was below 1°. For further details see CIBSE Guide J: *Weather, solar and illuminance data*.

A2.9   Climate change

There is ample evidence from the geological and historical record that the climate of the earth, and the UK in particular, has changed significantly in the past. Over recent decades, however, it has become clear that there is a global trend towards warmer temperatures.

The UK Climate Impacts Programme (www.ukcip.org.uk) helps UK organisations assess how they might be affected by climate change, so they can prepare for its impact.

Table A2.27 Monthly mean daily irradiation on inclined planes: London area (Bracknell) (1983–2002)

Month	Beam					Diffuse					Total					Ground reflected			
	0	30	45	60	90	0	30	45	60	90	0	30	45	60	90	30	45	60	90
(a) West																			
Jan	223	224	224	211	169	460	440	409	361	235	683	673	652	606	473	9	20	35	69
Feb	485	453	431	402	304	846	809	749	660	428	1332	1280	1219	1129	866	18	39	67	134
Mar	825	775	730	668	485	1410	1347	1248	1099	709	2235	2152	2044	1879	1417	30	66	112	224
Apr	1550	1503	1412	1283	917	2062	1996	1867	1662	1088	3611	3548	3385	3125	2367	48	106	181	362
May	2081	2025	1889	1701	1189	2565	2494	2337	2086	1370	4647	4581	4362	4019	3025	62	136	233	465
Jun	2190	2034	1851	1628	1083	2874	2744	2557	2260	1451	5064	4847	4557	4142	3042	68	149	254	508
Jul	2226	2080	1909	1690	1140	2702	2590	2412	2137	1378	4928	4737	4465	4073	3011	66	145	247	493
Aug	2013	1919	1784	1608	1133	2297	2224	2079	1856	1219	4310	4200	3990	3680	2783	58	126	216	432
Sep	1187	1193	1148	1067	804	1657	1619	1521	1354	897	2843	2850	2752	2564	1986	38	83	143	285
Oct	744	814	808	771	607	1001	997	944	850	576	1746	1834	1804	1708	1359	24	51	88	176
Nov	330	380	385	378	306	578	573	538	483	324	908	965	950	907	721	12	27	46	92
Dec	173	191	196	191	158	361	350	327	291	192	534	548	539	509	404	7	16	27	54
Mean	1169	1132	1064	966	691	1568	1515	1416	1258	822	2737	2684	2560	2362	1788	37	80	137	274
(b) South-west:																			
Jan	223	483	567	613	579	460	495	483	454	346	683	987	1071	1102	994	9	20	35	69
Feb	485	802	884	912	784	846	877	844	778	569	1332	1697	1768	1757	1486	18	39	67	134
Mar	825	1118	1166	1140	886	1410	1417	1342	1216	841	2235	2565	2574	2468	1951	30	66	112	224
Apr	1550	1846	1837	1715	1214	2062	2056	1944	1754	1189	3611	3950	3887	3650	2764	49	106	181	362
May	2081	2253	2151	1931	1238	2565	2523	2366	2115	1402	4647	4838	4652	4279	3106	62	136	233	465
Jun	2190	2217	2054	1788	1056	2874	2775	2578	2283	1480	5064	5059	4781	4325	3043	68	149	254	508
Jul	2226	2306	2166	1913	1171	2702	2624	2448	2173	1420	4928	4997	4758	4332	3084	66	145	247	493
Aug	2013	2277	2221	2037	1384	2297	2281	2153	1936	1303	4310	4616	4501	4189	3119	58	126	216	432
Sep	1187	1566	1620	1568	1204	1657	1687	1611	1471	1031	2843	3291	3315	3181	2520	38	84	143	285
Oct	744	1242	1374	1414	1220	1001	1078	1054	988	740	1746	2343	2480	2489	2136	24	51	88	175
Nov	330	694	811	872	817	578	636	630	597	462	908	1342	1467	1515	1371	12	27	46	92
Dec	173	424	511	562	549	361	401	399	380	298	534	833	925	969	901	7	16	27	54
Mean	1169	1436	1447	1372	1008	1568	1571	1488	1345	923	2737	3043	3015	2855	2206	37	80	137	274

Column header note: Mean irradiation (W·h·m⁻²) for stated inclination from horizontal (°)

Most of the climate modelling used by UKCIP to produce scenarios has been done by the Hadley Centre, which is part of the UK Met Office. (www.metoffice.com/research/hadleycentre/).

Development of future climate scenarios depends on:

(a) making assumptions about the emissions of CO_2 and other greenhouse gasses over the next century; the IPCC has published a range of standard scenarios, which depend on complex economic, technological and demographic factors

(b) calculating the relationships between greenhouse gas emissions and greenhouse gas concentrations in the atmosphere

(c) which particular global climate model is used to determine the geographic variation of changes; one of the leading models, widely used for UK climate scenarios, is the global Hadley Climate Model 3 (HadCM3); for regional scenarios, the Regional Model (HadRM3) has been used, relying on outputs from larger-scale models for its boundary conditions.

In early 2002, the UKCIP published four possible future climate scenarios, produced within this framework. These were felt to cover a large, but not exhaustive, part of the range of possible future changes. The change in global mean temperature (ΔT) and future CO_2 concentration are summarised for each scenario during three 30-year time periods centred on the 2020s (2011 to 2040), the 2050s

(2041 to 2070), and the 2080s (2071 to 2100) in Table A2.59.

A2.9.2 Climate change data

Tables A2.61 and A2.62 show 1-day near-extreme data selected on daily mean dry bulb temperature (1% exceedence (summer) and 99% exceedence (winter)) for London (Heathrow).

The percentage exceedence values are calculated using daily average temperatures.

A2.10 Heat island effect

The average air temperature in urban areas is generally higher than that in surrounding areas. This results from a multiplicity of differences between urban and rural areas, but the more important reasons are that urban areas have:

— greater heat capacity

— more effective absorption of solar radiation in 'street gorges' and less effective long-wave radiative cooling

— reduced wind speeds

— less vegetation.

Anthropogenic heat flux can also be important in some areas.

Table A2.59 Summary of the characteristics of the four UKCIP02 scenarios

Scenario	Climatic changes for stated period					
	2020s		2050s		2080s	
	$\Delta\theta$ / K	CO_2 / ppm	$\Delta\theta$ / K	CO_2 / ppm	$\Delta\theta$ / K	CO_2 / ppm
Low Emissions	0.79	422	1.41	489	2.00	525
Medium-Low Emissions	0.88	422	1.64	489	2.34	562
Medium-High Emissions	0.88	435	1.87	551	3.29	715
High Emissions	0.94	437	2.24	593	3.88	810

Table A2.61 Climate change dry bulb temperatures (1% exceedence) for London (Heathrow)

Hour	Dry bulb temperature (/ °C) for stated scenario*					
	1970s	2020s (A2 and B2)	2050s (B2)	2050s (A2)	2080s (B2)	2080s (A2)
0	18.2	19.6	20.8	21.1	21.8	23.3
1	18.7	19.9	21.0	21.3	21.9	23.3
2	18.2	19.4	20.4	20.7	21.3	22.6
3	16.8	18.0	19.1	19.4	20.0	21.3
4	17.2	18.4	19.5	19.8	20.4	21.7
5	18.3	19.5	20.6	21.0	21.6	23.0
6	19.9	21.2	22.4	22.7	23.5	24.9
7	21.8	23.3	24.6	24.9	25.7	27.4
8	23.3	25.0	26.6	27.0	27.9	29.8
9	24.5	26.4	28.1	28.6	29.7	31.8
10	25.5	27.7	29.6	30.1	31.3	33.6
11	26.5	28.8	30.8	31.4	32.6	35.1
12	27.1	29.6	31.7	32.4	33.6	36.3
13	27.6	30.1	32.3	33.0	34.3	37.0
14	27.7	30.3	32.5	33.2	34.5	37.3
15	27.7	30.3	32.4	33.1	34.4	37.2
16	27.7	30.1	32.3	32.9	34.2	36.9
17	27.4	29.8	31.8	32.4	33.6	36.2
18	26.8	29.1	31.0	31.5	32.7	35.1
19	25.8	27.9	29.7	30.2	31.3	33.5
20	24.4	26.3	28.0	28.5	29.5	31.5
21	22.7	24.4	26.0	26.4	27.3	29.3
22	20.9	22.5	23.9	24.3	25.2	27.0
23	19.3	20.8	22.1	22.5	23.3	24.9
24	18.2	19.6	20.8	21.1	21.8	23.3

* A1 = High emissions; A2 = Medium-High emissions; B1 = Low emissions; B2 = Medium-Low emissions

Table A2.62 Climate change dry bulb temperatures (99% exceedence) for London (Heathrow)

Hour	Dry bulb temperature (/ °C) for stated scenario*					
	1970s	2020s (A2 and B2)	2050s (B2)	2050s (A2)	2080s (B2)	2080s (A2)
0	−1.6	−0.8	−0.2	0.0	0.4	1.2
1	−2.7	−1.8	−1.0	−0.8	−0.4	0.6
2	−4.2	−3.2	−2.3	−2.0	−1.4	−0.2
3	−4.2	−3.2	−2.4	−2.1	−1.6	−0.6
4	−4.2	−3.2	−2.4	−2.1	−1.6	−0.6
5	−4.2	−3.2	−2.4	−2.1	−1.6	−0.6
6	−4.2	−3.2	−2.4	−2.1	−1.6	−0.6
7	−4.2	−3.2	−2.4	−2.1	−1.6	−0.6
8	−4.1	−3.1	−2.3	−2.0	−1.5	−0.5
9	−3.8	−2.8	−2.0	−1.7	−1.2	−0.1
10	−3.3	−2.3	−1.5	−1.2	−0.7	0.4
11	−2.7	−1.7	−0.9	−0.6	−0.1	1.0
12	−1.9	−1.0	−0.1	0.1	0.6	1.7
13	−1.1	−0.2	0.6	1.2	2.1	3.5
14	3.0	3.4	3.7	3.8	4.0	4.3
15	2.7	3.1	3.5	3.6	3.8	4.2
16	1.9	2.4	2.9	3.0	3.3	3.8
17	0.8	1.5	2.0	2.2	2.6	3.3
18	−0.2	0.6	1.3	1.5	1.9	2.7
19	−1.0	−0.1	0.7	0.9	1.4	2.3
20	−1.3	−0.4	0.4	0.6	1.1	2.0
21	−1.3	−0.4	0.3	0.5	1.0	1.9
22	−1.1	−0.4	0.3	0.5	0.9	1.7
23	−1.2	−0.4	0.2	0.4	0.8	1.6
24	−1.6	−0.8	−0.2	0.0	0.4	1.2

* A1 = High emissions; A2 = Medium-High emissions; B1 = Low emissions; B2 = Medium-Low emissions

A3 Thermal properties of building structures

A3.1 Introduction

A3.1.2 Calculation of heat losses/gains

The thermal transmittance (U-value) of the building envelope is the principal factor in the determination of the steady-state heat losses/gains. Hence, the capacity of the heating or cooling system required to maintain specified inside design conditions under design external conditions.

There are many different calculation procedures for determining the dynamic thermal behaviour of building structures. The parameters required for one of these, the admittance procedure, are given in Guide A Appendix 3.A6.

A3.1.3 Building Regulations

Part L of Schedule 1 to the Building Regulations 2000, which apply in England and Wales, requires that reasonable provision shall be made for the conservation of fuel and power in buildings. Ways of showing compliance with this requirement are given in Approved Document L1 for dwellings and Approved Document L2 for other buildings, although designers may choose to demonstrate compliance using other methods which are acceptable to the building control authority as providing equivalent performance. In terms of the thermal performance of the building structure, the aim of this part of the Regulations is to limit the heat loss and, where appropriate, maximise the heat gains through the fabric of the building.

In meeting this objective, Approved Documents L1 and L2 convey standards of fabric insulation which are set having regard to national standards of cost effectiveness, the need to avoid unacceptable technical risks and the need to provide flexibility for designers. However, for individual buildings, better standards of insulation can often be justified to clients using their own economic criteria and some guidance is given in BS 8207 and BS 8211.

A3.3   Heat losses from buildings

A3.3.1   General

In most cases the thermal properties of a building component are represented by its thermal transmittance, U (in $W \cdot m^{-2} \cdot K^{-1}$). The U-value multiplied by the area of the component gives the rate of heat loss through the component per unit of temperature difference between inside and outside.

Often it is convenient to characterise the whole building by a transmission heat loss coefficient, H_t, i.e:

$$H_t = \Sigma (A\, U) + \Sigma (L\, \Psi) \qquad (3.1)$$

where H_t is the transmission heat loss coefficient ($W \cdot K$), $\Sigma (A\, U)$ is the sum over all the components of the building (i.e. roof, walls, floor, windows) of the product of the area of each component and its U-value ($W \cdot m^{-2} \cdot K^{-1}$) and $\Sigma (L\, \Psi)$ is the sum over all thermal bridges of the product of the length of each thermal bridge (m) and its linear thermal transmittance ($W \cdot m^{-1} \cdot K^{-1}$).

Repeating thermal bridges (which occur at fixed intervals in the element, such as mortar joints or timber studding) are taken into account in the calculation of the U-value of the component and no further allowance is needed. Linear thermal transmittances (Ψ-values) arise at junctions between different components.

The transmission heat loss through a component is modified if there is an unheated space between the internal and external environments. One method of allowing for this is given in BS EN ISO 13789.

A3.3.2   Dimensions for heat loss calculations

The basis used in Building Regulations is the overall internal dimensions, measured between finished internal faces of external elements of the building and including the thickness of internal elements.

A3.3.3   Application of thermal insulation

There are a number of factors that must be considered in both the design and application of thermal insulation. Thermal insulation is most effective when applied as a continuous and even layer, without penetrations or breaks. Penetrations form thermal bridges and breaks permit air flow within and through the insulating layer, both of which reduce its effectiveness.

A3.3.4   Thermal resistance of materials

The thermal properties of a material are expressed in terms of its thermal resistance. For homogeneous, isotropic materials through which heat is transmitted by conduction only, the thermal resistance is directly proportional to the thickness and is given by:

$$R = d\, /\, \lambda \qquad (3.2)$$

where R is the thermal resistance ($m^2 \cdot K \cdot W^{-1}$), d is the thickness of material (m) and λ is the thermal conductivity ($W \cdot m^{-1} \cdot K^{-1}$).

A3.3.5   Thermal conductivity of masonry materials

For many types of masonry materials, including clay products and various types of aggregate and aerated concrete, the thermal conductivity is related to the bulk density and moisture content. Table A3.1 provides values of thermal conductivity for a range of densities at 'standard' values of moisture content, as defined in Table A3.2. 'Protected' includes internal partitions, inner leaves separated from outer leaves by a continuous air space, masonry protected by tile hanging, sheet cladding or other such protection, separated by a continuous air space. 'Exposed' covers rendered or unrendered masonry directly exposed to rain.

See Guide A for thermal conductivity of non-masonry materials and conversion coefficients.

A3.3.8   Thermal resistance of air spaces

Heat transfer across an air space is approximately proportional to the difference between the temperatures of the boundary surfaces. However, the thermal resistance depends upon various other factors such as the dimensions of the air space, the direction of heat flow, the emissivities of the inner surfaces and the extent to which the airspace is ventilated.

Tables A3.3 and A3.4 provide standardised values of thermal resistance for both continuous and divided air spaces. For air spaces of thicknesses greater than 25 mm see Guide A, equation 3.3.

Values for the thermal resistance of roof spaces are given in Table A3.5. Note that these values include an allowance for the thermal resistance of the roof construction but do not include the external surface resistance (R_{se}).

A3.3.9   Surface resistance

The inside and outside surface resistances are determined by the processes of heat transfer which occur at the boundary between a structural element and the air. Heat is transferred both by radiation interchange with other surfaces and by convective heat transfer at the air/surface interface.

A3.3.9.1   Heat transfer by radiation

Heat transfer by radiation is a complex process which depends upon the shape, temperature and emissivity of both the radiating surface and the surface or environment to which it radiates. A detailed description is contained in Guide C chapter 3. However, for practical purposes, the heat transfer by radiation is characterised by an emissivity factor, E, and a radiative heat transfer coefficient, h_r.

The emissivity factor depends upon the geometry of the room and the emissivities of the surfaces. However, for a

Table A3.1 Thermal conductivity of homogeneous masonry materials at 'standard' moisture content

Material	Dry density / kg.m^{-3}	Thermal conductivity / W·m^{-1}·K^{-1}		Material	Dry density / kg.m^{-3}	Thermal conductivity / W·m^{-1}·K^{-1}	
		Protected	Exposed			Protected	Exposed
Brick (fired clay)	1200	0.36	0.50	Pyro-processed colliery material concrete	1100	0.39	0.42
	1300	0.40	0.54		1200	0.41	0.44
	1400	0.44	0.60		1300	0.44	0.47
	1500	0.47	0.65		1400	0.46	0.49
	1600	0.52	0.71		1500	0.48	0.52
	1700	0.56	0.77	Pumice aggregate concrete	500	0.16	0.17
	1800	0.61	0.83		600	0.18	0.19
	1900	0.66	0.90		700	0.20	0.22
	2000	0.70	0.96		800	0.24	0.25
Brick (calcium silicate)	1700	0.77	1.05		900	0.27	0.29
	1800	0.89	1.22		1000	0.31	0.34
	1900	1.01	1.38		1100	0.36	0.38
	2000	1.16	1.58		1200	0.40	0.43
	2100	1.32	1.80		1300	0.46	0.49
	2200	1.51	2.06	Autoclaved aerated concrete	400	0.12	0.13
Dense aggregate concrete	1700	1.04	1.12		500	0.15	0.16
	1800	1.13	1.21		600	0.18	0.19
	1900	1.22	1.31		700	0.20	0.22
	2000	1.33	1.43		800	0.24	0.25
	2100	1.46	1.56		900	0.27	0.29
	2200	1.59	1.70	Other lightweight aggregate concrete	600	0.20	0.22
	2300	1.75	1.87		700	0.24	0.25
	2400	1.93	2.06		800	0.28	0.30
Blast furnace slag concrete	1000	0.19	0.20		900	0.31	0.34
	1100	0.24	0.25		1000	0.36	0.38
	1200	0.27	0.29		1100	0.40	0.43
	1300	0.32	0.35		1200	0.46	0.49
	1400	0.38	0.41		1300	0.52	0.55
	1500	0.45	0.48		1400	0.57	0.61
	1600	0.53	0.56		1500	0.63	0.67
	1700	0.60	0.65		1600	0.71	0.76

Note: these data have been derived from the values for the 90% fractile given in BS EN 1745 for the standard moisture contents given in Table 3.2. The value for mortar may be taken as 0.88 W·m^{-1}·K^{-1} (protected) and 0.94 W·m^{-1}·K^{-1} (exposed).

Table A3.2 'Standard' moisture contents for masonry

Material	Moisture content	
	Protected	Exposed
Brick (fired clay)	1% (by volume)	5% (by volume)
Brick (calcium silicate)	1% (by volume)	5% (by volume)
Dense aggregate concrete	3% (by volume)	5% (by volume)
Blast furnace slag concrete	3% (by weight)	5% (by weight)
Pumice aggregate concrete	3% (by weight)	5% (by weight)
Other lightweight aggregate concrete	3% (by weight)	5% (by weight)
Autoclaved aerated concrete	3% (by weight)	5% (by weight)

Note: % (by volume) = % (by weight) × density / 1000

Table A3.3 Thermal resistances for continuous unventilated air spaces

Air space thickness / mm	Surface emissivity†	Thermal resistance (/ m^2·K·W^{-1}) for heat flow in stated direction‡		
		Horizontal	Upward	Downward
5	High	0.11	0.11	0.11
	Low§	0.17	0.17	0.17
≥ 25	High	0.18	0.16	0.19
	Low§	0.44	0.34	0.50

† High emissivity: $\varepsilon > 0.8$; low emissivity: $\varepsilon \leq 0.2$

‡ Normal to the surface in the direction of heat flow

§ Assumes that the air space is bounded by one low emissivity surface and one high emissivity surface

Table A3.4 Thermal resistances for divided air spaces for horizontal heat flow

Air space thickness / mm	Thermal resistance (/ m^2·K·W^{-1}) for air space of stated breadth / mm				
	≥ 200	100	50	20	≤ 10
5	0.11	0.11	0.11	0.11	0.12
6	0.12	0.12	0.12	0.13	0.13
7	0.13	0.13	0.13	0.14	0.15
8	0.14	0.14	0.14	0.15	0.16
10	0.15	0.15	0.16	0.17	0.18
12	0.16	0.17	0.17	0.19	0.20
15	0.17	0.18	0.19	0.21	0.23
20	0.18	0.20	0.21	0.24	0.26
25	0.18	0.20	0.21	0.24	0.27

Notes: (1) applies to heat flow in horizontal direction only (see Guide A, Figure 3.2); (2) calculated in accordance with BS EN ISO 6946; (3) assumes high emissivity at surfaces.

Table A3.5 Thermal resistances for roof spaces (reproduced from BS EN ISO 6946 by permission of the British Standards Institution)

Item	Description	Thermal resistance / m^2·K·W^{-1}
1	Tiled roof with no felt, boards or similar	0.06
2	Sheeted roof or tiled roof with felt or boards or similar under the tiles	0.2
3	As 2 but with aluminium cladding or other low emissivity surface at underside of roof	0.3
4	Roof lined with boards and felt	0.3

cubical room with one exposed surface, all the internal surfaces having high emissivity, E may be expressed thus:

$$E = K \, \varepsilon \qquad (3.4)$$

where E is the emissivity factor, K is a constant related to room geometry and ε is the emissivity of the surface.

Values of the radiative heat transfer coefficient for a range of surface temperatures are given in Table A3.6. It should be noted that, for night time clear skies, the difference between the surface temperature and the 'sky' temperature can be very large, leading to underestimation of h_c in these circumstances. This is particularly important in the prediction of condensation.

Table A3.6 Radiative heat transfer coefficient, h_r

Mean temperature of surfaces / °C	Radiative heat transfer coefficient, $h_r / \mathrm{W \cdot m^{-2} \cdot K^{-1}}$
−10	4.1
0	4.6
10	5.1
20	5.7

A3.3.9.2   Heat transfer by convection

Heat transfer by convection is characterised by a heat transfer coefficient, h_c. This depends upon the temperature difference between the surface and the air, the surface roughness, the air velocity and the direction of heat flow. For still air conditions, values of the convective heat transfer coefficient are given in Table A3.7. Where significant air movement occurs, heat transfer by convection is more complex and reference should be made to Guide C chapter 3.

Table A3.7 Convective heat transfer coefficient, h_c

Direction of heat flow	Convective heat transfer coefficient†, $h_c / \mathrm{W \cdot m^{-2} \cdot K^{-1}}$
Horizontal	2.5
Upward	5.0
Downward	0.7

† Assumes still air conditions, i.e. air speed at the surface is not greater than 0.1 m·s⁻¹

A3.3.9.3   Internal surface resistance

The values for internal surface resistance used in BS EN ISO 6946 are shown in Table A3.8. These values represent a simplification of the heat transfer processes that occur at surfaces.

Table A3.8 Internal surface resistance, R_{si}

Building element	Direction of heat flow	Surface resistance / m²·K·W⁻¹
Walls	Horizontal	0.13
Ceilings or roofs (flat or pitched), floors	Upward	0.10
Ceilings or floors	Downward	0.17

A3.3.9.4   External surface resistance

The values for external surface resistance used in BS EN ISO 6946 are shown in Table A3.9, which are recommended for most design purposes. As with the Table A3.8, these values represent a simplification of the heat transfer processes that occur at surfaces.

Table A3.9 External surface resistance, R_{se}

Building element	Direction of heat flow	Surface resistance / m²·K·W⁻¹		
		BS EN ISO 6946 (normal design value)	Sheltered	Exposed
Wall	Horizontal	0.04	0.06	0.02
Roof	Upward	0.04	0.06	0.02
Floor	Downward	0.04	0.06	0.02

A3.3.10   Thermal transmittance for elements composed of plane homogenous layers

The thermal transmittance of a building element is obtained by combining the thermal resistances of its component parts and the adjacent air layers. Thermal transmittances of simple walls and roofs composed of parallel slabs are obtained by adding the thermal resistances and taking the reciprocal of the sum, thus:

$$U = 1 / (R_{si} + R_1 + R_2 + \dots + R_a + R_{se}) \qquad (3.10)$$

where U is the thermal transmittance ($\mathrm{W \cdot m^{-2} \cdot K^{-1}}$), R_{si} is the internal surface resistance ($\mathrm{m^2 \cdot K \cdot W^{-1}}$), R_1 and R_2 are the thermal resistances of components 1 and 2 ($\mathrm{m^2 \cdot K \cdot W^{-1}}$), R_a is the thermal resistance of the air spaces ($\mathrm{m^2 \cdot K \cdot W^{-1}}$) and R_{se} is the external surface resistance ($\mathrm{m^2 \cdot K \cdot W^{-1}}$).

Appendix 3.A8 of Guide A provides extensive tables of thermal transmittances for a wide range of typical building constructions which, for reasons of space, cannot be included in this Handbook.

A3.3.11   Thermal transmittance for elements composed of bridged layers

The method of calculation of thermal transmittance given in section 3.3.10 assumes that the direction of heat flow is perpendicular to the plane of the structure. This is true when the layers are of uniform thickness and the thermal conductivity is isotropic along this plane. Dissimilar thermal conductivities and thicknesses mean that heat flows are not unidirectional and thermal bridges are formed.

Guide A section 3.3.11 describes methods for calculating the thermal transmittance of bridged layers.

A3.4   Roofs

A3.4.1   Pitched roofs

For simple pitched roofs, the U-value is calculated normal to the plane of the roof. However, if the pitched roof includes a horizontal ceiling and an unheated loft, the U-value is defined with respect to the plane of the ceiling.

For heated lofts, the U-value of the roof is calculated in the normal way. However, in calculating the heat losses, the full surface area of the roof must be considered rather than the plan area. Building Regulations require that roof voids be ventilated. Standardised thermal resistances for loft spaces are given in Table A3.5 above.

A3.4.2 Flat roofs

The thermal transmittance of flat roofs is calculated using the methods given in sections A3.3.10 and A3.3.11.

A3.5 Ground floors and basements

A3.5.1 General

The heat loss through floors in contact with the ground is more complicated than that through above ground components. The heat flow is three-dimensional and the thermal performance is affected by various factors including the size and shape of the floor, the thickness of the surrounding wall and the presence of all-over or edge insulation. However, research has shown that the building dimensions affect the U-values of ground floors predominantly through the ratio of exposed perimeter of the floor to its area. This allows the U-value of a ground floor to be readily evaluated for a floor of any size or shape.

The information on ground floors is consistent with BS EN ISO 13370 and provides data for different soil types.

It should be noted that the heat flux density varies over the area of a floor, in general being greatest at the edges and least at the centre. The thermal transmittance of a floor is suitable for calculating the total heat transfer through the floor but cannot be used to obtain the heat flux density at a point on the floor surface or to calculate the surface temperature of the floor.

A3.5.2 Thermal transmittance of solid ground floors

Tables A3.15, A3.16 and A3.17 give U-values for solid ground floors in contact with the earth for the three types of soil in Table A3.14. The tables assume a wall thickness of 0.3 m. The U-values are given as a function of the ratio of exposed perimeter to floor area and the thermal resistance of the floor construction, R_f ($R_f = 0$ for an uninsulated floor). Linear interpolation may be used for values intermediate between those given in the tables.

The equations used to produce Tables A3.15, A3.16 and A3.17 are given in Guide A section 3.5.2.

The U-value of a solid floor in contact with the ground, see Figure A3.7, depends on a 'characteristic dimension' of the floor, B', and the 'total equivalent thickness', d_{ef}, of the factors that, in combination, restrict the heat flow (i.e. wall thickness, surface resistances, thermal insulation).

The characteristic dimension is defined thus:

$$B' = \frac{A_{fg}}{0.5\, p_f} \tag{3.19}$$

where B' is the characteristic dimension of the floor (m), A_{fg} is the area of floor in contact with the ground (m^2) and p_f is the exposed perimeter of the floor (m).

Table A3.14 Thermal conductivity of soils

Soil type	Thermal conductivity, λ_g / W·m^{-1}·K^{-1}
Clay or silt	1.5
Sand or gravel	2.0
Homogeneous rock	3.5

Table A3.15 U-values for solid ground floors on clay soil ($\lambda_g = 1.5$ W·m^{-1}·K^{-1})

Ratio p_f/A_{fg}	U-value (/ W·m^{-2}·K^{-1}) for stated thermal resistance, R_f (/ m^2·K·W^{-1})			
	0	0.5	1.0	2.0
0.05	0.13	0.11	0.10	0.08
0.10	0.22	0.18	0.16	0.13
0.15	0.30	0.24	0.21	0.17
0.20	0.37	0.29	0.25	0.19
0.25	0.44	0.34	0.28	0.22
0.30	0.49	0.38	0.31	0.23
0.35	0.55	0.41	0.34	0.25
0.40	0.60	0.44	0.36	0.26
0.45	0.65	0.47	0.38	0.27
0.50	0.70	0.50	0.40	0.28
0.55	0.74	0.52	0.41	0.28
0.60	0.78	0.55	0.43	0.29
0.65	0.82	0.57	0.44	0.30
0.70	0.86	0.59	0.45	0.30
0.75	0.89	0.61	0.46	0.31
0.80	0.93	0.62	0.47	0.32
0.85	0.96	0.64	0.47	0.32
0.90	0.99	0.65	0.48	0.32
0.95	1.02	0.66	0.49	0.33
1.00	1.05	0.68	0.50	0.33

Table A3.16 U-values for solid ground floors on sand or gravel ($\lambda_g = 2.0$ W·m^{-1}·K^{-1})

Ratio p_f/A_{fg}	U-value (/ W·m^{-2}·K^{-1}) for stated thermal resistance, R_f (/ m^2·K·W^{-1})			
	0	0.5	1.0	2.0
0.05	0.16	0.14	0.12	0.10
0.10	0.28	0.22	0.19	0.16
0.15	0.38	0.30	0.25	0.20
0.20	0.47	0.36	0.30	0.23
0.25	0.55	0.41	0.33	0.25
0.30	0.63	0.46	0.37	0.26
0.35	0.70	0.50	0.39	0.28
0.40	0.76	0.53	0.42	0.29
0.45	0.82	0.56	0.43	0.30
0.50	0.88	0.59	0.45	0.31
0.55	0.93	0.62	0.47	0.31
0.60	0.98	0.64	0.48	0.32
0.65	1.03	0.66	0.49	0.33
0.70	1.07	0.68	0.50	0.33
0.75	1.12	0.70	0.51	0.34
0.80	1.16	0.72	0.52	0.34
0.85	1.19	0.73	0.53	0.35
0.90	1.23	0.75	0.54	0.35
0.95	1.27	0.76	0.54	0.35
1.00	1.30	0.77	0.55	0.35

Table A3.17 U-values for solid ground floors on homogeneous rock ($\lambda_g = 3.5$ W·m^{-1}·K^{-1})

Ratio p_f/A_{fg}	U-value (/ W·m^{-2}·K^{-1}) for stated thermal resistance, R_f (/ m^2·K·W^{-1})			
	0	0.5	1.0	2.0
0.05	0.27	0.21	0.18	0.15
0.10	0.45	0.34	0.28	0.22
0.15	0.61	0.43	0.35	0.26
0.20	0.74	0.51	0.40	0.28
0.25	0.86	0.58	0.44	0.30
0.30	0.97	0.63	0.47	0.32
0.35	1.07	0.68	0.50	0.33
0.40	1.16	0.72	0.52	0.34
0.45	1.25	0.75	0.53	0.35
0.50	1.33	0.78	0.55	0.35
0.55	1.40	0.80	0.56	0.36
0.60	1.47	0.82	0.58	0.37
0.65	1.53	0.84	0.59	0.37
0.70	1.59	0.86	0.60	0.37
0.75	1.64	0.87	0.61	0.38
0.80	1.69	0.89	0.62	0.38
0.85	1.74	0.91	0.62	0.38
0.90	1.79	0.92	0.63	0.39
0.95	1.83	0.93	0.64	0.39
1.00	1.87	0.95	0.64	0.39

(a) Plan (not to scale)

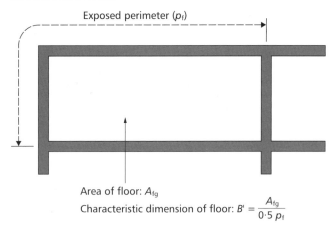

Area of floor: A_{fg}

Characteristic dimension of floor: $B' = \dfrac{A_{fg}}{0 \cdot 5\, p_f}$

(b) Section (not to scale)

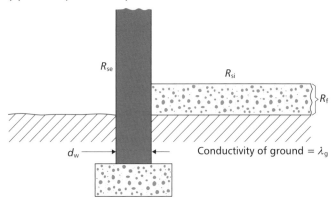

Total equivalent thickness of floor: $d_{ef} = d_w + \lambda_g\, (R_{si} + R_f + R_{se})$

Figure A3.7 Characteristic dimension and total equivalent thickness of solid ground floor

The total equivalent thickness is given by:

$$d_{ef} = d_w + \lambda_g\, (R_{si} + R_f + R_{se}) \qquad (3.20)$$

where d_{ef} is the total equivalent thickness of the floor (m), d_w is the thickness of the wall surrounding the ground floor (m), λ_g is the thermal conductivity of the ground ($W \cdot m^{-1} \cdot K^{-1}$), is the inside surface resistance ($m^2 \cdot K \cdot W^{-1}$), is the external surface resistance ($m^2 \cdot K \cdot W^{-1}$) and R_f is the thermal resistance of the floor ($m^2 \cdot K \cdot W^{-1}$). For calculation of heat losses through floors, R_{si} and R_{se} take values of $0.17\ m^2 \cdot K \cdot W^{-1}$ and $0.04\ m^2 \cdot K \cdot W^{-1}$ respectively .

A3.5.4 Thermal transmittance of solid ground floors with edge insulation

A slab-on-ground floor may be insulated by means of edge insulation placed either horizontally or vertically round the perimeter of the floor. The following equations are valid provided that no significant thermal bridging is introduced.

The U-value of an edge-insulated floor is given by:

$$U_{fi} = U_f + 2\, \Psi_{fi} / B' \qquad (3.23)$$

where U_{fi} is the thermal transmittance of the edge-insulated floor ($W \cdot m^{-2} \cdot K^{-1}$), U_f is the thermal transmittance of the same floor without insulation ($W \cdot m^{-2} \cdot K^{-1}$), Ψ_{fi} is a factor related to the floor edge insulation ($W \cdot m^{-1} \cdot K^{-1}$)

and B' is the characteristic dimension of the floor (m), see equation 3.19.

The edge insulation factor, Ψ_{fi}, depends on the thermal resistance of the edge insulation, on whether the edge insulation is placed horizontally or vertically and on its width (if horizontal) or depth (if vertical). Low-density foundations, of thermal conductivity less than that of the soil, are treated as vertical edge insulation.

A3.5.4.1 Horizontal edge insulation

Values of Ψ_{fi} for floors with horizontal edge insulation only are given in Table A3.18. The wall thickness is taken as 0.3 m.

A3.5.4.2 Vertical edge insulation

Values of Ψ_{fi} for floors with vertical edge insulation only are given in Table A3.19. The wall thickness is taken as 0.3 m.

Table A3.18 Edge insulation factor, Ψ_{fi}, for horizontal edge insulation

Soil type	Width of horizontal edge (floor) insulation, W_i / m	Edge insulation factor, Ψ_{fi} / $W \cdot m^{-1} \cdot K^{-1}$, for stated additional thermal resistance value, $R_i{'}$ / $m^2 \cdot K \cdot W^{-1}$			
		0.5	1.0	1.5	2.0
Clay/silt	0.50	−0.13	−0.18	−0.21	−0.22
	1.00	−0.20	−0.27	−0.32	−0.34
	1.50	−0.23	−0.33	−0.39	−0.42
Sand/gravel	0.50	−0.17	−0.23	−0.25	−0.27
	1.00	−0.26	−0.35	−0.40	−0.43
	1.50	−0.31	−0.43	−0.50	−0.54
Homogeneous rock	0.50	−0.25	−0.32	−0.35	−0.37
	1.00	−0.41	−0.53	−0.59	−0.62
	1.50	−0.52	−0.68	−0.76	−0.81

Table A3.19 Edge insulation factor, Ψ_{fi}, for vertical edge insulation

Soil type	Depth of vertical edge (floor) insulation, D_i / m	Edge insulation factor, Ψ_{fi} / $W \cdot m^{-1} \cdot K^{-1}$, for stated additional thermal resistance value, $R_i{'}$ / $m^2 \cdot K \cdot W^{-1}$			
		0.5	1.0	1.5	2.0
Clay/silt	0.25	−0.13	−0.18	−0.21	−0.22
	0.50	−0.20	−0.27	−0.32	−0.34
	0.75	−0.23	−0.33	−0.39	−0.42
	1.00	−0.26	−0.37	−0.43	−0.48
Sand/gravel	0.25	−0.17	−0.23	−0.25	−0.27
	0.50	−0.26	−0.35	−0.40	−0.43
	0.75	−0.31	−0.43	−0.50	−0.54
	1.00	−0.35	−0.49	−0.57	−0.62
Homogeneous rock	0.25	−0.25	−0.32	−0.35	−0.37
	0.50	−0.41	−0.53	−0.59	−0.62
	0.75	−0.52	−0.68	−0.76	−0.81
	1.00	−0.59	−0.79	−0.89	−0.95

A3.5.5.1 Uninsulated suspended floors

Table A3.20 gives U-values for uninsulated suspended floors for the following values of the relevant parameters:

— thermal resistance of floor: $R_f = 0.2\ m^2 \cdot K \cdot W^{-1}$

— ventilation opening: $\alpha = 0.0015$ or 0.003 m^2·m^{-1}

— average wind velocity: $v_w = 3$ m·s^{-1}

— wind shielding factor (average exposure): $f_w = 0.05$

— uninsulated under floor walls: $U_u = 1.7$ W·m^{-2}·K^{-1}

— height of floor above external ground level: $h_f = 0.5$ m.

Table A3.20 may be used in most cases to obtain the U-value of a suspended floor. However, if the parameters of the actual design differ significantly from the above values, the U-value should be calculated using the equations given in Guide A section 3.5.5.

Table A3.20 U-values for uninsulated suspended floors

Ratio p_f/A_{fg} (/ m^{-1})	U-value (/ W·m^{-2}·K^{-1}) for stated soil type and ventilation opening, α (/ m^2·m^{-1})					
	Clay/silt		Sand/gravel		Homogeneous rock	
	0.0015	0.003	0.0015	0.003	0.0015	0.003
0.05	0.16	0.17	0.19	0.20	0.27	0.28
0.10	0.27	0.29	0.32	0.33	0.43	0.44
0.15	0.36	0.38	0.42	0.43	0.54	0.55
0.20	0.44	0.46	0.49	0.51	0.63	0.64
0.25	0.50	0.52	0.56	0.58	0.70	0.71
0.30	0.56	0.58	0.62	0.64	0.76	0.77
0.35	0.61	0.63	0.67	0.69	0.81	0.82
0.40	0.65	0.68	0.72	0.74	0.85	0.87
0.45	0.69	0.72	0.76	0.78	0.89	0.91
0.50	0.73	0.76	0.79	0.82	0.92	0.94
0.55	0.76	0.79	0.83	0.85	0.95	0.97
0.60	0.79	0.83	0.86	0.88	0.98	1.00
0.65	0.82	0.85	0.88	0.91	1.00	1.02
0.70	0.85	0.88	0.91	0.94	1.03	1.05
0.75	0.87	0.91	0.93	0.96	1.05	1.07
0.80	0.90	0.93	0.95	0.98	1.06	1.09
0.85	0.92	0.95	0.97	1.00	1.08	1.11
0.90	0.94	0.97	0.99	1.02	1.10	1.12
0.95	0.96	0.99	1.01	1.04	1.11	1.14
1.00	0.98	1.01	1.03	1.06	1.13	1.15

A3.5.5.2 *U-values of insulated suspended floors*

For floors having thermal resistances other than 0.2 m^2·K·W^{-1}, the U-value can be obtained from:

$$U_{fsi} = [(1 / U_{fs}) - 0.2 + R_f]^{-1} \qquad (3.31)$$

where U_{fsi} is the thermal transmittance of the insulated suspended floor (W·m^{-2}·K^{-1}), U_{fs} is the combined thermal transmittance of the uninsulated floor (obtained from Table A3.20) (W·m^{-2}·K^{-1}) and R_f is the thermal resistance of the floor excluding surface resistances (m^2·K·W^{-1}).

A3.6 Windows

A3.6.1 General

The thermal transmittance of windows is made up of three components:

— centre-pane U-value of the glazing

— frame or sash

— interaction between glazing and frame, include the effect of the glazing spacer bars in multiple glazing (see Guide A section 3.6.4).

These components are determined separately as shown in the following sections. The overall U-value of the window is given by:

$$U_w = \frac{\Sigma (A_g U_g) + \Sigma (A_{wf} U_{wf}) + \Sigma (p_{wf} \Psi_s)}{\Sigma A_g + \Sigma A_{wf}} \qquad (3.35)$$

where U_w is the thermal transmittance of the window (W·m^{-2}·K^{-1}), A_g is the projected area of the glazing (m^2), A_{wf} is the projected area of the window frame or sash (m^2), U_g is the thermal transmittance of glazing (W·m^{-2}·K^{-1}), U_{wf} is the thermal transmittance of frame or sash (W·m^{-2}·K^{-1}), p_{wf} is the length of inner perimeter of frame or sash (m) and Ψ_s is the linear thermal transmittance for the glazing/frame (W·m^{-1}·K^{-1}).

The dimensions defined are shown in Figure A3.15.

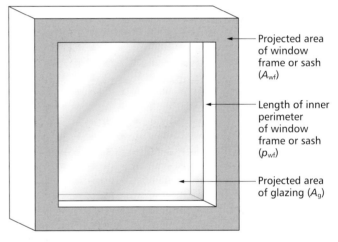

Projected area of window frame or sash (A_{wf})

Length of inner perimeter of window frame or sash (p_{wf})

Projected area of glazing (A_g)

Figure A3.15 Dimensions of window for calculation purposes

A3.6.2 Glazing (excluding frame or sash)

Tables A3.23 and A3.24 provide U-values for vertical, horizontal and near horizontal sloping glazing combinations for conventional and low-emissivity coated glasses, and for glazing units filled with argon gas. These values were calculated using the method given in BS EN 673.

Low emissivity coatings are highly transparent in the visual and solar parts of the spectrum but are reflective to radiation in the wavelength range 5 to 50 μm (i.e. far-infrared). To achieve a worthwhile improvement the emissivity must be less than 0.2 and accredited data must be obtained from the manufacturer to confirm that a particular product achieves this performance.

For the purposes of Building Regulations, 'vertical' includes glazing up to 20° from the vertical.

The tabulated values are based on a temperature difference of 15 K between the outer and inner glass surfaces and a mean temperature of 10 °C. The thermal conductivity of glass is approximately 1.0 W·m^{-1}·K^{-1}.

Table A3.23 *U*-values for vertical glazing

Type of glazing	Spacing / mm	*U*-value (/ W·m⁻²·K⁻¹) for stated exposure of panes†		
		Normal (0.13/0.04)	Sheltered (0.13/0.06)	Severe (0.13/0.02)
Single	—	5.75	5.16	6.49
Double	25	2.76	2.60	2.90
	20	2.74	2.60	2.90
	16	2.73	2.59	2.90
	12	2.85	2.70	3.02
	9	3.01	2.84	3.20
	6	3.28	3.08	3.51
Triple	25	1.72	1.67	1.78
	20	1.71	1.66	1.77
	16	1.78	1.72	1.84
	12	1.89	1.83	1.97
	9	2.04	1.96	2.12
	6	2.29	2.19	2.40
Coated double $\varepsilon = 0.2$	20	1.85	1.78	1.92
	16	1.82	1.76	1.89
	12	2.02	1.95	2.11
	9	2.29	2.19	2.39
	6	2.71	2.57	2.87
Coated double $\varepsilon = 0.1$	20	1.60	1.55	1.65
	16	1.57	1.53	1.63
	12	1.80	1.74	1.87
	9	2.10	2.01	2.19
	6	2.57	2.44	2.71
Coated double $\varepsilon = 0.05$	20	1.45	1.41	1.49
	16	1.42	1.38	1.46
	12	1.67	1.61	1.72
	9	1.98	1.91	2.06
	6	2.48	2.37	2.61
Coated double argon-filled $\varepsilon = 0.2$	20	1.65	1.60	1.71
	16	1.63	1.58	1.69
	12	1.76	1.70	1.82
	9	1.98	1.90	2.06
	6	2.35	2.24	2.46
Coated double argon-filled $\varepsilon = 0.1$	20	1.38	1.34	1.42
	16	1.36	1.32	1.40
	12	1.50	1.46	1.55
	9	1.75	1.69	1.81
	6	2.16	2.07	2.26
Coated double argon-filled $\varepsilon = 0.05$	20	1.21	1.18	1.24
	16	1.19	1.16	1.22
	12	1.34	1.31	1.38
	9	1.61	1.56	1.66
	6	2.05	1.97	2.14

† Internal and external surface resistances (m²·K·W⁻¹) respectively are given in parentheses

Table A3.24 *U*-values for horizontal and roof glazing

Type of glazing	Spacing / mm	*U*-value (/ W·m⁻²·K⁻¹) for stated exposure of panes†		
		Normal (0.13/0.04)	Sheltered (0.13/0.06)	Severe (0.13/0.02)
Single	—	6.94	6.10	8.07
Double	25	3.32	3.11	3.55
	20	3.34	3.23	3.58
	16	3.37	3.16	3.61
	12	3.41	3.19	3.66
	9	3.44	3.22	3.70
	6	3.63	3.39	3.92
Triple	25	2.06	1.98	2.15
	20	2.09	2.00	2.18
	16	2.11	2.02	2.20
	12	2.14	2.05	2.23
	9	2.17	2.08	2.27
	6	2.46	2.35	2.59
Coated double $\varepsilon = 0.2$	20	2.51	2.39	2.65
	16	2.56	2.43	2.69
	12	2.61	2.48	2.75
	9	2.67	2.53	2.82
	6	2.95	2.79	3.14
Coated double $\varepsilon = 0.1$	20	2.3	2.2	2.41
	16	2.35	2.24	2.46
	12	2.41	2.3	2.53
	9	2.47	2.35	2.6
	6	2.78	2.64	2.95
Coated double $\varepsilon = 0.05$	20	2.18	2.09	2.28
	16	2.22	2.13	2.33
	12	2.29	2.19	2.4
	9	2.35	2.25	2.47
	6	2.68	2.55	2.84
Coated double argon-filled $\varepsilon = 0.2$	20	2.20	2.10	2.30
	16	2.23	2.14	2.33
	12	2.28	2.18	2.39
	9	2.33	2.22	2.44
	6	2.52	2.40	2.66
Coated double argon-filled $\varepsilon = 0.1$	20	1.95	1.88	2.03
	16	2.00	1.91	2.07
	12	2.04	1.96	2.13
	9	2.09	2.02	2.19
	6	2.32	2.21	2.42
Coated double argon-filled $\varepsilon = 0.05$	20	1.80	1.74	1.87
	16	1.84	1.78	1.91
	12	1.90	1.83	1.97
	9	1.96	1.88	2.04
	6	2.19	2.10	2.29

† Internal and external surface resistances (m²·K·W⁻¹) respectively are given in parentheses

A3.6.3 Frames and sashes (excluding glazing)

The *U*-values given in Table A3.25 are based on data given in BS EN ISO 10077-1. Alternatively the *U*-value of window frames can be calculated by software conforming with BS EN ISO 10077-2.

A3.6.4 Spacer between panes (multiple glazing units)

In multiple glazing units, the thermal transmittance is increased due to interaction between the glazing and the frame, including the effect of the spacer bars. This allowed for by a linear thermal transmittance related to the perimeter length of the glazing.

The linear transmittance for particular glazing and frame combinations can be calculated by software conforming with BS EN ISO 10077-2. Table A3.26 gives default values that can be used in the absence of detailed information.

A3.6.5 Effect of blinds and curtains

A3.6.5.1 Internal blinds and curtains

Internal roller blinds or curtains provide additional insulation due to the air enclosed between the window and the blind. The degree of insulation depends strongly on the level of enclosure achieved. Roller blinds can achieve effective entrapment provided they run in side channels

Table A3.25 Thermal transmittances for various types of window frame and sash

Material	Description	U-value / $W \cdot m^{-2} \cdot K^{-1}$
Wood	Average thickness 30 mm	2.30
	Average thickness 40 mm	2.15
	Average thickness 50 mm	2.02
	Average thickness 60 mm	1.90
	Average thickness 70 mm	1.78
	Average thickness 80 mm	1.67
	Average thickness 90 mm	1.57
	Average thickness 100 mm	1.48
Plastic	Without metal reinforcement:	
	— polyurethane	2.8
	— PVC, two hollow chambers	2.2
	— PVC, three hollow chambers	2.0
Aluminium	Thermal barrier† with:	
	— 4 mm thermal break	4.4
	— 8 mm thermal break	3.9
	— 12 mm thermal break	3.5
	— 16 mm thermal break	3.2
	— 20 mm thermal break	3.0
Aluminium or steel	Without thermal barrier	6.9

† Thermal barrier must be continuous and totally isolate the interior side of the frame or frame sections from the exterior side

Table A3.26 Linear thermal transmittance, Ψ_s, for conventional sealed multiple glazing units

Frame type	Linear thermal transmittance (/ $W \cdot m^{-1} \cdot K^{-1}$) for stated glazing type	
	Double or triple glazing, uncoated glass, air or gas filled	Double or triple glazing, low-emissivity glass (1 pane coated for double glazing or 2 panes coated for triple glazing), air or gas filled
Wood or PVC	0.06	0.08
Metal with thermal break	0.08	0.11
Metal without thermal break	0.02	0.05

and are sealed at the top and bottom. With well-sealed blinds, further improvement can be achieved by using a material which has a low emissivity surface protected by layer transparent to infrared radiation. Values for the thermal resistance of internal blinds and curtains are given in Table A3.27.

A3.6.6 Indicative U-values for conceptual design

At the concept design stage, it is convenient to use indicative U-values for typical window configurations to enable an initial evaluation of the heat losses and energy consumption of the proposed building. Table A3.29 provides such values for these purposes.

A3.6.7 Indicative U-values for energy rating

Tables A3.30, A3.31 and A3.32 provide indicative U-values for windows, doors and rooflights for the purposes of energy rating.

Table A3.27 Thermal resistance of blinds and curtains

Description	Thermal resistance / $m^2 \cdot K \cdot W^{-1}$
Conventional roller blind, curtain or venetian blind (vertical slats)	0.05
Closely fitting curtain with pelmet	0.07
Roller blind:	
— bottom only sealed	0.09
— sides only sealed in channels	0.11
— sides and top sealed	0.15
— sides and bottom sealed	0.16
— fully sealed	0.18
Low emissivity roller blind, fully sealed	0.44

Table A3.29 Indicative U-values for windows for conceptual design

Type	Indicative U-value / $W \cdot m^{-2} \cdot K^{-1}$	
	Glazing only	Window (including frame or sash)
Single	5.7	5.0
Double	2.8	3.0
Double (low emissivity)	1.8	2.2
Triple	1.8	2.2

Table A3.30 Indicative U-values (/ $W \cdot m^{-2} \cdot K^{-1}$) for windows and rooflights with wood or PVC-U frames, and doors (Crown copyright, reproduced with the permission of the Controller of Her Majesty's Stationery Office and the Queen's Printer for Scotland)

Item	Indicative U-value (/ $W \cdot m^{-2} \cdot K^{-1}$) for stated gap between panes			Adjustment for rooflights in dwellings†
	6 mm	12 mm	≥16 mm	
Single glazing	4.8	—	—	+0.3
Double glazing (air filled):	3.1	2.8	2.7	+0.2
— low-E, $\varepsilon_n = 0.2$[1]	2.7	2.3	2.1	+0.2
— low-E, $\varepsilon_n = 0.15$	2.7	2.2	2.0	+0.2
— low-E, $\varepsilon_n = 0.1$	2.6	2.1	1.9	+0.2
— low-E, $\varepsilon_n = 0.05$	2.6	2.0	1.8	+0.2
Double glazing (argon filled[2]):	2.9	2.7	2.6	+0.2
— low-E, $\varepsilon_n = 0.2$	2.5	2.1	2.0	+0.2
— low-E, $\varepsilon_n = 0.15$	2.4	2.0	1.9	+0.2
— low-E, $\varepsilon_n = 0.1$	2.3	1.9	1.8	+0.2
— low-E, $\varepsilon_n = 0.05$	2.3	1.8	1.7	+0.2
Triple glazing:	2.4	2.1	2.0	+0.2
— low-E, $\varepsilon_n = 0.2$	2.1	1.7	1.6	+0.2
— low-E, $\varepsilon_n = 0.15$	2.0	1.7	1.5	+0.2
— low-E, $\varepsilon_n = 0.1$	2.0	1.6	1.5	+0.2
— low-E, $\varepsilon_n = 0.05$	1.9	1.5	1.4	+0.2
Triple glazing (argon filled[2]):	2.2	2.0	1.9	+0.2
— low-E, $\varepsilon_n = 0.2$	1.9	1.6	1.5	+0.2
— low-E, $\varepsilon_n = 0.15$	1.8	1.5	1.4	+0.2
— low-E, $\varepsilon_n = 0.1$	1.8	1.4	1.3	+0.2
— low-E, $\varepsilon_n = 0.05$	1.7	1.4	1.3	+0.2
Solid wooden door[3]	3.0	—	—	—

† No correction need be applied to rooflights in buildings other than dwellings

Notes: [1] The emissivities quoted are normal emissivities. (Corrected emissivity is used in the calculation of glazing U-values.) Uncoated glass is assumed to have a normal emissivity of 0.89. [2] The gas mixture is assumed to consist of 90% argon and 10% air. [3] For doors which are half-glazed the U-value of the door is the average of the appropriate window U-value and that of the non-glazed part of the door (e.g. 3.0 $W \cdot m^{-2} \cdot K^{-1}$ for a wooden door).

Table A3.31 Indicative U-values (/ $W \cdot m^{-2} \cdot K^{-1}$) for windows and fully-glazed doors with metal frames (4 mm thermal break) (Crown copyright, reproduced with the permission of the Controller of Her Majesty's Stationery Office and the Queen's Printer for Scotland)

Item	Indicative U-value (/ $W \cdot m^{-2} \cdot K^{-1}$) for stated gap between panes		
	6 mm	12 mm	16 mm or more
Single glazing	5.7	—	—
Double glazing (air filled):	3.7	3.4	3.3
— low-E, $\varepsilon_n = 0.2$[1]	3.3	2.8	2.6
— low-E, $\varepsilon_n = 0.15$	3.3	2.7	2.5
— low-E, $\varepsilon_n = 0.1$	3.2	2.6	2.4
— low-E, $\varepsilon_n = 0.05$	3.1	2.5	2.3
Double glazing (argon filled[2]):	3.5	3.3	3.2
— low-E, $\varepsilon_n = 0.2$	3.0	2.6	2.5
— low-E, $\varepsilon_n = 0.15$	3.0	2.5	2.4
— low-E, $\varepsilon_n = 0.1$	2.9	2.4	2.3
— low-E, $\varepsilon_n = 0.05$	2.8	2.3	2.1
Triple glazing:	2.9	2.6	2.5
— low-E, $\varepsilon_n = 0.2$)	2.6	2.1	2.0
— low-E, $\varepsilon_n = 0.15$)	2.5	2.1	2.0
— low-E, $\varepsilon_n = 0.1$)	2.5	2.0	1.9
— low-E, $\varepsilon_n = 0.05$)	2.4	1.9	1.8
Triple glazing (argon filled[2]):	2.8	2.5	2.4
— low-E, $\varepsilon_n = 0.2$	2.4	2.0	1.9
— low-E, $\varepsilon_n = 0.15$	2.3	1.9	1.8
— low-E, $\varepsilon_n = 0.1$	2.2	1.9	1.7
— low-E, $\varepsilon_n = 0.05$	2.2	1.8	1.7

[1] and [2]: see footnotes to Table A3.30

Table A3.32 Adjustments to U-values in Table A3.31 for frames with thermal breaks (Crown copyright, reproduced with the permission of the Controller of Her Majesty's Stationery Office and the Queen's Printer for Scotland)

Thermal break / mm	Adjustment to U-value (/ $W \cdot m^{-2} \cdot K^{-1}$)	
	Adjustment for thermal break	Additional adjustment for rooflights angled $< 70°$ to horizontal
0 (no break)	+0.3	+0.4
4	+0.0	+0.3
8	−0.1	+0.3
12	−0.2	+0.3
16	−0.2	+0.3
20	−0.3	+0.3
24	−0.3	+0.3
28	−0.3	+0.3
32	−0.4	+0.3
36	−0.4	+0.3

A3.8   Non-steady state thermal characteristics

A3.8.1   Admittance procedure

There are several methods available for assessing the non-steady state or dynamic performance of a structure. One of the simplest is the admittance procedure which is described in detail in Guide A chapter 5. The method of calculation of admittances and related parameters is defined in BS EN ISO 13786 and a summary is given in Guide A Appendix 3.A6.

A4   Ventilation and air infiltration

A4.2   Role of ventilation

A4.2.1   Background

Ventilation provides fresh air to occupants, and dilutes and removes concentrations of potentially harmful pollutants. It is also used to passively cool and distribute thermally conditioned air.

Energy losses from ventilation and general air exchange can account for more than half of the primary energy used in a building. These losses comprise space heating and refrigerative cooling losses as well as the electrical load associated with driving mechanical services.

A4.2.2   Minimum ventilation rates for air quality

The amount of ventilation required for air quality depends on:

— occupant density

— occupant activities

— pollutant emissions within a space.

BS EN 13779 provides basic definitions of air quality standards in occupied spaces and relates these to fresh air ventilation rates required for each occupant. These are summarised in Table 4.1.

Building Regulations Part F (2006) requires a minimum ventilation rate of 10 $L \cdot s^{-1}$ per person for most non-domestic applications. This fits between classes IDA2 and IDA3 in Table 4.1.

For guidance on ventilation techniques, see CIBSE Guide B.

Table A4.1 Ventilation and indoor air quality classification (BS EN 13779)

Classification	Indoor air quality standard	Ventilation range / ($L \cdot s^{-1}$/person)	Default value / ($L \cdot s^{-1}$/person)
IDA1	High	>15	20
IDA2	Medium	10–15	12.5
IDA3	Moderate	6–10	8
IDA4	Low	<6	5

A4.2.3   Ventilation rate and metabolic carbon dioxide

Carbon dioxide is emitted as part of the metabolic process and can be used as an estimate of the adequacy of ventilation. Guidelines related to CO_2 concentrations almost always refer to sedentary environments. It takes a finite period for CO_2 to reach a steady state level. Table A4.2 summarises CO_2 concentrations above the ambient outdoor concentration that reflect the air quality classifications of Table A4.1.

Table A4.2 Approximate maximum sedentary CO_2 concentrations associated with CEN indoor air quality standards (BS EN 13779)

Classification	Rise in indoor CO_2 concentration / ppm	Default value / ppm	Range in outdoor concentration / ppm	Total indoor value[*] / ppm
IDA1	<400	350	350–400	700–750
IDA2	400–600	500	350–400	850–900
IDA3	600–1000	800	350–400	1150–1200
IDA4	>1000	1200	350–400	1550–1600

[*] i.e. concentration rise plus outdoor value

A4.3 Ventilation techniques

Ventilation may be provided by natural, mechanical or mixed mode methods. .

A4.3.1 Natural ventilation

Natural ventilation is driven by the climatic forces of wind (wind effect) and temperature (stack effect). For this reason, natural ventilation is highly variable. Some basic calculation guidelines are given in section A4.7.3.

A4.3.2 Mechanical ventilation

Mechanical ventilation is applied by means of driving fans and a network of ducts. In large office buildings, mechanically supplied air is usually filtered and thermally conditioned by heating and cooling. Key types are:

(a)   supply-only ventilation

(b)   extract-only ventilation

(c)   balanced mechanical ventilation

A4.3.3 Mixed mode ventilation

Mixed mode ventilation utilises a combination of both natural and mechanical ventilation technology. The basic modes of operation are:

— *Supplementary*: mechanical ventilation is applied when natural driving forces are inadequate to meet ventilation need.

— *Complementary*: natural and mechanical ventilation work together to meet the ventilation needs of a building.

— *Alternate*: both natural and mechanical ventilation systems are provided; system use is dependent on current climate conditions and ventilation need.

A4.5 Outline of ventilation and air infiltration theory

A4.5.1 General

The rate of airflow through a building depends upon the areas and resistances of the various apertures (both intentionally provided and fortuitous) and the pressure difference between one end of the flow path and the other. This pressure difference may be due to:

— wind (wind-driven natural ventilation)

— differences in density of the air due to the indoor–outdoor temperature differences (commonly referred to as 'stack effect' or stack-driven ventilation)

— pressure differences created by mechanical ventilation fans

— a combination of the three above mechanisms.

These mechanisms are described in detail in Guide A section 4.5.

A4.6 Assessing natural ventilation and air infiltration rates

A4.6.1 Flow through openings

The magnitude of the airflow through small openings such as infiltration gaps and trickle ventilators is a function of the applied pressure difference across the opening and its length, cross-sectional area and internal geometry. This relationship is often described by the empirical power law:

$$q_v = C (\Delta p)^n \qquad (4.1)$$

where q_v is the volumetric flow rate through the opening ($m^3 \cdot s^{-1}$), C is the flow coefficient ($m^3 \cdot s^{-1} \cdot Pa^{-n}$), Δp is the pressure difference across the opening (Pa) and n is the flow exponent.

When considering infiltration through cracks, it is convenient to express the flow coefficient in terms of metre length of crack or opening. Equation 4.1 then becomes:

$$q_{vc} = l_c k_1 (\Delta p)^n \qquad (4.2)$$

where q_{vc} is the volumetric flow rate through the crack ($L \cdot s^{-1}$), l_c is the total length of crack or opening (m) and k_1 is the flow coefficient per unit length of opening ($L \cdot s^{-1} \cdot m^{-1} \cdot Pa^{-n}$). Note that, since k_1 is expressed in terms of $L \cdot s^{-1}$, the units for flow rate through the opening are $L \cdot s^{-1}$.

Note: air flow paths through mechanical systems may be treated in the same way as air flow path for natural ventilation and air infiltration openings, see section A4.6.2.

Tables A4.3 and A4.4 give typical values of flow coefficient (k_1) and exponent (n) for a range of door and window types when fully closed. However, these may not be the predominant leakage routes.

Table A4.3 Flow characteristics for doors (per unit length of joint)

Item	Flow coefficient per metre length of joint, k_1 / $L \cdot s^{-1} \cdot m^{-1} \cdot Pa^{-n}$, where $n = 0.6$			Size of sample
	Lower quartile	Median	Upper quartile	
External doors (weather stripped):				
— hinged	0.082	0.27	0.84	15
— sliding	—	—	—	0
— revolving (laboratory test)	1.0	1.5	2.0	4
External doors (non-weather stripped):				
— hinged	1.1	1.2	1.4	17
— sliding	—	0.20	—	1
Roller door per m² of surface (laboratory test)	3.3*	5.7*	10*	2*
Internal doors (non-weather stripped)	1.1	1.3	2.0	84
Loft hatches (non-weather stripped)	0.64	0.68	0.75	4

* Flow coefficient expressed in $L \cdot s^{-1} \cdot m^{-2} \cdot Pa^{-n}$

Table A4.4 Flow characteristics for windows (per unit length of joint)

Item	Flow coefficient per metre length of joint, k_1 / $L \cdot s^{-1} \cdot m^{-1} \cdot Pa^{-n}$, where $n = 0.6$			Size of sample
	Lower quartile	Median quartile	Upper	
Windows (weather stripped):				
— hinged	0.086	0.13	0.41	29
— sliding	0.079	0.15	0.21	19
Windows (non-weather stripped):				
— hinged	0.39	0.74	1.1	42
— sliding	0.18	0.23	0.37	36

A4.6.2 Representing flow through mechanical systems

The flow rate through the fan is a function of fan size, duct and component pressure losses (e.g. through filters, sound attenuators etc), diffuser and outlet characteristics, and the pressure developed in the space itself.

Provided that the correct fan is selected, small variations about the selected pressure drop can be represented by a constant flow rate to give a flow rate:

$$q_{vm} = \text{constant} \tag{4.4}$$

where q_{vm} is the volumetric flow rate for the mechanical ventilation system ($m^3 \cdot s^{-1}$).

This approximation enables flow through a mechanical system to be treated as an air flow path, as for natural ventilation and air infiltration openings.

A4.7 Estimation methods

A4.7.1 General

Guide A considers three methods for estimating air infiltration and natural ventilation: (1) empirical data, (2) tabular values, (3) standard formulae. For methods (1) and (2) see Guide A section 4.7.2. Method (3) is given in section A4.7.3, below.

A4.7.3 Method 3: Natural ventilation in simple building layouts

The assumption that ventilation openings can be represented by orifice flow equations enables estimates of ventilation rates using standard formulae for simple building layouts. These layouts and associated formulae are shown in Table A4.22 for a simple building with airflow through opposite sides and in Table A4.23 for a situation with openings in one wall only. Both wind-induced and temperature-induced ventilation are given.

The values of area A used in the formulae should be taken as the minimum cross-sectional area perpendicular to the direction of the airflow passing through the opening. Typical C_p values are given in Table A4.3.

The formulae given in Table A4.22 illustrate a number of general characteristics of natural ventilation, as follows:

— The effective area of a number of openings combined in parallel, across which the same pressure difference is applied, can be obtained by simple addition.

— The effective area of a number of openings combined in series (across which the same pressure difference is applied) can be obtained by adding the inverse squares of the individual areas and taking the inverse of the square root of the total (see Table A4.22(b)).

— When wind is the dominating mechanism the ventilation rate is proportional to wind speed and

Table A4.22 Standard formulae for estimating airflow rates for simple building layouts (openings on opposite sides)

Conditions	Schematic	Equations
(a) Wind only		$Q_w = C_d A_w v_r (\Delta C_p)^{0.5}$ $$\frac{1}{A_w^2} = \frac{1}{(A_1 + A_2)^2} + \frac{1}{(A_3 + A_4)^2}$$
(b) Temperature difference only		$Q_b = C_d A_b \left(\dfrac{2 \Delta \theta \, h_a g}{\bar{\theta} + 273} \right)^{0.5}$ $$\frac{1}{A_b^2} = \frac{1}{(A_1 + A_3)^2} + \frac{1}{(A_2 + A_4)^2}$$
(c) Wind and temperature difference together		$Q_t = Q_b$ for $(v_r / \sqrt{\Delta t}) < 0.26 (A_b/A_w)(h_a/\Delta C_p)^{0.5}$ $Q_t = Q_w$ for $(v_r / \sqrt{\Delta t}) > 0.26 (A_b/A_w)(h_a/\Delta C_p)^{0.5}$

to the square root of the difference in pressure coefficient. Thus, although ΔC_p may range between 0.1 and 1.0, this will result in a ratio of only about 1 to 3 in the predicted ventilation rates for the same wind speed

— When stack effect is the dominating mechanism the ventilation rate is proportional to the square root of both temperature difference and height between upper and lower openings. When wind and stack effect are of the same order of magnitude their interaction is complicated. However, for the simple case illustrated, the actual rate, to a first approximation, may be taken as equal to the larger of the rates for the two alternative approaches, considered separately. This is shown in Table A4.22(c).

Measurements have shown that, with normally sized windows, the magnitude of the resulting single-sided ventilation, while smaller than cross-ventilation with similar areas of opening under comparable conditions, can be large enough to contribute to natural cooling. Table A4.23 provides formulae that enable ventilation rates to be calculated for wind and stack effect. It is suggested that calculations be carried out using both formulae and the larger value taken. The formula for wind induced infiltration represents a minimum, which will be enhanced up to threefold for certain wind directions and windows with openings that tend to deflect inwards the impinging wind.

A5 Thermal response and plant sizing

A5.1 Introduction

Design is an iterative process that will normally be repeated at concept, detailed proposals (scheme) and final proposals (detail) design stages. While empirical rules of thumb may be appropriate at concept stage, later design stages will usually require better accuracy and quality, less uncertainty, a clear understanding of the sensitivity to assumptions and reduced risk.

The heating and cooling requirements are determined by:

— location of the building

— design internal and external temperatures

— design internal and external humidities

— thermal characteristics of the building

— ventilation rate

— type of system

— building usage patterns.

Table A4.23 Standard formulae for estimating airflow rates for simple building layouts (openings on one side only)

Conditions	Schematic	Equations
(a) Wind only		$Q = 0.025\,A\,V_r$
(b) Temperature difference only: two openings		$Q = C_d(A_1 + A_2)\left(\dfrac{\varepsilon\sqrt{2}}{(1+\varepsilon)(1+\varepsilon^2)^{0.5}}\right)\left(\dfrac{\Delta\theta\,h_a g}{\overline{\theta}+273}\right)^{0.5}$ where $\varepsilon = (A_1/A_2)$
(c) Temperature difference only: one openings		$Q = C_d(A/3)\left(\dfrac{\Delta\theta\,h_a g}{\overline{\theta}+273}\right)^{0.5}$ If opening light is present: $Q = C_d(A\,\mathcal{J}_\phi/3)\left(\dfrac{\Delta\theta\,h_a g}{\overline{\theta}+273}\right)^{0.5}$ where $\mathcal{J}_\phi$ is given by Figure 4.11

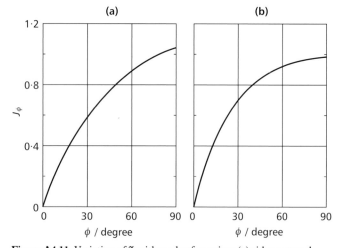

Figure A4.11 Variation of $\mathcal{J}_\phi$ with angle of opening; (a) side-mounted casement window, (b) centre-pivoted windows

A5.4 Selection of design parameters

Depending upon the building the parameters and data required to carry out the design are some, or all, of the following:

— location of the site

— internal design conditions (see Guide A chapter 1)

— appropriate overheating criteria (see Guide A chapter 1)

— external design conditions (see Guide A chapter 2 and CIBSE Guide J)

— infiltration and ventilation requirements (see Guide A chapter 4)

— internal gains and patterns of use (see Guide A chapter 6)

— building fabric properties (see Guide A chapter 3)

— building geometry.

A5.4.2 Overheating criteria

Where mechanical cooling is not provided, temperatures during hot periods of the year will usually exceed those deemed as comfortable for mechanically cooled spaces. While people will often accept these higher temperatures, it is necessary to make an assessment of what conditions will be like on hot days.

A5.4.3 External design conditions

Some or all of the following external design criteria are required in order to determine the plant capacity:

— winter dry and wet bulb temperatures

— summer dry and wet bulb temperatures

— solar irradiation

— longwave radiation loss

— sol-air temperatures

— wind speed and direction.

Summary data for the UK and elsewhere are given in Guide A chapter 2. More extensive data are contained in CIBSE Guide J.

Note: Climate change may require designers to 'future-proof' their designs. CIBSE Guide J provides some design data for future climates.

A5.4.3.1 Winter heating design criteria

External design dry bulb temperatures for the UK and sites worldwide are given in Guide A chapter 2. Where mechanical ventilation and/or air conditioning are used the fresh air plants should be sized using a lower temperature than that for the fabric heat loss calculation. This is because the air plant responds virtually instantaneously, whereas fabric storage has an averaging effect. The selection of a suitable design temperature will depend on the pattern of occupation for the building and the acceptable design risk.

A5.4.3.2 Summer design criteria

The maximum demand of an air conditioning system will depend on peak coincident zone loads. However, depending on the type of system, the peak external design dry and wet bulb temperatures will also have a significant influence on the installed plant capacity.

A5.4.4 Infiltration and ventilation

For systems employing mechanical ventilation minimum outside air quantities are given in Guide A chapter 1. Empirical values for air infiltration in naturally ventilated buildings in winter are given in Guide A chapter 4.

For the calculation of peak temperatures in summer where natural ventilation is to be used a maximum of 10 air changes per hour is not unreasonable, although this figure will depend upon the ventilation system, see Table 5.2. It is the responsibility of the designer to ensure that there is adequate provision for natural ventilation. Natural ventilation is considered in Guide A chapter 4 and CIBSE AM10: *Natural ventilation on non-domestic buildings*.

A5.4.5 Internal gains

These arise from the heat generated by the occupants, lighting and machines etc. used within the space. Depending upon the source sensible heat gains will be both convective and radiant in nature. Latent gains are mainly due to occupants; however there are some spaces such as swimming pools and kitchens where latent gains are more significant. In addition to being dependent upon the purpose of the building they may depend upon patterns of use. Diversity should therefore be considered, however this will need to be agreed with the client. Guide A chapter 6 provides information on the magnitude and nature of many sources of internal gain.

A5.6 Steady state models

The CIBSE recognises that different levels of detail may be required for different building types. A very simple approach will usually be sufficient where large temperature differences between surfaces are not anticipated, which is the case in most conventional buildings. The CIBSE Simple Model is described below; for more complex models refer to Guide A chapter 5.

A5.6.1 The approximate model

Prior to the publication of the 1999 edition of Guide A, the environmental temperature was used as the steady state design temperature for heating. In this model, the total heat loss is the sum of the fabric and ventilation losses, i.e:

$$\Phi_t = [\Sigma\,(A\,U) + C_v]\,(\theta_{ei} - \theta_{ao}) \tag{5.8}$$

where Φ_t is the total heat loss (W), $\Sigma\,(A\,U)$ is sum of the products of surface area and corresponding thermal transmittance over surfaces through which heat flow occurs (W·K^{-1}), C_v is the ventilation conductance (W·K^{-1}), θ_{ei} is the environmental temperature and θ_{ao} is the outside air temperature (°C).

The ventilation conductance is given by:

$$C_v = {}^1/_3\,N\,V \tag{5.9}$$

Where N is the number of room air changes for air entering the space at the outside air temperature (h^{-1}) and V is the room volume (m^3).

A5.6.2 CIBSE Simple Model

This model enables the designer to size emitters to achieve a specified operative temperature.

The total heat loss is the sum of the fabric and ventilation losses, i.e.:

$$\Phi_t = [F_{1cu}\,\Sigma\,(A\,U) + F_{2cu}\,C_v]\,(\theta_c - \theta_{ao}) \tag{5.10}$$

Table A5.2 Effective mean ventilation rates for openable windows

Location of openable windows	Usage of windows		Effective mean ventilation rate	
	Day	Night	Air changes per hour / h^{-1}	Ventilation loss / W·m^{-2}·K^{-1}
One side of building only	Closed	Closed	1	0.3
	Open	Closed	3	1.0
	Open	Open	10	3.3
More than one side of building	Closed	Closed	2	0.6
	Open	Closed	10	3.3
	Open	Open	30	10.0

where Φ_t is the total heat loss (W), F_{1cu} and F_{2cu} are factors related to characteristics of the heat source with respect to the operative temperature, $\Sigma(A\,U)$ is sum of the products of surface area and corresponding thermal transmittance over surfaces through which heat flow occurs (W·K^{-1}), C_v is the ventilation conductance (W·K^{-1}), θ_c is the operative temperature at centre of room (°C) and θ_{ao} is the outside air temperature (°C).

Where the fabric loss term contains heat loss through internal partitions, a modified U-value should be used:

$$U' = \frac{U(\theta_c - \theta_c{}')}{(\theta_c - \theta_{ao})} \tag{5.11}$$

where U' is the thermal transmittance modified for heat loss through internal partitions (W·m^{-2}·K^{-1}), and $\theta_c{}'$ is the operative temperature on the opposite side of partition through which heat flow occurs (°C).

F_{1cu} and F_{2cu} are calculated as follows (see Guide A Appendix 5.A5, equations 5.174 and 5.175):

$$F_{1cu} = \frac{3(C_v + 6\Sigma A)}{\Sigma(A\,U) + 18\,\Sigma A + 1.5\,R\,[3\,C_v - \Sigma(A\,U)]} \tag{5.12}$$

$$F_{2cu} = \frac{\Sigma(A\,U) + 18\,\Sigma A}{\Sigma(A\,U) + 18\,\Sigma A + 1.5\,R\,[3\,C_v - \Sigma(A\,U)]} \tag{5.13}$$

where R is the radiant fraction of the heat source, A is the total area through which heat flow occurs (m^2) and $\Sigma(A\,U)$ is the sum of the products of surface area and corresponding thermal transmittance over surfaces through which heat flow occurs (W·m^{-2}·K^{-1}). Typical values for R are given in Table A5.4.

However, in many cases the values of F_{1cu} and F_{2cu} are very close to unity, and the calculations can be done assuming this with little loss of accuracy. In this case equation 5.10 reduces to:

$$\Phi_t = [\Sigma(A\,U) + C_v]\,(\theta_c - \theta_{ao}) \tag{5.14}$$

Note this is the same as equation 5.8 except that θ_c is used for internal temperature instead of θ_{ei}

Table A5.4 Typical proportions of radiant (R) and convective heat from heat emitters

Emitter type	Proportion of emitted radiation	
	Convective	Radiative (R)
Forced warm air heaters	1.0	0
Natural convectors and convector radiators	0.9	0.1
Multi column radiators	0.8	0.2
Double and treble panel radiators, double column radiators	0.7	0.3
Single column radiators, floor warming systems, block storage heaters	0.5	0.5
Vertical and ceiling panel heaters	0.33	0.67
High temperature radiant systems	0.1	0.9

The corresponding air and mean surface temperatures are given by:

$$\theta_{ai} = \frac{\Phi_t(1 - 1.5\,R) + C_v\,\theta_{ao} + 6\,\Sigma A\,\theta_c}{C_v + 6\,\Sigma A} \tag{5.15}$$

$$\theta_m = 2\,\theta_c - \theta_{ai} \tag{5.16}$$

where θ_{ai} is the inside air temperature (°C), θ_m is the mean surface temperature (°C), θ_{ao} is the outside air temperature (°C) and θ_c is the operative temperature at the centre of the space (°C).

Note that the constants contained in the above equations assume standard heat transfer coefficients and emissivity values, i.e. $h_c = 3$ W·m^{-2}·K^{-1}, $h_r = 5.7$ W·m^{-2}·K^{-1}, $\varepsilon = 0.9$.

A5.7 Dynamic models

Dynamic model are considered in Guide A section 5.7.

A5.10 Application of CIBSE calculation methods

A5.10.1 Building/room dimensions

It is recommended that measurements be taken between internal wall surfaces (see Guide A section 3.3.2). Deviation from one-dimensional heat flow may be taken into account by modifying the thermal conductivity value for the wall. Consistency of surface dimensions is of particular importance when using software packages.

For manual calculation unventilated voids can be represented by their effect on the thermal properties of the surface. For manual cooling load calculations where the void is used for supply or extract, unless heat can flow from the void to an adjacent space, the effect of the void may be ignored. If the spaces above and below have similar characteristics to that under consideration heat loss will be compensated by heat gain and again the effect of the void may be ignored.

While the void may not have a significant effect upon the space-cooling load the same may not be true for space temperatures. For example, heat pick-up in a floor void will increase the temperature of any air flowing through the void. Thus in the case of a floor supply system where perhaps air is supplied to the void a few degrees below the desired room temperature any increase in supply temperature will reduce the available cooling capacity.

A5.10.2 Safety margins

Calculation of heating and cooling capacities in Guide A do not incorporate safety margins except where specifically stated and it is incumbent upon the designer to assess the plant margin required.

A5.10.3 Heating system design

The following calculation sequence is recommended:

— determine room heat emitter sizes

— apply corrections for local effects for example screening of emitters by furnishings

— apply corrections for intermittent operation

— assess heat losses from the distribution system, where appropriate

— assess diversity factor for central plant, where appropriate

— select central plant.

A5.10.3.2   Local effects

The size of the emitter will be affected by its position within the space and the characteristics of the space. Four important effects are:

— back losses from radiators

— stratification

— presence of furniture

— direct radiation incident on occupants.

Stratification

For heat loss calculations a uniform temperature is assumed throughout the height of the heated space. Some heating systems cause vertical temperature gradients across the space, which can lead to increased heat losses, particularly through the roof, see Figure A5.6.

Temperature gradients also depend on the height of the space. Some allowance can be made for the increase in fabric losses using Table A5.15, which provides percentage increases in fabric loss for various systems and for heated spaces of various heights.

A5.10.4   Cooling system design

The recommended calculation sequence is as follows:

— assess risk of overheating

— determine room cooling load

— apply corrections for intermittent plant operation, if appropriate

Table A5.15 Allowances for height of heated space

Type of heating system	Percentage increase in fabric loss for heated space of stated height / %		
	5 m	5–10 m	>10 m
Mainly radiant:			
— warm floor	0	0	0
— warm ceiling	0	0–5	—†
— medium and high temperature downward radiation from high level	0	0	0–5
Mainly convective:			
— natural warm air convection	0	0–5	—†
— forced warm air; cross flow at low level	0–5	5–15	15–30
— forced warm air; downward from high level	0–5	5–10	15–20
— medium and high temperature cross radiation from intermediate level	0	0–5	5–10

† System not appropriate to this application

Note: most conventional 'radiators' may be regarded as mainly convective

— apply corrections for fluctuations in control temperature, if appropriate

— assess the diversity factor for the central plant, if appropriate

— assess the heat gains/losses to the distribution system, if appropriate.

A5.10.4.1   Assessment of overheating risk

This should be carried out to determine if cooling is required. The method of assessment of overheating risk will differ according to the model chosen. If a transient model has been chosen then a period of hot days should be analysed. The exact overheating criteria and appropriate weather data must be agreed with the client.

Where the criterion is the number of hours of overheating, i.e. the hours for which a specified temperature will be exceeded, that prediction is very sensitive to the method of assessment and the climatic data used. For the UK, CIBSE recommends that the appropriate CIBSE Design Summer Year (DSY) be used.

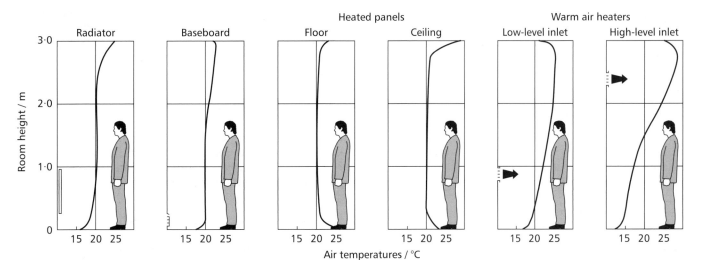

Figure A5.6 Vertical air temperature gradients

If it is found that overheating is likely to occur an assessment should be made to establish whether it could be reduced to an acceptable level by changes to the building fabric, increasing the natural ventilation, or by other means. Further information is given in Guide A section 5.10.4.1.

A5.11   Solar cooling load tables

Tables A5.19 and A5.20 provide solar cooling loads for SE England (Bracknell, 51° 33′N). Guide A section 5.11 provides similar tables for NW England (Manchester Aughton: 53° 33′N) and lowland Scotland (Edinburgh

Mylnefield: 56° 00′N). Table A5.19 is for buildings without shading and Table A5.20 is for buildings with intermittent shading.

The tabulated values apply to 'lightweight' buildings (i.e. those with a fast response to solar radiation) with single clear glass and assume that control of the cooling system will be based on the operative temperature. Multiplying factors are given at the foot of each table to adjust the tabulated cooling loads for application to buildings having a slow response to solar radiation and for other types of glazing.

Table A5.19 Solar cooling loads for fast-response building with single clear glazing: SE England; unshaded

Date	Orientation	Solar cooling load at stated sun time / W·m⁻²											Orientation
		07:30	08:30	09:30	10:30	11:30	12:30	13:30	14:30	15:30	16:30	17:30	
Jan 29	N	6	12	20	29	36	40	40	37	29	19	11	N
	NE	9	29	26	32	37	41	41	38	29	20	12	NE
	E	28	103	201	229	171	77	61	54	45	35	28	E
	SE	61	148	292	408	452	406	316	193	96	69	60	SE
	S	77	128	233	366	476	514	507	422	299	190	111	S
	SW	51	57	70	109	218	327	404	402	328	228	117	SW
	W	20	26	34	43	50	63	86	167	191	157	78	W
	NW	7	13	20	30	37	41	41	38	33	26	27	NW
	Horiz.	29	43	76	133	182	206	203	168	115	67	40	Horiz.
Feb 26	N	16	24	36	49	57	62	60	55	46	34	22	E
	NE	49	78	60	58	60	65	63	59	49	37	25	NE
	E	100	203	277	281	211	107	90	79	70	57	45	E
	SE	126	236	361	446	472	427	325	203	106	89	75	SE
	S	110	163	269	388	484	533	522	473	389	267	155	S
	SW	74	83	99	127	229	350	434	476	468	380	241	SW
	W	45	53	65	78	86	101	125	230	305	298	209	W
	NW	22	30	42	55	63	68	69	86	62	68	83	NW
	Horiz.	61	93	155	226	282	313	306	274	221	150	86	Horiz.
Mar 29	N	38	50	64	74	83	86	86	81	72	60	47	N
	NE	160	181	135	83	97	98	98	93	84	72	58	NE
	E	252	355	400	361	261	147	133	120	111	99	84	E
	SE	231	353	456	498	483	426	319	196	142	121	105	SE
	S	109	176	283	384	457	505	497	454	377	270	161	S
	SW	104	118	135	162	224	347	443	501	514	467	358	SW
	W	87	101	115	126	135	150	175	293	389	420	370	W
	NW	55	69	83	93	102	105	106	104	97	154	193	NW
	Horiz.	134	206	292	365	417	449	443	413	358	282	195	Horiz.
Apr 28	N	70	87	95	103	110	115	116	110	103	93	86	N
	NE	322	308	236	143	146	143	143	137	131	120	106	NE
	E	439	501	510	430	314	192	179	167	160	149	136	E
	SE	331	433	511	515	487	413	301	186	169	149	135	SE
	S	115	157	255	346	418	457	455	409	339	236	142	S
	SW	133	149	162	184	212	330	437	503	535	505	434	SW
	W	138	154	167	176	184	199	226	351	465	518	513	W
	NW	104	120	133	142	149	154	155	159	167	258	325	NW
	Horiz.	251	342	437	499	548	572	570	540	496	417	329	Horiz.
May 29	N	118	121	126	131	137	140	139	135	130	123	120	N
	NE	382	362	290	190	174	166	165	161	155	146	134	NE
	E	475	519	518	450	329	208	194	184	179	169	157	E
	SE	321	408	471	485	448	367	258	167	166	152	140	SE
	S	110	129	201	289	355	388	384	345	274	182	116	S
	SW	142	156	168	183	193	290	393	465	497	477	420	SW
	W	170	184	196	204	210	223	247	371	484	544	554	W
	NW	142	156	168	176	182	185	185	197	221	321	394	NW
	Horiz.	326	417	507	578	615	625	621	605	564	492	407	Horiz.
Jun 21	N	144	139	142	147	151	154	154	151	147	144	143	N
	NE	440	413	320	211	190	180	181	178	173	165	154	NE
	E	533	579	550	469	343	220	207	199	195	186	176	E
	SE	345	437	482	487	446	363	253	168	171	159	148	SE
	S	111	123	191	276	342	376	374	331	261	174	116	S
	SW	147	159	170	182	190	282	389	460	492	476	424	SW
	W	185	197	207	215	220	232	257	382	497	561	578	W
	NW	160	172	182	190	195	198	199	214	244	347	424	NW
	Horiz.	365	463	545	609	642	650	648	629	590	521	439	Horiz.

Table continues

Table A5.19 Solar cooling loads for fast-response building with single clear glazing: SE England; unshaded — *continued*

Date	Orien-tation	Solar cooling load at stated sun time / W·m⁻²											Orien-tation
		07:30	08:30	09:30	10:30	11:30	12:30	13:30	14:30	15:30	16:30	17:30	
Jul 4	N	126	126	130	136	142	146	146	141	136	130	127	N
	NE	394	372	294	196	179	171	171	166	161	152	139	NE
	E	480	525	509	437	323	210	196	187	182	172	160	E
	SE	314	400	450	458	422	346	244	162	162	149	136	SE
	S	102	118	184	265	328	359	360	320	253	168	108	S
	SW	135	149	160	174	184	272	372	438	467	453	401	SW
	W	168	182	192	202	209	221	245	360	467	529	542	W
	NW	144	157	168	177	183	187	188	200	226	322	394	NW
	Horiz.	329	420	503	565	599	606	608	590	551	487	407	Horiz.
Aug 4	N	81	92	99	107	113	117	117	115	106	97	91	N
	NE	316	314	244	153	148	143	144	141	132	123	109	NE
	E	414	486	487	420	309	189	176	167	159	149	135	E
	SE	302	406	471	484	459	378	270	173	160	144	130	SE
	S	107	137	223	311	382	410	405	367	298	203	122	S
	SW	125	139	152	170	189	294	393	460	490	452	372	SW
	W	134	148	161	170	176	189	215	334	440	480	454	W
	NW	105	120	132	141	147	150	152	161	171	257	303	NW
	Horiz.	261	354	442	509	557	567	560	539	498	417	325	Horiz.
Sep 4	N	43	55	65	78	86	88	87	82	74	64	54	N
	NE	241	244	167	97	109	107	106	101	93	83	70	NE
	E	365	462	465	394	277	159	144	132	124	114	101	E
	SE	304	433	508	521	482	410	310	189	147	129	116	SE
	S	106	175	283	379	439	470	478	439	362	257	151	S
	SW	110	124	138	165	215	329	436	502	520	481	375	SW
	W	99	112	124	137	146	158	183	306	408	450	404	W
	NW	65	78	91	103	111	113	113	112	109	181	225	NW
	Horiz.	171	258	345	413	453	471	477	451	398	321	230	Horiz.
Oct 4	N	19	30	42	52	59	64	64	61	53	40	28	N
	NE	91	132	87	66	67	71	70	68	59	47	35	NE
	E	172	324	381	351	236	119	103	94	86	73	61	E
	SE	183	348	472	535	504	415	315	200	115	104	89	SE
	S	120	194	315	435	499	507	499	460	383	266	165	S
	SW	79	90	105	124	222	332	419	470	473	395	285	SW
	W	54	64	76	86	94	109	134	243	324	325	266	W
	NW	28	38	50	61	68	73	73	72	74	90	117	NW
	Horiz.	82	136	216	293	337	347	342	316	264	188	120	Horiz.
Nov 4	N	7	13	22	32	38	42	43	39	31	21	13	N
	NE	12	43	34	37	40	44	44	41	33	23	14	NE
	E	37	153	279	288	196	85	70	61	53	43	35	E
	SE	73	203	391	501	507	447	328	204	105	81	70	SE
	S	89	158	295	439	527	566	527	457	352	235	132	S
	SW	58	64	79	117	233	356	421	438	395	298	151	SW
	W	25	31	40	50	56	69	95	187	235	214	110	W
	NW	8	14	23	33	39	44	44	41	37	35	37	NW
	Horiz.	36	55	105	173	223	247	234	200	147	90	50	Horiz.
Dec 4	N	4	5	12	21	28	32	32	27	20	11	4	N
	NE	5	6	23	23	28	32	32	27	20	11	5	NE
	E	17	26	139	209	156	63	48	39	32	23	17	E
	SE	50	62	219	395	448	403	306	191	92	57	50	SE
	S	70	79	190	362	478	518	495	429	314	159	70	S
	SW	48	49	62	109	221	329	392	405	342	179	48	SW
	W	16	16	24	32	40	50	73	154	185	112	16	W
	NW	5	5	13	21	28	32	32	27	23	22	5	NW
	Horiz.	20	22	45	96	143	164	158	129	84	39	20	Horiz.

Glazing configuration (inside to outside)	G-value	Correction factor for stated building response		Glazing configuration (inside to outside)	G-value	Correction factor for stated building response	
		Fast	Slow			Fast	Slow
Clear	0.84	1.00	0.88	Low-E/clear	0.66	0.79	0.68
Absorbing	0.62	0.80	0.69	Low-E/absorbing	0.46	0.59	0.50
Clear/clear	0.72	0.83	0.72	Low-E/clear/clear	0.60	0.69	0.59
Clear/reflecting	0.41	0.50	0.43	Low-E/clear/absorbing	0.40	0.49	0.42
Clear/absorbing	0.49	0.60	0.52				
Clear/clear/clear	0.64	0.71	0.60				
Clear/clear/reflecting	0.35	0.43	0.36				
Clear/clear/absorbing	0.42	0.50	0.42				
Air node correction factor		0.86	0.83				

Table A5.20 Solar cooling loads for fast-response building with single clear glazing: SE England; intermittent shading

Date	Orien-tation	Solar cooling load at stated sun time / W·m^{-2}											Orien-tation
		07:30	08:30	09:30	10:30	11:30	12:30	13:30	14:30	15:30	16:30	17:30	
Jan 29	N	6	11	18	26	33	37	37	35	27	18	11	N
	NE	7	27	24	30	34	38	38	36	28	19	12	NE
	E	11	164	149	131	41	62	47	40	33	24	16	E
	SE	22	210	238	287	276	225	74	155	62	36	27	SE
	S	29	71	305	281	324	331	291	214	74	142	67	S
	SW	18	22	31	140	183	245	263	228	165	54	83	SW
	W	16	21	28	36	43	52	67	234	50	148	74	W
	NW	7	11	18	27	34	38	38	36	31	24	27	NW
	Horiz.	20	31	60	113	248	142	55	153	104	59	32	Horiz.
Feb 26	N	15	22	33	45	52	57	56	52	44	33	21	N
	NE	42	72	56	53	55	60	59	55	47	35	24	NE
	E	73	287	191	161	55	87	71	61	53	42	31	E
	SE	77	321	271	304	291	234	80	162	68	53	39	SE
	S	48	180	210	283	328	335	310	261	186	67	98	S
	SW	33	41	54	71	301	262	301	308	267	181	64	SW
	W	25	33	43	55	63	74	181	189	204	161	56	W
	NW	20	28	39	51	58	63	62	82	55	61	79	NW
	Horiz.	34	60	117	297	200	204	188	157	59	122	61	Horiz.
Mar 29	N	34	46	58	68	76	79	80	76	68	57	45	N
	NE	144	167	129	76	90	90	91	86	78	68	55	NE
	E	216	262	256	202	77	118	105	93	85	74	61	E
	SE	297	271	315	318	290	228	83	147	94	75	60	SE
	S	47	201	214	271	311	318	297	253	187	68	106	S
	SW	58	71	85	105	282	267	316	337	319	258	99	SW
	W	45	58	71	81	89	100	222	230	268	252	188	W
	NW	51	64	77	87	95	98	99	98	83	138	180	NW
	Horiz.	76	240	211	252	280	285	270	238	191	74	142	Horiz.
Apr 28	N	64	80	87	95	101	106	107	102	96	86	80	N
	NE	223	189	85	121	124	121	122	117	111	101	90	NE
	E	325	347	312	242	104	150	139	127	121	111	99	E
	SE	261	322	341	331	292	224	93	138	122	103	91	SE
	S	59	177	194	248	284	293	271	230	166	62	92	S
	SW	68	83	95	112	238	249	304	335	329	291	216	SW
	W	74	89	101	109	115	127	258	269	320	332	285	W
	NW	72	87	99	107	114	118	119	122	209	206	214	NW
	Horiz.	264	244	294	332	355	362	347	321	274	215	94	Horiz.
May 29	N	109	111	116	121	126	129	129	125	120	114	109N	
	NE	263	227	107	163	148	140	139	135	130	122	111	NE
	E	344	355	325	255	116	163	150	140	136	127	116	E
	SE	251	301	323	310	265	197	88	122	122	109	98	SE
	S	70	80	253	217	248	254	236	195	74	143	79	S
	SW	80	93	104	117	205	222	280	312	310	280	223	SW
	W	96	109	120	128	133	141	269	280	334	354	330	W
	NW	92	105	116	123	129	132	132	139	260	243	266	NW
	Horiz.	349	293	347	382	396	398	390	368	324	269	124	Horiz.
Jun 21	N	134	128	131	135	140	142	143	140	136	133	129	N
	NE	303	255	124	182	161	152	152	150	146	138	129	NE
	E	388	385	343	268	128	173	160	153	149	142	132	E
	SE	272	314	328	311	264	195	90	123	127	116	107	SE
	S	74	77	239	209	240	248	229	187	73	137	79	S
	SW	85	97	106	117	198	220	277	309	309	283	229	SW
	W	107	119	128	136	140	148	276	289	345	369	350	W
	NW	106	117	127	134	139	141	142	152	284	264	291	NW
	Horiz.	251	311	360	391	404	406	397	375	334	280	218	Horiz.
Jul 4	N	117	116	120	125	131	135	135	131	126	121	115	N
	NE	272	233	113	169	153	144	145	140	136	128	116	NE
	E	350	354	319	251	119	165	153	144	139	131	120	E
	SE	250	294	310	296	253	107	204	122	123	111	100	SE
	S	66	74	231	201	230	238	220	181	69	132	73	S
	SW	80	92	102	115	114	328	267	296	297	271	219	SW
	W	96	109	119	127	133	142	265	271	325	346	327	W
	NW	94	107	117	125	131	135	135	142	265	245	269	NW
	Horiz.	355	294	342	373	385	389	382	360	321	269	126	Horiz.
Aug 4	N	74	85	91	99	104	108	108	106	99	91	84	N
	NE	225	193	88	130	126	121	122	120	112	104	91	NE
	E	314	332	303	238	104	148	135	127	120	111	99	E
	SE	244	298	320	313	270	203	86	127	116	101	88	SE
	S	64	84	281	233	262	267	249	210	79	160	83	S
	SW	67	81	92	108	212	224	278	309	299	253	187	SW
	W	75	88	99	108	113	122	248	257^{-2}	300	298	254	W
	NW	75	88	100	108	114	117	118	125	216	197	201	NW
	Horiz.	278	250	301	340	356	357	346	323	276	214	96	Horiz.

Table continues

Table A5.20 Solar cooling loads for fast-response building with single clear glazing: SE England; intermittent shading — *continued*

Date	Orien-tation	Solar cooling load at stated sun time / W·m⁻²											Orien-tation
		07:30	08:30	09:30	10:30	11:30	12:30	13:30	14:30	15:30	16:30	17:30	
Sep 4	N	39	51	60	71	79	81	81	76	69	60	51	N
	NE	180	77	158	87	100	97	97	93	86	77	66	NE
	E	294	318	288	219	88	127	113	102	95	86	75	E
	SE	252	317	341	326	285	224	88	140	101	83	71	SE
	S	46	203	213	263	291	303	288	244	179	65	99	S
	SW	51	63	75	96	250	248	304	328	315	257	180	SW
	W	52	64	75	87	95	103	226	240	284	272	220	W
	NW	45	57	68	80	88	90	90	89	77	236	148	NW
	Horiz.	105	305	244	278	296	305	295	264	217	87	171	Horiz.
Oct 4	N	18	27	38	47	54	59	59	57	50	38	27	N
	NE	78	122	82	60	61	65	65	63	56	44	33	NE
	E	261	240	242	183	60	90	75	67	60	48	37	E
	SE	248	273	333	334	286	221	76	151	67	57	44	SE
	S	55	227	244	302	319	318	299	256	184	67	107	S
	SW	38	47	60	68	285	251	295	310	274	207	75	SW
	W	32	41	52	62	68	79	190	201	220	194	70	W
	NW	26	35	46	56	63	68	68	67	66	80	111	NW
	Horiz.	44	92	279	209	223	224	211	182	68	150	87	Horiz.
Nov 4	N	6	12	20	29	35	39	40	37	30	21	13	N
	NE	8	40	32	34	36	40	41	38	31	22	14	NE
	E	14	241	194	155	48	67	53	45	38	28	20	E
	SE	25	296	302	330	306	238	78	160	65	42	32	SE
	S	27	183	238	312	352	342	302	238	161	58	76	S
	SW	20	26	35	147	198	257	281	265	212	70	114	SW
	W	12	18	26	35	41	49	147	149	152	51	98	W
	NW	8	13	21	30	36	40	41	38	34	31	37	NW
	Horiz.	22	37	82	238	163	163	61	178	129	76	37	Horiz.
Dec 4	N	4	4	11	19	25	29	30	25	19	11	4	N
	NE	5	5	22	21	26	29	30	25	19	11	5	NE
	E	10	10	211	122	38	53	39	30	24	16	10	E
	SE	16	92	213	279	271	217	142	44	57	23	16	SE
	S	24	24	262	279	325	324	290	223	74	114	24	S
	SW	18	18	26	145	187	241	263	240	78	149	18	SW
	W	12	12	18	26	33	40	55	222	46	108	12	W
	NW	5	5	11	19	26	29	30	25	21	22	5	NW
	Horiz.	20	20	39	86	131	153	149	123	82	39	20	Horiz.

Glazing configuration (inside to outside)	G-value	Correction factor for stated building response		Glazing configuration (inside to outside)	G-value	Correction factor for stated building response	
		Fast	Slow			Fast	Slow
Clear/blind	0.20	0.73	0.82	Low-E/clear/clear/blind	0.13	0.46	0.51
Absorbing/blind	0.17	0.58	0.62	Low-E/clear/blind/clear	0.23	0.55	0.57
				Low-E/clear/blind/absorbing	0.18	0.42	0.44
Clear/clear/blind	0.16	0.57	0.62	Low-E/clear/absorbing/blind	0.10	0.36	0.38
Clear/blind/clear	0.30	0.70	0.73				
Clear/blind/reflecting	0.21	0.46	0.47	Blind/clear	0.48	1.00	1.03
Clear/blind/absorbing	0.24	0.54	0.56	Blind/absorbing	0.40	0.81	0.83
Clear/reflecting/blind	0.11	0.35	0.38	Blind/clear/clear	0.49	0.95	0.95
Clear/absorbing/blind	0.13	0.41	0.45	Blind/clear/reflecting	0.31	0.61	0.61
Clear/clear/clear/blind	0.13	0.47	0.52	Blind/clear/absorbing	0.35	0.71	0.71
Clear/clear/blind/clear	0.24	0.56	0.58	Blind/low-E/clear	0.46	0.92	0.92
Clear/clear/blind/reflecting	0.16	0.37	0.38	Blind/low-E/absorbing	0.32	0.67	0.68
Clear/clear/blind/absorbing	0.19	0.42	0.43	Blind/clear/clear/clear	0.47	0.87	0.86
Clear/clear/reflecting/blind	0.09	0.29	0.32	Blind/clear/clear/reflecting	0.28	0.55	0.54
Clear/clear/absorbing/blind	0.10	0.34	0.37	Blind/clear/clear/absorbing	0.32	0.62	0.62
Low-E/clear/blind	0.15	0.54	0.58	Blind/low-E/clear/clear	0.45	0.85	0.84
Low-E/absorbing/blind	0.12	0.40	0.44	Blind/low-E/clear/absorbing	0.30	0.60	0.60

Air node correction factor:		
— internal blind	0.91	0.88
— mid-pane blind	0.87	0.83
— external blind	0.88	0.85

A6   Internal heat gains

A6.1   Introduction

Internal heat gain is the sensible and latent heat emitted within an internal space by:

—   bodies (human and animal)

—   lighting

—   computers and office equipment

—   electric motors

—   cooking appliances and other domestic equipment.

Designers can choose to estimate either the rate of internal heat gain, where sufficient is known about the use of the building, or use 'benchmark' values typical for the building.

A6.2   Benchmark values for internal heat gains

Benchmark values for internal heat gains are based on either surveys of measured internal heat gains from a number of buildings of particular types and usage, or empirical values found appropriate from experience and considered good practice in the industry.

A6.2.1   Office buildings

Figure A6.1, based on surveys of 30 air conditioned office buildings in the UK, shows that total internal heat gains are proportional to occupant density. The occupant densities in the surveys ranged from 4 to 24 m^2 per person.

Table A6.1 gives benchmark values for total internal heat gains for typical offices at various occupant densities.

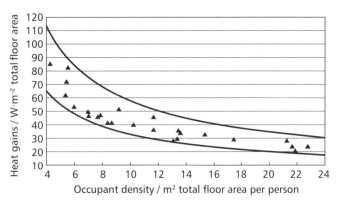

Figure A6.1 Variation of calculated total heat gains with occupation density

A6.2.2   Other building types

Table A6.2 provides typical internal heat gains for some common buildings and uses.

A6.3   Occupants

Table A6.3 provides representative heat emissions (sensible and latent) from an average adult male in different states of activity. The figures for a mixture of males and females assume typical percentages of men, women and children for the stated building type. A method for estimating the heat gains from animals is given in Guide A Appendix 6.A1.

Between 20 and 60% of the sensible heat emission, can be radiant depending on type of clothing, activity, mean radiant temperature and air velocity. Indicative values for high and low rates of air movement are shown in two columns on the right hand side of the table.

A6.4   Lighting

A6.4.1   General

All the electrical energy used by a lamp is ultimately released as heat. The energy is emitted by means of conduction, convection or radiation. When the light is switched on the luminaire itself absorbs some of the heat emitted by the lamp. Some of this heat may then be transmitted to the building structure, depending on the manner in which the luminaire is mounted. The radiant energy emitted (both visible and invisible) from a lamp will result in a heat gain to the space only after it has been absorbed by the room surfaces. This storage effect results in a time lag before the heat appears as a part of the cooling load.

In determining the internal heat gains due to artificial lighting the following must be known:

—   total electrical input power

—   fraction of heat emitted which enters the space

—   radiant, convective and conductive components.

Both the total electrical input power and the distribution of the heat output will vary with manufacturer. In particular, the optical properties of the luminaire can affect greatly the radiant/convective proportion emitted by the lamp. All figures quoted in the following section are typical. Manufacturers' data should be used where possible.

Table A6.1 Benchmark values for internal heat gains for offices (at 24 °C, 50% RH)

Building type	Use	Density of occupation / person·m⁻²	Sensible heat gain / W·m⁻²			Latent heat gain / W·m⁻²	
			People	Lighting	Equip't	People	Other
Office	General	4	20	12	25	15	—
		8	10	12	20	7.5	—
		12	6.7	12	15	5	—
		16	5	12	12	4	—
		20	4	12	10	3	—

Table A6.2 Benchmark allowances for internal heat gains in typical buildings

Building type	Use	Density of occupation / person·m⁻²	Sensible heat gain / W·m⁻²			Latent heat gain / W·m⁻²	
			People	Lighting*	Equip't†	People	Other
Offices	General	12	6.7	8–12	15	5	—
		16	5	8–12	12	4	—
	City centre	6	13.5	8–12	25	10	—
		10	8	8–12	18	6	—
	Trading/dealing	5	16	12–15	40+	12	—
	Call centre floor	5	16	8–12	60	12	—
	Meeting/conference	3	27	10–20	5	20	—
	IT rack rooms	0	0	8–12	200	0	—
Airports/stations‡	Airport concourse	0.83	75	12	5	4	—
	Check-in	0.83	75	12	5	50	—
	Gate lounge	0.83	75	15	5	50	—
	Customs /immigration	0.83	75	12	5	50	—
	Circulation spaces	10	9	12	5	6	—
Retail	Shopping malls	2–5	16–40	6	0	12–30	—
	Retail stores	5	16	25	5	12	—
	Food court	3	27	10	†	20	§
	Supermarkets	5	16	12	†	12	§
	Department stores:						
	— jewellery	10	8	55	5	6	—
	— fashion	10	8	25	5	6	—
	— lighting	10	8	200	5	6	—
	— china/glass	10	8	32	5	6	—
	— perfumery	10	8	45	5	6	—
	— other	10	8	22	5	6	—
Education	Lecture theatres	1.2	67	12	2	50	—
	Teaching spaces	1.5	53	12	10	40	—
	Seminar rooms	3	27	12	5	20	—
Hospitals	Wards	14	57	9	3	4.3	—
	Treatment rooms	10	8	15	3	6	—
	Operating theatres	5	16	25	60	12	—
Leisure	Hotel reception	4	20	10–20	5	15	—
	Banquet/conference	1.2	67	10–20	3	50	—
	Restaurant/dining	3	27	10–20	5	20	—
	Bars/lounges	3	27	10–20	5	20	—

* The internal heat gain allowance should allow for diversity of use of electric lighting coincident with peak heat gain and maximum temperatures. Lighting should be switched off in perimeter/window areas (up to say 4.5 m) and no allowance account for any dimming or other controls.

† Equipment gains do not allow for large duty local equipment such as heavy-duty photocopiers and vending machines.

‡ The exact density will depend upon airport and airplane capacity, the type of gate configuration (open or closed) and passenger throughput. Absolute passenger numbers if available would be a more appropriate design basis. Appropriate building scale diversities need to be derived based on airport passenger throughput.

§ Latent gains are likely but there are no benchmark allowances and heat gains need to be calculated from the sources, e.g. for meals, 15 W per meal served, of which 75% is sensible and 25% latent heat; see also CIBSE Guide A, Appendix 6.A2

Table A6.3 Typical rates at which heat is given off by human beings in different states of activity.

Degree of activity	Typical building	Total rate of heat emission for adult male / W	Rate of heat emission for mixture of males and females / W			Percentage of sensible heat that is radiant heat for stated air movement / %	
			Total	Sensible	Latent	High	Low
Seated at theatre	Theatre, cinema (matinee)	115	95	65	30	—	—
Seated at theatre, night	Theatre, cinema (night)	115	105	70	35	60	27
Seated, very light work	Offices, hotels, apartments	130	115	70	45	—	—
Moderate office work	Offices, hotels, apartments	140	130	75	55	—	—
Standing, light work; walking	Department store, retail store	160	130	75	55	58	38
Walking; standing	Bank	160	145	75	70	—	—
Sedentary work	Restaurant	145	160	80	80	—	—
Light bench work	Factory	235	220	80	140	—	—
Moderate dancing	Dance hall	265	250	90	160	49	35
Walking; light machine work	Factory	295	295	110	185	—	—
Bowling	Bowling alley	440	425	170	255	—	—
Heavy work	Factory	440	425	170	255	54	19
Heavy machine work; lifting	Factory	470	470	185	285	—	—
Athletics	Gymnasium	585	525	210	315	—	—

Source: ASHRAE Handbook: *Fundamentals* (2001)

A6.4.2   Total electrical power input

The total electrical power input to the lighting installation must be known. For lamps with associated control gear, it is important to add the power dissipated by the control gear to that dissipated by the lamp. The control gear power loss is likely to be about 10% of the lamp rating for electronic ballast and about 20% for conventional ballast.

Case studies carried out on a number of offices built or refurbished between 1977 and 1983 found that the lighting loads were between 10 and 32 W·m^{-2} for a maintained illuminance levels of 150–800 lux. Surveys carried out on newer buildings found that the lighting loads were in the range 8–18 W·m^{-2} for a maintained illuminance levels of 350–500 lux.

Where the actual installed power is not known reference should be made to Table A6.4, which provides target installed power densities for various task illuminances.

A6.4.3   Fraction of emitted heat entering the space

The proportion of heat entering the space depends upon the type and location of the light fittings.

Where the lamp or luminaire is suspended from the ceiling or wall-mounted or where uplighters or desk lamps are used, all the heat input will appear as an internal heat gain.

Where recessed or surface-mounted luminaires are installed below a false ceiling, some of the total input power will result in a heat gain to the ceiling void. An accurate assessment of the distribution of energy from particular types of luminaire should be obtained from the manufacturer.

Table A6.4 Lighting energy targets

Application	Lamp type	Task illuminance / lux	Average installed power density / W·m^{-2}
Commercial and similar applications (e.g. offices,shops*, schools)	Fluorescent-triphosphor	300	7
		500	11
		750	17
	Compact fluorescent	300	8
		500	14
		750	21
	Metal halide	300	11
		500	18
		750	27
Industrial and manufacturing	Fluorescent-triphosphor	300	6
		500	10
		750	14
		1000	19
	Metal halide	300	7
		500	12
		750	17
		1000	23
	High pressure sodium	300	6
		500	11
		750	16
		1000	21

* Excluding display lighting   Source: SLL *Code for Lighting* (2002)

manufacturer. In the absence of manufacturer's data, Table A6.5 provides an indication of the energy distribution for various arrangements of fluorescent lamp luminaires, based on laboratory measurements.

Table A6.5 Measured energy distribution for fluorescent fittings having four 70 W lamps

Type of fitting			Energy distribution / %	
Mounting	Schematic	Description	Upwards	Downwards
Recessed		Open	38	62
		Louvre	45	55
		Prismatic or opal diffuser	53	47
Surface		Open	12	88
		Enclosed prismatic or opal	22	78
		Enclosed prismatic on metal spine	6	94

A6.4.4 Radiant, convective and conductive components

Little information exists on the proportions of radiant, convective and conducted heat gain from lighting. Lamps radiate in both the visible and invisible wavebands and there will be a net gain of infrared radiation from the lamp and luminaire due to their radiant temperature being above the room mean radiant temperature. Table A6.6 provides approximate data for different lamp types and shows that a substantial proportion of the energy dissipated by all sources is emitted as radiant heat, which can cause discomfort to the occupants.

Table A6.6 Energy dissipation in lamps

Lamp type	Heat output / %		
	Radiant	Conducted/ convected*	Total
Fluorescent	30	70	100
Filament (tungsten)	85	15	100
High pressure mercury/ sodium, metal halide	50	50	100
Low pressure sodium	43	57	100

* The power loss of ballasts should be added to the conducted/convected heat.

A6.5 Personal computers and office equipment

A6.5.1 General

Personal computers (PCs) and associated office equipment result in heat gains to the room equal to the total power input. The internal heat gains for this equipment is normally allocated as an allowance in watts per square metre ($W \cdot m^{-2}$) of net usable floor area. Typical values are given in section A6.2 above.

The internal heat gains can be estimated from basic data but care must be taken to allow for diversity of use, idle operation and the effects of energy saving features of the equipment.

A6.5.2 Individual machine loads

It is well documented that nameplate power overstates the actual power and consequent heat gain. Research shows that with nameplate consumption of less than 1000 W the ratio of heat gain to nameplate power ranged from 25% to 50% and concluded the most accurate ratio for determining heat gain was 25%.

Tables A6.7 and A6.8 show typical heat gains from PCs and monitors in the continuous and energy saver modes. (Data for flat screen monitors have not been located.) Table A6.9 gives typical heat gains for laser printers. Typical heat gains from photocopiers are shown in Table A6.10. Table A6.11 gives heat outputs from some other items of office equipment.

Table A6.7 Typical heat gains from PCs

Nature of value	Value for stated mode / W	
	Continuous	Energy saving
Average	55	20
Conservative	65	25
Highly conservative	75	30

Table A6.8 Typical heat gains from PC monitors

Monitor size	Value for stated mode / W	
	Continuous	Energy saving
Small (13–15 inch)	55	0
Medium (16–18 inch)	70	0
Large (19–20 inch)	80	0

Table A6.9 Typical heat gains from laser printers

Printer size	Value for stated mode / W		
	Continuous	1-page/min.	Idle
Small desktop	130	75	10
Desktop	215	100	35
Small office	320	160	70
Large office	550	275	125

Table A6.10 Typical heat gains from photocopiers

Copier size	Value for stated mode / W		
	Continuous	1-page/min.	Idle
Desktop copier	400	85	20
Office copier	1100	400	300

Table A6.11 Typical heat gains from office equipment

Device	Value for stated mode / W	
	Continuous	Energy saving
Fax machine	30	15
Scanner	25	15
Dot matrix printer	50	25

A6.5.3   Diversity

Diversity is the factor that accounts for a percentage of equipment being idle or turned off. Figure A6.2 compares nameplate power (zero diversity) and the actual heat gain including diversity.

A6.5.4   Radiation, convection and conduction components

The electrical consumption of office equipment gives the total heat dissipated but it is also useful to know how that heat is transferred to the space. Heat that is convected or conducted is an instantaneous gain whereas that which is radiated is absorbed by the building mass and dissipated over time. Table A6.12 provides an indication of the likely breakdown of heat gains for a computer, monitor and laser printer. These figures should be used with caution since they were obtained from tests of a single computer, two monitors and one laser printer.

Table A6.12 Components of heat gain dissipated from office equipment

Device	Heat gain component / %	
	Convective/ conductive	Radiant
Desktop computer	86	14
Monitor	65	35
Laser printer	67	33

A6.6   Electric motors

A6.6.1   General

For situations where the motor and the motor driven equipment are both situated within the space (e.g. machinery in a workshop), the heat output is given by:

$$\Phi_g = P_a / \eta_t \qquad (6.1)$$

where Φ_g is the rate of heat gain to the space (W), P_a is the power at the equipment shaft (W) and η_t is the overall efficiency of transmission. The overall efficiency of transmission (η_t) is the product of the motor efficiency (η_m) and the drive efficiency (η_d).

For situations where the motor is situated within the space but the driven equipment is situated elsewhere:

$$\Phi_g = P_a [(1 / \eta_t) - 1] \qquad (6.2)$$

For motor driven equipment situated within, or related to the space (e.g. fans) but with the motor situated outside the space:

$$\Phi_g = P_a \qquad (6.3)$$

For precise details of efficiencies, which will vary with motor type, speed, performance and the character of the drive, reference should be made to manufacturers' data. For preliminary system design, in the absence of such data, reference may be made to Tables A6.13 and A6.14.

'High efficiency' motors are designed to minimise the inherent losses of the motor by using more copper in the stator and low-loss steel in the rotor. The improvement in efficiency is greatest at part-load, see Figure A6.3, particularly for loads below 50%.

Table A6.13 Average efficiencies for electric motors

Motor output rating	Average motor efficiencies, η_m / %			
	DC motors	AC motors		
		Single phase	Two-phase	Three-phase
0.75	76	65	73	74
3.75	83	78	84	85
7.50	86	81	87	88
15	88	83	88	90
38	90	85	91	91
56	92	86	92	92

Table A6.14 Average drive efficiencies

Drive	Drive efficiency, η_d / %
Plain bearings	95–98
Roller bearings	98
Ball bearings	99
Vee-belts	96–98
Spur gears	93
Bevel gears	92

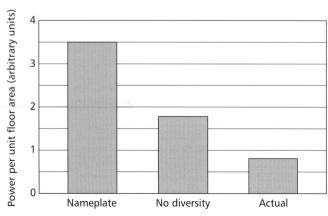

Figure A6.2 Load factor comparison

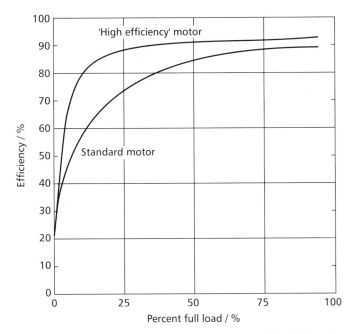

Figure A6.3 Comparison of efficiencies of standard and 'high efficiency' motors

A6.6.2 Escalator motors

It may be assumed that all the input power to the escalator motor will be converted to heat (ignoring the potential energy gained by ascending passengers). However, the motor will normally run at less than the motor rating and guidance should be sought from the manufacturer.

A6.6.3 Lift motors

It may be assumed that all the input power to the lift motor will be dissipated as heat within the lift motor room. The motor will not work continuously, nor at constant load. Table A6.15 may be used for preliminary systems design, in the absence of manufacturers' data.

A6.7 Cooking appliances

A6.7.1 General

Heat gain estimates for cooking appliances are subjective due to the variety of appliances, applications, time in use and types of installation. In estimating appliance loads, the probability of simultaneous use and operation for different appliances located in the same area must be considered.

To estimate heat gains from cooking appliances the actual energy input rating supplied by manufacturers should be used, suitably modified by appropriate usage factors, efficiencies or other judgmental factors. Guide A Appendix 6.A2 provides typical data for preliminary assessment prior to detailed design. Such preliminary assessments should be checked once manufacturers' information is available.

A6.7.2 Hooded appliances

Laboratory tests of hooded cooking appliances have indicated that the heat gains from effective hooded cooking appliances is primarily radiant, and that latent and convective heat are exhausted and do not enter the space.

The radiant heat gain from hooded cooking appliances varies from 15 to 45% of the actual energy consumption of the appliance. This may be expressed as a radiation factor, F_r, which depends on the appliance type and the fuel used by the appliance. The rate of heat gain to the space, Φ_h, is obtained by multiplying the average rate of energy consumption for the appliance by the radiation factor. The average rate of energy consumption for the appliance is obtained from the manufacturer's rated energy input, Φ_i, by applying a usage factor, F_u. Therefore:

$$\Phi_h = F_r (F_u \times \Phi_i) \tag{6.4}$$

where Φ_h is the rate of sensible heat gain to the space from a hooded appliance (W), Φ_i is the manufacturer's input rating or nameplate rating (W), F_r is the radiant factor and F_u is the usage factor.

Values for F_r and F_u for the main types of cooking equipment are given in Table A6.16.

Table A6.16 Useage and radiation factors for hooded cooking appliances

Appliance	Usage and radiation factors for appliances using stated fuel			
	Electrical appliance		Gas appliances	
	Usage factor (F_u)	Radiation factor (F_r)	Usage factor (F_u)	Radiation factor (F_r)
Griddle	0.16	0.45	0.25	0.25
Fryer	0.06	0.43	0.07	0.35
Convection oven	0.42	0.17	0.42	0.20
Charbroiler	0.83	0.29	0.62	0.18
Open top range, without oven	0.34	0.46	0.34	0.17
Hot-top range:				
— without oven	0.79	0.47	—	—
— with oven	0.59	0.48	—	—
Steam cooker	0.13	0.30	—	—

Table A6.15 Measured average power consumption of passenger lift motors

Drive type	Speed / m·s⁻¹	Number of passengers									
		8		10		13		16		21	
		Motor rating / kW	Average power / kW	Motor rating / kW	Average power / kW	Motor rating / kW	Average power / kW	Motor rating / kW	Average power / kW	Motor rating / kW	Average power / kW
Geared variable voltage	1.0	10	2.4	10	2.4	2.4	10	12	2.9	15	3.6
	1.6	15	3.6	15	3.6	15	3.6	17.6	4.2	22	5.3
Geared variable frequency	1.0	5.5	1.0	7.5	1.3	9.5	1.6	11	1.8	15	2.4
	1.6	9.5	1.6	11	1.8	13	2.2	18.5	3.0	22	3.6
Gearless static direct drive	2.5	—	—	—	—	—	3.8	—	4.2	—	5.2
	4.0	—	—	—	—	—	6.7	—	7.6	—	8.6

The usage factor, F_u, is the ratio of the standby or idle energy input to manufacturer's input rating. For appliances with a hood not listed in Table A6.16, typical values are 0.5 for types of equipment which cycle or require a constant temperature to be maintained, 0.4 for refrigerators and freezers and 1.0 for all other types of equipment.

The radiation factor, F_r, is the ratio of maximum room heat gain to the idle energy input of a hooded appliance. An average value is 0.32.

A6.7.3 Appliances without hoods

For cooking appliances not installed under an extract hood nor connected directly to an exhaust duct, a usage factor of 0.5 should be assumed, regardless of the type of energy or fuel used by the appliance. On average, 34% of the total heat gain may be assumed to be latent and 66% sensible heat. For the purposes of estimating cooling loads, appliances served by hoods which are not exhausted to outside should be treated as appliances without hoods.

A6.8 Hospital and laboratory equipment

Hospital and laboratory equipment can be major sources of heat gain in conditioned spaces. As this equipment is highly specialised, heat outputs for the specific pieces of equipment intended to occupy the space should be obtained from manufacturer. Care must be taken in evaluating the probability and duration of simultaneous usage when components are concentrated in one area.

For laboratories, the heat gains from equipment will vary widely according to the type of laboratory and the equipment likely to be installed and specific data should be obtained from the equipment suppliers. Heat gains of 50 to 200 $W \cdot m^{-2}$ are common for laboratories with high concentrations of equipment.

A7 Moisture transfer and condensation

A7.1 Introduction

Moisture gives rise to two types of problems:

— condensation, or more importantly, mould growth, on internal surfaces; as discussed in chapter 8, moulds and their spores are one of the most important causes of respiratory problems in buildings, especially in housing

— accumulation of moisture within a structure in areas where it may cause corrosion of metal components, decay of timber based components or reduction of the performance of insulants.

A7.3 Internal water vapour loads

In order to select the internal design conditions for condensation calculations, it is necessary to have some idea of the moisture content or vapour pressure of the air in a building. This will be determined mainly by the

Table A7.1 Sources of moisture within buildings

Source	Moisture produced
Combustion in room heaters/cookers without flues:	
— paraffin	0.1 $kg \cdot h^{-1} \cdot kW^{-1}$
— natural gas	0.16 $kg \cdot h^{-1} \cdot kW^{-1}$
— butane	0.12 $kg \cdot h^{-1} \cdot kW^{-1}$
— propane	0.13 $kg \cdot h^{-1} \cdot kW^{-1}$
Household activities:	
— cooking (3 meals)	0.9–3.0 $kg \cdot day^{-1}$
— dish washing (3 meals)	0.15–0.45 $kg \cdot day^{-1}$
— clothes washing	0.5–1.8 $kg \cdot day^{-1}$
— clothes drying (indoors)	2–5 $kg \cdot day^{-1}$
— baths/showers	0.2–0.5 $kg \cdot person^{-1} \cdot day^{-1}$
— floor washing	0.5–1.0 kg per 10 m^{-2}
— indoor plants	0.02–0.05 $kg \cdot plant^{-1} \cdot day^{-1}$
Perspiration and respiration of building occupants	0.04–0.06 $kg \cdot h^{-1} \cdot person^{-1}$

sources of moisture and the ventilation rate. Table A7.1 gives estimates for the amounts of moisture produced by various sources in housing.

BS 5250 suggests a typical daily moisture production rate of 6 kg for a five person family but clothes washing and the use of moisture-producing (i.e. non-electric) room heaters can increase this to 15 kg. The instantaneous moisture production will vary with the activities, e.g. a maximum will usually occur during cooking and clothes washing.

Industrial buildings present special problems due to the rate of production of moisture by some processes. The building services engineer should discuss the proposed use of the building with the client to enable any likely problems to be anticipated. For example, in the textiles industry it is estimated that about half a kilogram of water vapour is produced for each kilogram of wool that is scoured, dyed and washed.

Swimming pools have particularly high internal moisture loads because of the high air temperatures for the comfort of users, and the large exposed surface of heated water.

Animal houses need special consideration since chickens produce about 0.003 $kg \cdot h^{-1}$ (per bird) of moisture, sheep produce about 0.04 $kg \cdot h^{-1}$ (per animal) and pigs about 0.15 $kg \cdot h^{-1}$ (per animal).

A7.4 Moisture content of materials

Most materials will take up water when exposed to moist air, the equilibrium quantity depending on the nature of the material, its pore structure and the relative humidity of the air. This phenomenon is important when assessing the thermal conductivity of building and insulating materials. Equilibrium moisture contents for various materials are given in Table A7.2.

The moisture absorption is largely, though not solely, due to capillary forces. The vapour pressure over a concave surface is less than that over a plane surface. Water will condense on any surface having a radius of curvature such that the corresponding vapour pressure is less than that in the ambient air. If the radius is sufficiently small, condensation will occur from unsaturated atmospheres. Table

Table A7.2 Equilibrium moisture content of materials

Material	Density / kg·m⁻³	Moisture content at ambient air relative humidity of 50% / % by mass
Brick	1600	0.4
	2000	0.3
Cellular concrete	230	3
	640	4
Concrete	1200	4
	2300	1.5
Cement mortar	2000	2.5
Plaster:		
— lime sand	1750	1
— cement sand	2000	1
Limestone	2700	0.2
Sandstone	1800	2
Cork	200	5
Expanded Polystyrene	30	4
Glasswool slab	30	0.5
Mineral wool	30	0.5
Urethane foam	25	7
Hardwood	750	10
Softwood	420	10
Plywood	600	10
Strawboard	—	10
Woodwool/cement slab	360	10

Note: for newly constructed buildings, moisture contents will be higher than stated until 'drying-out' is completed

Table A7.3 Pore radius for hygroscopic equilibrium

Radius of curvature of pore / nm	Ambient air relative humidity for equilibrium / %
2.1	60
5	80
10	90
100	99

A7.3 shows the relative humidity of the ambient air that is in equilibrium with a concave surface.

A7.5 Mechanisms of moisture movement

A7.5.1 Surface moisture transfer

Mass transfer is analogous to heat transfer and the surface mass transfer coefficient is numerically related to the convective heat transfer coefficient, values of which can be derived from the appropriate expressions given in chapter 3 of CIBSE Guide C. Some common values are given in Table A7.4.

A7.5.2 Diffusion

Diffusion is the movement of molecules from high to low concentration. Most solid materials permit the diffusion of

Table A7.4 Values of convective heat transfer and surface mass transfer coefficients

Direction of heat flow	Convective heat transfer coefficient, h_c / W·m⁻²·K⁻¹	Surface mass transfer coefficient, β_v / m·s⁻¹
Downward	1.5	1.25×10^{-3}
Horizontal	3.0	2.5×10^{-3}
Upward	4.3	3.6×10^{-3}

water vapour to some extent and, whenever there is a difference in the vapour pressure across the material, a movement of water takes place. This is analogous to the flow of heat through a material when subjected to a temperature difference and this similarity is exploited in the calculation methods described in Guide A section 7.5.2.

Vapour resistivity values for common materials are given in Guide A chapter 3 and Appendix C of BS 5250.

Table A7.5 gives an indication of the likely resistivities of fibrous and open-celled materials and may be used in the absence of data for specific materials. It also gives a value for the vapour resistivity of still air in cavities within composite structures.

Table A7.5 Approximate values of vapour resistivity for fibrous or open-celled materials and for air spaces within structures

Density / kg·m⁻³	Vapour resistivity / MN·s·g⁻¹·m⁻¹
Air space	5
600	20
800	30
1000	40
1500	100
2000	220
2500	520

Vapour control layers are usually thin materials and it is more convenient to classify them by their vapour resistance rather than by their thickness and vapour resistivity. Table A7.6 gives approximate values of the vapour resistances of various membranes. It should be noted that these values apply to undamaged membranes and the presence of any perforations may reduce the vapour resistance considerably.

Table A7.6 Vapour resistance of membranes

Material	Thickness / mm	Vapour resistance / MN·s·g⁻¹
Polythene film	0.05	125
	0.1	200
	0.15	350
Mylar film	0.025	25
Gloss paint (average)	—	15
Interior paint	—	1
Varnish (phenolic, epoxy, polyurethane)	0.05	5
Roofing felt	—	400–1000
Aluminium foil	—	4000

A7.5.3 Air movement

Moisture is transferred by air movement through gaps at the junctions between elements of the construction and through cracks within the elements. In a typical masonry wall with windows or other openings, the mass flow of moisture due to air movement through gaps can be as much as an order of magnitude greater than that produced by diffusion. This is especially true in the case of pitched roofs, where the moisture transfers are dominated by wind and stack driven air flows from the house into the loft, through gaps in the ceiling and from the loft to outside via installed ventilators and laps in the undertiling membrane.

Certain buildings, such as operating theatres and clean rooms are deliberately operated at an overpressure to minimise ingress of contaminants. These are especially vulnerable to severe interstitial condensation caused by air infiltrating the structure.

A7.6 Surface condensation and mould growth

A7.6.1 Psychrometry of condensation of water vapour

The vapour pressures and temperatures at which water and air are in equilibrium are uniquely related by the saturation line, which applies whether the water vapour is present on its own or mixed with air. The equilibrium condition can be thought of in two ways:

(a)   when the temperature of the air equals the dew-point temperature corresponding to the partial pressure of the water vapour in the mixture

(b)   when the partial pressure of the water vapour equals the saturation pressure corresponding to the temperature of the mixture.

The first is useful when considering surface or superficial condensation on surfaces cooler than the room or ambient air. The second is more appropriate when considering internal or interstitial condensation within a building construction through which water vapour is moving under the influence of a difference between internal and external partial pressures.

Condensate frequently occurs on:

—   single glazing in bedrooms overnight or in kitchens and bathrooms at any time

—   double glazing, especially near to the frames, in rooms with high humidities

—   on WC cisterns or cold pipes in bathrooms or kitchens

—   on the walls of hallways and stairs in buildings of heavy masonry construction after a change from cold, dry weather to mild, wet weather

—   on massive floors in offices or industrial buildings, which remain cold after a change to warmer, more humid weather, or when heating is turned on in the morning.

Condensate is often only a nuisance. However, more serious consequences can result from, for example:

—   condensate from glazing promoting decay in the wooden window frames or condensate running from sills onto the wall below, damaging the décor

—   condensate dripping from roofs onto food preparation processes or sensitive electronic equipment

—   condensate on certain floor types, leading to a slip hazard.

A7.6.3 Mould growth

Mould growth is a source of health problems within buildings, increasing the incidence of asthma and other respiratory allergies. Mould spores exist in large numbers in the atmosphere and the critical factor for their germination and growth is the moisture conditions at surfaces and the length of time these conditions exist.

The surface relative humidity criterion of 80% for mould growth imposes a considerably more severe constraint on the thermal design of the building fabric than the 100% RH required for surface condensation. Table A7.7 shows the surface temperatures that must be achieved to avoid condensation and mould growth with an internal temperature of 20 °C and a range of internal relative humidities.

Table A7.7 Surface temperatures necessary to avoid condensation and mould assuming an internal air temperature of 20 °C and various internal relative humidities

Internal relative humidity / %	Surface temp. to avoid condensation / °C	Surface temp to avoid mould / °C
40	6.0	9.3
50	9.3	12.6
60	12.0	15.4
70	14.4	17.9

A7.7 Inside and outside design conditions

A7.7.1 Design conditions to avoid mould growth

The risk of mould growth on the internal surfaces of buildings depends on the combination of the internal surface temperature of external walls and the internal humidity. Because of the thermal inertia of structures and the time moulds take to germinate and grow, monthly mean conditions are often felt to be a sufficiently accurate predictor.

A7.7.2 Design conditions to avoid condensation on windows and their frames

Windows and their frames or other similar components with little thermal inertia, respond very rapidly to changes in outside temperature. The daily outside minimum temperature should therefore be used to calculate the risk of condensation. Table A7.10 shows the temperatures that

Table A7.10 Temperature that the daily minimum temperature falls below on various numbers of occasions per year (1983–2002)

No. of occasions	Temperature below which minimum daily temperature falls for stated number of occasions		
	London (Heathrow)	Manchester (Ringway)	Edinburgh (Turnhouse)
Minimum recorded temperature	−9.6	−11.1	−15.0
1 day/year	−6.1	−6.4	−9.3
2 days/year	−4.7	−5.0	−7.9
5 days/year	−3.4	−3.8	−5.7
10 days/year	−2.1	−2.6	−4.0
20 days/year	−0.6	−1.2	−2.5

the daily minimum falls below for different numbers of days per year at London, Manchester and Edinburgh. These can be used for design depending on the acceptable frequency of the occurrence of condensation.

Similar values can be derived from the available records for other locations.

A7.7.3 Design conditions to avoid interstitial condensation

The method for assessment of interstitial condensation is described in BS EN ISO 13788. For further information see Guide A section 7.7.3.

A7.8 Condensation calculations

A7.8.1 Calculations of the risk of surface condensation and mould growth

BS EN ISO 13788 specifies a procedure for design of structures to avoid mould growth, surface condensation or corrosion, where relevant. The principal steps in the design procedure are to determine the internal air humidity and then, based on the required relative humidity at the surface, to calculate the acceptable saturation vapour pressure, p_s, at the surface. From this value, a minimum surface temperature and hence a required 'thermal quality' of the building envelope (expressed by f_{Rsi}), is established. For further information see Guide A section 7.8.1.

A7.8.2 Calculations of the risk of interstitial condensation

BS EN ISO 13788 contains a method for establishing the annual moisture balance and calculating the maximum amount of accumulated moisture due to interstitial condensation within a structural element. For further information see Guide A section 7.8.2.

A8 Health issues

Guide A chapter 8 consists of extracts from CIBSE TM40: *Health issues in building services*, which may be downloaded from the members' area on the CIBSE website (http://www.cibse.org).

Guidance is provided on the following topics:

— thermal conditions for stress

— humidity

— air quality and ventilation

— visual environment

— electromagnetic effects

— noise and vibration.

For further information refer to Guide A chapter 8.

Guide A: abridgements and omissions

The extracts from CIBSE Guide A included above have been abridged for reasons of space. Reference should be made to CIBSE Guide A for the complete text and tables of data. In addition, the following sections have been omitted entirely from this Handbook:

Chapter 1: Environmental criteria for design:
— 1.2 Notation
— 1.5 Other factors potentially affecting comfort
— 1.6 The adaptive approach and field-studies of thermal comfort
— 1.8 Visual environment
— 1.10 Vibration
— 1.11 Electromagnetic and electrostatic environment
— Appendix 1.A1: Determination of predicted mean vote (PMV)
— Appendix 1.A2: Measuring operative temperature

Chapter 2: External design data:
— 2.2 Notation
— 2.8 Wind data

Chapter3: Thermal properties of buildings and components
— 3.2 Notation
— 3.7 Linear thermal transmittance
— Appendix 3.A1: Moisture content of masonry materials
— Appendix 3.A2: Thermal conductivity and thermal transmittance testing
— Appendix 3.A3: Heat transfer at surfaces
— Appendix 3.A4: Seasonal heat losses through ground floors
— Appendix 3.A5: Application of the combined method to multiple layer structures
— Appendix 3.A6: Calculation method for admittance, decrement factor and surface factor
— Appendix 3.A7: Properties of materials
— Appendix 3.A8: Thermal properties of typical constructions

Chapter 4: Ventilation and air infiltration
— 4.1 Introduction
— 4.4 Ventilation estimation techniques
— 4.8 Airtightness testing
— Appendix 4.A1: Air infiltration development algorithm (AIDA)

Chapter 5: Thermal response and plant sizing
— 5.2 Notation and glossary of terms
— 5.3 Quality assurance
— 5.5 Calculation methods
— 5.8 CIBSE cyclic model
— 5.9 Airflow modelling
— Appendix 5.A1: Quality assurance in building services software
— Appendix 5.A2: Overview of calculation methods
— Appendix 5.A3: Derivation of the thermal steady state models
— Appendix 5.A4: Comparison of thermal steady state models
— Appendix 5.A5: Equations for determination of sensible heating and cooling loads

Guide B: Heating, ventilating, air conditioning and refrigeration

B1   Heating

B1.2   Strategic design decisions

B1.2.2   Purpose of space heating systems

Heating systems are principally required to maintain comfortable conditions. As the human body exchanges heat with its surroundings by convection and radiation, comfort depends on the temperature of both the air and the exposed surfaces surrounding it and on air movement. Operative temperature, which combines air temperature and mean radiant temperature, has been used for assessing comfort. The predicted mean vote (PMV) index, as set out in the European Standard BS EN 7730, incorporates a range of factors contributing to thermal comfort. Methods for establishing comfort conditions are described in more detail in section B1.3.2 below.

B1.2.4   Legal, economic and general considerations

The design and performance of heating systems are covered by building regulations aimed at the conservation of fuel and power and ventilation; and regulations implementing the EU Boiler Directive set minimum efficiency levels for boilers. Heat producing appliances are also subject to regulations governing supply of combustion air, flues and chimneys, and emissions of gases and particles to the atmosphere, see section B1.5.5.1. Designers should also be aware of their obligations to comply with the Construction (Design and Management) Regulations and the Health and Safety at Work etc. Act.

Economic appraisal of different levels of insulation, heating systems, fuels, controls should be undertaken to show optimum levels of investment. Public sector procurement policies may specifically require life cycle costing.

B1.2.5   Interaction with building design, building fabric, services and facilities

The earlier the designer can be involved, the greater the scope for optimisation. The layout of the building, the size and orientation of windows, the extent and location of thermal mass within the building, and the levels of insulation can all have a significant effect on demand for heat. Airtightness of the building shell and the way in which it is ventilated are also important. Buildings that are very well insulated and airtight may have no net heating demand when occupied, which requires heating systems to be designed principally for pre-heating prior to occupancy.

B1.2.8   Making the strategic decisions

Each case must be considered on its own merits and rigorous option appraisal based on economic and environmental considerations should be undertaken. The flow charts shown in Figures B1.2 (heating systems) and B1.3 (fuels) are offered as general guidance.

B1.3   Design criteria

B1.3.1   General

Establishing the system design criteria starts by defining the indoor and outdoor climate requirements and the air change rates to maintain satisfactory air quality. A heat balance calculation is then used to determine the output required from the heating system under design condition, which in turn defines the heat output required in each room or zone of the building. This calculation may be done on a steady-state or dynamic basis.

B1.3.2   Internal climate requirements

Indoor climate may be defined in terms of temperature, humidity and air movement. The heat balance of the human body is discussed in CIBSE Guide A, section 1.4. The human body exchanges heat with its surroundings through radiation and convection in about equal measure. The perception of thermal comfort depends on the temperature of both the surrounding air and room surfaces. It also depends upon humidity and air movement. When defining temperature for heating under typical occupancy conditions, the generally accepted measure is the operative temperature, given by:

$$t_c = \{t_{ai}\sqrt{(10\,v)} + t_r\}/\{1 + \sqrt{(10\,v)}\} \tag{1.1}$$

where t_c is the operative temperature (°C), t_{ai} is the inside air temperature (°C), t_r is the mean radiant temperature (°C) and v is the mean air speed (m·s^{-1}).

For $v < 0.1$ m·s^{-1}:

$$t_c = (0.5\,t_{ai} + 0.5\,t_r) \tag{1.2}$$

Note: This selection chart is intended to give initial guidance only; it is not intended to replace more rigorous option appraisal

Constraints on combustion appliances in workplace?

Considering CHP, waste fuel or local community heating system available as source of heat?

Most areas have similar heating requirements in terms of times and temperatures?

Significant spot heating (>50% of heated space)?

Above average ventilation rates?

Non-sedentary workforce?

Radiant heat acceptable to process?

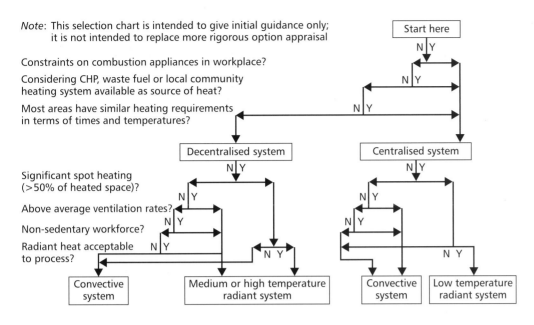

Figure B1.2 Selection chart: heating systems (reproduced from EEBPP Good Practice Guide GPG303; Crown copyright)

Waste fuel or local community heating available as source of heat?

Strategic need for back-up fuel supply?

Natural gas required?

Radiant heat required?

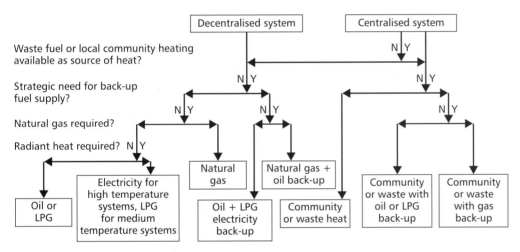

Figure B1.3 Selection chart: fuel (reproduced from EEBPP Good Practice Guide GPG303; Crown copyright)

As indoor air velocities are typically less than 0.1 m·s⁻¹, equation 1.2 generally applies.

Table A1.5 gives recommended winter operative temperatures for a range of building types and activities. These assume typical activity and clothing levels.

Temperature differences within the heated space may also affect the perception of thermal comfort. Vertical temperature differences are likely to arise from the buoyancy of warm air generated by convective heating. In general it is recommended that the vertical temperature difference should be no more than 3 K between head and feet. If air velocities are higher at floor level than across the upper part of the body, the gradient should be no more than 2 K·m⁻¹. Warm and cold floors may also cause discomfort to the feet. In general it is recommended that floor temperatures are maintained between 19 and 26 °C, but that may be increased to 29 °C for underfloor heating systems.

Asymmetric thermal radiation is a potential cause of thermal discomfort. It typically arises from:

— proximity to cold surfaces, such as windows

— proximity to hot surfaces, such as heat emitters, light sources and overhead radiant heaters

— exposure to solar radiation through windows.

CIBSE Guide A recommends that radiant temperature asymmetry should result in no more than 5% dissatisfaction, which corresponds approximately to vertical radiant asymmetry (for a warm ceiling) of less than 5 K and horizontal asymmetry (for a cool wall) of less than 10 K. The value for a cool ceiling is 14 K and for a warm wall is 23 K. It also gives recommended minimum comfortable distances from the centre of single glazed windows of different sizes.

The level of control achieved by the heating system directly affects occupant satisfaction with the indoor environment, see CIBSE Guide A. Although other factors also contribute to satisfaction (or dissatisfaction), the ability of the heating system and its controls to maintain dry resultant temperature close to design conditions is a necessary condition for satisfaction. Further guidance on comfort in naturally ventilated buildings may be found in CIBSE Applications Manual AM10: *Natural ventilation in non-domestic buildings*. The effect of temperatures on office worker performance is addressed in CIBSE TM24: *Environmental factors affecting office worker performance*.

Close control of temperature is often impractical in industrial and warehouse buildings, in which temperature variations of ±3 K may be acceptable. Also, in such buildings the requirements of processes for temperature control may take precedence over human comfort.

B1.3.3 Design room and building heat loss calculation

B1.3.3.1 Calculation principles

The first task is to estimate how much heat the system must provide to maintain the space at the required indoor temperature under the design external temperature conditions. Calculations are undertaken for each room or zone to allow the design heat loads to be assessed and for the individual heat emitters to be sized.

B1.3.3.2 External design conditions

The external design temperature depends upon geographical location, height above sea level, exposure and thermal inertia of the building. The method recommended in Guide A is based on the thermal response characteristics of buildings and the risk that design temperatures are exceeded. The degree of risk may be decided between designer and client, taking account of the consequences for the building, its occupants and its contents when design conditions are exceeded.

CIBSE Guide A section 2.3 gives guidance on the frequency and duration of extreme temperatures, including the 24- and 48-hour periods with an average below certain thresholds. It also gives data on the coincidence of low temperatures and high wind speeds. The information is available for a range of locations throughout the UK for which long term weather data are available.

The generally adopted external design temperature for buildings with low thermal inertia (capacity), see section B1.3.3.7, is that for which only one day on average in each heating season has a lower mean temperature. Similarly for buildings with high thermal inertia the design temperature selected is that for which only one two-day spell on average in each heating season has a lower mean temperature. Table B1.2 shows design temperatures derived on this basis for various location in the UK. In the absence of more localised information, data from the closest tabulated location may be used, decreased by 0.6 K for every 100 m by which the height above sea level of the site exceeds that of the location in the table. To determine design temperatures based on other levels of risk, see Guide A, section 2.3.

Table B1.2 Suggested design temperatures for various UK locations

Location	Altitude (m)	Design temperature*/ °C	
		Low thermal inertia	High thermal inertia
Belfast (Aldegrove)	68	−3	−1.5
Birmingham (Elmdon)	96	−4.5	−3
Cardiff (Rhoose)	67	−3	−2
Edinburgh (Turnhouse)	35	−4	−2
Glasgow (Abbotsinch)	5	−4	−2
London (Heathrow)	25	−3	−2
Manchester (Ringway)	75	−4	−2
Plymouth (Mountbatten)	27	−1	0

* Based on the lowest average temperature over a 24- or 48-hour period likely to occur once per year on average (derived from histograms in Guide A, section 2.3.1)

B1.3.3.3 Relationship between dry resultant, environmental and air temperatures

Thermal comfort is best assessed in terms of operative temperature, which depends on the combined effect of air and radiant temperatures. Steady-state heat loss calculations should be made using environmental temperature, which is the hypothetical temperature that determines the rate of heat flow into a room by both convection and radiation. For tightly built and well insulated buildings, differences between internal air temperature (t_{ai}), mean radiant temperature (t_r), operative temperature (t_c) and environmental temperature (t_e) are usually small in relation to the other approximations involved in plant sizing and may be neglected under steady-state conditions. This will apply to buildings built to current Building Regulations with minimum winter ventilation.

An estimate of the air temperature required to achieve a particular dry resultant temperature can be made using Guide A equation 5.15 (page 28). The difference between air and operative temperature is likely to be greater in a thermally massive building that is heated intermittently for short periods only, such as some church buildings.

B1.3.3.4 Structural or fabric heat loss

Structural heat loss occurs by conduction of heat through those parts of the structure exposed to the outside air or adjacent to unheated areas, often referred to as the 'building envelope'. The heat loss through each external element of the building can be calculated from:

$$\phi_f = U A (t_{en} - t_{ao}) \tag{1.3}$$

where ϕ_f is the heat loss through an external element of the building (W), U is the thermal transmittance of the building element (W·m^{-2}·K^{-1}), A is the area of the of building element (m$_2$), t_{en} is the indoor environmental temperature (°C) and t_{ao} is the outdoor temperature (°C).

Thermal bridges occur where cavities or insulation are crossed by components or materials with high thermal conductivity. They frequently occur around windows, doors and other wall openings through lintels, jambs and sills and can be particularly significant when a structural feature, such as a floor extending to a balcony, penetrates a wall. Guide A chapter 3 gives detailed information on thermal bridging. Other thermal bridging effects may be taken into account using the methods given in BS EN ISO 10211.

Heat losses through ground floors need to be treated differently from other losses as they are affected by the mass of earth beneath the floor and in thermal contact with it.

Tables A3.15 to A3.17 (page 17) gives U-values for solid ground floors on different soil types for a range of values of the ratio of the exposed floor perimeter p_f (m) and floor area A_f (m^2). The U-values are given as a function of the thermal resistance of the floor construction, R_f, where R_f = 0 for an uninsulated floor.

U-values for windows are normally quoted for the entire opening and therefore must include heat lost through both the frame and the glazing. Indicative U-values for typical glazing/frame combinations are given in Building Regulations Approved Documents L1 and L2.

U-values for typical constructions are given in Guide A, Appendix 3.A8. For other constructions the U-value must be calculated by summing the thermal resistances for the various elements, see section A3.3 (page 14).

Where adjacent rooms are to be maintained at the same temperature, there are neither heat losses nor heat gains either via the internal fabric or by internal air movement. However, where the design internal temperatures are not identical, heat losses between rooms should be taken into account in determining the heat requirements of each room.

B1.3.3.5   Ventilation heat loss

By convention, the conditions for the air are taken as the internal conditions, for which the density will not differ greatly from $\rho = 1.20$ kg·m^{-3}, and the specific heat capacity $c_p = 1.00$ kJ·kg^{-1}·K^{-1}. This leads to the following equations:

$$\phi_v = 1.2\, q_v\, (t_{ai} - t_{ao}) \tag{1.9}$$

or:

$$\phi_v = (N\, V\, /\, 3)\, (t_{ai} - t_{ao}) \tag{1.10}$$

where ϕ_v is the heat loss due to ventilation (W), q_v is the volume flow rate of air (litre·s^{-1}), t_{ai} is the inside air temperature (°C), t_{ao} the outside air temperature (°C), N is the number of air changes per hour (h^{-1}) and V is the volume of the room (m^3).

Ventilation heat losses may be divided into two distinct elements:

— purpose provided ventilation, either by mechanical or natural means

— air infiltration.

The amount of purpose-provided ventilation is decided according to how the building is to be used and occupied. Recommended air supply rates for a range of buildings and building uses are given in Table A1.5. More detailed guidance on ventilation is given in Guide B section 2.

When heat recovery is installed, the net ventilation load becomes:

$$\phi_v = 1.2\, q_v\, (t_{a2} - t_{ao}) \tag{1.11}$$

or:

$$\phi_v = q_m\, (h_{a2} - h_{ao}) \tag{1.12}$$

where t_{a2} is the extract air temperature after the heat recovery unit (°C) and h_{a2} is the extract air enthalpy after the heat recovery unit (J·kg^{-1}).

Air infiltration is the unintentional leakage of air through a building due to imperfections in its fabric. It is uncon-

Table B1.5 Recommended allowances for air infiltration for selected building types

Building/room type	Air infiltration allowance / air changes·h^{-1}	Building/room type	Air infiltration allowance / air changes·h^{-1}
Art galleries and museums	1	Hospitals (continued):	
Assembly and lecture halls	0.5	— wards and patient areas	2
Banking halls	1 to 1.5	— waiting rooms	1
Bars	1	Hotels:	
Canteens and dining rooms	1	— bedrooms	1
Churches and chapels	0.5 to 1	— public rooms	1
		— corridors	1.5
Dining and banqueting halls	0.5	— foyers	1.5
Exhibition halls	0.5	Laboratories	1
Factories:		Law courts	1
— up to 300 m^3 volume	1.5 to 2.5	Libraries:	
— 300 m^3 to 3000 m^3	0.75 to 1.5	— reading rooms	0.5 to 0.7
— 3000 m^3 to 10,000 m^3	0.5 to 1.0	— stack rooms	0.5
— over 10,000 m3	0.25 to 0.75	— storerooms	0.25
Fire stations	0.5 to 1	Offices:	
		— private	1
Gymnasia	0.75	— general	1
		— storerooms	0.5
Houses, flats and hostels:		Police cells	5
— living rooms	1		
— bedrooms	0.5	Restaurants, cafes	1
— bed-sitting rooms	1		
— bathrooms	2	Schools, colleges:	
— lavatories, cloakrooms	1.5	— classrooms	2
— service rooms	0.5	— lecture rooms	1
— staircases, corridors	1.5	— studios	1
— entrance halls, foyers	1.5	Sports pavilion changing rooms	1
— public rooms	1		
Hospitals:		Swimming pools:	
— corridors	1	— changing rooms	0.5
— offices	1	— pool hall	0.5
— operating theatres	0.5	Warehouses:	
— storerooms	0.5	— working and packing areas	0.5
		— storage areas	0.2

trolled and varies both with wind speed and the difference between indoor and outdoor temperatures. Table B1.5 gives empirical infiltration allowances for various types of building.

Building Regulations Approved Document L2 recommends that air permeability measured in accordance with CIBSE TM23: *Testing buildings for air leakage* should not be greater than 10 $m^3 \cdot h^{-1}$ per m^2 of external surface area at a pressure of 50 Pa. It also states that pressurisation tests should be used to show compliance with the Regulations for buildings with a floor area of 1000 m^2 or more. For buildings of less than 1000 m^2, pressurisation testing may also be used, but a report by a competent person giving evidence of compliance based on design and construction details may be accepted as an alternative.

B1.4   System selection

B1.4.1   Choice of heating options

B1.4.1.1   Heat emitters

Consideration must be given to the balance between convective and radiative output appropriate to the requirements of the building and activities to be carried out within it.

B1.4.1.2   Location of heat emitters

It is generally desirable to provide uniform temperatures throughout a room or zone. The position of the heat emitters can significantly affect comfort (e.g. locate emitters to counteract down-draughts). Locate heat emitters on external walls if the walls are poorly insulated.

B1.4.1.3   Distribution medium

Air and water are the most common; electricity is the most versatile. The choice of distribution medium should take account of the required balance between radiant and convective output. The relative merits of various distribution media are described in Table B1.6.

B1.4.2   Energy efficiency

B1.4.2.3   Seasonal boiler efficiency

Boiler efficiency is the principal determinant of system efficiency. Seasonal efficiency is the average efficiency of the boiler under varying conditions throughout the year. Typical values for various types of boiler are given in Table B1.7. For domestic boilers, seasonal efficiencies may be obtained from the SEDBUK database (http://www.sedbuk.com). Figure B1.4 shows how efficiency falls when operating at part load.

Table B1.7 Typical seasonal efficiencies for various boiler types

Boiler/system	Seasonal efficiency / %
Condensing boilers:	
— under-floor or warm water system	90
— standard size radiators, variable temperature circuit (weather compensation)	87
— standard fixed temperature emitters (83/72 °C flow/return)*	85
Non-condensing boilers:	
— modern high-efficiency non-condensing boilers	80–82
— good modern boiler design closely matched to demand	75
— typical good existing boiler	70
— typical existing oversized boiler (atmospheric, cast-iron sectional)	45–65

* Not permitted by current Building Regulations

B1.4.2.5   Controls

Heating system controls perform two distinct functions:

—   they maintain the temperature conditions required within the building when it is occupied, including pre-heating to ensure that those conditions are met at the start of occupancy periods

—   they ensure that the system itself operates safely and efficiently under all conditions.

Table B1.6 Characteristics of heat distribution media

Medium	Principal characteristics
Air	The main advantage of air is that no intermediate medium or heat exchanger is needed. The main disadvantage is the large volume of air required and the size of ductwork that results. This is due to the low density of air and the small temperature difference permissible between supply and return. High energy consumption required by fans can also be a disadvantage.
Low pressure hot water (LPHW)	LPHW systems operate at low pressures that can be generated by an open or sealed expansion vessel. They are generally recognised as simple to install and safe in operation but output is limited by system temperatures restricted to a maximum of about 85 °C.
Medium pressure hot water (MPHW)	Permits system temperatures up to 120 °C and a greater drop in water temperature around the system and thus smaller pipework. Only on a large system is this likely to be of advantage. This category includes pressurisation up to 5 bar absolute.
High pressure hot water (HPHW)	Even higher temperatures are possible in high pressure systems (up to 10 bar absolute), resulting in even greater temperature drops in the system, and thus even smaller pipework. Due to the inherent dangers, all pipework must be welded and to the standards applicable to steam pipework. This in unlikely to be a cost-effective choice except for the transportation of heat over long distances.
Steam	Exploits the latent heat of condensation to provide very high transfer capacity. Operates at high pressures, requiring high maintenance and water treatment. Principally used in hospitals and buildings with large kitchens or processes requiring steam.

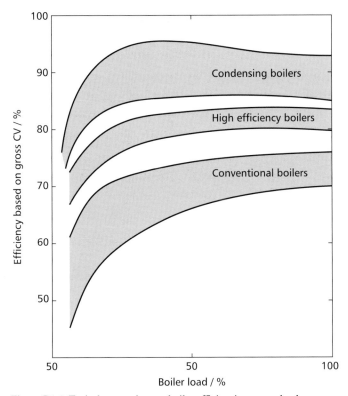

Figure B1.4 Typical seasonal LTHW boiler efficiencies at part load

B1.4.3 Hydronic systems

Hydronic systems use hot water for transferring heat from the heat generator to the heat emitters. They offer considerable flexibility in the type and location of the heat emitters.

B1.4.3.1 Operating temperatures for hydronic systems

Systems are generally classified according to the temperature and static pressure at which they operate, see Table B1.8. The operating temperature should be set low enough that exposed heat emitters do not present a burn hazard to building occupants.

LPHW systems are typically designed to operate with a maximum flow temperature of 82 °C and system temperature drop of 10 K. A minimum return temperature of 66 °C is specified by BS 5449 unless boilers are designed to

Table B1.8 Design water temperatures and pressures for hydronic heating systems

Category	System design water temperature / °C	Operating static pressure / bar (absolute)
Low pressure hot water (LPHW)	40 to 85	1 to 3
Medium pressure hot water (MPHW)	100 to 120	3 to 5
High pressure hot water (HPHW)	>120	5 to 10*

* Account must be taken of varying static pressure in a tall building

cope with condensation or are of the electric storage type. For condensing boilers, a low return temperature may be used with the benefit of improved operating efficiency. It may also be noted that the larger the difference between flow and return temperatures $(t_1 - t_2)$, the smaller the mass flow required, which tends to reduce pipe sizes and pumping power. The heat flux is given by:

$$\phi = q_m c_p (t_1 - t_2) \tag{1.14}$$

where ϕ is the heat flux (W), q_m is the mass flow rate (kg·s^{-1}), c_p is the specific heat capacity of the heat transfer fluid (J·kg^{-1}·K^{-1}), t_1 is the flow temperature (°C) and t_2 is the return temperature (°C).

Hence, the mass flow rate is given by:

$$q_m = \phi / [c_p (t_1 - t_2)] \tag{1.15}$$

The efficiency of a condensing boiler is more strongly influenced by the return temperature, rather than the flow temperature, which ought to be a further encouragement to use large values of $(t_1 - t_2)$. However, a larger temperature difference lowers the mean water temperature of the emitter, which reduces specific output and requires larger surface area. The effect of flow rate and return temperature on heat output is explored more fully in Guide B section 1.5.1.1.

B1.4.3.3 Choice of heat source

The choice of heat source will depend on the options available. These are summarised in Table B1.A.

Table B1.A Summary of information on boilers contained in CIBSE Guide B section 1.4.3.3 (This table does not appear in CIBSE Guide B)

Heat source	Notes
Boiler	Large range of types and sizes
	Good efficiency
	Good part load performance and seasonal efficiency
Heat pumps	Different forms to exploit sources of low grade heat
	Most widely used type is air-to-air, which can also provide cooling
Solar panels	Widely used for HWS; in UK, can provide up to 50% of annual requirement. Economically marginal in UK. Applicable for outdoor swimming pools
Community heating	Can be low cost and low environmental impact
Combined heat and power (CHP)	May be appropriate if no other heat supply
	Needs reasonable match between generated electrical output and demand
	Optimum ratio of heat demand to power demand generally lies between 1.3:1 and 2:1.

B1.4.3.4 Choice of heat emitter

Hydronic systems are capable of working with a wide variety of heat emitters. These are summarised in Table B1.B.

Table B1.B Summary of information on heat emitters contained in Guide B section 1.4.3.4 (This table does not appear in CIBSE Guide B)

Heat emitter	Notes
Radiators	Most frequent choice of emitter
	Usually pressed steel
	Wide variety of shapes, sizes and outputs
Natural convectors	Can be used instead of radiators or where radiators cannot be mounted (e.g. trench heating)
	Output varies with design
Fan coil convectors	High heat output from compact units
	Output is entirely convective
Floor heating	Embedded electric or hydronic systems available
	Insulation below heating elements is very important
	Floor surface temperature critical to comfort (21–28 °C)

B1.4.3.5   Pumping and pipework

The hydraulic requirements for a system are derived from parameters such as system operating temperature and the heat output required from emitters, which affect pipework layout. The design also needs to take account of the effect of water velocity on noise and corrosion, and the pressure and flow characteristics required of the circulation pump. The key design decisions include:

— system pressures

— whether to use an open or a sealed pressurisation method

— which material to use for pipes

— the flow velocity to be used

— how the system is to be controlled

— filling and air removal arrangements

— pumping requirements, i.e. variable or fixed flow rate.

Details of the characteristics of pipework and pumps are dealt with in sections B1.5.1.3 and B1.5.1.4.

B1.4.3.6   Energy storage

Energy storage may either be used to reduce peak loads or to take advantage of lower energy prices at certain times of day. Heat is stored using either solid cores or hot water vessels. The most common application of thermal storage is in dwellings, in which solid core storage is charged with heat at off-peak rates for a 7 or 8 hour period. Guidance for the design of such systems is contained in Electricity Association publication *Design of mixed storage heater/direct system*.

Thermal storage for larger buildings must rely on purpose-designed storage vessels with capacity and storage temperature optimised for the heat load. Other design parameters that must be considered are insulation of the storage vessel, arrangements for dealing with expansion and the control strategy for coupling the store to the rest of the system.

B1.4.3.7   Domestic hot water

In housing, where demand for hot water is a substantial proportion of the total heat load, a hydronic heating system is usually the most convenient and satisfactory means of producing hot water, using either a hot water storage cylinder or a combination boiler.

In buildings other than housing, the case for deriving domestic hot water from a hydronic heating system depends greatly on circumstances. In general, independent hot water generation is the more economical choice when relatively small amounts of hot water are required at positions distant from the boiler.

B1.4.3.8   Control for hydronic systems

Hydronic heating systems are capable of very close control over environmental conditions using a range of strategies. The choice of control system type will depend on the closeness of control required, the number of different zones that must be controlled independently and the times at which the building will be occupied and require heating.

Hydronic systems in larger buildings are likely to have more complex controls, including optimum start, and often incorporate weather compensation in which the system flow temperature is controlled in response to external temperature, according to a schedule derived for the building.

Comprehensive guidance on control system design is given in CIBSE Guide H: *Building control systems*.

B1.4.3.9   Water expansion

The density of water reduces significantly as temperature rises which results in significant expansion as a hydronic system warms up from cold. This must be accommodated without an excessive rise in system pressure. Table B1.9 shows the percentage expansion, calculated with reference to 4 °C at start-up for a range of operating temperatures using the expression:

$$(\Delta V / V_4) = (\rho_4 / \rho) - 1 \tag{1.16}$$

where ΔV is the change in volume resulting from change in temperature (m^3), V_4 is the volume at 4 °C (m^3), ρ_4 is the density at 4 °C (kg·m^{-3}) and ρ is the density (kg·m^{-3}) at a given temperature.

Allowance may also be made for the expansion of the pipework, but this is small for most materials.

Table B1.9 Percentage expansion of water heating up from 4 °C

Temperature / °C)	Expansion / %	Temperature / °C)	Expansion / %
40	0.79	130	7.00
50	1.21	140	8.00
60	1.71	150	9.10
70	2.27	160	10.2
80	2.90	170	11.4
90	3.63	180	12.8
100	4.34	190	14.2
110	5.20	200	15.7
120	6.00		

All hydronic systems must have provision for maintaining system operating pressure within a range that ensures safety and effective operation of the system.

An open system, relying on hydrostatic pressurisation normally has separate feed and open safety vent pipes, with the latter positioned to provide an unrestricted path for the relief of pressure and the escape of steam if the boiler thermostat were to fail and the system overheat.

Sealed pressurisation equipment for low pressure systems consists of an expansion vessel complying with BS 4814, a pressure gauge, a means for filling, and a non-adjustable safety valve.

Medium and high pressure systems may use a variety of techniques to maintain working pressure:

— pressurisation by expansion of water, in which the expansion of the water in the system is itself used to charge a pressure vessel

— pressurisation by an elevated header tank

— gas pressurisation with a spill tank, in which a pressure cylinder is partly filled with water and partly with a gas (usually nitrogen)

— hydraulic pressurisation with spill tank, in which pressure is maintained by a continuously running pump.

B1.4.4   Steam systems

Detailed information is given in Guide B section 1.4.4.

B1.4.7   Plant size ratio

B1.4.7.1   Definition of plant size ratio

Heating systems are designed to meet the maximum steady-state load likely to be encountered under design conditions. However, additional capacity is needed to overcome thermal inertia so that the building may reach equilibrium in a reasonable time, particularly if the building is heated intermittently.

Plant size ratio (PSR) is defined as:

$$\text{PSR} = \frac{\text{installed heat emission}}{\text{design heat load}}$$

The design heat load used in the calculation of PSR is the heat loss from the space or building under conditions of external design temperature and internal design temperature. For the purpose of specifying the heating system this condition should be calculated for the time of peak steady state load. The time at which this occurs will depend on the building or space, its services and its occupancy. Peak load normally occurs under one of the following conditions:

— *during occupancy*: taking account of any reliable internal heat gains, fabric heat losses and all ventilation heat losses

— *before occupancy*: taking account of any permanent internal heat gains (but not those occurring only during occupied periods), fabric heat losses and all

ventilation losses (unless ventilation systems operate during occupied periods only, in which case only infiltration losses are applicable).

B1.4.7.2   Intermittent heating

Intermittent occupancy permits a reduction in internal temperature while the building is unoccupied and a consequent reduction in fuel consumption. It is important to note that the building continues to lose heat during the off period and requires additional heat to bring the building back up to temperature during the 'pre-heat' period prior to the next period of occupancy. For many buildings, the pre-heat period can constitute the major energy consumption of the building. The shaded area in Figure B1.7 represents the accumulated temperature reduction (in degree-hours), which is directly related to the energy saved by the system due to the reduction in space temperature during the period of non-occupancy. A building having low thermal inertia, which cools to a lower temperature when the heating system is off, will experience greater economy as a result of intermittent heating, than a building of high thermal inertia, see Figure B1.8. However, it should be noted that high thermal inertia is beneficial in that it enables better utilisation of heat gains.

The necessary plant size ratio required to reach design temperature for a particular building depends on the occupancy and heating pattern. For many buildings, the most demanding situation arises on Monday morning after being unoccupied during the weekend. If the system is shut off completely during the weekend, the building may have to be heated up from a room temperature little higher than the outside temperature. The heating system may also be operated at a set-back temperature when it is not occupied, in which case less energy is required to restore it to design temperature. It may also be observed from Figure B1.8 that a building with low thermal inertia

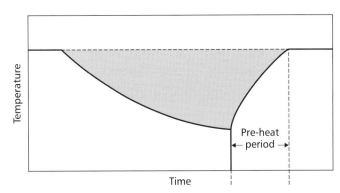

Figure B1.7 Temperature profile of a space during intermittent heating with the pre-heat period optimised to be as short as possible

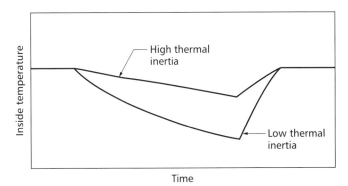

Figure B1.8 Profile of space temperature for buildings of high thermal inertia and low thermal inertia, each having the same plant size ratio

heats up more quickly than one with high thermal inertia and therefore a lower plant size ratio may be employed.

B1.4.7.3 Choice of plant size ratio

The shorter the pre-heat period, the greater is the saving in energy. This implies that the greater the plant size ratio, the greater the economy in energy consumption. However there are several disadvantages in over-sizing the heating system:

— greater capital cost

— more difficult to achieve stability of controls

— except during pre-heat, the plant will run at less than full load, generally leading to a lower seasonal efficiency.

The optimum plant size ratio is difficult to determine as it requires knowledge, or estimates, of:

— the occupancy pattern

— the thermal inertia or thermal response of the building areas

— the design internal temperature

— the minimum permissible internal temperature

— a record of the weather over a typical season

— the current fuel tariffs and estimates of future tariffs over the life of the system

— the capital and maintenance costs of different sizes of equipment.

For less complex buildings, CIBSE Guide A section 5.8.3.3 describes a method of calculating plant size ratio based on the admittance procedure:

$$F_3 = \frac{24 f_r}{H f_r + (24 - H)} \qquad (1.17)$$

where F_3 is the plant size ratio (or 'intermittency factor'), f_r is the thermal response factor (see equation 1.18) and H is the hours of plant operation (including preheat) (h).

The response factor may be calculated from:

$$f_r = \frac{\sum (A\,Y) + C_v}{\sum (A\,U) + C_v} \qquad (1.18)$$

where f_r is the thermal response factor, $\sum (A\,Y)$ is the sum of the products of surface areas and their corresponding thermal admittances ($W \cdot K^{-1}$), $\sum (A\,U)$ is the sum of the products of surface areas and their corresponding thermal transmittances over surfaces through which heat flow occurs ($W \cdot K^{-1}$) and C_v is the ventilation heat loss coefficient ($W \cdot K^{-1}$).

The ventilation heat loss coefficient is given by:

$$C_v = (c_p \, \rho \, N \, V) / 3600 \qquad (1.19)$$

where c_p is the specific heat capacity of air ($J \cdot kg^{-1} \cdot K^{-1}$), ρ is the density of air ($kg \cdot m^{-3}$), N is the number of air changes in the space (h^{-1}) and V is the room volume (m^3).

For air at ambient temperatures, $\rho \approx 1.20$ $kg \cdot m^{-3}$ and $c_p \approx 1000$ $J \cdot kg^{-1} \cdot K^{-1}$, hence:

$$C_v \approx N\,V / 3 \qquad (1.20)$$

Table B1.11 Plant size ratio calculated for different heating periods

Heating hours (including pre-heat period)	Thermal weight		
	Light ($f_r = 2$)	Medium ($f_r = 4$)	Heavy ($f_r = 8$)
6	1.6	—	—
7	1.5	—	—
8	1.5	2.0	—
9	1.5	1.9	—
10	1.4	1.8	2.0
11	1.4	1.7	1.9
12	1.3	1.6	1.8
13	1.3	1.5	1.7
14	1.3	1.5	1.6
15	1.2	1.4	1.5
16	1.2	1.3	1.4

Table 1.11 shows plant size ratios for a range of heating periods and thermal response factors. Structures with a response factor greater than 4 are referred to as slow response or 'heavyweight', and those with a response factor less than 4 as fast response or 'lightweight'. CIBSE Guide A recommends that when the calculation yields a result of less than 1.2, a plant size ratio of 1.2 should be used.

Plant sizing as described above is based on ensuring that the heating system is able to bring the building up to design temperature in the required time. In general, it may be observed that, unless rapid warm-up is essential, plant size ratio should be in the range 1.2 to 2.0. Optimum start control can ensure adequate pre-heat time in cold weather.

B1.5 Plant and equipment

B1.5.1 Equipment for hydronic systems

B1.5.1.1 Heat emitters

(a) Radiators and convectors

The effects of architectural features and surface finish on radiator output are summarised in Table B1.13. In general, heat output is reduced when airflow is restricted, such as by placing a shelf immediately above a radiator, or by an enclosure. It is also reduced by surface finishes with low emissivity, such as metallic paints or plating.

(b) Fan coil heaters

The characteristics of fan coil heaters are described in BS 4856, which gives test methods for heat output and air movement with and without attached ducting, and for noise levels without attached ducting. The heat output from fan coil heaters is approximately linear with the difference between system temperature and room air temperature, corresponding to $n = 1.0$ in equation 1.23; i.e:

$$\phi = K_m \, \Delta T^n \qquad (1.23)$$

where ϕ is the heat emission (W), K_m is a constant for a given height and design of emitter, ΔT is the excess temperature (K) and n is an index.

Table B1.13 Effects of finishes and architectural features on radiator output

Feature	Effect
Ordinary paint or enamel	No effect, irrespective of colour
Metallic paint such as aluminium and bronze	Reduces radiant output by 50% or more and overall output by between 10 and 25%. Emission may be substantially restored by applying two coats of clear varnish.
Open fronted recess	Reduces output by 10%.
Encasement with front grille	Reduces output by 20% or more, depending on design.
Radiator shelf	Reduces output by 10%.
Fresh air inlet at rear with baffle at front	May increase output by up to 10%. This increase should not be taken into account when sizing radiator but should be allowed for in pipe and boiler sizing. A damper should always be fitted.
Distance of radiator from wall	A minimum distance of 25 mm is recommended. Below this emission may be reduced due to restriction of air flow.
Height of radiator above floor	Little effect above a height of 100 mm. If radiators are mounted at high level, output will depend on temperature at that level and stratification may be increased.

(f) Heat emission from distribution pipework

Account needs to be taken of the heat emitted from distribution pipework when sizing both emitters and boilers. Tables B1.16 and B1.17 (page 54) give heat emissions per metre horizontal run for steel and copper pipes respectively. When pipes are installed vertically, heat emissions are different due to the differences in the boundary layer or air around the pipe surface. Table B1.18 gives correction factors for vertical pipes. When pipes are arranged in a horizontal bank, each pipe directly above another at close pitch, overall heat emission is reduced. Table B1.19 gives correction factors for such installations.

Table B1.18 Correction factors for for Tables B1.16 and B1.17 for heat emission from vertical pipes

Pipe size / mm	Correction factor
8	0.72
10	0.74
15	0.76
20	0.79
25	0.82
32	0.84
40	0.86
50	0.88
65	0.90
80	0.92
100	0.95
125	0.97
150	0.99
200	1.03
250	1.05
300	1.07

Table B1.19 Correction factors for Tables B1.16 and B1.17 for heat emission from horizontal pipes in banks

Number of pipes in bank	Correction factor
2	0.95
4	0.85
6	0.75
8	0.65

Heat emission from pipes and plane surfaces is covered in detail in CIBSE Guide C section 3.3.

B1.5.1.2   Heat sources

Boiler selection

The following factors need to be taken into account in selecting a boiler for a particular application:

— output in relation to calculated system requirements

— efficiency, particularly at part load

— hydraulic pressure at which the boiler must operate

— system operating temperature: it is particularly important that return water be maintained above the minimum recommended by the manufacturer for non-condensing oil-fired boilers to avoid corrosion from acid condensation in the flue system

— flue gas conditions, to comply with emission requirements

— corrosion and water treatment, taking account of the specific recommendations of the boiler manufacturer

— acoustic considerations, taking account of noise both inside and outside the boiler room

— floor temperature beneath the boiler: the temperature of a concrete floor should not be allowed to exceed 65 °C; this should not occur where the base of the boiler is water cooled, but may otherwise require a refractory hearth under the boiler

— space in the boiler house, especially with regard to access for maintenance

— access for initial installation and subsequent replacement.

B1.5.1.3   Pipework

The designer has considerable flexibility when determining pipework materials, installation costs and installation time. Table B16.1 (see page 55) gives examples of materials typically used for service piping. Table B16.2 (see page 55) lists the principal properties of a selection of materials used in the manufacture of piping. Table B16.4 (see page 55) gives the expansion per metre length for a range of pipe materials at various temperatures differences from that at which the pipe is assumed to be unstressed. This information was originally provided in section B16 of the 1986 edition of CIBSE Guide B. Table B16.1 has been reviewed to reflect current practice.

The designer also has considerable flexibility in choosing appropriate pipe sizes. A larger pipe diameter reduces the friction pressure drop and hence the pump power needed to achieve the design circulation. Even a small increase in diameter can have a significant effect, as the pressure drop is approximately proportional to the fifth power of diameter for the same mass flow.

The theoretical basis for calculating pressure drops in pipework is covered in detail in section (C)4, which also provides tables giving pressure drop per metre run for a range of pipe sizes and materials. Pipe sizes should ideally be selected to achieve minimum life cycle cost, taking

Table B1.16 Heat emission from single horizontal steel pipes with a surface emissivity of 0.9 and freely exposed to ambient air at temperatures between 10 and 20 °C

Nominal pipe size /mm	Heat emission / W·m⁻² for stated temperature difference between surface to surroundings / K																			
	40	45	50	55	60	65	70	75	80	100	120	140	160	180	200	220	240	260	280	300
15	42	48	55	62	69	77	84	92	100	135	173	215	261	311	366	425	490	560	635	717
20	51	59	67	75	84	93	103	112	122	164	211	262	318	380	447	520	600	686	780	881
25	62	71	81	92	102	114	125	137	149	200	257	320	389	465	547	637	735	842	957	1080
32	75	87	99	112	125	138	152	167	181	244	314	391	476	569	670	781	902	1030	1180	1330
40	84	98	111	125	140	155	170	186	203	273	352	438	534	638	753	878	1010	1160	1320	1500
50	106	118	135	152	169	188	206	226	246	331	427	532	648	776	916	1070	1240	1420	1620	1830
65	125	145	165	186	207	230	253	277	301	406	523	653	796	954	1130	1320	1520	1750	2000	2260
80	143	166	189	213	238	263	290	317	345	466	600	750	915	1100	1300	1510	1750	2010	2300	2610
100	179	207	236	266	297	329	362	396	431	582	750	937	1140	1370	1620	1900	2200	2530	2890	3280
125	214	247	281	317	354	392	432	473	515	696	897	1120	1370	1650	1950	2280	2650	3040	3480	3950
150	248	287	327	368	411	456	502	549	598	808	1040	1310	1600	1920	2270	2660	3090	3550	4060	4620
200	319	369	421	474	529	586	646	706	769	1040	1340	1680	2060	2480	2940	3450	4000	4610	5280	6010
250	389	449	512	577	644	714	786	860	937	1270	1640	2050	2520	3030	3600	4220	4900	5650	6470	7370
300	453	524	597	673	751	832	916	1000	1090	1480	1910	2400	2940	3540	4200	4930	5740	6620	7590	8650

Table B1.17 Heat emission from single horizontal copper pipes freely exposed to ambient air at temperatures of 20 °C

Nominal pipe size /mm	Heat emission / W·m⁻² for stated surface finish and temperature difference between surface and surroundings / K																			
	Painted pipe (ε = 0.95)										Tarnished pipe (ε = 0.5)									
	40	45	50	55	60	65	70	75	80	100	40	45	50	55	60	65	70	80	90	100
8	18	21	24	27	30	33	37	40	43	58	15	17	20	22	25	27	30	33	36	48
10	22	25	29	32	36	40	44	48	52	70	18	21	24	27	30	33	36	39	43	57
15	31	36	41	46	51	57	62	68	74	99	25	29	33	37	41	46	50	55	60	80
22	43	49	56	63	71	78	86	94	103	138	34	39	45	51	56	62	69	75	81	109
28	53	61	69	78	87	97	106	116	126	170	42	48	55	62	69	76	84	91	99	133
35	64	74	84	95	106	117	129	141	153	206	50	58	66	74	83	92	101	110	120	160
42	75	86	98	111	124	137	151	165	179	242	58	67	77	86	96	107	117	128	139	186
54	93	107	122	138	154	171	188	205	223	301	72	83	94	106	119	131	144	158	171	230
76	125	145	165	186	208	230	253	277	302	407	95	110	126	142	158	175	192	210	229	306
108	171	197	225	253	283	313	345	377	411	554	128	148	169	190	212	235	258	282	307	412
133	205	237	270	305	340	377	415	454	494	668	153	177	201	227	253	280	308	337	366	492
159	240	278	317	357	399	442	486	532	579	783	178	205	234	264	294	326	358	392	426	572

Table B16.1 Materials recommended for service piping

Service	Material
Compressed air	Galvanised steel, copper, ABS, PE-X, multi-layer
Condensate drainage	Copper, PVC-C, PVC-U, ABS, PE-X
Drains and wastes	Stainless steel, cast iron, silicon iron (spun), chemical stoneware, vitreous enamel, glazed fireclay, PVC-U, ABS, PP
Fuel oils	Heavy grade mild steel, copper, polyamide (externally coated with polyethylene)
Gas (natural)	Heavy grade mild steel, copper, HDPE
Heating	Heavy grade mild steel, copper, PVC-C, PE-X, PB, multi-layer, PP-R-fibre reinforced
Liquefied petroleum gas (LPG)	Copper, HDPE
Steam	Heavy grade mild steel, copper
Vacuum	Medium grade mild steel, copper, ABS, PE-X
Piped water supplies:	
— cold	Copper, galvanised steel, PVC-C, PVC-U, ABS, HDPE, PE-X, PB, PP, multi-layer, PP-R-fibre reinforced
— de-ionised, demineralised or softened	Stainless steel, PVC-C, PVC-U, ABS, HDPE, PE-X, PP
— hot	Copper, galvanised steel, PVC-C, PE-X, PB, multi-layer, PP-R-fibre reinforced

Note: ABS = acrylonitrile butadiene styrene; PE-X = cross-linked polyethylene; multi-layer = aluminium pipe between layers of HDPE or PE-X; PVC-C; PB = polybutylene; PP = polypropylene; PP-R-fibre reinforced = fibre reinforced polypropylene

Table B16.4 Expansion of pipes

Operating temperature difference* / K	Expansion for stated material / (mm·m⁻¹)				
	Mild/ carbon steel	Copper	Cast iron	Stainless steel	Polypropylene, HD poly-ethylene, CAB
	Coefficient of linear expansion per K × 10⁶ †				
	11.3	16.9	10.2	15.3	140.2
5	0.055	0.085	0.051	0.077	0.701
10	0.113	0.169	0.102	0.153	1.402
15	0.170	0.254	0.153	0.230	2.103
20	0.227	0.338	0.204	0.306	2.804
25	0.284	0.429	0.256	0.382	3.505
30	0.340	0.508	0.307	0.459	4.206
40	0.454	0.677	0.409	0.611	5.608
50	0.567	0.846	0.511	0.765	7.010
60	0.680	1.105	0.613	0.917	8.412‡
70	0.794	1.184	0.715	1.069	9.814‡
80	0.907	1.354	0.818	1.224	11.216‡
90	1.021	1.523	0.920	1.377	12.618‡
100	1.134	1.692	1.022	1.530	14.020‡
110	1.247	1.861	1.124	1.682	15.422‡
120	1.361	2.030	1.226	1.833	16.824‡
130	1.474	2.200	1.329	1.988	18.226‡
140	1.588	2.369	1.431	2.140	19.628‡
150	1.701	2.538	1.533	2.294	21.030‡

* Difference between temperature of medium and ambient temperature
† From Table B16.2
‡ Temperatures may exceed the limiting temperature for the material

Table B16.2 Comparative properties of piping materials

Material	Specific gravity	Specific heat capacity / kJ·kg⁻¹·K⁻¹	Softening point / °C	Heat distortion point (at 1.82 MN·m⁻²) / °C	Safe working temp. / °C	Coeff. of linear exp. per K × 10⁶	Thermal conductivity / W·m⁻²·K⁻¹	Weathering properties	Abrasion resistance
PVC:									
— normal impact	1.40	1.10	75	70.0	60	55.1	0.179	Excellent	Good
— high impact	1.37	1.10	73	65.0	49	75.1	0.189	Fair	Good
— flexible	1.37	—	70	—	—	—	—	—	—
Polythene:									
— low density	0.92	2.2–2.7	80	30.0	46	225.0	0.335	Fair	Moderate
— high density	0.95	2.5	110	45.0	49	140.2	0.490	Fair	Fair
Polypropylene	0.91	1.9	130	52.8	85	140.2	0.149	Good	Fair
ABS (acryonite butadiene styrene)	1.05	1.45	93	85.0	71	110.2	0.221	Fair	Good
Nylon	1.11	1.7–2.1	210	55.0	66	125.3	0.241	Fair	Good
CAB (cellulose acetate butyrate)	1.20	1.45	80	67.2	60	140.2	0.149	Good	Fair
PTFE	2.18	0.96	—	—	—	120.1	—	—	—
Polyester/glass fibre	1.80	1.25	—	141.1	141	—	—	Excellent	Good
Mild steel	7.85	0.485	—	—	—	11.3	47.6	Poor	—
Cast iron	7.40	0.405	—	—	—	10.2	47.6	Poor	—
Copper	8.91	0.390	—	—	—	16.9	172	Excellent	—
Aluminium	2.70	0.880	—	—	—	25.6	211	Excellent	—
Lead	11.21	0.135	—	—	—	29.0	34.6	Excellent	—
Stainless steel	7.93	0.522	—	—	—	15.3	16.0	Excellent	Excellent

account of both capital cost of pumps and pipework and the running cost to provide the pumping power required. In practice, the starting point for pipe sizing is usually based on flow velocity, ranging from <1 m·s^{-1} for small bore pipes to 3 m·s^{-1} for pipes with a diameter of greater than 50 mm. The pipe sizing tables generated by the spreadsheet contained on the CD-ROM that accompanies this Handbook are banded to show flow velocity. Another approach is to size for a particular pressure drop per unit length, typically between 200 to 300 Pa·m^{-1}.

B1.5.1.4 Pumps

(a) Pump characteristics

Centrifugal pumps are well suited to providing the necessary circulation in hydronic heating systems. They operate by using the energy imparted by a rotating impeller fitted in a carefully designed casing; liquid enters near the centre of the impeller and leaves at higher velocity at its perimeter. A typical centrifugal pump characteristic is shown in Figure B1.13, in which it may be observed that maximum pressure is produced at zero flow and maximum flow at zero pressure.

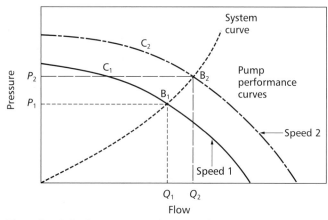

Figure B1.13 Performance curves for a centrifugal pump

Centrifugal pumps have the following characteristics:

— flow varies directly with the speed of rotation of the impeller

— pressure varies as the square of the speed

— power absorbed varies with cube of the speed.

If the diameter of the impeller is changed, but speed of rotation kept constant:

— flow varies as the cube of the impeller diameter

— pressure varies as the square of the impeller diameter

— power absorbed varies as the fifth power of the impeller diameter.

The flow available from a centrifugal pump in a circuit depends upon the resistance characteristics of the circuit. Figure B1.13 shows a typical system curve superimposed on the performance curves of the pump. The flow obtained at a given pump speed can be determined from the point at which the pump and system curves intersect. A pump speed is selected which can provide the required flow at the pressure drop around the path of the circuit with the highest pressure drop, otherwise known as the 'index' circuit.

(b) Variable speed pumping

Maximum flow and power are only required under design conditions in which all loads are calling for heat. As demand is satisfied, full flow is no longer required in parts of the circuit and pumping power can be reduced to match the system requirement at the time. The most effective method of controlling pump speed is by means of induction motors powered by variable frequency inverters; such a combination can maintain high efficiency over a wide range of speeds. Variable speed motors, which have a built-in inverter drive, are also available. Pump energy savings of 60–70% are possible, with payback times of around 2 years.

The design of variable speed pumping systems needs to allow two-port control valves to close without causing unwanted flow or pressure variations in other parts of the circuit. The most common method of controlling pump speed is to maintain a constant pressure differential between two points in the index circuit. BSRIA Application Guide AG 14/99 describes procedures for the design of systems with variable speed pumping.

B1.5.1.5 Controls

Guide B section 1.4.3.8 describes the general principles of control and control functions applied to hydronic systems. Guide B section 1.5.1.5 describes the key components required to implement those functions.

B1.5.5 Chimneys and flues

B1.5.5.1 Environmental legislation affecting chimneys and flues

Several different strands of legislation are relevant to the design of flues and chimneys, depending on the power of the plant they serve, the fuels used and where they are located.

The Environmental Protection Act 1990 gives powers to local authorities to control pollution from industrial and other processes, which includes the generation of heat and power. Large scale ('Part A') processes, with an output exceeding 50 MW, are subject to control by the Environment Agency. Local authorities control smaller scale ('Part B') processes, which may include large boilers and CHP units. One of the many requirements is for the use of 'best available techniques not entailing excessive cost' ('BATNEEC') to meet limits on levels of contaminants in flue discharges.

The Environment Act 1995 includes provisions for 'local air quality management' and sets air quality standards for seven key urban pollutants: nitrogen dioxide, carbon monoxide, sulphur dioxide, PM10 particles, benzene, 1,3-butadene and lead. An area where any of the standards are likely to be exceeded must be designated as an 'air quality management area' and action taken to reduce levels. This can lead to additional restrictions on development in those areas.

The legislation has an important impact on the design of chimneys and flues, particularly on the height at which combustion products are discharged to the atmosphere. Plant used for heating can for the most part be dealt with using published guidance. *The Clean Air Act Memorandum: Chimney Heights* (3rd edition) has long been recommended as a source of this guidance and remains valid. However, some types of plant require additional considerations to meet the requirements of the Environmental Protection Act; reference should be made to HMIP Guidance Note D1: *Guidelines for Discharge Stack Heights for Polluting Emissions*. CIBSE TM21 provides guidance on minimising pollution at air intakes, including the contribution made by chimneys and flues. For natural gas and other very low sulphur fuels, guidance may also be obtained from British Gas publication IM/11.

B1.5.5.2 The Building Regulations

Part J of the Building Regulations applies to all chimneys and flues, irrespective of the type of building, or the capacity of the appliance they serve. It includes the following requirements:

— that sufficient combustion air is supplied for proper operation of flues

— that combustion products are not hazardous to health

— that no damage is caused by heat or fire to the fabric of the building.

Similar requirements are contained in Part F of the Building Standards (Scotland) Regulations and the Building Regulations (Northern Ireland).

Approved Document J gives guidance on how to satisfy the requirements. It also makes clear that although Part J applies to all heat producing appliances, the guidance in the Approved Document itself deals mainly with domestic installations. Accordingly, the specific guidance it contains is limited to solid fuel installations of up to 50 kW rated output, gas installations of up to 70 kW net (77.7 kW gross) rated input and oil installations of up to 45 kW rated heat output.

For installations with ratings higher than those mentioned above, the guidance referred to in section B1.5.5.1 applies.

B1.5.5.3 Principles of flue and chimney design

A chimney or flue must produce sufficient suction to enable the installed plant to operate as intended and to disperse flue gases effectively. A natural draught chimney produces suction at its base by virtue of the difference in the density between the column of hot gas within the chimney and the outside air. This can be expressed by the formula:

$$\Delta p_d / H = (\rho_a - \rho_g) g \qquad (1.35)$$

where Δp_d is the pressure difference between top and bottom of chimney (Pa), H is the height of the chimney (m), ρ_a is the density of ambient air (kg·m^{-3}), ρ_g is the mean density of flue gases (kg·m^{-3}) and g is the acceleration due to gravity (m·s^{-2}).

The draught produced by a chimney is proportional to its height and the temperature of the gas within it. Figure B1.30 shows the draught available for typical winter and summer ambient conditions at various chimney temperatures. This gross draught is available to provide the energy required to move the flue gases through the particular boiler, flue and chimney system.

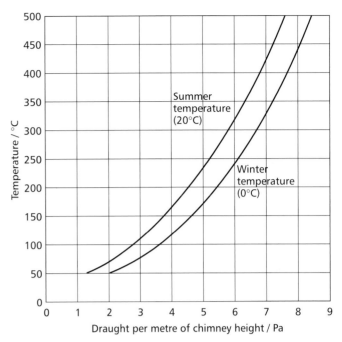

Figure B1.30 Chimney draught at summer and winter temperatures

(a) System resistance

The chimney/flue cross-sectional areas must be selected taking account of system resistance to gas flow and the required efflux velocity from the chimney terminal. It is important that the flue layout is carefully considered and designed to limit shock losses at bends etc. In general the following aspects should be observed in flue design:

— Position the boilers as close as possible to the chimney to limit friction and heat losses in the connecting flue system.

— Avoid all short radius 90° bends in flue systems.

— Avoid abrupt section changes and use transformation sections with 15° included angles.

— Arrange the entry section to slope at 45° or more to the horizontal

— Avoid protrusion of the flues beyond the inner face of the chimney or main flue connection.

— Make flues circular or square and avoid aspect (width to depth) ratios greater than 1.5 to 1.

— Slope flues up towards the chimney where possible.

— Provide clean-out doors at each bend in the flues, at the chimney base, and adjacent to fans and dampers to aid maintenance.

— Avoid long 'dead' chimney pockets under the flue entry points, which are corrosion zones, and can cause harmonic pulsation problems.

(b) Chimney efflux velocity

Chimney gas efflux velocities need to be high enough to avoid 'down-washing' of flue gases on the leeward side of the chimney. Guidance on chimney design is usually based on minimum full-load efflux velocities of 6 m·s^{-1} for natural draught and 7.5 m·s^{-1} for fan forced or induced draught installations. Low efflux velocities may also cause inversion, whereby cold air enters the top of the chimney and flows downward, reducing chimney internal skin temperatures below the acid dew-point and causing acid smut emission. The maintenance of an adequate efflux velocity at all loads is difficult where one chimney serves more than one boiler, particularly if each boiler has high/low or modulating firing.

It may not always be possible to achieve efflux velocities of 6 m·s^{-1} on natural draught plant, particularly if the whole flue and chimney system is designed on this velocity basis, due to the excessive system resistance involved. In such cases, the system can be designed for a lower velocity and a nozzle fitted at the chimney outlet to increase efflux velocity to the extent that the excess available draught allows.

(c) Flue corrosion and acid smut formation

Flue gases have a dew-point below which water vapour condenses. With sulphur bearing fuels, a second acid dew-point occurs at a higher temperature that depends on the type of fuel, amount of excess air, sulphur content and combustion intensity. The sulphur in the fuel is oxidised to SO_2 during the combustion process and a proportion of this is oxidised further to SO_3, with subsequent formation of sulphuric acid.

The peak rate of corrosion tends to occur some 30–40 °C below the acid dew-point and a dramatic increase in corrosion rate occurs below the water dew-point. Acid dew-points generally lie in the range 115–140 °C for the type of boiler plant used for heating but depend upon excess air used, flame temperature, sulphur content etc. A significant depression in acid dew-point temperature occurs where fuels have less than 0.5% sulphur content. It can also be reduced or eliminated by stoichiometric combustion conditions that can only be approached on very large plants.

A smut is an agglomeration of carbon particles resulting from a combination of stack solids and low temperature corrosion products. If the inner surface of any flue/chimney falls below the acid dew-point temperature of the waste gases, an acidic film forms on the surface. Stack solids adhere to this film and build up into loose layers, which are dislodged and ejected from the chimney as the firing rates change.

(d) Flue/chimney area and siting

Where chimneys are oversized, or where more than one boiler is used with one flue/chimney, the inner chimney surface temperatures may fall below acid dew-point conditions, even with insulation applied. To avoid these problems, it is strongly recommended to install one flue/chimney per boiler, correctly sized for maximum practicable full load flue gas.

Chimney outlets should not be positioned such that air inlets into the building are on the leeward side of the chimney for the prevailing wind direction. Generally internal chimneys have less heat dissipation than free-standing units but where external chimneys are used they should, where possible, be positioned on the leeward side of the building or site, considering the prevailing wind direction.

The chimney outlet should be at a minimum height of 3 m above the highest point of the adjacent building roof level in order to limit wind pressure variations on the flue outlet and present the minimum face area to the prevailing wind. Chimney heights must comply with environmental legislation and the Building Regulations. The sizing and height

of chimneys and flues is considered in detail in Guide B Appendix 1.A2.

(e) Cold air admission

The admission of cold air into the flue/chimney system reduces the flue gas temperatures and hence the available natural draught. Draught stabilisers deliberately introduce cold air to regulate the draught by this means. The use of draught stabilisers is not recommended when high sulphur fuels are used, as reduced flue gas temperature also produces corrosion and acid smut emissions.

Dampers for draught regulation should be fitted with safety interlocks to prevent firing against a closed damper. With high chimneys the damper should be arranged to close when the firing equipment is off-load, to isolate the boiler and limit cold air ingress to the system. This limits the cooling effect on the internal flue and chimney system, and the corrosion mechanism within the boiler gas-side heating surfaces.

(f) Heat loss

To enable the correct chimney construction to be selected it is necessary to predict the minimum internal surface temperature likely to be obtained at the chimney terminal under all loads. An approximate value may be obtained using the following method. It should be noted that average values are used for some parameters and that radiation from the gases to the chimney is ignored in order to simplify calculations.

The rate of heat loss from the chimney or duct is given by:

$$\phi_c = U A (t_g - t_{ao}) \qquad (1.36)$$

where ϕ_c is the heat loss rate (W), U is the overall thermal transmittance (W·m^{-2}·K^{-1}), A is the surface area (m^2), t_g is the mean waste gas temperature (°C) and t_{ao} is the outside air temperature (°C).

The overall thermal transmittance is given by:

$$\frac{1}{U} = \frac{1}{h_o} + \frac{l_1}{\lambda_1} + \frac{l_2}{\lambda_2} + ... \frac{1}{h_i} \qquad (1.37)$$

where h_o is the external film coefficient (W·m^{-2}·K^{-1}), l_1 etc. is the thickness of chimney layer 1 etc. (m), λ_1 is the thermal conductivity of chimney layer 1 and h_i is the internal film coefficient (W·m^2·K^{-1}).

Values of film coefficients h_o and h_i are given in Figures 1.31 and 1.32.

The heat loss may also be deduced from:

$$\phi_c = q_m c_p (t_{g1} - t_{g2}) \qquad (1.38)$$

where q_m is the mass flow rate of gases (kg·s^{-1}), c_p is the specific heat capacity at constant pressure of waste gases (J·kg^{-1}·K^{-1}), t_{g1} is the temperature of gases entering the bottom of the chimney (°C) and t_{g2} is the temperature of gases leaving the top of the chimney (°C).

Alternatively, the volume flow rate of waste gases (m^3·s^{-1}) may be used in conjunction with the specific heat capacity

$(J \cdot m^{-3} \cdot K^{-1})$. The specific heat is usually taken to be $1.22 \ kJ \cdot m^{-3} \cdot K^{-1}$ at 200 °C.

For thermal equilibrium, equations 1.36 and 1.38 must give the same heat loss, so they may be equated, i.e:

$$U A (t_g - t_{ao}) = q_m c_p (t_{g1} - t_{g2}) \qquad (1.39)$$

where t_g is given by:

$$t_g = \tfrac{1}{2} (t_{g1} + t_{g2}) \qquad (1.40)$$

If the temperature of the waste gases entering the chimney or duct is known or estimated, the temperature of the gases leaving the chimney may be determined from equation 1.39. The minimum surface temperature may then be established from:

$$h_i (t_{g2} - t_{si}) = U (t_{g2} - t_{ao}) \qquad (1.41)$$

where t_{si} is the temperature of the inside surface of chimney (°C).

B1.6 Fuels

B1.6.1 Classification and properties of fuels

See also section (C)5.

B1.6.1.1 Gaseous fuels

The main gaseous fuels are broadly classified as natural gas and liquefied petroleum gases (LPG). Natural gas consists predominantly of methane and is delivered by pipeline. LPG includes propane and butane, and is delivered as a liquid contained in a pressurised vessel. The key properties of the main gaseous fuels are shown in Table B1.23.

(a) Wobbe number

The Wobbe number (W) is designed to indicate the heat produced at a burner when fuelled by a particular gas, and is defined as:

$$W = h_g/d^{0.5} \qquad (1.42)$$

where W is the Wobbe number ($MJ \cdot m^{-3}$), h_g is the gross calorific value ($MJ \cdot m^{-3}$) and d is the relative density of the gas (relative to air at standard temperature and pressure).

(b) Supply/working pressure

Natural gas supplies are regulated at the metering point to an outlet pressure of 2100 Pa (21 mbar). This pressure may be reduced further at the appliance to provide the required pressure at the burner. LPG is supplied via tanks or cylinders, regulated to a pressure of 3700 Pa (37 mbar) for propane and 2800 Pa (28 mbar) for butane. This pressure is not normally reduced at the appliance.

(c) Landfill and sewage gas

Landfill gas is collected from wells inserted in land-fill sites, often complementing measures to prevent hazards arising from the escape of gas. It typically consists of between 40 and 60% methane by volume with the remainder mostly carbon dioxide and traces of many other gases. The calorific value of landfill gas is in the range 15 to 25 $MJ \cdot m^{-3}$, depending on its methane content.

Landfill gas is mostly used without processing, other than the removal of moisture and dust. Because of its low calorific value it is relatively expensive to transport and is most suitable for heat generation when it can be produced close to a heat load, which favoured its early exploitation for brick kilns adjacent to clay pits used for land fill. In other cases, it is used to generate electricity from gas turbines or reciprocating engines. The life expectancy of gas production from landfill sites is typically 15 to 30 years.

Sewage gas is produced from digestion of sewage sludge. Some of the gas produced is used to maintain optimum temperature for the digestion process. It is economic in many cases to use combined heat and power generation in this situation, and to export the surplus power to the grid.

B1.6.1.2 Liquid fuels

(a) Oil fuels

BS 2869 contains specifications for various classes of liquid fuels designated by the letters A to G. The fuels commonly used for heating are Class C2 (kerosene or burning oil), Class D (gas oil), Class E (light fuel oil), Class F (medium fuel oil) and Class G (heavy fuel oil). The key properties of these fuels are shown in Table B1.24. Further information can be found in CIBSE Guide C,

Table B1.23 Properties of commercial gas supplies at standard temperature and pressure

Property	Natural gas	Commercial propane	Commercial butane
Density relative to air	0.60	1.45 to 1.55	1.9 to 2.10
Gross calorific value ($MJ \cdot m^{-3}$)	38.7	93	122
Wobbe number ($MJ \cdot m^{-3}$)	45 to 55	73.5 to 87.5	73.5 to 87.5
Supply/working pressure (Pa)	1750 to 2750	3700	2800
Stoichiometric air to gas volume ratio	9.73	24	30
Flame speed ($m \cdot s^{-1}$)	0.43	0.47	0.38
Flammability limits (% gas in air)	5–15	2–10	2–9
Boiling point (°C)	—	−45	0
Latent heat of vaporisation ($kJ \cdot kg^{-1}$)	—	357	370
Flame temperature (°C)	1930	1950	—
Ignition temperature (°C)	704	530	470

Table B1.24 Key properties of typical petroleum fuels

Property	Class C2	Class D	Class E	Class F	Class G
Density at 15 °C (kg·m^{-3})	803	850	940	970	980
Minimum closed flash point (°C)	38	60	66	66	66
Kinematic viscosity (mm^2·s^{-1}) at 40 °C	1.0 to 2.0	1.5 to 5.5	—	—	—
Kinematic viscosity (mm^2·s^{-1}) at 100 °C	—	—	≤8.2	≤20.0	≤40.0
Maximum pour point (°C)	—	—	−6	24	30
Gross calorific value (MJ·kg^{-1})	46.4	45.5	42.5	41.8	42.7
Net calorific value (MJ·kg^{-1})	43.6	42.7	40.1	39.5	40.3
Maximum sulphur content by mass (%)	0.2	0.2	3.2	3.5	3.5
Mean specific heat 0–100 °C (MJ·kg^{-1})	2.1	2.06	1.93	1.89	1.89

section 5.5.2, including graphs showing the kinematic viscosity of fuel oils at different temperatures.

(b) Liquid biofuels

Fuels may be produced from crops grown specifically for the purpose. Historically, the principal fuel crop has been coppice wood for charcoal production. In recent decades, interest has been focussed on the production of liquid and gaseous fuels suitable for use in transport. The process and the crops used determine the type of fuel produced. Thermal processing (by combustion, gasification or pyrolysis) is best suited to dry materials. Anaerobic fermentation is better suited to wet bio-mass materials, which can yield both methane rich bio-gas and liquid fuels, according to the type of fermentation used. Ethanol has been produced commercially from sugar cane, notably in Brazil. In Europe, rape seed oil is used to produce bio-diesel, which has very similar properties to petroleum-derived diesel and can be used in existing engines without significant modification.

B1.6.1.3   Solid fuels

Coal is classified according to its chemical composition and graded according to size. CIBSE Guide C section 5.5 gives the properties of numerous varieties of coal, including moisture, ash and sulphur content. Gross calorific value ranges from 24 to 34 MJ·kg^{-1}.

Municipal waste may be burnt unprocessed, with heat extracted or electricity generated as part of the incineration process. Alternatively it may be used to produce refuse-derived fuel pellets, which may be used to fire some types of boiler plant. It has a calorific value about two thirds of that of coal and produces around 50% more ash.

Wood fuels are of interest because their use can result in a net decrease in greenhouse gas emissions. Forestry waste results from the normal processes of forestry management, which is has the principal objective of maximising the value of the timber crop. Waste wood is also available from industrial sources, particularly from saw-milling and furniture making. Its use as a fuel has a net benefit in greenhouse gas emissions, both by avoiding the need to burn a fossil fuel and by avoiding the production of methane that would result from decomposition on the forest floor or in landfill.

Wood fuel may be produced by growing arable coppice specifically for fuel production. The carbon dioxide released on combustion will have been sequestered during growth and there is no net contribution to CO_2 emissions. Notwithstanding its environmental advantages, wood is a low quality fuel, with a calorific value of around 19 MJ·kg^{-1} when dry and only around 10 MJ·kg^{-1} at the typical moisture content (55%) when harvested.

Straw is also used as a fuel, particularly since the phasing out of straw-burning on fields in the early 1990s. It is burnt in high temperature boilers and used to supply heat and hot water, usually on a fairly small scale.

B1.6.1.4   Electricity

Electricity is the most versatile form in which energy is delivered and may serve almost any end-use of energy, including those for which fuels are consumed directly. However, the high quality and versatility of electricity must be seen in the context of its high cost, which reflects the high primary energy input to electricity generation.

The shift towards gas generation has several important implications for UK electricity, apart from fuel supply considerations. Gas produces negligible emissions of sulphur dioxide to the atmosphere, and reduced concentrations of other atmospheric pollutants. As a result, UK sulphur dioxide emissions from power stations have declined by around two-thirds since 1990, contributing to a greater than 50% reduction in UK emissions from all sources. The amount of carbon dioxide released per unit of heat energy obtained from gas is also lower than for coal. The current generation of gas-fired power stations using combined cycle technology are more efficient than coal-fired stations. The overall effect is that the gas generated electricity is less than half as carbon intensive as coal-generated electricity.

B1.6.1.5   Renewable electricity generation

In addition to the use of bio-fuels described above, there are many possibilities for generating electricity directly from renewable sources of energy based on solar radiation, wind, tides, waves, hydropower and geothermal heat. The UK lacks the terrain to permit further exploitation of large-scale hydroelectric power, but there are numerous opportunities for small-scale exploitation. The UK also has very limited opportunities for exploiting geothermal power but has considerable resources for wind, wave and tidal power. A wide ranging assessment of the opportunities for renewable energy in the UK was undertaken by the Energy Technology Support Unit (ETSU) in the early 1990s.

Although the contribution to electricity generation by renewable sources is small at present, the government has ambitious targets for expanding it to reach 10% in 2010. In this context it should be noted that renewable generating capacity doubled in the four year period between 1996 and 2000. In the short term much of this expansion will come from wind and land-fill gas.

B1.6.2 Factors affecting fuel choice

B1.6.2.1 Fuel prices

The price of fuel remains a very important factor affecting fuel choice and a strong determinant of life-cycle cost.

The high price of electricity compared to fuels consumed at the point of use, which serves to illustrate why electricity should be reserved for purposes in which its special advantages are needed. This normally precludes its use as a principal source of space heating, although it can be economical for localised and occasional use, particularly as radiant spot heating.

B1.6.2.2 Environmental impact

Table B1.25 shows average CO_2 emissions, expressed in terms of carbon, attributable to each unit of energy used in the UK, taking account of upstream and overhead effects. This may be used to compare alternative options for fuel and shows the advantage of natural gas over other fuels. Electricity obtained from the public supply has an emission factor of about two and a half times that of gas.

Table B1.25 Carbon emission factors for UK in 2000–2005

Fuel	Carbon emission per unit of delivered energy/ $kgC \cdot (kW \cdot h)^{-1}$
Natural gas	0.053
LPG	0.068
Gas oil/burning oil	0.074
Coal	0.086
Electricity (average of public supply)	0.113

B2 Ventilation and air conditioning

B2.2 Integrated approach

B2.2.1 Introduction

The pursuance of an integrated design approach links the ventilation strategy with the design of the building fabric; all reasonable steps should be taken to maximise the potential of the building fabric. This is commonly referred to as the 'passive approach'. In particular, an appropriate degree of airtightness should be aimed at. The design process must be based on a clear understanding of client and end user needs and expectations and must be followed by effective commissioning, handover and building management. Close collaboration between the architect, services and structural engineers and the client is essential from the earliest stages of the outline design process.

B2.2.2 Establishing key performance requirements

The key performance requirements that need to be clarified before a ventilation strategy can be selected are summarised in Table B2.1. Ideally, where the issues highlighted in the table have not been covered within the specification documents, the design team should expect to agree requirements with the client at the outset of the project to optimise the choice of strategy. If the client is unable to advise on the precise needs, they must at least be made aware of any limitations of the chosen design in these respects.

The design team should also be able to advise the client of the cost implications (on a whole life basis if requested) of meeting their requirements. These may subsequently be adjusted over the course of the project to meet financial constraints or changing business needs. The design team must also be able to advise on the impact of any such changes on the ultimate building performance. An appreciation of the issues shown in Table B2.1 is an essential part of the briefing process. Further guidance on briefing as it applies to building services is given in BSRIA's *Project Management Handbook for Building Services*.

B2.2.3 Interaction with fabric/facilities

B2.2.3.1 Building fabric

The final ventilation rate is based on fresh air requirements and any additional ventilation required for comfort and cooling purposes based on estimates of:

— internal gains determined by the occupants, e.g. occupancy itself, lighting and small power loads

— internal gains determined by the fabric, e.g. insulation, glazing, thermal mass, as discussed below.

In order to engage effectively with the architect, the building services engineer must be able to enter into a dialogue on the issues introduced in Table B2.3, as a minimum. (Note that this table focuses solely on issues relating to the interaction between the building fabric and services. To these must be added, for example, consideration of the building function and broader issues. Where the ventilation strategy for the building depends on its thermal mass, early consultation with the structural engineer is also needed to consider, for example, the implications for roof design. At some point it may also be necessary to involve a façade specialist, who could advise the client accordingly.

For a detailed explanation of the role of the building fabric in contributing to an energy efficient solution see CIBSE Guide F and other publications referenced in Table B2.3. It is also important to consider the risks of air leakage through the building fabric and its subsequent impact on infiltration rates and heat loss calculations. The most common air-leakage risks are:

— at the junctions between the main structural elements, e.g. wall to roof, wall to floor, and wall to foundation

— at the joints between walling components, e.g. sealant or gasket joints between heavyweight or curtain walling panels, overlapping joints between

Table B2.1 Establishing performance requirements

Issue	Requirement/comments
Client brief	To be developed in the context of the other issues
Integrated design	Co-ordinated approach by the architect and other specialists from outline design, see Guide B2 section 2.3.1
Energy/environmental targets	Use of existing specifications or appropriate advice from the design team required, see Guide B2 see section 2.2.1 Compatibility with indoor environment standards
Indoor environmental standards	Use of existing standards or appropriate advice from the design team required, see see Guide B2 section 3 and CIBSE Guide A
	Areas or objects with special requirements
Provision of controls	Individual, local, team, zone or centralised basis
	Required closeness of control (e.g. of temperature, humidity, air quality, air flow)
	The required interaction of the end user with the building services, see see Guide B2 section 2.2.2
	The required basis of control, e.g. temperature, CO_2, CO or other
Demands of the building occupants and activities	The business process(es) to be undertaken in the building may demand specified levels of availability of ventilation
	Work patterns over space and over time (regularity, shifts, team structure)
	Cellular and open plan mix with associated partitioning strategy and likelihood of change
	Occupancy numbers and anticipated maximum occupancy over the building lifetime that might need to be taken into account
	Average occupancy density and any areas of high or low density
	Functions of space use, processes contained therein and subsequent internal loads (e.g. standard office space, meeting rooms, lecture theatres, photocopying rooms, sports hall, laboratories, manufacturing environments, retail space)
	Anticipated diversity of internal loads
Investment criteria	Constraints imposed by 'letability' requirements
Value engineering and whole life costs	Understanding of the client's priorities towards capital cost and issues of whole life costs
	Requirements for calculations to be carried out on systems or system elements and the basis for these calculations
	Has the client been involved in discussions of acceptable design risk?
	The importance of part load performance
Reliability	The business process(es) to be undertaken in the building may demand specified levels of reliability of the ventilation systems
Maintenance requirements	Understanding of the client's ability to carry out, or resource, maintenance
	Client willingness for maintenance to take place in the occupied space
	Any requirement for 'standard' or 'familiar' components
Associated systems	Implications of any particular requirements, e.g. fire, security, lighting, acoustic consideration.
Security	Restrictions on size and location of any openings
Future needs	Adaptability, i.e. the identified need to cope with future change of use
	Flexibility, i.e. the identified need to cope with future changes in work practices within the current building use
	Acceptable design margins: it is important to distinguish, in collaboration with the client, between design that is adequate for current requirements (which may not be currently accepted best practice), design which makes sensible agreed allowances for future changes and over-design
Aesthetic considerations	The need for system concealment
	Restriction on placement of grilles, diffusers etc.
	Restrictions imposed by local authorities, building listing etc.
Procurement issues	Time constraints.
	Programming constraints, particularly for refurbishment projects

lightweight sheet metal wall panels and boundaries of different cladding/walling systems

— around windows, doors and roof lights, e.g. between window or doorframes and walls or floors, between doors and windows and their frames, and between frames and sills

— through gaps in membranes, linings and finishes, e.g. in wall membranes and dry linings, in ceiling linings and boundaries with wall linings and gaps in floor finishes and around skirtings

— at service penetrations, e.g. electrical sockets and conduits, gas and electricity entry points, ventilation pipes for sanitary waste, overflow pipes and flues

Table B2.3 Issues influencing the choice of ventilation strategy

Issue	Comments
Location	Adjacent buildings can adversely affect wind patterns. The proximity of external sources of pollution can influence the feasibility of natural ventilation. The proximity of external sources of noise can impact on the feasibility of natural ventilation.
Pollution	Local levels of air pollution may limit the opportunity for natural ventilation. It may not be possible to provide air inlets at positions suitable for natural ventilation given the inability to filter the incoming air successfully.
Orientation	Buildings with their main facades facing north and south are much easier to protect from excessive solar gain in summer. West façade solar gain is the most difficult to control as high gains occur late in the day. Low sun angles occurring at certain times of year affect both east and west facing facades.
Form	At building depths greater than 15 m the ventilation strategy becomes more complex; the limit for daylighting and single-sided natural ventilation is often taken as 6 m. An atrium can enhance the potential for natural ventilation, see Guide B section 2.2.5.1.
	Tall buildings can affect the choice of ventilation system due to wind speeds and exposure. Adequate floor to ceiling heights are required for displacement ventilation and buoyancy driven natural ventilation; a minimum floor to ceiling height of 2.7 m is recommended, see see Guide B section 2.4.3.
Insulation	Insulation located on the external surface de-couples the mass of the structure from the external surface and enables it to stabilise the internal environment. In well-insulated buildings provision must be made for the removal of excess heat, for example through night cooling, see see Guide B section 2.4.7.
Infiltration	Ventilation strategies, whether natural or mechanically driven, depend on the building fabric being appropriately airtight. This implies a good practice standard of 5 $m^3 \cdot h^{-1}$ per m^2 of façade (excluding consideration of the ground floor) and requires suitable detailing. Site quality checks should be followed by air leakage pressure testing as part of the commissioning requirement.
Shading	The appropriate use of external planting or other features can reduce solar gain. In terms of effective reduction of solar gain, shading devices can be ranked in order of effectiveness as follows: external (most effective), mid pane, internal (least effective), see Guide B, Figure 2.3.
	Horizontal shading elements are most appropriate for reducing high angle solar gains, for example in summer time on south facing facades. Vertical shading devices are most appropriate for reducing low angle solar gain, e.g. on east and west facades. Control of solar shading devices should be linked with that of the ventilation system. Glare must be controlled to avoid a default to 'blinds-down' and 'lights-on' operation.
Window choice	Openable areas must be controllable in both summer and winter, e.g. large openings for still summer days and trickle ventilation for the winter time. Window shape can affect ventilation performance; deep windows can provide better ventilation than shallow. High level openings provide cross ventilation, low level openings provide local ventilation, although draughts should be avoided at working level. The location of the opening areas affects the ability of the window to contribute to night cooling (see see Guide B section 2 4.7). Window operation must not be affected by the choice of shading device. See see Guide B section 2 5.3 for details of window characteristics.
Glazing	Total solar heat transmission through window glazing can vary over a sixfold range, depending on the combination of glass and shading mechanisms selected. Guide B Figure 2.3 shows the relative effectiveness of eight glazing and shading systems. Guide B Figure 2.3 underlines the importance of decisions about glazing and shading to the overall ventilation strategy.
	At concept stage the percentage of glazed area (normally 20–40% of façade area) and selection of glazing type must balance thermal, ventilation and lighting needs. The choice includes single, double, triple glazing with selective coatings or gaseous fill. The type of coating may have a greater influence than the glazing type. Ideal glazing is transparent to long-wave radiation and reflective to short-wave radiation. Selective low-emissivity double-glazing is equivalent to air-filled triple-glazing.
	The use of tinted glazing may increase the use of supplementary electric lighting, increasing internal heat gains and energy use. Window frame construction and detailing must also be considered.
Thermal mass	Thermal mass is used to reduce peak cooling demands and stabilise internal radiant and air temperatures. The first 50 to 100 mm of the structure is most effective on a 24-hour basis. Thermal mass can be introduced into the ceiling/floor slab (most effective), walls or partitions, but must be 'accessible' in all cases. Heat transfer can be via the surface of the material or via cores/channels within it. The exposure of thermal mass has architectural and other servicing implications, although these effects can be reduced, e.g. by the use of perforated ceilings. See see Guide B section 2 4.7 for further details of incorporating thermal mass.

— around access and emergency openings, e.g. to roof space, to roof, to floors and to delivery points

— through some building materials, e.g. brickwork may be permeable especially where construction quality is low.

B2.2.5 Choice of ventilation strategy

Guide B section 2.2.5 gives an overview of the following strategies:

— natural ventilation

— mechanical ventilation

— comfort cooling

— air conditioning (which may be 'close control')

— mixed mode systems (i.e. a combination of natural and mechanical ventilation).

The selection of a strategy is affected by, amongst other factors, location, plan depth, heat gains, internal and external pollutant sources, economics, energy and environmental concerns and internal layout. Ultimately it is the use and occupancy of a space that determines the ventilation needs. There is no universal economic solution, although there are some best practice indicators that are considered in subsequent sections. Each ventilation system design must be evaluated on its merits, to suit the particular circumstances.

Table B2.9 Summary of recommendations

Building sector	Guide B section number	Recommendation
Animal husbandry	2.3.24.1	See Guide B2 Table 2.28
Assembly halls	2.3.3	See Guide B2 Table 2.14
Atria	2.3.4	See Guide B2 section 2.3.4.3
Broadcasting studios	2.3.5	6–10 ACH (but heat gain should be assessed)
Call centres	2.3.24.2	4–6 ACH (but heat gain should be assessed)
Catering (inc. commercial kitchens)	2.3.6	30–40 ACH
Cleanrooms	2.3.7	See Guide B2 Tables 2.19 and 2.20
Communal residential buildings	2.3.8	0.5–1 ACH
Computer rooms	2.3.9	See Guide B2 Table 2.21
Court rooms	2.3.24.3	As for typical naturally ventilated buildings
Darkrooms (photographic)	2.3.24.4	6–8 ACH (but heat gain should be assessed)
Dealing rooms	2.3.24.5	As offices for ventilation (but heat gain should be assessed)
Dwellings (inc. high-rise dwellings)	2.3.10	0.5–1 ACH
Factories and warehouses	2.3.11	See Guide B2 section 2.3.11.1 for regulatory requirements
High-rise (non-domestic) buildings	2.3.12	4–6 ACH for office areas; up to 10 ACH for meeting spaces
Horticulture	2.3.24.6	30–50 litre·s^{-1}·m^{-2} for greenhouses (45–60 ACH)
Hospitals and health care buildings	2.3.13	See Guide B2 Table 2.23
Hotels	2.3.14	10–15 ACH minimum for guest rooms with en-suite bathrooms
Industrial ventilation	2.3.15	Sufficient to minimise airborne contamination
Laboratories	2.3.16	6-15 ACH (allowance must be made for fume cupboards)
Museums, libraries and art galleries	2.3.17	Depends on nature of exhibits
Offices	2.3.2	See Guide B2 Tables 2.10 and 2.11
Plant rooms	2.3.18	Specific regulations apply, see Guide B2 section 2.3.18
Schools and educational buildings	2.3.19	See Guide B2 Table 2.26
Shops and retail premises	2.3.20	5–8 litre·s^{-1} per person
Sports centres (inc. swimming pools)	2.3.21	See Guide B2 Table 2.27
Standards rooms	2.3.24.7	45–60 ACH
Toilets	2.3.22	Building Regulations apply; opening windows of area 1/20th. of floor area or mechanical ventilation at 6 litre·s^{-1} per WC or 3 ACH minimum for non-domestic buildings; opening windows of area 1/20 th. of floor area (1/30th. in Scotland) or mechanical extract at 6 litre·s^{-1} (3 ACH in Scotland) minimum for dwellings
Transportation buildings (inc. car parks)	2.3.23	6 ACH for car parks (normal operation) 10 ACH (fire conditions)

Excessive air infiltration can destroy the performance of a ventilation strategy, hence good ventilation system design should be combined with optimum airtightness to achieve energy efficient ventilation.

B2.3   Requirements

B2.3.1   Introduction

A strategic consideration of requirements as part of an integrated approach to design is outlined in section B2.2. Specific requirements for various building sectors are summarised in Table B2.9.

B2.3.2   Offices

The following requirements apply to offices and to a wide range of other buildings. Requirements specific to other types of buildings are given in Guide B sections 2.3.3 to 2.3.24.

B2.3.2.1   *Indoor air quality: basic requirements for health and safety*

The issue of improving air quality in offices (and buildings in general) has previously been mainly related to sick building syndrome (SBS). However recent work has suggested that SBS is not linked to the type of ventilation or air conditioning system used but is more likely to be a function of how well systems are installed, managed and operated. It suggested that workspaces conforming to CIBSE guidelines on temperature and air movement should not suffer from SBS, unless there are aggravating work-related factors or extreme levels of pollution.

(a) Basis of requirements

Ventilation may be used to dilute or displace and remove airborne contaminants released in a space and which would otherwise rise to unacceptable concentrations. Within the Building Regulations, guidance on achieving compliance of relevance to the designer of ventilation systems includes:

— *Approved Document F: Ventilation*; Part F1: *Means of ventilation*; Part F2: *Condensation in roofs*

— *Approved Document J: Heat producing appliances*

— *Approved Document B: Fire safety*

— *Approved Document L: Conservation of fuel and power*

Note that if dilution is the main basis of control then the ventilation system should be designed to produce good mixing of the incoming air with the contaminant within the space. In situations where the contaminant release is from a fixed source then it is preferable to arrange the extract location as close to the source as possible so that direct removal is achieved. Requirements will also be affected by the ventilation efficiency, i.e. whether all the fresh air supplied is used or whether some is extracted prematurely. See Guide B section 2.4.2.2 for further consideration.

CIBSE Guide A chapter 1 should be consulted for the definition of, and requirements for achieving, suitable indoor air quality standards. It describes two methods for determining suitable outdoor air ventilation rates:

— a prescriptive method

— a calculation method for the control of a single known pollutant being released into the space at a known rate.

B2.4 Systems

B2.4.1 Introduction

Guide B section 2.4 provides details of the strategies and systems available to deliver the clients' requirements. Guide B sections 2.4.7 to 2.4.22 provide design guidelines for the various HVAC systems that can be utilised to achieve this objective. These are as follows:

— night cooling and thermal mass

— chilled ceilings/chilled beams

— cooled surfaces (floors and slabs)

— desiccant cooling systems

— dual duct (constant volume and variable air volume) and hot deck/cold deck systems

— evaporative cooling (direct and indirect)

— fan coil units

— ground cooling (air)

— ground cooling (water)

— heat pumps

— induction units

— room air conditioners

— single duct constant volume systems

— single duct variable air volume (VAV) systems

— split systems

— sea/river/lake water cooling.

Details of the constituent items of equipment within HVAC systems are given in Guide B section 2.5.

B2.5 Ventilation and air conditioning equipment

B2.5.1 Introduction

Guide B section 2.5 provides information about a wide range of equipment that is required for ventilation and air conditioning systems. It sets out critical design issues relating to the specific items of equipment and the key points to be considered in the selection of equipment. Where relevant, it provides references to key regulations and guidance relating specifically to the design, installation or use of the equipment.

The items of equipment considered are as follows:

— ventilation air intake and discharge points

— natural ventilation devices

— exhaust systems

— mixing boxes

— heat recovery devices

— air cleaners and filtration

— air heater batteries

— air cooler batteries

— humidifiers

— fans

— air control units

— air terminal devices.

B2.5.11 Fans

B2.5.11.2 Fan types and components

Table B2.53 provides a summary of fan types.

Table B2.53 Summary of fan types

Fan type	Efficiency / %		Advantages	Disadvantages	Applications
	Static	Total			
1 Axial-flow (without guide vanes	50–65	50–75	Very compact, straight-through flow. Suitable for installing in any position in run of ducting.	High tip speed. Relatively high noise level comparable with type 5. Low pressure development.	All low pressure atmospheric air applications.
2 Axial-flow (with guide vanes)	65–75	65–85	Straight-through flow. Suitable for vertical axis.	Same as type 1 but to lesser extent.	As for type 1, and large ventilation schemes such as tunnel ventilation.
3 Forward-curved or multivane centrifugal	45–60	45–70	Operates with low peripheral speed. Quiet and compact.	Severely rising power characteristic requires large motor margin.	All low and medium pressure atmospheric air and ventilation plants.
4 Straight or paddle-bladed centrifugal	45–55	45–70 60 (non-shrouded)	Strong, simple impeller. Least likely to clog. Easily cleaned and repaired.	Low efficiency. Rising power characteristic.	Material transport systems and any application where dust burden is high.
5 Backwards-curved or backwards-inclined blade centrifugal	65–75	65–85	Good efficiency. Non-over-loading power characteristic.	High tip speed. Relatively high noise level compared with type 3.	Medium and high pressure applications such as high velocity ventilation schemes.
6 Aerofoil-bladed centrifugal	80–85	80–90	Highest efficiency of all fan types. Non-overloading fan characteristic	Same as type 5.	Same as type 5 but higher efficiency justifies use for higher power applications.
7 Propeller	< 40	< 40	Low first cost and ease of installation.	Low efficiency and very low pressure development.	Mainly non-ducted low pressure atmospheric air applications. Pressure development can be increased by diaphragm mounting.
8 Mixed-flow	45–70	45–70	Straight-through flow. Suitable for installing in any position in run of ducting. Can be used for higher pressure duties than type 2. Lower blade speeds than types 1 or 2, hence lower noise.	Stator vanes are generally highly loaded due to higher pressure ratios. Maximum casing diameter is greater than either inlet or outlet diameters.	Large ventilation schemes where the higher pressures developed and lower noise levels give an advantage over type 2.
9 Cross-flow or tangential-flow	—	40–50	Straight across flow. Long, narrow discharge.	Low efficiency. Very low pressure development.	Fan coil units. Room conditioners. Domestic heaters.

Appendix B2.A2: Psychrometric processes

Table B2.A2.1 illustrates the basic psychrometric processes and lists the equipment concerned. See Guide B section 5 for details of the various items of equipment.

Table B2.A2.1 Basic psychrometric processes

Process	Method	Remarks	Psychrometric process
Heating	Electric	No additional plant required. High energy costs. Wiring and switch gear costs high for large duties. Usually only step control available.	
	Steam	Small heat transfer surface. Plant cost high unless steam required for other services. Condensate return can present difficulties. Modulating control available (2-way valve).	
	Hot water	Simple and reasonably cheap plant and distribution system. Integrates well with other heating systems. Some simplicity sacrificed to decrease heat surface with HTHW. Modulating control available (2- or 3-way valve).	
	Direct firing	Least expensive in specific cases. Can involve problems of combustion air and flue requirements. On/off control is common for smaller units while high/low flame is usually available for larger units.	
Humidification	Steam injection	Electrically heated, self-contained unit or unit supplied by mains steam. Water treatment advisable. Small space occupied. Mains units have modulating control (2-way valve), electric units are normally on/off. Mains units may require condensate drain.	
	Water injection	Involves atomising process (spinning disc, compressed air etc.). Some types are non-recirculatory and require drainage. Air is sensibly cooled as water evaporates. Contaminants from untreated water will enter airstream. Water treatment including biocidal control is essential. Space occupied depends on type. Some units mount on duct wall, other in duct line. Control is usually on/off by stopping atomiser or water supply; larger units in multiple form may be stepped. Normally modulation is not recommended unless water flow is large.	
	Spray washer	Bulky equipment requiring good access to tray and sprays. Also dehumidifies if supplied with chilled water (see Cooling — Air washer). Air sensibly cooled as water evaporates unless water is heated (not normal). Requires water treatment (including biocidal control) and bleed and recirculating pump. Removes both gaseous and particulate air contaminants but with low efficiency. Control indirect by modulation of inlet air condition (pre-heater or mixing dampers) or by by-pass and mixing. Saturation efficiencies range from approximately 70% for one bank facing upstream, to 85–90% for two banks opposed. Water quantity per bank is of the order of 0.4 litre·s^{-1} per m^3·s^{-1} of air flow. Air velocity is of the order of 2.5 m·s^{-1}.	
	Capillary washer	Similar to spray washer but less bulky and provides better air filtering. Has smaller cooling capacity than spray washer when used with chilled water. May require addition of cooling coil. Filtration efficiency is good.	

Table B2.A2.1 Basic psychrometric processes — *continued*

Process	Method	Remarks	Psychrometric process
Humidification	Sprayed cooling coil (not subject to refrigeration)	Utilises cooling coil as wetted pack for humidifying. Action as washer but sprays less prone to blocking. Eliminators not required unless air velocity to high.	
		Requires more space than non-sprayed coil but less space than washer. Water treatment advisable, bleed essential (see cooling coil). Control as for spray. Can be used to cool coil water circuit with low air on temperature, thus making t'_b greater than t'_a. This is sometimes used in an induction system primary plant. Saturation efficiency is of the order of 0.5–1.0 litre·s^{-1} per m^3·s^{-1} of air flow. Air velocity is of the order of 2.5 m·s^{-1}.	
Cooling	Indirect cooling coil	Supplied with chilled water or brine (usually 2 or 3 °C below apparatus dew-point required). As water is in closed circuit (except for head tank) there is no water contamination from air or evaporation. Contact factor depends on number of rows of pipes deep. Chilled water enters at air off-side. Drain is required. Control by modulating water temperature or flow rate (3-way valve). Normal to keep constant flow rate through chiller.	
	Direct cooling coil (direct expansion coil)	Coil is evaporator of refrigeration circuit. May be cheaper overall than indirect system, but usually involves refrigerant circuit site work. Control by steps, or modulated, depending on refrigeration system. May need special circuitry. Drain is required. Complex and costly for larger installations. May be excluded by local legislation for some applications.	
	Sprayed cooling coil (subject to refrigeration)	With spray off, coil operates exactly as cooling coil. Spray sometimes used to increase surface in contact with air, results in larger contact factor. Saturation efficiency of the order of 80–90%. Water quantity of the order of 0.5–1.0 litre·s^{-1} per m^3·s^{-1} of airflow. Air velocity of the order of 2.5 m·s^{-1}.	
	Air washer (spray washer)	See general remarks on Humidification — Spray washer. Sprays supplied with chilled water, which is liable to contamination through air washing and evaporation if also humidifying. Use with normal, non-cleanable direct expansion chiller not recommended. Overflow required. Contact factor determined by spray design and number of banks. Control by change of spray water temperature (diverting chilled water back to chiller). Saturation efficiencies range from approximately 70% for one bank facing upstream to 85–90% for two banks opposed. Water quantity per bank is of the order of 0.4 litre·s^{-1} per m^3·s^{-1} of air. Air velocity is of the order of 2.5 m·s^{-1}.	

B3 Ductwork

B3.1 Introduction

B3.1.1 General

Ductwork is considered to include all the components which contain pressurised air for ventilation and air conditioning purposes.

The quantitative data in this section apply to the flow of clean air in ducts, but these may also be used for vitiated air where the concentration of contaminant gas is low. The airflow data should not be applied to the conveyance of particulates in ducts.

Constructional aspects of ductwork are not covered in detail. For the UK, reference should be made to the ductwork specifications published by the Heating and Ventilating Contractors' Association.

B3.1.2.2 Definitions and abbreviations

AC/MV	Air conditioned/mechanically ventilated buildings
ACH	Air changes per hour
AHU	Air handling unit
Airflow generated noise	Noise produced by turbulence in the air flow, primarily where eddies are formed as the air flow separates from the surface

Aspect ratio	Ratio of width (w) to breadth (b) for a rectangular duct
Bend 'hard'	Rotation in the plane of the longer side of the cross section (see Figure (B3)3.2)
Bend 'soft'	Rotation in the plane of the shorter side of the cross section (see Figure (B3)3.2)
Fan gains	Increases in duct air temperature due to heat gains from fan/motor power dissipation
FCU	Fan coil unit
Hydraulic diameter (d_h)	Term used to calculate duct dimensions for non-circular shape:

$$d_h = \frac{4 \times (\text{cross-sectional area of duct})}{\text{length round periphery of cross section}}$$

Installation effects	Unsatisfactory or reduced fan performance due to poor inlet and outlet conditions at the fan system interface or other badly installed components
PSV	Passive stack ventilation
SFP	Specific fan power: the sum of the design total circuit watts including all losses through switchgear and controls such as inverters, of all fans that supply air and exhaust it back to outdoors (i.e. the sum of supply and extract fans) divided by the design ventilation rate through the building (see Appendix A6.2.2 for example calculation)
Static pressure (p)	The pressure exerted against the sides of a duct measured at right angles to the direction of flow
Total pressure (p_t)	The sum of the static and velocity pressures
VAV	Variable air volume
Velocity pressure (p_v)	The pressure created by the speed of the air-flow along the duct
VOCs	Volatile organic compounds

B3.2 Strategic design issues

B3.2.2 Classification of ductwork systems

Ductwork systems for ventilating and air conditioning applications can be divided into low, medium and high pressure systems.

Table B3.1 sets out the classification of ductwork systems adopted in the CIBSE Guide, using the design static pressure of the system, or part of the system. It is assumed that air is being transported. The classification follows that used in HVCA DW/144: *Specification for sheet metal ductwork*. The table also gives air leakage limits, see section B3.2.10.

The duct air velocity is not a major factor in the constructional specification of ductwork. Recommended velocities for particular applications using these three system classifications are given in Tables B3.2 and B3.3.

B3.2.3 Ductwork sections

B3.2.3.1 General

Ducting is generally available in rectangular, circular and flat oval sections, although other sections may be made for special situations. The majority of rectangular ductwork is made to order and available in any reasonable dimensions. Ductwork less than 0.0225 m² cross sectional area (e.g. 150 mm × 150 mm) will generally be more economic if made from circular section.

Table B3.1 Maximum positive and negative pressures and velocities for low, medium and high pressure ductwork

System classification	Design static pressure / Pa		Maximum air velocity / m·s⁻¹	Air leakage limit (per m² of duct surface area)* / litre·m²
	Maximum positive	Maximum negative		
Low pressure (Class A)	500	500	10	$0.027 \times p^{0.65}$
Medium pressure (Class B)	1000	750	20	$0.009 \times p^{0.65}$
High pressure (Class C)	2000	750	40	$0.003 \times p^{0.65}$

* where p is the static gauge pressure in the duct (Pa)

Table B3.2 Recommended maximum duct velocities for low pressure ductwork systems where noise generation is the controlling factor

Typical applications	Typical noise rating (NR)*	Velocity / m·s⁻¹		
		Main ducts	Branch	Runouts
Domestic buildings (bedrooms)	25	3.0	2.5	<2.0
Theatres, concert halls	20–25	4.0	2.5	<2.0
Auditoria, lecture halls, cinemas	25–30	4.0	3.5	<2.0
Bedrooms (non-domestic buildings)	20–30	5.0	4.5	2.5
Private offices, libraries	30–35	6.0	5.5	3.0
General offices, restaurants, banks	35–40	7.5	6.0	3.5
Department stores, supermarkets, shops, cafeterias	40–45	9.0	7.0	4.5
Industrial buildings	45–55	10.0	8.0	5.0

* See Table A1.1, and Table A1.17

Table B3.3 Recommended maximum duct velocities for medium and high pressure systems

Volume flow in duct / m³·s⁻¹	Velocity / m·s⁻¹	
	Medium pressure systems	High pressure systems
<0.1	8	9
0.1–0.5	9	11
0.5–1.5	11	15
>1.5	15	20

B3.2.4 Layout

The site will often dictate the main routing of ductwork systems but in general the design should seek to make the layout as symmetrical as possible; that is, the pressure loss in each branch should be as nearly equal as possible. This will aid regulation and may reduce the number and variety of duct fittings that are needed.

The number of duct fittings should be kept to a minimum and there should be a conscious attempt to achieve some standardisation of types and sizes. Increasing the numbers and variety of fittings in a system can markedly raise its overall cost.

The shorter the ductwork length, the lower is the pressure drop. Distribution lengths are influenced by:

— the shape of the building

— the number and location of plant rooms

— the provision of space for distribution.

B3.2.5 Spatial requirements

Provision of sufficient space for ductwork is essential and must be addressed at an early stage in the design process of the building. The designer should ensure that ductwork is co-ordinated with the other engineering services to be accommodated in the same space, particularly in false ceiling voids and riser spaces where there may be several distribution systems vying for restricted space.

Branches from vertical risers to serve horizontal distribution routes should be considered with care, as this is likely to be the most congested area of the service core.

Further information is available in BSRIA Technical Note TN10/92: *Spatial allowances for building services* and BS 8313: *Code of practice for accommodation of building services in ducts*.

B3.2.7 Approximate sizing

To make a preliminary estimate of a branch size, calculate the air flow rate required in the area served by multiplying the zone volume by the number of air changes per hour and divide by 3600 to obtain the zone flow rate in $m^3 \cdot s^{-1}$. Two air changes an hour may be appropriate for offices with a separate heating system for fabric losses. Where the air is used for heating, four air changes an hour may be required or six air changes or more for an air-conditioned space. Dividing this flow rate by the velocity given in Tables B3.1 and B3.2 gives the duct cross sectional area required. For conventional systems, the aspect ratio (long side to short side) of rectangular ducting should not exceed 3:1.

B3.2.9 Zoning

For a typical multiple zone system with heating and cooling application, the following should be noted:

— For a constant volume flow rate to be maintained to each zone, the system must be capable of supplying air at various temperatures at any one time; this may involve simultaneous heating and cooling of supply air.

— All rooms with similar solar gain patterns can be zoned together provided that other variables are in phase. However, the number and position of the zonal sensors will be important. Corner rooms pose further problems.

— North facing rooms experience less variation and can be grouped with internal zones for cooling provided that heating is dealt with by other means.

— Gains through poorly insulated roofs are similar to gains on south facing surfaces but, if adequately insulated, they may be treated as intermediate floors.

B3.2.10 Ductwork testing and air leakage limits

It is recommended as good practice that all significant installations (e.g. those with a fan capacity greater than $1 \ m^3 \cdot s^{-1}$) should be tested in accordance with HVCA specification DW/143: *A practical guide to ductwork leakage testing*. It should be noted that air leakage testing of low and medium pressure ductwork is not mandatory under HVCA specification DW/144. Air leakage testing of high pressure ductwork is mandatory. Refer to HVCA DW/143 for details of the testing procedure. Air leakage limits for the three classes of ductwork are given in Table B3.1. The leakage factors given for classes A, B and C are those for the classes similarly designated in draft European Standards prEN 12237 and BS prEN 1507.

B3.2.11 Fan power energy requirements

Building Regulations Approved Document L states maximum specific fan powers for buildings other than offices. Specific fan power (SFP) is defined as 'the sum of the design total circuit watts including all losses through switchgear and controls such as inverters, of all fans that supply air and exhaust it back to outdoors (i.e. the sum of supply and extract fans) divided by the design ventilation rate through the building'.

In new buildings, the SFP should be no greater than $2.0 \ W/(litre \cdot s^{-1})$ (e.g. $1.0 \ W/(litre \cdot s^{-1})$ supply; $0.8 \ W/(litre \cdot s^{-1})$ exhaust). In new AC/MV systems in refurbished buildings, or where an existing AC/MV system in an existing building is being substantially altered, the SFP should be no greater than $3.0 \ W/(litre \cdot s^{-1})$. Very energy efficient systems can achieve specific fan powers of $1 \ W/(litre \cdot s^{-1})$. The figures quoted apply to the Building Regulations for England and Wales; for Scotland the SFP is lower.

SFP is a useful benchmark for all types of buildings. However the performance criteria for use with offices is the Carbon Performance Rating which is a composite term that allows trade-off between solar control, fan, pump and chiller performance and the controls specification. Full details are provided in Approved Document L.

The formula for calculating fan power is:

$$P_{ef} = \frac{\Delta p_t \, q_v}{\eta_o} \tag{2.1}$$

where P_{ef} is the fan power (W), Δp_t is the difference in total pressure around the air circuit (Pa), q_v is the volume flow ($m^3 \cdot s^{-1}$) and η_o is the overall efficiency (%).

In general, centrifugal fans are more efficient, more controllable and quieter. Backward-curved centrifugal fans have high efficiency (up to 80%) with aerofoil backward curved fans providing even higher efficiency. Maximum efficiency for axial flow fans is about 75%. With all fans the efficiency varies with flow rate, so the chosen fan needs to have an operating point close to the point of peak efficiency. Table B2.53 gives a summary of different fan types showing their relative efficiencies. Detailed information on fan applications is provided in Guide B section 2.5.11.

Energy can be reduced in ventilation systems by:

— avoiding unnecessary bends

— using bends instead of mitred elbows

— having a 'shoe' on the branch fittings for tees

— avoiding reduced duct size (i.e. maintain cross sectional area)

— minimising duct length

— minimising the length of flexible ducting

— good inlet and outlet conditions either side of fan (see fan inlet and outlet below)

— using equipment with low pressure drops (i.e. filters, attenuators, heat exchangers).

B3.2.16 Cleaning

Dust will generally be deposited in operational ductwork over the lower surfaces of air distribution ducts, with the deposition increasing with distance from the fan.

Designers should take specialist advice and then stipulate their requirements for the periodic internal cleaning and maintenance of ductwork. Designers should also state any need for access for specialist cleaning equipment including size, type and location of the access openings required, with an indication of frequency of cleaning.

B3.3 Design criteria

B3.3.2 Duct air velocities

Recommended velocities for particular applications, using the HVCA system classifications, are given in Tables B3.2 and B3.3. These figures are a general guide and assume reasonable distances between the fittings (e.g. four times the duct hydraulic diameter). Higher velocities may be used if additional attenuation is employed. Maximum velocities, as stated in HVCA DW/144 are given in Table B3.1.

Table B3.4 gives recommended maximum air velocities for rectangular and circular ducts in risers and ceiling spaces. Table B3.5 gives recommended velocities for supply and return air openings.

B3.3.4 Health and safety

Two aspects of safety concerning ductwork need to be addressed:

— *during design*: that there are safe and secure means of access to the ductwork and associated plant and equipment (e.g. filter housings) for inspection, maintenance and cleaning

— *during installation*: by ensuring that the ductwork can be installed safely and securely.

Fibrous materials were often used as duct linings to provide sound absorption. However, they are not now generally used because:

— they can contribute to mould growth

— fibrous materials degrade with time

— fibres can erode from the surface and be carried in the air

— fibrous materials are difficult to clean.

Suitable alternative sound absorbing proprietary materials such as acoustic foam are now used and have the advantage of not requiring facings or edge treatment.

B3.3.5 Airflow in ducts

See also section (C)4.8, pages 142–145.

B3.3.5.1 General

Air in ducts follows natural laws of motion. While the detailed prediction of flow behaviour is very difficult, good design should ensure that the air follows the line of the duct with uniform velocities and that excessive turbulence is avoided. Ductwork fittings cause major pressure losses and good design is essential, particularly where higher velocities are used.

From the point of view of duct design the important aspects of the effects of disturbance to airflow are:

— increased pressure loss due to creation of eddies

— increased pressure loss as high velocity air mixes with low velocity air

— noise generated by the interaction on eddies with the inner surfaces of the ducts.

Table B3.4 Guide to maximum duct velocities in risers and ceilings

Duct location	Duct type	Maximum air velocity / m·s⁻¹ for stated room type		
		Critical	Normal	Non-critical
Riser or above plasterboard ceiling	Rectangular	5	7.5	10
	Circular	7	10	15
Above suspended ceiling	Rectangular	3	5	6
	Circular	5	7	10

Table B3.5 Maximum velocity for supply and return air openings (grilles and terminals)

Supply or return air	Permitted air velocity / m·s⁻¹		
	Critical	Normal	Uncritical
Supply	1.5	2.5	3
Return	2	3	4

B3.3.5.3 Bends

Figure B3.2 illustrates common bend types; their influence on the airflow is described below. Bends may be characterised as 'hard' or 'soft' according to whether the change of direction is in the plane of the longer or shorter side of the cross section, respectively (see Figure B3.3).

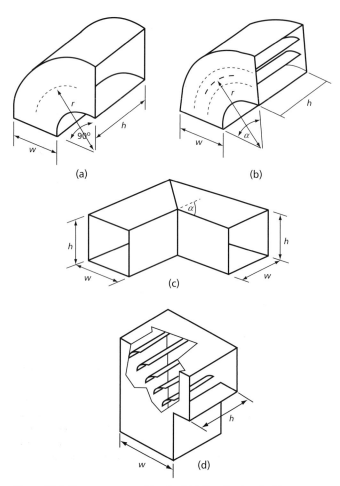

Figure B3.2 Common types of bends; (a) 90° radius bend without vanes, rectangular, (b) short radius bend with vanes (any angle), rectangular, (c) mitred elbow without vanes (any angle), (d) 90° mitred elbow with vanes

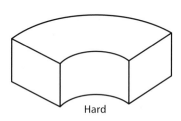 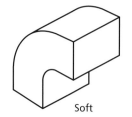

Figure B3.3 'Hard' and 'soft' bends

B3.3.5.4 Branches

There are many designs of branches and junctions in use. The important features are that the flow should be divided (or combined) with the minimum interference and disturbance, and that changes in duct sizes should not be made at the branch but at a short distance downstream (or upstream). Examples of good and economic branch design are shown in Guide B section 3.3.5.4. A good branch design cannot be effective if the flow entering the branch is not uniform across the section.

B3.3.6 Heat gains or losses

In a duct system, the air temperature change can be significant, e.g. when passing through an untreated space. This has the effect of reducing the heating or cooling capacity of the air and increasing the energy input to the system. The heat transmission to and from the surrounding space can be reduced by insulation of the ducts. The following notes give guidance on the estimation of temperature changes in ducted air due to heat gains or losses.

B3.3.7 Condensation and vapour barriers

B3.3.7.1 Surface condensation

Condensation of water vapour within air occurs whenever the temperature falls below the ambient dew-point. This can occur on the outside of the cold duct when the temperature of the duct air causes the duct itself to have a temperature below the dew-point of the surrounding air. Even when the ductwork is insulated, this can occur due to diffusion through the insulation of the more humid air external to the duct. In turn this can lead to corrosion of the ductwork as well as diminishing the thermal resistance of the insulation, leading to more condensation.

Vapour sealing will be required where the temperature of the air within the duct is at any time low enough to promote condensation on the exterior surface of the duct and cause moisture penetration through the thermal insulation.

BS 5970 warns of the risk of condensation within the layer of insulation which is primarily used to avoid condensation on its outside surfaces.

Further information and a worked example are provided in Guide B section 3.3.7.

B3.3.7.2 Vapour barriers

In extreme conditions the insulation thickness for vapour resistance may be larger than that for heat resistance. When cold ducts pass through areas of high dewpoint, carefully selected vapour barriers should be applied externally to the insulation. Well-installed vapour barriers with sealed joints will minimise vapour penetration and combat the risk of internal condensation in the insulation.

B3.3.8 Air leakage

B3.3.8.1 General

Leakage from sheet metal air ducts occurs at the seams and joints and is therefore proportional to the total surface area of the ductwork in the system. The level of leakage is similarly related to the air pressure in the duct system and, whilst there is no precise formula for calculating the level of air loss, it is generally accepted that leakage will increase in proportion to pressure to the power of 0.65.

The effect of air leakage from high pressure ductwork is critical in terms of system performance, energy consumption and the risk of high frequency noise associated with leakage. These problems are less critical with medium pressure systems, but should be considered. Low pressure ducts present the lowest risk in terms of the effect of leakage on the effective operation of the system.

For most ventilating and air conditioning applications, compliance with the construction and sealing requirements of DW/144 will ensure acceptably low leakage rates. For sheet metal ductwork the specification requires sealant to be applied to all longitudinal seams (except spirally wound, machine-made seams) and cross-joints; for plastic and resin bonded glass fibre ductwork similar sealing requirements are specified. The sheet metal specification also gives details of an air leakage test procedure. Recommended acceptable leakage rates in (litres·s^{-1}) per m^2 of surface area are given in Table B3.10.

Table B3.10 Ductwork air leakage limits

Ductwork pressure class	Air leakage limits / (l·s^{-1}) per m^2 of duct surface area
Low pressure (Class A)	$0.027 \times p^{0.65}$
Medium pressure (Class B)	$0.009 \times p^{0.65}$
High pressure (Class C)	$0.003 \times p^{0.65}$

Note: p = differential pressure / Pa

Table B3.A3.1 and Figure B3.A3.1 show these limits for a range of duct static pressure differentials. These rates are in accordance with the comparable classes in prEN 12237 and prEN 1507 but these provisional European Standards do not cover the full range of high pressure ductwork.

Items of equipment and plant installed in ductwork systems can also leak and particular attention should be paid to the sealing of these items. Where leakage testing is required, the designer should ensure that suppliers of these items can demonstrate that their equipment meets

Table B3.A3.1 Maximum permissible air leakage rates (reproduced from HCVA DW144 by permission of the Heating and Ventilating Contractors' Association)

Static pressure differential / Pa	Maximum permissible leakage of ductwork / (l·s^{-1}) per m^2 of surface area		
	Low pressure (Class A)	Medium pressure (Class B)	High pressure (Class C)
100	0.54	0.18	—
200	0.84	0.28	—
300	1.10	0.37	—
400	1.32	0.44	—
500	1.53	0.51	—
600	—	0.58	0.19
700	—	0.64	0.21
800	—	0.69	0.23
900	—	0.75	0.25
1000	—	0.80	0.27
1100	—	—	0.29
1200	—	—	0.30
1300	—	—	0.32
1400	—	—	0.33
1500	—	—	0.35
1600	—	—	0.36
1700	—	—	0.38
1800	—	—	0.39
1900	—	—	0.40
2000	—	—	0.42

Note: Recommended 'mean' test pressures are shown in italic type with the actual selection being left to the test operator.

the required airtightness standards. The designer should make adequate allowance in the fan selection for some air leakage so that the completed installation can meet its intended purpose without subsequent adjustments to the fan(s) and motor(s). Table B3.11 gives some recommendations for margins which should be included for complete installations (i.e. ductwork and equipment).

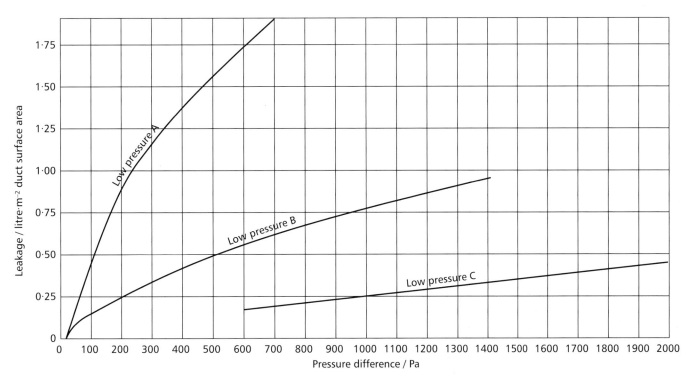

Figure B3.A3.1 Permitted leakage rates at various pressures (reproduced from HCVA DW144 by permission of the Heating and Ventilating Contractors' Association)

Table B3.11 Recommended air leakage margins for design figures

Margin	Value of margin for stated class of system		
	Low pressure	Medium pressure	High pressure
Volume flow rate margin (for leakage and balancing requirements)	+10%	+5%	+5%
System total pressure loss margin:			
(a) allowance for margin on volume flow rate	+10%	+5%	+5%
(b) allowance for uncertainty in calculation	+10%	+10%	+10%
(c) combined system total pressure loss margin (sum of (a) and (b))	+20%	+15%	+15%

B3.3.8.2   System leakage loss

There is no direct relationship between the volume of air conveyed and the surface area of the ductwork system. It is therefore difficult to express air leakage as a percentage of total air volume. Operating pressure will vary throughout the system and, since leakage is related to pressure, the calculations are complex. However, it is generally accepted that, in typical good quality systems, the leakage from each class of duct under operating conditions will be in the region of:

— low pressure (Class A): 6%

— medium pressure (Class B): 3%

— high pressure (Class C): 2%

B3.3.8.3   Designer's calculations

The designer can calculate with reasonable accuracy the predicted total loss from a system by:

(a)   calculating the operating pressure in each section of the system

(b)   calculating the surface area of the ductwork in each corresponding pressure section

(c)   calculating the allowable loss at the operating pressure for each section of the system (see above for indicative leakage figures).

This is illustrated in the duct sizing example shown in Guide B Appendix 3.A6.

B3.3.8.4   Variable pressures in systems

Designers can achieve significant cost savings by matching operating pressures throughout the system to constructional standards and appropriate air leakage testing. The practice of specifying construction standards for whole duct systems based on fan discharge pressures may incur unnecessary costs on a project.

For example, some large systems could well be classified for leakage limits as follows:

— plant room risers: Class C

— main floor distribution: Class B

— low pressure outlets: Class A

B3.3.9   Air leakage testing

B3.3.9.1   General

It is normal practice for leak testing to be a requirement for all or part of high pressure ductwork installations, but it is not a regular practice for medium or low pressure ductwork installations. It is recommended as good practice that all ductwork installations of significant size (e.g. with a fan capacity greater than 1 m$^3 \cdot$s^{-1}) should be leak tested in accordance with HVCA DW/143: *A practical guide to ductwork leakage testing*. It should be noted that air leakage testing of low and medium pressure ductwork is not obligatory under HVCA specification DW/144; this will therefore be an individual contractual matter.

Factors which should be taken into account in deciding whether leak testing of all or part of a ductwork installation is necessary are:

— whether adequate supervision of the installation can be provided and whether a final detailed examination of the system is feasible

— whether some sections need to be checked because access will be impracticable after the installation is complete

— safety hazards which may arise from leakage of contaminated air

— whether special circumstances make necessary more stringent control of leakage than is given in the existing specification

— the cost to the client of the leakage testing and the delays caused to the completion of the installation.

B3.3.9.5   Testing of plant items

Items of in-line plant will not normally be included in an air leakage test. The ductwork installation contractor may include such items in the test if the equipment has a certificate of conformity for the pressure class and air leakage classification for the system under test.

B3.3.10   Access for inspection, maintenance and cleaning

B3.3.10.1   General

Examples of space allowances, access problems and good practice are shown in Figures B3.A2.1 and B3.A2.2.

B3.3.10.2   Access/inspection openings

Due consideration should be given to access for inspection, maintenance and cleaning. Openings need to be safe and have sealed panels/covers designed so that they can be easily removed and refixed. Multiple setscrews are not recommended, and self-piercing screws are not acceptable as a method of fixing. Safety restraints should be connected to access panels located in riser ducts.

B3.3.10.4   Test holes for plant system commissioning

Test holes for in-duct airflow measurement are required, as follows:

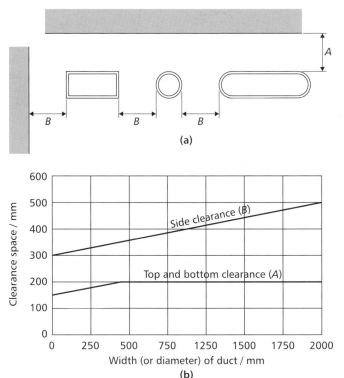

Figure B3.A2.1 Space allowance for rectangular, circular and flat oval ductwork (a) schematic, (b) recommended clearances (reproduced from BSRIA Technical Note TN10/92 by permission of the Building Services Research and Information Association)

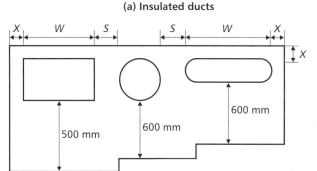

If W less than or equal to 1000 mm: X = 200 mm, S = 400 mm
If W greater than 1000 mm: X = 400 mm, S = 600 mm

(a) Insulated ducts

If W less than or equal to 1000 mm: X = 100 mm, S = 300 mm
If W greater than 1000 mm: X = 300 mm, S = 400 mm

(b) Uninsulated ducts

Figure B3.A2.2 Space allowance for rectangular, circular and flat oval ductwork; (a) insulated, (b) uninsulated (reproduced from MoD Design and Maintenance Guide 08; © Crown copyright)

— on both sides of the fans and heating and cooling coils (for pressure drop measurement)

— in the main ducts

— in all branches

— in centrifugal fan drive guards opposite the end of the fan spindle, for speed measurements.

The requirements for the nominal location and size of test holes are given in section Guide B section 3.6. Test holes are usually best drilled on site after installation is complete. The number and spacing of holes at a particular location are given in BSRIA Application Guide AG3/89.3: *Commissioning air systems in buildings*.

B3.3.11   Noise from ductwork and HVAC plant

See Guide B chapter 5.

B3.3.12   Fire issues

B3.3.12.1   General

Advice on fire protection systems is laid down in BS 5588: Part 9 and Association for Specialist Fire Protection publication *Fire rated and smoke outlet ductwork: An industry guide to design and installation*. Systems are required to be tested in accordance with BS 476: Part 20 and BS 476: Part 22 for fire and smoke dampers and BS 476: Part 24 (ISO 6944) for fire-rated ductwork. See also CIBSE Guide E: *Fire engineering* for general guidance on fire protection.

Building Regulations in the UK require that buildings be sub-divided, with fire resisting construction depending on size and use, to inhibit the spread of fire within the building. Advice on the degree of compartmentation and fire resisting periods are given in Building Regulations Approved Document B.

Fire and smoke containment and hazards are factors which influence the design and installation of ductwork systems. A design that is required to perform a particular action as part of a fire strategy is likely to combine electrical, mechanical and builders' work components which would be influenced by the normal day-to-day operations requirements. Some of the more common components are:

— ductwork

— fire dampers

— smoke extract fans.

B3.3.13   Supports and fixings

B3.3.13.1   General

Supports are an essential part of the ductwork system and their supply and installation are normally the responsibility of the ductwork contractor. The choice between available methods of fixing will depend on the type of building structure and on any limitations imposed by the structural design.

B3.4　System selection

B3.4.2　Duct sizing criteria

Recommended duct sizes are given in Appendix B3.A1 for rectangular, circular and flat oval duct. Rectangular ducting is available in any reasonable size since it is normally manufactured to order.

The basic equations for calculating pressure losses in ductwork and ductwork fittings, along with pressure loss factors, are given in Guide C chapter 4. Extracts are included herein, see pages 142–150 and 157–166. A worked example is provided in Guide B Appendix 3.A6.

B3.4.3　Principles of design

B3.4.3.1　General

Duct sizing and pressure loss calculations are normally carried out as a combined exercise to quantify the ductwork dimensions and provide data for specifying the fan duty. The duct sizing process and pressure loss calculations require the specification of system requirements, including:

— system type, i.e. low, medium, high pressure or industrial

— volume flow rates in all parts of the ductwork

— positions of fans, other plant items, supply and extract terminals

— special operating requirements, e.g. minimum conveying velocities in extract systems

— ductwork type, i.e. circular, rectangular, flat oval

— layout of the duct runs, including fittings, dampers and plant items

— duct material.

Before commencing duct sizing, a schematic of the air distribution system must be prepared. This should indicate the airflow directions and contain the following information:

(a)　system identification for each section

(b)　air volume flow rates in each section

(c)　the length of all straight sections

(d)　descriptions of fittings, dampers, plant items and terminals.

Items (a) and (b) are not needed specifically for sizing purposes but are needed to determine the system pressure loss and hence the fan duty specification.

An example schematic is shown in Guide B (Figure 3.11).

B3.4.3.2　Manual duct sizing methods

The most common method is based on constant pressure drops with maximum duct velocities as set out in Tables B3.2 and B3.3 for low, medium and high pressure systems. It is recommended that the calculated duct size be rounded to the nearest recommended duct size (see Appendix B3.A1) before the system resistance calculation is carried out.

(a)　*Velocity method*

This method is based on the selection of duct velocities by the designer. In a typical system the velocity at the fan connection is chosen, and this is progressively reduced in the duct run from the fan to the terminals. Tables B3.2 and B3.3 give some guidance on suitable maximum air velocities.

(b)　*Constant pressure drop (equal friction loss) method*

The basis for this method is to select a constant pressure loss per unit length for the duct runs and then to size the ducts at this rate, using Figure B3.12. The method is used for the sizing of very simple low pressure supply and extract systems, some medium pressure systems and also for variable air volume (VAV) systems. For low pressure systems, typical values used for the constant pressure loss rate are in the range $0.8–1.2$ Pa·m^{-1} with duct velocities not exceeding 10 m·s^{-1}. At large volume flow rates in low pressure systems the 10 m·s^{-1} duct velocity limit should override the constant pressure loss rate chosen, leading to somewhat lower pressure loss rates in the large ducts.

(c)　*Static regain method*

See Guide B section 3.4.3.2.

B3.4.3.3　Calculation of system pressure loss

The pressure loss in a ductwork system is made up of the pressure losses at plant items and terminal equipment, the friction loss in the straight ducts plus the losses due to duct fittings.

The losses due to both straight duct and fittings are directly related to the duct sizes, so that the determination of the system pressure loss follows the duct sizing process. The calculation as described, using data given in section 4.11 of CIBSE Guide C, gives the 'total pressure' loss and this can be used to assess the required fan total pressure for the system. The total pressure loss of plant items and fittings is related to the static pressure loss as follows:

$$\Delta p_t = \Delta p + p_{vi} - p_{vo} \qquad (3.18)$$

where Δp_t is the total pressure loss (Pa), Δp is the static pressure loss (Pa), p_{vi} is the inlet velocity pressure (Pa) and p_{vo} is the outlet velocity pressure (Pa).

Suitable air leakage margins are given in Table B3.11. The steps in the manual calculation of total pressure loss are described in Guide B section 3.4.3.3.

B3.4.7　Flow regulation

One of the basic requirements for an effective system is having the necessary dampers in the correct position. The main requirements for siting dampers are as follows:

— There should be a main damper for the air handling unit, preferably following it; an alternative is to use adjustable inlet guide vanes on the fan.

— There should be dampers on all terminals and in all branch and sub-branch ducts; Guide B includes an example basic schematic showing damper positions (Figure 3.20).

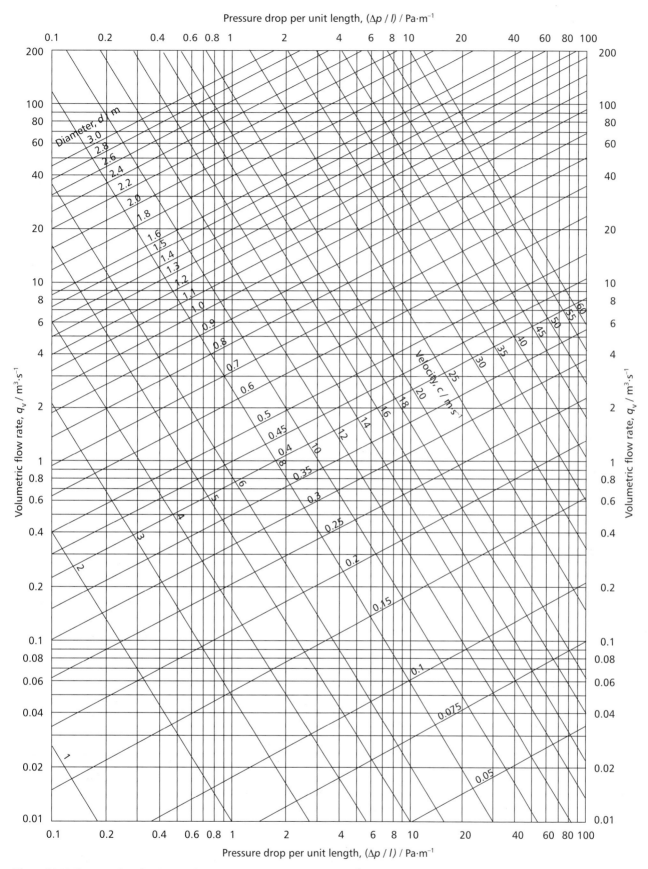

Figure B3.12 Pressure drop for air in galvanised circular ducts ($\rho = 1.2$ kg·m^{-3}; $T = 293$ K)

Further information on actuators and pressure, velocity, flow and air quality measurement sensors is available in CIBSE Guide H: *Building control systems*.

B3.4.8   Passive stack ventilation

A passive stack ventilation (PSV) system comprises vents connected to individual near-vertical circular or rectangular ducts which rise to ridge or tile terminals. Moist air is drawn through the ducts by a combination of stack and wind effects. The ducts should have no more than two bends at greater than 30° to the vertical to minimise the resistance to air flow, and be insulated where they pass through cold spaces to reduce the risk of condensation. Typical applications are in kitchens and bathrooms where ducts are normally 80–125 mm in diameter. This technique has also been applied to complete buildings such as communal residences, schools and other education buildings.

Effective commissioning of PSV systems is important. Further information on PSV systems is provided Guide B section 2.4.3.

suspended from a lightweight factory roof, Tables B3.16, B3.17, B3.18 and B3.19 may be used as a guide. Fittings may be taken as equivalent to the same length of straight duct. The weight of textile ducts may be taken as 230 g·m^{-2}, plus supports and hangers. Standard thicknesses for galvanised and aluminium sheet are given in Table B3.20.

B3.5 Ductwork materials and fittings

B3.5.1 Ductwork materials

The choice of materials to be used for the manufacture of a duct will take account of:

— the nature of the air or gas being conveyed through the duct

— the environment in which the duct will be placed and will operate

— the initial cost of the installation and the subsequent operation, maintenance and cleaning cost.

Factors influencing the selection of a material for a particular application are summarised in Table B3.15 (based on information published by SMACNA).

B3.5.2 Weights and thicknesses of ductwork materials

The weight of ductwork, in newtons, can be derived from the mass by multiplying the mass in kilograms by 9.81. This weight is normally insignificant, even when insulated, compared with most building materials, and its influence on structural calculations is usually negligible. However, if the weight of the ducting is requested, e.g. where it is to be

Table B3.16 Weight of galvanised steel ductwork

Thickness / mm	Weight per unit surface area of duct / kg·m^{-2}
0.5	3.9
0.6	4.7
0.7	5.4
0.8	6.2
0.9	7.0
1.0	7.8
1.2	9.4
1.6	12.5
2.0	15.6
2.5	19.6

Table B3.17 Weight of aluminium ductwork

Thickness / mm	Weight per unit surface area of duct / kg·m^{-2}
0.5	1.6
0.6	1.92
0.7	2.24
0.8	2.56
0.9	2.88
1.0	3.2
1.2	3.84
1.6	5.12
2.0	6.4
2.5	8.2

Table B3.18 Weight of stiffeners and joints

Angle section / (mm × mm × mm)	Weight per unit length / kg·m^{-1}	
	Steel	Aluminium
25 × 25 × 3	15	7
30 × 30 × 3	17	8
40 × 40 × 4	28	12
50 × 50 × 5	42	17

Note: values include 0.3 kg·m^{-1} for fastenings and sealant

Table B3.15 List of materials suitable for formation of ductwork

Material	Applications	Advantages	Limiting characteristics	Remarks
Galvanised steel	Most air handling systems	High strength, rigidity, durability, rust resistance, availability, non-porous, 'workability', 'weldability'	Weight, corrosion resistance for corrosive products or temperatures above 200 °C, ability to be painted	Widely used and available
Carbon steel (black iron)	Breeching, flues, stacks, hoods, high temperature systems, kitchens	High strength, rigidity, ability to be painted, non-porous	Corrosion resistance, weight	Steel when no minimum content specified
Aluminium	Moisture laden air (salt free), louvres, special exhausts, ornamental	Weight, resistance to corrosion due to moisture	Low strength, cost, difficult to weld, high thermal expansion	Various alloys available
Stainless steel	Kitchen exhaust, moisture laden air, fume exhaust	High corrosion resistance, high polish possible	Labour, cost, 'workability', availability	Various alloys available
Copper	Ductwork exposed to outside chemical attack, ornamental	Can be soldered, durable, resists corrosion, non-magnetic	Cost, electrolysis, stains, thermal expansion	Common for ornamental ductwork
Glass fibre reinforced plastic (GRP)	Chemical exhaust, scrubbers, underground ducts	Corrosion resistance, easily modified	Cost, weight, chemical and physical properties, fabrication	
Polyvinyl chloride (PVC)	Exhaust systems, underground ducts	Corrosion resistance, weight, easily modified	Cost, fabrication, thermal shock, weight, code acceptance	
Polyester (textile/fabric ducts)	Food and other process industries, warehousing, retail, sports/leisure, offices	Cost, weight, ease and speed of installation, low noise, not subject to condensation	Non-rigid, unsuitable for fire ductwork, damage during removal and/or replacement	

B3.5.3 Fittings, dampers and ancillaries

A wide range of fittings are available from the manufacturers of all types of ductwork, who can also provide design information. Examples of standard components for sheet metal ductwork are provided in DW/144. See also Guide B section 3.6.2.3.

Information on protective coverings, connections to building openings, and sensors is provided in Guide B sections 3.5.4, 3.5.5. and 3.5.6 respectively.

B3.6 Testing and commissioning

B3.6.1 Introduction

All ductwork systems should be tested and commissioned and those of significant size (e.g. with a fan capacity above $1 \ m^3 \cdot s^{-1}$) should also be leak tested, see Guide B section 3.2.10. The designer must accept the implications of the commissioning procedures to which the air distribution system will be subjected. Inadequate commissioning will result in poor environmental performance, energy wastage, draughts and noise.

B3.7 Maintenance and cleaning

B3.7.3 Maintenance

Ductwork systems should be clean on completion. HVCA DW/TM2: *Guide to good practice — internal cleanliness of*

new ductwork installations states that: 'where specific levels of cleanliness are required, ductwork shall be cleaned after installation by a specialist cleaning contractor.'

Special requirements apply to cleaning and maintenance of ductwork in applications such as food preparation (see HVCA DW/171: *Standard for kitchen ventilation systems*), process industries and plant rooms.

Detailed maintenance requirements for ductwork are set out in the HVCA Standard Maintenance Specification. A summary of these requirements is shown in Table B3.24.

B3.7.12 Cleaning methods

There are several methods by which cleaning contractors can remove dust, debris and other surface contaminants:

—   vacuum

—   steam

—   compressed air

—   rotary brush.

Cleaning methods are more fully described in HVCA Guide to Good Practice TR17 and BSRIA Technical Note TN18/92. Methods will vary according to the air distribution system. On the basis that the contaminants are dry, dry methods of cleaning are adequate for supply air and general extract systems. Wet methods are needed for air ducts in commercial kitchens and similar installations where extract air contains smoke, grease and other impurities.

Table B3.24 Summary of recommendations for maintenance of ductwork

Item	Frequency	Action
General: — access doors — flexible connections — insulation — anti-vibration mounts — internal cleanliness	12–monthly	Visual inspection for damage, security of fittings, deterioration and internal condition
Dampers: — volume control dampers — fire and smoke dampers — linkages — controls — electrical	6–monthly	Visual inspection, check action of moving parts and lubricate, check security of locking devices, check fusible links. Check for damage to electrical connections, tighten where required. Check integrity of electrical installation
Acoustics: — attenuators — support fixings	12–monthly	Inspect visually internally and externally. Repair sound insulation as required. Check all fixings are secure. Clean, de-rust, repaint as required
Grilles and diffusers	12–monthly	Examine, check mounting fittings, clean
Louvres, bird and insect screens	6–monthly	Clean, remove debris, check for damage, repair or replace

Appendix B3.A1: Recommended sizes for ductwork

Table B3.A1.1 Recommended sizes for rectangular ductwork, including equivalent diameter, hydraulic diameter, cross sectional area and perimeter (based on BS EN 1505)

Shorter side / mm

Longer side / mm	Parameter*	100	150	200	250	300	400	500	600	800	1000	1200	Parameter*
150	d_e	134	165										d_e
	P	0.5	0.6										P
	d_h	120.00	150.00										d_h
	A	0.015	0.0225										A
200	d_e	154	190	220									d_e
	P	0.6	0.7	0.8									P
	d_h	133.33	171.43	200.00									d_h
	A	0.02	0.03	0.04									A
250	d_e	171	212	246	275								d_e
	P	0.7	0.8	0.9	1.0								P
	d_h	142.86	187.50	222.22	250.00								d_h
	A	0.025	0.0375	0.05	0.0625								A
300	d_e	185	231	269	301	330							d_e
	P	0.8	0.9	1.0	1.1	1.2							P
	d_h	150.00	200.00	240.00	272.73	300.00							d_h
	A	0.03	0.045	0.06	0.075	0.09							A
400	d_e	211	264	308	346	387	441						d_e
	P	1.0	1.1	1.2	1.3	1.4	1.6						P
	d_h	160.00	218.18	266.67	307.69	342.86	400.00						d_h
	A	0.04	0.06	0.08	0.1	0.12	0.16						A
500	d_e		291	341	385	424	492	551					d_e
	P		1.3	1.4	1.5	1.6	1.8	2.0					P
	d_h		230.77	285.71	333.33	375.00	444.44	500.00					d_h
	A		0.075	0.1	0.125	0.15	0.2	0.25					A
600	d_e		316	371	419	462	537	603	661				d_e
	P		1.5	1.6	1.7	1.8	2.0	2.2	2.4				P
	d_h		240.00	300.00	352.94	400.00	480.00	545.45	600.00				d_h
	A		0.09	0.12	0.15	0.18	0.24	0.3	0.36				A
800	d_e			421	477	527	616	683	761	881			d_e
	P			2.0	2.1	2.2	2.4	2.6	2.8	3.2			P
	d_h			320.00	380.95	436.36	533.33	615.38	685.71	800.00			d_h
	A			0.16	0.2	0.24	0.32	0.4	0.48	0.64			A
1000	d_e				527	583	683	770	848	984	1101		d_e
	P				2.5	2.6	2.8	3.0	3.2	3.6	4.0		P
	d_h				400.00	461.54	571.43	666.67	750.00	888.89	1000.00		d_h
	A				0.25	0.3	0.4	0.5	0.6	0.8	1.0		A
1200	d_e					632	741	837	924	1075	1205	1322	d_e
	P					3.0	3.2	3.4	3.6	4.0	4.4	4.8	P
	d_h					480.00	600.00	705.88	800.00	960.00	1090.91	1200.00	d_h
	A					0.36	0.48	0.6	0.72	0.96	1.2	1.44	A

*d_e = equivalent diameter / mm; P = perimeter / m; d_h = hydraulic diameter / mm; A = cross sectional area / m²

Table continues

Table B3.A1.1 Recommended sizes for rectangular ductwork, including equivalent diameter, hydraulic diameter, cross sectional area and perimeter (based on BS EN 1505) — *continued*

Longer side / mm	Parameter*	Shorter side / mm										
		100	150	200	250	300	400	500	600	800	1000	1200
1400	d_e						794	898	992	1118	1299	1427
	P						3.6	3.8	4.0	4.4	4.8	5.2
	d_h						622.22	736.84	840.00	1018.18	1166.67	1292.31
	A						0.56	0.7	0.84	0.112	0.14	0.168
1600	d_e						843	954	1054	1231	1385	1523
	P						4.0	4.2	4.4	4.8	5.2	5.6
	d_h						640.00	761.90	872.73	1066.67	1230.77	1371.43
	A							0.8	0.96	1.28	1.6	1.92
1800	d_e							1006	1112	1256	1465	1612
	P							4.6	4.8	5.2	5.6	6.0
	d_h							782.61	900.00	1107.69	1285.71	1440.00
	A							0.9	1.08	1.44	1.8	2.16
2000	d_e							1053	1166	1365	1539	1695
	P							5.0	5.2	5.6	6.0	6.4
	d_h							800.00	923.08	1142.86	1333.33	1500.00
	A							1.0	1.2	1.6	2.0	2.4

* d_e = equivalent diameter / mm; P = perimeter / m; d_h = hydraulic diameter / mm; A = cross sectional area / m^2

Table B3.A1.3 Recommended sizes for flat oval ducting (from HVCA DW/144)

Perimeter / m	Width of duct (major axis) / mm for stated depth of duct (minor axis) / mm										
	75	100	125	150	200	250	300	350	400	450	500
0.718	320										
0.798		350	330	320							
0.878		390	370	360							
0.958		430	410	400							
1.037		470	450	440							
1.117	520	505	490	480							
1.197		545	530	520							
1.277				555	525						
1.436				635	605	580					
1.596				715	690	660	630				
1.756				800	770	740	710	685	655		
1.915				880	845	825	790	765	735	705	680
2.075				960	930	900	875	845	815	785	755
2.238				1040	1010	985	955	925	895	865	835
2.394				1120	1090	1065	1035	1005	975	945	915
2.553				1200	1170	1145	1115	1085	1055	1025	1000
2.873					1335	1305	1275	1245	1215	1190	1160
3.192						1465	1435	1405	1375	1350	1320
3.511						1625	1595	1570	1540	1510	1480
3.830						1785	1760	1730	1700	1670	1640

B4   Refrigeration and heat rejection

B4.1   Introduction

B4.1.1   General

Before using refrigeration and heat rejection systems, the designer should consider carefully the use of alternative free cooling and low energy techniques. Reasons for choosing such alternatives should be recorded and substantiated by the designer, see CIBSE Guide F: *Energy efficiency in buildings*.

B4.2   Strategic design decisions

B4.2.1   Introduction

Refrigeration is defined as the process of removing heat and heat rejection is defined as the discharge of heat to waste or atmosphere or to a system permitting reclaim or recovery.

Key factors to be considered are addressed in detail in Guide B section 4.2. Selected items are presented below.

B4.2.3   Energy efficiency and environmental issues

The UK government has introduced the Climate Change Levy, effectively a specific tax on energy use, and Enhanced Capital Allowances for certain energy efficient measures including some specific refrigeration plant, see *www.eca.gov.uk* for lists of eligible equipment. Approved Document L2 (ADL2) of the Building Regulations for England and Wales requires that refrigeration equipment and fans and pumps are reasonably efficient and appropriately sized. Guidance on specific requirements is given in Guide B section 4.3.5.

The chosen refrigeration and heat rejection strategy will influence, and will be influenced by, energy efficiency and environmental issues and any specific targets. Documents are available to assist in setting energy and environmental targets, including:

—   CIBSE TM22: *Energy Assessment and Reporting Method*

—   Energy Consumption Guides, now published by the Carbon Trust (provide energy benchmarks and targets for industrial buildings and sites, offices, public houses, hotels, hospitals, domestic properties, nursing and residential homes, and other non-domestic sectors)

—   the Building Research Establishment Environmental Assessment Method (BREEAM), which provides an environmental assessment methodology for industrial units, offices, superstores and supermarkets and housing.

Specific guidance on achieving energy targets is also given in CIBSE Guide F: *Energy efficiency in buildings*.

Refrigerant leakage can have an adverse impact on energy efficiency as operating a vapour compression system with either too much or too little refrigerant can cause a significant reduction in the cooling performance and energy efficiency of the system, see Guide B section 4.4.4.4.

Refrigeration and heat rejection systems also use other potentially environmentally harmful substances including water treatment chemicals required to minimise microbiological contamination and corrosion, see Guide B section 4.5.5.

B4.2.4   Interaction with building fabric, services and facilities

The building services engineer should enter into a dialogue with the architect on building fabric related issues that will impact on the cooling requirements, including the following:

—   location

—   pollution

—   orientation

—   form

—   insulation

—   infiltration

—   shading

—   window choice

—   glazing

—   thermal mass.

Specific guidance is given in CIBSE Guide A and in Guide B chapter 2. Some of these issues now have statutory requirements. For example, ADL2 requires that non-domestic buildings should be reasonably airtight, and that buildings of greater than 1000 m² are to be pressure tested in accordance with CIBSE TM23: *Testing buildings for air leakage*.

B4.2.5   Choice of refrigeration and heat rejection strategy

It is important that the requirement for cooling is minimised as this should reduce the energy consumption of the building, minimise maintenance costs (e.g. specialist refrigeration maintenance and water treatment costs), and in many cases reduce the life cycle costs of the building.

The requirement for cooling can also be minimised by selecting an appropriate building ventilation strategy that maximises the use of ambient air for ventilation and cooling instead of providing a full air conditioning system. Figure B4.2 shows a decision flow chart that may assist this selection process.

B4.2.10   Commissioning

Approved Document L2 requires that all building services systems are commissioned. The designer or procurer has to show that the design is commissionable, and show that

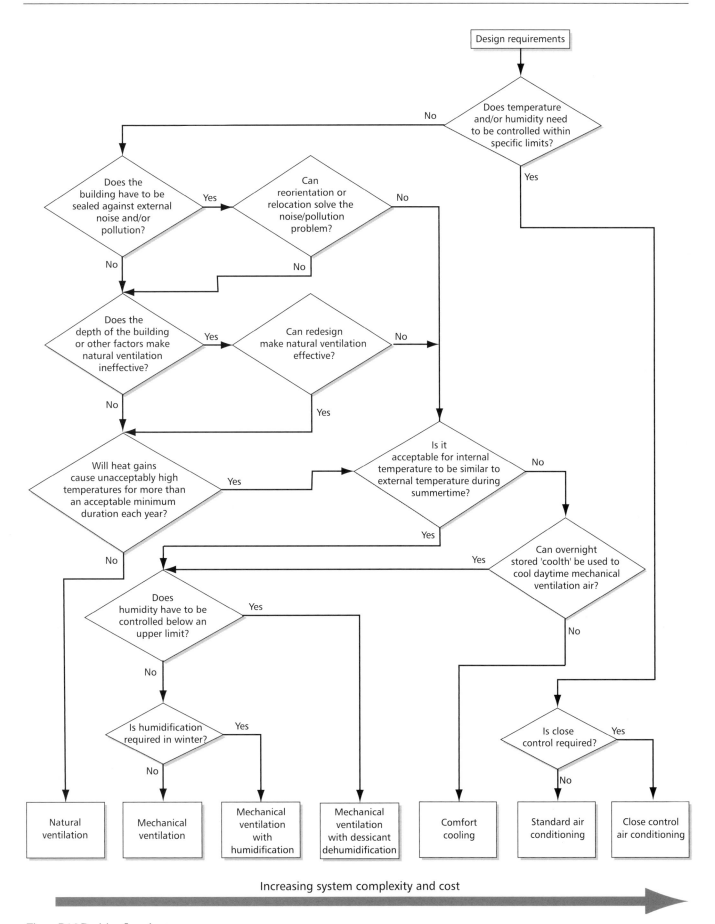

Figure B4.2 Decision flow chart

the systems have been commissioned, within reason, to the design specification.

It is particularly important for the success and feasibility of commissioning that the refrigeration system cooling capacity, controls and safety devices permit stable operation over the specified range of cooling load conditions. Oversizing should also be avoided and stand-by arrangements should be consistent with the design risk.

Key requirements for successfully commissioning a refrigeration and heat rejection system are given in Guide B section 4.3.6.2.

B4.2.11   Operation

The operational efficiency of the system depends on the ability and commitment of the end user.

It is therefore important to ensure that the relevant responsible person for the end user understands the system, and is also made aware of their responsibilities with regard to the operation of the plant. This is now a requirement of Approved Document L2 which requires that the owner and/or operator of the building is provided with a log book giving details of the installed building services and controls, their method of operation and maintenance, and other details that show how energy consumption can be monitored and controlled.

CIBSE TM31 provides specific guidance on the preparation of building log-books.

The need for specific user training should be considered in cases where the plant and systems are particularly complex or unusual.

Approved Document L2 also requires that sufficient sub-metering is provided so that the owner and/or operator can monitor and control energy use.

B4.3   Requirements

B4.3.2   Safety

B4.3.2.1   UK Health and Safety Legislation

Specific guidance on meeting the requirements of UK health and safety legislation for vapour compression refrigeration systems is given in The Institute of Refrigeration Safety Codes. The codes also give guidance on health and safety risk assessments for refrigeration systems. Guidance on compliance with the regulations with respect to the risk of exposure to *Legionella* bacteria is given in HSC Approved Code of Practice and Guidance L8: *Legionnaires' disease: The control of legionella bacteria in water systems*.

B4.3.2.2   Refrigerants

Refrigerants, their mixtures and combination with oils, water or other materials present in the refrigerating system can present risks to both people and property. Depending on the refrigerant used, the following risks can be caused by the escape of refrigerant from refrigeration systems:

—   fire

—   explosion

—   toxicity

—   caustic effects

—   freezing of skin

—   asphyxiation

—   panic.

Other risks related to refrigerants include bursting or explosion due to over pressure or failure of some part of the refrigeration system. These risks can be caused by poor system design, maintenance or operation and in the worst case can lead can lead to significant property damage and danger to people.

The risks associated with the escape of refrigerant and the risks of systems bursting or exploding due to over pressure of refrigerant or equipment failure should be minimised by complying with relevant regulations, codes and standards, some of which have been detailed in 4.3.2.1. In addition, it is CIBSE policy that the requirements of BS EN 378: *Refrigerating systems and heat pumps. Safety and environmental requirements* should also be complied with. The guidance given in CIBSE GN1 should also be followed. The Institute of Refrigeration Safety Codes provide specific guidance on the requirements of BS EN 378.

Safety requirements specific to particular refrigerants are given in section Guide B section 4.4.

B4.3.2.3   Legionella

Any system that contains water at between 20 °C and 45 °C is at risk of supporting colonies of *Legionella* bacteria. If the system has the means of creating and disseminating breathable water droplets or aerosols it is at risk of causing exposure to *Legionella* bacteria, the cause of a potentially fatal disease in humans. Cooling and heat rejection systems that incorporate a cooling tower or evaporative condenser are thus at particular risk of supporting the bacteria that could cause *Legionella* infection.

Practical guidance on complying with the relevant legislation is given in HSC Approved Code of Practice and Guidance L8 and CIBSE TM13.

The regulations impose specific legal duties on employers and building owners/operators to:

—   identify and assess all potential sources of *Legionella*

—   prepare a scheme for preventing or controlling the risk, implement, manage and monitor precautions

—   keep records of the precautions.

B4.3.3   Noise

Refrigeration and heat rejection plant produces noise pollution in the form of:

—   *mechanical vibration*: which can be transmitted through the building structure and generate noise in occupied rooms

— *airborne noise*: which can be a nuisance to the occupants of the building, to neighbouring buildings and also to operatives inside plant rooms.

Dealing with noise pollution is an important aspect of design and requirements for its control are given in Guide B chapter 5. Designers and employers should be aware that they have specific requirements under the Noise at Work Regulations 1990 relating to the exposure of employees to noise in the workplace. This is especially relevant to noise levels in refrigeration system plant rooms and requires a risk assessment and the implementation of measures to protect people from hazardous noise levels.

B4.3.4   Pollution

Many refrigerants, oils and other chemicals used in refrigeration systems may cause pollution to the environment. The system designer and the equipment specifier should be aware of any environmentally damaging substances or materials used in the refrigeration and heat rejection equipment. A major factor is the emission of environmentally damaging refrigerants, such as ozone-depleting CFCs and HCFCs, into the atmosphere due to leakage or spillage during servicing. The designer should be sure of the validity and reasoning behind the selection of potentially environmentally damaging materials.

The requirements of the following regulations must be met:

— EC Regulation No 2037/2000 on ozone depleting substances: as well as phasing-out and controlling use of CFCs and HCFC refrigerants this regulation also includes legal requirements for the minimisation and avoidance of refrigerant emissions and leakage, see section 4.3.4.1.

— Environmental Protection Act 1990: Section 33 of the Act states that it is illegal to 'treat, keep or dispose of controlled waste in a manner likely to cause pollution to the environment or harm human health'. Most refrigerants and oils come under the category of controlled waste. Section 34 places a duty of care on all those who handle controlled waste to ensure that it is legally and safety dealt with. This includes preventing its escape.

It is also considered good practice and CIBSE policy that the requirements of BS EN 378 are complied with as well as the above statutory regulations. The guidance given in CIBSE GN1 should also be followed.

B4.3.4.1   Ozone depleting substances

Full details including the Montreal Protocol and EC Regulation No. 2037/2000, greenhouse gases and global warming are given in Guide B section 4.3.4.

B4.3.5   Energy efficiency

Building Regulations Approved Document L2 includes specific energy efficiency provisions (see section B4.3.6), particularly for air conditioning systems in office buildings. The Energy Performance of Buildings Directive also requires specific energy efficiency targets to

be set for the design of most non-domestic buildings and periodic inspections and assessment of air conditioning systems. Information about the energy efficiency of specific types of vapour compression and absorption refrigeration systems is given in Guide B sections 4.4.4 and 4.4.5, and strategic design guidance on energy efficiency issues is given in Guide B section 4.2.3. Information and guidance on achieving energy targets is also given in CIBSE Guide F: *Energy efficiency in buildings*.

B4.3.5.1   Climate change levy

The levy was originally set at 0.15 p/kW·h for gas and 0.43 p/kW·h for electricity. At the time of writing the levy is offset by a cut in employers National Insurance Contributions and 100% first-year Enhanced Capital Allowances against tax for designated energy-saving equipment as an incentive for purchasers of equipment to choose more efficient equipment. Qualifying refrigeration related equipment includes:

— evaporative condensers
— liquid pressure amplification systems
— automatic air purgers
— automatic leak detection systems
— absorption chillers driven by qualifying combined heat and power (CHP) plant
— efficient compressors
— variable speed motor drives
— pipe insulation.

The list of qualifying equipment from particular manufacturers is subject to constant update and can be viewed at (www.eca.gov.uk).

B4.3.5.2   Total equivalent warming impact (TEWI)

Total equivalent warming impact (TEWI) is a way of assessing the overall impact of refrigeration systems from the direct refrigerant related and indirect fuel related emissions. Designers should seek to minimise TEWI through the selection of an appropriate refrigeration machine and refrigerant and by optimising equipment selection and system design for the best energy efficiency.

TEWI sums all emissions of greenhouse gases in tonnes or kilograms of CO_2 equivalent over the lifetime of the plant. It may be calculated using the following formula:

$$TEWI = Q \beta L + \frac{M L (l_1 + l_2 + s_1 + s_2)}{100} + M (1 - \alpha)$$

(4.1)

where TEWI is the total equivalent warming impact (kg CO_2), Q is the annual energy consumption (kW·h), β is the CO_2 emission factor for electricity (kg CO_2/ kW·h) (see Table B4.8 below), L is the life of the plant (years), M is the refrigerant charge (kg), l_1 is the annual leak rate (% of refrigerant charge), l_2 is the annual purge release factor (% of refrigerant charge), s_1 is the annual service release (% of refrigerant charge), s_2 is the probability factor for catastrophic failure (% refrigerant charge loss/year) and α is the refrigerant recovery efficiency factor.

For valid comparison between different refrigeration systems the annual energy consumption should include all of the circulation pumps, fans and related components that make up the whole refrigeration system.

Further guidance on the calculation of TEWI, including sample worksheets, is provided by the British Refrigerating Association (BRA). The BRA also provides sectorial release factors for calculating TEWI for new refrigeration systems that are manufactured, installed and maintained to current best practice standards. These factors are reproduced in Table B4.5.

Table B4.5 TEWI sectorial release factors for new systems to best practice standards

Sector	Lifetime, L (years)	Sectorial release factors				
		α	l_1	l_2	s_1	s_2
Commercial DX	10	0.95	5	n/a	0.25	n/a
Liquid chillers (flooded) and industrial plant	10	0.95	2	0.5	0.25	n/a
White goods:						
— commercial	10	0.6	0	0	0	0
— domestic	10	0.3	0	0	0	0

B4.3.6   Building Regulations

Approved Document L of the Building Regulations for England and Wales, and the equivalent for Scotland and Northern Ireland, provides guidance on building design to reduce energy consumption and carbon emissions.

The Building Regulations Approved Document L2 (ADL2) provides practical guidance with respect to the requirements of the regulations.

B4.3.6.2   Inspection and commissioning of the building services

The principal requirement of ADL2 is that the designer or procurer must provide a report that shows that the work complies with ADL2 and has been completed to a reasonable standard. The report must be produced by a competent person who's suitability should be agreed by the building control authority. The report should include:

—   A commissioning plan that shows that every system has been properly inspected and commissioned. A way of demonstrating compliance would be to follow the guidance in the CIBSE Commissioning Codes and BSRIA commissioning guides, see below. Guidance is also provided by the Commissioning Specialists Association.

—   The results of the commissioning tests, confirming that the performance is reasonably in accordance with the approved design.

Key recommendations for successfully commissioning a refrigeration and heat rejection system are given in Guide B section 4.3.6.2.

For further guidance see CIBSE Guides F and H, CIBSE Commissioning Code R: *Refrigerating systems* and BSRIA Application Guide AG02/89: *Commissioning of water systems in buildings*, and Commissioning Specialists Association Technical Memorandum No. 1: *Standard specification for the commissioning of mechanical engineering services installations for buildings*.

B4.3.6.3   Building log-book

The building owner should be provided with a log book, in which the installed plant and its function are described in simple language for the everyday use of the owner. The log book should be in addition to the more detailed information provided in the operation and maintenance manuals and the health and safety file.

A suitable template for the production of the building logbook is provided with CIBSE TM31: *Building log book toolkit*.

B4.3.6.4   Installation of energy meters

Adequate energy meters should be provided for the owner or occupier to measure their actual energy consumption. Sub-metering should be provided for significant individual items of plant such as chiller installations of greater than 20 kW rated input power, fan and pump motor control centers with a rated input power greater than 10 kW, or sub-tenanted areas of over 500 m^2. In some cases, such as the provision of chilled water service to tenants, heat metering may be required to measure the energy supplied.

The owners or occupiers should also be provided with instructions and a metering strategy, showing how to use the meters to account for at least 90% of the energy used with the building and how the results can be used to compare operating performance with published benchmarks. Guidance on metering strategies is given in CIBSE TM39: *Building energy metering*.

B4.3.6.5   EU Directive on the energy performance of buildings

The Energy Performance of Buildings Directive focuses on the ongoing performance of buildings after occupation and further development of the Building Regulations will be needed to support the aims of the Directive.

The Directive requires a number of specific procedures to be developed in EU countries:

—   development of a methodology for calculating the energy performance of buildings

—   minimum requirements for the energy performance of new buildings, and existing buildings undergoing major renovation

—   energy certification of buildings

—   regular inspection and assessment of boilers and air conditioning systems.

Under the Directive, regular inspection of air conditioning systems with a rated output of greater than 12 kW is required. The inspections should include an assessment of the of the air conditioning system efficiency and the sizing compared to the cooling requirements of the building. Appropriate advice should be provided to the users on possible improvement or replacement of the air conditioning system and on alternative solutions.

Guidance on inspection is given in CIBSE TM44: *Inspection of air conditioning systems*.

B4.4   System selection

B4.4.2   Refrigeration and heat rejection systems

Guidance on selecting cooling systems is given in Table B4.9 which summarises and classifies the main types of

systems according to BS EN 378-1. This is intended as an aid to understanding the types of equipment referred to later in Guide B sections 4.4 and 4.5.

Type (*a*) systems have the disadvantage that components that contain refrigerant are installed in the space or room being cooled. Distributed versions of (*a*) may contain large quantities of refrigerant. Most conventional chilled water based systems are based on systems (*d*) or (*e*) and use terminal units such as fan coil units, induction units or chilled beams and panels. With these systems the components that contain refrigerant are outside the space being cooled and this avoids the risk of refrigerant leaks into occupied areas.

Table B4.10 summarises the main types of heat rejection system and provides guidance on selection and cross-references to further information in section 4.5.

Table B4.9 Types of cooling system

System type	Description	Area to be cooled	Refrigerating or heat rejection system	Comments
(*a*) Direct system (direct expansion or 'DX' system)	The refrigeration system evaporator is in direct communication with the space to be cooled.			Most efficient cooling system but risk of refrigerant leaks in the occupied areas of the building. May have a relatively high refrigerant charge.
(*b*) Indirect open system	A refrigeration or heat rejection system cools a heat transfer medium which is in direct communication with the space to be cooled.			May use an air washer or spray coil to cool air. Hygiene risks mean that these systems are not widely used.
(*c*) Indirect vented open system	Similar to (*b*) but with open or vented tank.			
(*d*) Indirect closed system	A refrigeration or heat rejection system cools a heat transfer medium which passes through a closed circuit in direct communication with the space to be cooled.			Widely used with chilled water as heat transfer medium. Lower energy efficiency than (*a*), (*b*) or (*c*) due to additional heat transfer process. Safer than (*a*) because it keeps refrigerant-containing parts out of occupied areas.
(*e*) Indirect vented closed system	Similar to (*d*) but with open or vented tank.			
(*f*) Double indirect system (open or closed)	A combination of (*b*) and (*d*) where the cooled heat transfer medium passes through a second heat exchanger.			Two additional heat transfer processes make it least efficient system. Highest safety where toxic and/or flammable refrigerants are used, but little justification for its use.

Pipework containing refrigerant: ————   Pipework containing heat transfer medium: - - - - - - - - -

Table B4.10 Types of heat rejection system

System type	Description	Heat rejection system	Section	Comments
(a) Air cooled condenser	Fans induce air flow over finned tubing in which refrigerant condenses.		4.5.5.3	Convenient and common for chillers up to a few 100 k W. Free of hygiene risks and do not require water piping. Can be adapted to provide free cooling with thermosyphon systems.
(b) Dry air cooler	Similar to (a) but aqueous glycol solution of water is passed through the tubes instead of refrigerant.		4.5.5.4	Less efficient than (a) because an additional heat transfer process, and pumps, are required to reject heat from a refrigeration plant. May cool water sufficiently in winter to avoid need to operate a refrigeration plant – 'free cooling'.
(c) Cooling tower	Water is sprayed over a packing material. Airflow over the packing evaporates some of the water causing the water to be cooled.		4.5.5.5	More efficient than (a) or (b) because less air is required and water is cooled to a few degrees above the wet bulb temperature. May cool water sufficiently to avoid need to operate a refrigeration plant – 'free cooling'. High maintenance requirement.
(d) Evaporative condenser	Water is sprayed over tubing in which refrigerant condenses. Airflow across the tubing evaporates some of the water causing the water and the tubes to be cooled.		4.5.5.6	Most efficient method of rejecting heat from a refrigeration plant. Similar maintenance requirements as (c). Can be adapted to provide free cooling with thermosyphon systems.

Pipework containing refrigerant: ————   Pipework containing heat transfer medium: - - - - - - -

B4.4.3   Free cooling

The aim of 'free cooling' is to minimise or eliminate the need to provide and operate a refrigeration system. Most buildings or processes that require cooling throughout the year have the potential to use free-cooling during cool weather.

Free cooling usually requires the transport of air or water as a cooling medium and may also require the use of additional fans and pumps for heat rejection at a dry air cooler or cooling tower. Free cooling systems generally involve moving relatively large amounts of tempered or ambient air and cool water, compared with the smaller amounts of cold air or water distributed when a refrigeration system is operated.

The designer can maximise the opportunity for free-cooling by selecting a cooling system that requires air or chilled water at a relatively high temperature.

Further guidance on these systems is given in Guide B chapter 2.

In some systems the potential for free cooling may be increased by separating the latent and sensible loads. Free cooling may satisfy the sensible cooling load at quite high ambient temperatures, while a separate refrigeration system is provided for dehumidification as this function usually requires a lower coolant temperature.

B4.4.4   Vapour compression refrigeration

The vapour compression refrigeration cycle employs a volatile refrigerant fluid which vaporises or evaporates in a heat exchanger, cooling the surroundings through the absorption of heat. The vapour is then restored to the liquid phase by mechanical compression. The mechanical vapour compression refrigeration cycle is currently the dominant technique for refrigeration and air conditioning applications.

Figure B4.9 shows the basic components in a vapour compression circuit and Figure B4.10 illustrates the complete refrigeration cycle on a pressure–enthalpy diagram. The cycle shown is simplified and in particular ignores the effect of pressure drops in pipes and heat exchangers.

The stages in the cycle are as follows:

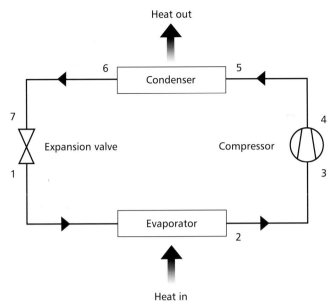

Figure B4.9 Vapour compression cycle: principal system components

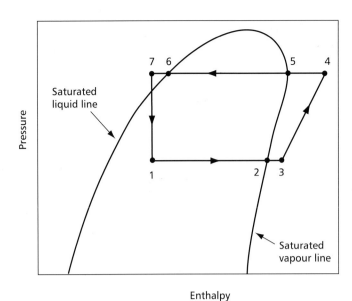

Figure B4.10 Vapour compression cycle : simple pressure–enthalpy diagram

— *Stage 1 to 2*: low pressure liquid refrigerant in the evaporator absorbs heat from the medium being cooled (usually water or air) at constant pressure while evaporating to become dry saturated vapour.

— *Stage 2 to 3*: the refrigerant vapour absorbs more heat while in the evaporator and while in the pipework joining the evaporator to the compressor, to become a superheated vapour.

— *Stage 3 to 4*: the superheated vapour is compressed, increasing its temperature and pressure.

— *Stage 4 to 5*: the hot superheated vapour enters the condenser where the first part of the process is de-superheating.

— *Stage 5 to 6*: the hot vapour is condensed back to a saturated liquid at constant temperature and pressure through being cooled by a coolant (usually air or water);

— *Stage 6 to 7*: further cooling may take place to sub-cool the liquid before it enters the expansion valve (this may occur in the condenser, a second heat exchanger or in the pipework connecting the condenser with the expansion valve).

— *Stage 7 to 1*: the high pressure sub-cooled liquid passes through an expansion device causing a reduction in its temperature and pressure at constant enthalpy.

Where a vapour compression system is intended to provide useful heating (from the heat rejected at the condenser) it is usually known as a heat pump. Heat pumps may also provide cooling. Figure B4.11 shows a reversible (refrigerant changeover) air-to-air heat pump that may be used for either heating or cooling. Water-to-water heat pumps employ a water changeover valve arrangement instead.

Modern vapour compression plant may use one of a variety of compressor types depending partly on the cooling capacity required. Information on compressors and other system components is given in Guide B section 4.5.2.

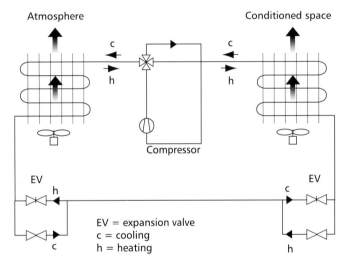

Figure B4.11 Reversible heat pump system for heating or cooling

The designer or specifier should take into account a number of factors when specifying a mechanical vapour compression plant including:

— refrigerant type

— safety requirements

— environmental requirements

— energy efficiency (coefficient of performance).

B4.4.4.1 Refrigerant selection

The basic requirement is that the fluid evaporates at the required cooling temperature at a reasonable pressure, and that it condenses at the temperature of a readily available cooling medium. However, commercial vapour compression refrigeration systems should be safe, practical and economic and generally the refrigerant should possess as many of the properties listed in Table B4.11 as possible.

No single refrigerant satisfies all of the desired refrigerant properties and a range of refrigerants are commercially available for standard refrigeration and air conditioning applications. Some key properties of these refrigerants are

Table B4.11 Key refrigerant section criteria

Refrigerant property	Selection criteria
Low toxicity	A desirable property especially for systems that may be installed in occupied parts of buildings, such as split and multi-split air conditioners. See section B4.4.4.2.
Zero ozone deletion potential	Ozone depleting substances are no longer acceptable as refrigerants. See Guide B section 4.3.4.1.
Low global warming potential	Substances with high global warming potential are likely to be restricted or phased out by some governments and some corporate environmental policies already restrict the use of refrigerants with high global warming potential. See Guide B section 4.3.4.2.
Non-flammable	A desirable property especially for systems that contain large quantities of refrigerant and are located in occupied parts of buildings. See section B4.4.4.2.
Chemically stable and compatible with conventional materials and compressor lubricants	Substances without these properties are unlikely to be used as commercial refrigerants.
Suitable pressure/temperature relationship	Excessively high operating pressures require the use of strong components, pipework and heat exchangers which increases the cost and weight of systems and increases the likelihood of leakage. Operating pressures below atmospheric pressure increase the risk of contamination and ingress of air. High pressure ratios reduce system energy efficiency.
High latent heat	This determines the mass flow of refrigerant that has to be circulated and although is a highly desirable property it can be offset by other properties.
High critical temperature	The critical temperature (the temperature above which a substance behaves like a permanent gas and cannot be liquefied) should normally be well above the required heat rejection temperature. Also, as the critical temperature is approached the latent heat of vapourisation decreases which tends to reduce the efficiency of the system. See section B4.4.4.5.
Low vapour specific heat ratio	The specific heat ratio determines the index of compression and hence the temperature rise during compression. Low indices of compression give low discharge temperatures which are desirable to minimise breakdown of refrigerant and lubricant.
Low temperature glide* (for blends)	This can either improve or reduce heat transfer coefficients in the evaporator and condenser, depending on their design. High glide can cause handling difficulties and cause preferential leakage (increasing the cost of maintenance). Refrigerants with a high glide are generally unsuitable for use in flooded evaporators due to large concentration changes in the evaporator leading to reductions in performance. High glide causes a reduction in the refrigerant temperature at the evaporator inlet for a given chilled water supply temperature. This may cause a risk of icing in systems supplying water at 6 °C or below and may require an anti-freeze additive.

*Non-azeotropic blends exhibit a change ('glide') in temperature during the evaporation and condensation process. The temperature of the evaporating refrigerant rises along the evaporator, and the temperature of the condensing vapour decreases along the condenser. The extent of the temperature glide is mainly dependent on the boiling points and proportions of the individual constituents.

summarised in Appendix B4.A1 and pressure–enthalpy charts are shown in Appendix B4.A2. The designer should select the most suitable refrigerant for a particular application taking into account the following factors:

—   *equipment size*: capacity required per machine, since the capacity of a compressor is affected by the type of refrigerant

—   *type of compressor*: reciprocating, centrifugal, screw or scroll

—   *operating temperature range*: air conditioning, process cooling

—   *economics*: first cost of the equipment and refrigerant, cost of servicing, refrigerant handling requirements and eventual cost of refrigerant disposal

—   *environmental and safety factors*: acceptability to the client (for example in relation to environmental policies and green labelling and certification), future refrigerant availability (government environmental regulation), safety requirements of relevant codes and standards.

B4.4.4.2   Safety

The selection of the system type and refrigerant should minimise hazards to persons, property and the environment. Specific requirements are detailed in BS EN 378, and theses are amplified in the Institute of Refrigeration safety Codes. Guidance on policy and refrigerant replacement issues are given in CIBSE GN1 and specific requirements for commissioning systems are given in CIBSE Commissioning Code R.

The purpose of BS EN 378 is to minimise possible hazards to persons, property and the environment from refrigerating systems and refrigerants. It stipulates specific requirements for different refrigerants, types of refrigeration systems, locations and type of building.

BS EN 378 classifies refrigerants into groups according to their influence on health and safety and these groupings are maintained in the the Institute of Refrigeration Safety Codes. Building occupancies are classified according to the safety of the occupants, who may be directly affected in case of abnormal operation operation of the refrigerating system (such as catastrophic leakage). Refrigerating systems are classified according to the method of cooling the space and heat rejection and broadly follows the classification given in Table B4.9.

Further guidance is given in Guide B section B4.4.4.2.

(a) Maximum charge of refrigerant

BS EN 378 limits the hazards from refrigerants by stipulating the maximum charge of refrigerant for given occupancy categories and refrigerant safety groups. Table B4.13 summarises maximum refrigerant charge and other restrictions for chillers (indirect closed systems) and direct (DX) systems. The latest version of BS EN 378 should always be consulted for full details. Maximum refrigerant charge is related to the 'practical limit' or maximum allowable short term refrigerant concentration should the entire charge be released into the space or the room occupied by the system (does not apply to systems located out of doors). Table B4.14 shows the practical limit and the corresponding maximum refrigerant charge for a range of common refrigerants.

Table B4.14 Maximum refrigerant charge derived from practical limits

Refrigerant	Practical limit ($/ \mathrm{kg \cdot m^{-3}}$)	Maximum refrigerant charge ($/ \mathrm{kg}$) for a direct system serving or installed in a 100 m³ room
R12	0.50	50
R22	0.30	30
R123	0.10	10
R134a	0.25	25
R407C	0.31	31
R410A	0.44	44
R717 (ammonia)	0.00035	0.035
R290 (propane)	0.008	0.8
R600a (isobutane)	0.008	0.8

Table B4.13 Summary of BS EN 378 requirements for maximum refrigerant charge (latest version of BS EN 378 should be consulted for full details)

Refrigerant	System type	Occupancy category A (e.g. residential, hotels, supermarkets etc.)		Occupancy category B (e.g. offices, shops, workplaces etc.)		Occupancy category C (e.g. manufacturing facilities, plant rooms or other areas with access limited to authorised persons)	
		Max. charge (per system)	Restrictions	Max. charge (per system)	Restrictions	Max. charge (per system)	Restrictions
L1 refrigerants (e.g. CFCS, HCFCS and HFCS)	DX	Practical limit × room vol.	Maximum charge limit may be relaxed*	No limit	If located below ground or on an upper floor without emergency exits then maximum charge is practical limit × room volume	No limit	If located below ground or on an upper floor without emergency exits then maximum charge is practical limit × room volume
	Chillers	No limit	Must be in open air or 'special machinery room'†	No limit	Must be in open air or 'special machinery room'†	No limit	Must be in open air or 'special machinery room'†
L2 refrigerants (e.g. ammonia)	DX	Practical limit × room vol. (2.5 kg limit)	Must be a sealed system. Not allowed if people are restricted in their movement	10 kg	—	10 kg	50 kg if occupancy less than 1 person per 10 m² and there are emergency exits
	Chillers	No limit	Must be in open air or 'special machinery room'† with an exit to open air and no direct access to cat. A	No limit	Must be in open air or 'special machinery room'† with no direct access to occupied rooms	No limit	—
L3 refrigerants (e.g. HCS)	DX	Practical limit × room vol. (1.5 kg limit)	Cannot be used for air conditioning or heating for human comfort. Refrigeration system must not have any sources of ignition (e.g. requires sealed electrics)	Practical limit × room vol. (2.5 kg limit)	Cannot be used for air conditioning or heating for human comfort. Practical limit × room vol. up to a maximum of 1 kg if below the ground	10 kg	Cannot be used for air conditioning or heating for human comfort. 1 kg limit if below ground level
	Chillers	5 kg	Must be in open air or 'special machinery room'†. 1 kg limit if below ground level	10 kg	Must be in open air or 'special machinery room'†. 1 kg limit if below ground level	No limit	Must be in open air or 'special machinery room'†. 1 kg limit if below ground level

* The total volume of all rooms cooled or heated by air from one system is used as the volume for calculation, provided the air supply to each room cannot be restricted below 25% of its full supply. If the space has a mechanical ventilation system that is always operating during operation then the effect of air change may be considered in calculating the volume. Other methods of ensuring safety in the event of a major release are permitted if they prevent concentrations exceeding the practical limit, or give adequate warning to occupants so that they may avoid excessive exposure time.

† Special machinery room is a plant room with special requirements. These include tight fitting and self-closing doors with at least 0.5 h fire resistance; all fabric elements and service entry points sealed; minimum specifications for ventilation; and refrigerant detectors. Additional requirements for ammonia include an at least one emergency exit opening into the open air or an escape passage way; mechanical ventilation and a remote switch for isolating all electrical equipment inside the plant room should ammonia be released into the plant room.

(b) Specific requirements for ammonia

Ammonia is highly toxic through direct contact and inhalation of concentrations above 1000 ppm. However, it has a highly pungent smell (detectable by nose down to about 10 ppm) which makes voluntary exposure highly unlikely. At these lower concentrations ammonia has no known long term or accumulative health effects although its pungency can induce panic and alarm. Ammonia is flammable at concentrations between 16% and 27% by volume, although in practise such high concentrations are only likely in the event of the most flagrant contravention of safety guidelines.

It is essential that relevant health and safety regulations, safety standards and codes and other industry guidance documents are complied with. These include:

—   relevant UK regulations (see section B4.3.2.1)

—   BS EN 378

—   Institute of Refrigeration's *Safety code for refrigerating systems utilizing ammonia refrigerant*

—   Health and Safety Executive Guidance Note PM81: *Safe management of ammonia refrigeration systems*

—   Institute of Refrigeration Guidance Note 10: *Working with ammonia.*

In addition to meeting the specific requirements of these standards and codes it is highly recommended that the following additional guidelines are followed:

—   Ammonia systems installed for air conditioning in buildings occupied by humans should be installed either in a special plant room within the building or inside a special enclosure which may be on the building roof. The advantages of such a plant room or enclosure are that any spilled or leaked liquid ammonia can be contained and that external gas discharge rates can be controlled.

—   The total quantity of ammonia used should be minimised through appropriate design such as the use of multiple chillers for large systems and the use of compact heat exchangers such as plate heat exchangers.

—   Relief valves should discharge in a safe place away from any building, such as a vertical pipe on the building roof.

—   An acceptable way of disposing of large quantities of spilt or leaked ammonia is through controlled atmospheric dispersion, ideally through a high fan-assisted stack away from people and other buildings.

—   The practice of spraying water onto pools of liquid ammonia is highly hazardous and should be avoided.

Further information on minimising ammonia hazards, including predicting gas concentrations in dispersing ammonia plumes is given in BRE Information Paper IP18/00.

(c) Specific requirements for hydrocarbons

Hydrocarbon (HC) refrigerants are highly flammable. However, they have very good refrigeration properties and may be used in a very wide range of refrigeration equipment.

It is essential that relevant health and safety regulations, safety standards and codes and other industry guidance documents are complied with. These include:

—   relevant UK regulations (see section B4.3.2.1)

—   BS EN 378

—   Institute of Refrigeration's *Safety code for refrigerating systems utilizing group A3 refrigerants*

—   ACRIB's *Guidelines for the use of hydrocarbon refrigerants in static refrigeration and air conditioning systems.*

The above standards and codes are designed to minimise hazards associated with the use of flammable hydrocarbon refrigerants and bring the degrees of risk in line with other types of refrigerant. It is also essential that safe working practices are adhered to during maintenance and servicing as refrigerant grades of hydrocarbons are odourless. In particular the following precautions are essential during maintenance and servicing:

—   Hydrocarbon vapour detectors should be used during maintenance and servicing to alert the technician to the presence of potentially flammable atmospheres.

—   No source of ignition should be present and special precautions should be taken prior to any brazing or welding.

—   Any person who is involved with working on or breaking into a refrigeration circuit should hold a current certificate from an industry accredited authority which certifies their competence to handle refrigerants (including hydrocarbons) safely in accordance with an industry recognised assessment specification.

(d) Refrigerant detection

Refrigerant detectors and alarms are required in all refrigeration equipment plant rooms to prevent the exposure of workers to refrigerant concentrations higher than the HSE occupational exposure limits (see HSE EH40) and to warn of higher toxic concentrations. Detectors are also required in plant rooms that contain hydrocarbon or ammonia systems to start emergency ventilation and shutdown any electrical equipment that is not suitable for operation in explosive atmospheres.

Further information is provided in Guide B section 4.4.4.2.

B4.4.4.3   Environmental impacts

The selection of a refrigerant and refrigeration system type should take account of the environmental impact of the refrigerant and the systems, and legal requirements. These are mainly related to the leakage of refrigerant to the atmosphere and the end of life disposal of refrigerants and compressor oil. It is a legal requirement that all used refrigerant and oils are recovered for recycling or disposal using an environmentally acceptable method. Legal and other environmental related requirements are detailed in section B4.3.4.

The selection of a refrigeration system and refrigerant should aim to minimise the total equivalent warming impact (TEWI) of the system over its expected lifetime. TEWI takes account of the direct global warming potential of the refrigerant and the global warming impact of the energy used to drive the system. Section B4.3.5.2. provides guidance on TEWI assessment.

B4.4.4.4 Refrigerant leakage

See Guide B section 4.4.4.4. Further guidance is given by the Institute of Refrigeration's *Code of practice for the minimization of refrigerant emissions from refrigerating systems*, Action Energy Good Practice Guide GPG178 and BRE Information Paper IP1/94.

B4.4.4.5 Coefficient of performance

The energy efficiency of a refrigeration system is defined as the coefficient of performance (COP):

$$\text{COP} = \frac{\text{Refrigeration effect (kW)}}{\text{Power input of the compressor (kW)}} \quad (4.2)$$

In practice the coefficient of system performance (COSP) is more useful for comparing different systems. COSP includes the power consumed by ancillary equipment associated with the refrigeration system, including condenser fan motors, condenser water pumps, electrical controls and cooling tower fans and pumps. COSP does not include the power consumed by the chilled water pumps or ventilation pumps.

$$\text{COP} = \frac{\text{Refrigeration effect (kW)}}{\begin{array}{c}\text{Power input of the compressor and}\\\text{ancillary motors and controls (kW)}\end{array}} \quad (4.3)$$

COSP depends on many factors although the temperature lift of the system is usually the most important factor. Temperature lift is the difference between the condensing and evaporating temperatures and is affected by factors such as the mode of heat rejection. Other factors include the compressor efficiency, motor efficiencies and the choice of refrigerant.

The COSP of a range of vapour compression chiller types with air-cooled and water-cooled condensers is shown in Table B4.15. The values shown are COSP values and are lower than COP values that might be quoted by a manufacturer.

Table B4.15 COSP for a range of vapour compression chiller types

Type	Cooling capacity / kW	Coefficient of system performance (COSP)*	
		Water-cooled condensers	Air-cooled condensers
Reciprocating	< 120	2.6	3.2
	> 120	2.8	3.4
Scroll	< 250	2.8	3.4
Screw	< 1800	2.6	3.6
Centrifugal	< 800	2.2	3.8
	> 800	2.3	4.0

*Values are typical for a packaged water chiller operating at chilled water temperature of +6 °C and dry bulb air temperature of 28 °C

The vapour compression cycle approximates to the reversed Rankine and Carnot cycles. The theoretical COP of the Carnot cycle is given by:

$$\text{COP} = \frac{T_1}{T_2 - T_1} \quad (4.4)$$

where T_1 is the evaporating temperature (K) and T_2 is the condensing temperature (K).

The COP of a practical vapour compression system is considerably lower than the COP of the theoretical Carnot cycle. However, equation 4.4 can be used by the designer to predict the relative change in COP from changes in the evaporating and condensing temperatures.

B4.4.5 Absorption refrigeration

See Guide B section 4.4.5.

B4.4.7 Secondary coolants

Secondary coolants (sometimes also known as heat transfer fluids, brines or secondary refrigerants) such as chilled water, brine or glycol mixes are generally used on larger plant where the volume of the primary refrigerant would be too large for environmental and/or cost reasons. The use of a secondary coolant involves an additional heat transfer process and therefore greater temperature difference, hence these systems are inherently less energy efficient than direct refrigeration systems.

Secondary coolants should ideally be non-toxic liquid with a high thermal conductivity, a high specific heat capacity and a low viscosity. For good heat transfer it is also desirable that the coolant velocity is high enough for turbulent flow. Table B4.19 summarises some of the key

Table B4.19 Properties of common secondary refrigerants

Substance	Concentration by weight / %	Viscosity / centipoise	Freezing point / °C	Flow rate per 100 kW for 5 K temp. rise
Water	100	1.55	0	4.8
NaCl	12	1.75	−8.0	5.1
CaCl₂	12	2.01	−7.2	5.2
Ethylene glycol	25	2.7	−10.6	5.1
Propylene glycol	30	5.0	−10.6	4.9
Polydimethylsiloxane	100	1.91	−111.0	14.5

properties of a range of common secondary refrigerants. Water has good heat transfer and transport properties and is the most widely used secondary coolant for applications above 0 °C, especially for air conditioning systems.

B4.5 Equipment

Details of refrigeration and heat rejection equipment required are contained in Guide B section 4.5. Table B4.A below, which does not appear in Guide B, summarises the main points given in Guide B section 4.5.

Table B4.A A summary of information contained in Guide B section 4.5 (This table does not appear in CIBSE Guide B)

Section number	Component	Construction	Advantages	Disadvantages
4.5.2.1	Evaporators:			
	— shell and tube (DX)	Steel vessel (shell) containing straight tubes, located between end tube plates, having removable end covers. Refrigerant flows through tubes. Used for water temp. down to 4 °C	Small refrigerant charge. Direct (only one heat transfer).	Coolant side inaccessible. Load fluctuations difficult to control.
	— flooded refrigerant	Similar to shell and tube but refrigerant in shell. Suitable for water temp. down to 4 °C.	Large load fluctuation without freezing. Higher rate of heat transfer than DX.	Large refrigerant charge. Higher cost than DX.
	— gasketed plate heat exchanger	Corrugated metal plates compressed between a frame plate. Plates sealed with gaskets directing fluid into alternate channels. Allows very low (> 2 °C) coolant and refrigerant temp. difference.	Low refrigerant charge. High rates of heat transfer.	Oil fouling can reduce heat transfer. Prone to freezing.
	— brazed plate heat exchanger	Variant of gasket type but cannot be dismantled.	As gasket type.	As gasket type.
	— air blown DX	Same as air cooled condenser, used as 'open unit' in cold rooms	—	—
4.5.2.2	Condensers:			
	— air cooled	Finned copper tubes in which refrigerant condenses. Temperature difference typically 20 °C.	Well suited to small packaged systems.	Size and inefficiency mean not suitable for cooling loads above 1000 kW.
	— water cooled shell and tube	Welded pressure vessel with plain or finned tubes between end plates. Often used with cooling towers or dry air coolers.	—	—
	— gasket/brazed plate heat exchangers	See under 'evaporators' above.	Significant reduction in size compared to shell and tube. High rates of heat transfer	Oil fouling can reduce heat transfer. Prone to freezing.
	— evaporative	Similar to forced draught cooling towers, but with refrigerant vapour condensed and circulated within the tubes.	Most energy efficient means of heat rejection to ambient air.	Need to be located close to compressor. Good water and cleaning essential.
	— low pressure receiver	Pressure vessel incorporating heat exchanger. Used in vapour compression systems. Allows evaporator to be operated more efficiently.	—	—
4.5.2.3	Expansion devices:			
	— capillary tube	Long, small bore capillary tube, used in domestic refrigerators and freezers.	Effective	Prone to blockage. No adjustment for superheat levels.
	— thermostatic expansion valve (TEV)	Automatic valve controlling rate of liquid refrigerant flow.	Ensures only gas is pumped	Require minimum pressure difference, in cold weather condensing temperature may have to be held artificially high.
	— electronic expansion valve	Relies on external electronic signal to provide closer control of superheat.	Operates with wider range of evaporating and condensing temps. than TEVs. Does not require condensing temp. to be held artificially high in cold weather.	More expensive than TEV and difficult to set up.
	— float valve regulator	Two types: high side and low side. High-side controls flow of liquid refrigerant. Low-side directly controls level of refrigerant in evaporator.	—	—

Table continues

Table B4.A A summary of information contained in Guide B section 4.5 — *continued*

Section number	Component	Construction	Advantages	Disadvantages
4.5.3	Direct expansion (DX) systems:			
	— general	Evaporator in which all refrigerant completely evaporates producing superheated vapour at exit.	Thermodynamically more efficient than indirect systems.	In practice, evaporator surface area and efficiencies of fans, compressor and condenser can affect overall efficiency.
	— through-the-wall DX	Packaged fan coil units (FCUs), room-air side evaporator and outside facing condenser coil. Many types operate as heat pump providing both heating and cooling.	—	Less suitable for large buildings due to high maintenance cost, potential control problems and limited air throw into deep plan rooms.
	— split DX	Similar to through-the-wall units except indoor and outdoor units are separate and connected by refrigerant pipes.	—	
	— variant refrigerant flow (VRF)	Multi-split systems with refrigerant flow distributor control device. Suitable for larger buildings.	Considerable installation flexibility.	Careful design and installation of interconnecting pipework is essential for reliable operation. Because of extensive pipework, have greater potential for refrigerant leakage. Particular care required when installed where people sleep.

B4.5.3.7 *Refrigerant pipework*

The design and installation of refrigerant pipework can critically affect the system performance and reliability and requires particular care for split and multi-split systems and any other site erected system.

— *Liquid line pressure drop*: should be kept to a minimum to ensure that there is no flash gas at the expansion device as this can significantly reduce the cooling capacity of the system. In liquid lines the liquid temperature is close to the refrigerant saturation temperature and the effect of pressure drop is to reduce the temperature difference increasing the risk of flash gas forming at the expansion valve.

— *Suction line pressure drop*: a balance has to be made between the effect on compressor performance and the minimum velocity required for oil return from the evaporator. Where the direction of refrigerant flow is upwards then the velocity must be high enough to entrain the oil. One way of accomplishing this is to use a double riser. One riser is fitted with an oil trap which will gradually accumulate oil until the line is completely blocked off. The suction gas is then taken by the second (smaller) line resulting in a temporary pressure drop which will suck the oil from the trap.

— *Cleanliness*: it is vital that ingress of dirt is avoided as this could lead to internal blockages, especially in systems with capillary tube expansion devices.

— *Refrigerant leakage*: demountable flare and screwed joints should be avoided wherever possible to minimise the risk of leakage. The number of joints should be minimised and where necessary should be brazed using competent personnel following industry good practice working methods. Pipework should not be installed where mechanical damage is likely.

B4.5.4 Water chillers

Factory built packaged chillers are generally preferable to site erected systems. Site erected systems increase the risk of refrigerant leakage and generally have longer runs of pipework which increases the refrigerant charge. There are considerable differences between chillers supplied by different manufacturers and the designer must make careful comparisons before choosing a supplier.

B4.5.4.1 *Vapour compression*

Table B4.20 gives an overview of the four basic types of compressor currently used in the refrigeration industry:

— reciprocating (piston cylinder)

— scroll

— screw

— centrifugal.

Current practice on very large installations is to use centrifugal or screw compressors. On medium to large plant scroll, reciprocating or screw semi-hermetic multi-compressors are used. These can be either equal or unequally sized.

(a) Reciprocating compressors

Reciprocating compressors are positive displacement machines with the refrigerant vapour compressed by pistons moving in a close fitting bore. Each cylinder has a suction and a discharge valve and the bearings are oil lubricated. Reciprocating compressors are available in a very wide range of sizes ranging from a single-cylinder type to eight cylinder or more compressors.

Table B4.20 Overview of vapour compression chillers

Type	Cooling range / kW	Refrigerant type and typical operating range	Capacity control*
Semi-hermetic:			
— reciprocating (2, 4, 6, 8, 10 and 12 cylinders)	20–1000	All types (–25 °C to +10 °C)	Cylinder, unloading
— single screw	200–2000	HCFC and HFC	Moving plate
— twin screw	200–3000	HCFC and HFC	Slider system
Hermetic:			
— twin screw	200–600	HCFC and HFC	Slider system, variable speed
— scroll	5–250	HCFC and HFC	—
— reciprocating (single-stage)	2–400	All types (–25 °C to +10 °C)	100%
— reciprocating (two-stage)	2–150	All types (–25 °C to +10 °C)	50/100% speed control
Centrifugal (multi-stage)	300–15000	HFC	Inlet guide vanes (all cases); variable speed (some cases)
Open-type reciprocating (2, 4, 6, 8, 10 and 12 cylinders)	100–1000	HFC and ammonia	Cylinder unloading
Open-type screw	200–3000	HFC and ammonia	Slider system, variable speed

* See Guide B section 4.5.6

(b) Screw compressors

Screw compressors are high-speed positive displacement machines, compression being obtained by the interaction of two screw-cut rotors or a single rotor meshing with two toothed wheels. They can generally operate over a wider pressure ratio range than reciprocating compressors.

Most screw compressors can be optionally equipped with an economiser which allows an additional charge of refrigerant gas to be pumped (a form of supercharging).

Screw compressors are cooled by oil injected into the machine to seal the running clearances between the rotors and casing. Oil separators are generally included in packaged units and in the case of hermetic machines within the hermetic housing.

(c) Centrifugal compressors

Hermetic units incorporate an induction motor and an internal gear which allows the impellers to run at speeds between 8000 and 10 000 revolutions per minute. Open-type machines can be driven by electric motors, steam turbines, gas turbines and gas engines. For capacities larger than about 7000 kW all machines are of the open type.

(d) Scroll compressors

Scroll compressors are hermetically sealed rotary positive displacement machines with one fixed and one orbiting scroll which progressively compresses refrigerant with a constant volume ratio. They have comparable or slightly higher efficiencies than reciprocating machines at typical air conditioning application temperatures. Some types of scroll compressor are compliant in that they allow some radial or axial movement of the scroll which allows them to cope with some liquid returned to the compressor. Noise and vibration levels are less than for reciprocating compressors.

B4.5.4.2 Absorption machines

Absorption machines are heat driven machines and do not have a compressor. They are larger and heavier than their vapour compression equivalents, hence the designer must confirm the weight and dimensions with the manufacturer.

Various types of absorption chiller are available but generally the choice of chiller type is determined by the temperature level of the available heat source and the temperature level of the load. Further information is given in section 4.4.5.

B4.5.4.3 Multiple chillers

For information on multiple chiller installations see Guide B section 4.5.4.3.

B4.5.5 Heat rejection and cooling water equipment

Heat rejection plant is required to cool the condenser; the efficiency of this process will affect the system COSP. Overall seasonal efficiencies are therefore influenced by energy efficient design of heat rejection systems. Where ever possible opportunities for free cooling should be sought, especially for systems that are operated throughout the year, see section 4.4.3.

The basic types of condenser (see Table 4.10, page 88) are:

— *direct*: air-cooled, direct water-cooled, or evaporative

— *indirect*: condenser heat is rejected via a water system by using cooling towers or dry air coolers or some other form of environmental cooling.

Information and guidance on the cost considerations of alternative forms of condenser cooling system are given in BSRIA TM 1/90 and BSRIA Technical Appraisal 1/93.

Table B4.21 gives a comparison of machine COPs together with the heat rejection which may be expected when evaporating at 5.0 °C and condensing at 35–40 °C. These are for water cooled systems; the COP would be lower for air cooled systems. The COPs are approximate and are for comparative purposes only.

B4.5.5.1 Sources of water cooling

In most air conditioning applications where water is used, the water is recirculated and cooled by an evaporative process; make-up losses are catered for by the use of a

Table B4.21 Approximate cops and heat rejection

Type	COP*	Heat rejection/ cooling† / kW
Reciprocating compressor	4	1.25
Scroll compressor	4	1.25
Centrifugal compressor	5.5	1.18
Screw compressor	5.5	1.18
Absorption machine (single effect)	0.68	2.47

Note: COP = cooling power (kW) / input power (kW)
* Evaporator temperature: 5 °C
† Condenser temperature: 35–40 °C

storage tank connected to the mains supply via a ballcock or similar device.

Environmental cooling may be used directly for cooling a building. If it is not cold enough then it may be used as a heat sink for heat rejected from the condensers. Examples of environmental cooling include:

— ambient air

— ground water

— rivers or lakes

— sea water.

Further information on these sources of cooling is given in Guide B section 4.4.3.1.

B4.5.5.2 Air cooled condensers

Air cooled condensers are the simplest form of condenser heat rejection plant, in which air is blown over finned tubes containing the condensed refrigerant. They are generally found on stand-alone plant such as packaged air conditioners, split systems or some packaged air handling plant. They lose efficiency by having to operate at a relatively high condensing temperature, since they do not have the benefit of evaporative water cooling on the outside of the coil. See Guide B section 4.5.2.2 for further information.

B4.5.5.3 Dry air coolers

Dry air coolers are heat exchangers of construction similar to that of an air cooled condenser. They are designed for cooling liquids (generally glycol–water) in a closed circuit. The freezing point of the liquid must usually be at least 5 K below the minimum winter ambient temperature of the site of installation. The cooling effect from night time sky radiation should also be considered where pipework is exposed.

Selection is normally to suit each individual case specifying maximum noise level, type of liquid, ambient temperature, liquid inlet temperature, liquid outlet temperature, maximum allowed pressure drop etc. They are simple in construction and operation with low installation and maintenance costs.

As the water distribution system is closed, atmospheric contamination cannot occur and microbiological control of water quality is simplified. Ambient air contamination could be a hazard and precautions similar to those for air-cooled condensers should be observed.

On some installations dry coolers have been used with sprayed water which improves their efficiency due to the evaporative cooling. These units are referred to as 'wet and dry coolers' or 'adiabatically enhanced' dry coolers. Local regulations regarding water treatment must be complied with.

B4.5.5.4 Wet cooling towers

A cooling tower cools the condenser water by evaporative cooling. There are two types of wet cooling tower:

— *Open circuit*: water from the condenser is pumped to the cooling tower and is cooled by the evaporation of some of the condenser water. This requires all the water passing through the condenser to be treated and results in increased water consumption due to drift losses.

— *Closed circuit*: condenser water is circulated in a closed loop and a separate water circuit is pumped through the cooling tower, cooling the condenser water by transferring heat through a heat exchanger. This minimises water treatment costs but it also reduces energy efficiency due to the temperature difference across the heat exchanger, although this effect can be minimised by specifying a high efficiency heat exchanger.

In a mechanical draught tower (see Table B4.22) the entering water is sprayed into the plastic fill packing and one or more fans force air through the packing to enhance evaporation and, hence, the cooling effect. The cooled water falls to the base reservoir and is pumped back to the condenser. Natural draught cooling towers are rarely used for building air conditioning applications due to their much greater height and high approach temperature.

(a) Specification

Table B4.22 describes the main types of mechanical draught cooling towers. Mechanical draught cooling towers use fans to move the air through the tower, thus providing absolute control over the air supply, as opposed to 'atmospheric' or 'natural draught' types. With the use of efficient eliminators, drift losses have been reduced to as little as 0.001% of water flow rate. The advantages of mechanical draught towers compared to natural draught towers include the following:

— compact (i.e. small plan area)

— close control over water temperature

— small static lift

— siting of tower is independent of prevailing wind direction (refer to HSE Approved Code of Practice L8: *Legionnaires' disease: the control of Legionella in water systems*)

— with efficient heat transfer packing, approach temperatures of 2–3 K are achievable, though 3–7 K is usually preferred.

The disadvantages include:

— fan powers can be higher than air cooled condenser equivalent (see Table B4.22 (*a*) and (*b*))

— recirculation of discharged air back into the air intake must be avoided or performance will suffer.

Table B4.22 Mechanical draught cooling towers

Type	Description
(a) Forced draught 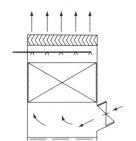	Fans are situated at the air intake and blow ambient air into the tower across the wet packing causing a portion of the water to be evaporated, thus removing heat from the remaining water. Advantages: — Fans located close to the ground, thus vibration is kept to a minimum. — Fractionally more efficient than induced draught since velocity pressure converted to static pressure does useful work, while the fan handles inlet cold air, and thus the weight of air per unit volume is greater than in the induced draught arrangement. — Fans and motors are situated in a comparatively dry air stream and are more easily accessible for maintenance. Disadvantages: — Limited fan size, thus a larger number of smaller fans of higher speed are needed compared with induced. draught arrangement, resulting in more noise (but tower itself provides some attenuation). — Tendency for ice to form on the fans in winter and block or throttle the intake. — Some types can be prone to recirculation of used air into the accessible low pressure fan inlet and resulting reduction in performance may be substantial; this occurs if outlet air velocities are low. The air may be ducted away at high velocity but at the expense of greater resistance and increased fan power requirements.
(b) Induced draught Counterflow Cross draught	Fans are situated in the air outlet from the tower, usually on the top, but sometimes in the side or in the ducting. Advantages: — Large fans possible (hence low speed and low noise). — Recirculation of air unlikely due to higher outlet velocity. — More compact plan area than (a) due to absence of fans on side. Disadvantages: — More prone to vibration since fan is mounted on superstructure. — Mechanical parts less readily accessible for maintenance. — Mechanical parts located in a hot, humid air stream. — High inlet velocities can draw in rubbish; air filters can be fitted. There are two types of induced draught cooling tower: 'counterflow' and 'cross draught'. (i) Counterflow Fans create vertical air movement up the tower across the packing in opposition to the water flow. Advantages: — Maximum performance arrangement as the coldest water is in contact with the driest air. — Up to three sides of the tower can be obstructed by adjacent buildings, provided that the remaining air inlet(s) are suitably increased in size. Disadvantages: — Mechanical parts and water distribution are not always easily accessible for maintenance. (ii) Cross draught Fans create horizontal air flow as the water falls across the air stream. Some types have a greater plan area than (c), but the air intakes can be full height of tower which is consequently of low silhouette, blending well with the architectural requirements. Rain ingress should be taken into account when considering water treatment dosage. Advantages: — Low silhouette. Disadvantages: — Some risk of recirculation of saturated vapour if sited in a confined space. — If uncovered, distribution basin will collect rubbish; a cover should be provided unless installation is indoors. — Location demands unobstructed air flow towards each end of tower.

Centrifugal fans are generally used to achieve low operating noise levels but variable fan speed motors should be considered for very noise sensitive locations.

The basic information required by the equipment manufacturer is as follows:

— design water flow rate

— design temperature range through which the water is to be cooled

— design ambient wet bulb temperature

— operational height above sea level

— any limitations on height, floor plan, weight, noise or appearance

— features which may affect the free flow of air to and from the unit

— preferably a drawing showing the tower location on site.

(b) *Selection of cooling tower site*

There should be sufficient free space around the tower to allow free flow of air both to the inlet and from the discharge outlet. Recirculation of the hot discharge back into the inlet must be avoided as it will substantially reduce performance. Discharge ducting or extended fan casings may be necessary to minimise recirculation risk and the effect of these components on fan power should be taken into account. The siting of the cooling tower should be such that the discharge air is not close to fresh air inlets and does not produce condensation upon nearby buildings and in the surrounding area.

The presence of exhaust heat from other equipment or of contaminated air from process plant (especially kitchen extract with high grease content), will reduce tower performance and may produce corrosive conditions. The tower should be sited as far away as possible, upwind of smoke stacks and other sources of pollution. Where local atmospheric air pollution is unavoidable, filters may be provided for cooling tower air inlets. The tower location should be carefully studied in relation to the noise created by the air and water.

The local authorities should always be consulted on the connection of mains water supplies to tanks and pumping circuits. In general it will be found that it is not permissible to connect pumps directly to the main and that a break tank must be interposed. Local fire regulations should be consulted when a tower is to be installed, particularly if any hazard or opportunity for ignition of the tower is present.

(c) Water treatment

Every water cooling tower requires an appropriate water quality management regime. This is essential to minimise the risk of legionellosis and to control corrosion and fouling (e.g. by bacterial growth, such as *Pseudomonous*). Biological contamination, however, can be controlled only through the use of biocides and such treatment should be initiated at system start-up and continued regularly thereafter. Poor water treatment can greatly increase energy and water costs. *Legionella* can be controlled if the tower is designed and operated in accordance with CIBSE TM13. The designer and owner/operator should ensure compliance with relevant UK regulations, see section B4.3.2.3. Compliance with the HSC's Approved Code of Practice (ACOP) L8 is mandatory. For information on corrosion and further information on water treatment see CIBSE Guide G: *Public health engineering*.

(d) Testing

Where cooling towers need to be site performance tested for confirmation of compliance with design conditions the relevant standard for the UK is BS 4485: Part 2.

B4.5.5.6 Evaporative condensers

An evaporative condenser is an extension of an air cooled condenser. As well as air being blown over the tubes, the tubes themselves are continuously wetted by a recirculating water system. They are able to achieve a similar performance to water cooled condensers and open-circuit cooling towers, but eliminate the condenser water pumps. See Guide B section 4.5.2.2 for further details.

B4.5.6 Controls

Appropriate and properly commissioned controls are essential to maintain the desired levels of performance and safety with good energy efficiency. Guidance on control systems is given by CIBSE Guide H: *Building control systems*.

B4.5.6.4 Safety devices

It is essential that safety devices should not be used to operate the plant under normal conditions. Safety devices are provided to ensure that, in the event of a fault developing, the plant shuts down in such a way that there is no risk of injury to personnel and equipment is protected from damage. Where particular operational conditions may result in frequent recycling, safety devices should be of the manual reset type. Table B4.23 lists types of safety devices and their function.

Although safety devices are usually dealt with by the equipment manufacturer, the designer should ensure that the provisions of BS EN 378-1 and the IoR Safety Codes, are complied with, e.g. refrigerant pressure relief devices should discharge to a safe place, and all cut-outs and switches should be tested during commissioning. It is recommended that, if the compressor/machine is fitted with capacity control, these tests be carried out with the compressor/machine at minimum capacity.

Table B4.23 Type and function of safety devices

Safety device	Function
Mechanical refrigeration:	
— high refrigerant pressure cut-out	Breaks circuit on excessive refrigerant pressure rise
— low refrigerant pressure cut-out	Breaks circuit on fall in refrigerant pressure
— low oil pressure cut-out	Protects against failure of lubricating system
— high oil temperature cut-out	Protects against failure of lubricating system or if bearing failure occurs
— low refrigerant temperature cut-out	Protects against low evaporating temperatures
— fusible plug	Protects against high refrigerant temperatures
— pressure relief device	Protects against high refrigerant pressure (static)
— low water temperature cut-out	Protects against evaporator freezing (in water chillers)
— flow switches	Protects against reduced fluid flow through evaporator or condenser
Absorption refrigeration:	
— low refrigerant temperature cut-out	Protects against evaporator freezing
— low chilled water temperature cut-out	Protects against evaporator freezing
— high solution temperature cut-out	Protects against over-concentration of the solution and consequent crystallisation
— low cooling water temperature cut-out	Protects against over-concentration of the solution and consequent crystallisation
— flow switches	Protects against reduced fluid flow through evaporator or condenser

Appendix B4.A1: Summary data for refrigerants

Group	Safety group	Refrigerant number	Description (composition = % weight)	Chemical formula	Practical limit / kg·m⁻³	Flammability (lower limit), concentration in air		GWP	ODP
						/ kg·m⁻³	/ % (vol.)		
L1	A1	R22	HCFC	$CHClF_2$	0.3	—	—	1700	0.055
L1	A1	R125	HFC	CF_3CHF_2	0.39	—	—	3200	0
L1	A1	R134a	HFC	CF_3CH_2F	0.25	—	—	1300	0
L1	A1/A1	R404A	R125/143a/134a (44/52/4)	$CF_3CHF_2 + CF3CH_3 + CF_3CH_2F$	0.48	—	—	3800	0
L1	A1/A1	R407C	R32/125/134a (23/25/52)	$CH_2F_2 + CF_3CHF_2 + CF_3CH_2F$	0.31	—	—	1600	0
L1	A1/A1	R410A	R32/125 (50/50)	$CH_2F_2 + CF_3CHF_2$	0.44	—	—	1900	0
L1	A1/A2	R413A	R134a/218/600a (88/9/3)	$CF_3CH_2F + C_3F_8 + CH(CH_3)_3$	0.25	—	—	1760	0
L1	A1/A1	R417A	R125/134a/600a (46.5/50/3.5)	$CF_3CHF_2 + CF_3CH_2F + CH_3CH_2CH_2CH_3$	0.31	—	—	1950	0
L2	B2	R123	HCFC	CF_3CHCl_2	0.1	—	—	93	0.02
L2	B2	R717	Ammonia	NH_3	0.00035	0.104	15	0	0
L3	A3	R290	Propane	$CH_3CH_2CH_3$	0.008	0.038	2.1	3	0
L3	A3	R600	Butane	$CH_3CH_2CH_2CH_3$	0.008	0.036	1.5	3	0
L3	A3	R600a	Isobutane	$CH(CH_3)_3$	0.008	0.043	1.8	3	0
L3	A3	R1270	Propylene	C_3H_6	0.008	0.043	2.5	3	0

Appendix B4.A2: Pressure–enthalpy charts for refrigerants

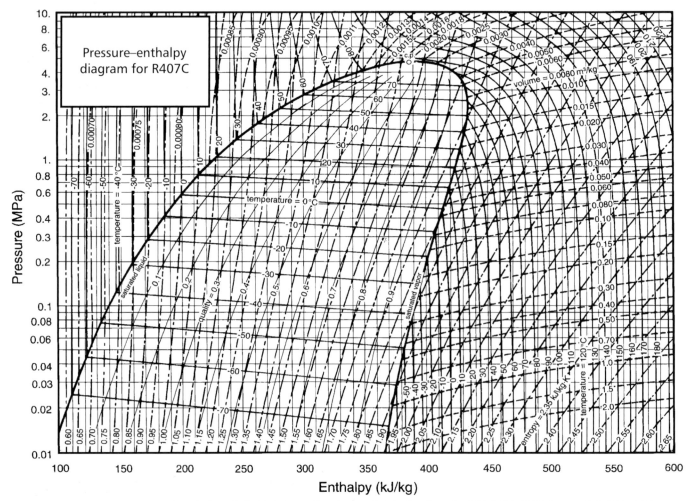

Figure B4.A2.5 Enthalpy–pressure chart for R407C (Guide B Appendix 4.A2 contains similar charts for R22, R134a, R290 (propane), R404A, R600a (isobutane) and R717A (ammonia))

B5   Noise and vibration control for HVAC

B5.1   Introduction

B5.1.3   Noise from HVAC systems

Noise from heating, ventilation and air conditioning (HVAC) systems is one of the problems of air conditioned and mechanically ventilated buildings. Naturally ventilated buildings require convected air currents which, originating in apertures to the exterior, may transmit unacceptable levels of external noise. Excessive noise contributes to discomfort, uneasiness, difficult communication and loss of productivity, since those who are not comfortable in their surroundings are not fully effective. However, some noise is useful in masking the sounds from colleagues and other sources. Masking noise is especially important in multi-occupied offices in order to provide privacy.

Most services components in a building interact with each other, or with the building through their attachments to it. The HVAC installation should be treated as a complete system, the separate parts of which influence other parts, see Figure B5.2. In this system, the air and noise travel from the fan through a number of components of the system, being affected by each one until they finally reach the occupants. During this process, one system may influence the performance of the preceding system.

Each component in the system either produces or reduces noise. The final noise level in the room is the summation of all these separate effects. The fan is the primary noise source, whilst airflow over duct fittings may generate aerodynamic noise. When the noise level exceeds criterion values additional noise control is required.

Noise in HVAC systems can be divided into three frequency ranges:

— low frequencies, characterised by 'rumble' noise, from about 31.5 Hz to 125 Hz on the octave band scale of measurement (see Appendix 5.A5); rumble is typically, but not exclusively, from large central plant fans

— mid frequencies, from about 125 Hz to 500 Hz, lead to 'roar', which might be from small fans located close to the occupied space

— higher frequencies contribute to hiss and whistle, which are often a result of diffuser noise.

An excess in any range leads to an unbalanced noise spectrum and the potential for complaints.

The primary path by which HVAC noise reaches occupants of the space being served is directly down the duct and out into the room, but this is not the only path. Other paths include the following:

— *Breakout noise from a duct*: occurs mostly near to the fan and is perceived as a throbbing, rumbly noise, or as a tonal noise if there is tone generation by the fan. Breakout noise often reduces downstream, because the noise has already broken out through the sides of the duct. Breakout can be a problem to occupants when a duct passes over their space.

— *Structure-borne noise*: results from poor vibration isolation of machinery, resulting in fluctuating forces acting directly into the structure and transmitting vibration through the building. The consequent vibration of surfaces radiates 'structure-borne' noise.

B5.2   Summary of noise and vibration problems from HVAC

B5.2.1   Typical sources of HVAC noise and their characteristics

Noise is produced by vibrating surfaces and by moving air streams. Sometimes the two interact, as in the case of fan blades. The primary source of the noise normally lies in the rotation of a machine, such as a motor, pump or fan. However, energy imparted to air or water can be converted into noise through interaction of fluid flow with solid objects, e.g. louvres in a duct termination. A very broad generalisation is that the 'noise conversion efficiency' of a machine is around 10^{-7} of its input power.

Different types of mechanical equipment produce noise over different frequency ranges. This is illustrated in Figure B5.3, which shows the frequencies most likely to be produced by equipment and gives a typical subjective terminology by which listeners might describe the noises.

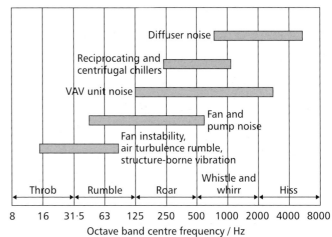

Figure B5.3 Frequencies at which different types of mechanical equipment generally control sound spectra (reproduced from ASHRAE *HVAC Applications Handbook* by permission of the American Society of Heating, Refrigerating and Air-Conditioning Engineers)

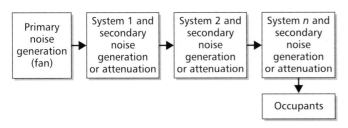

Figure B5.2 HVAC system in which the primary noise source is a fan

B5.2.3   Control of the transmission paths

The preferred way to control noise is to prevent it occurring in the first place, but some noise generation is unavoidable from realistic airflow velocities. In HVAC systems, controlling noise means:

— choosing the operating condition of the fan so that it is at a high efficiency point on its characteristic; this minimises fan noise

— ensuring good flow conditions for the air stream; the consequent benefits include components behaving more nearly as described in the manufacturer's data and reduced pressure losses, conserving energy and saving operating costs

— isolating vibrating components, including all machinery, ducts and pipework from the structure

— choosing an in-duct silencer or other means to control airborne noise in ducts; a full silencer may not be required, as lining bends with acoustic absorbent may be adequate, but this depends on the results of noise predictions (see Guide B section 5.10).

Noise control relies on attention to detail, both in the design and the implementation. It depends on choosing the correct components and ensuring that they are installed correctly.

There are many instances of problems which have resulted from inadequacies in design and installation, including:

— undersized fans, which could not accept the pressure loss of retrofit silencers

— oversized fans, which were working on an undesirable part of their characteristic

— vibration isolators which were by-passed by solid connections

— unsealed gaps left between spaces.

B5.3   Noise sources in building services

In the very early stages of a project, plant may not have been fully specified and, only under these temporary circumstances, generic information on noise may be used to give an initial overview of the noise of the project and to indicate space requirements for noise control, e.g. how much space to allow for in-duct silencers. Generic prediction information is given in Guide B Appendix 5.A2, which must be regarded as for temporary use only, until equipment-specific information is available. The uncertainties of generic information are at least ±5 dB, and often greater.

B5.3.1   Fans

Control of fan noise depends on:

— choosing an efficient operating point for the fan

— design of good flow conditions

— ensuring that the fan is vibration isolated from the structure

— ensuring that the fan is flexibly connected to the duct.

Where fan noise will be a problem, an in-duct attenuator should be used; these are described in detail in Guide B section 5.6.

B5.3.2   Variable air volume (VAV) systems

Noise from VAV systems depends on the method of control. Where the flow is adjusted by means of a damper or throttle valve, noise is mainly generated by turbulence at the obstruction to flow. Where control is by a fan, either cycled or modulated, the fan is the source of the noise, but modulation may affect the noise by changing the operating point of the fan. Improper air balancing must be avoided to ensure that the fan does not deliver at an unnecessarily high static pressure.

B5.3.3   Grilles and diffusers

Control of air velocity and flow conditions is the key to reducing this noise. Manufacturers' data should be consulted. Grilles and diffusers are the last stage in noise control because, once the sound has escaped into the room, there is no further attenuation other than by room surface absorption. Grilles and diffusers are considered in Guide B Appendix 5.A2.

B5.3.4   Roof-top units

Roof-top units have three main noise paths into the building space:

— through the duct

— breakout from the casing of the unit, which then transmits through the roof; this is most likely to occur underneath the unit, where the noise levels will be highest

— vibration transmission from the unit to the roof and consequent re-radiation of noise.

Noise through the duct is treated by absorptive material in the unit or by a silencer in the duct. Both supply and return may require treatment. Breakout, if a problem, is controlled by strengthening the underside of the casing or by adding sound attenuating material underneath the unit. Vibration transmission is reduced by well designed anti-vibration mounts.

B5.3.5   Fan coil units

These are an example of how noise sources are brought close to the occupants. Room perimeter units must be chosen for their low noise, by reference to manufacturers' information. Ceiling void units must be carefully mounted with inlet and discharge ducts designed to minimise the external resistance and with an adequate return air path ensured. A discharge silencer, or lined duct, may be required. Noise breakout through the casing must not be neglected. The sound power of the units will be provided by the manufacturer.

B5.3.6   Chillers, compressors and condensers

These produce both tonal and broadband noise. The tonal noise is typical of that from rotating or reciprocating machinery, linked to the rotational frequency. The broadband noise is from fluid flows, either liquid or gas. The tonal noise is often dominant, perceived as a whine or whirr, but the frequency range depends on the mode of operation. Reciprocating compressors have a relatively low-frequency fundamental tone, related to the oscillation frequency of the pistons. Screw compressors have strong tones in the octave bands between 250 Hz and 2000 Hz, and may require special attention to noise and vibration control, especially when they are located externally.

B5.3.7 Pumps

Pumps produce external noise from the motor, fluid-borne noise from the impeller and vibration into both the structure and the pipes. Noise problems may arise from the airborne noise, controlled by choosing a non-sensitive location or by an enclosure for the pump. If the pipes make solid contact with a radiating surface, there is the potential for both fluid-borne noise and pipe vibration to reappear as airborne noise at a distance from the pump. It is necessary to:

— use vibration isolators to isolate the pump from the building

— use a flexible connection from pump to pipes

— use resilient mountings for supporting the pipe to the structure.

B5.3.8 Stand-by generators

This noisy plant, which requires to be tested at regular intervals, is often housed in a separate generator room. A flow of fresh air is required both for the engine intake and for cooling. Noise problems arise from:

— the fresh air inlet

— the warm air discharge

— the engine exhaust

— the structure, due to vibration transmission.

The air inlet and discharge may require to be silenced by use of duct silencers, acoustic louvres or equivalent measures. The engine exhaust silencer will need to be selected to satisfy local requirements for environmental noise. Vibration isolation must be discussed with the supplier of the generator. It is common practice to line the generator room with acoustic absorbent in order to reduce the build-up of reverberant sound.

B5.3.9 Boilers

Hot water boilers may vary in size from a few hundred kilowatts, or lower, up to megawatts, depending on the heating requirement. Noise sources within the boiler room are from the air supply fan and the combustion. External noise is from the flue. A small boiler of about 200 kW capacity may have a spectrum peak at around 125 Hz and overall sound power level of 90 dBA. In general, the frequency of the peak drops with increasing boiler capacity so that, in the megawatt range, the spectrum peak is at 63 Hz or below. A large boiler, of several megawatt capacity, may have an overall sound power in excess of 100 dBA. Manufacturers' information should be consulted for octave band data. The presence of low frequencies leads to the total sound power being greater than the A-weighted sound power.

B5.3.10 Cooling towers

Cooling tower noise is mainly noise from the fan, details of which should be available from the manufacturer. See Guide B Appendix 5.A2 for fan noise prediction.

B5.3.11 Lifts

The intermittent operation of lifts, including door opening and closing, motor surges and operation of brakes, may cause disturbance in adjacent occupied spaces. Most of the noise is structure borne, for example impacts on door stops and lift machinery vibration. It is possible to reduce each of the noise sources by design and correct installation. Advice should be sought from the manufacturer.

B5.3.12 Escalators

Escalators are a source of noise and vibration from the motor and drive mechanism. This is not normally a problem provided that the equipment has been installed correctly. However, there is a possibility that vibration input from the motor will couple with a resonance on a surrounding floor or wall to produce a noticeable effect, which will then require correction.

B5.4 Noise control in plant rooms

B5.4.1 Health and safety

The Health and Safety Executive's guidance for employers on the Control of Noise at Work Regulations (2005) define action levels as follows:

(a) *Lower action level*: daily or weekly exposure of 80 dBA.

(b) *Upper action level*: daily or weekly exposure of 85 dBA.

Daily or weekly exposure levels must not exceed 87 Pa.

The peak action level refers to impulsive noise. A useful guide for steady noise is that, if it is necessary to raise one's voice to shouting level in order to communicate clearly with someone standing about 2 m away, the first action level has been exceeded, but this must be checked by measurement. If measurements show that the first action level has been reached, it is a requirement of the Noise at Work Regulations to make hearing protection available for employees who request it. When the second or peak action levels have been reached, there is an obligation to provide hearing protection for all exposed employees and to ensure that these are worn. Further details are given in the HSE's *Guidance on the Noise at Work Regulations*.

B5.4.2 Breakout noise from plant rooms

In order to reduce breakout noise the following steps must be taken:

— Isolate the equipment from the structural floor.

— Ensure that the separating walls give sufficient attenuation.

— Ensure that all penetrations of the plant room walls, floor or ceiling are carefully sealed.

— Pay proper attention to noise transmission through the plant room external walls and silencing of air inlets and outlets, louvres etc.

B5.4.3 Break-in noise in plant rooms

This refers to high levels of plant room noise entering the ducts and then being transmitted to occupied spaces. The problem is controlled by correct location of a duct silencer. The silencer should be placed to penetrate the plant room wall, so that all break-in noise to the duct is reduced along with other duct-borne noise.

B5.4.4 Estimation of noise levels in plant rooms

In a cramped plant room, the direct sound from the nearest item of plant is likely to control the local noise. However in a large uncrowded plant room, where a reverberant sound field may be assumed, the reverberant field is determined by approximation, see Guide B Appendix 5.A7.

B5.10 Noise prediction

Generic formulae for predicting noise from building services plant are given in Guide B Appendix 5.A2.

B5.10.1 System noise

System noise prediction follows a simple logical process, but this is sometimes lost in the complexities of real systems. The prediction process for the HVAC system is as follows:

(1) Obtain the noise power of the source in octave frequency bands from manufacturers' data.

(2) Determine the successive effects of system components on the noise as it propagates in the duct, adding the effects, which may be negative (noise reduction) or positive (noise regeneration). Data on component effects should be provided by manufacturers. The end result is the sound powers at the duct terminations, see Guide B Appendix 5.A2, section 5.A2.5.

(3) Determine breakout noise from ducts and central devices etc. above a room, see Guide B section 5.6.10 and manufacturers' data.

(4) Determine the total sound power input to the room.

(5) Finally obtain the sound level at the occupant, see Guide B section 5.7.2.

These steps are to be carried out at all frequencies required for the criterion used.

B5.10.2 Noise to atmosphere

This is most likely to occur from:

— a fan intake

— ventilation louvres in a plant room

— breakout through plant room roof or walls.

For the fan intake, the sound power at the opening is determined from the fan sound power and the attenuation that occurs between the fan and intake. Propagation effects to the outside are then included as in Guide B Appendix 5.A1, including directional radiation as appropriate.

The louvres in a plant room are treated similarly, but first the noise level in the plant room is estimated and this is assumed to be the level at the inside of the louvres. Louvre attenuation, as defined by the manufacturer, is then subtracted and the resulting propagation predicted.

Breakout through walls is treated similarly to louvres. Directivity of the sources should be included. These predictions are approximate and a more detailed analysis is given in BS EN 12354-4.

Guide B: abridgements and omissions

The extracts from CIBSE Guide B included above have been abridged for reasons of space. Reference should be made to CIBSE Guide B for the complete text and tables of data. In addition, the following sections have been omitted entirely from this Handbook:

Chapter 1: Heating:
— 1.1 Introduction
— Appendix 1.A1: Example calculations
— Appendix 1.A2: Sizing and height of chimneys and flues

Chapter 2: Ventilation and air conditioning:
— 2.1 Introduction
— Appendix 2.A1: Techniques for assessment of ventilation

Chapter 3: Ductwork:
— Appendix 3.A2: Space allowances
— Appendix 3.A3: Maximum permissible air leakage rates
— Appendix 3.A4: Summary of fan types and efficiencies (see chapter 2, Table B2.53)
— Appendix 3.A6: Example calculations

Chapter 4: Refrigeration and heat rejection:
— 4.1 Introduction

Chapter 5: Noise and vibration control for HVAC:
— 5.5 Airflow noise — regeneration of noise in ducts
— 5.6 Techniques for control of noise transmitted in ducts
— 5.7 Room sound levels
— 5.8 Transmission of noise to and from the outside
— 5.9 Criteria for noise in HVAC systems
— Appendix 5.A1: Acoustic terminology
— Appendix 5.A2: Generic formulae for predicting noise from building services plant
— Appendix 5.A3: Interpreting manufacturers' noise data
— Appendix 5.A4: Basic technique for prediction of room noise levels from HVAC systems
— Appendix 5.A5: Noise instrumentation
— Appendix 5.A6: Vibration instrumentation
— Appendix 5.A7: Direct and reverberant sound n a room
— Appendix 5.A8: Noise criteria

Guide B (1986): Installation and equipment data

B18: Owning and operating costs

(This section of Guide B is no longer available.)

Introduction

For designers, the selection of building services engineering systems will generally involve many options. The evaluation of these options to find the most economic and suitable choice requires the consideration of both capital and operational costs likely to be incurred during the life of the plant, and the operational requirements such as safety, reliability and maintainability. A further choice faced by the engineer where there is an existing plant or installation approaching the end of its economic life, is to decide whether it is better to continue to maintain the existing plant or to replace it.

Economic evaluation

There are many ways of evaluating engineering systems. The parameters most commonly assessed are:

(a)   Capital costs

(b)   Costs in use

(c)   Investment analysis (e.g. payback period)

(d)   Total life cycle cost

Capital costs

This is a simple method of cost comparison which, while appropriate for some investments, has serious limitations. The decision to select a particular configuration of plant is based purely on the capital expenditure and should only be taken when the investor is limited in the capital sum he can raise and consciously ignores operating costs and other behavioural aspects of the plant. The limitation of this approach is that plant which has high capital cost elements may result in long term operational benefits over the lifetime of the plant (e.g. higher reliability or lower running costs), a choice based on capital costs alone will disregard these potential benefits.

Capital cost of an installation may comprise many components. Some of these are:

(a)   Feasibility study, design and contracting costs

(b)   Capital cost of plant and equipment

(c)   Site acquisition (purchase or rent of land, plant room space etc.)

(d)   Other services required (e.g. gas, electricity, water)

Different designs and plant configurations generally lead to different cost combinations of these factors. A checklist of some of the factors affecting capital and operating costs is given in Table B18.1.

Table B18.1 Capital costs and costs in use — significant factors requiring consideration

Item	Influencing factors
Capital costs:	
— feasibility, design and contracting costs	Complexity and size of installation, level of design detail, total capital costs
— plant, equipment and construction costs	Design options, plant configurations, installation complexity, site location, safety requirements, fire requirements, need for standby etc.
— site acquisition costs	Space requirements (plant room, service, storage, accommodation etc.), rent or purchase, local restrictions (e.g. smoke emissions), fuel storage
— other service costs	Supply authority contributions, capacity of existing service mains, ducts and trenches etc. for mains
— builders' work costs	Design details, type of plant and equipment, method of construction
Costs in use:	
— operational costs	Method of plant operation (automatic, manual) and attendance, level of measurements, readings and logging
— preventative maintenance costs	Level of preventative maintenance selected, method and level of inspections and logging, complexity of plant, statutory and mandatory requirements, level of reliability expected, requirements for specialist labour
— corrective maintenance costs	Plant breakdown and tolerable downtime, requirement for specialist labour
— stores for spares	Degree of plant uniformity, tolerable downtime, requirement for specialist labour
— overheads	Maintenance management and administration, vehicles, building management systems etc.
— energy costs	
— insurance	

Costs in use

These can be used as the deciding factor for a suitable installation option. This would be appropriate should there be no capital restrictions but there is an allocation of revenue costs.

Again Table B18.1 may be used as a checklist of significant items requiring consideration in the assessment of costs in use.

Total life cycle costs

These are the total costs of acquiring and using a physical asset such as a heating installation or electrical distribution system. They include the capital, or first cost of designing, purchasing, installing and commissioning; the operational cost during the life of the asset for energy, labour, and operational materials; the maintenance costs associated with the asset principally comprising labour, materials and spares storage; the failure costs of breakdowns and providing alternative facilities and the disposal cost when the asset reaches the end of its life.

Typical applications for total life cycle costs are where:

(a)   energy costs of an asset are likely to be high throughout its life

(b)   an asset has a long life

(c)   investment costs are high

(d)   significant savings can be made by reducing maintenance or operational costs.

Plant maintenance costs have two components: preventive and corrective. Preventive maintenance, also known as planned maintenance, is carried out to reduce the incidence of breakdowns by careful inspection, adjustment and service of the plant.

Planned maintenance should reduce the need for corrective maintenance, however, a careful balance needs to be established to ensure that its costs do not exceed the benefits derived from it.

Economics are not the sole criterion for the level of maintenance. It is necessary to carry out a basic level of preventive maintenance to sustain essential plant operations, safety and to conform to statutory requirements.

Information on the economic life of plant is given in chapter 13 of the CIBSE Guide M: *Maintenance engineering and management*. This includes a comprehensive table of economic life factors, which is reproduced below as Appendix M13.A1.

CIBSE Guide M: *Maintenance engineering and management*, addresses how designers, installers, maintainers and building operators need to be aware of and how to approach the maintenance of building services. It provides guidance for designers, describes different types of maintenance, covers types of maintenance contracts, summaries energy efficiency issues (based on CIBSE Guide F). It also includes sections on controls, risk assessment, owning and operating costs, legislation compliance and health and safety.

Estimation of energy consumption for building services

Degree-days

Degree-days provide a means of comparing, over different periods, the variations in load sustained by heating plants in different parts of the UK. The standard method is to assess, for monthly periods, the daily difference in K between a base temperature of 15.5 °C and the 24-hour mean outside temperature. The monthly totals can then be used to compare monthly changes in the weather factor, or be added together for the heating season, enabling the severity and duration of the winter to be compared from year to year and from place to place.

Historical mean monthly and annual heating degree-day totals for various geographical areas are given in Table A2.17, see page 10. Current degree-day data are available from Degree Days Direct Ltd. (http://www.vesma.com/ddd).

For every building there are sources of heat gains other than the heating system (e.g. occupants, lighting, sunshine and equipment) and these represent a significant proportion of the heat input necessary to maintain comfort conditions. The average temperature rise which can be maintained by the miscellaneous heat gains alone is identified as d. Table B18.7 gives values of d for different building structures. In order to evaluate the effects of d it is convenient to quote the degree-day totals for a series of base temperatures. Table B18.9 gives the ratios of $D_d/D_{15.5}$ for the average degree-day total. From these, the value of D_d can be found for a specified indoor temperature in a given class of building.

Table B18.7 Values of d

Class of building	Building structure	d / K
1	Building with large areas of external glazing, much internal heat-producing equipment and densely populated	5 to 6
2	Buildings with one or two of the above factors	4 to 5
3	Traditional buildings with normal glazing, equipment and occupancy	3 to 4
4	Sparsely occupied buildings with little or no heat-producing equipment and small glazed area	2 to 3
5	Dwellings	5 to 8

Table B18.9 Ratio of $D_d / D_{15.5}$

Base temp. / K	$D_d / D_{15.5}$
10	0.33
12	0.57
14	0.82
15	0.94
15.5	1.00
16	1.06
17	1.18
18	1.30

Guide M: Maintenance engineering and management

Appendix M13.A1: Indicative life expectancy factors

Equipment item	Indicative life / years	Remarks	BCIS cost group	HVCA SFG/20 reference
(a) Heating source				
Boiler plant:				
— cast iron sectional boilers (MTHW/LTHW)	25		5E	05-14; 05-23
— condensing boilers (MTHW/LTHW)	20		5E	05-04; 05-12
— domestic boilers (combination)	10		—	—
— domestic boilers (condensing)	15		—	—
— electrode/electric boilers (MTHW/LTHW)	25	Water treatment is very important	5E	05-22
— electrode/electric boilers (steam and HTHW)	25	Water treatment is very important	5E	05-19; 05-20
— modular boilers	15		5E	05-11
— shell and tube boilers (MTHW/LTHW)	20	Water treatment is very important	5E	05-14; 05-23
— shell and tube boilers (steam and HTHW)	20	Water treatment is very important	5E	05-19; 05-20
— steel boilers (MTHW/LTHW)	20		5E	05-14; 05-23
— water tube boilers (MTHW/LTHW)	25	Water treatment is very important	5E	05-14; 05-23
— water tube boilers (steam and HTHW)	25	Water treatment is very important	5E	05-19; 05-20
Boiler plant auxiliaries:				
— boiler electrodes	8		5E	05-22
— chimney (brick or concrete) (outside)	40		5E	24-01
— chimney (brick or concrete) (inside)	50		5E	24-01
— chimney (steel) (outside)	30	Depends on thickness of metal and corrosion protection	5E	24-01
— combustion controls	12		5E	05-(15-20)
— dosing pots	15		5E	65-10
— fans (high temperature)	15		5E	20-08
— feed pumps	15		5E	45-04
— flue (mild steel)	15	Depends on thickness of metal and corrosion protection	5E	24-01
— flue (stainless steel)	30	Check quality of stainless steel	5E	24-01
— gas burners (atmospheric)	20		5E	05-(03-04); 06-01
— gas burners (forced air)	15		5E	05-(10-12); 06-03
— gas distribution system for boiler plant	40		5E	40-10
— instrumentation	10		5E	05-(15-18)
— oil burners (pressure jet)	15		5E	05-13; 06-(04-06)
— oil distribution system for boiler plant	40		5E	40-10
— oil storage tanks (external protection)	20	Depends on thickness of metal and corrosion protection	5E	56-05
— oil storage tanks (inside building)	30		5E	56-05
— oil storage tanks (underground)	15	Depends on thickness of metal and corrosion protection	5E	56-05
— water treatment equipment	15		5E	65-(01-10)
— solid fuel handling plant	15	Conveyor system up to 20 years	5E	05-(05-08)
(b) Cooling source				
Ancillaries:				
— refrigerant leak detector	10		5F	46-01
— trace heating	20		5F	40-03
Chillers (medium to large):				
— absorption	25	Depends on availability of refrigerant	5F	09-05
— centrifugal	20	Depends on availability of refrigerant	5F	09-02; 12-03
— reciprocating	20	Depends on availability of refrigerant	5F	09-02; 12-01
— screw	25	Depends on availability of refrigerant	5F	09-02; 12-02
External heat rejection for refrigeration plant:				
— air blast dry air coolers (epoxy treated metal)	20		5F	13-02
— air blast dry air coolers (plastic coated metal)	25	Consider thickness, bonding and quality of plastic coating	5F	13-02
— air blast dry air coolers (galvanised metal)	20	Consider thickness and quality of galvanising	5F	13-02
— air cooled condensers	20		5F	13-02
— evaporative condensers	20		5F	19-01; 13-02; 30-03

Equipment item	Indicative life / years	Remarks	BCIS cost group	HVCA SFG/20 reference
(b) Cooling source (*continued*)				
Open type cooling towers:				
— ceramic	35		5F	30-02
— epoxy treated metal	15			
— galvanised metal	12	Consider thickness and quality of galvanising	5F	30-02
— plastic coated metal	25	Consider thickness, bonding and quality of plastic coating	5F	30-02
— plastic construction	20	Consider thickness and quality of plastic	5F	30-02
— stainless steel	30	Consider quality and thickness of stainless steel	5F	30-02
— timber construction	10	Quality of timber preservation can extend life	5F	30-02
(c) Water and fuel installations				
Storage vessels:				
— chilled water storage vessel (copper)	20		5D (water)	56-02
— chilled water storage vessel (galvanised)	15	Not suitable for soft water or softened water	5D (water)	56-02
— chilled water storage vessel (mild steel)	20		5D (water)	56-02
— fuel oil storage tank (external, above ground)	20	Depends on thickness of metal and corrosion protection	5E	56-05
— fuel oil storage tank (external, below ground)	15	Depends on thickness of metal and corrosion protection	5E	56-05
— ice storage	15		5D (water)	56-02
— water cisterns (cast iron)	35		5D (water)	56-02
— water cisterns (galvanised)	15		5D (water)	56-02
— water cisterns (mild steel, treated)	25	Not for domestic or drinking water purposes	5D (water)	56-02
— water cisterns (plastic)	25	High quality structural support is necessary	5D (water)	56-02
(d) Calorifiers/heat exchangers				
Calorifiers:				
— copper	25		5D	32-(05-07)
— mild steel	20		5D	32-(05-07)
Heat exchangers:				
— plate	15	Subject to regular cleaning	5D	29-(05-07)
— shell and tube	25		5D	32-(05-07)
(e) Pumps				
Base mounted pumps	20		—	45-
Boiler feed pumps	15		—	—
Centrifugal pumps	20		—	45-03
Circulating pumps:				
— commercial (dual type)	20		—	45-02
— domestic	10		—	—
Condensate pumps	10		—	—
Glandless pumps	10		—	45-
Pipework mounted pumps	15		—	45-
Sump and well pumps	12	Consider mechanical damage and expansion	5D	45-10
(f) Pressurisation systems				
Chilled water pressurisation unit	20		5F	45-12
Combined heating/chilled water	20		—	45-12
Expansion vessel (unvented hot water)	15		—	—
Heating pressurisation unit	20		5E	45-12
(g) Water boosters				
Domestic booster	15		5D	45-11
Hose reel booster	20		—	23-02
Mains cold water booster	15		5F	45-12

Equipment item	Indicative life / years	Remarks	BCIS cost group	HVCA SFG/20 reference
(g) Water boosters (continued)				
Sprinkler	20		—	23-14
(h) Pipework systems and components				
Bellows:				
— expansion (steel)	10		—	—
— flexible (rubber)	8		—	—
— flexible (steel)	10		—	—
Condensate pipework system	12	Consider type of material, wall thickness and water treatment	5F	40-(04-06)
Condensate collecting vessel	12	Consider type of material, wall thickness and water treatment	5F	40-(04-06)
Expansion vessels:				
— open	10		—	—
— closed (with membrane)	15		—	—
Fuel pipework:				
— gas	50		—	—
— oil	50		—	—
Heating pipework system (plastic)	35		5E	40-01
Pipework systems (closed):				
— copper	45	Consider tube thickness and quality of copper	5E	40-01
— steel	25		5E	40-01
— steel (galvanised)	35		5E	40-01
Pipework systems (open):				
— copper	45	Consider tube thickness and quality of copper	5E	40-01
— steel	25		5E	40-01
— steel (galvanised)	25		5E	40-01
Refrigerant pipework systems	30		5F	46-01
Steam pipework system	25		5E	40-11
Water softeners:				
— base exchange	30		—	—
— de-alkalisation	20		—	—
— de-ionisation	20		—	—
Water treatment plant	15		—	65-(01-10)
Water treatment control and measurement equipment	10		—	65-(01-10)
(i) Insulation (pipework)				
Pipework thermal insulation:				
— moulded type	30	Consider fire and smoke rating	—	35-01
— blanket type	30	Consider fire and smoke rating	—	35-01
Vessel thermal insulation:				
— moulded type	30	Consider fire and smoke rating	—	35-01
— blanket type	30	Consider fire and smoke rating	—	35-01
Tank thermal insulation:				
— moulded type	30	Consider fire and smoke rating	—	35-01
— blanket type	30	Consider fire and smoke rating	—	35-01
Ductwork thermal insulation (blanket type)	30	Consider fire and smoke rating	—	35-01
Fire insulation (intumescent) for pipes and ducts	20	Inspection for damage required at frequent intervals	—	—
(j) Valves				
Commissioning valves	25		—	61-01
Draw-off taps	20		—	—
Fuel shut-off valves	25		—	61-01
Motorised control valves	15		—	62-(01-07)
Motorised control valve actuators	10		—	01-(01-08)
Shower mixer and head	10		—	61-05

Equipment item	Indicative life / years	Remarks	BCIS cost group	HVCA SFG/20 reference
(j) Valves (continued)				
Supply-side shut-off valve	25		—	—
Valves:				
— cast iron	30		—	—
— copper	30		—	—
— glandless	20			61-01
— glands	15			61-01
— mild steel	25		—	—
(k) Terminal units (wet systems)				
Ceiling heating:				
— hot water	25		5E	—
— electric	15		5E	—
Fan coil units (heating only)	15		5E	28-01
Natural convectors:				
— water	20		5E	—
— electric	10		5E	—
Radiant heaters:				
— steam and hot water	20		5E	28-01
— electric	10		5E	28-01
Radiators:				
— aluminium	20	Water condition and materials in the system are important	5E	28-01
— cast iron	25		5E	28-01
— steel	20	Water condition is important	5E	28-01
— steel (2 mm thick)	20	Water condition is important	5E	28-01
Radiator painting	5	Use correct type of paint	5E	28-01
Storage heaters (electric)	10		5E	—
Underfloor heating:				
— electric	20		5E	—
— plastic pipes (concrete encased)	30	Suggest a long-term bonded warranty is obtained; consider quality of plastic pipe	5E	—
— steel pipes (concrete encased)	25	Suggest a long-term bonded warranty is obtained; corrosion prevention required for steel pipes	5E	—
Unit heaters:				
— steam and hot water	15		5E	28-01
— gas and electric	10		5E	28-01
(l) Air handling and ventilation				
Air conditioning terminal units:				
— chilled ceiling panels	25	Flexible water pipework connections 10 years (depending on type)	5F	—
— chilled beams	20	Flexible water pipework connections 10 years (depending on type)	5F	—
— computer room air conditioning	15		5F	—
— double duct terminal units	15		5F	59-
— fan coil units (heating and cooling)	15		5F	59-06
— induction units	20		5F	59-05
— split systems	10		5F	—
— terminal reheat units	20		5F	59-(01-03)
— VAV terminal units (bellows type)	15		5F	59-(01-03)
— VAV terminal units (box type)	15		5F	59-(01-03)
— ventilated ceilings	25		5G	—
— VRV units	10		5F	—
— VVT fan powered terminal units	15		5F	—
Fans:				
— axial	15	Life likely to be reduced if fan motor in air stream	5E	20-04
— centrifugal	20	Life likely to be reduced if fan motor in air stream	5E	20-03
— centrifugal (heavy duty)	25	Life likely to be reduced if fan motor in air stream	5E	20-03
— extract (e.g. domestic)	10		—	—

Equipment item	Indicative life / years	Remarks	BCIS cost group	HVCA SFG/20 reference
(*l*) Air handling and ventilation (*continued*)				
Fans (*continued*):				
— high temperature (boiler combustion)	15		5E	—
— propellor	10		5E	20-05
— roof mounted units	15		5E	20-07
Ductwork:				
— galvanised (rectangular and circular)	40		5G	16-(01-04)
— plastic	15	Expansion and risk of mechanical damage and need to be considered	5G	16-(01-04)
— flexible (circular)	15	Risk of mechanical damage and cleaning difficulties needs to be considered	5G	16-(01-04)
Ductwork Ancillaries:				
— attenuators	25	Consider type of lining, adhesive and fixing of acoustic material	5G	16-04
— coils (aluminium fins) (cooling)	15	Consider quality and thickness of aluminium fins and exposure to adverse and wet external conditions	5E; 5F; 5G	29-01
— coils (aluminium fins) (heating)	15	Consider quality and thickness of aluminium fins and exposure to adverse external conditions	5E; 5F; 5G	29-01
— coils (copper fins) (cooling)	25	Consider operational duty (wet surfaces)	5E; 5F; 5G	29-01
— coils (copper fins) (heating)	25		5E; 5F; 5G	29-01
— coils (electric)	10		5G	29-02
— coils (galvanised) (heating	12		5E; 5F; 5G	29-01
— dampers (manual)	20		5G	16-03
— dampers (automatic)	15		5G	16-03
— eliminators (galvanised)	10		5G; 5F; 5G	16-02
— eliminators (plastic)	15		5G; 5F; 5G	16-02
— eliminators (stainless steel)	20		5G; 5F; 5G	16-02
— external louvres (anodised aluminium)	25	Regular cleaning is important to avoid possible breakdown of surface coating	5G	—
— external louvres (steel painted)	20	Early signs of corrosion must be dealt with	5G	26-02
— filters (automatic) (excluding media)	15		5G	21-02
— filters (panel) (excluding media)	20		5G	21-02
— filters (primary) (washable)	10	8 hours/day; 5 days/week	—	—
— filters (primary) (disposable)	0.5	8 hours/day; 5 days/week	—	—
— filters (secondary) (pleated and bag types)	1	8 hours/day; 5 days/week	—	—
— filters (electrostatic)	15		5G	21-03
— filters (activated carbon) (excluding media)	15		5G	21-02
— filters (high efficiency particulate air (HEPA))	2	8 hours/day; 5 days/week	5G	21-02
— fire dampers (curtain type)	10		5G	16-03
— grilles and diffusers (anodised aluminium)	25		5G	26-01
— grilles and diffusers (painted metal)	30		5G	26-01
— hoods	30		5G	—
— insulation (ductwork systems)	30		—	35-01
— plate recuperator	20		5G	29-03
— spray cooler coils (copper electro-tinned) and washers	15		5G; 5F; 5G	29-01
— thermal wheels	15		5G	29-04
Humidifiers:				
— chemical dehumidifiers (excluding medium)	15		5G	—
— pan type humidifier	10	Early signs of corrosion must be dealt with	5G	33-01
— steam (direct)	10	Maintenance is very important	5G	33-02
— steam (electrically generated)	8	Maintenance is very important	5G	33-02
— water spray	15	Early signs of corrosion must be dealt with	5G	33-01
Insulation (ductwork and vessel) (blanket type)	30	Consider type of fixing and risk of mechanical damage	5F; 5G	35-01
Packaged air handling/conditioning units:				
— external	15	Consider type of corrosion protection	5F; 5G	03-01
— internal	20		5F; 5G	03-01
Terminal units (air systems)	25			26-01
(*m*) Miscellaneous mechanical equipment and plant				
Air compressor	20		5M	40-08
Compressed air receiver	20		5M	40-09

Equipment item	Indicative life / years	Remarks	BCIS cost group	HVCA SFG/20 reference
(m) Miscellaneous mechanical equipment and plant (continued)				
Computer room air conditioning	15		5F	—
Domestic gas fired appliances:				
— warm air heaters	15		5E	—
— boilers	10		5E	—
— combination boilers	10		5E	—
— hot water (storage and continuous)	12		5E	—
— gas fires	8		5E	—
Drinking fountains	10		5D	—
Fire protection (pipes and ducts)	20	Damage to fire protection should be examined at frequent intervals	—	—
Food/container waste disposal	5		—	—
Furnaces (gas or oil fired)	15	Selection of heat exchanger material is important	5E	—
Hand dryers	5		—	—
Incinerators	15		—	—
Kitchen (cooking and support systems)	15		5B	—
Laundries (equipment and support systems)	20		5B	—
Sanitary towel disposal	10		—	—
Stair/lobby ventilation	20		5G	16-03
Tea rooms (equipment and support systems)	15		5D	—
Vending machines	8		—	—
Waste paper shredders/disposal	10		—	—
Water features	15	Water treatment is very important	5D	25-01
(n) Controls				
Building management systems (BMS):				
— head end (supervisor)	5		—	—
— outstations	10		5M	14-(01-16)
— plant controller	10		—	—
— operating system	5		5M	—
— remote display panels	10		5M	—
— communications network (hardwiring)	25	Should be 'future proofed' with additional cable wireways	5M	—
Electric/electronic controls:				
— electric controls	20		5M	14-(01-16)
— electronic controls	10		5M	14-(01-16)
— sensors	8	Periodic loop tuning and calibration should be considered	5M	50-(01-11)
— control valves	15		5M	62-(01-07)
— control dampers	15		5M	16-03
— hydraulic valve actuators	10		5M	01-05
— variable speed drives	15		—	—
Pneumatic controls:				
— air compressor	20		—	—
— pneumatic controls	20		5M	—
— pneumatic valve actuators	15		5M	01-04
— dryer (pneumatic controls)	20		—	—
— receiver	20		—	—
— valves, connections	20		—	—
— electronic/pneumatic interfaces	10		5M	—
— hydraulic valve actuators	10		5M	01-05
Leak detection:				
— gas	10		—	—
— refrigerant	10		—	—
— water	15		—	—
(o) Electrical installations				
Batteries and power storage:				
— battery chargers	20		5H	18-01
— lead–acid batteries (sealed)	5		5H	18-01
— nickel–alkaline batteries (vented)	20		5H	18-01

Equipment item	Indicative life / years	Remarks	BCIS cost group	HVCA SFG/20 reference
(o) Electrical installations (continued)				
Mains cable (permanent installations):				
— mineral insulated	35		5H	18-01
— paper insulated	35		5H	18-01
— thermoplastic	30		5H	18-01
— thermosetting (fire performance)	35		5H	18-01
Mains power supplies:				
— HV switchgear (external)	30		—	—
— HV switchgear (internal)	30		—	—
— LV switchgear (internal)	25		—	—
— main supply switchgear and distribution	30		5H	18-01
— transformers (dry type)	30		5H	18-01
— transformers (oil-filled type)	30		5H	18-01
Motors:				
— motor rating < 7.5 W	10		5H	18-01
— motor rating 7.5 W to 75 kW	15		5H	18-01
— motor rating > 75 kW	20		5H	18-01
Motor drives (variable speed)	15		5H	18-01
Power generation:				
— combined heat and power (CHP) (gas fired)	20		—	—
— combined heat and power (CHP) (diesel powered)	15		—	—
— continuously rated gas/oil engines (frequent use)	15		5H	18-01
— continuously rated gas/oil engines (standby)	25		5H	18-01
— continuously rated steam engines (frequent use)	25		5H	18-01
— continuously rated steam turbines (frequent use)	25		5H	18-01
— standby alternator plus prime mover	30		—	—
Protective installations:				
— earth bonding (major)	30		5H	18-01
— earth bonding (domestic)	25		5H	18-01
— lightning protection	25		5H	18-01
Sub-main distribution:				
— consumer units	20		5H	18-01
— distribution boards	20		5H	18-01
— feeder pillar	20		5H	18-01
— final circuits and outlets	20		5H	18-01
— inverter	20		5H	18-01
— lighting installations (luminaires) (external)	15		5H	18-01
— lighting installations (luminaires) (internal)	20		5H	18-01
— miniature circuit breaker (MCB)	20		—	—
— moulded case circuit breaker (MCCB)	25		—	—
— power distribution unit (PDU)	20		5H	18-01
— residual current breaker (RCB)	20		—	—
— switched socket outlet (SSO)	15		—	—
Uninterruptible power supplies (UPS)/back-up power:				
— battery chargers	20		5H	18-01
— lead–acid batteries (sealed)	5		5H	18-01
— nickel–alkaline batteries (vented)	20		5H	18-01
(p) Lighting				
Lamps:				
— compact fluorescent lamps	3	10 000 hours (based on 10 h/day, 6 days/week, 52 weeks/year	5H	36-(01-04)
— fluorescent tubes	2	7500 hours (based on 10 h/day, 6 days/week, 52 weeks/year	5H	36-(01-04)
— metal halide lamps	3	9000 hours (based on 10 h/day, 6 days/week, 52 weeks/year	5H	36-(01-04)
— SON lamps	4	12 000 hours (based on 10 h/day, 6 days/week, 52 weeks/year	5H	36-(01-04)
Lighting systems:				
— emergency lighting	25		5H	37-(01-02)
— lighting and luminaires (external)	15	Lamp life depends on usage	5H	36-(01-04)
— lighting and luminaires (internal)	20	Lamp life depends on usage	5H	36-(01-04)
— switches	10		—	—

Equipment item	Indicative life / years	Remarks	BCIS cost group	HVCA SFG/20 reference
(q) Drainage and sanitation				
Above ground rainwater drainage (plastic)	25	Includes guttering	5A	—
Below ground drainage:				
— salt glazed	40	Consider possibility of damage and structural movement	5A	—
— cast iron	45	Consider possibility of ground and structural movement	5A	—
— plastic	40	Consider mechanical damage	5A	—
Internal waste, foul and rainwater drainage:				
— cast iron	35		5C	—
— copper	40		5C	—
— plastic	20	Consider possibility of mechanical damage and requirements for expansion	5C	—
Sanitary ware	25		5A	—
(r) Metering and measurement				
Electricity	20		5M	14-03
Gas	20		5M	14-03
Water	20		5M	14-03
(s) Protection systems (fire and security)				
Access control	15		—	—
Call points (break glass)	15		5M	—
Closed circuit television (CCTV):				
— external	15		—	—
— internal	20		—	—
Computer room fire extinguishing system	15	Consider environmental impact and possible phasing out of fire extinguishing agent	—	23-05
Control panel	15		—	—
Dry risers	25		—	—
Fire alarms:				
— battery support	20		—	22-01
— electrical	20		—	22-01
Fire dampers (curtain type)	15		—	16-03
Fire protection (pipes and ducts)	20	Damage to fire protection should be examined at frequent intervals	—	—
Foam systems	15		—	23-07
Heat detectors	20		—	—
Hose reels (fire)	15		—	23-03
Hydrants (fire)	30		—	23-04
Infrared lighting	10		—	
Intruder detection	15		—	
Intruder system control panel	20		—	
Portable fire appliances	8		—	23-(08-13)
Risers:				
— dry	25		—	—
— wet	20		—	—
Smoke and heat detectors	10		—	—
Smoke curtain	20		—	—
Smoke ventilation systems	30		—	16-03
Wet risers	20		—	—
Sounder (bell)	15		—	—
Sprinklers:				
— alternate wet and dry	20	Consider corrosion	—	—
— wet	25	Consider corrosion	—	23-14

Equipment item	Indicative life / years	Remarks	BCIS cost group	HVCA SFG/20 reference
(s) Protection systems (fire and security) (continued)				
Sprinkler heads	30		—	—
(t) Miscellaneous electrical equipment and plant				
Air conditioner:				
— commercial ('through-the-wall' unit)	10		5H	—
— residential (single or split packaged unit)	10		5H	—
Batteries:				
— battery chargers	20		5H	—
— lead–acid batteries (sealed)	5		5H	—
— nickel–alkaline batteries (vented)	20		5H	—
Clock systems	15		5H	—
Closed circuit television (CCTV) and video	10		5H	—
Communication systems	20	Voice and data	5H	—
Continuous flow electrical heaters	12		5H	—
Electric floor heating	25		5H	—
Electrical heater (on peak)	8		5H	—
Electrical storage heaters with ventilation	20		5H	—
Electrical water heaters	12		5H	—
Heat pumps:				
— air-to-air (residential)	10		5H	—
— air-to-air (commercial)	15		5H	—
— water-to-air (commercial)	15		5H	—
Intruder alarms and intercommunications	10		5H	—
Lighting control and management systems	15		5H	—
Lightning protection	25		5H	—
Public address systems	20		5H	—
Television and satellite systems	15		5H	—
Uninterruptible power supply (UPS) systems	20		5H	—
Water cooled air conditioner	15		5H	—
Window unit air conditioner	8		5H	—
(u) Vertical and horizontal transportation				
Brake assembly	20		—	—
Car and landing cills	15		—	—
Car and landing door panels	10		—	—
Car door safety devices	15		—	—
Car frame	30		—	—
Controllers	15		—	—
Door operator	15		—	—
Electric traction lifts	20		—	—
Electric traction lifts (packaged)	15		—	—
Entrance doors:				
— two panel (with obstacle detector)	15		—	—
— single opening door (with obstacle detector)	20		—	—
Escalators (commercial, e.g. office, retail)	30		—	—
Floor selector	20		—	—
Governor rope	10		—	—
Guide rails	35		—	—
Hydraulic lifts:				
— lift installation	15		—	—
— hydraulic cylinder	15		—	—
— hydraulic oil	5	With filtration	—	—
— oil cooling system	10		—	—

Equipment item	Indicative life / years	Remarks	BCIS cost group	HVCA SFG/20 reference
(u) Vertical and horizontal transportation (continued)				
Machines:				
— geared	15		—	—
— gearless	20		—	—
Motor–generator	20		—	—
Motors (for drive units):				
— squirrel cage	10		—	—
— DC	25	Check for vibration	—	—
Suspension ropes	12		—	—
Traction sheave	15	Can be recut	—	—
Transportation systems:				
— airport terminal, bus or rail station	25		—	—
— high density mass transit	20		—	—
(v) Lifting equipment				
Atrium gantry	30		—	—
Eye bolt	30		—	—
Fork lift truck	10		—	—
Lifting beam	20		—	—
Pallet truck	15		—	—
Window cradle	25		—	—
(w) Other			—	—
Photovoltaic panels	25		—	53-01
Solar panels (water heating)	25		—	—
Swimming pool filtration system	20		—	—
Wind turbines	20		—	57-03

Guide C: Reference data

C1   Properties of humid air

C1.1.1   Basis of calculation

The method of formulation suggested by Goff and Gratch, based on the ideal gas laws with a modification to take account of intermolecular forces, has been adopted for calculating the thermodynamic properties of moist air. This approach remains in line with current practice.

C1.1.2   Standards adopted

All data are tabulated for an internationally agreed standard atmospheric pressure of 101.325 kPa.

The zero datum adopted by the National Engineering Laboratory for the expression of the thermodynamic properties of steam is the triple point of water, +0.01 °C.

The zero datum for the specific enthalpies of both dry air and liquid water has been taken here as 273.15 K (0 °C).

C1.1.3   Formulae used for calculations

The details of the formulae used for calculations and properties at non-standard barometric pressures are given in Guide C, section 1.1.3.

Tables of psychrometric data for dry bulb temperatures of –5, 0, 5, 10, 15, 16, 17, 18, 19, 20, 21, 22, 23, 24, 25, 30, 35 and 40 °C are provided here in truncated form for reasons of space. Full tables for dry bulb temperatures from –10 °C to +60 °C, in half-degree steps, are provided in Guide C, chapter 1.

−5 °C DRY BULB

Percentage saturation μ / %	Relative humidity ϕ / %	Value of stated parameter per kg dry air			Vapour pressure p_v / kPa	Dew point temperature θ_d / °C	Adiabatic saturation temperature $\theta^\star$ / °C	Wet bulb temperature	
		Moisture content, g / g·kg⁻¹	Specific enthalpy, h / kJ·kg⁻¹	Specific volume, v / m³·kg⁻¹				Screen θ'_{sc} / °C	Sling θ'_{sl} / °C
100	100.00	2.486	1.166	0.7621	0.4015	−5.0	−5.0	−5.0	−5.0
96	96.02	2.386	0.918	0.7620	0.3855	−5.5	−5.2	−5.1	−5.2
88	88.04	2.187	0.423	0.7618	0.3535	−6.5	−5.5	−5.5	−5.5
80	80.06	1.988	−0.073	0.7615	0.3215	−7.6	−5.9	−5.8	−5.9
72	72.08	1.790	−0.568	0.7613	0.2894	−8.8	−6.2	−6.1	−6.2
68	68.09	1.690	−0.816	0.7612	0.2734	−9.4	−6.4	−6.2	−6.4
64	64.09	1.591	−1.064	0.7611	0.2573	−10.1	−6.6	−6.4	−6.6
60	60.09	1.491	−1.311	0.7609	0.2413	−10.8	−6.8	−6.5	−6.7
56	56.10	1.392	−1.559	0.7608	0.2252	−11.6	−7.0	−6.7	−6.9
52	52.10	1.292	−1.807	0.7607	0.2092	−12.4	−7.2	−6.8	−7.1
48	48.10	1.193	−2.055	0.7606	0.1931	−13.3	−7.4	−7.0	−7.3
44	44.10	1.094	−2.302	0.7605	0.1771	−14.3	−7.5	−7.1	−7.5
40	40.09	0.994	−2.550	0.7603	0.1610	−15.3	−7.7	−7.3	−7.6
36	36.09	0.895	−2.798	0.7602	0.1449	−16.4	−7.9	−7.5	−7.8
32	32.09	0.795	−3.045	0.7601	0.1288	−17.7	−8.1	−7.6	−8.0
28	28.08	0.696	−3.293	0.7600	0.1127	−19.1	−8.3	−7.8	−8.2
20	20.06	0.497	−3.789	0.7597	0.0806	−22.6	−8.7	−8.1	−8.6
12	12.04	0.298	−4.284	0.7595	0.0484	−27.7	−9.1	−8.4	−8.9
8	8.03	0.199	−4.532	0.7594	0.0322	−31.6	−9.3	−8.6	−9.1
0	0.00	0.000	−5.027	0.7591	0.0000	—	−9.7	−8.9	−9.5

0 °C DRY BULB

Percentage saturation μ / %	Relative humidity ϕ / %	Value of stated parameter per kg dry air			Vapour pressure p_v / kPa	Dew point temperature θ_d / °C	Adiabatic saturation temperature $\theta^\star$ / °C	Wet bulb temperature	
		Moisture content, g / g·kg⁻¹	Specific enthalpy, h / kJ·kg⁻¹	Specific volume, v / m³·kg⁻¹				Screen θ'_{sc} / °C	Sling θ'_{sl} / °C
100	100.00	3.789	9.475	0.7780	0.6108	0.0	0.0	0.0	0.0
96	96.02	3.637	9.096	0.7778	0.5865	−0.5	−0.2	−0.2	−0.2
88	88.06	3.334	8.338	0.7775	0.5379	−1.5	−0.7	−0.6	−0.7
80	80.10	3.031	7.580	0.7771	0.4892	−2.7	−1.1	−1.0	−1.1
72	72.12	2.728	6.822	0.7767	0.4405	−3.9	−1.6	−1.4	−1.6
68	68.13	2.576	6.443	0.7765	0.4161	−4.6	−1.9	−1.6	−1.8
64	64.14	2.425	6.064	0.7763	0.3918	−5.3	−2.1	−1.8	−2.0
60	60.14	2.273	5.685	0.7761	0.3674	−6.0	−2.4	−2.0	−2.3
56	56.15	2.122	5.306	0.7760	0.3429	−6.8	−2.6	−2.2	−2.5
52	52.15	1.970	4.927	0.7758	0.3185	−7.7	−2.8	−2.5	−2.8
48	48.15	1.819	4.548	0.7756	0.2941	−8.6	−3.1	−2.7	−3.0
44	44.15	1.667	4.169	0.7754	0.2696	−9.6	−3.4	−2.9	−3.3
40	40.14	1.516	3.790	0.7752	0.2452	−10.7	−3.6	−3.1	−3.5
36	36.14	1.364	3.411	0.7750	0.2207	−11.8	−3.9	−3.3	−3.8
32	32.13	1.212	3.032	0.7748	0.1962	−13.1	−4.1	−3.5	−4.0
28	28.12	1.061	2.653	0.7747	0.1718	−14.6	−4.4	−3.8	−4.3
20	20.10	0.758	1.895	0.7743	0.1228	−18.2	−4.9	−4.2	−4.8
12	12.06	0.455	1.137	0.7739	0.0737	−23.5	−5.5	−4.7	−5.3
8	8.04	0.303	0.758	0.7737	0.0491	−27.6	−5.7	−4.9	−5.5
0	0.00	0.000	0.000	0.7733	0.0000	—	−6.3	−5.3	−6.1

5 °C DRY BULB

Percentage saturation μ / %	Relative humidity ϕ / %	Value of stated parameter per kg dry air			Vapour pressure p_v / kPa	Dew point temperature θ_d / °C	Adiabatic saturation temperature $\theta^\star$ / °C	Wet bulb temperature	
		Moisture content, g / g·kg⁻¹	Specific enthalpy, h / kJ·kg⁻¹	Specific volume, v / m³·kg⁻¹				Screen θ'_{sc} / °C	Sling θ'_{sl} / °C
100	100.00	5.422	18.64	0.7944	0.8719	5.0	5.0	5.0	5.0
96	96.03	5.206	18.10	0.7941	0.8373	4.4	4.7	4.8	4.7
88	88.09	4.772	17.01	0.7935	0.7681	3.2	4.2	4.3	4.2
80	80.14	4.338	15.92	0.7930	0.6987	1.9	3.6	3.8	3.6
72	72.17	3.904	14.83	0.7925	0.6293	0.4	3.0	3.2	3.1
68	68.19	3.687	14.29	0.7922	0.5945	−0.3	2.7	3.0	2.8
64	64.20	3.470	13.74	0.7919	0.5598	−1.0	2.4	2.7	2.5
60	60.21	3.254	13.20	0.7916	0.5250	−1.8	2.1	2.5	2.2
56	56.21	3.037	12.65	0.7914	0.4901	−2.6	1.8	2.2	1.9
52	52.22	2.820	12.11	0.7911	0.4553	−3.5	1.5	1.9	1.6
48	48.22	2.603	11.56	0.7908	0.4204	−4.5	1.2	1.7	1.3
44	44.21	2.386	11.02	0.7905	0.3855	−5.5	0.9	1.4	1.0
40	40.21	2.169	10.47	0.7903	0.3506	−6.6	0.6	1.1	0.7
36	36.20	1.952	9.930	0.7900	0.3156	−7.8	0.3	0.9	0.4
32	32.19	1.735	9.385	0.7897	0.2806	−9.1	−0.4	0.6	0.1
28	28.17	1.518	8.841	0.7895	0.2456	−10.6	−0.7	0.3	−0.6
20	20.14	1.084	7.752	0.7889	0.1756	−14.4	−1.4	−0.6	−1.2
12	12.09	0.651	6.663	0.7884	0.1054	−19.8	−2.1	−1.2	−1.9
8	8.06	0.434	6.119	0.7881	0.0703	−24.0	−2.5	−1.5	−2.2
0	0.00	0.000	5.030	0.7875	0.0000	—	−3.2	−2.1	−2.9

10 °C DRY BULB

Percentage saturation μ / %	Relative humidity ϕ / %	Value of stated parameter per kg dry air			Vapour pressure p_v / kPa	Dew point temperature θ_d / °C	Adiabatic saturation temperature $\theta^\star$ / °C	Wet bulb temperature	
		Moisture content, g / g·kg^{-1}	Specific enthalpy, h / kJ·kg^{-1}	Specific volume, v / m^3·kg^{-1}				Screen θ'_{sc} / °C	Sling θ'_{sl} / °C
100	100.00	7.659	29.35	0.8116	1.227	10.0	10.0	10.0	10.0
96	96.05	7.352	28.58	0.8112	1.180	9.4	9.7	9.7	9.7
88	88.13	6.740	27.04	0.8104	1.081	8.1	9.0	9.1	9.0
80	80.19	6.127	25.50	0.8096	0.9841	6.7	8.3	8.5	8.3
72	72.24	5.514	23.95	0.8088	0.8866	5.2	7.6	7.8	7.6
68	68.26	5.208	23.18	0.8084	0.8377	4.4	7.2	7.5	7.3
64	64.28	4.902	22.41	0.8080	0.7888	3.6	6.9	7.2	6.9
60	60.29	4.595	21.64	0.8076	0.7398	2.7	6.5	6.9	6.6
56	56.30	4.289	20.86	0.8072	0.6909	1.7	6.1	6.5	6.2
52	52.30	3.983	20.09	0.8069	0.6419	0.7	5.7	6.2	5.8
48	48.30	3.676	19.32	0.8065	0.5928	−0.4	5.4	5.9	5.5
44	44.30	3.370	18.55	0.8061	0.5436	−1.4	5.0	5.5	5.1
40	40.29	3.064	17.78	0.8057	0.4945	−2.5	4.6	5.2	4.7
36	36.28	2.757	17.00	0.8053	0.4452	−3.8	4.2	4.8	4.3
32	32.27	2.451	16.23	0.8049	0.3960	−5.2	3.8	4.5	3.9
28	28.25	2.144	15.46	0.8045	0.3466	−6.7	3.4	4.1	3.5
20	20.20	1.532	13.92	0.8037	0.2478	−10.5	2.5	3.4	2.7
12	12.13	0.919	12.38	0.8029	0.1488	−16.1	1.7	2.7	1.9
8	8.09	0.613	11.60	0.8025	0.0993	−20.4	1.2	2.3	1.4
0	0.00	0.000	10.06	0.8018	0.0000	—	0.3	1.6	0.6

15 °C DRY BULB

Percentage saturation μ / %	Relative humidity ϕ / %	Value of stated parameter per kg dry air			Vapour pressure p_v / kPa	Dew point temperature θ_d / °C	Adiabatic saturation temperature $\theta^\star$ / °C	Wet bulb temperature	
		Moisture content, g / g·kg^{-1}	Specific enthalpy, h / kJ·kg^{-1}	Specific volume, v / m^3·kg^{-1}				Screen θ'_{sc} / °C	Sling θ'_{sl} / °C
100	100.00	10.697	42.11	0.8299	1.704	15.0	15.0	15.0	15.0
96	96.06	10.260	41.03	0.8293	1.637	14.4	14.6	14.6	14.6
88	88.18	9.405	38.87	0.8282	1.503	13.1	13.8	13.9	13.8
80	80.27	8.550	36.71	0.8271	1.368	11.6	13.0	13.2	13.0
72	72.34	7.695	34.55	0.8260	1.233	10.1	12.2	12.4	12.2
68	68.37	7.268	33.47	0.8254	1.165	9.2	11.7	12.0	11.8
64	64.39	6.840	32.28	0.8249	1.097	8.3	11.3	11.6	11.4
60	60.41	6.413	31.30	0.8243	1.030	7.4	10.9	11.2	10.9
56	56.42	5.985	30.22	0.8237	0.9616	6.4	10.4	10.8	10.5
52	52.43	5.558	29.14	0.8232	0.8935	5.4	9.9	10.4	10.0
48	48.43	5.130	28.06	0.8226	0.8253	4.2	9.5	10.0	9.6
44	44.42	4.703	26.98	0.8221	0.7570	3.0	9.0	9.6	9.1
40	40.41	4.275	25.90	0.8215	0.6887	1.7	8.5	9.2	8.6
36	36.39	3.848	24.82	0.8210	0.6202	0.2	8.0	8.7	8.1
32	32.37	3.420	23.74	0.8204	0.5517	−1.2	7.5	8.3	7.7
28	28.35	2.993	22.66	0.8198	0.4831	−2.8	7.0	7.9	7.2
20	20.27	2.138	20.49	0.8187	0.3455	−6.7	6.0	6.9	6.1
12	12.18	1.282	18.33	0.8176	0.2076	−12.5	4.9	6.0	5.1
8	8.13	0.855	17.25	0.8171	0.1385	−16.9	4.3	5.5	4.5
0	0.00	0.000	15.09	0.8159	0.0000	—	3.2	4.6	3.4

16 °C DRY BULB

Percentage saturation μ / %	Relative humidity ϕ / %	Value of stated parameter per kg dry air			Vapour pressure p_v / kPa	Dew point temperature θ_d / °C	Adiabatic saturation temperature $\theta^\star$ / °C	Wet bulb temperature	
		Moisture content, g / g·kg^{-1}	Specific enthalpy, h / kJ·kg^{-1}	Specific volume, v / m^3·kg^{-1}				Screen θ'_{sc} / °C	Sling θ'_{sl} / °C
100	100.00	11.41	44.96	0.8337	1.817	16.0	16.0	16.0	16.0
96	96.07	10.95	43.81	0.8331	1.746	15.4	15.6	15.6	15.6
88	88.19	10.04	41.50	0.8319	1.603	14.0	14.8	14.9	14.8
80	80.29	9.127	39.19	0.8307	1.459	12.6	14.0	14.1	14.0
72	72.37	8.214	36.88	0.8295	1.315	11.0	13.1	13.3	13.1
68	68.40	7.758	35.73	0.8289	1.243	10.2	12.6	12.9	12.7
64	64.42	7.302	34.57	0.8283	1.171	9.3	12.2	12.5	12.2
60	60.44	6.845	33.42	0.8277	1.098	8.4	11.7	12.1	11.8
56	56.45	6.389	32.26	0.8271	1.026	7.4	11.3	11.7	11.3
52	52.46	5.933	31.11	0.8265	0.9532	6.3	10.8	11.3	10.9
48	48.46	5.476	29.95	0.8259	0.8805	5.1	10.3	10.8	10.4
44	44.48	5.020	28.80	0.8254	0.8077	3.9	9.8	10.4	9.9
40	40.44	4.564	27.64	0.8248	0.7348	2.6	9.3	10.0	9.4
36	36.42	4.107	26.49	0.8242	0.6618	1.1	8.8	9.5	8.9
32	32.40	3.651	25.33	0.8236	0.5887	−0.4	8.3	9.1	8.4
28	28.37	3.194	24.17	0.8230	0.5155	−2.0	7.7	8.6	7.9
20	20.29	2.282	21.87	0.8218	0.3688	−6.0	6.6	7.6	6.8
12	12.19	1.369	19.56	0.8206	0.2216	−11.8	5.5	6.7	5.7
8	8.13	0.912	18.40	0.8200	0.1478	−16.2	4.9	6.2	5.1
0	0.00	0.000	16.10	0.8188	0.0000	—	3.7	5.1	4.0

17 °C DRY BULB

Percentage saturation μ / %	Relative humidity ϕ / %	Value of stated parameter per kg dry air			Vapour pressure p_v / kPa	Dew point temperature θ_d / °C	Adiabatic saturation temperature $\theta^\star$ / °C	Wet bulb temperature	
		Moisture content, g / g·kg^{-1}	Specific enthalpy, h / kJ·kg^{-1}	Specific volume, v / m^3·kg^{-1}				Screen θ'_{sc} / °C	Sling θ'_{sl} / °C
100	100.00	12.17	47.93	0.8376	1.936	17.0	17.0	17.0	17.0
96	96.07	11.69	46.69	0.8370	1.860	16.4	16.6	16.6	16.6
88	88.20	10.71	44.23	0.8357	1.708	15.0	15.8	15.9	15.8
80	80.31	9.739	41.76	0.8344	1.555	13.6	14.9	15.1	14.9
72	72.39	8.765	39.30	0.8331	1.402	12.0	14.0	14.3	14.0
68	68.42	8.278	38.06	0.8325	1.325	11.2	13.5	13.8	13.6
64	64.45	7.791	36.83	0.8318	1.248	10.3	13.1	13.4	13.1
60	60.47	7.304	35.60	0.8312	1.171	9.3	12.6	13.0	12.7
56	56.48	6.817	34.36	0.8306	1.094	8.3	12.1	12.6	12.2
52	52.49	6.330	33.13	0.8299	1.016	7.2	11.6	12.1	11.7
48	48.49	5.843	31.90	0.8293	0.9390	6.1	11.1	11.7	11.2
44	44.48	5.356	30.66	0.8287	0.8614	4.8	10.6	11.2	10.7
40	40.47	4.869	29.43	0.8280	0.7837	3.5	10.1	10.7	10.2
36	36.45	4.382	28.20	0.8274	0.7058	2.0	9.6	10.3	9.7
32	32.43	3.896	26.97	0.8267	0.6279	0.4	9.0	9.8	9.1
28	28.39	3.409	25.73	0.8261	0.5498	−1.3	8.5	9.3	8.6
20	20.31	2.435	23.27	0.8248	0.3934	−5.2	7.3	8.3	7.5
12	12.21	1.461	20.80	0.8235	0.2364	−11.1	6.1	7.3	6.3
8	8.14	0.974	19.57	0.8229	0.1577	−15.5	5.5	6.8	5.7
0	0.00	0.000	17.10	0.8216	0.0000	—	4.3	5.7	4.5

18 °C DRY BULB

Percentage saturation μ / %	Relative humidity ϕ / %	Value of stated parameter per kg dry air			Vapour pressure p_v / kPa	Dew point temperature θ_d / °C	Adiabatic saturation temperature $\theta^\star$ / °C	Wet bulb temperature	
		Moisture content, g / g·kg^{-1}	Specific enthalpy, h / kJ·kg^{-1}	Specific volume, v / m^3·kg^{-1}				Screen θ'_{sc} / °C	Sling θ'_{sl} / °C
100	100.00	12.98	51.01	0.8416	2.063	18.0	18.0	18.0	18.0
96	96.08	12.46	49.69	0.8409	1.982	17.4	17.6	17.6	17.6
88	88.22	11.43	47.06	0.8395	1.820	16.0	16.7	16.8	16.7
80	80.33	10.39	44.43	0.8381	1.657	14.6	15.8	16.0	15.9
72	72.42	9.348	41.80	0.8368	1.494	13.0	14.9	15.2	15.0
68	68.45	8.829	40.48	0.8361	1.412	12.1	14.4	14.7	14.5
64	64.48	8.309	39.16	0.8354	1.330	11.2	14.0	14.3	14.0
60	60.50	7.790	37.85	0.8347	1.248	10.3	13.5	13.9	13.5
56	56.51	7.271	36.53	0.8340	1.166	9.2	13.0	13.4	13.0
52	52.52	6.751	35.22	0.8334	1.083	8.2	12.5	13.0	12.5
48	48.52	6.232	33.90	0.8327	1.001	7.0	11.9	12.5	12.0
44	44.51	5.713	32.58	0.8320	0.9182	5.7	11.4	12.0	11.5
40	40.50	5.193	31.27	0.8313	0.8354	4.4	10.9	11.5	11.0
36	36.48	4.674	29.95	0.8306	0.7525	2.9	10.3	11.0	10.4
32	32.45	4.155	28.64	0.8299	0.6694	1.3	9.7	10.5	9.9
28	28.42	3.635	27.32	0.8293	0.5862	−0.5	9.2	10.0	9.3
20	20.33	2.597	24.69	0.8279	0.4194	−4.5	8.0	9.0	8.2
12	12.22	1.558	22.06	0.8265	0.2521	−10.3	6.7	7.9	6.9
8	8.15	1.039	20.74	0.8258	0.1682	−14.8	6.1	7.4	6.3
0	0.00	0.000	18.11	0.8245	0.0000	—	4.8	6.3	5.0

19 °C DRY BULB

Percentage saturation μ / %	Relative humidity ϕ / %	Value of stated parameter per kg dry air			Vapour pressure p_v / kPa	Dew point temperature θ_d / °C	Adiabatic saturation temperature $\theta^\star$ / °C	Wet bulb temperature	
		Moisture content, g / g·kg^{-1}	Specific enthalpy, h / kJ·kg^{-1}	Specific volume, v / m^3·kg^{-1}				Screen θ'_{sc} / °C	Sling θ'_{sl} / °C
100	100.00	13.84	54.21	0.8456	2.196	19.0	19.0	19.0	19.0
96	96.08	13.29	52.81	0.8449	2.110	18.4	18.6	18.6	18.6
88	88.23	12.18	50.00	0.8434	1.938	17.0	17.7	17.8	17.7
80	80.35	11.07	47.19	0.8419	1.765	15.5	16.8	17.0	16.8
72	72.44	9.966	44.39	0.8405	1.591	13.9	15.8	16.1	15.9
68	68.48	9.412	42.98	0.8397	1.504	13.1	15.3	15.6	15.4
64	64.51	8.859	41.58	0.8390	1.417	12.2	14.8	15.2	14.9
60	60.53	8.305	40.17	0.8383	1.329	11.2	14.3	14.7	14.4
56	56.55	7.751	38.77	0.8375	1.242	10.2	13.8	14.3	13.9
52	52.55	7.198	37.37	0.8368	1.154	9.1	13.3	13.8	13.4
48	48.55	6.644	35.96	0.8361	1.066	7.9	12.8	13.3	12.8
44	44.55	6.090	34.56	0.8354	0.9782	6.7	12.2	12.8	12.3
40	40.53	5.537	33.15	0.8346	0.8902	5.3	11.6	12.3	11.8
36	36.51	4.983	31.75	0.8339	0.8018	3.8	11.1	11.8	11.2
32	32.48	4.429	30.35	0.8332	0.7134	2.2	10.5	11.3	10.6
28	28.45	3.876	28.94	0.8324	0.6248	0.3	9.9	10.8	10.0
20	20.36	2.768	26.13	0.8310	0.4470	−3.7	8.7	9.7	8.8
12	12.24	1.661	23.33	0.8295	0.2687	−9.6	7.4	8.6	7.6
8	8.16	1.107	21.92	0.8288	0.1792	−14.1	6.7	8.0	6.9
0	0.00	0.000	19.11	0.8273	0.0000	—	5.3	6.8	5.6

20 °C DRY BULB

Percentage saturation μ / %	Relative humidity ϕ / %	Value of stated parameter per kg dry air			Vapour pressure p_v / kPa	Dew point temperature θ_d / °C	Adiabatic saturation temperature $\theta^\star$ / °C	Wet bulb temperature	
		Moisture content, g / g·kg^{-1}	Specific enthalpy, h / kJ·kg^{-1}	Specific volume, v / m^3·kg^{-1}				Screen θ'_{sc} / °C	Sling θ'_{sl} / °C
100	100.00	14.75	57.55	0.8497	2.337	20.0	20.0	20.0	20.0
96	96.09	14.16	56.05	0.8489	2.246	19.4	19.6	19.6	19.6
88	88.25	12.98	53.06	0.8473	2.062	18.0	18.7	18.8	18.7
80	80.37	11.80	50.06	0.8458	1.878	16.5	17.7	17.9	17.7
72	72.47	10.62	47.07	0.8442	1.694	14.9	16.7	17.0	16.8
68	68.51	10.03	45.57	0.8434	1.601	14.0	16.2	16.5	16.3
64	64.54	9.441	44.08	0.8427	1.508	13.1	15.7	16.1	15.8
60	60.56	8.851	42.58	0.8419	1.415	12.1	15.2	15.6	15.3
56	56.58	8.260	41.08	0.8411	1.322	11.1	14.7	15.1	14.7
52	52.59	7.670	39.58	0.8403	1.229	10.0	14.1	14.6	14.2
48	48.59	7.080	38.09	0.8395	1.136	8.8	13.6	14.1	13.7
44	44.58	6.490	36.59	0.8388	1.042	7.6	13.0	13.6	13.1
40	40.57	5.900	35.09	0.8380	0.9480	6.2	12.4	13.1	12.5
36	36.55	5.310	33.60	0.8372	0.8541	4.7	11.8	12.6	12.0
32	32.52	4.720	32.10	0.8364	0.7600	3.0	11.2	12.0	11.4
28	28.48	4.130	30.60	0.8356	0.6656	1.2	10.6	11.5	10.7
20	20.38	2.950	27.61	0.8341	0.4763	−3.0	9.3	10.4	9.5
12	12.25	1.770	24.61	0.8325	0.2863	−8.9	8.0	9.2	8.2
8	8.17	1.180	23.11	0.8317	0.1910	−13.4	7.3	8.6	7.5
0	0.00	0.000	20.11	0.8301	0.0000	—	5.8	7.3	6.1

21 °C DRY BULB

Percentage saturation μ / %	Relative humidity ϕ / %	Value of stated parameter per kg dry air			Vapour pressure p_v / kPa	Dew point temperature θ_d / °C	Adiabatic saturation temperature $\theta^\star$ / °C	Wet bulb temperature	
		Moisture content, g / g·kg^{-1}	Specific enthalpy, h / kJ·kg^{-1}	Specific volume, v / m^3·kg^{-1}				Screen θ'_{sc} / °C	Sling θ'_{sl} / °C
100	100.00	15.71	61.03	0.8539	2.486	21.0	21.0	21.0	21.0
96	96.09	15.09	59.43	0.8530	2.389	20.4	20.6	20.6	20.6
88	88.26	13.83	56.24	0.8514	2.194	19.0	19.6	19.7	19.6
80	80.40	12.57	53.05	0.8497	1.998	17.5	18.7	18.8	18.7
72	72.50	11.31	49.86	0.8480	1.802	15.9	17.7	17.9	17.7
68	68.54	10.69	48.26	0.8472	1.704	15.0	17.1	17.4	17.2
64	64.58	10.06	46.66	0.8464	1.605	14.1	16.6	17.0	16.7
60	60.60	9.428	45.07	0.8455	1.506	13.1	16.1	16.5	16.1
56	56.62	8.800	43.47	0.8447	1.407	12.1	15.5	16.0	15.6
52	52.63	8.171	41.88	0.8439	1.308	11.0	15.0	15.5	15.0
48	48.63	7.542	40.28	0.8430	1.209	9.8	14.4	14.9	14.5
44	44.62	6.914	38.68	0.8422	1.109	8.5	13.8	14.4	13.9
40	40.60	6.285	37.09	0.8413	1.009	7.1	13.2	13.9	13.3
36	36.58	5.657	35.49	0.8405	0.9093	5.6	12.6	13.3	12.7
32	32.55	5.028	33.89	0.8397	0.8091	3.9	12.0	12.8	12.1
28	28.51	4.400	32.30	0.8388	0.7087	2.1	11.3	12.2	11.5
20	20.40	3.143	29.11	0.8372	0.5072	−2.2	10.0	11.0	10.1
12	12.27	1.886	25.91	0.8355	0.3049	−8.2	8.6	9.8	8.8
8	8.19	1.257	24.32	0.8347	0.2035	−12.7	7.8	9.2	8.1
0	0.00	0.000	21.13	0.8330	0.0000	—	6.3	7.9	6.6

22 °C DRY BULB

Percentage saturation μ / %	Relative humidity ϕ / %	Value of stated parameter per kg dry air			Vapour pressure p_v / kPa	Dew point temperature θ_d / °C	Adiabatic saturation temperature $\theta^\star$ / °C	Wet bulb temperature	
		Moisture content, g / g·kg^{-1}	Specific enthalpy, h / kJ·kg^{-1}	Specific volume, v / m^3·kg^{-1}				Screen θ'_{sc} / °C	Sling θ'_{sl} / °C
100	100.00	16.73	64.65	0.8581	2.643	22.0	22.0	22.0	22.0
96	96.10	16.06	62.95	0.8572	2.540	21.3	21.5	21.6	21.5
88	88.28	14.72	59.55	0.8555	2.333	20.0	20.6	20.7	20.6
80	80.42	13.39	56.15	0.8537	2.125	18.5	19.6	19.8	19.6
72	72.53	12.05	52.75	0.8519	1.917	16.8	18.6	18.8	18.6
68	68.58	11.38	51.05	0.8510	1.812	16.0	18.1	18.3	18.1
64	64.61	10.71	49.35	0.8501	1.707	15.0	17.5	17.9	17.6
60	60.64	10.04	47.64	0.8492	1.602	14.0	17.0	17.3	17.0
56	56.66	9.370	45.94	0.8483	1.497	13.0	16.4	16.8	16.5
52	52.67	8.701	44.24	0.8474	1.392	11.9	15.8	16.3	15.9
48	48.67	8.032	42.54	0.8465	1.286	10.7	15.2	15.8	15.3
44	44.66	7.362	40.84	0.8457	1.180	9.4	14.6	15.2	14.7
40	40.64	6.693	39.14	0.8448	1.074	8.0	14.0	14.7	14.1
36	36.62	6.024	37.44	0.8439	0.9677	6.5	13.4	14.1	13.5
32	32.58	5.354	35.74	0.8430	0.8611	4.8	12.7	13.5	12.8
28	28.54	4.685	34.04	0.8421	0.7542	2.9	12.0	12.9	12.2
20	20.43	3.346	30.64	0.8403	0.5399	−1.5	10.6	11.7	10.8
12	12.28	2.008	27.24	0.8385	0.3246	−7.5	9.2	10.4	9.4
8	8.20	1.339	25.53	0.8376	0.2166	−12.0	8.4	9.8	8.6
0	0.00	0.000	22.13	0.8358	0.0000	—	6.8	8.4	7.1

23 °C DRY BULB

Percentage saturation μ / %	Relative humidity ϕ / %	Value of stated parameter per kg dry air			Vapour pressure p_v / kPa	Dew point temperature θ_d / °C	Adiabatic saturation temperature $\theta^\star$ / °C	Wet bulb temperature	
		Moisture content, g / g·kg⁻¹	Specific enthalpy, h / kJ·kg⁻¹	Specific volume, v / m³·kg⁻¹				Screen θ'_{sc} / °C	Sling θ'_{sl} / °C
100	100.00	17.81	68.43	0.8625	2.808	23.0	23.0	23.0	23.0
96	96.11	17.10	66.62	0.8615	2.699	22.3	22.5	22.6	22.5
88	88.30	15.67	63.00	0.8596	2.479	21.0	21.6	21.7	21.6
80	80.45	14.25	59.37	0.8577	2.259	19.5	20.6	20.7	20.6
72	72.57	12.82	55.75	0.8558	2.038	17.8	19.5	19.7	19.5
68	68.61	12.11	53.94	0.8549	1.927	16.9	19.0	19.2	19.0
64	64.65	11.40	52.13	0.8539	1.815	16.0	18.4	18.7	18.5
60	60.68	10.69	50.31	0.8530	1.704	15.0	17.8	18.2	17.9
56	56.70	9.974	48.50	0.8520	1.592	13.9	17.2	17.7	17.3
52	52.71	9.262	46.69	0.8511	1.480	12.8	16.7	17.1	16.7
48	48.71	8.549	44.88	0.8501	1.368	11.6	16.0	16.6	16.1
44	44.70	7.837	43.07	0.8392	1.255	10.3	15.4	16.0	15.5
40	40.68	7.124	41.26	0.8482	1.142	8.9	14.8	15.4	14.9
36	36.66	6.412	39.44	0.8473	1.029	7.4	14.1	14.9	14.2
32	32.62	5.699	37.63	0.8463	0.9160	5.7	13.4	14.3	13.6
28	28.58	4.987	35.82	0.8453	0.8024	3.8	12.7	13.6	12.9
20	20.46	3.562	32.20	0.8434	0.5745	−0.7	11.3	12.4	11.5
12	12.30	2.137	28.57	0.8415	0.3455	−6.8	9.8	11.0	10.0
8	8.21	1.425	26.76	0.8406	0.2306	−11.3	9.0	10.3	9.2
0	0.00	0.000	23.14	0.8387	0.0000	—	7.3	8.9	7.6

24 °C DRY BULB

Percentage saturation μ / %	Relative humidity ϕ / %	Value of stated parameter per kg dry air			Vapour pressure p_v / kPa	Dew point temperature θ_d / °C	Adiabatic saturation temperature $\theta^\star$ / °C	Wet bulb temperature	
		Moisture content, g / g·kg⁻¹	Specific enthalpy, h / kJ·kg⁻¹	Specific volume, v / m³·kg⁻¹				Screen θ'_{sc} / °C	Sling θ'_{sl} / °C
100	100.00	18.95	72.37	0.8669	2.983	24.0	24.0	24.0	24.0
96	96.11	18.19	70.44	0.8659	2.867	23.3	23.5	23.6	23.5
88	88.31	16.68	66.59	0.8639	2.634	21.9	22.5	22.6	22.5
80	80.48	15.16	62.73	0.8619	2.400	20.4	21.5	21.7	21.5
72	72.60	13.64	58.87	0.8598	2.165	18.8	20.4	20.7	20.5
68	68.65	12.89	56.94	0.8588	2.048	17.9	19.9	20.2	19.9
64	64.69	12.13	55.01	0.8578	1.930	16.9	19.3	19.6	19.3
60	60.72	11.37	53.08	0.8568	1.811	15.9	18.7	19.1	18.8
56	56.74	10.61	51.15	0.8558	1.692	14.9	18.1	18.5	18.2
52	52.75	9.855	49.22	0.8547	1.573	13.8	17.5	18.0	17.6
48	48.75	9.097	47.29	0.8537	1.454	12.6	16.9	17.4	16.9
44	44.75	8.339	45.37	0.8527	1.335	11.3	16.2	16.8	16.3
40	40.73	7.580	43.44	0.8517	1.215	9.8	15.6	16.2	15.7
36	36.70	6.822	41.51	0.8507	1.095	8.3	14.9	15.6	15.0
32	32.66	6.064	39.58	0.8497	0.9741	6.6	14.2	15.0	14.3
28	28.61	5.306	37.65	0.8486	0.8534	4.7	13.4	14.4	13.6
20	20.49	3.790	33.79	0.8466	0.6111	−0.0	11.9	13.0	12.1
12	12.32	2.274	29.93	0.8446	0.3675	−6.0	10.4	11.6	10.6
8	8.22	1.516	28.00	0.8435	0.2453	−10.7	9.5	10.9	9.8
0	0.00	0.000	24.14	0.8415	0.0000	—	7.8	9.4	8.1

25 °C DRY BULB

Percentage saturation μ / %	Relative humidity ϕ / %	Value of stated parameter per kg dry air			Vapour pressure p_v / kPa	Dew point temperature θ_d / °C	Adiabatic saturation temperature $\theta^\star$ / °C	Wet bulb temperature	
		Moisture content, g / g·kg⁻¹	Specific enthalpy, h / kJ·kg⁻¹	Specific volume, v / m³·kg⁻¹				Screen θ'_{sc} / °C	Sling θ'_{sl} / °C
100	100.00	20.16	76.49	0.8715	3.166	25.0	25.0	25.0	25.0
96	96.12	19.35	74.43	0.8704	3.044	24.3	24.5	24.5	24.5
88	88.33	17.74	70.33	0.8682	2.797	22.9	23.5	23.6	23.5
80	80.51	16.13	66.22	0.8661	2.549	21.4	22.4	22.6	22.5
72	72.64	14.51	62.11	0.8639	2.300	19.7	21.3	21.6	21.4
68	68.69	13.71	60.06	0.8628	2.175	18.8	20.8	21.1	20.8
64	64.74	12.90	58.01	0.8617	2.050	17.9	20.2	20.5	20.2
60	60.77	12.10	55.95	0.8606	1.924	16.9	19.6	20.0	19.6
56	56.79	11.29	53.90	0.8596	1.798	15.8	19.0	19.4	19.0
52	52.80	10.48	51.85	0.8585	1.672	14.7	18.3	18.8	18.4
48	48.80	9.676	49.79	0.8574	1.545	13.5	17.7	18.2	17.8
44	44.79	8.870	47.74	0.8563	1.418	12.2	17.0	17.6	17.1
40	40.77	8.063	45.69	0.8552	1.291	10.8	16.3	17.0	16.4
36	36.74	7.257	43.63	0.8541	1.163	9.2	15.6	16.4	15.7
32	32.70	6.450	41.58	0.8530	1.036	7.5	14.9	15.7	15.0
28	28.65	5.644	39.52	0.8520	0.9072	5.6	14.2	15.1	14.3
20	20.52	4.032	35.42	0.8498	0.6497	0.9	12.6	13.7	12.8
12	12.34	2.419	31.31	0.8476	0.3908	−5.3	10.9	12.2	11.2
8	8.24	1.613	29.26	0.8465	0.2609	−10.0	10.1	11.5	10.3
0	0.00	0.000	25.15	0.8443	0.0000	—	8.2	9.9	8.5

30 °C DRY BULB

Percentage saturation μ / %	Relative humidity ϕ / %	Value of stated parameter per kg dry air			Vapour pressure p_v / kPa	Dew point temperature θ_d / °C	Adiabatic saturation temperature $\theta^\star$ / °C	Wet bulb temperature	
		Moisture content, g / g·kg⁻¹	Specific enthalpy, h / kJ·kg⁻¹	Specific volume, v / m³·kg⁻¹				Screen θ'_{sc} / °C	Sling θ'_{sl} / °C
100	100.00	27.31	99.98	0.8959	4.242	30.0	30.0	30.0	30.0
96	96.16	26.22	97.19	0.8944	4.079	29.3	29.5	29.5	29.5
88	88.45	24.03	91.61	0.8915	3.752	27.9	28.4	28.4	28.4
80	80.69	21.85	86.02	0.8885	3.423	26.3	27.2	27.3	27.2
72	72.87	19.66	80.44	0.8855	3.091	24.6	26.0	26.2	26.0
68	68.94	18.57	77.65	0.8840	2.924	23.7	25.3	25.6	25.4
64	65.00	17.48	74.85	0.8825	2.757	22.7	24.7	25.0	24.7
60	61.04	16.39	72.06	0.8810	2.589	21.7	24.0	24.4	24.0
56	57.07	15.29	69.27	0.8795	2.421	20.6	23.3	23.7	23.4
52	53.08	14.20	66.48	0.8780	2.252	19.4	22.6	23.0	22.6
48	49.08	13.11	63.69	0.8765	2.092	18.1	21.8	22.4	21.9
44	45.07	12.02	60.89	0.8750	1.912	16.8	21.1	21.7	21.2
40	41.05	10.92	58.10	0.8735	1.741	15.3	20.3	20.9	20.4
36	37.00	9.832	55.31	0.8720	1.570	13.7	19.4	20.2	19.6
32	32.95	8.739	52.52	0.8705	1.398	12.0	18.6	19.4	18.7
28	28.88	7.647	49.73	0.8690	1.225	10.0	17.7	18.6	17.9
20	20.70	5.462	44.14	0.8660	0.8782	5.1	15.9	17.0	16.0
12	12.47	3.277	38.56	0.8630	0.5288	−1.7	13.8	15.2	14.1
8	8.32	2.185	35.77	0.8615	0.3531	−6.5	12.8	14.3	13.0
0	0.00	0.000	30.18	0.8585	0.0000	—	10.5	12.3	10.8

35 °C DRY BULB

Percentage saturation μ / %	Relative humidity ϕ / %	Value of stated parameter per kg dry air			Vapour pressure p_v / kPa	Dew point temperature θ_d / °C	Adiabatic saturation temperature $\theta^\star$ / °C	Wet bulb temperature	
		Moisture content, g / g·kg⁻¹	Specific enthalpy, h / kJ·kg⁻¹	Specific volume, v / m³·kg⁻¹				Screen θ'_{sc} / °C	Sling θ'_{sl} / °C
100	100.00	36.73	129.4	0.9238	5.622	35.0	35.0	35.0	35.0
96	96.21	35.26	125.6	0.9218	5.409	34.3	34.4	34.5	34.4
88	88.60	32.32	118.1	0.9177	4.981	32.8	33.2	33.3	33.2
80	80.91	29.38	110.6	0.9136	4.549	31.2	32.0	32.1	32.0
72	73.15	26.44	103.0	0.9095	4.113	29.5	30.6	30.8	30.7
68	69.25	24.97	99.27	0.9075	3.893	28.5	29.9	30.2	30.0
64	65.33	23.51	95.50	0.9055	3.673	27.5	29.2	29.5	29.2
60	61.38	22.04	91.74	0.9034	3.451	26.5	28.4	28.8	28.5
56	57.42	20.57	87.97	0.9014	3.228	25.3	27.7	28.1	27.7
52	53.45	19.10	84.20	0.8993	3.005	24.1	26.9	27.3	26.9
48	49.45	17.63	80.43	0.8973	2.780	22.8	26.0	26.5	26.1
44	45.44	16.16	76.66	0.8952	2.554	21.4	25.1	25.7	25.2
40	41.40	14.69	72.90	0.8932	2.328	19.9	24.2	24.9	24.4
36	37.35	13.22	69.13	0.8912	2.100	18.3	23.3	24.0	23.4
32	33.27	11.75	65.36	0.8891	1.871	16.5	22.3	23.1	22.5
28	29.18	10.28	61.59	0.8871	1.641	14.4	21.3	22.2	21.4
20	20.94	7.346	54.06	0.8830	1.177	9.4	19.1	20.2	19.3
12	12.63	4.407	46.52	0.8789	0.7098	2.1	16.7	18.1	16.9
8	8.44	2.938	42.75	0.8768	0.4743	−3.0	15.4	17.0	15.7
0	0.00	0.000	35.22	0.8727	0.0000	—	12.6	14.6	12.9

40 °C DRY BULB

Percentage saturation μ / %	Relative humidity ϕ / %	Value of stated parameter per kg dry air			Vapour pressure p_v / kPa	Dew point temperature θ_d / °C	Adiabatic saturation temperature $\theta^\star$ / °C	Wet bulb temperature	
		Moisture content, g / g·kg⁻¹	Specific enthalpy, h / kJ·kg⁻¹	Specific volume, v / m³·kg⁻¹				Screen θ'_{sc} / °C	Sling θ'_{sl} / °C
100	100.00	49.10	166.6	0.9563	7.375	40.0	40.0	40.0	40.0
96	96.28	47.13	161.6	0.9535	7.101	39.3	39.4	39.4	39.4
88	88.78	43.21	151.5	0.9480	6.548	37.8	38.1	38.2	38.1
80	81.20	39.28	141.3	0.9424	5.989	36.1	36.8	36.9	36.8
72	73.52	35.35	131.2	0.9369	5.422	34.3	35.3	35.5	35.4
68	69.64	33.39	126.2	0.9341	5.137	33.4	34.6	34.8	34.6
64	65.75	31.42	121.1	0.9314	4.849	32.4	33.8	34.0	33.8
60	61.83	29.46	116.1	0.9286	4.560	31.3	32.9	33.3	33.0
56	57.88	27.49	111.0	0.9258	4.269	30.1	32.1	32.5	32.2
52	53.91	25.53	106.0	0.9230	3.976	28.9	31.2	31.6	31.3
48	49.92	23.57	100.9	0.9203	3.682	27.6	30.3	30.8	30.4
44	45.90	21.60	95.85	0.9175	3.385	26.1	29.3	29.9	29.4
40	41.86	19.64	90.80	0.9147	3.087	24.6	28.3	28.9	28.4
36	37.79	17.67	85.74	0.9119	2.787	22.9	27.2	27.9	27.4
32	33.69	15.71	80.69	0.9092	2.485	21.0	26.1	26.9	26.3
28	29.57	13.75	75.63	0.9064	2.181	18.9	25.0	25.8	25.1
20	21.26	9.819	65.52	0.9008	1.568	13.7	22.4	23.5	22.6
12	12.83	5.892	55.41	0.8953	0.9466	6.2	19.6	21.0	19.8
8	8.58	3.928	50.36	0.8925	0.6330	0.5	18.0	19.6	18.3
0	0.00	0.000	40.25	0.8869	0.0000	—	14.6	16.6	14.9

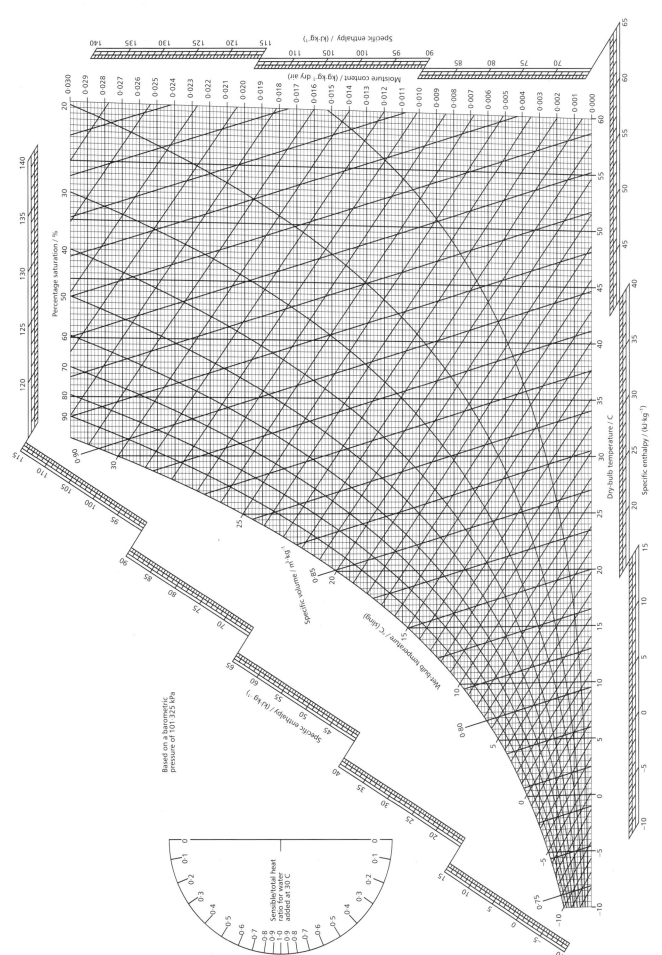

Figure C1.2 CIBSE psychrometric chart (−10 to +60 °C) (CIBSE Guide C includes charts for temperature ranges −10 to +60 °C and +10 to 110 °C)

C2   Properties of water and steam

C2.1   Introduction

The data presented in Tables 2.1, 2.2, and 2.3 are based upon the tables prepared by the National Engineering Laboratory, augmented as necessary by further values obtained by interpolation from the tables of Mayhew and Rogers.

The units and symbols used are as follows:

c_f Specific heat capacity ($kJ \cdot kg^{-1} \cdot K^{-1}$)

h_f Specific enthalpy (saturated liquid) ($kJ \cdot kg^{-1}$)

h_g Specific enthalpy (saturated vapour) ($kJ \cdot kg^{-1}$)

h_{fg} Specific latent heat of evaporation ($kJ \cdot kg^{-1}$)

p Absolute pressure (kPa)

p_s Absolute saturation pressure (kPa)

v Specific volume ($m^3 \cdot kg^{-1}$)

$(Pr)_f$ Prandtl number (saturated liquid)

$(Pr)_g$ Prandtl number (saturated vapour)

θ Temperature (°C)

θ_s Temperature (saturation) (°C)

μ_f Dynamic viscosity (saturated liquid) ($\mu Pa \cdot s$)

ρ Density (specific mass) ($kg \cdot m^{-3}$)

Table 2.1 lists values of saturation temperature, specific volume, specific enthalpies of saturated liquid and vapour and the specific latent heat of evaporation at round values of absolute pressure.

The values quoted were in all cases derived from NEL Table 2, except for Prandtl numbers, which were obtained by Lagrangian interpolation from Mayhew and Rogers, page 10.

Table 2.2 lists values of the saturation vapour pressure, specific heat capacity, dynamic viscosity, density (specific mass) and of the specific enthalpy and Prandtl numbers of the saturated liquid and vapour at round values of temperature.

The values quoted were derived as follows:

—   vapour pressure, density (as reciprocal of volume) and specific enthalpy from NEL Table 1.

—   specific heat capacity, dynamic viscosity and Prandtl numbers (all by Lagrangian interpolation) from Mayhew and Rogers, page 10.

Table 2.3 lists values of specific enthalpy for superheated steam at round values of absolute pressure for a restricted range of final temperatures.

The values quoted were in all cases derived from NEL Table 3.

Table C2.1 Properties of saturated steam

Absolute pressure p / kPa	Temperature t_s / °C	Specific enthalpy			Specific volume v / (m³·kg⁻¹)	Specific heat capacity of vapour c_f / (kJ·kg⁻¹·K⁻¹)	Prandtl number $(Pr)_g$	Absolute pressure p / kPa
		In saturated liquid h_f / (kJ·kg⁻¹)	Latent heat of evaporation h_{fg} / (kJ·kg⁻¹)	In saturated vapour h_g / (kJ·kg⁻¹)				
1	6.98	29.3	2484.3	2513.6	129.205	1.86	1.03	1
2	17.51	73.5	2459.5	2533.0	67.010	1.87	1.03	2
4	28.98	121.4	2432.4	2553.9	34.805	1.88	1.02	4
6	36.18	151.5	2415.3	2566.8	23.742	1.88	1.02	6
8	41.53	173.9	2402.5	2576.4	18.104	1.89	1.02	8
10	45.83	191.8	2392.2	2584.1	14.673	1.89	1.03	10
20	60.09	251.5	2357.7	2609.1	7.648	1.91	1.03	20
30	69.13	289.3	2335.4	2624.8	5.228	1.93	1.03	30
40	75.89	317.7	2318.6	2636.3	3.992	1.94	1.03	40
50	81.35	340.6	2304.9	2645.4	3.239	1.95	1.04	50
60	85.95	359.9	2293.2	2653.1	2.731	1.96	1.04	60
70	89.96	376.8	2282.9	2659.7	2.364	1.97	1.04	70
80	83.51	391.7	2273.7	2665.4	2.087	1.98	1.04	80
90	96.71	405.2	2265.4	2670.6	1.869	1.99	1.04	90
100	99.63	417.5	2257.7	2675.2	1.694	2.01	1.04	100
110	102.32	428.8	2250.6	2679.5	1.549	2.02	1.05	110
120	104.81	439.3	2244.0	2683.3	1.428	2.03	1.05	120
130	107.13	449.2	2237.8	2686.9	1.325	2.04	1.05	130
140	109.32	458.4	2231.9	2690.3	1.237	2.05	1.05	140
150	111.37	367.5	2226.3	2693.4	1.159	2.05	1.05	150
160	113.32	475.4	2221.0	2696.4	1.091	2.06	1.06	160
170	115.17	483.2	2215.9	2699.1	1.031	2.07	1.06	170
180	116.93	490.7	2211.1	2701.8	0.977	2.07	1.06	180
190	118.62	497.9	2206.4	2704.2	0.929	2.08	1.06	190
200	120.23	504.7	2201.9	2706.6	0.886	2.09	1.06	200
210	121.78	511.3	2197.6	2708.9	0.846	2.10	1.06	210
220	123.27	517.6	2193.4	2711.0	0.810	2.11	1.07	220
230	124.71	523.7	2189.3	2713.1	0.777	2.12	1.07	230
240	126.09	529.6	2185.4	2715.0	0.747	2.13	1.07	240
250	127.43	535.4	2181.6	2716.9	0.719	2.13	1.07	250
260	128.73	540.9	2177.8	2718.7	0.693	2.14	1.07	260
270	129.99	546.2	2174.2	2720.5	0.669	2.15	1.08	270
280	131.21	551.5	2170.7	2722.2	0.646	2.16	1.08	280
290	132.39	556.5	2167.3	2723.8	0.625	2.16	1.08	290
300	133.54	561.4	2163.9	2725.4	0.606	2.17	1.08	300
310	134.66	566.2	2160.6	2726.9	0.587	2.18	1.09	310
320	135.76	570.9	2157.4	2728.4	0.570	2.19	1.09	320
330	136.82	575.5	2154.3	2729.8	0.554	2.20	1.09	330
340	137.86	579.9	2151.2	2731.1	0.539	2.20	1.09	340
350	138.88	584.3	2148.2	2732.5	0.524	2.21	1.10	350
360	139.87	588.5	2145.2	2733.8	0.510	2.21	1.10	360
370	140.84	592.7	2142.3	2735.0	0.497	2.22	1.10	370
380	141.79	596.8	2139.5	2736.3	0.485	2.22	1.10	380
390	142.72	600.8	2136.7	2737.5	0.473	2.23	1.11	390
400	143.63	604.7	2133.9	2738.6	0.462	2.24	1.11	400
410	144.52	608.5	2131.2	2739.8	0.452	2.24	1.11	410
420	145.39	612.3	2128.6	2740.9	0.442	2.25	1.11	420
430	146.25	616.0	2125.9	2741.9	0.432	2.26	1.11	430
440	147.09	619.6	2123.4	2743.0	0.423	2.27	1.12	440
450	147.92	623.2	2120.8	2744.0	0.414	2.28	1.12	450
460	148.73	626.7	2118.2	2745.0	0.405	2.28	1.12	460
470	149.53	630.1	2115.8	2746.0	0.397	2.29	1.13	470
480	150.31	633.5	2113.4	2746.9	0.389	2.29	1.13	480
490	151.09	636.8	2111.0	2747.8	0.382	2.30	1.13	490
500	151.85	640.1	2108.6	2748.7	0.375	2.31	1.13	500

Table continues

Table C2.1 Properties of saturated steam — *continued*

Absolute pressure p / kPa	Temperature t_s / °C	Specific enthalpy			Specific volume v / (m³·kg⁻¹)	Specific heat capacity of vapour c_f / (kJ·kg⁻¹·K⁻¹)	Prandtl number $(Pr)_g$	Absolute pressure p / kPa
		In saturated liquid h_f / (kJ·kg⁻¹)	Latent heat of evaporation h_{fg} / (kJ·kg⁻¹)	In saturated vapour h_g / (kJ·kg⁻¹)				
520	153.33	646.5	2104.0	2750.5	0.361	2.32	1.13	520
540	154.77	652.8	2099.4	2752.2	0.349	2.33	1.14	540
560	156.16	658.8	2095.0	2753.8	0.337	2.34	1.14	560
580	157.52	664.7	2090.7	2755.4	0.326	2.35	1.14	580
600	158.84	670.4	2086.4	2756.8	0.316	2.37	1.14	600
620	160.12	676.0	2082.3	2758.3	0.306	2.38	1.15	620
640	161.38	681.5	2078.2	2759.9	0.297	2.39	1.15	640
660	162.60	686.8	2074.2	2761.0	0.288	2.40	1.16	660
680	163.79	692.0	2070.3	2762.3	0.280	2.41	1.16	680
700	164.96	697.1	2066.4	2763.5	0.273	2.43	1.16	700
720	166.10	702.0	2062.7	2764.7	0.266	2.44	1.17	720
740	167.21	706.9	2058.9	2765.8	0.259	2.45	1.17	740
760	168.30	711.7	2055.3	2767.0	0.252	2.47	1.17	760
780	169.37	716.4	2051.7	2768.0	0.246	2.48	1.18	780
800	170.41	720.9	2048.2	2769.1	0.240	2.49	1.18	800
820	171.44	725.4	2044.7	2770.1	0.235	2.51	1.18	820
840	172.45	729.8	2041.2	2771.1	0.229	2.52	1.19	840
860	173.43	734.2	2037.8	2772.0	0.224	2.53	1.19	860
880	174.40	738.4	2034.5	2772.9	0.220	2.55	1.20	880
900	175.36	742.6	2031.2	2773.8	0.215	2.56	1.21	900
920	176.29	746.8	2028.0	2774.7	0.210	2.57	1.21	920
940	177.21	750.8	2024.7	2775.6	0.206	2.58	1.21	940
960	178.12	754.8	2021.6	2776.4	0.202	2.60	1.22	960
980	179.01	758.7	2018.4	2777.2	0.198	2.61	1.22	980
1000	179.88	762.6	2015.3	2777.9	0.194	2.62	1.23	1000
1100	184.06	781.1	2000.4	2781.5	0.177	2.67	1.25	1100
1200	187.96	798.4	1986.2	2784.6	0.163	2.71	1.26	1200
1300	191.60	814.7	1972.6	2787.3	0.151	2.76	1.27	1300
1400	195.04	830.0	1959.6	2789.7	0.141	2.81	1.29	1400
1500	198.28	844.6	1947.1	2791.8	0.132	2.86	1.30	1500
1600	201.37	858.5	1935.1	2793.6	0.124	2.91	1.31	1600
1700	204.30	871.8	1923.4	2795.2	0.117	2.96	1.33	1700
1800	207.10	884.5	1912.1	2796.6	0.110	3.01	1.35	1800
1900	209.79	896.8	1901.1	2797.8	0.105	3.07	1.36	1900
2000	212.37	908.6	1890.4	2798.9	0.100	3.13	1.37	2000
2200	217.24	930.0	1869.7	2800.6	0.091	3.19	1.39	2200
2400	221.78	951.9	1850.0	2801.9	0.083	3.25	1.41	2400
2600	226.03	971.7	1831.0	2802.7	0.077	3.36	1.43	2600
2800	230.04	990.5	1812.7	2903.2	0.071	3.45	1.44	2800
3000	233.84	1008.3	1795.0	2803.4	0.067	3.53	1.46	3000
3200	237.44	1025.4	1777.9	2803.3	0.062	3.60	1.49	3200
3400	240.88	1041.8	1761.2	2803.0	0.059	3.68	1.53	3400
3600	244.16	1057.6	1744.9	2802.4	0.055	3.77	1.57	3600
3800	247.31	1072.7	1728.9	2802.1	0.052	3.86	1.59	3800
4000	250.33	1087.4	1713.4	2801.7	0.050	3.94	1.60	4000

Table C2.2 Properties of water at saturation

Temperature t_s / °C	Absolute vapour pressure p_s / kPa	Specific heat capacity c_r / (kJ·kg⁻¹·K⁻¹)	Dynamic viscosity μ_f / (μPa·s)	Density ρ / (kg·m⁻³)	Specific enthalpy of liquid h_f / (kJ·kg⁻¹)	Prandtl number $(Pr)_g$	Temperature t_s / °C
0.01	0.61	4.2100	1782	999.8	0.00	13.61	0.01
1	0.66	4.2096	1724	999.8	4.17	13.11	1
2	0.71	4.2088	1669	999.9	8.39	12.64	2
3	0.76	4.2075	1616	999.9	12.60	12.18	3
4	0.81	4.2059	1565	999.9	16.80	11.75	4
5	0.87	4.2040	1517	999.9	21.01	11.33	5
6	0.93	4.2019	1471	999.9	25.21	10.93	6
7	1.00	4.1997	1427	999.9	29.41	10.55	7
8	1.07	4.1974	1385	999.8	33.61	10.19	8
9	1.15	4.1952	1344	999.7	37.81	9.85	9
10	1.23	4.1930	1306	999.7	42.00	9.52	10
11	1.31	4.1913	1269	999.6	46.19	9.21	11
12	1.40	4.1897	1234	999.4	50.38	8.92	12
13	1.50	4.1883	1201	999.3	54.57	8.64	13
14	1.60	4.1871	1169	999.2	58.75	8.37	14
15	1.70	4.1860	1138	999.0	62.94	8.12	15
16	1.82	4.1852	1108	998.9	67.13	7.88	16
17	1.94	4.1845	1080	998.7	71.31	7.64	17
18	2.06	4.1839	1053	998.6	75.49	7.42	18
19	2.20	4.1834	1027	998.4	79.68	7.20	19
20	2.34	4.1830	1002	998.2	83.86	7.00	20
21	2.49	4.1826	978	997.9	88.04	6.81	21
22	2.64	4.1821	955	997.7	92.23	6.62	22
23	2.81	4.1817	932	997.5	96.41	6.44	23
24	2.98	4.1814	911	997.2	100.59	6.27	24
25	3.17	4.1810	890	997.0	104.77	6.11	25
26	3.36	4.1806	870	996.7	108.95	5.95	26
27	3.56	4.1801	851	996.5	113.13	5.80	27
28	3.78	4.1797	833	996.2	117.31	5.66	28
29	4.00	4.1794	815	995.9	121.49	5.52	29
30	4.24	4.1790	798	995.6	125.67	5.39	30
31	4.49	4.1787	781	995.3	129.85	5.26	31
32	4.75	4.1784	765	995.0	134.03	5.14	32
33	5.01	4.1782	749	994.6	138.20	5.02	33
34	5.32	4.1781	734	994.3	142.38	4.91	34
35	5.62	4.1780	719	994.0	146.56	4.80	35
36	5.94	4.1781	705	993.6	150.74	4.69	36
37	6.27	4.1782	692	993.3	154.92	4.59	37
38	6.62	4.1784	678	993.0	159.09	4.49	38
39	6.99	4.1787	666	992.6	163.27	4.39	39
40	7.38	4.1790	653	992.2	167.45	4.30	40
41	7.78	4.1794	641	991.8	171.63	4.21	41
42	8.20	4.1798	629	991.4	175.81	4.13	42
43	8.64	4.1802	618	991.0	179.99	4.05	43
44	9.10	4.1806	606	990.6	184.17	3.97	44
45	9.58	4.1810	596	990.2	188.35	3.89	45
46	10.09	4.1812	586	989.8	192.53	3.81	46
47	10.61	4.1815	576	989.3	196.71	3.74	47
48	11.16	4.1817	566	988.9	200.90	3.67	48
49	11.74	4.1818	556	988.5	205.08	3.60	49
50	12.33	4.1820	547	988.0	209.26	3.53	50
51	12.96	4.1822	538	987.6	213.44	3.47	51
52	13.61	4.1823	529	987.2	217.62	3.40	52
53	14.29	4.1825	521	986.7	221.81	3.35	53
54	15.00	4.1828	512	986.2	225.99	3.29	54

Table continues

Table C2.2 Properties of water at saturation — *continued*

Temperature t_s / °C	Absolute vapour pressure p_s / kPa	Specific heat capacity c_r / (kJ·kg⁻¹·K⁻¹)	Dynamic viscosity μ_f / (μPa·s)	Density ρ / (kg·m⁻³)	Specific enthalpy of liquid h_f / (kJ·kg⁻¹)	Prandtl number $(Pr)_g$	Temperature t_s / °C
55	15.74	4.1830	504	985.7	230.17	3.23	55
56	16.51	4.1833	496	985.2	234.35	3.17	56
57	17.31	4.1837	489	984.7	238.54	3.12	57
58	18.15	4.1841	481	984.3	242.72	3.06	58
59	19.02	4.1845	474	983.7	246.81	3.01	59
60	19.92	4.1850	467	983.2	251.09	2.96	60
61	20.86	4.1856	460	982.7	255.27	2.91	61
62	21.84	4.1861	453	982.1	259.46	2.87	62
63	22.85	4.1867	447	981.6	263.65	2.82	63
64	23.91	4.1874	440	981.1	267.83	2.78	64
65	25.01	4.1880	434	980.5	272.02	2.74	65
66	26.15	4.1886	428	979.9	276.21	2.70	66
67	27.33	4.1892	422	979.4	280.40	2.66	67
68	28.56	4.1898	416	978.9	284.59	2.62	68
69	29.84	4.1904	410	978.3	288.78	2.58	69
70	31.16	4.1910	404	977.7	292.97	2.54	70
71	32.53	4.1916	399	977.1	297.16	2.50	71
72	33.96	4.1921	394	976.6	301.35	2.47	72
73	35.43	4.1927	388	976.0	305.54	2.43	73
74	36.96	4.1934	383	975.4	309.74	2.39	74
75	38.55	4.1940	378	974.9	313.93	2.36	75
76	40.19	4.1947	373	974.3	318.12	2.33	76
77	41.89	4.1955	369	973.6	322.32	2.30	77
78	43.65	4.1962	364	973.1	326.52	2.27	78
79	45.47	4.1971	359	972.5	330.71	2.24	79
80	47.36	4.1980	355	971.8	334.91	2.21	80
81	49.31	4.1990	350	971.2	339.11	2.18	81
82	51.33	4.1999	346	970.6	343.31	2.15	82
83	53.42	4.2009	342	969.9	347.51	2.12	83
84	55.57	4.2020	338	969.3	351.71	2.10	84
85	57.80	4.2030	334	968.6	355.91	2.07	85
86	60.11	4.2040	330	968.0	360.11	2.05	86
87	62.49	4.2050	326	967.3	364.32	2.02	87
88	64.95	4.2060	322	966.7	368.52	2.00	88
89	67.49	4.2070	318	966.0	372.73	1.97	89
90	70.11	4.2080	314	965.3	376.94	1.95	90
91	72.82	4.2090	311	964.7	381.15	1.93	91
92	75.61	4.2099	307	964.0	385.36	1.90	92
93	78.49	4.2109	304	963.3	389.57	1.88	93
94	81.46	4.2120	300	962.7	393.78	1.85	94
95	84.53	4.2130	297	961.9	397.99	1.83	95
96	87.69	4.2141	294	961.2	402.30	1.81	96
97	90.94	4.2153	291	960.5	406.42	1.79	97
98	94.30	4.2165	287	959.8	410.63	1.77	98
99	97.76	4.2177	284	959.1	414.84	1.76	99
100	101.33	4.2190	281	958.3	419.06	1.74	100
102	108.78	4.2217	275	956.9	427.50	1.70	102
104	116.68	4.2246	269	955.5	435.95	1.67	104
106	125.04	4.2274	264	954.0	444.40	1.63	106
108	133.90	4.2302	259	952.6	452.86	1.60	108
110	143.26	4.2330	253	951.0	461.32	1.57	110
112	153.16	4.2357	248	949.5	469.79	1.54	112
114	163.61	4.2386	243	948.0	478.26	1.51	114
116	174.64	4.2414	239	946.3	486.74	1.48	116
118	186.28	4.2445	234	944.7	495.20	1.45	118

Table continues

Table C2.2 Properties of water at saturation — *continued*

Temperature t_s / °C	Absolute vapour pressure p_s / kPa	Specific heat capacity c_r / (kJ·kg⁻¹·K⁻¹)	Dynamic viscosity μ_f / (μPa·s)	Density ρ / (kg·m⁻³)	Specific enthalpy of liquid h_f / (kJ·kg⁻¹)	Prandtl number $(Pr)_g$	Temperature t_s / °C
120	198.53	4.2480	230	943.1	503.70	1.42	120
122	211.44	4.2527	226	941.5	512.20	1.40	122
124	225.03	4.2576	223	939.9	520.70	1.38	124
126	239.32	4.2621	219	938.3	529.20	1.36	126
128	254.34	4.2661	216	936.5	537.80	1.34	128
130	270.12	4.2700	212	934.8	546.30	1.32	130
132	286.68	4.2740	209	933.1	554.90	1.30	132
134	304.05	4.2780	206	931.4	563.40	1.28	134
136	322.27	4.2820	202	929.6	572.00	1.26	136
138	341.36	4.2860	199	927.9	580.50	1.25	138
140	361.36	4.2900	196	926.1	589.10	1.23	140
142	382.28	4.2934	193	924.3	597.70	1.21	142
144	404.18	4.2975	191	922.5	606.30	1.20	144
146	427.07	4.3029	189	920.6	614.90	1.18	146
148	450.99	4.3102	187	918.8	623.50	1.17	148
150	475.97	4.3200	185	916.9	632.20	1.17	150
152	502.05	4.3250	183	915.1	640.80	1.16	152
154	529.26	4.3320	181	913.2	649.40	1.15	154
156	557.64	4.3380	178	911.2	658.10	1.13	156
158	587.23	4.3440	176	909.3	666.80	1.12	158
160	618.05	4.3500	174	907.4	675.50	1.11	160
162	650.14	4.3557	172	905.4	684.20	1.10	162
164	683.55	4.3614	170	903.4	692.90	1.09	164
166	718.31	4.3674	167	901.5	701.60	1.07	166
168	754.45	4.3735	165	899.4	710.40	1.06	168
170	792.03	4.3800	163	897.3	719.1	1.05	170
172	831.07	4.3875	161	895.3	727.9	1.04	172
174	871.61	4.3954	159	893.3	736.7	1.03	174
176	913.71	4.4034	157	891.2	745.5	1.02	176
178	957.39	4.4117	155	889.1	754.3	1.01	178
180	1002.7	4.4200	153	886.9	763.1	1.00	180
182	1049.7	4.4277	151	884.8	772.0	0.99	182
184	1098.4	4.4354	150	882.6	780.8	0.99	184
186	1148.9	4.4434	148	880.4	789.7	0.98	186
188	1201.1	4.4515	146	879.7	798.6	0.98	188
190	1255.2	4.4600	145	876.0	807.5	0.97	190
192	1311.2	4.4695	144	873.8	816.4	0.96	192
194	1369.2	4.4794	142	781.5	825.4	0.96	194
196	1429.1	4.4894	141	869.3	834.4	0.95	196
198	1491.0	4.4997	139	867.0	843.4	0.95	198
200	1555.1	4.5100	138	864.7	852.4	0.94	200
205	1724.5	4.5337	134	858.8	875.0	0.92	205
210	1908.0	4.5600	131	852.8	897.7	0.91	210
215	2106.3	4.5937	128	846.6	920.6	0.90	215
220	2320.1	4.6300	125	840.3	943.7	0.90	220
225	2550.4	4.6644	122	833.9	966.9	0.90	225
230	2797.0	4.7000	120	827.3	990.3	0.89	230
235	3063.5	4.7387	118	820.6	1013.8	0.89	235
240	3348.0	4.7800	115	813.6	1037.6	0.88	240
245	3652.4	4.8231	112	806.5	1061.6	0.87	245
250	3977.6	4.8700	110	799.2	1085.8	0.87	250

Table C2.3 Enthalpy of superheated steam

Absolute pressure p / kPa	Saturation temperature t_s / °C	Enthalpy of superheated steam / kJ·kg^{-1} for stated final steam temperature / °C															
		100	120	140	160	180	200	220	240	260	280	300	320	340	360	380	400
100	99.6	2676	2717	2757	2797	2836	2876	2915	2955	2995	3034	3075	3115	3155	3196	3237	3278
120	104.8		2715	2755	2796	2835	2875	2914	2954	2994	3034	3074	3114	3155	3196	3237	3278
140	109.3		2713	2754	2794	2834	2874	2914	2953	2993	3033	3074	3114	3155	3195	3236	3278
160	113.3		2711	2752	2793	2833	2873	2913	2953	2993	3033	3073	3114	3154	3195	3236	3277
180	116.9		2708	2751	2792	2832	2872	2912	2952	2992	3032	3073	3113	3154	3195	3236	3277
200	120.2			2749	2790	2831	2871	2911	2951	2992	3032	3072	3113	3153	3194	3235	3277
220	123.3			2747	2789	2830	2870	2911	2951	2991	3031	3072	3112	3153	3194	3235	3276
240	126.1			2745	2787	2829	2969	2910	2950	2990	3031	3071	3112	3153	3194	3235	3276
260	128.7			2743	2786	2827	2868	2909	2949	2990	3030	3071	3111	3152	3193	3234	3276
280	131.2			2742	2785	2826	2867	2908	2949	2989	3030	3070	3111	3152	3193	3234	3275
300	133.5			2740	2783	2825	2866	2907	2948	2988	3029	3070	3110	3151	3192	3234	3275
340	137.9			2736	2780	2823	2865	2906	2947	2987	3028	3069	3110	3151	3192	3233	3274
380	141.8				2777	2820	2863	2904	2945	2986	3027	3068	3109	3150	3191	3232	3274
420	145.4				2774	2818	2861	2902	2944	2985	3026	3067	3108	3149	3190	3232	3273
460	148.7				2771	2816	2859	2901	2942	2984	3025	3066	3107	3148	3189	3231	3273
500	151.8				2768	2813	2857	2899	2941	2982	3024	3065	3106	3147	3189	3230	3272
600	158.8				2759	2807	2851	2895	2937	2979	3021	3062	3104	3145	3187	3229	3270
700	165.0					2800	2846	2890	2933	2976	3018	3060	3102	3143	3185	3227	3269
800	170.4					2793	2840	2886	2930	2973	3015	3057	3099	3141	3183	3225	3267
900	175.4					2785	2835	2881	2926	2969	3012	3055	3097	3139	3181	3223	3266
1000	179.9					2778	2829	2876	2922	2966	3009	3052	3095	3137	3179	3222	3264
1200	188.0						2817	2867	2914	2959	3003	3047	3090	3133	3176	3218	3261
1400	195.0						2803	2856	2905	2952	2997	3042	3085	3129	3172	3215	3257
1600	201.4							2846	2897	2945	2991	3036	3081	3124	3168	3211	3254
1800	207.1							2834	2888	2937	2985	3031	3076	3120	3164	3207	3251
2000	212.4							2822	2878	2930	2978	3025	3071	3116	3160	3204	3248
2500	223.9								2853	2909	2961	3011	3058	3105	3150	3195	3239
3000	233.8								2825	2888	2943	2995	3045	3093	3140	3185	3231
3500	242.5									2864	2925	2980	3031	3081	3129	3176	3222
4000	250.3									2838	2904	2963	3017	3069	3118	3166	3214
4500	257.4									2809	2883	2946	3003	3056	3107	3156	3205
5000	263.9										2859	2927	2988	3043	3096	3146	3196
6000	275.6										2806	2887	2955	3016	3072	3126	3177
7000	285.8											2841	2919	2987	3048	3104	3158
8000	295.0											2787	2880	2955	3021	3082	3139
9000	303.3												2835	2921	2993	3058	3118
10000	311.0												2784	2884	2964	3033	3097

C3 Heat transfer

C3.2 Heat transfer principles

The mechanisms of heat transfer are convection, conduction, radiation and mass transfer.

C3.2.1 Convection

Convection is a mode of heat transfer between a moving fluid and a solid, liquid or gas. Convection can be free or forced. Many complications can arise due to the following reasons:

(a) The flow can be laminar (having smooth and orderly streamlines) or turbulent (having irregularly interwoven streamlines) or separated (having a reversed flow along the fluid boundary, as with cylinders in cross flow with vortex shedding). There is a transitional state between laminar and turbulent flow.

(b) There is a boundary layer between the fluid and the other medium.

(c) At the base of the boundary layer the fluid is stationary with respect to the other medium. This means that there is a thin layer in which only conduction and mass transfer can take place.

(d) For heat to be transferred within any substance, a temperature gradient must exist. In a fluid, therefore, there are density gradients which cause buoyancy forces.

Convection can be free (primarily due to buoyancy forces) or forced (due to mechanical means).

C3.2.1.1 Free convection over surfaces

Table C3.2 presents correlations for the average Nu number for free convection over various geometries for a range of Ra numbers. The appropriate characteristic length is also given. The flow regime is determined by

Table C3.2 Empirical correlations for the average Nusselt number for free convection over surfaces (adapted from *Introduction to Thermodynamics and Heat Transfer* by Y A Cengel (1997) by permission of The McGraw-Hill Companies)

Geometry	Characteristic length	Ra range	Nusselt number, Nu	
Vertical plate	D	10^4–10^9 10^9–10^{13}	$Nu = 0.59\,Ra^{1/4}$ $Nu = 0.1\,Ra^{1/3}$	(3.1) (3.2)
		Entire range	$Nu = \left(0.825 + \dfrac{0.387\,Ra^{1/6}}{[1 + (0.492\,/\,Pr)^{9/16}]^{8/27}} \right)^2$ (complex but more accurate)	(3.3)
Inclined plate	D		Use vertical plate equations as a first degree of approximation Replace g with $g \cos\theta$ in the formula for Gr, see page 3-1, for $Ra < 10^9$	
Horizontal plate (surface area = A and perimeter = P)	A/P			
(a) Upper surface of a hot plate or lower surface of a cold plate		10^4–10^7 10^7–10^{11}	$Nu = 0.54\,Ra^{1/4}$ $Nu = 0.15\,Ra^{1/3}$	(3.4) (3.5)
(b) Lower surface of a hot plate or upper surface of a cold plate		10^5–10^{11}	$Nu = 0.27\,Ra^{1/4}$	(3.6)
Vertical cylinder	D		A vertical cylinder can be treated as a vertical plate when: $d \geq \dfrac{35\,D}{Gr^{1/4}}$	(3.7)
Horizontal cylinder	d	10^5–10^{12}	$Nu = \left(0.6 + \dfrac{0.387\,Ra^{1/6}}{[1 + (0.559\,/\,Pr)^{9/16}]^{8/27}} \right)^2$	(3.8)
Sphere	$\pi\,d/2$	$Ra \leq 10^{11}$ $Pr \geq 0.7$	$Nu = 2 + \dfrac{0.589\,Ra^{1/4}}{[1 + (0.469\,/\,Pr)^{9/16}]^{4/9}}$	(3.9)

calculating the Ra number for a particular situation; note that the power of the Ra number is usually 0.25 for laminar flow and 0.33 for turbulent flow. All fluid properties are evaluated at the average of the surface temperature (θ_s) and the free stream fluid temperature (θ_f).

Further information is given in Guide C section 3.2, including empirical correlations for free convection inside enclosures and forced convection over circular and non-circular cylinders.

C3.2.2   Conduction

Conduction is the transfer of heat within substances from positions of higher temperature to positions of lower temperature. Within all substances, except metals, conduction is primarily due to molecular movements although internal radiation can be significant. Within metals, most heat is transferred by free electrons.

Complications arise when heat is conducted through porous materials; this is because they are rarely dry, so that there are transient periods at the end and beginning of heat transfer during which moisture is also transferred. Eventually, equilibrium states are reached, though sometimes only after many months. CIBSE Guide A chapter 3 deals with the problem of moisture content in more detail.

C3.2.3   Radiation

Radiation, in the context of heating, is the emission, from a source, of electromagnetic waves having wavelengths between those of visible light and those of radio waves. Radiation heat transfer is governed by the Stefan-Boltzmann law for black bodies which can be written:

$$\phi = \sigma T^4 \tag{3.56}$$

where ϕ is the heat exchange per unit area (W·m^{-2}), σ is the Stefan-Boltzmann constant (5.67×10^{-8}) (W·m^{-2}·K^{-4}) and T is the absolute temperature (K).

A black body is defined as one which absorbs totally all radiation falling onto its surface. A grey body has a surface which absorbs all wavelengths equally but does not absorb all the radiation. Emissivity is defined as the ratio of the total emissive power of a body to the total emissive power of a black body at the same temperature. Some values of emissivity are given in Tables 3.7, 3.8 and 3.9.

C3.2.4   Mass transfer

Mass transfer can be described as the diffusion of one substance into another. Most commonly, a liquid vapourises into, or condenses from, a gas with an accompanying variation of vapour concentration, i.e. partial pressure, within the gas. This variation occurs within a boundary layer.

In buildings and building services systems, the most common examples of mass transfer are condensation, humidification and evaporation. These examples can all take place within air conditioning equipment and cooling towers but the first and last examples often occur within structures, such as during the drying out period of buildings and condensation on walls and windows. For

these examples, the previous heat transfer equations are not applicable.

Calculations for most mass transfer problems are quite complex although generally the equations follow the form of the convection heat transfer equations.

C3.3   Heat transfer practice

C3.3.1   External environment

At the external surfaces of buildings, heat transfer takes place via the processes of convection and radiation. While radiation heat loss is a function of surface temperature and emissivity, convection heat loss is more complex, being a function of a number of variables such as wind speed and direction, flow regime and surface roughness. This makes difficult the accurate determination of heat transfer at a building surface.

Further information is given in Guide C section 3.3.

C3.3.4   Equipment and components

C3.3.4.3   Insulated pipes

If the external surface temperature of insulation concentric to a pipe is known, then the theoretical heat emission may be calculated in the same way as for an exposed pipe. In practice, however, it is the surface temperature of the pipe itself which can be more readily ascertained so that an equation relating the temperature difference between this and ambient air is more useful. The main variables are the thermal conductivity of the insulation material, its thickness and the nature of the final surface finish. The data are, therefore, given per unit area of pipe.

The heat exchange from insulated pipes is given by:

$$\phi = U\,(\theta_s - \theta_a) \tag{3.109}$$

or, more conveniently, per metre run of pipe by:

$$\Phi / l = \pi\,d_{op}\,(\theta_s - \theta_a) \tag{3.110}$$

where ϕ is the heat exchange per unit area (W·m^{-2}), U is the overall thermal transmittance (W·m^{-2}·K^{-1}), θ_s is the surface temperature (°C), θ_a is the air temperature (°C), Φ / l is the heat exchange per unit length of pipe (W·m^{-1}) and d_{op} is the outside diameter of the pipe (m).

The overall thermal transmittance is given by:

$$U = \cfrac{1}{R_n + \cfrac{d_{op}}{h_{so}\,d_{on}}} \tag{3.111}$$

where U is the overall thermal transmittance (W·m^{-2}·K^{-1}) R_n is the thermal resistance of the insulation (m^2·K·W^{-1}), d_{on} is the outside diameter of insulation (m) and h_{so} is the outside surface heat transfer coefficient (or film coefficient) (W·m^{-2}·K^{-1}).

Table C3.7 Absorptivity and emissivity: impermeable materials

Material	Condition (where known)	Absorptivity	Emissivity
Aluminium	Polished	0.10–0.40	0.03–0.06
	Dull/rough polish	0.40–0.65	0.18–0.30
	Anodised	—	0.72
Aluminium surfaced roofing		—	0.216
Asphalt	Newly laid	0.91–0.93	—
	Weathered	0.82–0.89	—
	Block	0.85–0.98	0.90–0.98
Asphalt pavement		0.852–0.928	—
Bitumen/felt roofing		0.86–0.89	0.91
Bitumen pavement		0.86–0.89	0.90–0.98
Brass	Polished	0.30–0.50	0.03–0.05
	Dull	0.40–0.065	0.20–0.30
	Anodised	—	0.59–0.61
Bronze		0.34	—
Copper	Polished	0.18–0.50	0.02–0.05
	Dull	0.40–0.065	0.20–0.30
	Anodised	0.64	0.60
Glass	Normal	★	0.88
	Hemispherical	★	0.84
Iron	Unoxidised	—	0.05
	Bright/polished	0.40–0.65	0.20–0.377
	Oxidised	—	0.736–0.74
	Red rusted	—	0.61–0.65
	Heavily rusted	0.737	0.85–0.94
Iron, cast	Unoxidised/polished	—	0.21–0.24
	Oxidised	—	0.64–0.78
	Strongly oxidised	—	0.95
Iron, galvanised	New	0.64–0.66	0.22–0.28
	Old/very dirty	0.89–0.92	0.89
Lead	Unoxidised	—	0.05–0.075
	Old/oxidised	0.77–0.79	0.28–0.281
Rubber	Hard/glossy	—	0.945
	Grey/rough	—	0.859
Steel	Unoxidised/polished/stainless	0.20	0.074–0.097
	Oxidised	0.20	0.79–0.82
Tin	Highly polished/unoxidised	0.10–0.40	0.043–0.084
Paint:			
— aluminium		0.30–0.55	0.27–0.67
— zinc		0.30	0.95
Polyvinylchloride (pvc)		—	0.90–0.92
Tile	Light colour	0.3–0.5	0.85–0.95
Varnish		—	0.80–0.98
Zinc	Polished	0.55	0.045–0.053
	Oxidised	0.05	0.11–0.25

★ See manufacturers' data

The thermal resistance of the insulation is given by:

$$R = \frac{d_{op}}{2\,\lambda_n} \ln\left(\frac{d_{on}}{d_{op}}\right) \qquad (3.112)$$

where R is the thermal resistance ($\mathrm{m^2 \cdot K \cdot W^{-1}}$) and λ_n is the thermal conductivity of the insulation ($\mathrm{W \cdot m^{-1} \cdot K^{-1}}$).

(a) Thicknesses of insulation

Minimum thicknesses of insulation for the prevention of freezing or condensation are given in BS 5422 for a range of applications and conditions.

In some circumstances it is important to relate the thickness of insulation to the financial cost involved. Methods for calculating these costs and hence determining the economic thickness of insulation are given in BS 5422. The economic thickness is defined in BS 5422 as the thickness of insulation that gives a minimum total cost over a chosen evaluation period.

The costs to be considered are:

— the cost of heat lost from the insulated surfaces during the evaluation period

— the cost of the insulation system during the evaluation period.

Table C3.8 Absorptivity and emissivity: inorganic, porous materials

Material	Condition (where known)	Absorptivity	Emissivity
Asbestos:			
— board	—		0.96
— paper	—		0.93–0.94
— cloth	—		0.90
— cement	New	0.61	0.95–0.96
	Very dirty	0.83	0.95–0.96
Brick	Glazed/light	0.25–0.36	0.85–0.95
	Light	0.36–0.62	0.85–0.95
	Dark	0.63–0.89	0.85–0.95
Cement mortar, screed		0.73	0.93
Clay tiles	Red, brown	0.60–0.69	0.85–0.95
	Purple/dark	0.81–0.82	0.85–0.95
Concrete		0.65–0.80	0.85–0.95
— tile		0.65–0.80	0.85–0.95
— block		0.56–0.69	0.94
Plaster		0.30–0.50	0.91
Stone:			
— granite (red)		0.55	0.90–0.93
— limestone		0.33–0.53	0.90–0.93
— marble		0.44–0.592	0.90–0.93
— quartz		—	0.90
— sandstone		0.54–0.76	0.90–0.93
— slate		0.79–0.93	0.85–0.98

Table C3.9 Absorptivity and emissivity: hygroscopic materials

Material	Condition (where known)	Absorptivity	Emissivity
Paper	—		0.091–0.94
— white, bond		0.25–0.28	—
Cloth:			
— cotton, black		0.67–0.98	—
— cotton, deep blue		0.82–0.83	—
— cotton, red		0.562	—
— wool, black		0.75–0.88	—
— felt, black		0.775–0.861	—
— fabric (unspecified)		—	0.89–0.92
Wood:			
— beach		—	0.94
— oak		—	0.89–0.90
— spruce		—	0.82
— walnut		—	0.83

(b) Temperature changes in insulated pipes

In a piping system, the heat gains or losses of the fluid can be significant, especially when passing through an untreated space. The temperature change in the fluid passing through a pipe is given by:

$$\Delta\theta = \theta_u - \theta_d = \frac{\theta_u - \theta_a}{0.5 + f} \qquad (3.115)$$

where $\Delta\theta$ is the temperature change (K), θ_u is the temperature at the upstream end of pipe or duct section (°C) and θ_d is the temperature at down stream end of pipe or duct section (°C).

The function f is given by:

$$f = \frac{M c_p \times 10^3}{\pi l d_{op} U} \qquad (3.116)$$

where M is the mass flow rate (kg·s^{-1}), c_p is the specific heat capacity at constant pressure (kJ·kg^{-1}·K^{-1}), l is the length of pipe (m), d_{op} is the outside diameter of the pipe (m) and U is the overall thermal transmittance (W·m^{-2}·K^{-1}).

For water, c_p = 4.19 kJ·kg^{-1}·K^{-1} and the loss per metre run is approximately:

$$\Delta\theta_m = \frac{U(\theta_u - \theta_a) d_{op}}{1330 M} \qquad (3.117)$$

Equation 3.117 is illustrated in Figure C3.9 for various values of overall transmittance. The *U*-values for various thermal conductivities, thicknesses of insulation and pipe sizes may be found by dividing the values in Table C3.26 by πd_{op} or by using equation 3.111.

C3.3.4.4   *Buried pipes*

The heat emission from underground piping, whether buried in ducts, pressure-tight casings, insulating materials *in situ* or laid directly in the earth, varies from that of the insulated pipe exposed freely to ambient air; this is the result of the additional insulating effect of the air gap within the duct or outer pipe, where present, and that of the earth cover. Equation 3.110 may be adapted to each of these cases with sufficient accuracy for practical purposes, bearing in mind the thermal resistance of the air gap is not greatly significant and that of the earth cover will vary dependent upon its wetness. BS 4508 describes methods for the determination of heat losses.

The heat loss per metre run of buried pipe is given by the following expression:

$$\Phi / l = \pi d_{op} U (\theta_s + \theta_e) \qquad (3.118)$$

where Φ/l is the heat loss per unit length of pipe (W·m^{-1}), d_{op} is the outside diameter of the pipe (m), U is the overall thermal transmittance (W·m^{-2}·K^{-1}), θ_e is the ground temperature (°C) and θ_s is the surface temperature of the pipe (°C).

The overall thermal transmittance is given by:

$$U = \frac{1}{R_n + R_a + R_e} \qquad (3.119)$$

where R_n is the thermal resistance of the insulation (m^2·K·W^{-1}), R_a is the thermal resistance of the air gap (m^2·K·W^{-1}) and R_e is the thermal resistance of the earth (m^2·K·W^{-1}).

The thermal resistance of the insulation is given by:

$$R_n = \frac{d_{op}}{2 \lambda_n} \ln\left(\frac{d_{on}}{d_{op}}\right) \qquad (3.120)$$

where d_{on} is the outside diameter of insulation (m) and λ_n is the thermal conductivity of the insulation (W·m^{-1}·K^{-1}).

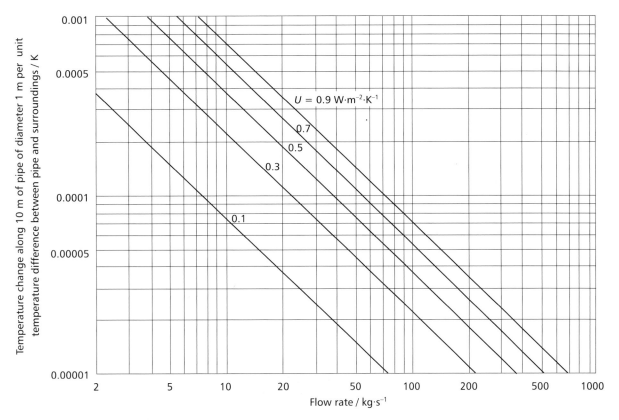

Figure C3.9 Temperature change along insulated pipes in air

Table C3.26 Heat emission or absorption from insulated pipes per unit length and per unit temperature difference

Nominal pipe size	Heat emission or absorption from insulated pipework per unit temperature difference (/ W·m⁻¹ K⁻¹) for stated thermal conductivity of insulation (/ W·m⁻¹ K⁻¹) and thickness of insulation (/ mm)																			
	0.025					0.040					0.055					0.070				
	12.5	19	25	38	50	12.5	19	25	38	50	12.5	19	25	38	50	12.5	19	25	38	50
15	0.18	0.14	0.12	0.10	0.09	0.27	0.22	0.19	0.16	0.14	0.34	0.29	0.25	0.21	0.19	0.41	0.35	0.31	0.27	0.24
20	0.21	0.16	0.14	0.11	0.10	0.31	0.25	0.22	0.18	0.16	0.40	0.33	0.29	0.24	0.21	0.47	0.40	0.36	0.30	0.26
25	0.25	0.19	0.16	0.13	0.11	0.36	0.29	0.25	0.20	0.18	0.47	0.38	0.33	0.27	0.24	0.56	0.46	0.41	0.34	0.30
32	0.29	0.22	0.19	0.15	0.13	0.43	0.34	0.29	0.23	0.20	0.55	0.45	0.39	0.31	0.27	0.66	0.54	0.47	0.38	0.34
40	0.32	0.25	0.21	0.16	0.14	0.48	0.37	0.32	0.25	0.21	0.61	0.49	0.42	0.33	0.29	0.72	0.59	0.52	0.42	0.36
50	0.39	0.29	0.24	0.18	0.16	0.57	0.44	0.37	0.29	0.24	0.73	0.58	0.49	0.39	0.33	0.86	0.70	0.60	0.48	0.41
65	0.47	0.35	0.29	0.22	0.18	0.69	0.55	0.44	0.34	0.28	0.88	0.69	0.58	0.45	0.38	1.04	0.83	0.71	0.56	0.48
80	0.54	0.40	0.33	0.24	0.20	0.79	0.60	0.50	0.38	0.32	1.0	0.78	0.66	0.50	0.43	1.19	0.94	0.80	0.63	0.53
100	0.67	0.49	0.40	0.29	0.24	0.98	0.74	0.61	0.45	0.38	1.25	0.96	0.80	0.61	0.51	1.47	1.16	0.98	0.75	0.63
125	0.81	0.58	0.47	0.34	0.28	1.18	0.88	0.72	0.53	0.44	1.49	1.14	0.95	0.71	0.59	1.76	1.38	1.16	0.88	0.73
150	0.96	0.69	0.55	0.40	0.32	1.37	1.02	0.83	0.61	0.50	1.74	1.32	1.09	0.81	0.67	2.05	1.59	1.33	1.01	0.84
200	1.22	0.88	0.70	0.50	0.40	1.78	1.32	1.07	0.77	0.63	2.26	1.70	1.40	1.03	0.84	2.66	2.05	1.71	1.27	1.05
250	1.50	1.07	0.86	0.60	0.48	2.19	1.61	1.30	0.94	0.75	2.77	2.09	1.71	1.25	1.01	3.27	2.51	2.08	1.54	1.26
300	1.77	1.26	1.00	0.70	0.56	2.58	1.89	1.52	1.09	0.87	3.26	2.44	2.00	1.45	1.17	3.84	2.94	2.48	1.79	1.46

Note: the pipes sizes are to BS EN 10255: 2004 and BS EN 545: 2006. It is assumed that the outside surface of the insulation has been painted, is in still air at 20 °C and h_{so} = 10 W·m⁻²·K⁻¹

The thermal resistance of the air gap is given by:

$$R_a = \frac{d_{op}}{h_{so}\,d_{on}} + \frac{d_{op}}{h_{si}\,d_{ic}} \qquad (3.121)$$

where h_{so} is the outside surface heat transfer coefficient (or film coefficient) (W·m⁻²·K⁻¹), h_{si} is the inside surface heat transfer coefficient (or film coefficient) (W·m⁻²·K⁻¹) and d_{ic} is the inside diameter of the casing (m).

The thermal resistance of the earth cover is given by:

$$R_e = \frac{d_{op}}{2\,\lambda_e} \ln\left(\left(\frac{2\,m}{d_{ic}}\right)\left\{1 + \left[1 - \left(\frac{d_{ic}}{2\,m}\right)^2\right]\right\}\right)^{0.5} \qquad (3.122)$$

where m is the burial depth (m).

C4　Flow of fluids in pipes and ducts

C4.3　Fluid flow in straight pipes and ducts

C4.3.1　General

The D'Arcy equation for pressure loss due to friction may be given as:

$$\Delta p = \lambda \frac{l}{d} \, {}^{1}\!/_{2} \, \rho \, c^2 \qquad (4.1)$$

where Δp is pressure difference (Pa), λ is the friction coefficient, l is the length of duct (m), d is the diameter of the duct (m), ρ is density (kg·m^{-3}) and c is the fluid velocity (m·s^{-1}).

The friction factor, λ, may be obtained mathematically or from the Moody chart, Figure C4.1, and depends upon the values of Reynolds number, Re, and relative roughness.

The Reynolds number is given by:

$$Re = \frac{\rho \, c \, d}{\eta} = \frac{c \, d}{v} \qquad (4.2)$$

where η is the dynamic viscosity (kg·m^{-1}·s^{-1}) and v is the kinematic viscosity (m^2·s^{-1}).

Relative roughness $= k / d$. Values of roughness k are given in Table C4.1.

Values of internal diameters of pipes, d, are given in Tables C4.2, C4.3 and C4.4. For copper pipes (Table 4.3), the sizes listed are the preferred sizes given in BS EN 1057: 2006. Although manufacturers may not as yet supply the entire range, they may be manufacturing other sizes as a transitional arrangement. CEN has defined the recommended dimensions as a first step towards rationalisation. It is aiming for not more than three wall thicknesses for any diameter, and to have a restricted number of diameters. Three categories of pipe are given: R220 (annealed), R250 (half hard) and R290 (hard). Specification involves two numbers: e.g. 28 × 1.2 means that the outside diameter is 28 mm and the wall thickness is 1.2 mm.

For pipes of PVC-U, grey Imperial (inch) pipes are still available. The internal diameters given in Table 4.4 were obtained from Annex B of BS EN 1452-2: 1999.

Values of ρ, η, and v for some fluids are given in Appendix 4.A1.

C4.3.2　Laminar flow

Laminar flow occurs for values of Reynolds number less than 2000. This is most unlikely to occur for water flow or air flow, but is very likely for more viscous fluids such as oil. Rather than use Figure C4.1, the value of λ is more easily obtained from the Poisseuille equation:

For $Re < 2000$:

$$\lambda = \frac{64}{Re} \qquad (4.3)$$

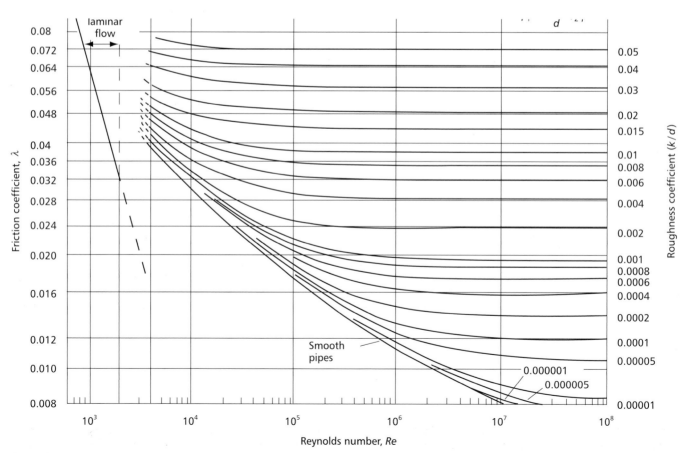

Figure C4.1 Moody chart: variation of friction coefficient (λ) with Reynolds number (Re) and relative roughness (k / d)

Table C4.1 Values of equivalent roughness, k, for various pipe and duct materials

Type of material	Condition	Roughness, k / mm	Source
Seamless copper, brass, lead	Commercially smooth	0.0015–0.0100	Idelchik
Cast iron	New	0.25–1.00	Idelchik
	Corroded	1.00–1.25	Idelchik
	With appreciable deposits	2.0–4.0	Idelchik
	Heavily corroded	up to 3.0	Idelchik
Steel pipe, seamless	New	0.02–0.10	Idelchik
	Old but cleaned	0.04	Idelchik
	Moderately corroded	0.4	Idelchik
	Water pipelines, used	1.2–1.5	Idelchik
	Encrusted	0.8–0.9	Lamont
	Poor condition	> 5.0	Idelchik
Steel pipe, welded	New	0.04–1.0	Idelchik
	With small deposits	1.5	Idelchik
	With appreciable deposits	2.0–4.0	Idelchik
	Poor condition	> 5.0	Idelchik
Steel pipe, galvanised	Bright galvanisation, new	0.07–0.10	Idelchik
	Ordinary galvanisation	0.10–0.15	Idelchik
Steel duct, galvanised	Longitudinal seams	0.05–0.10	ASHRAE
	Spiral seams	0.06–0.12	ASHRAE
Coated steel	Glass enamel	0.001–0.01	Idelchik
	Asphalt	0.12–0.30	Idelchik
Glass		0.0015–0.010	Idelchik
Brick	Fair-faced brickwork	1.5–7.5	Schneider
	Rough	3.5–40	Schneider
Plaster	New	0.05–0.15	Idelchik
Concrete pipes	New	0.25–0.34	Idelchik
	Carefully smoothed	0.5	Idelchik
	Brushed, air-placed	2.3	Idelchik
	Non-smoothed, air-placed	3.0–6.0	Idelchik
Polymers:			
— PVC-U	New	0.0015–0.010*	Schneider
— poly-butylene (PB)		0.0015–0.010	Schneider
— poly-ethylene (PE-X)		0.0015–0.010	Schneider
— ABS		0.007*	
Aluminium		0.05	ASHRAE
Flexible duct	Fully extended	1.0–4.6	ASHRAE
Fibrous glass duct	Spray coated	4.5	ASHRAE
Rock tunnels	Blast-hewed, little jointing	100–140	Idelchik
	Roughly cut, highly uneven surface	500–1500	Idelchik

* No original source has been found for the surface roughness of PVC-U or ABS, their values being generally assumed to be identical to that of PB and PE-X. The values of $k = 0.007$ mm quoted above are merely those used by manufacturers in their calculations of pressure drop. In this range, the surface is so 'smooth' that the value chosen has little effect on the pressure drop calculation.

With increasing velocity, Re increases and λ is seen to decrease. Nevertheless when substituted into equation 4.1, it will be found that the pressure drop increases with increasing velocity. With laminar flow, the pressure drop is directly proportional to velocity. This type of flow sometimes occurs for air passing through HEPA filters where the air passageways are particularly small, and with liquids of high viscosity.

Surface roughness of the duct or pipe is found to have no effect.

C4.3.3   Turbulent flow

This occurs for values of Re greater than 3000. Since air flow in ducts is more likely to have a Reynolds number in the region of 100 000 (i.e. 10^5), it is clear that air flow is almost invariably turbulent. Water flow is also likely to be turbulent.

It will be seen from Figure 4.1 that the friction coefficient depends upon values of both Reynolds number and relative roughness, k/d. The family of curves on the chart was generated from the following equation, developed by Colebrook–White, which may be used directly instead of using the chart:

$$\frac{1}{\sqrt{\lambda}} = -2 \log \left(\frac{2.51}{Re \sqrt{\lambda}} + \frac{k/d}{3.7} \right) \tag{4.4}$$

Note that the square of the above equation might appear more elegant, but the essential negative sign would thereby be lost. It is $\sqrt{\lambda}$ that is needed for the iteration.

Table C4.2 Internal diameters of steel and iron pipes

Nominal pipe size	Non-alloy steel (BS EN 10255)			Ductile iron (BS EN 545)			Seamless and welded steel 'Series 1' (BS EN 10220)*		
	Specified outside diameter / mm	Inside diameter / mm		Nominal outside diameter / mm	Inside diameter / mm		Outside diameter / mm	Wall thickness / mm	Inside diameter / mm
		'Medium'	'Heavy'		'Class 40'	'Type K9'			
6	10.2	6.2	5.0	—	—	—	10.2	1.4	7.4
8	13.5	9.0	7.8	—	—	—	13.5	1.6	10.3
10	17.2	12.5	11.3	—	—	—	17.2	1.8	13.6
15	21.3	16.2	15.0	—	—	—	21.3	2.0	17.3
20	26.9	21.7	20.5	—	—	—	26.9	2.3	29.1
25	33.7	27.4	25.8	—	—	—	33.7	2.3	22.3
32	42.4	36.1	34.5	—	—	—	42.4	2.3	37.8
40	48.3	42.0	40.4	56	46.4	44.0	48.3	2.6	43.1
50	60.3	53.1	51.3	66	56.4	54.0	60.3	2.6	55.1
60	—	—	—	77	67.4	65.0	76.1	2.6	70.9
65	76.1	68.8	67.0	82	72.4	70.0	—	—	—
80	88.9	80.8	78.8	98	88.4	86.0	88.9	2.6	83.7
100	114.3	105.1	103.3	118	108.4	106.0	114.3	2.9	108.5
125	139.7	129.7	128.9	144	134.4	132.0	139.7	3.2	133.3
150	165.1	155.2	154.4	170	160.0	158.0	168.3	3.2	161.9
200	—	—	—	222	211.2	209.4	219.1	3.6	211.9
250	—	—	—	274	262.4	260.4	273.0	3.6	265.8
300	—	—	—	326	313.6	311.6	323.9	4.0	315.9
350	—	—	—	378	364.0	362.6	355.6	4.0	347.6
400	—	—	—	429	413.4	412.8	406.4	4.0	398.4
450	—	—	—	480	—	462.8	457.0	4.5	448.0
500	—	—	—	532	—	514.0	508.0	4.5	499.0
600	—	—	—	635	—	615.2	610.0	4.5	601.0
700	—	—	—	738	—	716.4	711.0	5.0	701.0
800	—	—	—	842	—	818.6	813.0	5.0	803.0
900	—	—	—	945	—	919.8	914.0	5.0	904.0
1000	—	—	—	1048	—	1021.0	1016.0	5.0	1006.0
1100	—	—	—	1152	—	1123.2	1067.0	5.4	1056.2
1200	—	—	—	1255	—	1224.4	1118.0	5.4	1107.2
1400	—	—	—	1462	—	1427.8	1219.0	5.4	1208.2
1500	—	—	—	1565	—	1529.0	1422.0	5.6	1410.8
1600	—	—	—	1668	—	1630.2	1626.0	6.3	1613.4
1800	—	—	—	1875	—	1833.6	—	—	—
2000	—	—	—	2082	—	2037.0	—	—	—

* BS EN 10220 quotes such a wide range of possible sizes for large steel pipes that the values given should only be regarded as typical.

Table C4.3 Wall thickness and internal diameters of copper pipes (BS EN 1057) (The pipes tabulated are those marked 'R' in BS EN 1057 but all might not be readily available in the UK.)

Nominal pipe size / mm	Combinations of nominal wall thickness, ε (/ mm), and mean internal diameter, d_i (/ mm)									
	ε	d_i	ε	d_i	ε	d_i	ε	d_i	ε	d_i
6	0.6	4.8	0.8	4.4	1.0	4.0	—	—	—	—
8	0.6	6.8	0.8	6.4	1.0	6.0	—	—	—	—
10	0.6	8.8	0.7	8.6	0.8	8.4	1.0	8.0	—	—
12	0.6	10.8	0.7	10.6	0.8	10.4	1.0	10.0	—	—
15	0.7	13.6	0.8	13.4	1.0	13.0	—	—	—	—
16	1.0	14.0	—	—	—	—	—	—	—	—
18	0.8	16.4	1.0	16.0	—	—	—	—	—	—
22	0.9	20.2	1.0	20.0	1.1	19.8	1.2	19.6	1.5	19.0
28	0.9	26.2	1.0	26.0	1.2	25.6	1.5	25.0	—	—
35	1.0	33.0	1.2	32.6	1.5	32.0	—	—	—	—
42	1.0	40.0	1.2	39.6	1.5	39.0	—	—	—	—
54	1.0	52.0	1.2	51.6	1.5	51.0	2.0	50.0	—	—
66.7	1.2	64.3	2.0	62.7	—	—	—	—	—	—
76.1	1.5	73.1	2.0	72.1	—	—	—	—	—	—
88.9	2.0	84.9	—	—	—	—	—	—	—	—
108	1.5	105	2.5	103	—	—	—	—	—	—
133	1.5	130	3.0	127	—	—	—	—	—	—
159	2.0	155	3.0	153	—	—	—	—	—	—
219	3.0	210	—	—	—	—	—	—	—	—
267	3.0	261	—	—	—	—	—	—	—	—

Table C4.4 Internal diameters of polymer pipes

PVC-U (BS EN 1452-2)

Nom. outside diam. / mm	Nom. internal diameter / mm							
	PN 6	PN 8	PN 10	PN 12.5	PN 16	PN 20	—	—
12	—	—	—	—	—	9.0		
16	—	—	—	—	—	13.0		
20	—	—	—	—	17.0	16.2		
25	—	—	—	22.0	21.2	20.4		
32	—	29.0	28.8	28.2	27.2	26.2		
40	37.0	36.8	36.2	35.2	34.0	32.6		
50	46.8	46.0	45.2	44.0	42.6	40.8		
63	59.0	58.0	57.0	55.4	53.6	51.4		
75	70.4	69.2	67.8	66.0	63.8	61.4		
90	84.4	83.0	81.4	79.2	76.6	73.6		
	PN 6	PN 7.5	PN 8	PN 10	PN 12.5	PN 16	PN 20	PN 25
110	104.6	103.6	103.2	101.6	99.4	96.8	93.8	90.0
125	118.8	117.6	117.2	115.4	113.0	110.2	106.6	102.2
140	133.0	131.8	131.4	129.2	126.6	123.4	119.4	114.6
160	152.0	150.6	150.2	147.6	144.6	141.0	136.4	130.8
180	171.2	169.4	169.0	166.2	162.8	158.6	153.4	147.2
200	190.2	188.2	187.6	184.6	180.8	176.2	170.6	163.6
225	214.0	211.8	211.2	207.8	203.4	198.2	187.8	—
250	237.6	235.4	234.6	230.8	226.2	220.4	213.2	—
280	266.2	263.6	262.8	258.6	253.2	246.8	238.8	—
315	299.6	296.6	295.6	290.8	285.0	277.6	268.6	—
355	337.6	334.2	333.2	327.8	321.2	312.8	302.8	—
400	380.4	376.6	375.4	369.4	361.8	352.6	341.2	—
450	428.0	423.6	422.4	415.6	407.0	396.6	383.8	—
500	475.4	470.8	469.4	461.8	452.2	440.6	426.4	—
560	532.6	527.2	525.6	517.2	506.6	—	—	—
630	599.2	593.2	591.4	581.8	570.0	—	—	—
710	675.2	668.6	666.4	655.6	—	—	—	—
800	760.8	753.4	751.0	738.8	—	—	—	—
900	856.0	847.4	844.8	—	—	—	—	—
1000	951.0	941.6	938.8	—	—	—	—	—

PVC-U (Annex B) (Imperial)

Nom. outside diam. / inch	Nom. internal diameter / mm		
	PN 8	PN 12	PN 15
3/8	—	—	14.2
1/2	—	—	18.0
3/4	—	—	23.0
1	—	—	29.2
1 1/4	—	37.9	36.9
1 1/2	—	43.3	42.1
2	55.4	54.2	52.6
3	81.9	79.7	77.5
4	105.3	102.3	99.7
6	155.1	150.7	146.7
8	203.5	198.5	187.7
10	253.6	247.4	235.6
12	300.9	293.5	277.1
16	377.4	368.4	—
18	424.6	414.4	—
20	471.8	—	—
24	566.2	—	—

PB and PE-X (BS 7291/BS EN 1057)

Nom. outside diam. / mm	Nom. int. diam. / mm
0	6.7
12	8.7
15	11.7
18	14.2
22	17.7
28	22.5
35	28.3

PB and PE-X (BS 7291/BS ISO 4065)

Nom. outside diam. / mm	Nom. int. diam. / mm
10	6.8
12	8.8
16	12.3
20	16.0
25	20.2
32	26.0
PB	
40	32.0
50	40.2
63	50.8
75	60.6
90	72.6
110	88.8

ABS (BS 2782-11 /BS ISO 4065)

Nom. outside diam. / mm	PN	Nom. int. diam. / mm
16	10	13.0
20	10	16.8
25	10	21.2
32	10	27.8
40	10	34.6
50	10	43.2
63	10	54.6
75	10	65.0
90	10	78.0
110	10	95.4
125	10	108.6
140	10	121.4
160	10	139.0
200	10	173.6
225	10	195.4
250	10	217.8
315	8	273.4

Note: PVC-U = unplasticized polyvinyl chloride; PB = polybutene; PE-X = cross-linked polyethylene; ABS = acrylonitrile butadiene styrene

The Colebrook–White equation, (equation 4.4), gives values of λ which are some 2 to 4 per cent greater than others and so can be considered to include a small margin of safety. The Moody chart was constructed using this equation.

Since λ appears on both sides of equation 4.4, values can only be obtained iteratively. Altshul was the first to derive an equation to give λ directly. Since then, Haaland has provided an even more useful equation:

$$\frac{1}{\sqrt{\lambda}} = -1.8 \log \left[\frac{6.9}{Re} + \left(\frac{k/d}{3.71} \right)^{1.11} \right] \qquad (4.5)$$

Relative to the Colebrook-White equation, the Haaland equation gives values which differ by no more than $\pm$ 1.5%. In the light of this, the use of equation 4.5 is recommended.

C4.3.4   Unpredictable flow

In the region $2000 < Re < 3000$ the flow may be laminar or turbulent depending upon upstream conditions. The nature of the flow may even be unstable and oscillate between laminar and turbulent. Applying caution in pressure drop estimates, it would appear prudent to base calculations on turbulent flow in this region.

C4.3.5   Flexible steel-reinforced smooth rubber hoses

As these hoses are usually used under pressure, the internal diameter will extend slightly with pressure. For instance, a nominal internal diameter of 50 mm may extend to 55 mm at a pressure of 150 kPa. If these dimensional changes are known they should be included in the calculation using equation 4.1. Since lengths are not likely to be great, only a few guidance figures are given in Table C4.5, taken from Idelchik at a pressure of 150 kPa.

Table C4.5 Values of λ for flexible rubber hose (from Idelchik)

Nominal diameter / mm	d / mm	λ
25	25	0.051–0.057
32	32.2	0.053–0.066
38	40.5	0.072–0.090
50	55	0.083–0.094
65	67.4	0.085–0.100

C4.3.6   Non-circular ducts

Equation C4.1 needs to be rewritten in terms of hydraulic mean diameter (d_h) instead of diameter; d_h is given by:

$$d_h = \frac{4A}{P} \qquad (4.6)$$

where A is the cross-sectional area (m²) and P is the perimeter of the duct (m). (For a circular duct the hydraulic diameter d_h is equal to the actual diameter d.)

Then:

$$\Delta p = \lambda \frac{l}{d_h} {}^1/_2 \, \rho \, c^2 \qquad (4.7)$$

For airflow through ducts, improved equations for 'equivalent diameter' are given in section C4.8.

C4.4   Components and fittings

C4.4.1   Pressure loss factor, ζ

To obtain the extra pressure loss due to the installation of any fitting, data are generally presented in terms of a pressure loss factor, ζ. The data obtained experimentally are complex but a simplified collection of the data is available in Guide C sections 4.9 and 4.10.

Whether for liquids in pipes, or gases in ducts, the same fundamental equation applies:

$$\Delta p = \zeta \, {}^1/_2 \, \rho \, c^2 \qquad (4.11)$$

In particular it should be noted that where velocity changes occur due either to changes in section or flow splitting in tees, there may be instances where the static pressure increases despite a loss in total pressure due to friction. Δp is always the drop in total pressure:

$$\Delta p = (p_1 + {}^1/_2 \, \rho \, c_1{}^2) - (p_2 + {}^1/_2 \, \rho \, c_2{}^2) \qquad (4.12)$$

C4.4.2   Capacity, K

Most valve manufacturers and damper manufacturers quote the performance of their components in terms of capacity, K, defined in the following relationship:

$$q_v = K \sqrt{\Delta p} \qquad (4.13)$$

K is useful when dealing with the authority of a valve, and in the prediction of flows in complex circuits. Further information is given in Guide C Appendix 4.A3.

C4.5   Water flow in pipes

C4.5.1   Pipe sizing: desirable velocities

There are no rules concerning pipe sizing. The most cost effective will be the design based on life-cycle costing including the pumping costs. The smaller the pipework, the greater the pumping power and energy consumption. Increasing the pipe diameter by one size can have a large effect in decreasing pumping power: smaller friction pressure drops of the basic circuit will require smaller pressure drops through control valves, for the same value of valve authority. The optimum sizing from the point of view of life-cycle costing must consider the length of the system, the capital cost, the mean pressure drop, the running time at full and partial flow, the efficiency of the pump–motor combination, and anticipated electrical tariffs (i.e. 'on-peak' or 'off-peak' operation).

To give a starting point in selecting pipe sizes, rule of thumb water velocities are given in Table C4.6. An alternative starting point might be to consider a typical

Table C4.6 Typical water velocities for pipework (BSRIA)

Situation/diameter	Velocity / m·s⁻¹	Total pressure drop / kPa
Small bore	<1.0	—
Diam. 15 to 50 mm	0.75–1.15	—
Diam. > 50 mm	1.25–3.0	—
Heating/cooling coils	0.5–1.5	28

pressure drop per unit length of 360 Pa·m⁻¹ or 250 Pa·m⁻¹, but this is arbitrary.

C4.5.5 Water expansion

Between a heating system being cold (usually under the 'fill' situation), and warm under the design running condition, the water contained in the system will expand. The expansion, as a percentage, has been calculated with reference to a cold situation of 4 °C using:

$$\frac{\Delta V}{V_4} = \left(\frac{\rho_4}{\rho} - 1 \right) \qquad (4.14)$$

The volumetric expansion of the pipework may be deduced from the volumetric expansion of the water, if desired. Values of the density of water are given in Table C4.7. Pre-calculated values for the expansion of water are given in Table C4.8.

C4.5.7 Pipe-sizing

Earlier editions of CIBSE Guide C provided tables of pressure-loss data for water at two temperatures. Since the much simpler, but still accurate, equation of Haaland (equation 4.5) is now available, pipe sizing can be carried out directly on a simple spreadsheet for any temperature and, indeed, for any fluid. A Microsoft® Excel spreadsheet is provided on the CD-ROM that accompanies CIBSE Guide C. This enables fluid velocities, pressure losses and velocity pressures to be calculated for water and water–glycol mixtures at various temperatures in pipes of various materials and sizes. Pre-calculated pressure-drop tables are therefore no longer needed. However, for the purposes of this Handbook, the spreadsheet has been used to generate pipe sizing tables for water at 10 °C and 75 °C in pipes of various materials. These tables appear herein as Appendix C4.A0 (pages 167 to 194). Note that these tables do not appear in CIBSE Guide C.

It should be noted that, particularly for small pipes, the flow is sometimes in the laminar regime, $Re < 2000$. For $Re > 3000$ the flow is almost invariably turbulent. In the intermediate zone, the flow may be either laminar or turbulent depending upon upstream conditions. Thus in the zone $2000 < Re < 3000$ the pressure drop conditions are impossible to predict.

C4.5.8 Pipework fittings; water flow

The calculation of the extra pressure drop due to components is obtained using equation 4.11 with appropriate values of ζ. Some values of the velocity pressure ($\frac{1}{2} \rho c^2$)

Table C4.7 Properties of water: density, dynamic and kinematic viscosity

Temperature θ / °C	Density ρ / kg·m⁻³	Dynamic viscosity η / 10^{-6} kg·m⁻¹·s⁻¹	Kinematic viscosity v / 10^{-6} m²·s⁻¹
0.001	999.8	1752	1.7524
4	1000.0	1551	1.5510
10	999.7	1300	1.3004
20	999.8	1002	1.0022
30	995.6	797	0.8005
40	992.2	651	0.6561
50	988.0	544	0.5506
60	983.2	463	0.4709
70	977.8	400	0.4091
80	971.8	351	0.3612
90	965.3	311	0.3222
100	958.4	279	0.2911
110	950.6	252	0.2651
120	943.4	230	0.2438
130	934.6	211	0.2258
140	925.9	195	0.2106
150	916.6	181	0.1975
160	907.4	169	0.1862
170	897.7	158	0.1760
180	886.5	149	0.1681
190	875.6	141	0.1610
200	864.3	134	0.1550

Table C4.8 Percentage expansion of water at different temperatures, relative to the volume at 4 °C

Temp. / °C	Expansion / %	Temp. / °C	Expansion / %
40	0.786	130	7.00
50	1.21	140	8.00
60	1.71	150	9.10
70	2.27	160	10.2
80	2.90	170	11.4
90	3.63	180	12.8
100	4.34	190	14.2
110	5.20	200	15.7
120	6.00		

of water are given in Table C4.10, but these are valid only for water at 10 °C.

The values of velocity pressure in Table C4.10 may be corrected for different temperatures by dividing by the density of water at 10 °C (= 999.7 kg·m⁻³) and multiplying by the density at the required temperature.

Values of ζ for pipework given in Guide C sections 4.9 and 4.10. Since the additional pressure drop caused by a fitting is largely due to the internal friction of the fluid suffering an abrupt change of direction, rusting and scaling have traditionally been considered not to have a significant effect on pressure drop. However, for elbows, the values of ζ are found to vary considerably with diameter, which implies that surface effects are significant. An allowance for ageing is therefore needed.

C4.6 Flow of steam in pipes

Due to the considerable variation in steam conditions which may be encountered, and the fact that the steam conditions themselves (notably temperature and pressure) do not remain constant as the steam flows along the pipe, this is a very complex subject. Specialist advice should be sought.

Table C4.10 Velocity pressures, p_v $(= \frac{1}{2} \rho c^2)$, for water at 10 °C

c / m·s^{-1}	p_v / Pa	c / m·s^{-1}	p_v / Pa
0.01	0.049 99	0.85	361.152
0.02	0.199 95	0.9	404.891
0.03	0.449 88	0.95	451.128
0.04	0.799 78	1	499.865
0.05	1.249 66	1.1	604.837
0.06	1.799 51	1.2	719.806
0.07	2.449 34	1.3	844.772
0.08	3.199 14	1.4	979.735
0.09	4.048 91	1.5	1124.69
0.10	4.999	1.6	1279.65
0.15	11.247	1.7	1444.61
0.25	31.242	1.8	1619.56
0.30	44.988	1.9	1804.51
0.35	61.233	2	1999.46
0.40	79.978	2.5	3124.2
0.45	101.223	3	4498.8
0.50	124.966	3.5	6123.3
0.55	151.209	4	7997.8
0.6	179.951	4.5	10 122.3
0.65	211.193	5	12 496.6
0.7	244.934	5.5	15 120.9
0.75	281.174	6	17 995.1
0.8	319.914	6.5	21 119.3

Some property data are is given in Guide C Appendix 4.A4. It should be remembered that density varies with temperature.

C4.7   Natural gas in pipes

In the UK, natural gas consists predominantly of methane. It should be noted that gases are highly compressible and that the density therefore varies considerably with pressure and temperature. Although the viscosity varies little with pressure, that too varies with temperature. Thus pressure drops are therefore best obtained by direct calculation using the method explained in section C4.3. Although section C4.3 assumes incompressible flow (ρ = constant), the method may be used with reasonable accuracy so long as the drop in pressure along the pipe does not exceed 10% of the initial (absolute) inlet pressure.

Some data are given in Guide C Appendix 4.A1. It should be remembered that the density varies considerably with pressure.

C4.8   Air flow in ducts

C4.8.1   Duct sizing: desirable velocities

The smaller the ductwork, the greater the fan power and energy consumption. Increasing the duct size can have a large effect in decreasing fan power: smaller friction pressure drops of the basic circuit will require smaller pressure drops through control dampers, for the same value of control authority thus leading to a further saving. The optimum sizing from the point of view of life-cycle costing must consider the length of the system, the capital cost, the mean pressure drop, the running time at full and partial flow, the efficiency of the fan–motor combination and anticipated electrical tariffs (i.e. 'on-peak', 'off-peak' operation).

To provide a starting point in selecting duct sizes, rule of thumb air velocities are given in Table C4.11. An alternative starting point might be to consider a typical pressure drop per unit length of 1 Pa·m^{-1} for low velocity systems and 8 Pa·m^{-1} for high velocity systems. Typical air velocities for air handling and other components are given in Table C4.12.

Table C4.11 Typical air velocities for ductwork

System type	Velocity / m·s^{-1}	Maximum pressure drop per unit length / Pa·m^{-1}	Total pressure drop / kPa
Low velocity	3–6	1	0.900 (supply) 0.400 (extract)
High velocity	7.5–15	8	1.5–2.0 (supply)

Table C4.12 Typical air velocities (face velocities) for air handling units and other components

Situation	Velocity / m·s^{-1}	Pressure drop / Pa
Heating system	2.5–4 (through face area)	50–125
Cooling system	1.5–2.5 (through face area)	60–180
Inlet louvres	2.5 (through free area)	35 max.
Extract louvres	2.5 (through free area)	60 max.
Filters:		
— flat panel	As duct	—
— pleated	< 3.8	—
— HEPA	1.3	—
— moving curtain viscous	2.5	
— moving curtain dry	1.0	—
— electronic, ionising	0.8–1.8	—

C4.8.2   Noise

The major source of duct-generated noise is caused by the vortices created in diffusers, grilles, fittings and the fan itself. Higher air velocities will create more noise. The ductwork and sharp elbows can have an attenuating effect especially of the higher frequencies. Frequently a noise problem may be due to noise from one zone being able to be propagated to another either via grilles and the ductwork, or by 'break-in' to the ductwork itself or 'break-out'. For detailed consideration, see Guide B chapter 5.

C4.8.3   Pressure drop for circular ducts

The pressure drop per unit length can be calculated for any duct material, and for any air condition using the pressure loss factor λ, as explained in section C4.3.

Repeating the D'Arcy equation for pressure loss due to friction (equation 4.1):

Table C4.13 Some properties of air at a relative humidity of 50% and at a pressure of 1.013 25 bar

Temperature, θ / °C	Density, ρ / kg·m⁻³	Dynamic viscosity, η / 10⁻⁶ kg·m⁻¹·s⁻¹	Specific heat capacity, c_p / kJ·kg⁻¹·K⁻¹
0	1.29	17.15	1.006
5	1.27	17.39	1.009
10	1.24	17.63	1.011
15	1.22	17.88	1.014
20	1.20	18.12	1.018
25	1.18	18.36	1.022
30	1.16	18.55	1.030
35	1.14	18.78	1.039
40	1.11	19.01	1.050

$$\Delta p = \lambda \frac{l}{d} \, \frac{1}{2} \rho c^2 \qquad (4.1)$$

Useful property values for air are given in Table C4.13, and in Guide C Appendix 4.A1.

Note that values of density, being the reciprocal of the specific volume, are best obtained from the psychrometric chart which covers any value of humidity.

The variation of density with pressure can be obtained using a value ρ_0 from Table C4.13 or from the psychrometric chart, and the ideal gas equation:

$$\rho = \rho_0 \left(\frac{p}{1.01325} \right) \qquad (4.15)$$

where p is pressure (bar).

Values of viscosity and specific thermal capacity do not vary significantly with pressure.

C4.8.4 Pre-calculated values of pressure drop for circular ducts

Until recently, the best curve-fit for pressure drop data was the equation of Colebrook-White (equation 4.4), which could only be solved by iteration. To help with duct-sizing, a chart is provided (Figure C4.2), but this is valid only for one condition of air, see (a) below. However, using the Haaland equation (equation 4.5), duct-sizing can be carried out directly on a simple spreadsheet for any temperature and air density. The mathematical steps required for the spreadsheet calculations are given in Guide C Appendix 4.A2, where a worked example is included. A Microsoft® Excel spreadsheet is provided on the CD-ROM that accompanies Guide C. This enables air velocities, pressure losses and velocity pressures to be calculated at various temperatures in various types and sizes of duct.

The chart (Figure C4.2) was produced using values for the appropriate variables as follows:

(a)   air at 20 °C, 101.325 kPa, 43% saturation

(b)   density, $\rho = 1.200$ kg·m⁻³

(c)   viscosity, $\eta = 18.2 \times 10^{-6}$ kg·m⁻¹·s⁻¹

(d)   roughness, $k = 0.15$ mm (longitudinal seams).

Compared with values from equation 4.5 (for $k = 0.075$ mm), the chart gives slightly greater pressure drops, reading +1.5% high, over much of the chart.

For air at a temperature other than 20 °C, the pressure loss read from the chart may be corrected by use of the following expression, where T must be in kelvins:

$$\Delta p = \Delta p_{20} \left(\frac{293}{T} \right)^{0.86} \qquad (4.16)$$

C4.8.6 Ducts of other materials

Using the values for surface roughness given in Table 4.1, and Haaland's equation (equation 4.5) a duct friction factor λ is easily obtained for any material.

C4.8.7 Flexible ductwork

Flexible ductwork has an equivalent roughness which is appreciably more than for galvanised steel ductwork (see Table 4.1). This alone causes a much greater pressure drop. If the flexible duct is not fully extended then, according to ASHRAE, if the length is only 70% of the extended length, the pressure loss can be greater by a factor of 4.

Based on a worst case of roughness $k = 4.6$ mm, and extended to only 70% of full length, Table 4.15 gives the multiplying factor to be applied to the equivalent rigid circular galvanised duct.

Table C4.15 Correction factors to be applied to the pressure drop of a rigid duct (obtained from Figure C4.2) for flexible duct having a roughness of 4.6 mm and extended to only 70% of full length (from ASHRAE)

Velocity, c / m·s⁻¹	Correction factor for flexible duct of stated diameter, d / mm		
	100	200	500
2.5	6.70	7.47	8.3
4.5	7.35	8.05	8.7
6.0	7.66	8.21	8.9

C4.8.8 Non-circular ducts

C4.8.8.1 Direct calculation

For ducts of non-circular cross section, the use of equation 4.1 necessitates the use of a value for a 'diameter' characteristic of the non-circular duct. For this, hydraulic mean diameter has traditionally been used, defined by:

$$d_h = \frac{4A}{P} \qquad (4.17)$$

where A is the cross-sectional area (m²) and P is the perimeter (m²) of the duct. (For a circular duct the hydraulic diameter d_h is equal to the actual diameter d.)

The pressure loss is then given by:

$$\Delta p = \lambda \frac{l}{d_h} \, \frac{1}{2} \rho c^2 \qquad (4.18)$$

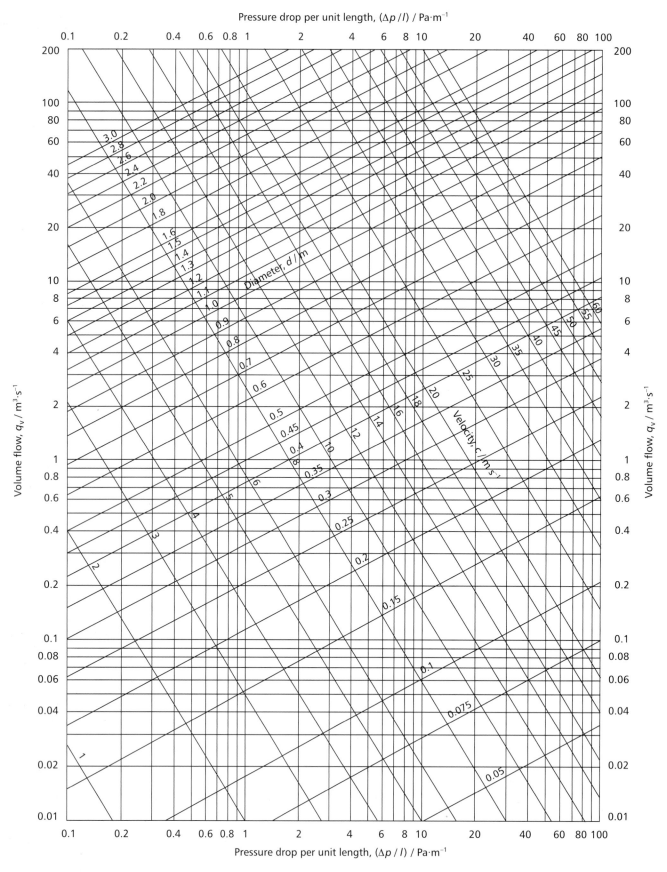

Figure C4.2 Pressure drop for air in galvanised circular ducts ($\rho = 1.2\ \text{kg·m}^{-3}$; $T = 293\ \text{K}$)

To obtain a value of λ, the Haaland equation (4.5) should be used. For this the hydraulic diameter d_h should be used for obtaining relative roughness k/d and Re. The use of equation 4.18 then gives the pressure drop for any condition of air and duct material. A worked example is given in Guide C Appendix 4.A2.2.

The concept of using hydraulic diameter is nevertheless fundamentally flawed. For ductwork having particularly sharp apex angles, it has been shown that the use of equation 4.17 does not give a good correlation.

C4.8.8.2 Manual method using charts and tables

Prior to the use of the Haaland equation, engineers preferred to use pre-calculated tables or charts to obtain the pressure drop along a duct, even though these were for only one condition of air, one ductwork material, and only for circular ducts. To enable the use of these charts for non-circular ducts, the concept of an 'equivalent diameter' (d_e) was conceived, relating to an equivalent circular duct. The most convenient form of equivalent diameter is that which will give the same pressure drop per unit length and for the same volume flow.

When hydraulic diameter is used in conjunction with equation 4.18 to determine a circular equivalent for a non-circular duct, to give the same pressure drop for the same volume flow, the following equation is easily derived:

$$d_e = 1.453 \frac{A^{0.6}}{P^{0.2}} \qquad (4.19)$$

Once the equivalent diameter has been obtained, using equation 4.19, it may be used in conjunction with pre-calculated tables for a circular duct, or with Figure 4.2. Care must be taken to use such circular duct data only with the same volume flow q_v.

(a) Rectangular ducts

The direct calculation approach should be used as explained above. Table C4.16 was obtained using equation 4.19, and gives pre-calculated values of equivalent diameter for rectangular ductwork of preferred sizes.

(b) Flat-oval spirally wound ducts

The direct calculation approach should therefore be used as explained above. Table C4.17 gives values of perimeter P and area A. The pre-calculated values of d_e given in Table C4.18 have been obtained using equation 4.19.

C4.8.9 Components and fittings

Whether for liquids in pipes or gasses in ducts, the same fundamental equation applies:

$$\Delta p_f = \zeta \, \tfrac{1}{2} \rho \, c^2 \qquad (4.23)$$

Values for ζ for some ductwork components are given in sections C4.11 and C4.11. Data for a more comprehensive range of fittings are given in Guide C sections 4.10 and 4.11.

Values of $\tfrac{1}{2} \rho c^2$ for air at 20 °C, normal atmospheric pressure, and 50% saturation are given in Table C4.19. Values of $\tfrac{1}{2} \rho c^2$ are easily calculated for other conditions.

C4.9 Pressure loss factors

An extensive review of pressure loss factors has been undertaken. Many sources give conflicting information, much derived from research results of many years ago. The data presented are those that are considered most reliable.

The pressure loss due to the insertion of a component such as an elbow is predominantly due to the vortices created downstream. Practical measurements close to the component would therefore be highly unrepeatable, and therefore unreliable. Experimental measurements of pressure are therefore made well upstream and downstream of the disturbance (i.e. 20 diameters upstream/downstream). The results are always quoted as the 'extra pressure drop due to the insertion of the component'.

The pressure drop calculated for a component is always to be added to the pressure drop of the full length of the pipework or ducting (unless otherwise stated).

If the distance between one component and another (entries and exits included) is less than 20 diameters, there is an interaction between the components. Thus the pressure drop could be more or less than the calculated figure depending on the type of component and the type of flow disturbances created, especially by the upstream component.

The predominant source of friction pressure drop has traditionally been attributed to the flow separation and vortices downstream of an elbow or bend. However, with pipework in particular, surface effects play an important part, the pressure drop being very dependent upon the surface roughness and shape of the inner surface. Thus it is found that the values of ζ depend upon the diameter and the material. Since even a small change in the internal shape of a pipe fitting can cause an appreciable difference in friction effects, it is clear that for small diameters, the pressure loss factor could also be manufacturer-dependent. This applies principally to elbows in pipework but also to elbows in ductwork.

With tees, the predominant friction pressure drop is due to the turbulence created by the mixing or separation of flows. In the past it was convenient to consider that surface effects would not play such an important part with tees and that therefore the values of ζ might not vary with diameter. This would appear doubtful in the light of recent work on tees in pipework. There is an indication that larger diameter tees give smaller values of ζ but the effect is easily swamped by manufacturing details.

It had previously been assumed that any possible variation with diameter would not apply to ductwork components due to the larger diameters. Recent work on circular ductwork shows this not to be the case. For bends in ductwork, ζ is strongly diameter-dependent. Work done on rectangular bends showed that size effects are appreciable for square bends of long radius and for those having a low aspect ratio (h/w).

Table C4.16 Equivalent diameters for rectangular ductwork, to give the same pressure drop for the same volume flow, surface roughness and friction coefficient λ; calculated from equation 4.19

Dimen. of side, h	100	125	150	175	200	225	250	300	350	400	450	500	550	600	650	700	750	800	850	900	Dimen. of side, h
100	110	123	134	145	154	163	171	185	199	211	222	232	242	251	260	268	276	284	291	298	100
		138	151	162	173	183	192	209	225	238	251	263	275	285	295	305	314	323	331	339	125
			165	178	190	201	212	231	248	264	278	291	304	316	327	338	348	358	368	377	150
				193	206	218	230	251	269	287	302	317	331	344	357	369	380	391	401	411	175
					220	234	246	269	289	308	325	341	356	371	384	397	409	421	433	444	200
						248	261	286	308	328	346	364	380	395	410	424	437	450	462	474	225
							275	301	325	346	366	385	402	419	434	449	463	477	490	503	250
								330	357	381	403	424	443	462	479	496	512	527	542	556	300
									385	412	436	459	481	501	520	539	556	573	589	605	350
125	347									440	467	492	515	537	558	578	597	616	633	650	400
150	386	394																			150
175	421	430	440								496	522	547	571	594	615	636	655	674	693	450
200	454	464	474	484								551	577	603	627	650	672	693	713	732	500
													606	632	658	682	706	728	749	770	550
225	485	496	507	517	527									661	688	713	738	761	784	806	600
250	515	527	538	549	560	570									716	743	768	793	817	840	650
300	570	583	596	608	620	632	643														300
350	620	635	649	662	676	689	701	713									771	798	824	849	873	700
400	667	682	698	713	727	741	755	768	794									826	853	879	904	750
																		881	908	934	800
450	710	727	744	760	776	791	805	820	848	874									936	963	850
500	751	770	787	804	821	837	853	868	898	927	954									991	900
550	790	809	828	846	864	881	898	915	946	976	1005	1033									550
600	827	847	867	887	905	923	941	958	992	1024	1054	1084	1112								600
650	862	884	905	925	944	964	982	1000	1035	1069	1101	1132	1162	1191							650
700	896	918	940	961	982	1002	1022	1041	1077	1112	1146	1179	1210	1240	1269						700
750	928	952	974	997	1018	1039	1059	1079	1118	1154	1189	1223	1256	1287	1318	1347					750
800	959	984	1007	1030	1053	1075	1096	1116	1156	1195	1231	1266	1300	1333	1365	1396	1425				800
850	989	1015	1039	1063	1086	1109	1131	1152	1194	1234	1272	1308	1343	1378	1410	1442	1473	1503			850
900	1018	1044	1070	1095	1119	1142	1165	1187	1230	1271	1311	1349	1385	1420	1455	1488	1520	1551	1581		900
950	1046	1073	1100	1125	1150	1174	1198	1221	1265	1308	1349	1388	1426	1462	1497	1532	1565	1597	1629	1659	950
1000		1101	1128	1155	1180	1205	1230	1253	1299	1343	1385	1426	1465	1503	1539	1574	1609	1642	1675	1706	1000
1050			1156	1183	1210	1236	1261	1285	1332	1378	1421	1463	1503	1542	1580	1616	1651	1686	1719	1752	1050
1100				1211	1238	1265	1291	1316	1365	1411	1456	1499	1540	1580	1619	1657	1693	1728	1763	1796	1100
1150					1266	1294	1320	1346	1396	1444	1490	1534	1576	1618	1657	1696	1733	1770	1805	1840	1150
1200						1321	1349	1375	1426	1476	1523	1568	1612	1654	1695	1735	1773	1810	1847	1882	1200
1250							1376	1404	1456	1507	1555	1601	1646	1690	1732	1772	1812	1850	1887	1924	1250
1300								1432	1485	1537	1586	1634	1680	1724	1767	1809	1850	1889	1927	1964	1300
1400									1542	1596	1647	1697	1745	1792	1837	1880	1923	1964	2004	2043	1400
1500										1652	1706	1758	1808	1856	1903	1949	1993	2036	2078	2119	1500
1600											1762	1816	1868	1919	1967	2015	2061	2106	2149	2191	1600
1700												1872	1926	1978	2029	2078	2126	2172	2218	2262	1700
1800													1982	2036	2089	2140	2189	2237	2284	2330	1800
1900														2092	2146	2199	2250	2300	2348	2395	1900
2000															2202	2257	2309	2361	2411	2459	2000
2100																2312	2367	2420	2471	2521	2100
2200																	2423	2477	2530	2581	2200
2300																		2533	2587	2640	2300
2400																			2643	2697	2400
2500																				2753	2500
Dimen. of side, h	950	1000	1050	1100	1150	1200	1250	1300	1400	1500	1600	1700	1800	1900	2000	2100	2200	2300	2400	2500	Dimen. of side, h

$$d_e = \frac{1.453\,A^{0.6}}{P^{0.2}}$$

Table C4.17 Areas and perimeters for flat-oval ductwork; the dimensions are those of the preferred sizes of ductwork

Dimension	Area, A (/ mm²), for stated width, w (/ mm), and height, h / mm											Perimeter, P / mm
	75	100	125	150	200	250	300	350	400	450	500	
w	320											720
A	22793											
w	360	350	330	320								808
A	25793	32854	37897	43171								
w	400	390	370	360								888
A	28793	36854	42897	49171								
w	440	430	410	400								968
A	31793	40854	47897	55171								
w	480	470	450	440								1048
A	34793	44854	52897	61171								
w	520	505	490	480								1126
A	37793	48354	57897	67171								
w		545	530	520								1206
A		52354	62897	73171								
w				555	525							1280
A				78421	96416							
w				635	605	580						1442
A				90421	112416	131587						
w				715	690	660	630					1604
A				102241	129416	151587	169686					
w				800	770	740	710	685	655			1767
A				115171	145416	171587	193686	213461	227664			
w				880	845	825	790	765	735	705	680	1927
A				127171	160416	192837	217686	241461	259664	273793	286350	
w				960	930	900	875	845	815	785	755	2067
A				139171	177416	211587	243186	269461	291664	309793	323850	
w				1040	1010	985	955	925	895	865	835	2249
A				151171	193416	232837	267186	297461	323664	345793	363850	
w				1120	1090	1065	1035	1005	975	945	915	2409
A				163171	209416	252837	291186	325461	355664	381793	403850	
w				1200	1170	1145	1115	1085	1055	1025	1000	2570
A				175171	225416	272837	315186	353461	387664	417793	446350	
w					1335	1305	1275	1245	1215	1190	1160	2892
A					258416	312837	363186	409461	451664	492043	526350	
w						1465	1435	1405	1375	1350	1320	3211
A						352837	411186	465461	515664	564043	606350	
w						1625	1595	1570	1540	1510	1480	3535
A						392837	459186	523211	581664	636043	686350	
w						1785	1760	1730	1700	1670	1640	3856
A						432837	508686	579211	645664	708043	766350	

Table C4.18 Equivalent diameters for flat-oval ductwork to give the same pressure drop for the same volume flow, surface roughness and friction coefficient λ; values of d_e have been obtained using equation 4.19; the dimensions are those of the preferred sizes of ductwork

$$d_e = \frac{1.453\,A^{0.6}}{P^{0.2}}$$

Dimension	Equivalent diameter, d_e (/ mm) for stated width, w (/ mm), and height, h / mm											Perimeter, P / mm
	75	100	125	150	200	250	300	350	400	450	500	
w	320											720
d_e	160											
w	360	350	330	320								808
d_e	169	195	213	230								
w	400	390	370	360								888
d_e	177	205	225	244								
w	440	430	410	400								968
d_e	185	215	236	257								
w	480	470	450	440								1048
d_e	192	223	247	269								
w	520	505	490	480								1126
d_e	199	230	257	281								
w		545	530	520								1206
d_e		238	266	291								
w				555	525							1280
d_e				300	340							
w				635	605	580						1442
d_e				319	364	400						
w				715	690	660	630					1604
d_e				337	388	426	456					
w				800	770	740	710	685	655			1767
d_e				354	408	450	484	513	534			
w				880	845	825	790	765	735	705	680	1927
d_e				370	425	475	510	543	567	586	602	
w				960	930	900	875	845	815	785	755	2067
d_e				384	444	494	537	571	599	621	638	
w				1040	1010	985	955	925	895	865	835	2249
d_e				398	461	515	560	597	628	653	674	
w				1120	1090	1065	1035	1005	975	945	915	2409
d_e				411	477	534	581	621	655	684	707	
w				1200	1170	1145	1115	1085	1055	1025	1000	2570
d_e				423	492	552	602	645	681	713	741	
w					1335	1305	1275	1245	1215	1190	1160	2892
d_e					522	585	640	688	729	768	799	
w						1465	1435	1405	1375	1350	1320	3211
d_e						616	675	727	773	816	852	
w						1625	1595	1570	1540	1510	1480	3535
d_e						644	708	765	815	860	901	
w						1785	1760	1730	1700	1670	1640	3856
d_e						671	739	799	853	902	946	

Table C4.19 Velocity pressure, p_v ($= \frac{1}{2} \rho c^2$), for air having a density $\rho = 1.20$ kg·m^{-3}; this is the case at 20 °C, 50% saturation and pressure of 101.325 bar

Velocity c / m·s^{-1}	Velocity pressure, p_v (/ Pa), for stated velocity, c / m.s^{-1}									
	0.0	0.1	0.2	0.3	0.4	0.5	0.6	0.7	0.8	0.9
0	0.00	0.01	0.02	0.05	0.10	0.15	0.22	0.29	0.38	0.49
1	0.60	0.73	0.86	1.01	1.18	1.35	1.54	1.73	1.94	2.17
2	2.40	2.65	2.90	3.17	3.46	3.75	4.06	4.37	4.70	5.05
3	5.40	5.77	6.14	6.53	6.94	7.35	7.78	8.21	8.66	9.13
4	9.60	10.09	10.58	11.09	11.62	12.15	12.70	13.25	13.82	14.41
5	15.00	15.61	16.22	16.85	17.50	18.15	18.82	19.49	20.18	20.89
6	21.60	22.33	23.06	23.81	24.58	25.35	26.14	26.93	27.74	28.57
7	29.40	30.25	31.10	31.97	32.86	33.75	34.66	35.57	36.50	37.45
8	38.40	39.37	40.34	41.33	42.34	43.35	44.38	45.41	46.46	47.53
9	48.60	49.69	50.78	51.89	53.02	54.15	55.30	56.45	57.62	58.81
10	60.00	61.21	62.42	63.65	64.90	66.15	67.42	68.69	69.98	71.29
11	72.60	73.93	75.26	76.61	77.98	79.35	80.74	82.13	83.54	84.97
12	86.40	87.85	89.30	90.77	92.26	93.75	95.26	96.77	98.30	99.85
13	101.40	102.97	104.54	106.13	107.74	109.35	110.98	112.61	114.26	115.93
14	117.60	119.29	120.98	122.69	124.42	126.15	127.90	129.65	131.42	133.21
15	135.00	136.81	138.62	140.45	142.30	144.15	146.02	147.89	149.78	151.69
16	153.60	155.53	157.46	159.41	161.38	163.35	165.34	167.33	169.34	171.37
17	173.40	175.45	177.50	179.57	181.66	183.75	185.86	187.97	109.10	192.25
18	194.40	196.57	198.74	200.93	203.14	205.35	207.58	209.81	212.06	214.33
19	216.60	218.89	221.18	223.49	225.82	228.15	230.50	232.85	235.22	237.61
20	240.00	242.41	244.82	247.25	249.70	252.15	254.62	257.09	259.58	262.09
21	264.60	367.13	269.66	272.21	274.78	277.35	279.94	282.53	285.14	287.77
22	290.40	293.05	295.70	298.37	301.06	303.75	306.46	309.17	311.90	413.65
23	317.40	320.17	322.94	325.73	328.54	331.35	334.18	337.01	339.86	342.73
24	345.60	348.49	351.38	354.29	357.22	360.15	363.10	366.05	369.02	372.01
25	375.00	378.01	381.02	384.05	387.10	390.15	393.22	396.29	399.38	402.49
26	405.60	408.73	411.86	415.01	418.18	421.35	424.54	427.37	430.94	434.17
27	437.40	440.65	443.90	447.17	450.46	453.75	457.06	460.37	463.70	467.05
28	470.40	473.77	477.14	480.53	483.94	487.35	490.78	494.21	497.66	501.13
29	504.60	508.09	511.58	515.09	518.62	522.15	525.70	529.25	532.82	536.41
30	540.00	543.61	547.22	550.85	554.50	558.15	561.82	565.49	569.18	572.89
31	576.60	580.33	584.06	587.81	591.58	595.35	599.14	602.93	606.74	610.57
32	614.40	618.25	622.10	625.97	629.86	633.75	637.66	641.57	645.50	649.45
33	653.40	657.37	661.34	665.33	669.34	673.35	677.38	681.41	685.46	689.53
34	693.60	697.69	701.78	705.89	710.02	714.15	718.30	722.45	726.62	730.81
35	735.00	739.21	743.42	747.65	751.90	756.15	760.42	764.69	768.98	773.29
36	777.60	781.93	786.26	790.61	794.98	799.35	803.74	808.13	812.54	816.97
37	821.40	825.85	830.30	834.77	839.26	843.75	848.26	852.77	857.30	861.85
38	866.40	870.97	875.54	880.13	884.74	889.35	893.98	898.61	903.26	907.93
39	912.60	917.29	921.98	926.69	931.42	936.15	940.90	945.65	950.42	955.21
40	960.00	964.81	969.62	974.45	979.30	984.15	989.02	993.78	998.78	1003.69

With tees, there are three flows and three velocity pressures. To avoid confusion, all the pressure loss coefficients are quoted in relation to the velocity pressure of the combined flow.

C4.10 Pressure loss factors for pipework components

C4.10.1 Elbows and bends

C4.10.1.1 Laminar flow

As with the friction factor λ for straight pipes, the pressure loss factor ζ for elbows/bends is found to be much higher in the laminar flow regime. This fact, generally overlooked, is important since pipes may often carry fluids of high viscosity which results in laminar flow.

Using Idelchik, to quote a simplistic value of ζ for laminar flow ($Re < 1000$), suggests that:

— $\zeta = 2.30$ could be taken for smooth elbows (laminar)

— $\zeta = 2.35$ could be taken for rough elbows (laminar).

Note that in the laminar flow regime neither relative roughness nor pipe diameter have any great effect on the value of ζ.

C4.10.1.2 Turbulent flow

Recent data are given in Table C4.20 and show the variation of ζ with diameter and velocity. The PVC-U elbows tested were all proprietary sharp elbows, except one where the 90° bend was made up of two 45° elbows glued together. This fabrication results in a bend of increased r/d, the effect of which is a reduction in the values of ζ far greater than any adverse effect from the discontinuity of the glued joint. Table C4.21 gives more comprehensive data, and shows the variation of ζ with size.

Table C4.20 Elbows: values of ζ varying with velocity; (a) screwed joint, malleable iron, (b) welded joint, forged steel, (c) and (d) PVC-U (derived from Rahmeyer)

Type and material	Diameter, d / mm	Velocity, c / m·s^{-1}								
		0.5	1	1.5	2	2.5	3	3.5	4	5
Short radius ($r/d = 1.0$):										
(a) Screwed joint, malleable iron	50	0.52	0.58	0.63	0.66	0.68	0.71	0.72	—	—
(b) Welded joint, forged steel	100	0.41	0.38	0.36	0.35	0.34	0.33	0.33	—	—
Long radius ($r/d = 1.5$):										
(b) Welded joint, forged steel	100	0.28	0.26	0.25	0.25	0.24	0.24	0.24	0.23	0.23
	300*	*0.18*	*0.16*	*0.15*	*0.15*	*0.14*	*0.14*	*0.14*	*0.13*	*0.13*
	400	0.15	0.13	0.12	0.12	0.12	0.11	0.11	0.11	0.11
	500	0.13	0.12	0.11	0.11	0.12	0.10	0.10	0.10	0.10
	600	0.11	0.10	0.10	0.10	0.09	0.09	0.09	0.08	0.08

	Diameter†, d / mm	Velocity, c / m·s^{-1}								
		0.85	1	1.5	2	3	4	5	6	7.5
Sharp inner edge ($r/d = 0.5$):										
(c) PVC-U	51	1.077	1.490	0.990	0.976	0.956	0.938	0.925	0.914	0.901
	102	0.978	0.955	0.914	0.902	0.886	0.873	0.863	0.855	0.844
	153*	0.887	0.869	*0.835*	*0.826*	*0.815*	*0.805*	0.797	0.789	—
	204	0.794	0.782	0.759	0.753	0.745	0.738	0.732	0.727	—
Glued 45° elbows giving 90° bend ($r/d \approx 1.0$):										
(d) PVC-U	204	0.462	0.448	0.419	0.412	0.402	0.394	0.387	0.382	—

* Experimental readings for this size were unreliable. Figures in italics were obtained by interpolation, and should be considered as 'best advice' only.

† 51 mm = nominal 2-inch, 102 mm = nominal 4-inch, 153 mm = nominal 6-inch, 204 mm = nominal 8-inch.

Note: accuracy: (a) ±22% for d = 50 mm; (b) ±10% for d = 400 mm and 500 mm; (c) ±1.3% for d = 51–204 mm

Table C4.21 Elbows: values of ζ varying with diameter (derived from ASHRAE and Miller)

Type	Diameter, d / mm								
	10	15	20	25	32	40	50	75	100
(a) Elbows:									
— screwed fitting*	2.5	2.1	1.7	1.5	1.3	1.2	1.0	0.82	0.70
— rough, sharp inner edge	1.56	1.45	1.35	1.3	1.24	1.18	1.15	1.10	1.10
— smooth radiussed inner	1.10	0.93	0.75	0.8	0.75	0.72	0.70	0.70	0.70
(b) Bends:									
— screwed fitting†	—	—	0.92	0.78	0.65	0.54	0.42	0.33	0.24
— smooth, $r/d > 1.5$	0.57	0.53	0.49	0.46	0.43	0.42	0.40	0.40	0.40

* Accuracy ± 40% for d < 50 mm, ± 20% for d > 50 mm; † accuracy ± 25%

C4.10.2   Elbows in close proximity

See Figure C4.3. When components are in close proximity, the flow disturbance created by the first will interact with the second. The pressure drop will not then be the same as for the two components in isolation. Table C4.22 contains values for a 'coefficient of close proximity', C_{cp} to be used in the following equations.

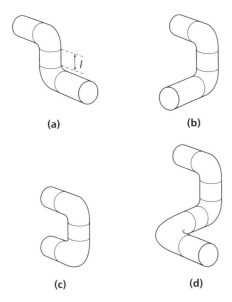

Figure C4.3 Elbows in close proximity; configurations for Table 4.22: (*a*) two elbows in same plane, (*b*) two elbows in different planes, (*c*) two elbows in same plane ('U'), (*d*) three elbows (swing)

For two components:

$$\Delta p = C_{cp} \, 2 \, \zeta_1 \, {}^1\!/_2 \, \rho \, c^2 \qquad (4.24)$$

For three components:

$$\Delta p = C_{cp} \, 3 \, \zeta_1 \, {}^1\!/_2 \, \rho \, c^2 \qquad (4.25)$$

where ζ_1 is the pressure loss coefficient for one of the components in isolation.

C4.10.3   Expanding and contracting elbows

See Figure C4.4 and Tables C4.23 and C4.24. Values of ζ are to be used with the velocity pressure at the smallest dimension.

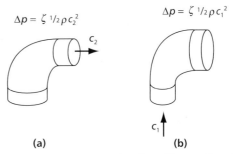

Figure C4.4 (*a*) Contracting elbow, (*b*) expanding elbow

Table C4.23 Contracting elbows: values of ζ varying with velocity; the value of ζ is with reference to the downstream velocity pressure

Type and diameter, d	Area ratio A_2/A_1	Velocity, c_2 / m·s⁻¹					
		1	2	3	4	5	6
Screwed joint, 50 mm > 37 mm	0.548	0.237	0.250	0.268	0.274	0.280	0.286
welded joint 100 mm > 76 mm	0.578	0.230	0.192	0.173	0.159	0.146	0.137

Note: the 50 mm fitting is of malleable iron, contracting round the elbow from 50 mm to 37 mm; the 100 mm fitting is of forged steel, contracting round the elbow from 100 mm to 76 mm. Both are of long radius.

Table C4.24 Expanding elbows: values of ζ varying with velocity; the value of ζ is with reference to the upstream velocity pressure

Type and diameter, d	Area ratio A_2/A_1	Velocity, c_1 / m·s⁻¹						
		0.5	1	1.5	2	2.5	3	3.5
Screwed joint, 37 mm < 50 mm	1.83	0.662	0.61	0.521	0.55	0.532	0.521	0.508
welded joint 76 mm < 100 mm	1.73	0.285	0.276	0.272	0.269	0.267	0.265	0.263

Note: the 37 mm fitting is of malleable iron, expanding round the elbow from 37 mm to 50 mm; the 76 mm fitting is of forged steel, expanding round the elbow from 76 mm to 100 mm. Both are of long radius.

C4.10.4   Gradual changes of section

See Figure C4.5 and Tables C4.25 and C4.26. Values of ζ are to be used with the velocity pressure at the smallest dimension.

C4.10.4.1   Contractions

Rahmeyer tested contractions of two types, the results of which are reproduced in Table C4.25. The smaller size, with screw threads, gave the highest values of ζ. It is not

Table C4.22 Elbows in close proximity: values of correction factor C_{cp} (Rahmeyer; ASHRAE *Transactions* **108** (1) 2002 © American Society of Heating, Refrigerating and Air-Conditioning Engineers Inc. (www.ashrae.org))

Configuration (see Figure 4.3)	Ratio of separation to diameter, l/d							
	0	1	2	3	4	5	10	20
Diameter, d = 51 mm ('2-inch'):								
(*a*) Two elbows in plane	0.90	0.88	0.86	0.89	0.88	0.88	1.00	1.01
(*b*) Two elbows out of plane	0.87	0.88	0.88	0.85	0.87	0.88	0.97	1.00
(*c*) Two elbows in plane ('U')	0.60	0.65	0.70	0.72	0.77	0.83	1.00	1.00
(*d*) Three elbows (swing)	0.70	0.72	0.74	0.72	0.75	0.77	0.99	0.99
Diameter, d = 102 mm ('4-inch'):								
(*a*) Two elbows in plane	0.95	0.93	0.90	0.90	0.92	0.94	0.98	1.00
(*b*) Two elbows out of plane	0.73	0.79	0.86	0.85	0.88	0.90	0.97	0.99
(*c*) Two elbows in plane ('U')	0.82	0.86	0.71	0.85	0.89	0.93	0.97	0.99
(*d*) Three elbows (swing)	0.86	0.87	0.87	0.87	0.88	0.90	0.95	0.99

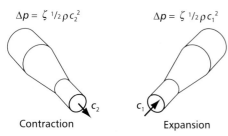

$\Delta p = \zeta \, {}^{1}/_{2} \rho c_2^{2}$ $\Delta p = \zeta \, {}^{1}/_{2} \rho c_1^{2}$

Contraction   Expansion

Figure C4.5 Gradual changes of section

known how much of this is due to the smaller size, and how much due to the screwed joint, as both are known to increase the value of ζ.

C4.10.4.2 Expansions

Rahmeyer tested expansions of two types, the results of which are reproduced in Table C4.26. The smaller size, with screwed joints, gave the highest values of ζ. It is not known how much of this is due to the smaller size, and how much due to the screwed joint, as both are known to increase the value of ζ.

C4.10.5 Abrupt changes of section

See Figure C4.6 and Table C4.27. Values of ζ are to be used with the velocity pressure at the smallest dimension.

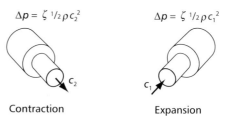

$\Delta p = \zeta \, {}^{1}/_{2} \rho c_2^{2}$ $\Delta p = \zeta \, {}^{1}/_{2} \rho c_1^{2}$

Contraction   Expansion

Figure C4.6 (*a*) Sudden contraction, (*b*) sudden expansion

C4.10.5.1 Sudden contractions

There will be a range when flow is in the laminar range upstream of the contraction, whilst turbulent downstream. In the intermediate zone, it is anticipated that the disturbance of the sudden contraction will trigger downstream turbulence at $Re_2 < 3 \times 10^3$, possibly as low as $Re_2 = 2 \times 10^3$, see Figure C4.1.

Table C4.25 Contractions: values of ζ (derived from Rahmeyer)

Type and diameters	Area ratio A_2/A_1	Velocity, c_2 / m·s⁻¹						
		0.5	1	2	3	4	5	7
(*a*) Screwed joint, malleable iron:								
— 50 mm > 37 mm	0.548	0.45	0.34	0.20	0.14	0.11	0.09	—
(*b*) Welded joint, forged steel:								
— 100 mm > 75 mm	0.562	0.17	0.14	0.09	0.05	0.04	0.04	—
(*c*) PVC-U:								
— 150 mm > 100 mm	0.444	0.18	0.16	0.13	0.11	0.10	0.10	0.10

Note: spread between items of different manufacturers: (*a*) $\Delta\zeta = \pm 0.020$, $\pm 22\%$ at $c_2 = 2$ m·s⁻¹; (*b*) $\Delta\zeta = \pm 0.022$, $\pm 55\%$ at $c_2 = 4$ m·s⁻¹; (*c*) $\Delta\zeta = \pm 0.028$, $\pm 27\%$ at $c_2 = 5$ m·s⁻¹

Table C4.26 Expansions: values of ζ (derived from Rahmeyer)

Type and diameters	Area ratio A_2/A_1	Velocity, c_1 / m·s⁻¹							
		0.3	0.5	1	1.5	2	2.5	3	3.7
(*a*) Screwed joint, malleable iron:									
— 37 mm < 50 mm	1.83	0.25	0.21	0.17	0.15	0.14	0.13	0.12	0.12
(*b*) Welded joint, forged steel:									
— 75 mm < 100 mm	1.78	0.14	0.13	0.13	0.12	0.11	0.11	0.11	0.11
(*c*) Wrought steel, butt-welded:									
— 254 mm < 305 mm	1.44	$\zeta = 0.111$ for 0.5 m·s⁻¹ $< c <$ 6 m·s⁻¹							
— 305 mm < 406 mm	1.78	$\zeta = 0.075$ for 0.5 m·s⁻¹ $< c <$ 6 m·s⁻¹							
— 406 mm < 508 mm	1.56	$\zeta = 0.022$ for 0.5 m·s⁻¹ $< c <$ 6 m·s⁻¹							
— 508 mm < 610 mm	1.44	$\zeta = 0.020$ for 0.5 m·s⁻¹ $< c <$ 6 m·s⁻¹							

Note: accuracy: (*a*) $\pm 14\%$; (*b*) $\pm 13\%$

Table C4.27 Abrupt contraction: values of ζ; for $Re_2 < 10^4$ (from diagram 4-10 of Idelchik)

Area ratio, A_2/A_1	Reynolds number, Re_2									
	40	50	100	200	500	1000	2000	4000	5000	10 000
0.1	2.00	1.80	1.30	1.04	0.82	0.64	0.50	*0.80*	*0.75*	0.50
0.2	1.84	1.62	1.20	0.95	0.70	0.50	0.40	*0.60*	0.60	0.40
0.3	1.70	1.50	1.10	0.85	0.60	0.44	0.30	0.55	0.55	0.35
0.4	1.60	1.40	1.00	0.78	0.50	0.35	0.25	0.45	0.50	0.30
0.5	1.46	1.30	0.90	0.65	0.42	0.30	0.20	0.40	0.42	0.25
0.6	1.35	1.20	0.80	0.56	0.35	0.24	0.15	0.35	0.35	0.20

Note: figures in italics are for conditions where, although turbulent flow occurs downstream of the contraction, laminar conditions occur upstream.

For flow in the laminar regime, values of ζ are appreciably larger than for turbulent flow. The value varies considerably with Reynolds number in a very non-linear manner; e.g. for a value of $Re = 10$, $\zeta < 4.9$, referring to the velocity pressure at the smaller dimension.

For turbulent flow, the Idelchik data suggest that for $Re > 10^5$, variation of ζ with Re is trivial and the following equation has been found to fit best the available data for $Re > 10^4$:

$$\zeta = 0.5\left(1 - \frac{A_2}{A_1}\right)^{0.75} \qquad (4.26)$$

However, this equation takes no account of size effects and Reynolds number effects, which are in evidence for the more recent data of Table C4.25 for gradual contractions. Standard pipe fittings would normally have a more rounded transition and give a slightly lower pressure drop than the values given in Table C4.27.

C4.10.5.2   Sudden enlargements

The Borda–Carnot equation may be used for $Re > 10^4$:

$$\zeta = 0.5\left(1 - \frac{A_1}{A_2}\right)^2 \qquad (4.27)$$

However this equation takes no account of size effects and Reynolds number effects which are in evidence for the more recent data of Table C4.26 for gradual expansions. Standard pipe fittings would normally have a more rounded transition and give a slightly lower pressure drop.

C4.10.5.3   Sudden entry/exit of a pipe to/from a vessel

For a sudden entry to a pipe from a vessel, $\zeta = 0.5$.

For a sudden exit from a pipe into vessel, $\zeta = 1.0$

C4.10.6   Tees

See Figures C4.7 to C4.9 and Tables C4.28 to C4.34.

Although for elbows there is considerable evidence that values of ζ vary with diameter, there is no clear evidence that this is also the case for tees.

Note that all values of ζ must be used with the velocity pressure of the combined flow.

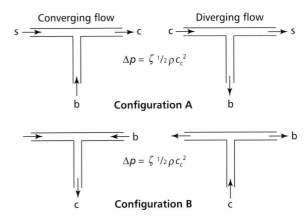

Figure C4.7 Equal tees: configurations (Tables C4.28 to C4.30)

C4.10.6.2   Tees: laminar flow

In the laminar region, ζ is sensibly constant for flow to or from a branch, being rather higher than for turbulent flow.

Summarised from Idelchik it could be said that for $Re < 2000$:

— for laminar flow, converging flow branch: $\zeta = 2.5$

— laminar flow, diverging flow branch: $\zeta = 3.4$

Surprisingly, compared with turbulent flow, it is the pressure loss factor for the straight flow across the tee which is said to be most complex. Idelchik gives very

Table C4.28 Equal tees, converging flow, configuration A (see Figure C4.7): values for the straight factor, $\zeta_{s\text{-}c}$ (derived from Rahmeyer)

Type and diameter	Relative straight flow, q_s / q_c									
	0.1	0.2	0.3	0.4	0.5	0.6	0.7	0.8	0.9	1.0
(a) Screwed joint, malleable iron:										
— 50 mm	0.43	0.48	0.51	0.52	0.52	0.50	0.46	0.40	0.32	0.23
(b) Welded joint, forged steel:										
— 100 mm	−0.15	≠ −0.07	−0.01	0.05	0.11	0.15	0.17	0.16	0.12	0.06
(c) Butt-welded, wrought steel:										
— 300 mm	−0.05	0.02	0.08	0.14	0.18	0.20	0.21	0.18	0.13	0.07
— 400 mm	0.01	0.09	0.15	0.20	0.22	0.21	0.19	0.14	0.09	0.03
(d) PVC-U, moulded:										
— 50 mm	0.18	0.24	0.28	0.31	0.34	0.35	0.34	0.31	0.26	0.20
— 100 mm	0.22	0.26	0.30	0.32	0.33	0.33	0.31	0.27	0.21	0.13
— 150 mm	0.38	0.40	0.41	0.40	0.38	0.35	0.31	0.25	0.17	0.07
— 200 mm	0.24	0.27	0.30	0.31	0.30	0.28	0.25	0.21	0.15	0.07
(e) PVC-U, segmented:										
— 200 mm	0.64	0.68	0.70	0.67	0.63	0.57	0.48	0.37	0.26	0.14

Note: scatter between different manufacturers: (a) (b) (c) = ± 0.2; (d) (e) = ± 0.1; figures in italics are extrapolated values

Table C4.29 Equal tees, converging flow, configuration A (see Figure C4.7): values for the branch factor, $\zeta_{\text{b-c}}$ (derived from Rahmeyer)

Type and diameter	Relative branch flow, q_b/q_c									
	0.1	0.2	0.3	0.4	0.5	0.6	0.7	0.8	0.9	1.0
(a) Screwed joint, malleable iron:										
— 50 mm	−0.22	−0.06	0.10	0.27	0.43	0.59	0.74	0.88	1.00	1.10
(b) Welded joint, forged steel:										
— 100 mm	−0.65	−0.48	−0.34	−0.20	−0.06	0.08	0.20	0.30	0.42	0.54
(c) Butt–welded, wrought steel:										
— 300 mm	*−0.55*	*−0.39*	−0.23	−0.09	0.05	0.19	0.33	0.79	0.60	0.71
— 400 mm	*−0.49*	*−0.32*	−0.18	−0.02	0.12	0.26	0.39	0.51	0.63	0.75
(d) PVC–U, moulded:										
— 50 mm to 200 mm	−0.53	−0.30	−0.09	0.11	0.29	0.42	0.56	0.70	0.85	1.00

Note: scatter between different manufacturers: (a) (b) (c) = ± 0.2; (d) = ± 0.1; figures in italics are extrapolated values

Table C4.30 Equal tees, diverging flow, configuration A (see Figure C4.7): values for the straight factor, $\zeta_{\text{s-c}}$ (derived from Rahmeyer)

Type and diameter	Relative straight flow, q_s/q_c									
	0.1	0.2	0.3	0.4	0.5	0.6	0.7	0.8	0.9	1.0
(a) Screwed joint, malleable iron:										
— 50 mm	0.25	0.18	0.13	0.08	0.04	0.02	0.02	0.05	0.12	0.21
(b) Welded joint, forged steel:										
— 100 mm	0.45	0.35	0.26	0.18	0.11	0.06	0.03	0.01	0.02	0.06
(c) Butt-welded, wrought steel:										
— 300 mm	*0.30*	*0.21*	0.14	0.08	0.04	0.02	0.02	0.03	0.05	0.09
(d) PVC-U, moulded:										
— 50 mm	*0.22*	*0.17*	0.13	0.09	0.06	0.04	0.04	0.07	0.13	0.21
— 100 mm	*0.35*	*0.28*	0.22	0.16	0.11	0.07	0.04	0.05	0.08	0.14
— 150 mm	*0.34*	*0.27*	0.20	0.14	0.09	0.05	0.03	0.03	0.06	0.10
— 200 mm	*0.32*	*0.23*	0.16	0.10	0.06	0.03	0.02	0.02	0.04	0.07
(e) PVC-U, segmented:										
— 200 mm	*0.35*	*0.27*	0.21	0.16	0.11	0.07	0.06	0.06	0.09	0.13

Note: scatter between different manufacturers: (a) (b) (c) = ± 0.4; (d) (e) = ± 0.5; figures in italics are extrapolated values

Table C4.31 Equal tees, diverging flow, configuration A (see Figure C4.7): values for the branch factor, $\zeta_{\text{c-b}}$ (derived from Rahmeyer)

Type and diameter	Relative branch flow, q_b/q_c									
	0.1	0.2	0.3	0.4	0.5	0.6	0.7	0.8	0.9	1.0
(a) Screwed joint, malleable iron:										
— 50 mm	0.74	0.69	0.63	0.62	0.63	0.65	0.70	0.76	0.83	0.90
(b) Welded joint, forged steel:										
— 100 mm	0.93	0.82	0.74	0.67	0.62	0.60	0.61	0.64	0.68	0.74
(c) Butt–welded, wrought steel:										
— 300 mm	*0.80*	*0.72*	0.66	0.61	0.57	0.56	0.57	0.59	0.62	0.66
— 400 mm	*0.75*	*0.67*	0.60	0.54	0.51	0.50	0.51	0.52	0.53	0.54
(d) PVC–U, moulded:										
— 50 mm	*0.95*	*0.92*	0.90	0.89	0.90	0.95	1.02	1.10	1.18	1.26
— 100 mm	0.95	0.87	0.82	0.79	0.79	0.81	0.85	0.89	0.95	1.02
— 150 mm	*0.85*	*0.78*	0.73	0.70	0.69	0.72	0.75	0.79	0.84	0.89
(e) PVC–U, segmented:										
— 200 mm	*1.24*	*1.18*	1.14	1.12	1.12	1.15	1.20	1.27	1.36	1.47

Note: scatter between different manufacturers: (a) (b) (c) = ± 0.15; (d) (e) = ± 0.12; figures in italics are extrapolated values

Table C4.32 Equal tees, converging and diverging flow, configuration B (see Figure C4.7): values of ζ (derived from Rahmeyer)

Type	Flow ratio, q_b/q_c									
	0.1	0.2	0.3	0.4	0.5	0.6	0.7	0.8	0.9	1.0
Converging flow ($\zeta_{\text{b-c}}$)	0.09	0.26	0.45	0.56	0.55	0.47	0.39	0.37	0.49	0.80
Diverging flow ($\zeta_{\text{c-b}}$)	0.64	0.64	0.63	0.64	0.67	0.71	0.77	0.84	0.95	1.10

complex relationships depending on the relative branch size, the relative flows and the Reynolds number. Carrying out a sample calculation for $Re = 100$, and with 50 per cent of the flow to or from a branch of the same diameter, revealed that, approximately:

— for converging flow, straight ζ is four times that for turbulent flow

— for diverging flow, straight ζ is four times that for turbulent flow.

C4.10.6.3   Tees: turbulent flow

The value of ζ is seen to vary considerably with the ratio of the respective flows so no simplistic values can be given. The friction loss differs considerably between converging and diverging flows. The effect of branch diameter relative to the diameter of the part carrying the combined flow, d_b / d_c, is appreciable and cannot be ignored but there are few data on this effect.

For flows straight across the tee, the values of ζ do not vary greatly with the relative flows, q_b / q_c.

A clear distinction is made between converging and diverging flows as follows.

(a) Converging flows

There is little information on the effect of the upstream type of connection. However Idelchik reports that when the flow from the branch is less than 80% of the combined flow, screwed branches give losses 10–20% more than for smooth connections. Conversely it would appear that when the branch flow is greater than 80% of the total, screwed branches give losses 10–20% less than for smooth connections.

It will be observed that in the case of converging flows, it is possible under certain flow conditions for the flow from the branch to experience a negative pressure loss factor, i.e. to experience a pressure gain.

(b) Diverging flows

For losses round to the branch, there is little difference between tees of smooth joints and those of screwed joints.

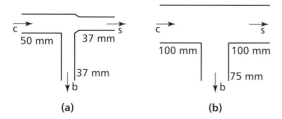

(a)   **(b)**

Figure C4.8 Unequal tees, diverging flow: configurations (Table C4.33)

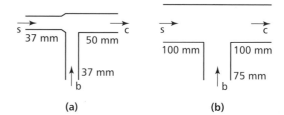

(a)   **(b)**

Figure C4.9 Unequal tees, converging flow: configurations (Table C4.34)

Table C4.33 Unequal tees, diverging flow: values of ζ; (a) for $d_c = 50$ mm, $d_s = 37$ mm, $d_b = 37$ mm, (b) $d_c = 100$ mm, $d_s = 100$ mm, $d_b = 75$ mm (see Figure C4.8) (derived from Rahmeyer)

Type	Flow ratio, q_b / q_c										
	0	0.1	0.2	0.3	0.4	0.5	0.6	0.7	0.8	0.9	1.0
Branch factors, $\zeta_{c\text{-}b}$:											
(a) 50 mm, screwed	—	0.78	0.78	0.86	1.04	1.30	1.64	2.05	2.55	3.11	3.75
(b) 100 mm, welded	—	0.91	0.89	0.90	0.94	1.11	1.33	1.64	2.06	2.59	3.26
Straight factors, $\zeta_{c\text{-}s}$:											
(a) 50 mm, screwed	2.55	2.02	1.56	1.16	0.83	0.57	0.38	0.25	0.20	0.22	—
(b) 100 mm, welded	0.04	0	0.01	0.01	0.05	0.11	0.17	0.24	0.31	0.39	—

Table C4.34 Unequal tees, converging flow: values of ζ; for (a) $d_c = 50$ mm, $d_s = 37$ mm, $d_b = 37$ mm, (b) $d_c = 100$ mm, $d_s = 100$ mm, $d_b = 75$ mm (see Figure C4.9) (derived from Rahmeyer)

Type	Flow ratio, q_b / q_c										
	0	0.1	0.2	0.3	0.4	0.5	0.6	0.7	0.8	0.9	1.0
Branch factors, $\zeta_{b\text{-}c}$:											
(a) 50 mm, screwed	—	2.26	2.54	2.73	2.86	2.98	3.08	3.174	3.24	3.30	3.36
(b) 100 mm, welded	—	−1.18	−0.82	−0.60	−0.55	−0.35	0.26	0.55	1.00	1.45	1.60
Straight factors, $\zeta_{s\text{-}c}$:											
(a) 50 mm, screwed	1.59	1.60	1.60	1.61	1.62	1.63	1.64	1.66	1.68	1.73	—
(b) 100 mm, welded	0.07	0.21	0.20	0.19	0.17	0.04	−0.04	−0.06	−0.14	−0.16	—

C4.10.7 Valves

The following approximate data are given to help in initial design calculations. The actual values, supplied by the manufacturer, should be used as soon as they are available.

A single value can only be given for the valve in the fully open position. (The value of ζ will be infinite when the valve is closed.) For regulating valves therefore, the manufacturer will generally prefer to give a value of the valve capacity (K) for the valve fully open, supplemented by a graph of the variation of the relative capacity with relative valve opening. (The value of K will be 0 when the valve is closed.) This is more useful than ζ when establishing the valve authority and overall control characteristic. The pressure drop due to the valve is easily calculated from equation 4.13 (see section C4.4.2), i.e:

$$q_v = K \sqrt{\Delta p}$$

C4.10.7.1 Globe valves

See Table C4.35. Values of ζ are for the valve fully open. These vary with the internal design of the valve so are included here only for guidance and should be used with care.

C4.10.7.2 Gate valves

These should be installed for use in the fully open position. They are designed to give a clear bore when fully open. In operation, therefore, the pressure drop through them should be quite small.

Although designs may vary, the following provides a rough estimate of the pressure drop:

— spherical-seal gates: $\zeta = 0.03$

— plain-parallel gates: $\zeta = 0.3$

C4.10.7.3 Non-return valves

See Tables C4.36 and C4.37. A single value of ζ cannot be given.

Table C4.36 Non-return valves: approximate values of ζ (taken from Idelchik)

Type	Angle of opening / degree						
	20	30	40	50	60	70	75
Non-return valve	1.7	3.2	6.6	14	30	62	90

Table C4.37 Spring-loaded non-return valves: approximate values of K

Type	Value of K (/ m³·h⁻¹·bar⁻⁰·⁵) for stated diameter / mm		
	25	38	50
Spring-loaded non-return valve	15	38	55

For the gravity flap type, the greater the flow, the more the valve flap opens and the lower becomes the value of ζ.

Spring-loaded non-return valves also behave in a very non-linear fashion, and so the manufacturer's characteristic must be used. The data in Table C4.37, taken from part of the performance characteristic of valves of a single manufacturer, may be used for the purpose of first estimates. It does not state what flow would result in these values of K.

C4.10.8 Pipe joints

C4.10.8.1 Welded and screwed metal tubes

The joints do not have a great effect and will generally be small in relation to the long tube lengths used. Therefore only brief guidance is given in Table C4.38. Screwed joints give a greater pressure drop due to the appreciable discontinuity of the surface at the joint, but no clear data are available.

C4.10.8.2 Plastic joints

Tubes are likely to be shorter and smaller and the effects of joints can be significant. All of the values in Table C4.38 are taken from Idelchik for Re values: $1.8 \times 10^5 < Re < 5 \times 10^5$.

Table C4.35 Globe valves: approximate values of ζ (taken from Idelchik)

Type	Value of ζ for stated diameter / mm							
	20	40	60	80	100	150	200	300
Standard globe valve, angular dividing walls	8	4.9	—	4	4.1	4.4	4.7	5.4
Angle globe valve	—	—	2.7	2.4	2.2	1.86	1.65	1.4

Table C4.38 Pipe joints: values of ζ for $1.8 \times 10^5 < Re < 5 \times 10^5$ (from Idelchik)

Type	Pipe diameter / mm									
	50	75	100	150	200	250	300	400	500	600
Metal pipe, welded joints	—	—	—	—	0.026	—	0.0135	0.009	0.006	0.004
Plastic pipe:										
— welded joints	0.411	0.224	0.146	0.079	0.057	0.037	0.028	—	—	—
— flanged joints	0.131	0.13	0.114	0.096	0.079	0.062	0.045	—	—	—

Table C4.39 Sharp-edged orifice: values of ζ calculated from equation 4.28; for $Re_o > 10^5$ (Idelchik)

Type	Diameter ratio, d_o/d										
	0.15	0.2	0.25	0.3	0.35	0.4	0.5	0.6	0.7	0.8	0.9
Orifice	5565	1714	678	313	160	88.2	30.8	11.8	4.67	1.73	0.49

C4.10.9 Orifices

See Figure C4.10 and Table C4.39.

Orifice plates are generally used for flow measurement but may sometimes be installed to aid the balancing of flow. Although there is a gradual pressure recovery downstream of the orifice, they do incur a permanent pressure loss and permanent pumping costs. Thus if used for balancing purposes, consideration should be given to reducing the resistance of the parallel circuit instead.

Idelchik gives data for various shapes of orifice and for the combination with a sudden contraction. In Table C4.39 the data for only one are given, namely for a thin sharp-edged orifice for which Re_o (within the orifice) $\geq 10^5$ and $\delta/d_o \leq 0.0075$, where δ is the plate thickness. Note that the values of ζ are to be used with the velocity pressure in the main pipe.

ζ is given by:

$$\zeta = \left(\frac{A}{A_o}\right)^2 \left[\left(1 - \frac{A_o}{A}\right) + 0.707\left(1 - \frac{A_o}{A}\right)^{0.375}\right]^2 \quad (4.28)$$

$$\Delta p = \zeta \; {}^1\!/_2 \rho c^2$$

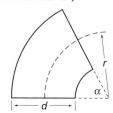

Diameter = d
Area = A
Velocity = c

Figure C4.10 Orifice

C4.11 Pressure loss factors for ductwork components

Guide C section 4.11 provides pressure loss factors for a wide range of components and fittings associated with both rectangular and circular ductwork. The following extracts provide data for some of the more common components and fittings.

C4.11.2 Pressure loss factors for ductwork components: circular

C4.11.2.1 Smooth radius round bends (HVCA 127: 'pressed bend')

See Tables C4.40, C4.41 and C4.42.

Table C4.40 Smooth bends: variation of ζ with Reynolds number; for $d = 250$ mm, $r/d = 1.0$ (derived from European Programme Report and Koch)

Bend angle, α / degree	Reynolds number, Re ($/10^5$)							
	0.5	1	1.5	2	2.5	3	3.5	4
30	—	—	0.048	0.044	0.044	0.043	0.043	0.042
45	0.119	0.101	0.094	0.087	0.086	0.085	0.084	0.083
60	0.221	0.187	0.175	0.161	0.160	0.158	0.156	0.155
75	0.298	0.252	0.238	0.217	0.216	0.213	0.211	0.209
90	0.343	0.290	0.271	0.250	0.248	0.245	0.242	0.240

Note: figures in italics were obtained by interpolation

Table C4.41 Smooth bends of any angle: value of ζ relative to that of a 90° bend; for $d = 250$ mm, $r/d = 1.0$; $1.0 \times 10^5 < Re < 2 \times 10^5$ (derived from the European Programme Report and Koch)

Type	Value of ζ relative to 90° bend for stated bend angle, α				
	30°	45°	60°	75°	90°
Smooth bend	0.177	0.347	0.645	0.870	1

Note: figures in italics were obtained by interpolation

Table C4.42 Smooth 90° bends: variation of ζ with diameter; for Reynolds number = 1×10^5 (adapted from UMC)

Ratio, r/d	Diameter, d / mm							
	63	80	100	125	150	180	200	250
1.5	(0.35)	(0.28)	(0.21)	0.16	0.14	0.115	0.11	0.11

Notes: UMC also provides data for $r/d = 1.0$, but where a cross reference with Table C4.41 is possible a large contradiction is evident; these have therefore been omitted so as to avoid any confusion. Figures in parentheses were obtained by extrapolation. UMC gives the variation with diameter but gives no data on the variation with Re.

C4.11.2.2 Pleated bends

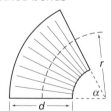

The only data available are for 90° bends, see Table C4.43. For bends of other angles (α) see Figure C4.11.

Table C4.43 Pleated 90° bends: variation of ζ with diameter; for $r/d = 1.5$, Reynolds number unknown (adapted from ASHRAE Handbook: *Fundamentals* 2005, chapter 35. © American Society of Heating, Refrigerating and Air-Conditioning Engineers Inc. (www.ashrae.org))

Type	Diameter, d / mm								
	100	125	150	180	200	250	300	350	400
Pleated 90° bend	0.57	0.495	0.43	0.375	0.34	0.28	0.26	0.11	0.25

Note: figures in italics were obtained by interpolation

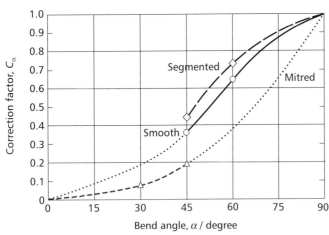

Figure C4.11 Variation of correction factor with bend angle (from Koch); duct diameter $d = 250$ mm. Valid for $1.0 \times 10^5 < Re < 4.0 \times 10^5$; segmented and smooth bends ($r/d = 1.0$)

C4.11.2.3   Segmented bends (HVCA 128)

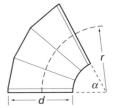

See Tables C4.44 to C4.48. Data from SMACNA show that the greater the number of segments, the smoother is the bend, and the lower is the value of ζ. Five or more segments are only likely to be used for large radius bends.

Table C4.44 Segmented 90° bends: variation of ζ with diameter; for $Re = 1 \times 10^5$ (adapted from UMC)

Ratio, r/d	Diameter, d / mm										
	80	100	125	150	200	250	300	400	500	800	1200
1.5 (5-segments)	(0.48)	(0.40)	(0.325)	0.28	0.23	0.20	0.18	0.16	0.14	0.12	0.12

Note: similar data are also provided for $r/d = 2.5$ (7-segments) by UMC and for $r/d = 1.0$ (5-segments) by ASHRAE but the values contradict those of Table 4.48 for $d = 250$ mm; to avoid confusion, these are omitted. Figures in parenthesis are extrapolated values.

Table C4.45 Segmented bends: variation of ζ with Reynolds number; for $r/d = 1.0$ (derived from European Programme Report and Koch)

Diameter, d / mm	Bend angle, α / degree	Reynolds number, Re (/ 10^5)								
		0.5	1.0	1.5	2.0	2.5	3.0	4.0	5.0	6.0
250	45	0.159	0.143	0.129	0.122	0.120	0.118	0.114	—	—
	60	0.243	0.218	0.197	0.186	0.183	0.180	0.175	—	—
	75	*0.303*	*0.272*	*0.245*	*0.232*	*0.228*	*0.225*	*0.217*	—	—
	90	0.340	0.305	0.275	0.260	0.256	0.252	0.244	—	—
400	45	0.12	0.105	0.09	0.083	0.078	0.073	0.068	0.064	0.064
400	60	0.21	0.183	0.170	0.160	0.152	0.147	0.142	0.135	0.13
400	90	—	—	—	0.20*	—	—	—	—	—

* estimated value

Note: figures in italics were obtained by interpolation

Table C4.46 Segmented bends of any angle: value of ζ relative to that of a 90° bend; for $d = 250$ mm, $r/d = 1.0$; $1.0 \times 10^5 < Re < 4 \times 10^5$ (derived from the European Programme Report and Koch)

Type	Value of ζ relative to 90° bend for stated bend angle, α			
	45°	60°	75°	90°
Segmented bend	0.44	0.73	*0.90*	1

Note: figure in italics was obtained by interpolation

Table C4.47 Segmented bends (4 segments): variation of ζ with relative bend ratio (r/d); for $\alpha = 90°$, $d = 250$ mm; $Re = 2 \times 10^5$ (adapted from the European Programme Report)

Type	Relative bend ratio, r/d						
	0.7	1.0	1.5	2.0	2.5	3.0	5.0
Segmented bend (4 segments)	0.44	0.26	0.20	0.195	0.21	0.23	0.31

Table C4.48 Segmented bends: variation of ζ with Reynolds number, in terms of a multiplying factor C_{Re} to be applied to the values of Table 4.45; for $\alpha = 90°$, $d = 250$ mm (adapted from the European Programme Report)

Aspect ratio, r/d	Multiplying factor, C_{Re}, for stated Reynolds number, Re / 10^5						
	0.5	1.0	1.5	2.0	2.5	3.0	4.0
0.7	1.30	1.15	1.05	1.0	0.95	0.95	0.95
1.0	1.31	1.17	1.08	1.0	0.93	0.92	0.93
1.5	1.44	1.24	1.10	1.0	0.92	0.87	0.84
≥ 2.0	1.51	1.24	1.08	1.0	0.92	0.86	0.87

C4.11.2.4   Mitred elbow (HVCA 128)

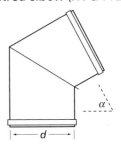

See Tables C4.49 to C4.51.

Table C4.49 Mitred elbows: variation of ζ with diameter; Re unknown (derived from UMC)

Bend angle, α / degree	Diameter, d / mm										
	80	100	125	150	200	250	300	400	500	800	1200
90	(1.44)	(1.4)	(1.36)	1.31	1.26	1.23	1.20	1.17	1.15	1.14	1.12

Note: figures in parentheses were obtained by extrapolation

Table C4.50 Mitred elbows: variation of ζ with Reynolds number; for d = 250 mm (derived from European Programme Report and Koch)

Diam., d / mm	Bend angle, α / degree	Reynolds number, Re (/ 10^5)						
		0.5	1.0	1.5	2.0	2.5	3.0	4.0
250	30	0.131	0.121	0.115	0.112	0.110	0.109	0.107
	45	0.269	0.253	0.239	0.233	0.229	0.227	0.223
	60	*0.526*	*0.488*	*0.461*	*0.450*	*0.448*	*0.432*	*0.431*
	75	*0.901*	*0.835*	*0.790*	*0.770*	*0.757*	*0.750*	*0.737*
	90	1.38	1.28	1.23	1.18	1.16	1.15	1.13
400	30	0.08	0.061	0.045	0.039	0.035	0.034	0.032

Note: figures in italics were obtained by interpolation

Table C4.51 Mitred elbows of any angle: values of ζ relative to that of a 90° elbow; for d = 250 mm; $1.0 \times 10^5 < Re < 4 \times 10^5$ (derived from European Programme Report and Koch)

Type	Value of ζ relative to that of a 90° elbow, for stated elbow angle, α / degree					
	22.5	30	45	60	75	90
Mitred elbow	*0.05*	0.095	0.197	*0.381*	*0.653*	1

Note: figures in italics were obtained by interpolation

C4.11.2.5 Bends and elbows in close proximity, in same plane ('gooseneck')

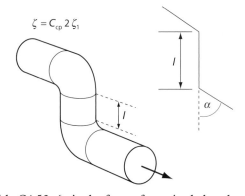

$$\zeta = C_{cp} \, 2 \, \zeta_1$$

See Table C4.52; ζ_1 is the factor for a single bend.

The data given in Table C4.52 do not include the pressure drop of the length of separation. The separation (l) should be added to the length of straight ductwork of the same size.

C4.11.2.6 Bends and elbows in close proximity, through perpendicular plane

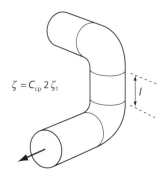

$$\zeta = C_{cp} \, 2 \, \zeta_1$$

See Table C4.53; ζ_1 is the factor for a single bend.

The data given in Table C4.53 do not include the pressure drop of the length of separation. The separation l should be added to the length of straight ductwork of the same size.

Table C4.52 Two bends in close proximity in the same plane; values of interaction factor C_{cp}; for d = 250 mm, r/d = 1 (from European Programme Report and Koch)

Bend angle, α, and type	Ratio, l/d	Value of C_{cp} for stated Reynolds number, Re / 10^5						
		0.5	1.0	1.5	2.0	2.5	3.0	4.0
30° mitred	$1 < l/d < 5$	0.83	0.82	0.82	0.82	0.82	0.81	0.80
30° smooth	$l/d = 1$	—	—	0.95	0.88	0.84	0.73	0.73
	$3 < l/d < 5$	—	—	1.12	1.02	0.93	0.87	0.79
45° segmented	$1 < l/d < 5$	1.45	1.16	1.10	1.07	1.04	1.02	0.96
45° smooth	$1 < l/d < 5$	0.96	0.99	0.97	0.92	0.88	0.84	0.85
60° segmented	$1 < l/d < 5$	1.03	1.11	1.10	1.07	1.08	1.09	1.09
60° smooth	$1 < l/d < 5$	1.05	0.94	0.93	0.87	0.86	0.84	0.83
75° segmented	$l/d = 1$	1.11	1.11	1.04	1.02	1.04	0.99	1.01
	$1 < l/d < 5$	1.10	0.97	0.93	0.93	0.95	0.93	0.81
75° smooth	$1 < l/d < 5$	1.07	1.00	0.96	0.92	0.92	0.91	0.89
90° smooth and segmented	$1 < l/d < 5$	1.07	0.96	0.95	1.02	1.04	1.02	1.10

Note: factors for close proximity C_{cp} are applied to the values of ζ_1 obtained from Tables C4.40 to C4.51, as appropriate.

Table C4.53 Two 90° bends in close proximity, out of plane: values of interaction factor C_{cp}; for d = 250 mm, r/d = 1 (derived from European Programme Report)

Type	Ratio, l/d	Value of C_{cp} for stated Reynolds number, Re (/ 10^5)						
		0.5	1.0	1.5	2.0	2.5	3.0	4.0
Smooth	1	1.14	0.91	0.83	0.82	0.83	0.83	0.84
	3	1.04	0.95	0.90	0.89	0.89	0.88	0.87
	5	1.16	0.96	0.90	0.89	0.89	0.89	0.89
Segmented	1	0.87	0.93	0.98	1.04	1.10	1.09	1.01
	3	0.94	0.99	1.04	1.09	1.15	1.15	1.02
	5	0.98	1.05	1.08	1.14	1.19	1.20	1.08

C4.11.2.15   90° branch tees, circular from circular (HVCA 139) and pressed equal tee (HVCA 130)

(a) Converging flows ($A_c = A_s$)

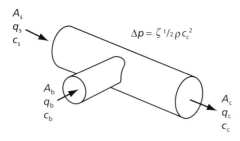

See Tables C4.63 and C4.64. Re_c is based on the value for the combined flow.

It is now evident that the value of both the straight factor and the branch factor vary with the size of the tee (i.e. with the diameters of the main parts of the tee: A_c, A_s), and with Reynolds number. Values of the straight factor ζ_{s-c} appear generally to vary little with Re and not in a regular manner. In the interests of simplicity, the values of ζ_{s-c} given in Table C4.63 are mean values over the range $1 \times 10^5 < Re_c < 5 \times 10^5$. Values for $Re_c = 0.5 \times 10^5$ can be as much as 25% greater.

It is now evident that the value of the branch factor ζ_{b-c} varies with the size of the tee (i.e. with the diameters of the main parts of the tee: d_s, d_c), and with Reynolds number. For $Re > 1 \times 10^5$, the variation is not very great. In the interests of simplicity, the values of ζ_{b-c} given in Table 4.64 are mean values over the range $1 \times 10^5 < Re_c < 2 \times 10^5$. Values for $Re_c = 0.5 \times 10^5$ are generally about 8% greater.

(b) Diverging flows ($A_c = A_s$)

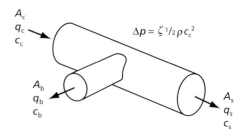

See Tables C4.65 and C4.66. Values of the straight factor ζ_{s-c} appear generally to vary little with Reynolds number, and not in a regular manner. Mean values are therefore given below. Any possible variation with diameter is inconclusive at present.

It is now evident that the value of the branch factor ζ_{s-b} varies with the size of the tee (i.e. with the diameters of the main parts of the tee: d_c, d_s), and with Reynolds number. Re is based on the value for the combined flow. For $Re_c > 1 \times 10^5$, the variation is not very great. In the interests of simplicity, the values of ζ given in Table C4.66 are mean values over the range $1.0 \times 10^5 < Re_c < 5 \times 10^5$. Values for $Re_c = 0.5 \times 10^5$ are generally about 8% greater.

Table C4.63 90° tees, converging flow: values for the straight factor ζ_{s-c} (derived from the European Programme Report and Koch)

Area ratio, A_b/A_c	Relative straight flow, q_s/q_c									
	0.1	0.2	0.3	0.4	0.5	0.6	0.7	0.8	0.9	1.0
(a) Main duct size: $d_s = d_c = 400$ mm										
0.0625*	0.45	0.60	0.80	1.1	1.4	0.85	0.55	0.25	0.04	0
0.10	1.2	1.1	1.15	1.08	1.0	0.60	0.35	0.22	0.10	0
0.1406*	1.65	1.5	1.25	1.0	0.74	0.50	0.31	0.20	0.09	0
0.20	1.4	1.3	1.10	0.83	0.62	0.43	0.285	0.19	0.10	0
0.25*	1.0	1.0	0.86	0.72	0.55	0.41	0.27	0.18	0.10	0
0.30	0.80	0.75	0.70	0.60	0.47	0.38	0.26	0.175	0.10	0
0.3906*	0.56	0.54	0.47	0.42	0.34	0.30	0.24	0.17	0.10	0
(b) Main duct size: $d_s = d_c = 250$ mm										
0.16†	1.55	1.7	1.6	1.53	1.09	0.87	0.56	0.4	0.2	0.02
0.2	1.50	1.5	1.4	1.2	1.0	0.75	0.55	0.39	0.21	0.02
0.3	1.3	1.2	1.05	0.90	0.75	0.60	0.47	0.36	0.22	0.03
0.36†	1.18	1.08	0.93	0.78	0.67	0.55	0.47	0.60	0.30	0.04
0.4	1.12	1.02	0.9	0.79	0.66	0.53	0.43	0.335	0.215	0.04
0.5	0.98	0.90	0.80	0.73	0.62	0.52	0.415	0.32	0.21	0.05
0.6	0.87	0.80	0.74	0.68	0.59	0.51	0.405	0.305	0.20	0.05
0.64†	0.84	0.78	0.68	0.66	0.58	0.49	0.43	0.31	0.19	0.05
0.7	0.81	0.75	0.71	0.66	0.58	0.50	0.40	0.30	0.17	0.05
0.8	0.78	0.74	0.70	0.65	0.58	0.50	0.40	0.30	0.14	0.06
1.00†	0.74	0.72	0.70	0.64	0.58	0.49	0.41	0.30	0.19	0.07

* Values obtained using a main duct size: $d_s = d_c = 400$ mm; other values obtained by interpolation
† Values obtained using a main duct size: $d_s = d_c = 250$ mm; other values obtained by interpolation

Table C4.64 90° tees, converging flow: values for the branch factor ζ_{b-c}; for $1 \times 10^5 < Re < 2 \times 10^5$ (derived from the European Programme Report and Koch)

Area ratio, A_b/A_c	Relative branch flow, q_b/q_c									
	0.1	0.2	0.3	0.4	0.5	0.6	0.7	0.8	0.9	1.0
(a) Main duct size: $d_s = d_c = 400$ mm										
0.0625*	1.5	10	22	40	69	100	140	180	230	283
0.1	1.0	3.5	7.5	15	25	42	60	80	102	125
0.1406*	0.10	1.0	3.3	6.5	10.5	16	22.6	30.4	39.7	49.4
0.20	0	0.50	1.8	3.3	5.0	7.5	11	15	19	24
0.25*	0	0.43	1.1	2.0	3.3	5.1	7.2	9.5	12.2	14.7
0.30	0.10	0.30	0.70	1.3	2.0	3.0	4.4	6.1	8.0	10
0.3906*	−0.20	0	0.30	0.73	1.3	2.0	2.85	3.76	4.8	6.0
(b) Main duct size: $d_s = d_c = 250$ mm										
0.16†	0.05	1.2	3.24	6.1	10.4	15.5	22.5	30.3	39	46.7
0.2	0.40	0.85	2.0	3.5	6.1	9.6	13	17	23	30
0.3	0.40	0.30	0.90	1.8	2.8	4.0	5.2	6.8	8.2	9.8
0.36†	0	0.21	0.65	1.20	1.91	2.83	3.89	5.22	6.61	7.74
0.4	−0.20	0.17	0.55	1.0	1.6	2.3	3.2	4.35	5.2	6.3
0.5	0	0.13	0.40	0.78	1.15	1.6	2.3	3.0	3.8	4.5
0.6	0	0.85	0.30	0.61	0.9	1.2	1.7	2.2	2.6	3.0
0.64†	−0.12	0.07	0.27	0.55	0.82	1.10	1.43	1.87	2.26	2.61
0.7	−0.10	0.05	0.25	0.50	0.72	1.0	1.3	1.7	2.0	2.3
0.8	0	0.05	0.20	0.42	0.63	0.9	1.2	1.5	1.72	1.93
1.00†	−0.59	-0.24	0.15	0.36	0.56	0.76	0.95	1.07	1.19	1.26

* Values obtained using a main duct size: $d_s = d_c = 400$ mm; other values obtained by interpolation
† Values obtained using a main duct size: $d_s = d_c = 250$ mm; other values obtained by interpolation

Table C4.65 90° tees, diverging flow; values for the straight factor ζ_{c-s} (derived from the European Programme Report and Koch)

Diam. d_c, ($= d_s$) / mm	Relative straight flow, q_s/q_c									
	0.1	0.2	0.3	0.4	0.5	0.6	0.7	0.8	0.9	1.0
250	0.24	0.20	0.14	0.08	0.04	0.01	−0.01	0	0.03	0.11
400	0.29	0.22	0.15	0.09	0.04	0.01	−0.01	−0.03	−0.02	0

Table C4.66 90° tees, diverging flow: values for the branch factor ζ_{c-b} (derived from the European Programme Report and Koch)

Area ratio, A_b/A_c	Relative branch flow, q_b/q_c									
	0.1	0.2	0.3	0.4	0.5	0.6	0.7	0.8	0.9	1.0
(a) Main duct size: $d_s = d_c = 400$ mm										
0.0625*	2.0	3.0	3.6	4.2	4.5	6.0	9.0	12.0	16	21
0.1	1.5	1.8	2.4	3.0	3.4	4.5	6.0	8.1	10.4	12.5
0.1406*	1.25	1.3	1.7	2.2	2.7	3.4	4.3	5.4	6.6	7.8
0.20	1.1	1.2	1.4	1.65	2.0	2.3	2.7	3.3	3.75	4.5
0.25*	1.08	1.2	1.3	1.4	1.65	1.75	2.0	2.3	2.65	3.1
0.30	1.05	1.1	1.18	1.25	1.37	1.48	1.6	1.8	2.05	2.4
0.3906*	0.99	0.99	1.0	1.02	1.05	1.1	1.18	1.3	1.45	1.6
(b) Main duct size: $d_s = d_c = 250$ mm										
0.16†	1.6	2.3	3.0	4.0	5.7	7.9	10	13	16.8	21.5
0.2	1.45	2.0	2.5	3.3	4.4	6.5	7.6	9.0	10.5	14
0.3	1.25	1.5	1.8	2.2	2.7	3.3	4.1	5.0	6.0	7.0
0.36†	1.18	1.3	1.48	1.8	2.16	2.6	3.1	3.7	4.4	5.0
0.4	1.14	1.2	1.35	1.6	1.9	2.2	2.6	3.1	3.8	4.4
0.5	1.06	1.05	1.15	1.2	1.4	1.7	1.9	2.2	2.5	3.0
0.6	1.01	1.01	1.05	1.04	1.15	1.3	1.5	1.65	1.8	2.2
0.64†	1.0	1.0	1.0	1.0	1.1	1.2	1.35	1.5	1.7	2.0
0.7	0.98	0.98	0.98	0.98	1.05	1.1	1.2	1.3	1.5	1.7
0.8	0.97	0.97	0.97	0.97	1.0	1.0	1.1	1.15	1.3	1.4
1.00†	0.97	0.95	0.95	0.95	0.95	0.95	1.0	1.08	1.15	1.24

* Values obtained using a main duct size: $d_s = d_c = 400$ mm; other values obtained by interpolation
† Values obtained using a main duct size: $d_s = d_c = 250$ mm; other values obtained by interpolation

C4.11.2.30   Angled off-sets, circular (HVCA 134)

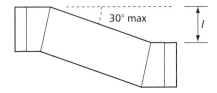

There are no specific data on mitred elbows in close proximity. A good approximation would be to use the sum of two mitres, and the length of straight duct between them. The value of ζ for mitre elbows of small angles can be obtained from Table C4.51 and Figure C4.11.

C4.11.3   Pressure loss factors for ductwork components: flat-oval

C4.11.3.1   90° segmented bends

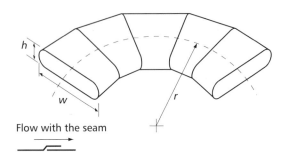

Flow with the seam

See Table C4.106. Smith and Jones found that having the seams against the flow gave rise to an additional 0.06 in the value of ζ in comparison with the value when the flow is with the seam (approximately 23% extra). The values in Table C4.106 are for flow 'with the seam'. The values of ζ are greater than for a bend of circular cross section (see Table C4.47). It is to be expected that values of ζ for other values of r/w will be similarly greater than the circular equivalent.

For bends having the same aspect ratio h/w, the larger ducts have a slightly lower value of ζ.

C4.11.3.2   Tees, flow diverging

All tees are circular off the oval duct, with branch diameter equal to the height of the oval duct ($d_b = h$). No data are available for the straight factor $\zeta_{c\text{-}s}$, nor for converging flow.

(a) 90° tee

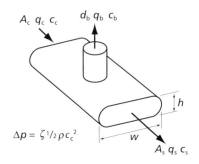

$\Delta p = \zeta \frac{1}{2} \rho c_c^2$

See Table C4.107.

(b) 45° tee

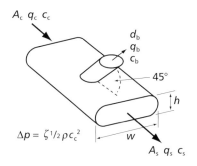

$\Delta p = \zeta \frac{1}{2} \rho c_c^2$

See Table C4.108.

Table C4.106 90° segmented bends, flat-oval ($r/w = 1.5$): values of ζ; for $4 \times 10^5 < Re < 29 \times 10^5$ and 419 mm $< d_e <$ 794 mm (derived from Smith and Jones)

Item	Ratio, h/w									
	'Hard' ($w > h$)					'Easy' ($w < h$)				
	0.25	0.33	0.4	0.5	0.75	1	2	3	4	5
Seg. bend (flat-oval)	0.239	0.220	0.204	*0.192*	*0.171*	*0.170*	0.171	0.182	0.197	*0.214*

The figures in italics were obtained by interpolation

Table C4.107 90° tee, flat-oval, diverging: values of the branch factor, $\zeta_{c\text{-}b}$; for $4 \times 10^5 < Re_c < 29 \times 10^5$, and 255 mm $< d_{ec} <$ 550 mm (derived from Smith and Jones)

Aspect, ratio, w/h	Equivalent diameter, d_{ec} / mm	Branch diameter, d_b / mm	Area ratio, A_b/A_c	Relative branch flow, q_b/q_c							
				0.1	0.2	0.3	0.4	0.5	0.6	0.7	0.8
2.0	255	150	0.279	0.921	1.05	1.21	1.53	1.95	2.42	3.03	—
3.2	300	150	0.196	0.958	1.17	1.64	2.26	3.12	—	—	—
4.1	550	150	0.157	1.00	1.37	2.11	3.12	—	—	—	—
2.0	423	250	0.282	0.937	1.04	1.26	1.53	1.90	2.37	3.00	3.69
2.9	484	250	0.210	0.947	1.16	1.53	2.11	2.84	3.69	—	—
4.1	550	250	0.159	1.00	1.37	2.05	3.03	—	—	—	—

Table C4.108 45° tee, flat-oval, diverging: values of the branch factor, $\zeta_{\text{c-b}}$; for $4 \times 10^5 < Re_c < 29 \times 10^5$, and 255 mm $< d_{ec} <$ 550 mm (derived from Smith and Jones)

Aspect, ratio, w/h	Equivalent diameter, d_{ec} / mm	Branch diameter, d_b / mm	Area ratio, A_b/A_c	Relative branch flow, q_b/q_c							
				0.1	0.2	0.3	0.4	0.5	0.6	0.7	0.8
2.0	255	150	0.279	0.684	0.505	0.542	0.789	1.48	3.32	—	—
3.2	300	150	0.196	0.579	0.526	0.921	1.59	2.82	—	—	—
4.1	550	150	0.157	0.505	0.658	1.42	2.79	—	—	—	—
2.0	423	250	0.282	0.658	0.484	0.432	0.553	0.916	1.42	2.1	2.97
2.9	484	250	0.210	0.526	0.421	0.553	0.980	1.79	3.65	—	—
4.1	550	250	0.159	0.484	0.431	1.00	2.05	3.66	—	—	—

C4.11.4 Pressure loss factors for ductwork components : rectangular

When Reynolds number is required for rectangular ducts, the hydraulic diameter (d_h) is to be used, being four times the hydraulic radius:

$$d_h = \frac{2\,w\,h}{(w + h)} \qquad (4.35)$$

$$Re = \frac{\rho\,c\,d_h}{\eta} \qquad (4.36)$$

where w and h are the width (mm) and height (mm) of the duct section.

C4.11.4.1 90° radius bends without vanes (HVCA 86, 87)

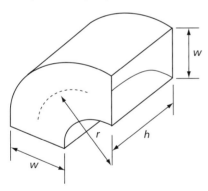

See Tables C4.109 and C4.110. The values in Table C4.109 are for $Re = 2 \times 10^5$.

Table C4.109 90° bends, rectangular: values of ζ; for $Re = 2 \times 10^5$ (derived from Miller)

Ratio, r/w	Aspect ratio, h/w				
	0.5	0.75	1.0	1.5	2.0
0.8	—	—	—	—	0.359
1.0	0.232	0.248	0.254	0.253	0.243
1.5	0.180	0.177	0.174	0.164	0.137
2.0	0.164	0.160	0.155	0.142	0.121
2.5	0.166	0.158	0.151	0.137	0.124
3	0.170	0.158	0.150	0.137	0.128
4	—	—	—	—	0.135
6	—	—	—	—	0.153

Note: w is believed to be approximately 300 mm.

Figures in italics obtained by interpolation

Table C4.110 90° bends, rectangular: values of C_{Re} (derived from the European Programme Report)

Item	Value of C_{Re} for stated Reynolds number, $Re / 10^5$						
	0.5	1.0	1.5	2.0	3	4	10
90° bend, rect.	1.37	1.16	1.084	1.0	0.98	0.96	0.948

Table C4.111 Radius bends, rectangular: values of angle factor C_α; for $Re = 2 \times 10^5$ (derived from Miller)

Aspect ratio, h/w	Ratio, r/w	Value of C_α for stated bend angle, α					
		15°	30°	45°	60°	75°	90°
0.5	1	0.150	0.264	0.395	0.636	0.873	1
	2	0.219	0.400	0.568	0.742	0.897	1
	3	0.224	0.422	0.609	0.776	0.908	1
1.0	1	0.124	0.237	0.328	0.498	0.784	1
	2	0.170	0.367	0.531	0.701	0.857	1
	3	0.204	0.430	0.613	0.775	0.880	1
2.0	1	0.088	0.189	0.357	0.617	0.877	1
	2	0.183	0.391	0.583	0.722	0.852	1
	3	0.182	0.388	0.554	0.711	0.860	1

Figures in italics are interpolated values

For values of Re other than 2×10^5 the tabulated values should be multiplied by the correction factor C_{Re} given in Table C4.110.

Appreciable savings in pressure drop are obtained by employing a radius r/d of 1.5 or greater. For 'tight' bends where $r/d \leq 1$, consideration should be given to using a guide vane (see section C4.11.4.2).

For bends of angles (α) other than 90°, Table C4.111 gives the angle factor, C_α, relative to the values of ζ for 90° bends.

C4.11.4.2 Short radius bends with vanes (splitters) : rectangular (HVCA 88)

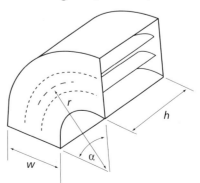

See Table C4.112.

These data were published before size and Re were known to have an effect. Preferred positions for splitters are given in Table C4.113.

For bends of other angles, it is suggested that the angle factors given in Table C4.111 be used.

Table C4.112 Short radius 90° bends, rectangular, with vanes: values of ζ (reproduced from *HVAC Systems Duct Design* by permission of the Sheet Metal and Air-Conditioning Contractors' National Association (SMACNA), Chantilly, Virginia, USA)

Ratio, r/w	Aspect ratio, h/w										
	0.25	0.5	1.0	1.5	2.0	3.0	4.0	5.0	6.0	7.0	8.0
(a) 1 turning vane											
0.55	0.52	0.40	0.43	0.49	0.55	0.66	0.75	0.84	0.93	1.01	1.09
0.60	0.36	0.27	0.25	0.28	0.30	0.35	0.39	0.42	0.46	0.49	0.52
0.65	0.28	0.21	0.18	0.19	0.20	0.22	0.25	0.26	0.28	0.30	0.32
0.70	0.22	0.16	0.14	0.14	0.15	0.16	0.17	0.18	0.19	0.20	0.21
0.75	0.18	0.13	0.11	0.11	0.11	0.12	0.13	0.14	0.14	0.15	0.15
0.80	0.15	0.11	0.09	0.09	0.09	0.09	0.10	0.10	0.11	0.11	0.12
0.90	0.11	0.08	0.07	0.06	0.06	0.06	0.06	0.07	0.07	0.07	0.07
1.00	0.09	0.06	0.05	0.05	0.04	0.04	0.04	0.05	0.05	0.05	0.05
(b) 2 turning vanes											
0.55	0.26	0.20	0.22	0.25	0.28	0.33	0.37	0.41	0.45	0.48	0.51
0.60	0.17	0.13	0.11	0.12	0.13	0.15	0.16	0.17	0.19	0.20	0.21
0.65	0.12	0.09	0.08	0.08	0.08	0.09	0.10	0.10	0.11	0.11	0.11
0.70	0.09	0.07	0.06	0.05	0.06	0.06	0.06	0.06	0.07	0.07	0.07
0.75	0.08	0.05	0.04	0.04	0.04	0.04	0.05	0.05	0.05	0.05	0.05
0.80	0.06	0.04	0.03	0.03	0.03	0.03	0.03	0.03	0.04	0.04	0.04
0.90	0.05	0.03	0.03	0.02	0.02	0.02	0.02	0.02	0.02	0.02	0.02
1.00	0.03	0.02	0.02	0.02	0.02	0.01	0.01	0.01	0.01	0.01	0.01
(c) 3 turning vanes											
0.55	0.11	0.10	0.12	0.13	0.14	0.16	0.18	0.19	0.21	0.22	0.23
0.60	0.07	0.05	0.06	0.06	0.06	0.07	0.07	0.08	0.08	0.08	0.09
0.65	0.05	0.04	0.04	0.04	0.04	0.04	0.04	0.04	0.04	0.05	0.05
0.70	0.03	0.03	0.03	0.03	0.03	0.03	0.03	0.03	0.03	0.03	0.03
0.75	0.03	0.02	0.02	0.02	0.02	0.02	0.02	0.02	0.02	0.02	0.02
0.80	0.03	0.02	0.02	0.02	0.02	0.01	0.01	0.01	0.01	0.01	0.01
0.90	0.02	0.01	0.01	0.01	0.01	0.01	0.01	0.01	0.01	0.01	0.01
1.00	0.01	0.01	0.01	0.01	0.01	0.01	0.01	0.01	0.01	0.01	0.01

Table C4.113 Short radius 90° bends, rectangular: recommended positions for splitters (from HVCA DW/144)

Dimension, w / mm	No. of splitters	Splitter position		
		1	2	3
400–800	1	$w/3$	—	—
801–1600	2	$w/4$	$w/2$	—
1601–2000	3	$w/8$	$w/3$	$w/2$

C4.11.4.4   Elbow, mitred, rectangular, any angle

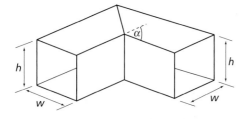

See Table C4.115. This table has been derived from data of Idelchik. These data were published before size and Re were known to have an effect.

Table C4.115 Mitred elbow, rectangular: values of ζ (from Idelchik)

Bend angle, α	Aspect ratio, h/w										
	0.25	0.5	0.75	1	1.5	2	3	4	5	6	8
20°	0.14	0.13	0.13	0.12	0.12	0.11	0.10	0.10	0.09	0.09	0.09
30°	0.17	0.17	0.16	0.16	0.15	0.14	0.13	0.12	0.12	0.11	0.11
45°	0.35	0.34	0.33	0.32	0.3	0.29	0.26	0.25	0.24	0.23	0.22
60°	0.61	0.59	0.58	0.56	0.53	0.50	0.46	0.43	0.42	0.40	0.39
75°	0.89	0.86	0.84	0.81	0.77	0.73	0.67	0.63	0.60	0.58	0.56
90°	1.31	1.27	1.24	1.19	1.13	1.07	0.99	0.93	0.89	0.86	0.83

With the exception of small angles, similar values of ζ may be obtained using the following algorithm, being adapted from curve-fits by Idelchik:

$$\zeta = \left(0.97 - 0.13 \ln \frac{h}{w}\right)\left(0.89 + \frac{40}{\alpha} \cos^2 (\alpha - 45)\right)$$

$$\times \left(0.95 \sin^2 \left(\frac{\alpha}{2}\right) + 2.05 \sin^4 \left(\frac{\alpha}{2}\right)\right) \qquad (4.37)$$

C4.11.4.7   Rectangular mitred elbows with vanes

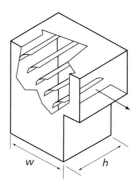

No reliable data available. It is suggested that the values of Table C4.115 might be halved.

C4.11.4.8   Bends in close proximity, rectangular ('gooseneck')

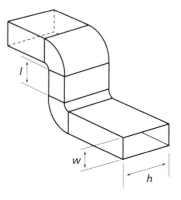

No data are available for the interaction factor C_{cp} of rectangular ductwork installed in close proximity. It is to be expected that C_{cp} would depend upon r/w and h/w of each bend as well as the separation l/w. We can also expect that it will vary with Reynolds number, and possibly also with size w.

Data for 'gooseneck' bends for circular ductwork are given in section C4.11.2.5 for close coupling of bends with $d = 250$ mm, and $r/d = 1.0$. Thus for close coupling of square bends of sides approximately 250 mm and with $r/d = 1.0$, it would seem reasonable to use the values of C_{cp} given in Table C4.52, in conjunction with values of ζ_1 from Table C4.109 in the equation:

$$\Delta p = 2\, C_{cp}\, \zeta_1\, \tfrac{1}{2}\, \rho\, c^2 \qquad (4.39)$$

Note that the above does not include for the pressure drop of the length of separation. The separation (l) should be added to the length of straight ductwork of the same size.

C4.11.4.12   90° rectangular tees (HVCA 104 and 106)

The values given in Tables C4.120 to C4.123 should be treated as 'best advice'. In the rectangular tees tested, w of the main duct remained constant ($w = h_c = h_s$), whereas $h_c \geq h_b$. Miller tested for various sizes of the shoe, b. The greater the size of the shoe the greater the reduction in ζ. The reduction in the values of ζ due to the installation of a trailing or leading bevel ($\Delta\zeta$) is shown in the tables.

It is to be expected that values of ζ will vary considerably with A_b/A_c, as occurs for circular tees. It is expected that ζ will depend on the aspect ratios of both the main duct (h_c/w) and of the branch (h_b/w_b), and a little upon size but no experimental data are available.

(a) *Converging flow*

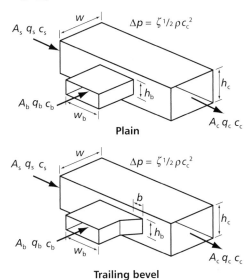

Plain

Trailing bevel

See Tables C4.120 and C4.121.

Table C4.120 90° rectangular tees, converging flow: values for the straight factor ζ_{s-c} and reduction in ζ obtained by inclusion of trailing bevel; for $w = h_c = h_s = 300$ mm, $Re_c > 10^5$ (derived from Miller)

Area ratio, A_b/A_c	Relative straight flow, q_s/q_c						
	0.2	0.3	0.4	0.5	0.6	0.7	0.8
0.79	0.75	0.71	0.66	0.60	0.53	0.44	0.35
1.00	0.74	0.70	0.65	0.59	0.52	0.43	0.33
	Bevel length, b	Reduction in straight factor, $\Delta\zeta_{s-c}$, due to trailing bevel					
0.79	$w/8$	0.26	0.24	0.22	0.20	0.17	0.15	0.11
1.00	$w/8$	0.26	0.24	0.25	0.26	0.19	0.11	0.06
1.00	$w/2$	0.54	0.45	0.35	0.27	0.19	0.11	0.06

Table C4.121 90° rectangular tees, converging flow: values for the branch factor ζ_{b-c} and reduction in ζ obtained by inclusion of trailing bevel; for $w = h_c = h_s = 300$ mm, $Re_c > 10^5$ (derived from Miller)

Area ratio, A_b/A_c	Relative branch flow, q_b/q_c						
	0.2	0.3	0.4	0.5	0.6	0.7	0.8
0.79	0.18	0.34	0.51	0.71	0.94	1.23	1.52
1.00	−0.10	0.19	0.42	0.62	0.83	1.01	1.13
	Bevel length, b	Reduction in branch factor, $\Delta\zeta_{b-c}$, due to trailing bevel					
0.79	$w/8$	—	0.23	0.21	0.23	0.25	0.27	0.30
1.00*	$w/8$	—	0.15	0.22	0.25	0.27	0.25	0.26
1.00	$w/2$	—	0.19	0.26	0.32	0.40	0.49	0.57

* Raw data is out of step with other data

(b) *Diverging flow*

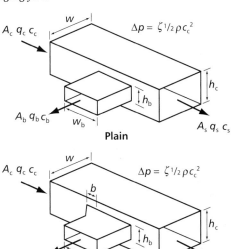

Plain

Leading bevel

See Tables C4.122 and C4.123.

Table C4.122 90° rectangular tees, diverging flow: values for the straight factor ζ_{c-s} and reduction in ζ obtained by inclusion of leading bevel; for $w = h_c = h_s = 300$ mm, $Re_c > 10^5$ (derived from Miller)

Area ratio, A_b/A_c	Relative straight flow, q_s/q_c						
	0.2	0.3	0.4	0.5	0.6	0.7	0.8
1.00	0.31	0.21	0.13	0.07	0.025	0	0
	Bevel length, b	Reduction in straight factor, $\Delta\zeta_{s-c}$, due to leading bevel					
1.00	$w/8$	No noticeable effect					
1.00	$w/2$	No noticeable effect					

Table C4.123 90° rectangular tees, diverging flow: values for the branch factor ζ_{c-b} and reduction in ζ obtained by inclusion of leading bevel; for $w = h_c = h_s = 300$ mm, $Re_c > 10^5$ (derived from Miller)

Area ratio, A_b/A_c	Relative branch flow, q_b/q_c						
	0.2	0.3	0.4	0.5	0.6	0.7	0.8
1.00*	*0.87*	*0.82*	*0.82*	*0.84*	*0.89*	*0.94*	*1.02*
	Bevel length, b	Reduction in branch factor, $\Delta\zeta_{b-c}$, due to leading bevel					
1.00	$w/8$	0.04	0.04	0.07	0.09	0.13	0.16	0.21
1.00	$w/2$	0.095	0.16	0.23	0.31	0.39	0.48	0.58

* Figures in italics are Miller's readings. They would be expected to be greater than for a circular tee (Table C4.66), but he did not make this comparison. The values as presented conflict with those for circular tees, thus there is possibly some doubt about these values.

C4.11.4.16   90° swept branch tee

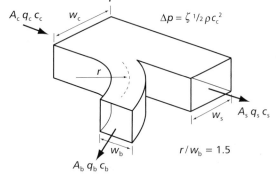

See Tables C4.124 and C4.125.

The values of the branch factor $\zeta_{c\text{-}b}$ ought to depend on the aspect ratio h_b/w_b. The only available data are from ASHRAE.

Table C4.124 90° swept tees, rectangular, diverging flow: values for the straight factor $\zeta_{c\text{-}s}$; for $h_b = h_c = h_s, A_b + A_s \geq A_c$ (from ASHRAE Handbook: *Fundamentals* 2005, ch. 35. © American Society of Heating, Refrigerating and Air-Conditioning Engineers Inc. (www.ashrae.org))

A_s/A_c	A_b/A_c	Relative straight flow, q_s/q_c								
		0.1	0.2	0.3	0.4	0.5	0.6	0.7	0.8	0.9
0.50	0.25	8.75	1.62	0.50	0.17	0.05	0.00	−0.02	−0.02	0.00
	0.50	7.50	1.12	0.25	0.06	0.05	0.09	0.14	0.19	0.22
	1.00	5.00	0.62	0.17	0.08	0.08	0.09	0.12	0.15	0.19
0.75	0.25	19.13	3.38	1.00	0.28	0.05	−0.02	−0.02	0.00	0.06
	0.50	20.81	3.23	0.75	0.14	−0.02	−0.05	−0.05	−0.02	0.03
	1.00	16.88	2.81	0.63	0.11	−0.02	−0.05	0.01	0.00	0.07
1.00	0.25	46.00	9.50	3.22	1.31	0.52	0.14	−0.02	−0.05	−0.01
	0.50	35.00	6.75	2.11	0.75	0.24	0.00	−0.10	−0.09	−0.04
	1.00	38.00	7.50	2.44	0.81	0.24	−0.03	−0.08	−0.06	−0.02

Table C4.125 90° swept tees, rectangular, diverging flow: values for the branch factor $\zeta_{c\text{-}b}$; for $h_w = h_c = h_s, A_b + A_s \geq A_c$ (from ASHRAE Handbook: *Fundamentals* 2005, ch. 35. © American Society of Heating, Refrigerating and Air-Conditioning Engineers Inc. (www.ashrae.org))

A_s/A_c	A_b/A_c	Relative branch flow, q_b/q_c								
		0.1	0.2	0.3	0.4	0.5	0.6	0.7	0.8	0.9
0.50	0.25	3.44	0.70	0.30	0.20	0.17	0.16	0.16	0.17	0.18
	0.50	11.00	2.37	1.06	0.64	0.52	0.47	0.47	0.47	0.48
	1.00	60.00	13.00	4.78	2.06	0.96	0.47	0.31	0.27	0.26
0.75	0.25	2.19	0.55	0.35	0.31	0.33	0.35	0.36	0.37	0.39
	0.50	13.00	2.50	0.89	0.47	0.34	0.31	0.32	0.36	0.43
	1.00	70.00	15.00	5.67	2.62	1.36	0.78	0.53	0.41	0.36
1.00	0.25	3.44	0.78	0.42	0.33	0.30	0.31	0.40	0.42	0.46
	0.50	15.50	3.00	1.11	0.62	0.48	0.42	0.40	0.42	0.46
	1.00	67.00	13.75	5.11	2.31	1.28	0.81	0.59	0.47	0.46

C4.11.4.18   Opposed blade dampers

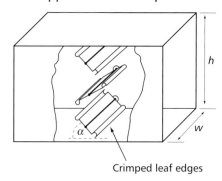

Crimped leaf edges

See Table C4.126. The parameter x is determined from:

$$x = \frac{n\,w}{2\,(h + w)} \tag{4.40}$$

where n is the number of blades.

Table C4.126 Opposed blade damper: values of ζ from ASHRAE Handbook: *Fundamentals* 2005, ch. 35. © American Society of Heating, Refrigerating and Air-Conditioning Engineers Inc. (www.ashrae.org))

Value of x	Value of ζ for stated blade angle, α								
	0°	10°	20°	30°	40°	50°	60°	70°	80°
0.3	0.52	0.79	1.91	3.77	8.55	19.5	70.1	295	807
0.4	0.52	0.85	2.07	4.61	10.4	26.7	92.9	346	926
0.5	0.52	0.93	2.25	5.44	12.3	34.0	119	393	1045
0.6	0.52	1.00	2.46	5.99	14.1	41.3	144	440	1163
0.8	0.52	1.08	2.66	6.96	18.2	56.5	194	520	1325
1.0	0.52	1.17	2.91	7.31	20.2	71.7	245	576	1521
1.5	0.52	1.38	3.16	9.51	27.6	104.4	361	717	1804

Appendix C4.A0 : Pipe sizing tables

q_m	= mass flow rate	kg/s
c	= velocity	m/s
$\Delta p/l$	= pressure loss per unit length	Pa/m

COPPER (OLD TABLE X)

WATER AT 10 °C

$\Delta p/l$	c	10 mm		12 mm		15 mm		22 mm		28 mm		35 mm		42 mm		c	$\Delta p/l$
		q_m	c	q_m	c	q_m	c	q_m	c	q_m	c	q_m	c	q_m	c		
0.1												0.002	0.00	0.004	0.00		0.1
0.2										0.001	0.00	0.004	0.00	0.009	0.01		0.2
0.3										0.002	0.00	0.006	0.01	0.013	0.01		0.3
0.4								0.001	0.00	0.003	0.01	0.008	0.01	0.018	0.01		0.4
0.5								0.001	0.00	0.004	0.01	0.010	0.01	0.023	0.02		0.5
0.6								0.001	0.00	0.005	0.01	0.012	0.01	0.027	0.02		0.6
0.7								0.002	0.01	0.006	0.01	0.014	0.02	0.032	0.03		0.7
0.8								0.002	0.01	0.007	0.01	0.017	0.02	0.037	0.03		0.8
0.9								0.002	0.01	0.008	0.01	0.019	0.02	0.041	0.03		0.9
1.0								0.003	0.01	0.008	0.01	0.021	0.03	0.046	0.04	0.05	1.0
1.5								0.004	0.01	0.013	0.02	0.032	0.04	0.069	0.06		1.5
2.0						0.001	0.01	0.006	0.02	0.017	0.03	0.042	0.05	0.080	0.06		2.0
2.5						0.001	0.01	0.007	0.02	0.022	0.04	0.053	0.06	0.080	0.06		2.5
3.0						0.001	0.01	0.009	0.03	0.026	0.05	0.064	0.08	0.085	0.07		3.0
3.5						0.002	0.01	0.011	0.03	0.031	0.06	0.066	0.08	0.093	0.08		3.5
4.0				0.001	0.01	0.002	0.01	0.012	0.04	0.035	0.06	0.066	0.08	0.101	0.08		4.0
4.5				0.001	0.01	0.002	0.01	0.014	0.04	0.040	0.07	0.066	0.08	0.108	0.09		4.5
5.0				0.001	0.01	0.003	0.02	0.015	0.05	0.044	0.08	0.066	0.08	0.115	0.09		5.0
5.5				0.001	0.01	0.003	0.02	0.017	0.05	0.049	0.09	0.070	0.08	0.122	0.10		5.5
6.0				0.001	0.01	0.003	0.02	0.018	0.06	0.053	0.10	0.074	0.09	0.128	0.10		6.0
6.5				0.001	0.01	0.004	0.03	0.020	0.06	0.053	0.10	0.078	0.09	0.135	0.11		6.5
7.0				0.001	0.01	0.004	0.03	0.022	0.07	0.053	0.10	0.082	0.10	0.141	0.11		7.0
7.5				0.001	0.01	0.004	0.03	0.023	0.07	0.053	0.10	0.085	0.10	0.147	0.12		7.5
8.0				0.002	0.02	0.005	0.03	0.025	0.08	0.053	0.10	0.088	0.11	0.153	0.12		8.0
8.5				0.002	0.02	0.005	0.03	0.026	0.08	0.053	0.10	0.092	0.11	0.158	0.13		8.5
9.0		0.001	0.02	0.002	0.02	0.005	0.03	0.028	0.09	0.053	0.10	0.095	0.11	0.164	0.13		9.0
9.5		0.001	0.02	0.002	0.02	0.006	0.04	0.029	0.09	0.053	0.10	0.098	0.12	0.169	0.14		9.5
10.0		0.001	0.02	0.002	0.02	0.006	0.04	0.031	0.10	0.055	0.10	0.101	0.12	0.174	0.14	0.15	10.0
12.5		0.001	0.02	0.003	0.03	0.008	0.06	0.039	0.12	0.062	0.11	0.116	0.14	0.199	0.16		12.5
15.0		0.001	0.02	0.003	0.03	0.009	0.06	0.041	0.13	0.070	0.13	0.129	0.15	0.221	0.18		15.0
17.5		0.001	0.02	0.004	0.04	0.011	0.08	0.041	0.13	0.077	0.14	0.141	0.17	0.242	0.20		17.5
20.0		0.002	0.03	0.005	0.05	0.012	0.08	0.041	0.13	0.083	0.15	0.153	0.18	0.262	0.21		20.0
22.5		0.002	0.03	0.005	0.05	0.014	0.10	0.043	0.13	0.089	0.16	0.164	0.20	0.281	0.23		22.5
25.0		0.002	0.03	0.006	0.07	0.016	0.11	0.046	0.14	0.095	0.18	0.175	0.21	0.299	0.24		25.0
27.5		0.003	0.05	0.007	0.08	0.017	0.12	0.048	0.15	0.100	0.19	0.185	0.22	0.316	0.26		27.5
30.0		0.003	0.05	0.007	0.08	0.019	0.13	0.051	0.16	0.106	0.20	0.194	0.23	0.332	0.27		30.0
32.5		0.003	0.05	0.008	0.09	0.020	0.14	0.054	0.17	0.111	0.21	0.204	0.24	0.348	0.28		32.5
35.0	0.05	0.003	0.05	0.008	0.09	0.022	0.15	0.056	0.17	0.116	0.21	0.213	0.25	0.364	0.30	0.30	35.0
37.5		0.004	0.07	0.009	0.10	0.024	0.17	0.058	0.18	0.121	0.22	0.222	0.27	0.378	0.31		37.5
40.0		0.004	0.07	0.010	0.11	0.025	0.17	0.061	0.19	0.126	0.23	0.230	0.28	0.393	0.32		40.0
42.5		0.004	0.07	0.010	0.11	0.027	0.19	0.063	0.20	0.130	0.24	0.238	0.28	0.407	0.33		42.5
45.0		0.005	0.08	0.011	0.12	0.027	0.19	0.065	0.20	0.135	0.25	0.247	0.30	0.421	0.34		45.0
47.5		0.005	0.08	0.012	0.13	0.027	0.19	0.067	0.21	0.139	0.26	0.255	0.31	0.434	0.35		47.5
50.0		0.005	0.08	0.012	0.13	0.027	0.19	0.069	0.21	0.143	0.26	0.262	0.31	0.447	0.36		50.0
52.5		0.005	0.08	0.013	0.14	0.027	0.19	0.071	0.22	0.147	0.27	0.270	0.32	0.460	0.37		52.5
55.0		0.006	0.10	0.014	0.15	0.027	0.19	0.073	0.23	0.152	0.28	0.277	0.33	0.472	0.38		55.0
57.5		0.006	0.10	0.014	0.15	0.027	0.19	0.075	0.23	0.156	0.29	0.285	0.34	0.485	0.39		57.5
60.0		0.006	0.10	0.015	0.16	0.027	0.19	0.077	0.24	0.160	0.30	0.292	0.35	0.497	0.40		60.0
62.5		0.007	0.12	0.016	0.17	0.027	0.19	0.079	0.25	0.163	0.30	0.299	0.36	0.509	0.41		62.5
65.0		0.007	0.12	0.016	0.17	0.027	0.19	0.081	0.25	0.167	0.31	0.306	0.37	0.520	0.42		65.0
67.5		0.007	0.12	0.017	0.19	0.027	0.19	0.083	0.26	0.171	0.32	0.312	0.37	0.532	0.43		67.5
70.0		0.007	0.12	0.017	0.19	0.028	0.19	0.085	0.26	0.175	0.32	0.319	0.38	0.543	0.44		70.0
72.5		0.008	0.13	0.018	0.20	0.028	0.19	0.087	0.27	0.178	0.33	0.326	0.39	0.554	0.45		72.5
75.0		0.008	0.13	0.019	0.21	0.029	0.20	0.088	0.27	0.182	0.34	0.332	0.40	0.565	0.46		75.0
77.5		0.008	0.13	0.019	0.21	0.029	0.20	0.090	0.28	0.185	0.34	0.338	0.40	0.576	0.47		77.5
80.0		0.009	0.15	0.020	0.22	0.030	0.21	0.092	0.29	0.189	0.35	0.345	0.41	0.586	0.48		80.0
82.5		0.009	0.15	0.021	0.23	0.031	0.21	0.094	0.29	0.192	0.36	0.351	0.42	0.597	0.48		82.5
85.0		0.009	0.15	0.021	0.23	0.031	0.21	0.095	0.30	0.196	0.36	0.357	0.43	0.607	0.49		85.0
87.5		0.009	0.15	0.022	0.24	0.032	0.22	0.097	0.30	0.199	0.37	0.363	0.43	0.617	0.50	0.50	87.5
90.0		0.010	0.16	0.022	0.24	0.032	0.22	0.099	0.31	0.202	0.37	0.369	0.44	0.627	0.51		90.0

q_m = mass flow rate — kg/s
c = velocity — m/s
$\Delta p/l$ = pressure loss per unit length — Pa/m

COPPER (OLD TABLE X)

WATER AT 10 °C

$\Delta p/l$	c	10 mm q_m	10 mm c	12 mm q_m	12 mm c	15 mm q_m	15 mm c	22 mm q_m	22 mm c	28 mm q_m	28 mm c	35 mm q_m	35 mm c	42 mm q_m	42 mm c	c	$\Delta p/l$
92.5		0.010	0.16	0.022	0.24	0.033	0.23	0.100	0.31	0.206	0.38	0.375	0.45	0.637	0.52		92.5
95.0		0.010	0.16	0.022	0.24	0.033	0.23	0.102	0.32	0.209	0.39	0.381	0.46	0.647	0.52		95.0
97.5		0.011	0.18	0.022	0.24	0.034	0.23	0.103	0.32	0.212	0.39	0.386	0.46	0.657	0.53		97.5
100		0.011	0.18	0.022	0.24	0.034	0.23	0.105	0.33	0.215	0.40	0.392	0.47	0.667	0.54		100
120		0.013	0.21	0.022	0.24	0.038	0.26	0.117	0.36	0.239	0.44	0.436	0.52	0.740	0.60		120
140		0.015	0.25	0.022	0.24	0.042	0.29	0.128	0.40	0.262	0.49	0.476	0.57	0.808	0.66		140
160		0.017	0.28	0.024	0.26	0.046	0.32	0.138	0.43	0.283	0.52	0.514	0.61	0.872	0.71		160
180		0.017	0.28	0.026	0.28	0.049	0.34	0.148	0.46	0.303	0.56	0.550	0.66	0.933	0.76		180
200		0.017	0.28	0.027	0.29	0.052	0.36	0.158	0.49	0.322	0.60	0.584	0.70	0.991	0.80		200
220		0.017	0.28	0.029	0.32	0.055	0.38	0.167	0.52	0.340	0.63	0.617	0.74	1.040	0.84		220
240		0.017	0.28	0.030	0.33	0.058	0.40	0.175	0.55	0.357	0.66	0.649	0.78	1.090	0.88		240
260	0.30	0.018	0.30	0.032	0.35	0.061	0.42	0.184	0.57	0.374	0.69	0.679	0.81	1.150	0.93		260
280		0.019	0.31	0.033	0.36	0.064	0.44	0.192	0.60	0.391	0.72	0.708	0.85	1.190	0.97	1.00	280
300		0.019	0.31	0.035	0.38	0.067	0.46	0.200	0.62	0.406	0.75	0.737	0.88	1.240	1.01		300
320		0.020	0.33	0.036	0.39	0.069	0.48	0.207	0.64	0.422	0.78	0.764	0.91	1.290	1.05		320
340		0.021	0.35	0.038	0.41	0.072	0.50	0.215	0.67	0.437	0.81	0.791	0.95	1.330	1.08		340
360		0.022	0.36	0.039	0.43	0.074	0.51	0.222	0.69	0.451	0.84	0.817	0.98	1.380	1.12		360
380		0.022	0.36	0.040	0.44	0.077	0.53	0.229	0.71	0.465	0.86	0.843	1.01	1.420	1.15		380
400		0.023	0.38	0.041	0.45	0.079	0.54	0.236	0.74	0.479	0.89	0.868	1.04	1.460	1.18		400
420		0.024	0.39	0.043	0.47	0.081	0.56	0.243	0.76	0.493	0.91	0.892	1.07	1.500	1.22		420
440		0.025	0.41	0.044	0.48	0.084	0.58	0.249	0.78	0.506	0.94	0.916	1.10	1.540	1.25		440
460		0.025	0.41	0.045	0.49	0.086	0.59	0.256	0.80	0.519	0.96	0.940	1.12	1.580	1.28		460
480		0.026	0.43	0.046	0.50	0.088	0.61	0.262	0.82	0.532	0.99	0.963	1.15	1.620	1.31		480
500		0.027	0.44	0.047	0.51	0.090	0.62	0.268	0.83	0.545	1.01	0.985	1.18	1.660	1.35		500
520		0.027	0.44	0.049	0.54	0.092	0.63	0.274	0.85	0.557	1.03	1.000	1.20	1.700	1.38		520
540		0.028	0.46	0.050	0.55	0.094	0.65	0.280	0.87	0.569	1.05	1.020	1.22	1.730	1.40		540
560		0.028	0.46	0.051	0.56	0.096	0.66	0.286	0.89	0.581	1.08	1.050	1.26	1.770	1.44		560
580		0.029	0.48	0.052	0.57	0.098	0.67	0.292	0.91	0.593	1.10	1.070	1.28	1.810	1.47		580
600		0.030	0.49	0.053	0.58	0.100	0.69	0.298	0.93	0.604	1.12	1.090	1.30	1.840	1.49	1.50	600
620	0.50	0.030	0.49	0.054	0.59	0.102	0.70	0.304	0.95	0.616	1.14	1.110	1.33	1.870	1.52		620
640		0.031	0.51	0.055	0.60	0.104	0.72	0.309	0.96	0.627	1.16	1.130	1.35	1.910	1.55		640
660		0.031	0.51	0.056	0.61	0.106	0.73	0.315	0.98	0.638	1.18	1.150	1.38	1.940	1.57		660
680		0.032	0.53	0.057	0.62	0.108	0.74	0.320	1.00	0.649	1.20	1.170	1.40	1.980	1.61		680
700		0.033	0.54	0.058	0.63	0.110	0.76	0.326	1.02	0.660	1.22	1.190	1.42	2.010	1.63		700
720		0.033	0.54	0.059	0.64	0.112	0.77	0.331	1.03	0.670	1.24	1.210	1.45	2.040	1.65		720
740		0.034	0.56	0.060	0.66	0.113	0.78	0.336	1.05	0.681	1.26	1.230	1.47	2.070	1.68		740
760		0.034	0.56	0.061	0.67	0.115	0.79	0.341	1.06	0.691	1.28	1.240	1.48	2.100	1.70		760
780		0.035	0.58	0.062	0.68	0.117	0.81	0.346	1.08	0.702	1.30	1.260	1.51	2.130	1.73		780
800		0.035	0.58	0.063	0.69	0.119	0.82	0.352	1.10	0.712	1.32	1.280	1.53	2.160	1.75		800
820		0.036	0.59	0.064	0.70	0.120	0.83	0.357	1.11	0.722	1.34	1.300	1.56	2.190	1.78		820
840		0.036	0.59	0.065	0.71	0.122	0.84	0.361	1.12	0.732	1.36	1.320	1.58	2.220	1.80		840
860		0.037	0.61	0.065	0.71	0.124	0.85	0.366	1.14	0.742	1.37	1.330	1.59	2.250	1.82		860
880		0.037	0.61	0.066	0.72	0.125	0.86	0.371	1.16	0.751	1.39	1.350	1.61	2.280	1.85		880
900		0.038	0.62	0.067	0.73	0.127	0.87	0.376	1.17	0.761	1.41	1.370	1.64	2.310	1.87		900
920		0.038	0.62	0.068	0.74	0.129	0.89	0.381	1.19	0.771	1.43	1.390	1.66	2.340	1.90		920
940		0.039	0.64	0.069	0.75	0.130	0.90	0.386	1.20	0.780	1.45	1.400	1.67	2.370	1.92		940
960		0.039	0.64	0.070	0.76	0.132	0.91	0.390	1.21	0.789	1.46	1.420	1.70	2.400	1.95		960
980		0.040	0.66	0.071	0.78	0.134	0.92	0.395	1.23	0.799	1.48	1.440	1.72	2.430	1.97		980
1000		0.040	0.66	0.071	0.78	0.135	0.93	0.399	1.24	0.808	1.50	1.450	1.73	2.450	1.99	2.00	1000
1100		0.043	0.71	0.076	0.83	0.143	0.98	0.422	1.31	0.853	1.58	1.530	1.83	2.590	2.10		1100
1200		0.045	0.74	0.080	0.87	0.150	1.03	0.443	1.38	0.896	1.66	1.610	1.93	2.720	2.21		1200
1300		0.047	0.77	0.083	0.91	0.157	1.08	0.464	1.45	0.937	1.74	1.680	2.01	2.840	2.30		1300
1400		0.049	0.81	0.087	0.95	0.164	1.13	0.484	1.51	0.977	1.81	1.760	2.11	2.960	2.40		1400
1500		0.051	0.84	0.091	0.99	0.171	1.18	0.503	1.57	1.010	1.87	1.830	2.19	3.080	2.50		1500
1600		0.053	0.87	0.094	1.03	0.177	1.22	0.522	1.63	1.050	1.95	1.890	2.26	3.190	2.59		1600
1700		0.055	0.90	0.098	1.07	0.184	1.27	0.540	1.68	1.090	2.02	1.960	2.34	3.300	2.68		1700
1800		0.057	0.94	0.101	1.10	0.190	1.31	0.558	1.74	1.120	2.07	2.020	2.42	3.410	2.77		1800
1900		0.059	0.97	0.104	1.14	0.196	1.35	0.576	1.79	1.160	2.15	2.090	2.50	3.510	2.85		1900
2000		0.061	1.00	0.107	1.17	0.202	1.39	0.593	1.85	1.190	2.20	2.150	2.57	3.620	2.94		2000

q_m = mass flow rate — kg/s
c = velocity — m/s
$\Delta p/l$ = pressure loss per unit length — Pa/m

COPPER (OLD TABLE X)

WATER AT 10 °C

$\Delta p/l$	c	54 mm		67 mm		76 mm		108 mm		133 mm		159 mm		mm		c	$\Delta p/l$
		q_m	c	q_m	c	q_m	c	q_m	c	q_m	c	q_m	c	q_m	c		
0.1		0.013	0.01	0.032	0.01	0.054	0.01	0.214	0.02	0.307	0.02	0.503	0.03				0.1
0.2		0.026	0.01	0.064	0.02	0.108	0.03	0.256	0.03	0.466	0.04	0.760	0.04				0.2
0.3		0.040	0.02	0.096	0.03	0.149	0.04	0.327	0.04	0.593	0.04	0.964	0.05			0.05	0.3
0.4		0.053	0.03	0.128	0.04	0.149	0.04	0.388	0.04	0.702	0.05	1.140	0.06				0.4
0.5		0.067	0.03	0.131	0.04	0.161	0.04	0.443	0.05	0.801	0.06	1.300	0.07				0.5
0.6		0.080	0.04	0.131	0.04	0.180	0.04	0.494	0.06	0.891	0.07	1.440	0.08				0.6
0.7		0.093	0.04	0.137	0.04	0.198	0.05	0.541	0.06	0.975	0.07	1.580	0.08				0.7
0.8		0.105	0.05	0.149	0.05	0.214	0.05	0.585	0.07	1.050	0.08	1.700	0.09				0.8
0.9		0.105	0.05	0.160	0.05	0.230	0.05	0.627	0.07	1.120	0.08	1.820	0.10				0.9
1.0	0.05	0.105	0.05	0.170	0.05	0.245	0.06	0.667	0.08	1.200	0.09	1.940	0.10				1.0
1.5		0.117	0.06	0.217	0.07	0.312	0.07	0.845	0.10	1.510	0.11	2.450	0.13				1.5
2.0		0.139	0.07	0.257	0.08	0.370	0.09	0.999	0.12	1.790	0.13	2.890	0.15			0.15	2.0
2.5		0.160	0.08	0.294	0.09	0.422	0.10	1.130	0.13	2.030	0.15	3.280	0.17				2.5
3.0		0.178	0.09	0.327	0.10	0.469	0.11	1.260	0.15	2.260	0.17	3.640	0.19				3.0
3.5		0.195	0.09	0.358	0.11	0.514	0.12	1.380	0.16	2.470	0.19	3.980	0.21				3.5
4.0		0.211	0.10	0.388	0.12	0.556	0.13	1.490	0.17	2.660	0.20	4.290	0.23				4.0
4.5		0.226	0.11	0.416	0.13	0.595	0.14	1.590	0.18	2.850	0.21	4.590	0.24				4.5
5.0		0.241	0.12	0.442	0.14	0.633	0.15	1.690	0.20	3.030	0.23	4.870	0.26				5.0
5.5		0.255	0.12	0.467	0.14	0.669	0.16	1.790	0.21	3.190	0.24	5.140	0.27				5.5
6.0		0.269	0.13	0.492	0.15	0.704	0.17	1.880	0.22	3.360	0.25	5.400	0.29				6.0
6.5		0.281	0.13	0.515	0.16	0.737	0.18	1.970	0.23	3.510	0.26	5.660	0.30			0.30	6.5
7.0		0.294	0.14	0.538	0.17	0.769	0.18	2.050	0.24	3.670	0.28	5.900	0.31				7.0
7.5	0.15	0.306	0.15	0.560	0.17	0.801	0.19	2.130	0.25	3.810	0.29	6.130	0.32				7.5
8.0		0.318	0.15	0.581	0.18	0.831	0.20	2.220	0.26	3.950	0.30	6.360	0.34				8.0
8.5		0.330	0.16	0.602	0.19	0.861	0.20	2.290	0.26	4.090	0.31	6.580	0.35				8.5
9.0		0.341	0.16	0.623	0.19	0.890	0.21	2.370	0.27	4.230	0.32	6.800	0.36				9.0
9.5		0.352	0.17	0.642	0.20	0.918	0.22	2.440	0.28	4.360	0.33	7.010	0.37				9.5
10.0		0.363	0.17	0.662	0.20	0.946	0.22	2.520	0.29	4.490	0.34	7.210	0.38				10.0
12.5		0.413	0.20	0.753	0.23	1.070	0.25	2.860	0.33	5.090	0.38	8.180	0.43				12.5
15.0		0.459	0.22	0.837	0.26	1.190	0.28	3.170	0.37	5.650	0.43	9.070	0.48			0.50	15.0
17.5		0.502	0.24	0.914	0.28	1.300	0.31	3.460	0.40	6.160	0.46	9.890	0.52				17.5
20.0		0.543	0.26	0.987	0.30	1.400	0.33	3.730	0.43	6.640	0.50	10.600	0.56				20.0
22.5		0.581	0.28	1.050	0.32	1.500	0.36	3.990	0.46	7.100	0.54	11.300	0.60				22.5
25.0	0.30	0.618	0.30	1.120	0.35	1.600	0.38	4.240	0.49	7.530	0.57	12.000	0.64				25.0
27.5		0.653	0.31	1.180	0.36	1.680	0.40	4.470	0.52	7.940	0.60	12.700	0.67				27.5
30.0		0.686	0.33	1.240	0.38	1.770	0.42	4.700	0.54	8.340	0.63	13.300	0.71				30.0
32.5		0.719	0.34	1.300	0.40	1.850	0.44	4.910	0.57	8.730	0.66	13.900	0.74				32.5
35.0		0.750	0.36	1.360	0.42	1.930	0.46	5.120	0.59	9.100	0.69	14.500	0.77				35.0
37.5		0.780	0.37	1.410	0.43	2.010	0.48	5.330	0.62	9.460	0.71	15.100	0.80				37.5
40.0		0.810	0.39	1.460	0.45	2.090	0.50	5.520	0.64	9.800	0.74	15.700	0.83				40.0
42.5		0.838	0.40	1.520	0.47	2.160	0.51	5.710	0.66	10.100	0.76	16.200	0.86				42.5
45.0		0.866	0.41	1.570	0.48	2.230	0.53	5.900	0.68	10.400	0.78	16.700	0.89				45.0
47.5		0.894	0.43	1.620	0.50	2.300	0.55	6.080	0.70	10.700	0.81	17.200	0.91				47.5
50.0		0.920	0.44	1.660	0.51	2.370	0.56	6.260	0.72	11.100	0.84	17.700	0.94				50.0
52.5		0.946	0.45	1.710	0.53	2.430	0.58	6.440	0.74	11.400	0.86	18.200	0.96				52.5
55.0		0.972	0.46	1.760	0.54	2.500	0.59	6.610	0.76	11.700	0.88	18.700	0.99			1.00	55.0
57.5		0.997	0.48	1.800	0.56	2.560	0.61	6.770	0.78	12.000	0.90	19.200	1.02				57.5
60.0		1.020	0.49	1.850	0.57	2.630	0.62	6.940	0.80	12.300	0.93	19.600	1.04				60.0
62.5	0.50	1.040	0.50	1.890	0.58	2.690	0.64	7.100	0.82	12.500	0.94	20.100	1.07				62.5
65.0		1.060	0.51	1.930	0.60	2.750	0.65	7.260	0.84	12.800	0.96	20.500	1.09				65.0
67.5		1.090	0.52	1.970	0.61	2.810	0.67	7.410	0.86	13.100	0.99	21.000	1.11				67.5
70.0		1.110	0.53	2.010	0.62	2.870	0.68	7.560	0.87	13.400	1.01	21.400	1.13				70.0
72.5		1.130	0.54	2.050	0.63	2.920	0.69	7.710	0.89	13.600	1.02	21.800	1.16				72.5
75.0		1.160	0.55	2.090	0.64	2.980	0.71	7.860	0.91	13.900	1.05	22.200	1.18				75.0
77.5		1.180	0.56	2.130	0.66	3.040	0.72	8.010	0.93	14.100	1.06	22.600	1.20				77.5
80.0		1.200	0.57	2.170	0.67	3.090	0.73	8.150	0.94	14.400	1.09	23.100	1.22				80.0
82.5		1.220	0.58	2.210	0.68	3.150	0.75	8.290	0.96	14.600	1.10	23.400	1.24				82.5
85.0		1.240	0.59	2.250	0.69	3.200	0.76	8.430	0.97	14.900	1.12	23.800	1.26				85.0
87.5		1.260	0.60	2.290	0.71	3.250	0.77	8.570	0.99	15.100	1.14	24.200	1.28				87.5
90.0		1.280	0.61	2.320	0.72	3.300	0.78	8.710	1.01	15.400	1.16	24.600	1.30				90.0

q_m	= mass flow rate	kg/s
c	= velocity	m/s
$\Delta p/l$	= pressure loss per unit length	Pa/m

COPPER (OLD TABLE X)

WATER AT 10 °C

$\Delta p/l$	c	54 mm		67 mm		76 mm		108 mm		133 mm		159 mm		mm		c	$\Delta p/l$
		q_m	c	q_m	c	q_m	c	q_m	c	q_m	c	q_m	c	q_m	c		
92.5		1.30	0.6	2.36	0.7	3.36	0.8	8.84	1.0	15.60	1.2	25.00	1.3					92.5
95.0		1.32	0.6	2.40	0.7	3.41	0.8	8.97	1.0	15.80	1.2	25.40	1.3					95.0
97.5		1.34	0.6	2.43	0.7	3.46	0.8	9.10	1.1	16.10	1.2	25.70	1.4					97.5
100		1.36	0.6	2.47	0.8	3.51	0.8	9.23	1.1	16.30	1.2	26.10	1.4					100
120		1.51	0.7	2.73	0.8	3.89	0.9	10.20	1.2	18.00	1.4	28.90	1.5			1.5		120
140		1.65	0.8	2.98	0.9	4.24	1.0	11.10	1.3	19.70	1.5	31.40	1.7					140
160		1.78	0.9	3.22	1.0	4.57	1.1	12.00	1.4	21.20	1.6	33.90	1.8					160
180		1.90	0.9	3.44	1.1	4.88	1.2	12.80	1.5	22.60	1.7	36.10	1.9					180
200	1.0	2.02	1.0	3.65	1.1	5.18	1.2	13.50	1.6	24.00	1.8	38.30	2.0			2.0		200
220		2.13	1.0	3.85	1.2	5.46	1.3	14.30	1.7	25.30	1.9	40.40	2.1					220
240		2.24	1.1	4.04	1.2	5.73	1.4	15.00	1.7	26.50	2.0	42.40	2.2					240
260		2.34	1.1	4.23	1.3	6.00	1.4	15.70	1.8	27.70	2.1	44.30	2.3					260
280		2.44	1.2	4.41	1.4	6.25	1.5	16.30	1.9	28.90	2.2	46.10	2.4					280
300		2.54	1.2	4.58	1.4	6.50	1.5	17.00	2.0	30.00	2.3	47.90	2.5					300
320		2.63	1.3	4.75	1.5	6.73	1.6	17.60	2.0	31.10	2.3	49.60	2.6					320
340		2.73	1.3	4.91	1.5	6.97	1.7	18.20	2.1	32.20	2.4	51.30	2.7					340
360		2.82	1.3	5.07	1.6	7.19	1.7	18.80	2.2	33.20	2.5	53.00	2.8					360
380		2.90	1.4	5.23	1.6	7.41	1.8	19.40	2.2	34.20	2.6	54.60	2.9					380
400		2.99	1.4	5.38	1.7	7.63	1.8	19.90	2.3	35.20	2.7	56.10	3.0			3.0		400
420		3.07	1.5	5.53	1.7	7.84	1.9	20.50	2.4	36.10	2.7	57.60	3.1					420
440		3.15	1.5	5.67	1.7	8.04	1.9	21.00	2.4	37.10	2.8	59.10	3.1					440
460	1.5	3.23	1.5	5.82	1.8	8.24	2.0	21.50	2.5	38.00	2.9	60.60	3.2					460
480		3.31	1.6	5.96	1.8	8.44	2.0	22.00	2.5	38.90	2.9	62.00	3.3					480
500		3.39	1.6	6.09	1.9	8.64	2.1	22.50	2.6	39.80	3.0	63.40	3.4					500
520		3.46	1.7	6.23	1.9	8.83	2.1	23.00	2.7	40.60	3.1	64.80	3.4					520
540		3.54	1.7	6.36	2.0	9.01	2.1	23.50	2.7	41.50	3.1	66.20	3.5					540
560		3.61	1.7	6.49	2.0	9.20	2.2	24.00	2.8	42.30	3.2	67.50	3.6					560
580		3.68	1.8	6.62	2.0	9.38	2.2	24.50	2.8	43.20	3.3	68.80	3.6					580
600		3.75	1.8	6.74	2.1	9.56	2.3	24.90	2.9	44.00	3.3	70.10	3.7					600
620		3.82	1.8	6.87	2.1	9.73	2.3	25.40	2.9	44.80	3.4	71.40	3.8					620
640		3.89	1.9	6.99	2.2	9.90	2.4	25.80	3.0	45.60	3.4	72.60	3.8					640
660		3.96	1.9	7.11	2.2	10.00	2.4	26.30	3.0	46.30	3.5	73.90	3.9					660
680		4.02	1.9	7.23	2.2	10.20	2.4	26.70	3.1	47.10	3.5	75.10	4.0					680
700		4.09	2.0	7.35	2.3	10.40	2.5	27.10	3.1	47.90	3.6	76.30	4.0					700
720		4.15	2.0	7.46	2.3	10.50	2.5	27.60	3.2	48.60	3.7	77.50	4.1					720
740		4.22	2.0	7.58	2.3	10.70	2.5	28.00	3.2	49.30	3.7	78.60	4.2					740
760	2.0	4.28	2.0	7.69	2.4	10.90	2.6	28.40	3.3	50.10	3.8	79.80	4.2					760
780		4.34	2.1	7.80	2.4	11.00	2.6	28.80	3.3	50.80	3.8	80.90	4.3					780
800		4.41	2.1	7.92	2.4	11.20	2.7	29.20	3.4	51.50	3.9	82.10	4.4					800
820		4.47	2.1	8.02	2.5	11.30	2.7	29.60	3.4	52.20	3.9	83.20	4.4					820
840		4.53	2.2	8.13	2.5	11.50	2.7	30.00	3.5	52.90	4.0	84.30	4.5					840
860		4.59	2.2	8.24	2.5	11.60	2.8	30.40	3.5	53.60	4.0	85.40	4.5					860
880		4.65	2.2	8.35	2.6	11.80	2.8	30.80	3.6	54.30	4.1	86.50	4.6					880
900		4.70	2.2	8.45	2.6	11.90	2.8	31.20	3.6	54.90	4.1	87.50	4.6					900
920		4.76	2.3	8.55	2.6	12.10	2.9	31.50	3.6	55.60	4.2	88.60	4.7					920
940		4.82	2.3	8.66	2.7	12.20	2.9	31.90	3.7	56.30	4.2	89.60	4.7					940
960		4.88	2.3	8.76	2.7	12.40	2.9	32.30	3.7	56.90	4.3	90.70	4.8					960
980		4.93	2.4	8.86	2.7	12.50	3.0	32.70	3.8	57.60	4.3	91.70	4.9					980
1000		4.99	2.4	8.96	2.8	12.60	3.0	33.00	3.8	58.20	4.4	92.70	4.9					1000
1100		5.26	2.5	9.45	2.9	13.30	3.2	34.80	4.0	61.30	4.6	97.70	5.2					1100
1200		5.52	2.6	9.91	3.1	14.00	3.3	36.50	4.2	64.30	4.8	102.00	5.4					1200
1300		5.77	2.8	10.30	3.2	14.60	3.5	38.20	4.4	67.20	5.1	107.00	5.7					1300
1400		6.02	2.9	10.80	3.3	15.20	3.6	39.70	4.6	70.00	5.3	111.00	5.9					1400
1500	3.0	6.25	3.0	11.20	3.5	15.80	3.8	41.30	4.8	72.70	5.5	115.00	6.1					1500
1600		6.48	3.1	11.60	3.6	16.40	3.9	42.80	4.9	75.30	5.7	119.00	6.3					1600
1700		6.70	3.2	12.00	3.7	17.00	4.0	44.20	5.1	77.80	5.9	123.00	6.5					1700
1800		6.92	3.3	12.40	3.8	17.50	4.2	45.60	5.3	80.30	6.1	127.00	6.7					1800
1900		7.13	3.4	12.70	3.9	18.00	4.3	47.00	5.4	82.70	6.2	131.00	6.9					1900
2000		7.33	3.5	13.10	4.0	18.50	4.4	48.30	5.6	85.00	6.4	135.00	7.2					2000

q_m = mass flow rate — kg/s
c = velocity — m/s
$\Delta p/l$ = pressure loss per unit length — Pa/m

COPPER (OLD TABLE X)

WATER AT 75 °C

$\Delta p/l$	c	10 mm		12 mm		15 mm		22 mm		28 mm		35 mm		42 mm		c	$\Delta p/l$
		q_m	c	q_m	c	q_m	c	q_m	c	q_m	c	q_m	c	q_m	c		
0.1								0.001	0.00	0.002	0.00	0.007	0.01	0.015	0.01		0.1
0.2								0.002	0.01	0.005	0.01	0.014	0.02	0.023	0.02		0.2
0.3								0.003	0.01	0.008	0.02	0.019	0.02	0.026	0.02		0.3
0.4								0.004	0.01	0.011	0.02	0.019	0.02	0.032	0.03		0.4
0.5						0.001	0.01	0.005	0.02	0.014	0.03	0.021	0.03	0.036	0.03		0.5
0.6						0.001	0.01	0.006	0.02	0.015	0.03	0.023	0.03	0.040	0.03		0.6
0.7						0.001	0.01	0.007	0.02	0.015	0.03	0.026	0.03	0.044	0.04		0.7
0.8						0.001	0.01	0.008	0.03	0.015	0.03	0.028	0.03	0.048	0.04		0.8
0.9						0.001	0.01	0.009	0.03	0.016	0.03	0.030	0.04	0.051	0.04		0.9
1.0						0.002	0.01	0.010	0.03	0.017	0.03	0.032	0.04	0.055	0.05	0.05	1.0
1.5				0.001	0.01	0.003	0.02	0.012	0.04	0.022	0.04	0.040	0.05	0.070	0.06		1.5
2.0				0.001	0.01	0.004	0.03	0.012	0.04	0.026	0.05	0.048	0.06	0.083	0.07		2.0
2.5				0.002	0.02	0.005	0.04	0.014	0.04	0.030	0.06	0.055	0.07	0.094	0.08		2.5
3.0		0.001	0.02	0.002	0.02	0.006	0.04	0.016	0.05	0.033	0.06	0.061	0.07	0.105	0.09		3.0
3.5		0.001	0.02	0.003	0.03	0.007	0.05	0.017	0.05	0.036	0.07	0.067	0.08	0.114	0.09		3.5
4.0		0.001	0.02	0.003	0.03	0.008	0.06	0.019	0.06	0.039	0.07	0.072	0.09	0.124	0.10		4.0
4.5		0.001	0.02	0.003	0.03	0.008	0.06	0.020	0.06	0.042	0.08	0.078	0.10	0.132	0.11		4.5
5.0		0.001	0.02	0.004	0.04	0.008	0.06	0.022	0.07	0.045	0.09	0.083	0.10	0.141	0.12		5.0
5.5		0.002	0.03	0.004	0.04	0.008	0.06	0.023	0.07	0.048	0.09	0.087	0.11	0.149	0.12		5.5
6.0		0.002	0.03	0.005	0.06	0.008	0.06	0.024	0.08	0.050	0.09	0.092	0.11	0.156	0.13		6.0
6.5		0.002	0.03	0.005	0.06	0.008	0.06	0.025	0.08	0.053	0.10	0.096	0.12	0.164	0.14		6.5
7.0		0.002	0.03	0.006	0.07	0.008	0.06	0.027	0.09	0.055	0.10	0.100	0.12	0.171	0.14		7.0
7.5		0.002	0.03	0.006	0.07	0.009	0.06	0.028	0.09	0.057	0.11	0.105	0.13	0.178	0.15	0.15	7.5
8.0		0.003	0.05	0.006	0.07	0.009	0.06	0.029	0.09	0.059	0.11	0.108	0.13	0.185	0.15		8.0
8.5		0.003	0.05	0.006	0.07	0.010	0.07	0.030	0.10	0.061	0.12	0.112	0.14	0.191	0.16		8.5
9.0		0.003	0.05	0.006	0.07	0.010	0.07	0.031	0.10	0.064	0.12	0.116	0.14	0.198	0.16		9.0
9.5		0.003	0.05	0.006	0.07	0.010	0.07	0.032	0.10	0.066	0.13	0.120	0.15	0.204	0.17		9.5
10.0	0.05	0.003	0.05	0.006	0.07	0.011	0.08	0.033	0.11	0.068	0.13	0.123	0.15	0.210	0.17		10.0
12.5		0.004	0.07	0.006	0.07	0.012	0.08	0.037	0.12	0.077	0.15	0.140	0.17	0.239	0.20		12.5
15.0		0.005	0.08	0.007	0.08	0.014	0.10	0.042	0.13	0.086	0.16	0.156	0.19	0.265	0.22		15.0
17.5		0.005	0.08	0.008	0.09	0.015	0.11	0.046	0.15	0.094	0.18	0.170	0.21	0.289	0.24		17.5
20.0		0.005	0.08	0.008	0.09	0.016	0.11	0.049	0.16	0.101	0.19	0.184	0.23	0.312	0.26		20.0
22.5		0.005	0.08	0.009	0.10	0.017	0.12	0.053	0.17	0.108	0.21	0.197	0.24	0.334	0.28		22.5
25.0		0.005	0.08	0.010	0.11	0.019	0.13	0.056	0.18	0.115	0.22	0.209	0.26	0.354	0.29	0.30	25.0
27.5		0.005	0.08	0.010	0.11	0.020	0.14	0.060	0.19	0.122	0.23	0.221	0.27	0.374	0.31		27.5
30.0		0.006	0.10	0.011	0.12	0.021	0.15	0.063	0.20	0.128	0.24	0.232	0.28	0.393	0.33		30.0
32.5		0.006	0.10	0.011	0.12	0.022	0.16	0.066	0.21	0.134	0.25	0.243	0.30	0.411	0.34		32.5
35.0		0.006	0.10	0.012	0.13	0.023	0.16	0.069	0.22	0.140	0.27	0.253	0.31	0.429	0.36		35.0
37.5		0.007	0.12	0.012	0.13	0.024	0.17	0.071	0.23	0.145	0.28	0.263	0.32	0.446	0.37		37.5
40.0		0.007	0.12	0.013	0.15	0.025	0.18	0.074	0.24	0.151	0.29	0.273	0.33	0.462	0.38		40.0
42.5		0.007	0.12	0.013	0.15	0.026	0.18	0.077	0.25	0.156	0.30	0.283	0.35	0.478	0.40		42.5
45.0		0.008	0.13	0.014	0.16	0.026	0.18	0.079	0.25	0.161	0.31	0.292	0.36	0.494	0.41		45.0
47.5		0.008	0.13	0.014	0.16	0.027	0.19	0.082	0.26	0.166	0.32	0.301	0.37	0.509	0.42		47.5
50.0		0.008	0.13	0.015	0.17	0.028	0.20	0.084	0.27	0.171	0.32	0.310	0.38	0.524	0.44		50.0
52.5	0.15	0.008	0.13	0.015	0.17	0.029	0.20	0.087	0.28	0.176	0.33	0.319	0.39	0.539	0.45		52.5
55.0		0.009	0.15	0.016	0.18	0.030	0.21	0.089	0.28	0.181	0.34	0.327	0.40	0.553	0.46		55.0
57.5		0.009	0.15	0.016	0.18	0.031	0.22	0.091	0.29	0.186	0.35	0.336	0.41	0.567	0.47		57.5
60.0		0.009	0.15	0.016	0.18	0.031	0.22	0.094	0.30	0.190	0.36	0.344	0.42	0.581	0.48		60.0
62.5		0.009	0.15	0.017	0.19	0.032	0.23	0.096	0.31	0.195	0.37	0.352	0.43	0.594	0.49	0.50	62.5
65.0		0.010	0.17	0.017	0.19	0.033	0.23	0.098	0.31	0.199	0.38	0.360	0.44	0.608	0.51		65.0
67.5		0.010	0.17	0.018	0.20	0.034	0.24	0.100	0.32	0.203	0.39	0.368	0.45	0.621	0.52		67.5
70.0		0.010	0.17	0.018	0.20	0.034	0.24	0.102	0.33	0.208	0.40	0.375	0.46	0.634	0.53		70.0
72.5		0.010	0.17	0.018	0.20	0.035	0.25	0.104	0.33	0.212	0.40	0.383	0.47	0.646	0.54		72.5
75.0		0.010	0.17	0.019	0.21	0.036	0.25	0.107	0.34	0.216	0.41	0.390	0.48	0.659	0.55		75.0
77.5		0.011	0.19	0.019	0.21	0.036	0.25	0.109	0.35	0.220	0.42	0.398	0.49	0.671	0.56		77.5
80.0		0.011	0.19	0.019	0.21	0.037	0.26	0.111	0.35	0.224	0.43	0.405	0.50	0.683	0.57		80.0
82.5		0.011	0.19	0.020	0.22	0.038	0.27	0.113	0.36	0.228	0.43	0.412	0.51	0.695	0.58		82.5
85.0		0.011	0.19	0.020	0.22	0.038	0.27	0.114	0.36	0.232	0.44	0.419	0.51	0.707	0.59		85.0
87.5		0.011	0.19	0.021	0.24	0.039	0.28	0.116	0.37	0.236	0.45	0.426	0.52	0.718	0.60		87.5
90.0		0.012	0.20	0.021	0.24	0.040	Pa/m	0.118	0.38	0.240	0.46	0.432	0.53	0.730	0.61		90.0

q_m = mass flow rate — kg/s
c = velocity — m/s
$\Delta p/l$ = pressure loss per unit length — Pa/m

COPPER (OLD TABLE X)

WATER AT 75 °C

Δp/l	c	10 mm qm	10 mm c	12 mm qm	12 mm c	15 mm qm	15 mm c	22 mm qm	22 mm c	28 mm qm	28 mm c	35 mm qm	35 mm c	42 mm qm	42 mm c	c	Δp/l
92.5		0.012	0.20	0.021	0.24	0.040	0.28	0.120	0.38	0.243	0.46	0.439	0.54	0.741	0.62		92.5
95.0		0.012	0.20	0.022	0.25	0.041	0.29	0.122	0.39	0.247	0.47	0.446	0.55	0.752	0.63		95.0
97.5		0.012	0.20	0.022	0.25	0.042	0.30	0.124	0.40	0.251	0.48	0.452	0.55	0.763	0.63		97.5
100		0.012	0.20	0.022	0.25	0.042	0.30	0.126	0.40	0.254	0.48	0.459	0.56	0.774	0.64		100
120		0.014	0.24	0.025	0.28	0.047	0.33	0.139	0.44	0.282	0.54	0.508	0.62	0.857	0.71		120
140		0.015	0.25	0.027	0.30	0.051	0.36	0.152	0.49	0.308	0.59	0.554	0.68	0.934	0.78		140
160		0.017	0.29	0.029	0.32	0.056	0.40	0.164	0.52	0.332	0.63	0.598	0.73	1.000	0.83		160
180	0.30	0.018	0.30	0.032	0.36	0.060	0.42	0.176	0.56	0.354	0.67	0.638	0.78	1.070	0.89		180
200		0.019	0.32	0.034	0.38	0.063	0.44	0.186	0.59	0.376	0.71	0.677	0.83	1.130	0.94		200
220		0.020	0.34	0.035	0.39	0.067	0.47	0.197	0.63	0.397	0.75	0.714	0.88	1.200	1.00	1.00	220
240		0.021	0.35	0.037	0.41	0.070	0.49	0.207	0.66	0.417	0.79	0.750	0.92	1.260	1.05		240
260		0.022	0.37	0.039	0.44	0.074	0.52	0.216	0.69	0.436	0.83	0.784	0.96	1.310	1.09		260
280		0.023	0.39	0.041	0.46	0.077	0.54	0.226	0.72	0.454	0.86	0.817	1.00	1.370	1.14		280
300		0.024	0.40	0.042	0.47	0.080	0.56	0.235	0.75	0.472	0.90	0.849	1.04	1.420	1.18		300
320		0.025	0.42	0.044	0.49	0.083	0.59	0.243	0.78	0.490	0.93	0.880	1.08	1.470	1.22		320
340		0.026	0.44	0.046	0.52	0.086	0.61	0.252	0.81	0.506	0.96	0.910	1.12	1.530	1.27		340
360		0.027	0.46	0.047	0.53	0.089	0.63	0.260	0.83	0.523	0.99	0.940	1.15	1.570	1.31		360
380		0.028	0.47	0.049	0.55	0.092	0.65	0.268	0.86	0.539	1.02	0.968	1.19	1.620	1.35		380
400		0.028	0.47	0.050	0.56	0.094	0.66	0.276	0.88	0.555	1.05	0.996	1.22	1.670	1.39		400
420		0.029	0.49	0.052	0.58	0.097	0.68	0.283	0.90	0.570	1.08	1.020	1.25	1.720	1.43		420
440	0.50	0.030	0.51	0.053	0.59	0.099	0.70	0.291	0.93	0.585	1.11	1.050	1.29	1.760	1.46		440
460		0.031	0.52	0.054	0.60	0.102	0.72	0.298	0.95	0.600	1.14	1.070	1.31	1.800	1.50	1.50	460
480		0.032	0.54	0.056	0.63	0.105	0.74	0.306	0.98	0.614	1.17	1.100	1.35	1.850	1.54		480
500		0.032	0.54	0.057	0.64	0.107	0.76	0.313	1.00	0.628	1.19	1.120	1.37	1.890	1.57		500
520		0.033	0.56	0.058	0.65	0.109	0.77	0.320	1.02	0.642	1.22	1.150	1.41	1.930	1.61		520
540		0.034	0.57	0.060	0.67	0.112	0.79	0.326	1.04	0.656	1.25	1.170	1.44	1.970	1.64		540
560		0.035	0.59	0.061	0.68	0.114	0.81	0.333	1.06	0.669	1.27	1.200	1.47	2.010	1.67		560
580		0.035	0.59	0.062	0.69	0.116	0.82	0.340	1.09	0.682	1.30	1.220	1.50	2.050	1.70		580
600		0.036	0.61	0.063	0.71	0.119	0.84	0.346	1.11	0.695	1.32	1.240	1.52	2.090	1.74		600
620		0.037	0.62	0.065	0.73	0.121	0.85	0.353	1.13	0.708	1.35	1.270	1.56	2.130	1.77		620
640		0.037	0.62	0.066	0.74	0.123	0.87	0.359	1.15	0.721	1.37	1.290	1.58	2.160	1.80		640
660		0.038	0.64	0.067	0.75	0.125	0.88	0.365	1.17	0.733	1.39	1.310	1.61	2.200	1.83		660
680		0.039	0.66	0.068	0.76	0.127	0.90	0.371	1.19	0.745	1.42	1.330	1.63	2.240	1.86		680
700		0.039	0.66	0.069	0.77	0.130	0.92	0.378	1.21	0.757	1.44	1.350	1.66	2.270	1.89		700
720		0.040	0.67	0.070	0.78	0.132	0.93	0.383	1.22	0.769	1.46	1.380	1.69	2.310	1.92		720
740		0.041	0.69	0.071	0.80	0.134	0.95	0.389	1.24	0.781	1.48	1.400	1.72	2.350	1.95		740
760		0.041	0.69	0.073	0.82	0.136	0.96	0.395	1.26	0.793	1.51	1.420	1.74	2.380	1.98	2.00	760
780		0.042	0.71	0.074	0.83	0.138	0.97	0.401	1.28	0.804	1.53	1.440	1.77	2.410	2.00		780
800		0.043	0.73	0.075	0.84	0.140	0.99	0.407	1.30	0.816	1.55	1.460	1.79	2.450	2.04		800
820		0.043	0.73	0.076	0.85	0.142	1.00	0.412	1.32	0.827	1.57	1.480	1.82	2.480	2.06		820
840		0.044	0.74	0.077	0.86	0.144	1.02	0.418	1.34	0.838	1.59	1.500	1.84	2.510	2.09		840
860		0.044	0.74	0.078	0.87	0.146	1.03	0.423	1.35	0.849	1.61	1.520	1.86	2.550	2.12		860
880		0.045	0.76	0.079	0.88	0.147	1.04	0.429	1.37	0.860	1.63	1.540	1.89	2.580	2.15		880
900		0.046	0.78	0.080	0.90	0.149	1.05	0.434	1.39	0.871	1.65	1.560	1.91	2.610	2.17		900
920		0.046	0.78	0.081	0.91	0.151	1.07	0.440	1.41	0.881	1.67	1.570	1.93	2.640	2.20		920
940		0.047	0.79	0.082	0.92	0.153	1.08	0.445	1.42	0.892	1.69	1.590	1.95	2.680	2.23		940
960		0.047	0.79	0.083	0.93	0.155	1.09	0.450	1.44	0.902	1.71	1.610	1.97	2.710	2.25		960
980		0.048	0.81	0.084	0.94	0.157	1.11	0.455	1.45	0.913	1.73	1.630	2.00	2.740	2.28		980
1000		0.048	0.81	0.085	0.95	0.158	1.12	0.461	1.47	0.923	1.75	1.650	2.02	2.770	2.30		1000
1100		0.051	0.86	0.090	1.01	0.167	1.18	0.486	1.55	0.973	1.85	1.740	2.13	2.920	2.43		1100
1200		0.054	0.91	0.094	1.05	0.176	1.24	0.510	1.63	1.020	1.94	1.820	2.23	3.060	2.54		1200
1300		0.056	0.94	0.098	1.10	0.184	1.30	0.533	1.70	1.060	2.01	1.910	2.34	3.200	2.66		1300
1400	1.00	0.059	1.00	0.103	1.15	0.191	1.35	0.555	1.77	1.110	2.11	1.980	2.43	3.330	2.77		1400
1500		0.061	1.03	0.107	1.20	0.199	1.41	0.577	1.84	1.150	2.18	2.060	2.53	3.460	2.88		1500
1600		0.063	1.06	0.111	1.24	0.206	1.45	0.598	1.91	1.190	2.26	2.140	2.63	3.580	2.98	3.00	1600
1700		0.066	1.11	0.115	1.29	0.214	1.51	0.618	1.97	1.230	2.34	2.210	2.71	3.700	3.08		1700
1800		0.068	1.15	0.118	1.32	0.220	1.55	0.638	2.04	1.270	2.41	2.280	2.80	3.820	3.18		1800
1900		0.070	1.18	0.122	1.37	0.227	1.60	0.658	2.10	1.310	2.49	2.350	2.88	3.930	3.27		1900
2000		0.072	1.21	0.126	1.41	0.234	1.65	0.677	2.16	1.350	2.56	2.410	2.96	4.040	3.36		2000

q_m = mass flow rate   kg/s
c = velocity   m/s
$\Delta p/l$ = pressure loss per unit length   Pa/m

COPPER (OLD TABLE X)

WATER AT 75 °C

$\Delta p/l$	c	54 mm q_m	54 mm c	67 mm q_m	67 mm c	76 mm q_m	76 mm c	108 mm q_m	108 mm c	133 mm q_m	133 mm c	159 mm q_m	159 mm c	mm q_m	mm c	c	$\Delta p/l$
0.1		0.030	0.01	0.054	0.02	0.077	0.02	0.210	0.02	0.379	0.03	0.613	0.03				0.1
0.2		0.044	0.02	0.081	0.03	0.117	0.03	0.315	0.04	0.565	0.04	0.913	0.05			0.05	0.2
0.3		0.056	0.03	0.103	0.03	0.148	0.04	0.399	0.05	0.714	0.06	1.150	0.06				0.3
0.4		0.066	0.03	0.122	0.04	0.175	0.04	0.471	0.06	0.841	0.06	1.350	0.07				0.4
0.5		0.076	0.04	0.139	0.04	0.200	0.05	0.535	0.06	0.955	0.07	1.530	0.08				0.5
0.6		0.085	0.04	0.155	0.05	0.222	0.05	0.594	0.07	1.060	0.08	1.700	0.09				0.6
0.7		0.093	0.05	0.170	0.05	0.243	0.06	0.648	0.08	1.150	0.09	1.860	0.10				0.7
0.8		0.100	0.05	0.183	0.06	0.262	0.06	0.700	0.08	1.240	0.10	2.000	0.11				0.8
0.9	0.05	0.107	0.05	0.196	0.06	0.281	0.07	0.749	0.09	1.330	0.10	2.140	0.12				0.9
1.0		0.114	0.06	0.209	0.07	0.298	0.07	0.795	0.09	1.410	0.11	2.270	0.12				1.0
1.5		0.145	0.07	0.264	0.08	0.376	0.09	1.000	0.12	1.780	0.14	2.850	0.15			0.15	1.5
2.0		0.171	0.08	0.311	0.10	0.444	0.11	1.170	0.14	2.090	0.16	3.350	0.18				2.0
2.5		0.195	0.10	0.354	0.11	0.504	0.12	1.330	0.16	2.370	0.18	3.800	0.21				2.5
3.0		0.216	0.11	0.393	0.12	0.559	0.14	1.480	0.18	2.620	0.20	4.210	0.23				3.0
3.5		0.236	0.12	0.429	0.14	0.611	0.15	1.610	0.19	2.860	0.22	4.590	0.25				3.5
4.0		0.255	0.12	0.463	0.15	0.659	0.16	1.740	0.21	3.080	0.24	4.940	0.27				4.0
4.5		0.273	0.13	0.495	0.16	0.704	0.17	1.860	0.22	3.290	0.25	5.280	0.29				4.5
5.0		0.290	0.14	0.526	0.17	0.748	0.18	1.970	0.23	3.490	0.27	5.600	0.30			0.30	5.0
5.5	0.15	0.306	0.15	0.555	0.18	0.789	0.19	2.080	0.25	3.690	0.29	5.900	0.32				5.5
6.0		0.322	0.16	0.583	0.18	0.829	0.20	2.180	0.26	3.870	0.30	6.190	0.34				6.0
6.5		0.337	0.17	0.610	0.19	0.867	0.21	2.280	0.27	4.050	0.31	6.470	0.35				6.5
7.0		0.352	0.17	0.636	0.20	0.904	0.22	2.380	0.28	4.220	0.33	6.750	0.37				7.0
7.5		0.366	0.18	0.661	0.21	0.940	0.23	2.470	0.29	4.380	0.34	7.010	0.38				7.5
8.0		0.379	0.19	0.686	0.22	0.975	0.24	2.560	0.30	4.540	0.35	7.270	0.40				8.0
8.5		0.393	0.19	0.710	0.22	1.000	0.24	2.650	0.31	4.700	0.36	7.510	0.41				8.5
9.0		0.406	0.20	0.733	0.23	1.040	0.25	2.740	0.32	4.850	0.37	7.760	0.42				9.0
9.5		0.418	0.20	0.756	0.24	1.070	0.26	2.820	0.33	5.000	0.39	7.990	0.43				9.5
10.0		0.431	0.21	0.778	0.25	1.100	0.27	2.900	0.34	5.140	0.40	8.220	0.45			0.45	10.0
12.5		0.489	0.24	0.883	0.28	1.250	0.30	3.290	0.39	5.820	0.45	9.300	0.51				12.5
15.0		0.542	0.27	0.978	0.31	1.380	0.34	3.640	0.43	6.440	0.50	10.200	0.55				15.0
17.5	0.30	0.591	0.29	1.060	0.34	1.510	0.37	3.970	0.47	7.020	0.54	11.200	0.61				17.5
20.0		0.638	0.31	1.150	0.36	1.630	0.40	4.270	0.51	7.550	0.58	12.000	0.65				20.0
22.5		0.682	0.33	1.220	0.39	1.740	0.42	4.560	0.54	8.060	0.62	12.800	0.70				22.5
25.0		0.723	0.35	1.300	0.41	1.840	0.45	4.840	0.57	8.550	0.66	13.600	0.74				25.0
27.5		0.763	0.37	1.370	0.43	1.940	0.47	5.100	0.60	9.010	0.70	14.300	0.78				27.5
30.0		0.802	0.39	1.440	0.46	2.040	0.50	5.350	0.63	9.450	0.73	15.000	0.82				30.0
32.5		0.838	0.41	1.500	0.47	2.140	0.52	5.590	0.66	9.880	0.76	15.700	0.85				32.5
35.0		0.874	0.43	1.570	0.50	2.230	0.54	5.830	0.69	10.200	0.79	16.400	0.89				35.0
37.5		0.909	0.45	1.630	0.52	2.310	0.56	6.060	0.72	10.600	0.82	17.000	0.92				37.5
40.0		0.942	0.46	1.690	0.53	2.400	0.58	6.280	0.74	11.000	0.85	17.600	0.96				40.0
42.5		0.975	0.48	1.750	0.55	2.480	0.60	6.490	0.77	11.400	0.88	18.200	0.99			1.00	42.5
45.0		1.000	0.49	1.810	0.57	2.560	0.62	6.700	0.79	11.800	0.91	18.800	1.02				45.0
47.5	0.50	1.030	0.50	1.860	0.59	2.640	0.64	6.900	0.82	12.100	0.94	19.400	1.05				47.5
50.0		1.060	0.52	1.910	0.60	2.710	0.66	7.100	0.84	12.500	0.97	19.900	1.08				50.0
52.5		1.090	0.53	1.970	0.62	2.790	0.68	7.290	0.86	12.800	0.99	20.500	1.11				52.5
55.0		1.120	0.55	2.020	0.64	2.860	0.70	7.480	0.89	13.100	1.01	21.000	1.14				55.0
57.5		1.150	0.56	2.070	0.65	2.930	0.71	7.670	0.91	13.500	1.04	21.500	1.17				57.5
60.0		1.180	0.58	2.120	0.67	3.000	0.73	7.850	0.93	13.800	1.07	22.000	1.20				60.0
62.5		1.200	0.59	2.170	0.69	3.070	0.75	8.030	0.95	14.100	1.09	22.500	1.22				62.5
65.0		1.230	0.60	2.220	0.70	3.140	0.76	8.200	0.97	14.400	1.11	23.000	1.25				65.0
67.5		1.260	0.62	2.260	0.71	3.210	0.78	8.380	0.99	14.700	1.14	23.500	1.28				67.5
70.0		1.280	0.63	2.310	0.73	3.270	0.80	8.550	1.01	15.000	1.16	23.900	1.30				70.0
72.5		1.310	0.64	2.360	0.75	3.340	0.81	8.710	1.03	15.300	1.18	24.400	1.33				72.5
75.0		1.330	0.65	2.400	0.76	3.400	0.83	8.880	1.05	15.600	1.21	24.900	1.35				75.0
77.5		1.360	0.67	2.440	0.77	3.460	0.84	9.040	1.07	15.900	1.23	25.300	1.38				77.5
80.0		1.380	0.68	2.490	0.79	3.520	0.86	9.200	1.09	16.200	1.25	25.800	1.40				80.0
82.5		1.410	0.69	2.530	0.80	3.580	0.87	9.350	1.11	16.400	1.27	26.200	1.42				82.5
85.0		1.430	0.70	2.570	0.81	3.640	0.89	9.510	1.13	16.700	1.29	26.600	1.45				85.0
87.5		1.450	0.71	2.610	0.83	3.700	0.90	9.660	1.14	17.000	1.31	27.100	1.47				87.5
90.0		1.480	0.73	2.660	0.84	3.760	0.92	9.810	1.16	17.200	1.33	27.500	1.49				90.0

q_m = mass flow rate   kg/s
c = velocity   m/s
$\Delta p/l$ = pressure loss per unit length   Pa/m

COPPER (OLD TABLE X)

WATER AT 75 °C

$\Delta p/l$	c	54 mm q_m	c	67 mm q_m	c	76 mm q_m	c	108 mm q_m	c	133 mm q_m	c	159 mm q_m	c	mm q_m	c	c	$\Delta p/l$
92.5		1.50	0.7	2.70	0.9	3.82	0.9	9.96	1.2	17.50	1.4	27.90	1.5				92.5
95.0		1.52	0.7	2.74	0.9	3.88	0.9	10.10	1.2	17.80	1.4	28.30	1.5				95.0
97.5		1.55	0.8	2.78	0.9	3.93	1.0	10.20	1.2	18.00	1.4	28.70	1.6				97.5
100		1.57	0.8	2.82	0.9	3.99	1.0	10.40	1.2	18.30	1.4	29.10	1.6				100
120		1.74	0.9	3.12	1.0	4.41	1.1	11.40	1.4	20.20	1.6	32.20	1.8				120
140		1.89	0.9	3.39	1.1	4.80	1.2	12.50	1.5	22.00	1.7	35.00	1.9				140
160	1.0	2.04	1.0	3.65	1.2	5.17	1.3	13.40	1.6	23.60	1.8	37.60	2.0			2.0	160
180		2.17	1.1	3.90	1.2	5.51	1.3	14.30	1.7	25.20	1.9	40.10	2.2				180
200		2.30	1.1	4.13	1.3	5.84	1.4	15.20	1.8	26.70	2.1	42.50	2.3				200
220		2.43	1.2	4.35	1.4	6.16	1.5	16.00	1.9	28.10	2.2	44.70	2.4				220
240		2.55	1.2	4.57	1.4	6.46	1.6	16.70	2.0	29.50	2.3	46.90	2.5				240
260		2.66	1.3	4.77	1.5	6.75	1.6	17.50	2.1	30.80	2.4	49.00	2.7				260
280		2.78	1.4	4.97	1.6	7.03	1.7	18.20	2.2	32.00	2.5	51.00	2.8				280
300		2.88	1.4	5.16	1.6	7.30	1.8	18.90	2.2	33.30	2.6	52.90	2.9				300
320	1.5	2.99	1.5	5.35	1.7	7.56	1.8	19.60	2.3	34.50	2.7	54.80	3.0			3.0	320
340		3.09	1.5	5.53	1.7	7.82	1.9	20.20	2.4	35.60	2.8	56.60	3.1				340
360		3.19	1.6	5.71	1.8	8.07	2.0	20.90	2.5	36.70	2.8	58.40	3.2				360
380		3.29	1.6	5.88	1.9	8.31	2.0	21.50	2.5	37.80	2.9	60.10	3.3				380
400		3.38	1.7	6.05	1.9	8.55	2.1	22.10	2.6	38.90	3.0	61.80	3.4				400
420		3.47	1.7	6.21	2.0	8.78	2.1	22.70	2.7	39.90	3.1	63.50	3.5				420
440		3.56	1.7	6.37	2.0	9.00	2.2	23.30	2.8	41.00	3.2	65.10	3.5				440
460		3.65	1.8	6.53	2.1	9.22	2.2	23.90	2.8	41.90	3.2	66.70	3.6				460
480		3.74	1.8	6.68	2.1	9.44	2.3	24.40	2.9	42.90	3.3	68.20	3.7				480
500		3.82	1.9	6.83	2.2	9.65	2.4	25.00	3.0	43.90	3.4	69.70	3.8				500
520		3.90	1.9	6.98	2.2	9.86	2.4	25.50	3.0	44.80	3.5	71.20	3.9				520
540		3.99	2.0	7.13	2.3	10.00	2.4	26.00	3.1	45.70	3.5	72.70	4.0				540
560		4.07	2.0	7.27	2.3	10.20	2.5	26.60	3.2	46.70	3.6	74.10	4.0				560
580	2.0	4.15	2.0	7.41	2.3	10.40	2.5	27.10	3.2	47.50	3.7	75.50	4.1				580
600		4.22	2.1	7.55	2.4	10.60	2.6	27.60	3.3	48.40	3.7	76.90	4.2				600
620		4.30	2.1	7.69	2.4	10.80	2.6	28.10	3.3	49.30	3.8	78.30	4.3				620
640		4.38	2.1	7.82	2.5	11.00	2.7	28.60	3.4	50.10	3.9	79.60	4.3				640
660		4.45	2.2	7.95	2.5	11.20	2.7	29.00	3.4	51.00	3.9	81.00	4.4				660
680		4.52	2.2	8.08	2.6	11.40	2.8	29.50	3.5	51.80	4.0	82.30	4.5				680
700		4.60	2.3	8.21	2.6	11.60	2.8	30.00	3.6	52.60	4.1	83.60	4.5				700
720		4.67	2.3	8.34	2.6	11.70	2.9	30.40	3.6	53.40	4.1	84.90	4.6				720
740		4.74	2.3	8.47	2.7	11.90	2.9	30.90	3.7	54.20	4.2	86.10	4.7				740
760		4.81	2.4	8.59	2.7	12.10	2.9	31.30	3.7	55.00	4.3	87.40	4.8				760
780		4.88	2.4	8.71	2.8	12.30	3.0	31.80	3.8	55.80	4.3	88.60	4.8				780
800		4.94	2.4	8.83	2.8	12.40	3.0	32.20	3.8	56.60	4.4	89.80	4.9				800
820		5.01	2.5	8.95	2.8	12.60	3.1	32.70	3.9	57.30	4.4	91.00	4.9				820
840		5.08	2.5	9.07	2.9	12.80	3.1	33.10	3.9	58.10	4.5	92.20	5.0				840
860		5.14	2.5	9.19	2.9	12.90	3.1	33.50	4.0	58.80	4.5	93.40	5.1				860
880		5.21	2.6	9.30	2.9	13.10	3.2	33.90	4.0	59.50	4.6	94.50	5.1				880
900		5.27	2.6	9.42	3.0	13.20	3.2	34.30	4.1	60.30	4.7	95.70	5.2				900
920		5.34	2.6	9.53	3.0	13.40	3.3	34.80	4.1	61.00	4.7	96.80	5.3				920
940		5.40	2.6	9.64	3.0	13.60	3.3	35.20	4.2	61.70	4.8	97.90	5.3				940
960		5.46	2.7	9.76	3.1	13.70	3.3	35.60	4.2	62.40	4.8	99.00	5.4				960
980		5.53	2.7	9.87	3.1	13.90	3.4	36.00	4.3	63.10	4.9	100.00	5.4				980
1000		5.59	2.7	9.97	3.2	14.00	3.4	36.40	4.3	63.80	4.9	101.00	5.5				1000
1100		5.88	2.9	10.50	3.3	14.80	3.6	38.30	4.5	67.10	5.2	106.00	5.8				1100
1200	3.0	6.17	3.0	11.00	3.5	15.50	3.8	40.10	4.8	70.30	5.4	111.00	6.0				1200
1300		6.45	3.2	11.50	3.6	16.20	3.9	41.90	5.0	73.40	5.7	116.00	6.3				1300
1400		6.71	3.3	11.90	3.8	16.80	4.1	43.60	5.2	76.40	5.9	121.00	6.6				1400
1500		6.97	3.4	12.40	3.9	17.50	4.3	45.20	5.4	79.30	6.1	125.00	6.8				1500
1600		7.22	3.5	12.80	4.0	18.10	4.4	46.80	5.5	82.10	6.3	130.00	7.1				1600
1700		7.46	3.7	13.30	4.2	18.70	4.6	48.40	5.7	84.80	6.6	134.00	7.3				1700
1800		7.69	3.8	13.70	4.3	19.30	4.7	49.90	5.9	87.40	6.8	138.00	7.5				1800
1900		7.92	3.9	14.10	4.5	19.90	4.8	51.30	6.1	90.00	7.0	142.00	7.7				1900
2000		8.15	4.0	14.50	4.6	20.40	5.0	52.80	6.3	92.40	7.1	146.00	7.9				2000

q_m = mass flow rate — kg/s
c = velocity — m/s
$\Delta p/l$ = pressure loss per unit length — Pa/m

HEAVY GRADE STEEL

WATER AT 10 °C

$\Delta p/l$	c	10 mm		15 mm		20 mm		25 mm		32 mm		40 mm		50 mm		c	$\Delta p/l$
		q_m	c	q_m	c	q_m	c	q_m	c	q_m	c	q_m	c	q_m	c		
0.1										0.002	0.00	0.005	0.00	0.013	0.01		0.1
0.2								0.001	0.00	0.005	0.01	0.010	0.01	0.026	0.01		0.2
0.3						0.001	0.00	0.002	0.00	0.008	0.01	0.015	0.01	0.039	0.02		0.3
0.4						0.001	0.00	0.003	0.01	0.010	0.01	0.020	0.02	0.052	0.03		0.4
0.5						0.001	0.00	0.004	0.01	0.013	0.01	0.025	0.02	0.065	0.03		0.5
0.6						0.002	0.01	0.005	0.01	0.016	0.02	0.030	0.02	0.078	0.04		0.6
0.7						0.002	0.01	0.005	0.01	0.018	0.02	0.035	0.03	0.091	0.04		0.7
0.8						0.002	0.01	0.006	0.01	0.021	0.02	0.040	0.03	0.104	0.05		0.8
0.9						0.003	0.01	0.007	0.01	0.024	0.03	0.045	0.04	0.104	0.05		0.9
1.0						0.003	0.01	0.008	0.02	0.026	0.03	0.050	0.04	0.104	0.05	0.05	1.0
1.5				0.001	0.01	0.005	0.02	0.012	0.02	0.040	0.04	0.075	0.06	0.114	0.06		1.5
2.0				0.001	0.01	0.006	0.02	0.016	0.03	0.053	0.06	0.082	0.06	0.136	0.07		2.0
2.5				0.002	0.01	0.008	0.02	0.020	0.04	0.066	0.07	0.082	0.06	0.155	0.08		2.5
3.0				0.002	0.01	0.010	0.03	0.025	0.05	0.070	0.07	0.089	0.07	0.173	0.08		3.0
3.5		0.001	0.01	0.003	0.02	0.011	0.03	0.029	0.06	0.070	0.07	0.097	0.08	0.190	0.09		3.5
4.0		0.001	0.01	0.003	0.02	0.013	0.04	0.033	0.06	0.070	0.07	0.105	0.08	0.205	0.10		4.0
4.5		0.001	0.01	0.004	0.02	0.015	0.05	0.037	0.07	0.072	0.08	0.113	0.09	0.220	0.11		4.5
5.0		0.001	0.01	0.004	0.02	0.016	0.05	0.041	0.08	0.077	0.08	0.120	0.09	0.234	0.11		5.0
5.5		0.001	0.01	0.005	0.03	0.018	0.05	0.045	0.09	0.082	0.09	0.127	0.10	0.248	0.12		5.5
6.0		0.001	0.01	0.005	0.03	0.020	0.06	0.050	0.10	0.086	0.09	0.134	0.10	0.261	0.13		6.0
6.5		0.002	0.02	0.006	0.03	0.021	0.06	0.052	0.10	0.090	0.10	0.141	0.11	0.273	0.13		6.5
7.0		0.002	0.02	0.006	0.03	0.023	0.07	0.052	0.10	0.094	0.10	0.147	0.11	0.285	0.14		7.0
7.5		0.002	0.02	0.007	0.04	0.025	0.08	0.052	0.10	0.098	0.10	0.153	0.12	0.297	0.14		7.5
8.0		0.002	0.02	0.007	0.04	0.026	0.08	0.052	0.10	0.102	0.11	0.159	0.12	0.308	0.15		8.0
8.5		0.002	0.02	0.008	0.05	0.028	0.08	0.052	0.10	0.106	0.11	0.165	0.13	0.319	0.15	0.15	8.5
9.0		0.002	0.02	0.008	0.05	0.030	0.09	0.052	0.10	0.110	0.12	0.170	0.13	0.330	0.16		9.0
9.5		0.002	0.02	0.009	0.05	0.031	0.09	0.052	0.10	0.113	0.12	0.176	0.14	0.341	0.17		9.5
10.0		0.003	0.03	0.009	0.05	0.033	0.10	0.052	0.10	0.117	0.13	0.181	0.14	0.351	0.17		10.0
12.5		0.003	0.03	0.011	0.06	0.041	0.12	0.059	0.11	0.133	0.14	0.207	0.16	0.399	0.19		12.5
15.0		0.004	0.04	0.014	0.08	0.041	0.12	0.066	0.13	0.148	0.16	0.230	0.18	0.443	0.21		15.0
17.5	0.05	0.005	0.05	0.016	0.09	0.041	0.12	0.072	0.14	0.162	0.17	0.251	0.20	0.484	0.23		17.5
20.0		0.006	0.06	0.019	0.11	0.041	0.12	0.078	0.15	0.175	0.19	0.271	0.21	0.522	0.25		20.0
22.5		0.006	0.06	0.021	0.12	0.044	0.13	0.084	0.16	0.188	0.20	0.290	0.23	0.559	0.27		22.5
25.0		0.007	0.07	0.023	0.13	0.047	0.14	0.089	0.17	0.200	0.21	0.308	0.24	0.593	0.29		25.0
27.5		0.008	0.08	0.026	0.15	0.049	0.15	0.094	0.18	0.211	0.23	0.326	0.25	0.626	0.30	0.30	27.5
30.0		0.009	0.09	0.028	0.16	0.052	0.16	0.099	0.19	0.222	0.24	0.342	0.27	0.658	0.32		30.0
32.5		0.010	0.10	0.030	0.17	0.055	0.17	0.104	0.20	0.232	0.25	0.359	0.28	0.688	0.33		32.5
35.0		0.010	0.10	0.030	0.17	0.057	0.17	0.109	0.21	0.243	0.26	0.374	0.29	0.718	0.35		35.0
37.5		0.011	0.11	0.030	0.17	0.059	0.18	0.113	0.22	0.252	0.27	0.389	0.30	0.746	0.36		37.5
40.0		0.012	0.12	0.030	0.17	0.062	0.19	0.117	0.22	0.262	0.28	0.404	0.32	0.774	0.37		40.0
42.5		0.013	0.13	0.030	0.17	0.064	0.19	0.122	0.23	0.271	0.29	0.418	0.33	0.801	0.39		42.5
45.0		0.013	0.13	0.030	0.17	0.066	0.20	0.126	0.24	0.280	0.30	0.431	0.34	0.827	0.40		45.0
47.5		0.014	0.14	0.030	0.17	0.068	0.21	0.130	0.25	0.289	0.31	0.445	0.35	0.852	0.41		47.5
50.0	0.15	0.015	0.15	0.030	0.17	0.070	0.21	0.134	0.26	0.297	0.32	0.458	0.36	0.877	0.42		50.0
52.5		0.016	0.16	0.030	0.17	0.072	0.22	0.137	0.26	0.306	0.33	0.471	0.37	0.901	0.44		52.5
55.0		0.016	0.16	0.031	0.18	0.075	0.23	0.141	0.27	0.314	0.34	0.483	0.38	0.925	0.45		55.0
57.5		0.017	0.17	0.032	0.18	0.076	0.23	0.145	0.28	0.322	0.34	0.496	0.39	0.948	0.46		57.5
60.0		0.018	0.18	0.033	0.19	0.078	0.24	0.148	0.28	0.330	0.35	0.508	0.40	0.971	0.47		60.0
62.5		0.019	0.19	0.033	0.19	0.080	0.24	0.152	0.29	0.338	0.36	0.519	0.40	0.994	0.48		62.5
65.0		0.020	0.20	0.034	0.19	0.082	0.25	0.155	0.30	0.345	0.37	0.531	0.41	1.010	0.49		65.0
67.5		0.020	0.20	0.035	0.20	0.084	0.25	0.159	0.30	0.353	0.38	0.542	0.42	1.030	0.50	0.50	67.5
70.0		0.021	0.21	0.036	0.20	0.086	0.26	0.162	0.31	0.360	0.39	0.554	0.43	1.050	0.51		70.0
72.5		0.022	0.22	0.036	0.20	0.088	0.27	0.166	0.32	0.367	0.39	0.565	0.44	1.070	0.52		72.5
75.0		0.023	0.23	0.037	0.21	0.089	0.27	0.169	0.32	0.374	0.40	0.576	0.45	1.100	0.53		75.0
77.5		0.023	0.23	0.038	0.22	0.091	0.28	0.172	0.33	0.381	0.41	0.586	0.46	1.120	0.54		77.5
80.0		0.023	0.23	0.039	0.22	0.093	0.28	0.175	0.33	0.388	0.42	0.597	0.47	1.140	0.55		80.0
82.5		0.023	0.23	0.039	0.22	0.094	0.28	0.178	0.34	0.395	0.42	0.607	0.47	1.150	0.56		82.5
85.0		0.023	0.23	0.040	0.23	0.096	0.29	0.181	0.35	0.402	0.43	0.617	0.48	1.170	0.57		85.0
87.5		0.023	0.23	0.041	0.23	0.098	0.30	0.184	0.35	0.408	0.44	0.627	0.49	1.190	0.58		87.5
90.0		0.023	0.23	0.041	0.23	Pa/m 0.099	0.30	0.187	0.36	0.415	0.44	0.637	0.50	1.210	0.59		90.0

q_m = mass flow rate kg/s

c = velocity m/s

$\Delta p/l$ = pressure loss per unit length Pa/m

HEAVY GRADE STEEL

WATER AT 10 °C

$\Delta p/l$	c	10 mm		15 mm		20 mm		25 mm		32 mm		40 mm		50 mm		c	$\Delta p/l$
		q_m	c	q_m	c	q_m	c	q_m	c	q_m	c	q_m	c	q_m	c		
92.5		0.023	0.23	0.042	0.24	0.101	0.31	0.190	0.36	0.421	0.45	0.647	0.50	1.230	0.60		92.5
95.0		0.023	0.23	0.043	0.24	0.102	0.31	0.193	0.37	0.428	0.46	0.657	0.51	1.250	0.60		95.0
97.5		0.023	0.23	0.043	0.24	0.104	0.32	0.196	0.38	0.434	0.46	0.667	0.52	1.270	0.61		97.5
100		0.023	0.23	0.044	0.25	0.106	0.32	0.199	0.38	0.440	0.47	0.676	0.53	1.290	0.62		100
120		0.023	0.23	0.049	0.28	0.117	0.35	0.221	0.42	0.488	0.52	0.748	0.58	1.420	0.69		120
140		0.024	0.24	0.054	0.31	0.128	0.39	0.241	0.46	0.531	0.57	0.815	0.64	1.550	0.75		140
160		0.026	0.26	0.058	0.33	0.138	0.42	0.260	0.50	0.572	0.61	0.877	0.68	1.670	0.81		160
180		0.028	0.28	0.062	0.35	0.148	0.45	0.277	0.53	0.611	0.65	0.936	0.73	1.780	0.86		180
200	0.30	0.030	0.30	0.066	0.37	0.157	0.48	0.294	0.56	0.648	0.69	0.992	0.77	1.880	0.91		200
220		0.032	0.32	0.070	0.40	0.166	0.50	0.310	0.59	0.683	0.73	1.040	0.81	1.980	0.96	1.00	220
240		0.033	0.33	0.074	0.42	0.174	0.53	0.326	0.62	0.716	0.77	1.090	0.85	2.080	1.01		240
260		0.035	0.35	0.077	0.44	0.182	0.55	0.341	0.65	0.748	0.80	1.140	0.89	2.170	1.05		260
280		0.036	0.36	0.080	0.45	0.190	0.58	0.355	0.68	0.780	0.83	1.190	0.93	2.260	1.09		280
300		0.038	0.38	0.084	0.48	0.197	0.60	0.369	0.71	0.810	0.87	1.230	0.96	2.350	1.14		300
320		0.039	0.39	0.087	0.49	0.204	0.62	0.382	0.73	0.839	0.90	1.280	1.00	2.430	1.18		320
340		0.041	0.41	0.090	0.51	0.212	0.64	0.395	0.76	0.867	0.93	1.320	1.03	2.510	1.21		340
360		0.042	0.42	0.093	0.53	0.218	0.66	0.408	0.78	0.894	0.96	1.360	1.06	2.590	1.25		360
380		0.044	0.44	0.096	0.54	0.225	0.68	0.420	0.80	0.921	0.99	1.400	1.09	2.660	1.29		380
400		0.045	0.45	0.098	0.55	0.232	0.70	0.432	0.83	0.947	1.01	1.440	1.12	2.740	1.33		400
420		0.046	0.46	0.101	0.57	0.238	0.72	0.444	0.85	0.973	1.04	1.480	1.15	2.810	1.36		420
440		0.047	0.47	0.104	0.59	0.244	0.74	0.456	0.87	0.998	1.07	1.520	1.19	2.880	1.39		440
460		0.049	0.49	0.107	0.61	0.250	0.76	0.467	0.89	1.020	1.09	1.560	1.22	2.950	1.43		460
480	0.50	0.050	0.50	0.109	0.62	0.256	0.78	0.478	0.91	1.040	1.11	1.590	1.24	3.020	1.46		480
500		0.051	0.51	0.112	0.63	0.262	0.79	0.489	0.94	1.060	1.13	1.630	1.27	3.090	1.50	1.50	500
520		0.052	0.52	0.114	0.65	0.268	0.81	0.499	0.95	1.090	1.17	1.660	1.30	3.150	1.52		520
540		0.053	0.53	0.117	0.66	0.273	0.83	0.510	0.98	1.110	1.19	1.700	1.33	3.220	1.56		540
560		0.054	0.54	0.119	0.67	0.279	0.85	0.520	0.99	1.130	1.21	1.730	1.35	3.280	1.59		560
580		0.056	0.56	0.121	0.68	0.284	0.86	0.530	1.01	1.150	1.23	1.760	1.37	3.340	1.62		580
600		0.057	0.57	0.124	0.70	0.290	0.88	0.540	1.03	1.180	1.26	1.800	1.40	3.400	1.65		600
620		0.058	0.58	0.126	0.71	0.295	0.89	0.550	1.05	1.200	1.28	1.830	1.43	3.460	1.67		620
640		0.059	0.59	0.128	0.72	0.300	0.91	0.559	1.07	1.220	1.31	1.860	1.45	3.520	1.70		640
660		0.060	0.60	0.130	0.74	0.305	0.92	0.569	1.09	1.240	1.33	1.890	1.47	3.580	1.73		660
680		0.061	0.61	0.133	0.75	0.310	0.94	0.578	1.11	1.260	1.35	1.920	1.50	3.640	1.76		680
700		0.062	0.62	0.135	0.76	0.315	0.95	0.587	1.12	1.280	1.37	1.950	1.52	3.690	1.79		700
720		0.063	0.63	0.137	0.78	0.320	0.97	0.596	1.14	1.300	1.39	1.980	1.55	3.750	1.81		720
740		0.064	0.64	0.139	0.79	0.325	0.98	0.605	1.16	1.320	1.41	2.010	1.57	3.810	1.84		740
760		0.065	0.65	0.141	0.80	0.330	1.00	0.614	1.17	1.340	1.43	2.040	1.59	3.860	1.87		760
780		0.066	0.66	0.143	0.81	0.335	1.02	0.623	1.19	1.350	1.44	2.070	1.62	3.910	1.89		780
800		0.067	0.67	0.145	0.82	0.339	1.03	0.631	1.21	1.370	1.47	2.100	1.64	3.970	1.92		800
820		0.068	0.68	0.147	0.83	0.344	1.04	0.640	1.22	1.390	1.49	2.120	1.65	4.020	1.95		820
840		0.069	0.69	0.149	0.84	0.349	1.06	0.648	1.24	1.410	1.51	2.150	1.68	4.070	1.97		840
860		0.069	0.69	0.151	0.85	0.353	1.07	0.657	1.26	1.430	1.53	2.180	1.70	4.120	1.99	2.00	860
880		0.070	0.70	0.153	0.87	0.358	1.08	0.665	1.27	1.450	1.55	2.210	1.72	4.170	2.02		880
900		0.071	0.71	0.155	0.88	0.362	1.10	0.673	1.29	1.460	1.56	2.230	1.74	4.220	2.04		900
920		0.072	0.72	0.157	0.89	0.366	1.11	0.681	1.30	1.480	1.58	2.260	1.76	4.270	2.07		920
940		0.073	0.73	0.159	0.90	0.371	1.12	0.689	1.32	1.500	1.61	2.280	1.78	4.320	2.09		940
960		0.074	0.74	0.161	0.91	0.375	1.14	0.697	1.33	1.510	1.62	2.310	1.80	4.370	2.11		960
980		0.075	0.75	0.162	0.92	0.379	1.15	0.705	1.35	1.530	1.64	2.340	1.83	4.420	2.14		980
1000		0.076	0.76	0.164	0.93	0.383	1.16	0.712	1.36	1.550	1.66	2.360	1.84	4.460	2.16		1000
1100		0.080	0.80	0.173	0.98	0.404	1.22	0.750	1.44	1.630	1.74	2.480	1.94	4.690	2.27		1100
1200		0.084	0.84	0.182	1.03	0.423	1.28	0.786	1.50	1.710	1.83	2.600	2.03	4.910	2.38		1200
1300		0.088	0.88	0.190	1.08	0.442	1.34	0.820	1.57	1.780	1.90	2.710	2.11	5.130	2.48		1300
1400		0.091	0.91	0.198	1.12	0.460	1.39	0.853	1.63	1.850	1.98	2.820	2.20	5.330	2.58		1400
1500		0.095	0.95	0.205	1.16	0.477	1.45	0.885	1.69	1.920	2.05	2.930	2.29	5.530	2.68		1500
1600	1.00	0.098	0.98	0.213	1.21	0.494	1.50	0.916	1.75	1.990	2.13	3.030	2.36	5.720	2.77		1600
1700		0.102	1.02	0.220	1.25	0.511	1.55	0.947	1.81	2.050	2.19	3.130	2.44	5.900	2.86		1700
1800		0.105	1.05	0.227	1.28	0.527	1.60	0.976	1.87	2.120	2.27	3.220	2.51	6.080	2.94	3.00	1800
1900		0.108	1.08	0.233	1.32	0.542	1.64	1.000	1.91	2.180	2.33	3.320	2.59	6.250	3.02		1900
2000		0.111	1.11	0.240	1.36	0.557	1.69	1.030	1.97	2.240	2.40	3.410	2.66	6.420	3.11		2000

q_m = mass flow rate — kg/s
c = velocity — m/s
$\Delta p/l$ = pressure loss per unit length — Pa/m

HEAVY GRADE STEEL

WATER AT 10 °C

$\Delta p/l$	c	65 mm		80 mm		100 mm		125 mm		150 mm		mm		mm		c	$\Delta p/l$
		q_m	c	q_m	c	q_m	c	q_m	c	q_m	c	q_m	c	q_m	c		
0.1		0.038	0.01	0.072	0.01	0.210	0.03	0.299	0.02	0.497	0.03						0.1
0.2		0.076	0.02	0.145	0.03	0.244	0.03	0.453	0.03	0.749	0.04						0.2
0.3		0.114	0.03	0.160	0.03	0.311	0.04	0.576	0.04	0.950	0.05					0.05	0.3
0.4		0.136	0.04	0.173	0.04	0.369	0.04	0.682	0.05	1.120	0.06						0.4
0.5		0.136	0.04	0.198	0.04	0.421	0.05	0.777	0.06	1.270	0.07						0.5
0.6		0.140	0.04	0.221	0.05	0.469	0.06	0.865	0.07	1.420	0.08						0.6
0.7		0.153	0.04	0.242	0.05	0.514	0.06	0.946	0.07	1.550	0.08						0.7
0.8		0.166	0.05	0.262	0.05	0.556	0.07	1.020	0.08	1.670	0.09						0.8
0.9		0.178	0.05	0.281	0.06	0.595	0.07	1.090	0.08	1.790	0.10						0.9
1.0	0.05	0.190	0.05	0.299	0.06	0.633	0.08	1.160	0.09	1.900	0.10						1.0
1.5		0.242	0.07	0.380	0.08	0.802	0.10	1.460	0.11	2.400	0.13						1.5
2.0		0.287	0.08	0.450	0.09	0.947	0.11	1.730	0.13	2.830	0.15					0.15	2.0
2.5		0.327	0.09	0.512	0.11	1.070	0.13	1.960	0.15	3.210	0.17						2.5
3.0		0.364	0.10	0.569	0.12	1.190	0.14	2.180	0.17	3.560	0.19						3.0
3.5		0.398	0.11	0.622	0.13	1.300	0.16	2.380	0.18	3.880	0.21						3.5
4.0		0.430	0.12	0.672	0.14	1.400	0.17	2.570	0.20	4.190	0.22						4.0
4.5		0.461	0.13	0.720	0.15	1.500	0.18	2.740	0.21	4.480	0.24						4.5
5.0		0.490	0.14	0.764	0.16	1.600	0.19	2.910	0.22	4.750	0.25						5.0
5.5		0.518	0.15	0.807	0.17	1.680	0.20	3.070	0.24	5.010	0.27						5.5
6.0	0.15	0.544	0.15	0.849	0.17	1.770	0.21	3.230	0.25	5.260	0.28						6.0
6.5		0.570	0.16	0.889	0.18	1.850	0.22	3.370	0.26	5.500	0.29					0.30	6.5
7.0		0.595	0.17	0.927	0.19	1.930	0.23	3.520	0.27	5.730	0.31						7.0
7.5		0.619	0.18	0.964	0.20	2.010	0.24	3.660	0.28	5.960	0.32						7.5
8.0		0.642	0.18	1.000	0.21	2.080	0.25	3.790	0.29	6.170	0.33						8.0
8.5		0.665	0.19	1.030	0.21	2.160	0.26	3.920	0.30	6.390	0.34						8.5
9.0		0.687	0.19	1.070	0.22	2.230	0.27	4.050	0.31	6.590	0.35						9.0
9.5		0.709	0.20	1.100	0.23	2.300	0.27	4.170	0.32	6.790	0.36						9.5
10.0		0.730	0.21	1.130	0.23	2.360	0.28	4.290	0.33	6.990	0.37						10.0
12.5		0.829	0.24	1.280	0.26	2.680	0.32	4.860	0.37	7.910	0.42						12.5
15.0		0.919	0.26	1.420	0.29	2.970	0.35	5.380	0.41	8.750	0.47					0.50	15.0
17.5	0.30	1.000	0.28	1.550	0.32	3.230	0.39	5.860	0.45	9.520	0.51						17.5
20.0		1.080	0.31	1.670	0.34	3.480	0.42	6.310	0.48	10.200	0.54						20.0
22.5		1.150	0.33	1.790	0.37	3.720	0.44	6.730	0.52	10.900	0.58						22.5
25.0		1.220	0.35	1.900	0.39	3.940	0.47	7.140	0.55	11.500	0.61						25.0
27.5		1.290	0.37	2.000	0.41	4.150	0.50	7.520	0.58	12.200	0.65						27.5
30.0		1.350	0.38	2.100	0.43	4.360	0.52	7.890	0.61	12.700	0.68						30.0
32.5		1.420	0.40	2.200	0.45	4.560	0.54	8.240	0.63	13.300	0.71						32.5
35.0		1.480	0.42	2.290	0.47	4.750	0.57	8.580	0.66	13.900	0.74						35.0
37.5		1.530	0.43	2.380	0.49	4.930	0.59	8.910	0.68	14.400	0.77						37.5
40.0		1.590	0.45	2.470	0.51	5.110	0.61	9.230	0.71	14.900	0.80						40.0
42.5		1.650	0.47	2.550	0.52	5.280	0.63	9.540	0.73	15.400	0.82						42.5
45.0		1.700	0.48	2.630	0.54	5.450	0.65	9.840	0.75	15.900	0.85						45.0
47.5	0.50	1.750	0.50	2.710	0.56	5.610	0.67	10.100	0.77	16.400	0.88						47.5
50.0		1.800	0.51	2.790	0.57	5.770	0.69	10.400	0.80	16.800	0.90						50.0
52.5		1.850	0.52	2.870	0.59	5.930	0.71	10.700	0.82	17.300	0.92						52.5
55.0		1.900	0.54	2.940	0.60	6.080	0.73	10.900	0.84	17.700	0.95						55.0
57.5		1.950	0.55	3.010	0.62	6.230	0.74	11.200	0.86	18.200	0.97						57.5
60.0		1.990	0.56	3.080	0.63	6.380	0.76	11.500	0.88	18.600	0.99					1.00	60.0
62.5		2.040	0.58	3.150	0.65	6.520	0.78	11.700	0.90	19.000	1.02						62.5
65.0		2.080	0.59	3.220	0.66	6.660	0.79	12.000	0.92	19.400	1.04						65.0
67.5		2.130	0.60	3.290	0.67	6.800	0.81	12.200	0.94	19.800	1.06						67.5
70.0		2.170	0.62	3.360	0.69	6.930	0.83	12.500	0.96	20.200	1.08						70.0
72.5		2.210	0.63	3.420	0.70	7.070	0.84	12.700	0.97	20.600	1.10						72.5
75.0		2.250	0.64	3.490	0.72	7.200	0.86	12.900	0.99	21.000	1.12						75.0
77.5		2.300	0.65	3.550	0.73	7.330	0.87	13.200	1.01	21.300	1.14						77.5
80.0		2.340	0.66	3.610	0.74	7.460	0.89	13.400	1.03	21.700	1.16						80.0
82.5		2.380	0.68	3.670	0.75	7.580	0.90	13.600	1.04	22.100	1.18						82.5
85.0		2.410	0.68	3.730	0.77	7.710	0.92	13.800	1.06	22.400	1.20						85.0
87.5		2.450	0.70	3.790	0.78	7.830	0.93	14.100	1.08	22.800	1.22						87.5
90.0		2.490	0.71	3.850	0.79	7.950	0.95	14.300	1.10	23.100	1.23						90.0

q_m	= mass flow rate	kg/s
c	= velocity	m/s
$\Delta p/l$	= pressure loss per unit length	Pa/m

HEAVY GRADE STEEL

WATER AT 10 °C

$\Delta p/l$	c	65 mm		80 mm		100 mm		125 mm		150 mm		mm		mm		c	$\Delta p/l$
		q_m	c	q_m	c	q_m	c	q_m	c	q_m	c	q_m	c	q_m	c		
92.5		2.53	0.7	3.91	0.8	8.07	1.0	14.50	1.1	23.50	1.3						92.5
95.0		2.57	0.7	3.97	0.8	8.18	1.0	14.70	1.1	23.80	1.3						95.0
97.5		2.60	0.7	4.02	0.8	8.30	1.0	14.90	1.1	24.10	1.3						97.5
100		2.64	0.7	4.08	0.8	8.41	1.0	15.10	1.2	24.50	1.3						100
120		2.92	0.8	4.51	0.9	9.28	1.1	16.70	1.3	27.00	1.4					1.5	120
140		3.17	0.9	4.90	1.0	10.00	1.2	18.10	1.4	29.30	1.6						140
160		3.41	1.0	5.27	1.1	10.80	1.3	19.40	1.5	31.40	1.7						160
180	1.0	3.64	1.0	5.61	1.2	11.50	1.4	20.70	1.6	33.40	1.8						180
200		3.85	1.1	5.94	1.2	12.20	1.5	21.90	1.7	35.40	1.9						200
220		4.05	1.1	6.25	1.3	12.80	1.5	23.00	1.8	37.20	2.0					2.0	220
240		4.25	1.2	6.55	1.3	13.40	1.6	24.10	1.8	38.90	2.1						240
260		4.44	1.3	6.84	1.4	14.00	1.7	25.20	1.9	40.60	2.2						260
280		4.62	1.3	7.11	1.5	14.60	1.7	26.20	2.0	42.20	2.3						280
300		4.79	1.4	7.38	1.5	15.10	1.8	27.10	2.1	43.80	2.3						300
320		4.96	1.4	7.64	1.6	15.60	1.9	28.10	2.2	45.30	2.4						320
340		5.12	1.5	7.89	1.6	16.10	1.9	29.00	2.2	46.80	2.5						340
360		5.28	1.5	8.13	1.7	16.60	2.0	29.90	2.3	48.20	2.6						360
380	1.5	5.44	1.5	8.37	1.7	17.10	2.0	30.70	2.4	49.60	2.6						380
400		5.59	1.6	8.60	1.8	17.60	2.1	31.60	2.4	50.90	2.7						400
420		5.73	1.6	8.83	1.8	18.00	2.1	32.40	2.5	52.20	2.8						420
440		5.88	1.7	9.05	1.9	18.50	2.2	33.20	2.5	53.50	2.9						440
460		6.02	1.7	9.26	1.9	18.90	2.3	34.00	2.6	54.80	2.9						460
480		6.16	1.7	9.47	1.9	19.40	2.3	34.70	2.7	56.00	3.0					3.0	480
500		6.29	1.8	9.68	2.0	19.80	2.4	35.50	2.7	57.20	3.1						500
520		6.42	1.8	9.88	2.0	20.20	2.4	36.20	2.8	58.40	3.1						520
540		6.55	1.9	10.00	2.1	20.60	2.5	37.00	2.8	59.50	3.2						540
560		6.68	1.9	10.20	2.1	21.00	2.5	37.70	2.9	60.70	3.2						560
580		6.81	1.9	10.40	2.1	21.40	2.6	38.40	2.9	61.80	3.3						580
600		6.93	2.0	10.60	2.2	21.80	2.6	39.00	3.0	62.90	3.4						600
620		7.05	2.0	10.80	2.2	22.10	2.6	39.70	3.0	64.00	3.4						620
640	2.0	7.17	2.0	11.00	2.3	22.50	2.7	40.40	3.1	65.00	3.5						640
660		7.29	2.1	11.20	2.3	22.90	2.7	41.00	3.1	66.10	3.5						660
680		7.40	2.1	11.30	2.3	23.20	2.8	41.70	3.2	67.10	3.6						680
700		7.52	2.1	11.50	2.4	23.60	2.8	42.30	3.2	68.10	3.6						700
720		7.63	2.2	11.70	2.4	24.00	2.9	42.90	3.3	69.10	3.7						720
740		7.74	2.2	11.90	2.4	24.30	2.9	43.60	3.3	70.10	3.7						740
760		7.85	2.2	12.00	2.5	24.60	2.9	44.20	3.4	71.10	3.8						760
780		7.96	2.3	12.20	2.5	25.00	3.0	44.80	3.4	72.10	3.9						780
800		8.07	2.3	12.40	2.5	25.30	3.0	45.40	3.5	73.00	3.9						800
820		8.17	2.3	12.50	2.6	25.60	3.1	45.90	3.5	74.00	4.0						820
840		8.28	2.3	12.70	2.6	26.00	3.1	46.50	3.6	74.90	4.0						840
860		8.38	2.4	12.80	2.6	26.30	3.1	47.10	3.6	75.80	4.0						860
880		8.48	2.4	13.00	2.7	26.60	3.2	47.70	3.7	76.70	4.1						880
900		8.58	2.4	13.10	2.7	26.90	3.2	48.20	3.7	77.60	4.1						900
920		8.68	2.5	13.30	2.7	27.20	3.2	48.80	3.7	78.50	4.2						920
940		8.78	2.5	13.40	2.7	27.50	3.3	49.30	3.8	79.40	4.2						940
960		8.88	2.5	13.60	2.8	27.80	3.3	49.90	3.8	80.20	4.3						960
980		8.97	2.5	13.70	2.8	28.10	3.4	50.40	3.9	81.10	4.3						980
1000		9.07	2.6	13.90	2.9	28.40	3.4	50.90	3.9	82.00	4.4						1000
1100		9.53	2.7	14.60	3.0	29.90	3.6	53.50	4.1	86.10	4.6						1100
1200		9.98	2.8	15.30	3.1	31.30	3.7	56.00	4.3	90.00	4.8						1200
1300	3.0	10.40	3.0	15.90	3.3	32.60	3.9	58.30	4.5	93.80	5.0						1300
1400		10.80	3.1	16.60	3.4	33.90	4.0	60.60	4.6	97.50	5.2						1400
1500		11.20	3.2	17.20	3.5	35.10	4.2	62.80	4.8	101.00	5.4						1500
1600		11.60	3.3	17.80	3.7	36.30	4.3	64.90	5.0	104.00	5.6						1600
1700		11.90	3.4	18.30	3.8	37.40	4.5	67.00	5.1	107.00	5.7						1700
1800		12.30	3.5	18.90	3.9	38.60	4.6	69.00	5.3	110.00	5.9						1800
1900		12.60	3.6	19.40	4.0	39.70	4.7	70.90	5.4	114.00	6.1						1900
2000		13.00	3.7	19.90	4.1	40.70	4.9	72.80	5.6	117.00	6.3						2000

q_m	= mass flow rate	kg/s
c	= velocity	m/s
$\Delta p/l$	= pressure loss per unit length	Pa/m

HEAVY GRADE STEEL

WATER AT 75 °C

$\Delta p/l$	c	10 mm		15 mm		20 mm		25 mm		32 mm		40 mm		50 mm		c	$\Delta p/l$
		q_m	c	q_m	c	q_m	c	q_m	c	q_m	c	q_m	c	q_m	c		
0.1						0.001	0.00	0.002	0.00	0.008	0.01	0.016	0.01	0.030	0.01		0.1
0.2						0.002	0.01	0.005	0.01	0.017	0.02	0.023	0.02	0.043	0.02		0.2
0.3						0.003	0.01	0.008	0.02	0.020	0.02	0.028	0.02	0.054	0.03		0.3
0.4				0.001	0.01	0.004	0.01	0.011	0.02	0.021	0.02	0.033	0.03	0.065	0.03		0.4
0.5				0.001	0.01	0.005	0.02	0.014	0.03	0.024	0.03	0.038	0.03	0.074	0.04		0.5
0.6				0.001	0.01	0.006	0.02	0.015	0.03	0.027	0.03	0.042	0.03	0.082	0.04		0.6
0.7				0.002	0.01	0.007	0.02	0.015	0.03	0.030	0.03	0.046	0.04	0.090	0.04		0.7
0.8				0.002	0.01	0.008	0.02	0.015	0.03	0.032	0.04	0.050	0.04	0.097	0.05		0.8
0.9				0.002	0.01	0.010	0.03	0.015	0.03	0.034	0.04	0.054	0.04	0.104	0.05		0.9
1.0		0.001	0.01	0.003	0.02	0.011	0.03	0.016	0.03	0.037	0.04	0.057	0.05	0.110	0.05	0.05	1.0
1.5		0.001	0.01	0.004	0.02	0.012	0.04	0.020	0.04	0.047	0.05	0.072	0.06	0.139	0.07		1.5
2.0		0.002	0.02	0.006	0.03	0.013	0.04	0.024	0.05	0.055	0.06	0.085	0.07	0.164	0.08		2.0
2.5		0.002	0.02	0.008	0.05	0.014	0.04	0.028	0.05	0.063	0.07	0.097	0.08	0.187	0.09		2.5
3.0		0.003	0.03	0.008	0.05	0.016	0.05	0.031	0.06	0.070	0.08	0.108	0.09	0.207	0.10		3.0
3.5		0.003	0.03	0.008	0.05	0.018	0.06	0.034	0.07	0.076	0.08	0.118	0.09	0.226	0.11		3.5
4.0		0.004	0.04	0.008	0.05	0.019	0.06	0.037	0.07	0.082	0.09	0.127	0.10	0.243	0.12		4.0
4.5		0.004	0.04	0.008	0.05	0.021	0.07	0.039	0.08	0.088	0.10	0.136	0.11	0.260	0.13		4.5
5.0		0.005	0.05	0.009	0.05	0.022	0.07	0.042	0.08	0.093	0.10	0.144	0.12	0.276	0.14		5.0
5.5	0.05	0.005	0.05	0.009	0.05	0.023	0.07	0.044	0.09	0.099	0.11	0.152	0.12	0.291	0.14		5.5
6.0		0.006	0.06	0.010	0.06	0.024	0.07	0.047	0.09	0.104	0.11	0.160	0.13	0.305	0.15	0.15	6.0
6.5		0.006	0.06	0.010	0.06	0.026	0.08	0.049	0.10	0.108	0.12	0.167	0.13	0.319	0.16		6.5
7.0		0.006	0.06	0.011	0.06	0.027	0.08	0.051	0.10	0.113	0.12	0.174	0.14	0.333	0.17		7.0
7.5		0.006	0.06	0.011	0.06	0.028	0.09	0.053	0.10	0.118	0.13	0.181	0.14	0.346	0.17		7.5
8.0		0.006	0.06	0.012	0.07	0.029	0.09	0.055	0.11	0.122	0.13	0.188	0.15	0.358	0.18		8.0
8.5		0.006	0.06	0.012	0.07	0.030	0.09	0.057	0.11	0.126	0.14	0.194	0.16	0.371	0.18		8.5
9.0		0.006	0.06	0.013	0.08	0.031	0.10	0.059	0.12	0.130	0.14	0.200	0.16	0.382	0.19		9.0
9.5		0.006	0.06	0.013	0.08	0.032	0.10	0.061	0.12	0.134	0.15	0.206	0.16	0.394	0.20		9.5
10.0		0.006	0.06	0.014	0.08	0.033	0.10	0.062	0.12	0.138	0.15	0.212	0.17	0.405	0.20		10.0
12.5		0.007	0.07	0.016	0.09	0.038	0.12	0.071	0.14	0.157	0.17	0.240	0.19	0.458	0.23		12.5
15.0		0.008	0.08	0.017	0.10	0.042	0.13	0.079	0.16	0.173	0.19	0.266	0.21	0.506	0.25		15.0
17.5		0.008	0.08	0.019	0.11	0.046	0.14	0.086	0.17	0.189	0.21	0.290	0.23	0.551	0.27		17.5
20.0		0.009	0.09	0.021	0.12	0.049	0.15	0.092	0.18	0.203	0.22	0.312	0.25	0.592	0.29	0.30	20.0
22.5		0.010	0.10	0.022	0.13	0.052	0.16	0.099	0.19	0.217	0.24	0.332	0.27	0.631	0.31		22.5
25.0		0.010	0.10	0.023	0.13	0.056	0.17	0.105	0.21	0.230	0.25	0.352	0.28	0.668	0.33		25.0
27.5		0.011	0.11	0.025	0.15	0.059	0.18	0.110	0.22	0.242	0.27	0.371	0.30	0.704	0.35		27.5
30.0		0.012	0.12	0.026	0.15	0.062	0.19	0.116	0.23	0.254	0.28	0.389	0.31	0.738	0.37		30.0
32.5		0.012	0.12	0.027	0.16	0.065	0.20	0.121	0.24	0.266	0.29	0.406	0.32	0.770	0.38		32.5
35.0		0.013	0.13	0.028	0.16	0.067	0.21	0.126	0.25	0.276	0.30	0.423	0.34	0.801	0.40		35.0
37.5		0.013	0.13	0.030	0.17	0.070	0.22	0.131	0.26	0.287	0.31	0.439	0.35	0.832	0.41		37.5
40.0		0.014	0.14	0.031	0.18	0.073	0.23	0.136	0.27	0.297	0.33	0.454	0.36	0.861	0.43		40.0
42.5		0.014	0.14	0.032	0.19	0.075	0.23	0.140	0.27	0.307	0.34	0.469	0.38	0.889	0.44		42.5
45.0		0.015	0.15	0.033	0.19	0.077	0.24	0.145	0.28	0.317	0.35	0.484	0.39	0.917	0.46		45.0
47.5	0.15	0.015	0.15	0.034	0.20	0.080	0.25	0.149	0.29	0.326	0.36	0.498	0.40	0.944	0.47		47.5
50.0		0.016	0.16	0.035	0.20	0.082	0.25	0.153	0.30	0.335	0.37	0.512	0.41	0.970	0.48		50.0
52.5		0.016	0.16	0.036	0.21	0.084	0.26	0.157	0.31	0.344	0.38	0.526	0.42	0.995	0.49	0.50	52.5
55.0		0.017	0.17	0.037	0.21	0.087	0.27	0.161	0.32	0.353	0.39	0.539	0.43	1.020	0.51		55.0
57.5		0.017	0.17	0.038	0.22	0.089	0.28	0.165	0.32	0.362	0.40	0.552	0.44	1.040	0.52		57.5
60.0		0.018	0.18	0.039	0.23	0.091	0.28	0.169	0.33	0.370	0.41	0.565	0.45	1.060	0.53		60.0
62.5		0.018	0.18	0.039	0.23	0.093	0.29	0.173	0.34	0.378	0.41	0.577	0.46	1.090	0.54		62.5
65.0		0.018	0.18	0.040	0.23	0.095	0.30	0.177	0.35	0.386	0.42	0.590	0.47	1.110	0.55		65.0
67.5		0.019	0.19	0.041	0.24	0.097	0.30	0.181	0.36	0.394	0.43	0.602	0.48	1.130	0.56		67.5
70.0		0.019	0.19	0.042	0.24	0.099	0.31	0.184	0.36	0.402	0.44	0.614	0.49	1.160	0.58		70.0
72.5		0.020	0.20	0.043	0.25	0.101	0.31	0.188	0.37	0.410	0.45	0.625	0.50	1.180	0.59		72.5
75.0		0.020	0.20	0.044	0.26	0.103	0.32	0.191	0.37	0.417	0.46	0.637	0.51	1.200	0.60		75.0
77.5		0.020	0.20	0.045	0.26	0.105	0.33	0.195	0.38	0.425	0.47	0.648	0.52	1.220	0.61		77.5
80.0		0.021	0.21	0.045	0.26	0.106	0.33	0.198	0.39	0.432	0.47	0.659	0.53	1.240	0.62		80.0
82.5		0.021	0.21	0.046	0.27	0.108	0.34	0.201	0.39	0.439	0.48	0.670	0.54	1.260	0.63		82.5
85.0		0.021	0.21	0.047	0.27	0.110	0.34	0.205	0.40	0.446	0.49	0.680	0.54	1.280	0.64		85.0
87.5		0.022	0.23	0.048	0.28	0.112	0.35	0.208	0.41	0.453	0.50	0.691	0.55	1.300	0.65		87.5
90.0		0.022	0.23	0.048	0.28	0.113	0.35	0.211	0.41	0.460	0.50	0.701	0.56	1.320	0.66		90.0

q_m	= mass flow rate	kg/s
c	= velocity	m/s
$\Delta p/l$	= pressure loss per unit length	Pa/m

HEAVY GRADE STEEL

WATER AT 75 °C

$\Delta p/l$	c	10 mm q_m	c	15 mm q_m	c	20 mm q_m	c	25 mm q_m	c	32 mm q_m	c	40 mm q_m	c	50 mm q_m	c	c	$\Delta p/l$
92.5		0.022	0.23	0.049	0.28	0.115	0.36	0.214	0.42	0.467	0.51	0.712	0.57	1.340	0.67		92.5
95.0		0.023	0.24	0.050	0.29	0.117	0.36	0.217	0.43	0.474	0.52	0.722	0.58	1.360	0.67		95.0
97.5		0.023	0.24	0.051	0.30	0.118	0.37	0.220	0.43	0.480	0.53	0.732	0.59	1.380	0.68		97.5
100		0.023	0.24	0.051	0.30	0.120	0.37	0.223	0.44	0.487	0.53	0.742	0.59	1.400	0.69		100
120		0.026	0.27	0.057	0.33	0.133	0.41	0.246	0.48	0.536	0.59	0.817	0.65	1.540	0.76		120
140	0.30	0.028	0.29	0.062	0.36	0.144	0.45	0.267	0.52	0.582	0.64	0.886	0.71	1.670	0.83		140
160		0.031	0.32	0.066	0.38	0.155	0.48	0.287	0.56	0.624	0.68	0.951	0.76	1.790	0.89		160
180		0.033	0.34	0.071	0.41	0.165	0.51	0.306	0.60	0.664	0.73	1.010	0.81	1.900	0.94		180
200		0.035	0.36	0.075	0.44	0.174	0.54	0.323	0.63	0.702	0.77	1.060	0.85	2.010	1.00	1.00	200
220		0.036	0.37	0.079	0.46	0.184	0.57	0.340	0.67	0.738	0.81	1.120	0.90	2.110	1.05		220
240		0.038	0.39	0.083	0.48	0.192	0.60	0.356	0.70	0.773	0.85	1.170	0.94	2.210	1.10		240
260		0.040	0.41	0.086	0.50	0.201	0.62	0.371	0.73	0.806	0.88	1.220	0.98	2.300	1.14		260
280		0.042	0.43	0.090	0.52	0.209	0.65	0.386	0.76	0.838	0.92	1.270	1.02	2.390	1.19		280
300		0.043	0.44	0.093	0.54	0.217	0.67	0.401	0.79	0.868	0.95	1.320	1.06	2.480	1.23		300
320		0.045	0.46	0.097	0.56	0.224	0.70	0.414	0.81	0.898	0.99	1.360	1.09	2.570	1.28		320
340		0.046	0.47	0.100	0.58	0.231	0.72	0.428	0.84	0.927	1.02	1.400	1.12	2.650	1.32		340
360		0.048	0.49	0.103	0.60	0.238	0.74	0.441	0.87	0.955	1.05	1.450	1.16	2.730	1.35		360
380	0.50	0.049	0.50	0.106	0.62	0.245	0.76	0.454	0.89	0.982	1.08	1.490	1.19	2.800	1.39		380
400		0.051	0.52	0.109	0.63	0.252	0.78	0.466	0.91	1.000	1.10	1.530	1.22	2.880	1.43		400
420		0.052	0.53	0.112	0.65	0.259	0.80	0.478	0.94	1.030	1.13	1.570	1.26	2.950	1.46		420
440		0.053	0.54	0.115	0.67	0.265	0.82	0.490	0.96	1.060	1.16	1.610	1.29	3.020	1.50	1.50	440
460		0.055	0.56	0.117	0.68	0.271	0.84	0.501	0.98	1.080	1.19	1.640	1.31	3.090	1.53		460
480		0.056	0.57	0.120	0.70	0.277	0.86	0.512	1.00	1.100	1.21	1.680	1.34	3.160	1.57		480
500		0.057	0.58	0.123	0.71	0.283	0.88	0.523	1.03	1.130	1.24	1.720	1.38	3.230	1.60		500
520		0.058	0.59	0.125	0.73	0.289	0.90	0.534	1.05	1.150	1.26	1.750	1.40	3.300	1.64		520
540		0.059	0.60	0.128	0.74	0.295	0.92	0.545	1.07	1.170	1.28	1.790	1.43	3.360	1.67		540
560		0.061	0.62	0.130	0.75	0.301	0.94	0.555	1.09	1.200	1.32	1.820	1.46	3.420	1.70		560
580		0.062	0.63	0.133	0.77	0.306	0.95	0.566	1.11	1.220	1.34	1.850	1.48	3.490	1.73		580
600		0.063	0.64	0.135	0.78	0.312	0.97	0.576	1.13	1.240	1.36	1.890	1.51	3.550	1.76		600
620		0.064	0.65	0.137	0.80	0.317	0.99	0.586	1.15	1.260	1.38	1.920	1.54	3.610	1.79		620
640		0.065	0.66	0.140	0.81	0.323	1.00	0.595	1.17	1.280	1.40	1.950	1.56	3.670	1.82		640
660		0.066	0.68	0.142	0.82	0.328	1.02	0.605	1.19	1.300	1.43	1.980	1.58	3.730	1.85		660
680		0.067	0.69	0.144	0.84	0.333	1.03	0.614	1.20	1.320	1.45	2.010	1.61	3.780	1.88		680
700		0.068	0.70	0.147	0.85	0.338	1.05	0.624	1.22	1.340	1.47	2.040	1.63	3.840	1.91		700
720		0.069	0.71	0.149	0.86	0.343	1.07	0.633	1.24	1.360	1.49	2.070	1.66	3.900	1.94		720
740		0.070	0.72	0.151	0.88	0.348	1.08	0.642	1.26	1.380	1.51	2.100	1.68	3.950	1.96		740
760		0.071	0.73	0.153	0.89	0.353	1.10	0.651	1.28	1.400	1.54	2.130	1.70	4.010	1.99	2.00	760
780		0.072	0.74	0.155	0.90	0.358	1.11	0.660	1.30	1.420	1.56	2.160	1.73	4.060	2.01		780
800		0.073	0.75	0.157	0.91	0.362	1.13	0.668	1.31	1.440	1.58	2.190	1.75	4.110	2.04		800
820		0.074	0.76	0.159	0.92	0.367	1.14	0.677	1.33	1.460	1.60	2.220	1.78	4.170	2.07		820
840		0.075	0.77	0.161	0.93	0.372	1.16	0.685	1.34	1.480	1.62	2.240	1.79	4.220	2.09		840
860		0.076	0.78	0.163	0.95	0.376	1.17	0.694	1.36	1.490	1.64	2.270	1.82	4.270	2.12		860
880		0.077	0.79	0.165	0.96	0.381	1.18	0.702	1.38	1.510	1.66	2.300	1.84	4.320	2.14		880
900		0.078	0.80	0.167	0.97	0.385	1.20	0.710	1.39	1.530	1.68	2.320	1.86	4.370	2.17		900
920		0.079	0.81	0.169	0.98	0.390	1.21	0.718	1.41	1.550	1.70	2.350	1.88	4.420	2.19		920
940		0.080	0.82	0.171	0.99	0.394	1.22	0.726	1.42	1.560	1.71	2.380	1.90	4.470	2.22		940
960		0.081	0.83	0.173	1.00	0.398	1.24	0.734	1.44	1.580	1.73	2.400	1.92	4.520	2.24		960
980		0.082	0.84	0.175	1.02	0.403	1.25	0.742	1.46	1.600	1.76	2.430	1.94	4.560	2.26		980
1000		0.083	0.85	0.177	1.03	0.407	1.26	0.750	1.47	1.620	1.78	2.450	1.96	4.610	2.29		1000
1100		0.087	0.89	0.186	1.08	0.428	1.33	0.788	1.55	1.700	1.87	2.580	2.06	4.840	2.40		1100
1200		0.091	0.93	0.194	1.13	0.447	1.39	0.824	1.62	1.770	1.94	2.690	2.15	5.060	2.51		1200
1300	1.00	0.095	0.97	0.203	1.18	0.466	1.45	0.859	1.69	1.850	2.03	2.810	2.25	5.270	2.62		1300
1400		0.099	1.01	0.211	1.22	0.484	1.50	0.892	1.75	1.920	2.11	2.920	2.34	5.470	2.71		1400
1500		0.102	1.04	0.218	1.27	0.502	1.56	0.924	1.81	1.990	2.18	3.020	2.42	5.670	2.81		1500
1600		0.106	1.08	0.226	1.31	0.519	1.61	0.955	1.87	2.060	2.26	3.120	2.50	5.860	2.91		1600
1700		0.109	1.11	0.233	1.35	0.535	1.66	0.986	1.93	2.120	2.33	3.220	2.58	6.040	3.00	3.00	1700
1800		0.112	1.15	0.240	1.39	0.551	1.71	1.010	1.98	2.180	2.39	3.310	2.65	6.220	3.09		1800
1900		0.116	1.19	0.247	1.43	0.567	1.76	1.040	2.04	2.250	2.47	3.410	2.73	6.400	3.18		1900
2000		0.119	1.22	0.253	1.47	0.582	1.81	1.070	2.10	2.300	2.52	3.500	2.80	6.560	3.26		2000

q_m = mass flow rate　　　　kg/s
c = velocity　　　　　　　　m/s
$\Delta p/l$ = pressure loss per unit length　　Pa/m

HEAVY GRADE STEEL

WATER AT 75 °C

$\Delta p/l$	c	65 mm		80 mm		100 mm		125 mm		150 mm		mm		mm		c	$\Delta p/l$
		q_m	c	q_m	c	q_m	c	q_m	c	q_m	c	q_m	c	q_m	c		
0.1		0.060	0.02	0.094	0.02	0.200	0.02	0.367	0.03	0.602	0.03						0.1
0.2		0.090	0.03	0.142	0.03	0.299	0.04	0.546	0.04	0.893	0.05					0.05	0.2
0.3		0.115	0.03	0.179	0.04	0.377	0.05	0.688	0.05	1.120	0.06						0.3
0.4		0.136	0.04	0.212	0.04	0.444	0.05	0.810	0.06	1.320	0.07						0.4
0.5		0.154	0.04	0.241	0.05	0.504	0.06	0.918	0.07	1.490	0.08						0.5
0.6		0.171	0.05	0.267	0.06	0.559	0.07	1.010	0.08	1.650	0.09						0.6
0.7	0.05	0.187	0.05	0.292	0.06	0.610	0.07	1.100	0.09	1.800	0.10						0.7
0.8		0.202	0.06	0.315	0.07	0.658	0.08	1.190	0.09	1.940	0.11						0.8
0.9		0.216	0.06	0.337	0.07	0.703	0.09	1.270	0.10	2.070	0.11						0.9
1.0		0.230	0.07	0.358	0.08	0.745	0.09	1.350	0.11	2.200	0.12						1.0
1.5		0.289	0.08	0.450	0.09	0.935	0.11	1.690	0.13	2.750	0.15					0.15	1.5
2.0		0.340	0.10	0.528	0.11	1.090	0.13	1.980	0.16	3.220	0.18						2.0
2.5		0.386	0.11	0.599	0.13	1.240	0.15	2.240	0.18	3.640	0.20						2.5
3.0		0.427	0.12	0.662	0.14	1.370	0.17	2.480	0.20	4.020	0.22						3.0
3.5		0.466	0.14	0.722	0.15	1.490	0.18	2.690	0.21	4.370	0.24						3.5
4.0	0.15	0.502	0.15	0.777	0.16	1.600	0.20	2.900	0.23	4.690	0.26						4.0
4.5		0.536	0.16	0.829	0.17	1.710	0.21	3.090	0.24	5.000	0.27						4.5
5.0		0.568	0.17	0.879	0.18	1.810	0.22	3.270	0.26	5.300	0.29					0.30	5.0
5.5		0.599	0.17	0.926	0.19	1.910	0.23	3.440	0.27	5.580	0.31						5.5
6.0		0.628	0.18	0.971	0.20	2.000	0.24	3.610	0.28	5.840	0.32						6.0
6.5		0.656	0.19	1.010	0.21	2.090	0.26	3.770	0.30	6.100	0.33						6.5
7.0		0.684	0.20	1.050	0.22	2.180	0.27	3.920	0.31	6.350	0.35						7.0
7.5		0.710	0.21	1.090	0.23	2.260	0.28	4.070	0.32	6.590	0.36						7.5
8.0		0.736	0.21	1.130	0.24	2.340	0.29	4.220	0.33	6.820	0.37						8.0
8.5		0.760	0.22	1.170	0.25	2.420	0.30	4.360	0.34	7.040	0.39						8.5
9.0		0.785	0.23	1.210	0.25	2.490	0.30	4.490	0.35	7.260	0.40						9.0
9.5		0.808	0.24	1.240	0.26	2.570	0.31	4.620	0.36	7.480	0.41						9.5
10.0		0.831	0.24	1.280	0.27	2.640	0.32	4.750	0.37	7.680	0.42						10.0
12.5		0.938	0.27	1.440	0.30	2.980	0.36	5.360	0.42	8.650	0.47					0.50	12.5
15.0	0.30	1.030	0.30	1.590	0.33	3.280	0.40	5.900	0.46	9.530	0.52						15.0
17.5		1.120	0.33	1.730	0.36	3.560	0.44	6.410	0.50	10.300	0.56						17.5
20.0		1.210	0.35	1.860	0.39	3.830	0.47	6.880	0.54	11.000	0.60						20.0
22.5		1.280	0.37	1.980	0.42	4.070	0.50	7.320	0.58	11.800	0.65						22.5
25.0		1.360	0.40	2.100	0.44	4.310	0.53	7.740	0.61	12.400	0.68						25.0
27.5		1.430	0.42	2.210	0.46	4.530	0.55	8.130	0.64	13.100	0.72						27.5
30.0		1.500	0.44	2.310	0.49	4.740	0.58	8.520	0.67	13.700	0.75						30.0
32.5		1.570	0.46	2.410	0.51	4.950	0.61	8.880	0.70	14.300	0.78						32.5
35.0		1.630	0.47	2.510	0.53	5.150	0.63	9.230	0.73	14.800	0.81						35.0
37.5	0.50	1.690	0.49	2.600	0.55	5.340	0.65	9.570	0.75	15.400	0.84						37.5
40.0		1.750	0.51	2.690	0.57	5.520	0.68	9.900	0.78	15.900	0.87						40.0
42.5		1.810	0.53	2.780	0.58	5.700	0.70	10.200	0.80	16.400	0.90						42.5
45.0		1.860	0.54	2.870	0.60	5.880	0.72	10.500	0.83	16.900	0.93						45.0
47.5		1.920	0.56	2.950	0.62	6.040	0.74	10.800	0.85	17.400	0.95						47.5
50.0		1.970	0.57	3.030	0.64	6.210	0.76	11.100	0.87	17.900	0.98						50.0
52.5		2.020	0.59	3.110	0.65	6.370	0.78	11.400	0.90	18.300	1.00					1.00	52.5
55.0		2.070	0.60	3.190	0.67	6.530	0.80	11.700	0.92	18.800	1.03						55.0
57.5		2.120	0.62	3.260	0.69	6.680	0.82	11.900	0.94	19.200	1.05						57.5
60.0		2.170	0.63	3.340	0.70	6.830	0.84	12.200	0.96	19.700	1.08						60.0
62.5		2.220	0.65	3.410	0.72	6.980	0.85	12.500	0.98	20.100	1.10						62.5
65.0		2.260	0.66	3.480	0.73	7.120	0.87	12.700	1.00	20.500	1.12						65.0
67.5		2.310	0.67	3.550	0.75	7.270	0.89	13.000	1.02	20.900	1.15						67.5
70.0		2.350	0.68	3.620	0.76	7.400	0.91	13.200	1.04	21.300	1.17						70.0
72.5		2.400	0.70	3.690	0.78	7.540	0.92	13.500	1.06	21.700	1.19						72.5
75.0		2.440	0.71	3.750	0.79	7.680	0.94	13.700	1.08	22.100	1.21						75.0
77.5		2.480	0.72	3.820	0.80	7.810	0.96	13.900	1.09	22.500	1.23						77.5
80.0		2.520	0.73	3.880	0.82	7.940	0.97	14.200	1.12	22.800	1.25						80.0
82.5		2.570	0.75	3.940	0.83	8.070	0.99	14.400	1.13	23.200	1.27						82.5
85.0		2.610	0.76	4.010	0.84	8.190	1.00	14.600	1.15	23.600	1.29						85.0
87.5		2.650	0.77	4.070	0.86	8.320	1.02	14.800	1.16	23.900	1.31						87.5
90.0		2.690	0.78	4.130	0.87	8.440	1.03	15.100	1.19	24.300	1.33						90.0

q_m = mass flow rate   kg/s
c = velocity   m/s
$\Delta p/l$ = pressure loss per unit length   Pa/m

HEAVY GRADE STEEL

WATER AT 75 °C

$\Delta p/l$	c	65 mm		80 mm		100 mm		125 mm		150 mm		mm		mm		c	$\Delta p/l$
		q_m	c	q_m	c	q_m	c	q_m	c	q_m	c	q_m	c	q_m	c		
92.5		2.72	0.8	4.19	0.9	8.56	1.0	15.30	1.2	24.60	1.3						92.5
95.0		2.76	0.8	4.25	0.9	8.68	1.1	15.50	1.2	24.90	1.4						95.0
97.5		2.80	0.8	4.30	0.9	8.80	1.1	15.70	1.2	25.30	1.4						97.5
100		2.84	0.8	4.36	0.9	8.91	1.1	15.90	1.3	25.60	1.4						100
120		3.12	0.9	4.80	1.0	9.80	1.2	17.50	1.4	28.10	1.5					1.5	120
140	1.0	3.38	1.0	5.20	1.1	10.60	1.3	18.90	1.5	30.50	1.7						140
160		3.63	1.1	5.57	1.2	11.30	1.4	20.30	1.6	32.60	1.8						160
180		3.86	1.1	5.92	1.2	12.00	1.5	21.60	1.7	34.70	1.9						180
200		4.07	1.2	6.25	1.3	12.70	1.6	22.80	1.8	36.60	2.0					2.0	200
220		4.28	1.2	6.57	1.4	13.40	1.6	23.90	1.9	38.40	2.1						220
240		4.48	1.3	6.87	1.4	14.00	1.7	25.00	2.0	40.20	2.2						240
260		4.67	1.4	7.16	1.5	14.60	1.8	26.00	2.0	41.80	2.3						260
280		4.85	1.4	7.44	1.6	15.10	1.8	27.00	2.1	43.50	2.4						280
300		5.02	1.5	7.71	1.6	15.70	1.9	28.00	2.2	45.00	2.5						300
320	1.5	5.19	1.5	7.97	1.7	16.20	2.0	28.90	2.3	46.50	2.5						320
340		5.36	1.6	8.22	1.7	16.70	2.0	29.90	2.4	48.00	2.6						340
360		5.52	1.6	8.46	1.8	17.20	2.1	30.70	2.4	49.40	2.7						360
380		5.68	1.7	8.70	1.8	17.70	2.2	31.60	2.5	50.80	2.8						380
400		5.83	1.7	8.93	1.9	18.20	2.2	32.40	2.5	52.10	2.9						400
420		5.98	1.7	9.16	1.9	18.60	2.3	33.30	2.6	53.40	2.9						420
440		6.12	1.8	9.38	2.0	19.10	2.3	34.10	2.7	54.70	3.0					3.0	440
460		6.26	1.8	9.60	2.0	19.50	2.4	34.80	2.7	56.00	3.1						460
480		6.40	1.9	9.81	2.1	19.90	2.4	35.60	2.8	57.20	3.1						480
500		6.53	1.9	10.00	2.1	20.30	2.5	36.40	2.9	58.40	3.2						500
520		6.67	1.9	10.20	2.1	20.80	2.5	37.10	2.9	59.60	3.3						520
540		6.80	2.0	10.40	2.2	21.20	2.6	37.80	3.0	60.70	3.3						540
560	2.0	6.93	2.0	10.60	2.2	21.60	2.6	38.50	3.0	61.90	3.4						560
580		7.05	2.1	10.80	2.3	22.00	2.7	39.20	3.1	63.00	3.5						580
600		7.17	2.1	10.90	2.3	22.30	2.7	39.90	3.1	64.10	3.5						600
620		7.30	2.1	11.10	2.3	22.70	2.8	40.60	3.2	65.10	3.6						620
640		7.42	2.2	11.30	2.4	23.10	2.8	41.20	3.2	66.20	3.6						640
660		7.53	2.2	11.50	2.4	23.40	2.9	41.90	3.3	67.20	3.7						660
680		7.65	2.2	11.70	2.5	23.80	2.9	42.50	3.3	68.30	3.7						680
700		7.76	2.3	11.80	2.5	24.20	3.0	43.10	3.4	69.30	3.8						700
720		7.88	2.3	12.00	2.5	24.50	3.0	43.80	3.4	70.30	3.9						720
740		7.99	2.3	12.20	2.6	24.90	3.0	44.40	3.5	71.30	3.9						740
760		8.10	2.4	12.40	2.6	25.20	3.1	45.00	3.5	72.20	4.0						760
780		8.20	2.4	12.50	2.6	25.50	3.1	45.60	3.6	73.20	4.0						780
800		8.31	2.4	12.70	2.7	25.90	3.2	46.20	3.6	74.10	4.1						800
820		8.42	2.4	12.80	2.7	26.20	3.2	46.80	3.7	75.10	4.1						820
840		8.52	2.5	13.00	2.7	26.50	3.2	47.30	3.7	76.00	4.2						840
860		8.62	2.5	13.20	2.8	26.80	3.3	47.90	3.8	76.90	4.2						860
880		8.73	2.5	13.30	2.8	27.10	3.3	48.50	3.8	77.80	4.3						880
900		8.83	2.6	13.50	2.8	27.50	3.4	49.00	3.9	78.70	4.3						900
920		8.93	2.6	13.60	2.9	27.80	3.4	49.60	3.9	79.60	4.4						920
940		9.02	2.6	13.80	2.9	28.10	3.4	50.10	3.9	80.40	4.4						940
960		9.12	2.7	13.90	2.9	28.40	3.5	50.60	4.0	81.30	4.5						960
980		9.22	2.7	14.10	3.0	28.70	3.5	51.20	4.0	82.20	4.5						980
1000		9.31	2.7	14.20	3.0	29.00	3.5	51.70	4.1	83.00	4.5						1000
1100		9.78	2.8	14.90	3.1	30.40	3.7	54.30	4.3	87.10	4.8						1100
1200	3.0	10.20	3.0	15.60	3.3	31.80	3.9	56.70	4.5	91.00	5.0						1200
1300		10.60	3.1	16.30	3.4	33.10	4.1	59.00	4.6	94.80	5.2						1300
1400		11.00	3.2	16.90	3.6	34.40	4.2	61.30	4.8	98.40	5.4						1400
1500		11.40	3.3	17.50	3.7	35.60	4.4	63.50	5.0	101.00	5.5						1500
1600		11.80	3.4	18.10	3.8	36.80	4.5	65.60	5.2	105.00	5.8						1600
1700		12.20	3.5	18.60	3.9	37.90	4.6	67.60	5.3	108.00	5.9						1700
1800		12.50	3.6	19.20	4.0	39.00	4.8	69.60	5.5	111.00	6.1						1800
1900		12.90	3.8	19.70	4.1	40.10	4.9	71.50	5.6	114.00	6.2						1900
2000		13.20	3.8	20.20	4.2	41.20	5.0	73.40	5.8	117.00	6.4						2000

q_m	= mass flow rate	kg/s	
c	= velocity	m/s	
$\Delta p/l$	= pressure loss per unit length	Pa/m	

PE-X

WATER AT 10 °C

$\Delta p/l$	c	10 mm		12 mm		16 mm		20 mm		25 mm		32 mm		mm		c	$\Delta p/l$
		q_m	c	q_m	c	q_m	c	q_m	c	q_m	c	q_m	c	q_m	c		
0.1																	0.1
0.2												0.001	0.00				0.2
0.3												0.002	0.00				0.3
0.4										0.001	0.00	0.003	0.01				0.4
0.5										0.001	0.00	0.004	0.01				0.5
0.6										0.001	0.00	0.005	0.01				0.6
0.7										0.002	0.01	0.006	0.01				0.7
0.8										0.002	0.01	0.006	0.01				0.8
0.9								0.001	0.00	0.002	0.01	0.007	0.01				0.9
1.0								0.001	0.00	0.003	0.01	0.008	0.02				1.0
1.5								0.001	0.00	0.004	0.01	0.012	0.02				1.5
2.0								0.002	0.01	0.006	0.02	0.017	0.03				2.0
2.5						0.001	0.01	0.003	0.01	0.007	0.02	0.021	0.04				2.5
3.0						0.001	0.01	0.003	0.01	0.009	0.03	0.025	0.05			0.05	3.0
3.5						0.001	0.01	0.004	0.02	0.010	0.03	0.030	0.06				3.5
4.0						0.001	0.01	0.004	0.02	0.012	0.04	0.034	0.06				4.0
4.5						0.001	0.01	0.005	0.02	0.014	0.04	0.038	0.07				4.5
5.0						0.002	0.02	0.006	0.03	0.015	0.05	0.043	0.08				5.0
5.5						0.002	0.02	0.006	0.03	0.017	0.05	0.047	0.09				5.5
6.0						0.002	0.02	0.007	0.03	0.018	0.06	0.051	0.10				6.0
6.5						0.002	0.02	0.008	0.04	0.020	0.06	0.053	0.10				6.5
7.0						0.003	0.03	0.008	0.04	0.021	0.07	0.053	0.10				7.0
7.5						0.003	0.03	0.009	0.04	0.023	0.07	0.053	0.10				7.5
8.0						0.003	0.03	0.009	0.04	0.025	0.08	0.053	0.10				8.0
8.5						0.003	0.03	0.010	0.05	0.026	0.08	0.053	0.10				8.5
9.0				0.001	0.02	0.003	0.03	0.011	0.05	0.028	0.09	0.053	0.10				9.0
9.5				0.001	0.02	0.004	0.03	0.011	0.05	0.029	0.09	0.053	0.10				9.5
10.0				0.001	0.02	0.004	0.03	0.012	0.06	0.031	0.10	0.053	0.10				10.0
12.5				0.001	0.02	0.005	0.04	0.015	0.07	0.039	0.12	0.061	0.11				12.5
15.0				0.001	0.02	0.006	0.05	0.018	0.09	0.041	0.13	0.068	0.13				15.0
17.5				0.001	0.02	0.007	0.06	0.021	0.10	0.041	0.13	0.075	0.14				17.5
20.0				0.002	0.03	0.008	0.07	0.024	0.12	0.041	0.13	0.081	0.15			0.15	20.0
22.5				0.002	0.03	0.009	0.08	0.027	0.13	0.043	0.13	0.087	0.16				22.5
25.0		0.001	0.03	0.002	0.03	0.010	0.08	0.030	0.15	0.045	0.14	0.093	0.18				25.0
27.5		0.001	0.03	0.003	0.05	0.011	0.09	0.032	0.16	0.048	0.15	0.098	0.18				27.5
30.0		0.001	0.03	0.003	0.05	0.012	0.10	0.032	0.16	0.051	0.16	0.103	0.19				30.0
32.5		0.001	0.03	0.003	0.05	0.014	0.12	0.032	0.16	0.053	0.17	0.108	0.20				32.5
35.0		0.001	0.03	0.003	0.05	0.015	0.13	0.032	0.16	0.056	0.17	0.113	0.21				35.0
37.5		0.001	0.03	0.004	0.07	0.016	0.13	0.032	0.16	0.058	0.18	0.118	0.22				37.5
40.0		0.001	0.03	0.004	0.07	0.017	0.14	0.032	0.16	0.060	0.19	0.122	0.23				40.0
42.5		0.001	0.03	0.004	0.07	0.018	0.15	0.032	0.16	0.063	0.20	0.127	0.24				42.5
45.0		0.001	0.03	0.005	0.08	0.019	0.16	0.033	0.16	0.065	0.20	0.131	0.25				45.0
47.5	0.05	0.001	0.03	0.005	0.08	0.020	0.17	0.035	0.17	0.067	0.21	0.135	0.25				47.5
50.0		0.002	0.06	0.005	0.08	0.021	0.18	0.036	0.18	0.069	0.22	0.140	0.26				50.0
52.5		0.002	0.06	0.005	0.08	0.022	0.19	0.037	0.18	0.071	0.22	0.144	0.27				52.5
55.0		0.002	0.06	0.006	0.10	0.023	0.19	0.038	0.19	0.073	0.23	0.148	0.28				55.0
57.5		0.002	0.06	0.006	0.10	0.024	0.20	0.039	0.19	0.075	0.23	0.152	0.29				57.5
60.0		0.002	0.06	0.006	0.10	0.025	0.21	0.040	0.20	0.077	0.24	0.155	0.29				60.0
62.5		0.002	0.06	0.007	0.12	0.025	0.21	0.041	0.20	0.079	0.25	0.159	0.30			0.30	62.5
65.0		0.002	0.06	0.007	0.12	0.025	0.21	0.042	0.21	0.081	0.25	0.163	0.31				65.0
67.5		0.002	0.06	0.007	0.12	0.025	0.21	0.043	0.21	0.083	0.26	0.166	0.31				67.5
70.0		0.002	0.06	0.007	0.12	0.025	0.21	0.044	0.22	0.084	0.26	0.170	0.32				70.0
72.5		0.002	0.06	0.008	0.13	0.025	0.21	0.045	0.22	0.086	0.27	0.174	0.33				72.5
75.0		0.003	0.08	0.008	0.13	0.025	0.21	0.046	0.23	0.088	0.27	0.177	0.33				75.0
77.5		0.003	0.08	0.008	0.13	0.025	0.21	0.047	0.23	0.090	0.28	0.181	0.34				77.5
80.0		0.003	0.08	0.009	0.15	0.025	0.21	0.047	0.23	0.091	0.28	0.184	0.35				80.0
82.5		0.003	0.08	0.009	0.15	0.025	0.21	0.048	0.24	0.093	0.29	0.187	0.35				82.5
85.0		0.003	0.08	0.009	0.15	0.025	0.21	0.049	0.24	0.095	0.30	0.191	0.36				85.0
87.5	0.15	0.003	0.08	0.009	0.15	0.025	0.21	0.050	0.25	0.096	0.30	0.194	0.37				87.5
90.0		0.003	0.08	0.010	0.16	0.025	0.21	0.051	0.25	0.098	0.31	0.197	0.37				90.0

q_m	= mass flow rate	kg/s
c	= velocity	m/s
$\Delta p/l$	= pressure loss per unit length	Pa/m

PE-X	
WATER AT 10 °C	

$\Delta p/l$	c	10 mm q_m	c	12 mm q_m	c	16 mm q_m	c	20 mm q_m	c	25 mm q_m	c	32 mm q_m	c	mm q_m	c	c	$\Delta p/l$
92.5		0.003	0.08	0.010	0.16	0.025	0.21	0.052	0.26	0.100	0.31	0.200	0.38				92.5
95.0		0.003	0.08	0.010	0.16	0.025	0.21	0.053	0.26	0.101	0.32	0.203	0.38				95.0
97.5		0.003	0.08	0.011	0.18	0.025	0.21	0.053	0.26	0.103	0.32	0.206	0.39				97.5
100		0.004	0.11	0.011	0.18	0.026	0.22	0.054	0.27	0.104	0.32	0.209	0.39				100
120		0.004	0.11	0.013	0.21	0.029	0.24	0.061	0.30	0.116	0.36	0.233	0.44				120
140	0.15	0.005	0.14	0.015	0.25	0.032	0.27	0.066	0.33	0.127	0.40	0.255	0.48			0.50	140
160		0.006	0.17	0.017	0.28	0.034	0.29	0.072	0.36	0.137	0.43	0.275	0.52				160
180		0.007	0.19	0.017	0.28	0.037	0.31	0.077	0.38	0.147	0.46	0.294	0.55				180
200		0.008	0.22	0.017	0.28	0.039	0.33	0.082	0.41	0.156	0.49	0.313	0.59				200
220		0.008	0.22	0.017	0.28	0.042	0.35	0.087	0.43	0.165	0.52	0.330	0.62				220
240		0.009	0.25	0.017	0.28	0.044	0.37	0.091	0.45	0.174	0.54	0.347	0.65				240
260		0.010	0.28	0.018	0.30	0.046	0.39	0.096	0.48	0.182	0.57	0.364	0.69				260
280	0.30	0.011	0.30	0.019	0.31	0.048	0.40	0.100	0.50	0.190	0.59	0.379	0.71				280
300		0.012	0.33	0.019	0.31	0.050	0.42	0.104	0.52	0.198	0.62	0.395	0.74				300
320		0.012	0.33	0.020	0.33	0.052	0.44	0.108	0.54	0.205	0.64	0.409	0.77				320
340		0.013	0.36	0.021	0.35	0.054	0.45	0.112	0.56	0.213	0.66	0.424	0.80				340
360		0.013	0.36	0.022	0.36	0.056	0.47	0.116	0.58	0.220	0.69	0.438	0.83				360
380		0.013	0.36	0.022	0.36	0.058	0.49	0.120	0.60	0.227	0.71	0.452	0.85				380
400		0.013	0.36	0.023	0.38	0.059	0.50	0.123	0.61	0.234	0.73	0.465	0.88				400
420		0.013	0.36	0.024	0.39	0.061	0.51	0.127	0.63	0.240	0.75	0.478	0.90				420
440		0.013	0.36	0.024	0.39	0.063	0.53	0.130	0.65	0.247	0.77	0.491	0.93				440
460		0.013	0.36	0.025	0.41	0.064	0.54	0.134	0.67	0.253	0.79	0.503	0.95				460
480		0.013	0.36	0.026	0.43	0.066	0.56	0.137	0.68	0.259	0.81	0.516	0.97				480
500		0.013	0.36	0.026	0.43	0.068	0.57	0.140	0.70	0.266	0.83	0.528	0.99			1.00	500
520		0.013	0.36	0.027	0.44	0.069	0.58	0.143	0.71	0.272	0.85	0.540	1.02				520
540		0.013	0.36	0.028	0.46	0.071	0.60	0.147	0.73	0.277	0.86	0.551	1.04				540
560		0.013	0.36	0.028	0.46	0.072	0.61	0.150	0.75	0.283	0.88	0.563	1.06				560
580		0.014	0.39	0.029	0.48	0.074	0.62	0.153	0.76	0.289	0.90	0.574	1.08				580
600		0.014	0.39	0.030	0.49	0.075	0.63	0.156	0.78	0.295	0.92	0.585	1.10				600
620		0.014	0.39	0.030	0.49	0.077	0.65	0.159	0.79	0.300	0.94	0.596	1.12				620
640		0.015	0.41	0.031	0.51	0.078	0.66	0.162	0.81	0.306	0.96	0.607	1.14				640
660		0.015	0.41	0.031	0.51	0.080	0.67	0.165	0.82	0.311	0.97	0.618	1.16				660
680		0.015	0.41	0.032	0.53	0.081	0.68	0.167	0.83	0.317	0.99	0.628	1.18				680
700		0.015	0.41	0.032	0.53	0.082	0.69	0.170	0.85	0.322	1.01	0.639	1.20				700
720		0.016	0.44	0.033	0.54	0.084	0.71	0.173	0.86	0.327	1.02	0.649	1.22				720
740		0.016	0.44	0.033	0.54	0.085	0.72	0.176	0.88	0.332	1.04	0.659	1.24				740
760		0.016	0.44	0.034	0.56	0.087	0.73	0.178	0.89	0.337	1.05	0.669	1.26				760
780		0.017	0.47	0.035	0.58	0.088	0.74	0.181	0.90	0.342	1.07	0.679	1.28				780
800		0.017	0.47	0.035	0.58	0.089	0.75	0.184	0.92	0.347	1.08	0.689	1.30				800
820		0.017	0.47	0.036	0.59	0.090	0.76	0.186	0.93	0.352	1.10	0.698	1.32				820
840		0.017	0.47	0.036	0.59	0.092	0.77	0.189	0.94	0.357	1.11	0.708	1.33				840
860		0.018	0.50	0.037	0.61	0.093	0.78	0.192	0.96	0.362	1.13	0.717	1.35				860
880		0.018	0.50	0.037	0.61	0.094	0.79	0.194	0.97	0.367	1.15	0.727	1.37				880
900		0.018	0.50	0.038	0.62	0.096	0.81	0.197	0.98	0.371	1.16	0.736	1.39				900
920	0.50	0.018	0.50	0.038	0.62	0.097	0.82	0.199	0.99	0.376	1.17	0.745	1.40				920
940		0.019	0.52	0.039	0.64	0.098	0.83	0.202	1.00	0.381	1.19	0.754	1.42				940
960		0.019	0.52	0.039	0.64	0.099	0.83	0.204	1.01	0.385	1.20	0.763	1.44				960
980		0.019	0.52	0.040	0.66	0.100	0.84	0.207	1.03	0.390	1.22	0.772	1.45				980
1000		0.019	0.52	0.040	0.66	0.102	0.86	0.209	1.04	0.394	1.23	0.781	1.47			1.50	1000
1100		0.020	0.55	0.042	0.69	0.107	0.90	0.221	1.10	0.416	1.30	0.824	1.55				1100
1200		0.022	0.61	0.045	0.74	0.113	0.95	0.232	1.15	0.437	1.36	0.865	1.63				1200
1300		0.023	0.63	0.047	0.77	0.118	0.99	0.243	1.21	0.457	1.43	0.904	1.70				1300
1400		0.024	0.66	0.049	0.81	0.123	1.04	0.253	1.26	0.477	1.49	0.943	1.78				1400
1500		0.025	0.69	0.051	0.84	0.128	1.08	0.263	1.31	0.496	1.55	0.980	1.85				1500
1600		0.026	0.72	0.053	0.87	0.133	1.12	0.273	1.36	0.514	1.60	1.010	1.90				1600
1700		0.027	0.74	0.055	0.90	0.138	1.16	0.283	1.41	0.532	1.66	1.050	1.98			2.00	1700
1800		0.028	0.77	0.057	0.94	0.142	1.20	0.292	1.45	0.549	1.71	1.080	2.03				1800
1900		0.028	0.77	0.058	0.95	0.147	1.24	0.301	1.50	0.566	1.77	1.110	2.09				1900
2000		0.029	0.80	0.060	0.99	0.151	1.27	0.310	1.54	0.583	1.82	1.150	2.17				2000

q_m = mass flow rate　　kg/s
c = velocity　　m/s
$\Delta p/l$ = pressure loss per unit length　　Pa/m

PE-X

WATER AT 75 °C

$\Delta p/l$	c	10 mm q_m	c	12 mm q_m	c	16 mm q_m	c	20 mm q_m	c	25 mm q_m	c	32 mm q_m	c	mm q_m	c	c	$\Delta p/l$
0.1										0.001	0.00	0.002	0.00				0.1
0.2										0.002	0.01	0.005	0.01				0.2
0.3								0.001	0.01	0.003	0.01	0.008	0.02				0.3
0.4								0.001	0.01	0.004	0.01	0.011	0.02				0.4
0.5								0.002	0.01	0.005	0.02	0.014	0.03				0.5
0.6								0.002	0.01	0.006	0.02	0.015	0.03				0.6
0.7						0.001	0.01	0.002	0.01	0.007	0.02	0.015	0.03				0.7
0.8						0.001	0.01	0.003	0.02	0.008	0.03	0.015	0.03				0.8
0.9						0.001	0.01	0.003	0.02	0.009	0.03	0.015	0.03				0.9
1.0						0.001	0.01	0.004	0.02	0.010	0.03	0.017	0.03				1.0
1.5						0.002	0.02	0.006	0.03	0.011	0.04	0.021	0.04				1.5
2.0						0.002	0.02	0.008	0.04	0.012	0.04	0.025	0.05			0.05	2.0
2.5						0.003	0.03	0.009	0.05	0.014	0.04	0.029	0.06				2.5
3.0				0.001	0.02	0.004	0.03	0.009	0.05	0.016	0.05	0.032	0.06				3.0
3.5				0.001	0.02	0.005	0.04	0.009	0.05	0.017	0.05	0.035	0.07				3.5
4.0				0.001	0.02	0.005	0.04	0.010	0.05	0.019	0.06	0.038	0.07				4.0
4.5				0.001	0.02	0.006	0.05	0.010	0.05	0.020	0.06	0.041	0.08				4.5
5.0				0.001	0.02	0.007	0.06	0.011	0.06	0.022	0.07	0.044	0.09				5.0
5.5				0.002	0.03	0.007	0.06	0.012	0.06	0.023	0.07	0.046	0.09				5.5
6.0				0.002	0.03	0.007	0.06	0.012	0.06	0.024	0.08	0.049	0.09				6.0
6.5				0.002	0.03	0.007	0.06	0.013	0.07	0.025	0.08	0.051	0.10				6.5
7.0				0.002	0.03	0.007	0.06	0.014	0.07	0.026	0.08	0.053	0.10				7.0
7.5		0.001	0.03	0.002	0.03	0.007	0.06	0.014	0.07	0.027	0.09	0.056	0.11				7.5
8.0		0.001	0.03	0.003	0.05	0.007	0.06	0.015	0.08	0.029	0.09	0.058	0.11				8.0
8.5		0.001	0.03	0.003	0.05	0.007	0.06	0.015	0.08	0.030	0.10	0.060	0.12				8.5
9.0		0.001	0.03	0.003	0.05	0.007	0.06	0.016	0.08	0.031	0.10	0.062	0.12				9.0
9.5		0.001	0.03	0.003	0.05	0.008	0.07	0.016	0.08	0.032	0.10	0.064	0.12				9.5
10.0		0.001	0.03	0.003	0.05	0.008	0.07	0.017	0.09	0.033	0.11	0.066	0.13				10.0
12.5	0.05	0.001	0.03	0.004	0.07	0.009	0.08	0.019	0.10	0.037	0.12	0.075	0.14			0.15	12.5
15.0		0.002	0.06	0.005	0.08	0.010	0.09	0.022	0.11	0.041	0.13	0.083	0.16				15.0
17.5		0.002	0.06	0.005	0.08	0.011	0.09	0.024	0.12	0.045	0.14	0.091	0.18				17.5
20.0		0.002	0.06	0.005	0.08	0.012	0.10	0.026	0.13	0.049	0.16	0.098	0.19				20.0
22.5		0.003	0.08	0.005	0.08	0.013	0.11	0.027	0.14	0.053	0.17	0.105	0.20				22.5
25.0		0.003	0.08	0.005	0.08	0.014	0.12	0.029	0.15	0.056	0.18	0.112	0.22				25.0
27.5		0.003	0.08	0.005	0.08	0.015	0.13	0.031	0.16	0.059	0.19	0.118	0.23				27.5
30.0		0.004	0.11	0.006	0.10	0.015	0.13	0.033	0.17	0.062	0.20	0.124	0.24				30.0
32.5		0.004	0.11	0.006	0.10	0.016	0.14	0.034	0.17	0.065	0.21	0.130	0.25				32.5
35.0		0.004	0.11	0.006	0.10	0.017	0.15	0.036	0.18	0.068	0.22	0.136	0.26				35.0
37.5		0.004	0.11	0.007	0.12	0.018	0.16	0.037	0.19	0.071	0.23	0.141	0.27				37.5
40.0		0.004	0.11	0.007	0.12	0.018	0.16	0.039	0.20	0.073	0.23	0.146	0.28				40.0
42.5		0.004	0.11	0.007	0.12	0.019	0.16	0.040	0.20	0.076	0.24	0.151	0.29				42.5
45.0		0.004	0.11	0.008	0.13	0.020	0.17	0.041	0.21	0.079	0.25	0.156	0.30			0.30	45.0
47.5		0.004	0.11	0.008	0.13	0.020	0.17	0.043	0.22	0.081	0.26	0.161	0.31				47.5
50.0		0.004	0.11	0.008	0.13	0.021	0.18	0.044	0.22	0.083	0.27	0.166	0.32				50.0
52.5		0.004	0.11	0.008	0.13	0.022	0.19	0.045	0.23	0.086	0.28	0.171	0.33				52.5
55.0		0.004	0.11	0.009	0.15	0.022	0.19	0.046	0.23	0.088	0.28	0.175	0.34				55.0
57.5		0.004	0.11	0.009	0.15	0.023	0.20	0.048	0.24	0.090	0.29	0.180	0.35				57.5
60.0		0.004	0.11	0.009	0.15	0.023	0.20	0.049	0.25	0.093	0.30	0.184	0.36				60.0
62.5		0.004	0.11	0.009	0.15	0.024	0.21	0.050	0.26	0.095	0.30	0.188	0.36				62.5
65.0		0.004	0.11	0.009	0.15	0.025	0.22	0.051	0.26	0.097	0.31	0.193	0.37				65.0
67.5		0.004	0.11	0.010	0.17	0.025	0.22	0.052	0.27	0.099	0.32	0.197	0.38				67.5
70.0		0.005	0.14	0.010	0.17	0.026	0.22	0.053	0.27	0.101	0.32	0.201	0.39				70.0
72.5		0.005	0.14	0.010	0.17	0.026	0.22	0.054	0.28	0.103	0.33	0.205	0.40				72.5
75.0		0.005	0.14	0.010	0.17	0.027	0.23	0.056	0.29	0.105	0.34	0.209	0.40				75.0
77.5		0.005	0.14	0.011	0.19	0.027	0.23	0.057	0.29	0.107	0.34	0.213	0.41				77.5
80.0		0.005	0.14	0.011	0.19	0.028	0.24	0.058	0.30	0.109	0.35	0.217	0.42				80.0
82.5		0.005	0.14	0.011	0.19	0.028	0.24	0.059	0.30	0.111	0.36	0.220	0.43				82.5
85.0		0.005	0.14	0.011	0.19	0.029	0.25	0.060	0.31	0.113	0.36	0.224	0.43				85.0
87.5		0.005	0.14	0.011	0.19	0.029	0.25	0.061	0.31	0.115	0.37	0.228	0.44				87.5
90.0		0.005	0.14	0.012	0.20	0.030	0.26	0.062	0.32	0.117	0.37	0.231	0.45				90.0

q_m = mass flow rate   kg/s
c = velocity   m/s
$\Delta p/l$ = pressure loss per unit length   Pa/m

PE-X

WATER AT 75 °C

$\Delta p/l$	c	10 mm q_m	c	12 mm q_m	c	16 mm q_m	c	20 mm q_m	c	25 mm q_m	c	32 mm q_m	c	mm q_m	c	c	$\Delta p/l$
92.5	0.15	0.005	0.14	0.012	0.20	0.030	0.26	0.063	0.32	0.119	0.38	0.235	0.45				92.5
95.0		0.006	0.17	0.012	0.20	0.031	0.27	0.064	0.33	0.120	0.38	0.239	0.46				95.0
97.5		0.006	0.17	0.012	0.20	0.031	0.27	0.065	0.33	0.122	0.39	0.242	0.47				97.5
100		0.006	0.17	0.012	0.20	0.032	0.28	0.066	0.34	0.124	0.40	0.246	0.48			0.50	100
120		0.006	0.17	0.014	0.24	0.035	0.30	0.073	0.37	0.137	0.44	0.272	0.53				120
140		0.007	0.20	0.015	0.25	0.039	0.34	0.079	0.40	0.150	0.48	0.296	0.57				140
160		0.008	0.23	0.016	0.27	0.042	0.36	0.086	0.44	0.162	0.52	0.319	0.62				160
180		0.008	0.23	0.018	0.30	0.045	0.39	0.092	0.47	0.173	0.55	0.341	0.66				180
200		0.009	0.25	0.019	0.32	0.047	0.41	0.097	0.49	0.183	0.59	0.362	0.70				200
220		0.009	0.25	0.020	0.34	0.050	0.43	0.103	0.53	0.193	0.62	0.381	0.74				220
240		0.010	0.28	0.021	0.35	0.053	0.46	0.108	0.55	0.203	0.65	0.400	0.77				240
260	0.30	0.010	0.28	0.022	0.37	0.055	0.47	0.113	0.58	0.212	0.68	0.418	0.81				260
280		0.011	0.31	0.023	0.39	0.057	0.49	0.118	0.60	0.221	0.71	0.436	0.84				280
300		0.011	0.31	0.024	0.40	0.060	0.52	0.122	0.62	0.230	0.74	0.453	0.88				300
320		0.012	0.34	0.025	0.42	0.062	0.54	0.127	0.65	0.238	0.76	0.469	0.91				320
340		0.012	0.34	0.025	0.42	0.064	0.55	0.131	0.67	0.246	0.79	0.485	0.94				340
360		0.013	0.37	0.026	0.44	0.066	0.57	0.135	0.69	0.254	0.81	0.500	0.97				360
380		0.013	0.37	0.027	0.46	0.068	0.59	0.140	0.71	0.262	0.84	0.516	1.00			1.00	380
400		0.014	0.40	0.028	0.47	0.070	0.60	0.144	0.73	0.269	0.86	0.530	1.02				400
420		0.014	0.40	0.029	0.49	0.072	0.62	0.148	0.76	0.277	0.89	0.545	1.05				420
440		0.014	0.40	0.030	0.51	0.074	0.64	0.152	0.78	0.284	0.91	0.559	1.08				440
460		0.015	0.42	0.030	0.51	0.076	0.66	0.155	0.79	0.291	0.93	0.573	1.11				460
480		0.015	0.42	0.031	0.52	0.078	0.67	0.159	0.81	0.298	0.95	0.586	1.13				480
500		0.016	0.45	0.032	0.54	0.080	0.69	0.163	0.83	0.305	0.98	0.599	1.16				500
520		0.016	0.45	0.033	0.56	0.082	0.71	0.166	0.85	0.311	1.00	0.612	1.18				520
540		0.016	0.45	0.033	0.56	0.083	0.72	0.170	0.87	0.318	1.02	0.625	1.21				540
560		0.017	0.48	0.034	0.57	0.085	0.73	0.173	0.88	0.324	1.04	0.638	1.23				560
580		0.017	0.48	0.035	0.59	0.087	0.75	0.177	0.90	0.331	1.06	0.650	1.26				580
600	0.50	0.017	0.48	0.035	0.59	0.088	0.76	0.180	0.92	0.337	1.08	0.662	1.28				600
620		0.018	0.51	0.036	0.61	0.090	0.78	0.183	0.93	0.343	1.10	0.674	1.30				620
640		0.018	0.51	0.037	0.62	0.092	0.79	0.187	0.95	0.349	1.12	0.686	1.33				640
660		0.018	0.51	0.037	0.62	0.093	0.80	0.190	0.97	0.355	1.14	0.697	1.35				660
680		0.019	0.54	0.038	0.64	0.095	0.82	0.193	0.98	0.361	1.16	0.709	1.37				680
700		0.019	0.54	0.039	0.66	0.096	0.83	0.196	1.00	0.367	1.17	0.720	1.39				700
720		0.019	0.54	0.039	0.66	0.098	0.85	0.199	1.02	0.372	1.19	0.731	1.41				720
740		0.020	0.56	0.040	0.67	0.099	0.85	0.202	1.03	0.378	1.21	0.742	1.43				740
760		0.020	0.56	0.041	0.69	0.101	0.87	0.205	1.05	0.384	1.23	0.753	1.45				760
780		0.020	0.56	0.041	0.69	0.102	0.88	0.208	1.06	0.389	1.25	0.764	1.48				780
800		0.020	0.56	0.042	0.71	0.104	0.90	0.211	1.08	0.395	1.26	0.774	1.50			1.50	800
820		0.021	0.59	0.042	0.71	0.105	0.91	0.214	1.09	0.400	1.28	0.785	1.52				820
840		0.021	0.59	0.043	0.73	0.107	0.92	0.217	1.11	0.405	1.30	0.795	1.54				840
860		0.021	0.59	0.043	0.73	0.108	0.93	0.220	1.12	0.411	1.32	0.805	1.56				860
880		0.022	0.62	0.044	0.74	0.110	0.95	0.223	1.14	0.416	1.33	0.815	1.57				880
900		0.022	0.62	0.045	0.76	0.111	0.96	0.225	1.15	0.421	1.35	0.825	1.59				900
920		0.022	0.62	0.045	0.76	0.112	0.97	0.228	1.16	0.426	1.36	0.835	1.61				920
940		0.022	0.62	0.046	0.78	0.114	0.98	0.231	1.18	0.431	1.38	0.845	1.63				940
960		0.023	0.65	0.046	0.78	0.115	0.99	0.233	1.19	0.436	1.40	0.855	1.65				960
980		0.023	0.65	0.047	0.79	0.116	1.00	0.236	1.20	0.441	1.41	0.864	1.67				980
1000		0.023	0.65	0.047	0.79	0.118	1.02	0.239	1.22	0.446	1.43	0.874	1.69				1000
1100		0.025	0.71	0.050	0.84	0.124	1.07	0.252	1.29	0.470	1.50	0.920	1.78				1100
1200		0.026	0.73	0.052	0.88	0.130	1.12	0.264	1.35	0.492	1.57	0.964	1.86				1200
1300		0.027	0.76	0.055	0.93	0.136	1.17	0.276	1.41	0.514	1.65	1.000	1.93			2.00	1300
1400		0.028	0.79	0.057	0.96	0.142	1.23	0.287	1.46	0.535	1.71	1.040	2.01				1400
1500		0.029	0.82	0.059	1.00	0.147	1.27	0.298	1.52	0.556	1.78	1.080	2.09				1500
1600		0.030	0.85	0.062	1.05	0.152	1.31	0.309	1.58	0.575	1.84	1.120	2.16				1600
1700		0.032	0.90	0.064	1.08	0.158	1.36	0.319	1.63	0.595	1.90	1.160	2.24				1700
1800		0.033	0.93	0.066	1.11	0.163	1.41	0.329	1.68	0.613	1.96	1.190	2.30				1800
1900		0.034	0.96	0.068	1.15	0.168	1.45	0.339	1.73	0.631	2.02	1.230	2.38				1900
2000		0.035	0.99	0.070	1.18	0.172	1.48	0.349	1.78	0.649	2.08	1.260	2.43				2000

q_m = mass flow rate — kg/s
c = velocity — m/s
$\Delta p/l$ = pressure loss per unit length — Pa/m

PVC-U PN10

WATER AT 10 °C

$\Delta p/l$	c	32 mm		40 mm		50 mm		63 mm		75 mm		90 mm		110 mm		c	$\Delta p/l$
		q_m	c	q_m	c	q_m	c	q_m	c	q_m	c	q_m	c	q_m	c		
0.1		0.001	0.00	0.003	0.00	0.007	0.00	0.019	0.01	0.039	0.01	0.082	0.02	0.210	0.03		0.1
0.2		0.002	0.00	0.006	0.01	0.015	0.01	0.039	0.02	0.079	0.02	0.165	0.03	0.244	0.03		0.2
0.3		0.003	0.00	0.009	0.01	0.023	0.01	0.059	0.02	0.119	0.03	0.166	0.03	0.311	0.04		0.3
0.4		0.005	0.01	0.012	0.01	0.031	0.02	0.079	0.03	0.138	0.04	0.190	0.04	0.370	0.04		0.4
0.5		0.006	0.01	0.016	0.02	0.039	0.02	0.099	0.04	0.138	0.04	0.217	0.04	0.422	0.05	0.05	0.5
0.6		0.007	0.01	0.019	0.02	0.047	0.03	0.116	0.05	0.145	0.04	0.243	0.05	0.470	0.06		0.6
0.7		0.009	0.01	0.022	0.02	0.055	0.03	0.116	0.05	0.159	0.04	0.266	0.05	0.515	0.06		0.7
0.8		0.010	0.02	0.025	0.02	0.063	0.04	0.116	0.05	0.173	0.05	0.288	0.06	0.557	0.07		0.8
0.9		0.011	0.02	0.029	0.03	0.070	0.04	0.116	0.05	0.185	0.05	0.309	0.06	0.597	0.07		0.9
1.0		0.012	0.02	0.032	0.03	0.078	0.05	0.121	0.05	0.197	0.05	0.329	0.06	0.635	0.08		1.0
1.5		0.019	0.03	0.048	0.05	0.092	0.06	0.155	0.06	0.252	0.07	0.418	0.08	0.805	0.10		1.5
2.0		0.025	0.04	0.064	0.06	0.096	0.06	0.184	0.07	0.298	0.08	0.495	0.10	0.952	0.11		2.0
2.5	0.05	0.032	0.05	0.073	0.07	0.110	0.07	0.210	0.08	0.341	0.09	0.565	0.11	1.080	0.13		2.5
3.0		0.038	0.06	0.073	0.07	0.122	0.08	0.234	0.09	0.379	0.11	0.628	0.12	1.200	0.14	0.15	3.0
3.5		0.045	0.07	0.073	0.07	0.134	0.08	0.257	0.10	0.415	0.11	0.687	0.13	1.310	0.16		3.5
4.0		0.051	0.08	0.078	0.08	0.145	0.09	0.278	0.11	0.449	0.12	0.742	0.14	1.420	0.17		4.0
4.5		0.058	0.09	0.084	0.08	0.156	0.10	0.298	0.12	0.481	0.13	0.795	0.15	1.520	0.18		4.5
5.0		0.058	0.09	0.089	0.09	0.166	0.10	0.317	0.12	0.511	0.14	0.845	0.16	1.610	0.19		5.0
5.5		0.058	0.09	0.094	0.09	0.176	0.11	0.335	0.13	0.541	0.15	0.893	0.17	1.700	0.20		5.5
6.0		0.058	0.09	0.100	0.10	0.185	0.12	0.353	0.14	0.569	0.16	0.939	0.18	1.790	0.21		6.0
6.5		0.058	0.09	0.104	0.10	0.194	0.12	0.370	0.15	0.596	0.17	0.983	0.19	1.870	0.22		6.5
7.0		0.058	0.09	0.109	0.11	0.203	0.13	0.386	0.15	0.622	0.17	1.020	0.20	1.950	0.23		7.0
7.5		0.060	0.09	0.114	0.11	0.212	0.13	0.402	0.16	0.648	0.18	1.060	0.20	2.030	0.24		7.5
8.0		0.062	0.10	0.118	0.11	0.220	0.14	0.417	0.16	0.672	0.19	1.100	0.21	2.110	0.25		8.0
8.5		0.064	0.10	0.123	0.12	0.228	0.14	0.432	0.17	0.696	0.19	1.140	0.22	2.180	0.26		8.5
9.0		0.067	0.10	0.127	0.12	0.236	0.15	0.447	0.18	0.720	0.20	1.180	0.23	2.260	0.27		9.0
9.5		0.069	0.11	0.131	0.13	0.243	0.15	0.461	0.18	0.743	0.21	1.220	0.23	2.330	0.28		9.5
10.0		0.071	0.11	0.135	0.13	0.251	0.16	0.475	0.19	0.765	0.21	1.260	0.24	2.400	0.29	0.30	10.0
12.5		0.081	0.12	0.154	0.15	0.286	0.18	0.541	0.21	0.870	0.24	1.430	0.27	2.720	0.33		12.5
15.0		0.091	0.14	0.172	0.17	0.318	0.20	0.601	0.24	0.966	0.27	1.580	0.30	3.020	0.36		15.0
17.5	0.15	0.100	0.15	0.188	0.18	0.348	0.22	0.657	0.26	1.050	0.29	1.730	0.33	3.290	0.39		17.5
20.0		0.108	0.17	0.204	0.20	0.376	0.23	0.710	0.28	1.130	0.31	1.870	0.36	3.550	0.42		20.0
22.5		0.116	0.18	0.218	0.21	0.403	0.25	0.760	0.30	1.210	0.34	2.000	0.38	3.800	0.45		22.5
25.0		0.123	0.19	0.232	0.23	0.428	0.27	0.807	0.32	1.290	0.36	2.120	0.41	4.030	0.48	0.50	25.0
27.5		0.130	0.20	0.246	0.24	0.452	0.28	0.853	0.33	1.360	0.38	2.240	0.43	4.250	0.51		27.5
30.0		0.137	0.21	0.258	0.25	0.476	0.30	0.896	0.35	1.430	0.40	2.350	0.45	4.470	0.53		30.0
32.5		0.144	0.22	0.271	0.26	0.498	0.31	0.938	0.37	1.500	0.42	2.460	0.47	4.670	0.56		32.5
35.0		0.150	0.23	0.283	0.28	0.520	0.32	0.979	0.38	1.560	0.43	2.570	0.49	4.870	0.58		35.0
37.5		0.156	0.24	0.294	0.29	0.541	0.34	1.010	0.40	1.630	0.45	2.670	0.51	5.060	0.61		37.5
40.0		0.163	0.25	0.306	0.30	0.562	0.35	1.050	0.41	1.690	0.47	2.770	0.53	5.250	0.63		40.0
42.5		0.168	0.26	0.316	0.31	0.581	0.36	1.090	0.43	1.750	0.48	2.870	0.55	5.430	0.65		42.5
45.0		0.174	0.27	0.327	0.32	0.601	0.37	1.130	0.44	1.800	0.50	2.960	0.57	5.610	0.67		45.0
47.5		0.180	0.28	0.338	0.33	0.620	0.39	1.160	0.45	1.860	0.52	3.050	0.59	5.780	0.69		47.5
50.0		0.185	0.28	0.348	0.34	0.638	0.40	1.200	0.47	1.920	0.53	3.140	0.60	5.950	0.71		50.0
52.5		0.191	0.29	0.358	0.35	0.657	0.41	1.230	0.48	1.970	0.55	3.230	0.62	6.120	0.73		52.5
55.0	0.30	0.196	0.30	0.368	0.36	0.674	0.42	1.260	0.49	2.020	0.56	3.310	0.64	6.280	0.75		55.0
57.5		0.201	0.31	0.377	0.37	0.692	0.43	1.290	0.51	2.070	0.57	3.400	0.65	6.430	0.77		57.5
60.0		0.206	0.32	0.386	0.38	0.709	0.44	1.330	0.52	2.120	0.59	3.480	0.67	6.590	0.79		60.0
62.5		0.211	0.32	0.396	0.38	0.725	0.45	1.360	0.53	2.170	0.60	3.560	0.68	6.740	0.81		62.5
65.0		0.216	0.33	0.405	0.39	0.742	0.46	1.390	0.54	2.220	0.62	3.640	0.70	6.890	0.82		65.0
67.5		0.221	0.34	0.414	0.40	0.758	0.47	1.420	0.56	2.270	0.63	3.720	0.72	7.040	0.84		67.5
70.0		0.226	0.35	0.422	0.41	0.774	0.48	1.450	0.57	2.320	0.64	3.800	0.73	7.180	0.86		70.0
72.5		0.230	0.35	0.431	0.42	0.790	0.49	1.480	0.58	2.360	0.65	3.870	0.74	7.320	0.88		72.5
75.0		0.235	0.36	0.440	0.43	0.805	0.50	1.510	0.59	2.410	0.67	3.950	0.76	7.460	0.89		75.0
77.5		0.239	0.37	0.448	0.44	0.820	0.51	1.530	0.60	2.450	0.68	4.020	0.77	7.600	0.91		77.5
80.0		0.244	0.37	0.456	0.44	0.835	0.52	1.560	0.61	2.500	0.69	4.090	0.79	7.740	0.93		80.0
82.5		0.248	0.38	0.464	0.45	0.850	0.53	1.590	0.62	2.540	0.70	4.160	0.80	7.870	0.94		82.5
85.0		0.252	0.39	0.472	0.46	0.865	0.54	1.620	0.64	2.590	0.72	4.230	0.81	8.000	0.96		85.0
87.5		0.257	0.39	0.480	0.47	0.879	0.55	1.640	0.64	2.630	0.73	4.300	0.83	8.130	0.97		87.5
90.0		0.261	0.40	0.488	0.47	0.893	0.56	1.670	0.65	2.670	0.74	4.370	0.84	8.260	0.99		90.0

q_m	= mass flow rate	kg/s
c	= velocity	m/s
$\Delta p/l$	= pressure loss per unit length	Pa/m

PVC-U PN10

WATER AT 10 °C

$\Delta p/l$	c	32 mm		40 mm		50 mm		63 mm		75 mm		90 mm		110 mm		c	$\Delta p/l$
		q_m	c	q_m	c	q_m	c	q_m	c	q_m	c	q_m	c	q_m	c		
92.5		0.265	0.41	0.496	0.48	0.907	0.57	1.700	0.67	2.710	0.75	4.440	0.85	8.390	1.00		92.5
95.0		0.269	0.41	0.504	0.49	0.921	0.57	1.720	0.67	2.750	0.76	4.500	0.86	8.520	1.02		95.0
97.5		0.273	0.42	0.511	0.50	0.935	0.58	1.750	0.69	2.790	0.77	4.570	0.88	8.640	1.03		97.5
100		0.277	0.43	0.519	0.50	0.949	0.59	1.770	0.69	2.830	0.78	4.640	0.89	8.760	1.05		100
120	0.50	0.308	0.47	0.576	0.56	1.050	0.65	1.970	0.77	3.140	0.87	5.130	0.99	9.700	1.16		120
140		0.337	0.52	0.629	0.61	1.140	0.71	2.140	0.84	3.420	0.95	5.590	1.07	10.500	1.26		140
160		0.364	0.56	0.678	0.66	1.230	0.77	2.310	0.91	3.690	1.02	6.030	1.16	11.300	1.35		160
180		0.389	0.60	0.725	0.70	1.320	0.82	2.470	0.97	3.940	1.09	6.440	1.24	12.100	1.45	1.50	180
200		0.414	0.64	0.770	0.75	1.400	0.87	2.620	1.03	4.180	1.16	6.820	1.31	12.800	1.53		200
220		0.437	0.67	0.813	0.79	1.480	0.92	2.760	1.08	4.410	1.22	7.190	1.38	13.500	1.61		220
240		0.459	0.70	0.854	0.83	1.550	0.97	2.900	1.14	4.630	1.28	7.550	1.45	14.200	1.70		240
260		0.480	0.74	0.894	0.87	1.620	1.01	3.040	1.19	4.840	1.34	7.890	1.52	14.800	1.77		260
280		0.501	0.77	0.932	0.91	1.690	1.05	3.160	1.24	5.040	1.40	8.220	1.58	15.400	1.84		280
300		0.521	0.80	0.969	0.94	1.760	1.10	3.290	1.29	5.240	1.45	8.540	1.64	16.000	1.91		300
320		0.541	0.83	1.000	0.97	1.830	1.14	3.410	1.34	5.430	1.50	8.850	1.70	16.600	1.99	2.00	320
340		0.560	0.86	1.040	1.01	1.890	1.18	3.530	1.38	5.610	1.55	9.150	1.76	17.200	2.06		340
360		0.578	0.89	1.070	1.04	1.950	1.22	3.640	1.43	5.800	1.61	9.450	1.82	17.700	2.12		360
380		0.596	0.92	1.100	1.07	2.010	1.25	3.750	1.47	5.970	1.65	9.730	1.87	18.300	2.19		380
400		0.614	0.94	1.140	1.11	2.070	1.29	3.860	1.51	6.140	1.70	10.000	1.92	18.800	2.25		400
420		0.631	0.97	1.170	1.14	2.130	1.33	3.970	1.56	6.310	1.75	10.200	1.96	19.300	2.31		420
440	1.00	0.648	1.00	1.200	1.17	2.180	1.36	4.070	1.60	6.480	1.80	10.500	2.02	19.800	2.37		440
460		0.664	1.02	1.230	1.20	2.240	1.40	4.170	1.63	6.640	1.84	10.800	2.08	20.300	2.43		460
480		0.681	1.05	1.260	1.22	2.290	1.43	4.270	1.67	6.800	1.88	11.000	2.11	20.800	2.49		480
500		0.697	1.07	1.290	1.25	2.340	1.46	4.370	1.71	6.950	1.93	11.300	2.17	21.200	2.54		500
520		0.712	1.09	1.320	1.28	2.400	1.50	4.470	1.75	7.100	1.97	11.500	2.21	21.700	2.60		520
540		0.728	1.12	1.340	1.30	2.450	1.53	4.560	1.79	7.250	2.01	11.800	2.27	22.200	2.65		540
560		0.743	1.14	1.370	1.33	2.500	1.56	4.650	1.82	7.400	2.05	12.000	2.31	22.600	2.70		560
580		0.757	1.16	1.400	1.36	2.550	1.59	4.740	1.86	7.540	2.09	12.200	2.35	23.000	2.75		580
600		0.772	1.19	1.430	1.39	2.590	1.61	4.830	1.89	7.690	2.13	12.500	2.40	23.500	2.81		600
620		0.786	1.21	1.450	1.41	2.640	1.65	4.920	1.93	7.830	2.17	12.700	2.44	23.900	2.86		620
640		0.801	1.23	1.480	1.44	2.690	1.68	5.010	1.96	7.960	2.21	12.900	2.48	24.300	2.91		640
660		0.815	1.25	1.510	1.47	2.740	1.71	5.100	2.00	8.100	2.24	13.100	2.52	24.700	2.95		660
680		0.828	1.27	1.530	1.49	2.780	1.73	5.180	2.03	8.230	2.28	13.400	2.58	25.100	3.00	3.00	680
700		0.842	1.29	1.560	1.52	2.830	1.76	5.260	2.06	8.370	2.32	13.600	2.61	25.500	3.05		700
720		0.856	1.31	1.580	1.54	2.870	1.79	5.350	2.10	8.500	2.36	13.800	2.65	25.900	3.10		720
740		0.869	1.33	1.600	1.56	2.920	1.82	5.430	2.13	8.630	2.39	14.000	2.69	26.300	3.15		740
760		0.882	1.35	1.630	1.58	2.960	1.85	5.510	2.16	8.750	2.42	14.200	2.73	26.700	3.19		760
780		0.895	1.37	1.650	1.60	3.000	1.87	5.590	2.19	8.880	2.46	14.400	2.77	27.100	3.24		780
800		0.908	1.39	1.680	1.63	3.050	1.90	5.670	2.22	9.000	2.49	14.600	2.81	27.500	3.29		800
820		0.920	1.41	1.700	1.65	3.090	1.93	5.740	2.25	9.130	2.53	14.800	2.84	27.800	3.32		820
840		0.933	1.43	1.720	1.67	3.130	1.95	5.820	2.28	9.250	2.56	15.000	2.88	28.200	3.37		840
860		0.945	1.45	1.750	1.70	3.170	1.98	5.900	2.31	9.370	2.60	15.200	2.92	28.600	3.42		860
880		0.958	1.47	1.770	1.72	3.210	2.00	5.970	2.34	9.490	2.63	15.400	2.96	28.900	3.46		880
900	1.50	0.970	1.49	1.790	1.74	3.250	2.03	6.050	2.37	9.600	2.66	15.600	3.00	29.300	3.50		900
920		0.982	1.51	1.810	1.76	3.290	2.05	6.120	2.40	9.720	2.69	15.800	3.04	29.600	3.54		920
940		0.994	1.53	1.830	1.78	3.330	2.08	6.190	2.43	9.830	2.72	15.900	3.06	30.000	3.59		940
960		1.000	1.54	1.860	1.81	3.370	2.10	6.260	2.45	9.950	2.76	16.100	3.09	30.300	3.62		960
980		1.010	1.55	1.880	1.83	3.410	2.13	6.340	2.49	10.000	2.77	16.300	3.13	30.700	3.67		980
1000		1.020	1.57	1.900	1.85	3.450	2.15	6.410	2.51	10.100	2.80	16.500	3.17	31.000	3.71		1000
1100		1.080	1.66	2.000	1.94	3.630	2.26	6.750	2.65	10.700	2.96	17.400	3.34	32.600	3.90		1100
1200		1.130	1.74	2.100	2.04	3.810	2.38	7.080	2.78	11.200	3.10	18.200	3.50	34.200	4.09		1200
1300		1.190	1.83	2.200	2.14	3.980	2.48	7.400	2.90	11.700	3.24	19.000	3.65	35.700	4.27		1300
1400		1.240	1.90	2.290	2.23	4.150	2.59	7.710	3.02	12.200	3.38	19.800	3.81	37.200	4.45		1400
1500	2.00	1.290	1.98	2.380	2.31	4.310	2.69	8.000	3.14	12.600	3.49	20.600	3.96	38.600	4.62		1500
1600		1.330	2.04	2.460	2.39	4.470	2.79	8.290	3.25	13.100	3.63	21.300	4.09	40.000	4.78		1600
1700		1.380	2.12	2.550	2.48	4.620	2.88	8.570	3.36	13.500	3.74	22.000	4.23	41.300	4.94		1700
1800		1.420	2.18	2.630	2.56	4.760	2.97	8.840	3.47	14.000	3.88	22.700	4.36	42.600	5.09		1800
1900		1.470	2.26	2.710	2.63	4.910	3.06	9.100	3.57	14.400	3.99	23.400	4.50	43.800	5.24		1900
2000		1.510	2.32	2.790	2.71	5.050	3.15	9.360	3.67	14.800	4.10	24.000	4.61	45.100	5.39		2000

q_m = mass flow rate   kg/s
c = velocity   m/s
$\Delta p/l$ = pressure loss per unit length   Pa/m

PVC-U PN10

WATER AT 10 °C

$\Delta p/l$	c	125 mm q_m	c	140 mm q_m	c	160 mm q_m	c	180 mm q_m	c	200 mm q_m	c	225 mm q_m	c	250 mm q_m	c	c	$\Delta p/l$
0.1		0.239	0.02	0.317	0.02	0.461	0.03	0.640	0.03	0.856	0.03	1.180	0.03	1.580	0.04		0.1
0.2		0.348	0.03	0.480	0.04	0.696	0.04	0.965	0.04	1.280	0.05	1.780	0.05	2.370	0.05	0.05	0.2
0.3		0.444	0.04	0.610	0.04	0.884	0.05	1.220	0.05	1.630	0.06	2.250	0.06	3.000	0.07		0.3
0.4	0.05	0.527	0.05	0.723	0.05	1.040	0.06	1.440	0.06	1.920	0.07	2.660	0.08	3.540	0.08		0.4
0.5		0.601	0.06	0.824	0.06	1.190	0.07	1.640	0.07	2.190	0.08	3.020	0.09	4.030	0.09		0.5
0.6		0.669	0.06	0.917	0.07	1.320	0.07	1.830	0.08	2.430	0.09	3.360	0.10	4.470	0.10		0.6
0.7		0.732	0.07	1.000	0.07	1.440	0.08	2.000	0.09	2.660	0.10	3.670	0.10	4.880	0.11		0.7
0.8		0.792	0.07	1.080	0.08	1.560	0.09	2.160	0.10	2.870	0.10	3.960	0.11	5.270	0.12		0.8
0.9		0.848	0.08	1.160	0.09	1.670	0.09	2.310	0.10	3.070	0.11	4.240	0.12	5.640	0.13		0.9
1.0		0.902	0.08	1.230	0.09	1.780	0.10	2.450	0.11	3.260	0.12	4.500	0.13	5.990	0.14	0.15	1.0
1.5		1.140	0.11	1.560	0.12	2.250	0.13	3.100	0.14	4.110	0.15	5.670	0.16	7.540	0.17		1.5
2.0		1.340	0.12	1.840	0.14	2.650	0.15	3.650	0.16	4.850	0.18	6.680	0.19	8.870	0.21		2.0
2.5	0.15	1.530	0.14	2.090	0.15	3.010	0.17	4.150	0.19	5.500	0.20	7.580	0.22	10.000	0.23		2.5
3.0		1.700	0.16	2.320	0.17	3.340	0.19	4.600	0.21	6.100	0.22	8.400	0.24	11.100	0.26		3.0
3.5		1.860	0.17	2.540	0.19	3.650	0.21	5.020	0.22	6.660	0.24	9.170	0.26	12.100	0.28		3.5
4.0		2.010	0.19	2.740	0.20	3.940	0.22	5.420	0.24	7.180	0.26	9.880	0.28	13.100	0.30	0.30	4.0
4.5		2.150	0.20	2.930	0.22	4.210	0.24	5.790	0.26	7.670	0.28	10.500	0.30	14.000	0.32		4.5
5.0		2.280	0.21	3.110	0.23	4.470	0.25	6.150	0.27	8.150	0.29	11.200	0.32	14.800	0.34		5.0
5.5		2.410	0.22	3.280	0.24	4.720	0.27	6.490	0.29	8.590	0.31	11.800	0.34	15.600	0.36		5.5
6.0		2.530	0.23	3.450	0.25	4.950	0.28	6.810	0.30	9.030	0.33	12.400	0.35	16.400	0.38		6.0
6.5		2.650	0.25	3.610	0.27	5.180	0.29	7.130	0.32	9.440	0.34	12.900	0.37	17.200	0.40		6.5
7.0		2.760	0.26	3.770	0.28	5.410	0.31	7.430	0.33	9.840	0.36	13.500	0.39	17.900	0.41		7.0
7.5		2.870	0.27	3.920	0.29	5.620	0.32	7.730	0.34	10.200	0.37	14.000	0.40	18.600	0.43		7.5
8.0		2.980	0.28	4.060	0.30	5.830	0.33	8.010	0.36	10.600	0.38	14.500	0.41	19.300	0.45		8.0
8.5		3.080	0.29	4.200	0.31	6.030	0.34	8.290	0.37	10.900	0.39	15.000	0.43	20.000	0.46		8.5
9.0	0.30	3.190	0.30	4.340	0.32	6.230	0.35	8.560	0.38	11.300	0.41	15.500	0.44	20.600	0.48		9.0
9.5		3.290	0.31	4.480	0.33	6.420	0.36	8.830	0.39	11.600	0.42	16.000	0.46	21.200	0.49		9.5
10.0		3.380	0.31	4.610	0.34	6.610	0.37	9.080	0.40	12.000	0.43	16.500	0.47	21.800	0.50	0.50	10.0
12.5		3.840	0.36	5.230	0.39	7.500	0.42	10.300	0.46	13.600	0.49	18.700	0.53	24.700	0.57		12.5
15.0		4.260	0.39	5.800	0.43	8.310	0.47	11.400	0.51	15.000	0.54	20.700	0.59	27.400	0.63		15.0
17.5		4.640	0.43	6.320	0.47	9.060	0.51	12.400	0.55	16.400	0.59	22.500	0.64	29.800	0.69		17.5
20.0		5.010	0.46	6.810	0.50	9.760	0.55	13.300	0.59	17.700	0.64	24.300	0.69	32.100	0.74		20.0
22.5	0.50	5.350	0.50	7.280	0.54	10.400	0.59	14.300	0.64	18.900	0.68	25.900	0.74	34.300	0.79		22.5
25.0		5.680	0.53	7.720	0.57	11.000	0.62	15.100	0.67	20.000	0.72	27.500	0.79	36.400	0.84		25.0
27.5		5.990	0.56	8.150	0.60	11.600	0.65	15.900	0.71	21.100	0.76	29.000	0.83	38.300	0.89		27.5
30.0		6.290	0.58	8.550	0.63	12.200	0.69	16.700	0.74	22.100	0.80	30.400	0.87	40.200	0.93		30.0
32.5		6.580	0.61	8.940	0.66	12.800	0.72	17.500	0.78	23.100	0.84	31.800	0.91	42.000	0.97	1.00	32.5
35.0		6.860	0.64	9.320	0.69	13.300	0.75	18.200	0.81	24.100	0.87	33.100	0.95	43.800	1.01		35.0
37.5		7.130	0.66	9.690	0.71	13.800	0.78	19.000	0.85	25.100	0.91	34.400	0.98	45.500	1.05		37.5
40.0		7.390	0.69	10.000	0.74	14.300	0.81	19.600	0.87	26.000	0.94	35.600	1.02	47.200	1.09		40.0
42.5		7.650	0.71	10.300	0.76	14.800	0.84	20.300	0.91	26.900	0.97	36.900	1.05	48.800	1.13		42.5
45.0		7.890	0.73	10.700	0.79	15.300	0.86	21.000	0.94	27.700	1.00	38.000	1.09	50.300	1.16		45.0
47.5		8.140	0.75	11.000	0.81	15.800	0.89	21.600	0.96	28.600	1.03	39.200	1.12	51.800	1.20		47.5
50.0		8.370	0.78	11.300	0.83	16.200	0.91	22.200	0.99	29.400	1.06	40.300	1.15	53.300	1.23		50.0
52.5		8.600	0.80	11.600	0.86	16.700	0.94	22.900	1.02	30.200	1.09	41.400	1.18	54.800	1.27		52.5
55.0		8.830	0.82	11.900	0.88	17.100	0.97	23.400	1.04	31.000	1.12	42.500	1.21	56.200	1.30		55.0
57.5		9.050	0.84	12.200	0.90	17.500	0.99	24.000	1.07	31.800	1.15	43.500	1.24	57.600	1.33		57.5
60.0		9.270	0.86	12.500	0.92	18.000	1.02	24.600	1.10	32.500	1.18	44.600	1.27	58.900	1.36		60.0
62.5		9.480	0.88	12.800	0.94	18.400	1.04	25.200	1.12	33.300	1.21	45.600	1.30	60.300	1.40		62.5
65.0		9.690	0.90	13.100	0.97	18.800	1.06	25.700	1.15	34.000	1.23	46.600	1.33	61.600	1.43		65.0
67.5		9.900	0.92	13.400	0.99	19.200	1.08	26.300	1.17	34.700	1.26	47.600	1.36	62.900	1.46		67.5
70.0		10.100	0.94	13.700	1.01	19.600	1.11	26.800	1.20	35.400	1.28	48.500	1.38	64.100	1.48	1.50	70.0
72.5		10.300	0.96	13.900	1.03	19.900	1.12	27.300	1.22	36.100	1.31	49.500	1.41	65.400	1.51		72.5
75.0		10.500	0.97	14.200	1.05	20.300	1.15	27.800	1.24	36.800	1.33	50.400	1.44	66.600	1.54		75.0
77.5		10.600	0.98	14.500	1.07	20.700	1.17	28.300	1.26	37.400	1.35	51.300	1.46	67.800	1.57		77.5
80.0	1.00	10.800	1.00	14.700	1.08	21.100	1.19	28.800	1.28	38.100	1.38	52.200	1.49	69.000	1.60		80.0
82.5		11.000	1.02	15.000	1.11	21.400	1.21	29.300	1.31	38.700	1.40	53.100	1.52	70.200	1.62		82.5
85.0		11.200	1.04	15.200	1.12	21.800	1.23	29.800	1.33	39.400	1.43	54.000	1.54	71.400	1.65		85.0
87.5		11.400	1.06	15.500	1.14	22.100	1.25	30.300	1.35	40.000	1.45	54.800	1.56	72.500	1.68		87.5
90.0		11.600	1.08	15.700	1.16	22.500	1.27	30.800	1.37	40.600	1.47	55.700	1.59	73.600	1.70		90.0

q_m	= mass flow rate	kg/s
c	= velocity	m/s
$\Delta p/l$	= pressure loss per unit length	Pa/m

PVC-U PN10

WATER AT 10 °C

$\Delta p/l$	c	125 mm		140 mm		160 mm		180 mm		200 mm		225 mm		250 mm		c	$\Delta p/l$
		q_m	c	q_m	c	q_m	c	q_m	c	q_m	c	q_m	c	q_m	c		
92.5		11.70	1.1	16.00	1.2	22.80	1.3	31.30	1.4	41.30	1.5	56.50	1.6	74.7	1.7		92.5
95.0		11.90	1.1	16.20	1.2	23.20	1.3	31.70	1.4	41.90	1.5	57.40	1.6	75.8	1.8		95.0
97.5		12.10	1.1	16.40	1.2	23.50	1.3	32.20	1.4	42.50	1.5	58.20	1.7	76.9	1.8		97.5
100		12.30	1.1	16.70	1.2	23.80	1.3	32.60	1.5	43.10	1.6	59.00	1.7	78.0	1.8		100
120		13.60	1.3	18.40	1.4	26.30	1.5	36.10	1.6	47.60	1.7	65.20	1.9	86.2	2.0	2.0	120
140		14.80	1.4	20.10	1.5	28.70	1.6	39.30	1.8	51.80	1.9	70.90	2.0	93.7	2.2		140
160	1.5	15.90	1.5	21.60	1.6	30.90	1.7	42.20	1.9	55.70	2.0	76.30	2.2	100.0	2.3		160
180		17.00	1.6	23.10	1.7	32.90	1.9	45.00	2.0	59.40	2.1	81.40	2.3	107.0	2.5		180
200		18.00	1.7	24.40	1.8	34.90	2.0	47.70	2.1	63.00	2.3	86.20	2.5	113.0	2.6		200
220		19.00	1.8	25.80	1.9	36.80	2.1	50.30	2.2	66.30	2.4	90.70	2.6	119.0	2.8		220
240		19.90	1.8	27.00	2.0	38.50	2.2	52.70	2.4	69.50	2.5	95.10	2.7	125.0	2.9		240
260		20.80	1.9	28.20	2.1	40.30	2.3	55.10	2.5	72.60	2.6	99.40	2.8	131.0	3.0	3.0	260
280	2.0	21.70	2.0	29.40	2.2	41.90	2.4	57.30	2.6	75.60	2.7	103.00	2.9	136.0	3.1		280
300		22.50	2.1	30.50	2.2	43.50	2.5	59.50	2.7	78.50	2.8	107.00	3.1	141.0	3.3		300
320		23.30	2.2	31.60	2.3	45.10	2.5	61.70	2.8	81.30	2.9	111.00	3.2	146.0	3.4		320
340		24.10	2.2	32.70	2.4	46.60	2.6	63.70	2.8	84.00	3.0	114.00	3.3	151.0	3.5		340
360		24.90	2.3	33.70	2.5	48.10	2.7	65.70	2.9	86.70	3.1	118.00	3.4	156.0	3.6		360
380		25.60	2.4	34.70	2.6	49.50	2.8	67.70	3.0	89.20	3.2	122.00	3.5	161.0	3.7		380
400		26.40	2.4	35.70	2.6	50.90	2.9	69.60	3.1	91.80	3.3	125.00	3.6	165.0	3.8		400
420		27.10	2.5	36.70	2.7	52.30	3.0	71.50	3.2	94.20	3.4	128.00	3.7	170.0	3.9		420
440		27.80	2.6	37.60	2.8	53.70	3.0	73.30	3.3	96.60	3.5	132.00	3.8	174.0	4.0		440
460		28.50	2.6	38.60	2.8	55.00	3.1	75.10	3.3	99.00	3.6	135.00	3.9	178.0	4.1		460
480		29.10	2.7	39.50	2.9	56.20	3.2	76.80	3.4	101.00	3.7	138.00	3.9	182.0	4.2		480
500		29.80	2.8	40.40	3.0	57.50	3.2	78.60	3.5	103.00	3.7	141.00	4.0	186.0	4.3		500
520		30.40	2.8	41.20	3.0	58.70	3.3	80.30	3.6	105.00	3.8	144.00	4.1	190.0	4.4		520
540		31.10	2.9	42.10	3.1	60.00	3.4	81.90	3.7	107.00	3.9	147.00	4.2	194.0	4.5		540
560		31.70	2.9	42.90	3.2	61.20	3.5	83.50	3.7	110.00	4.0	150.00	4.3	198.0	4.6		560
580	3.0	32.30	3.0	43.70	3.2	62.30	3.5	85.10	3.8	112.00	4.1	153.00	4.4	202.0	4.7		580
600		32.90	3.1	44.60	3.3	63.50	3.6	86.70	3.9	114.00	4.1	156.00	4.5	205.0	4.7		600
620		33.50	3.1	45.40	3.3	64.60	3.6	88.30	3.9	116.00	4.2	158.00	4.5	209.0	4.8		620
640		34.10	3.2	46.10	3.4	65.70	3.7	89.80	4.0	118.00	4.3	161.00	4.6	213.0	4.9		640
660		34.70	3.2	46.90	3.5	66.80	3.8	91.30	4.1	120.00	4.3	164.00	4.7	216.0	5.0		660
680		35.20	3.3	47.70	3.5	67.90	3.8	92.80	4.1	122.00	4.4	167.00	4.8	220.0	5.1		680
700		35.80	3.3	48.40	3.6	69.00	3.9	94.20	4.2	124.00	4.5	169.00	4.8	223.0	5.2		700
720		36.30	3.4	49.20	3.6	70.10	4.0	95.70	4.3	126.00	4.6	172.00	4.9	227.0	5.3		720
740		36.90	3.4	49.90	3.7	71.10	4.0	97.10	4.3	127.00	4.6	174.00	5.0	230.0	5.3		740
760		37.40	3.5	50.70	3.7	72.10	4.1	98.50	4.4	129.00	4.7	177.00	5.1	233.0	5.4		760
780		37.90	3.5	51.40	3.8	73.20	4.1	99.90	4.5	131.00	4.7	179.00	5.1	237.0	5.5		780
800		38.50	3.6	52.10	3.8	74.20	4.2	101.00	4.5	133.00	4.8	182.00	5.2	240.0	5.6		800
820		39.00	3.6	52.80	3.9	75.20	4.2	102.00	4.5	135.00	4.9	184.00	5.3	243.0	5.6		820
840		39.50	3.7	53.50	3.9	76.10	4.3	104.00	4.6	136.00	4.9	187.00	5.3	246.0	5.7		840
860		40.00	3.7	54.20	4.0	77.10	4.4	105.00	4.7	138.00	5.0	189.00	5.4	249.0	5.8		860
880		40.50	3.8	54.80	4.0	78.10	4.4	106.00	4.7	140.00	5.1	191.00	5.5	252.0	5.8		880
900		41.00	3.8	55.50	4.1	79.00	4.5	107.00	4.8	142.00	5.1	194.00	5.5	255.0	5.9		900
920		41.50	3.8	56.20	4.1	80.00	4.5	109.00	4.9	143.00	5.2	196.00	5.6	258.0	6.0		920
940		42.00	3.9	56.80	4.2	80.90	4.6	110.00	4.9	145.00	5.2	198.00	5.7	261.0	6.0		940
960		42.50	3.9	57.50	4.2	81.80	4.6	111.00	4.9	147.00	5.3	200.00	5.7	264.0	6.1		960
980		42.90	4.0	58.10	4.3	82.70	4.7	112.00	5.0	148.00	5.4	203.00	5.8	267.0	6.2		980
1000		43.40	4.0	58.80	4.3	83.60	4.7	114.00	5.1	150.00	5.4	205.00	5.9	270.0	6.2		1000
1100		45.70	4.2	61.90	4.6	88.00	5.0	120.00	5.4	158.00	5.7	216.00	6.2	284.0	6.6		1100
1200		47.90	4.4	64.80	4.8	92.30	5.2	125.00	5.6	165.00	6.0	226.00	6.5	298.0	6.9		1200
1300		50.00	4.6	67.70	5.0	96.30	5.4	131.00	5.8	173.00	6.3	236.00	6.7	311.0	7.2		1300
1400		52.10	4.8	70.40	5.2	100.00	5.6	136.00	6.1	179.00	6.5	245.00	7.0	323.0	7.5		1400
1500		54.00	5.0	73.10	5.4	104.00	5.9	141.00	6.3	186.00	6.7	254.00	7.3	335.0	7.8		1500
1600		55.90	5.2	75.70	5.6	107.00	6.0	146.00	6.5	193.00	7.0	263.00	7.5	347.0	8.0		1600
1700		57.80	5.4	78.20	5.8	111.00	6.3	151.00	6.7	199.00	7.2	272.00	7.8	358.0	8.3		1700
1800		59.60	5.5	80.60	5.9	114.00	6.4	156.00	7.0	205.00	7.4	280.00	8.0	369.0	8.5		1800
1900		61.40	5.7	83.00	6.1	118.00	6.7	160.00	7.1	211.00	7.6	289.00	8.3	380.0	8.8		1900
2000		63.10	5.9	85.30	6.3	121.00	6.8	165.00	7.4	217.00	7.9	297.00	8.5	391.0	9.0		2000

q_m = mass flow rate   kg/s
c = velocity   m/s
$\Delta p/l$ = pressure loss per unit length   Pa/m

PVC-U PN10
WATER AT 75 °C

$\Delta p/l$	c	32 mm		40 mm		50 mm		63 mm		75 mm		90 mm		110 mm		c	$\Delta p/l$
		q_m	c	q_m	c	q_m	c	q_m	c	q_m	c	q_m	c	q_m	c		
0.1		0.004	0.01	0.010	0.01	0.026	0.02	0.038	0.02	0.062	0.02	0.104	0.02	0.200	0.02		0.1
0.2		0.008	0.01	0.021	0.02	0.030	0.02	0.058	0.02	0.094	0.03	0.156	0.03	0.300	0.04		0.2
0.3		0.013	0.02	0.021	0.02	0.038	0.02	0.074	0.03	0.120	0.03	0.198	0.04	0.380	0.05		0.3
0.4		0.017	0.03	0.024	0.02	0.046	0.03	0.088	0.04	0.142	0.04	0.234	0.05	0.448	0.05	0.05	0.4
0.5		0.017	0.03	0.028	0.03	0.052	0.03	0.100	0.04	0.161	0.05	0.266	0.05	0.509	0.06		0.5
0.6		0.017	0.03	0.031	0.03	0.058	0.04	0.111	0.04	0.179	0.05	0.296	0.06	0.566	0.07		0.6
0.7		0.018	0.03	0.034	0.03	0.064	0.04	0.122	0.05	0.196	0.06	0.324	0.06	0.618	0.08		0.7
0.8		0.019	0.03	0.037	0.04	0.069	0.04	0.132	0.05	0.212	0.06	0.349	0.07	0.666	0.08		0.8
0.9		0.021	0.03	0.040	0.04	0.074	0.05	0.141	0.06	0.227	0.06	0.374	0.07	0.713	0.09		0.9
1.0		0.022	0.03	0.042	0.04	0.079	0.05	0.150	0.06	0.241	0.07	0.397	0.08	0.757	0.09		1.0
1.5		0.028	0.04	0.054	0.05	0.100	0.06	0.190	0.08	0.305	0.09	0.501	0.10	0.952	0.12		1.5
2.0	0.05	0.034	0.05	0.064	0.06	0.118	0.08	0.224	0.09	0.359	0.10	0.590	0.12	1.120	0.14	0.15	2.0
2.5		0.039	0.06	0.073	0.07	0.135	0.09	0.254	0.10	0.408	0.12	0.670	0.13	1.270	0.16		2.5
3.0		0.043	0.07	0.081	0.08	0.150	0.10	0.282	0.11	0.453	0.13	0.743	0.15	1.400	0.17		3.0
3.5		0.047	0.07	0.089	0.09	0.164	0.10	0.308	0.12	0.494	0.14	0.810	0.16	1.530	0.19		3.5
4.0		0.051	0.08	0.096	0.10	0.177	0.11	0.333	0.13	0.533	0.15	0.874	0.17	1.650	0.20		4.0
4.5		0.055	0.09	0.103	0.10	0.189	0.12	0.356	0.14	0.570	0.16	0.934	0.18	1.760	0.22		4.5
5.0		0.058	0.09	0.109	0.11	0.201	0.13	0.378	0.15	0.605	0.17	0.991	0.20	1.870	0.23		5.0
5.5		0.062	0.10	0.116	0.12	0.212	0.14	0.399	0.16	0.638	0.18	1.040	0.21	1.970	0.24		5.5
6.0		0.065	0.10	0.122	0.12	0.223	0.14	0.419	0.17	0.670	0.19	1.090	0.21	2.070	0.25		6.0
6.5		0.068	0.11	0.127	0.13	0.234	0.15	0.439	0.18	0.701	0.20	1.140	0.22	2.170	0.27		6.5
7.0		0.071	0.11	0.133	0.13	0.244	0.16	0.458	0.18	0.731	0.21	1.190	0.23	2.260	0.28		7.0
7.5		0.074	0.12	0.138	0.14	0.254	0.16	0.476	0.19	0.760	0.22	1.240	0.24	2.350	0.29		7.5
8.0		0.077	0.12	0.144	0.14	0.263	0.17	0.494	0.20	0.788	0.22	1.290	0.25	2.430	0.30	0.30	8.0
8.5		0.079	0.12	0.149	0.15	0.272	0.17	0.511	0.21	0.816	0.23	1.330	0.26	2.520	0.31		8.5
9.0		0.082	0.13	0.154	0.15	0.281	0.18	0.528	0.21	0.842	0.24	1.370	0.27	2.600	0.32		9.0
9.5		0.085	0.13	0.159	0.16	0.290	0.19	0.544	0.22	0.868	0.25	1.420	0.28	2.680	0.33		9.5
10.0	0.15	0.087	0.14	0.163	0.16	0.299	0.19	0.560	0.23	0.894	0.25	1.460	0.29	2.750	0.34		10.0
12.5		0.099	0.16	0.186	0.19	0.339	0.22	0.635	0.26	1.010	0.29	1.650	0.33	3.120	0.38		12.5
15.0		0.110	0.17	0.206	0.21	0.376	0.24	0.703	0.28	1.120	0.32	1.830	0.36	3.450	0.42		15.0
17.5		0.121	0.19	0.225	0.22	0.410	0.26	0.767	0.31	1.220	0.35	1.990	0.39	3.760	0.46		17.5
20.0		0.130	0.20	0.242	0.24	0.442	0.28	0.826	0.33	1.310	0.37	2.140	0.42	4.040	0.50	0.50	20.0
22.5		0.139	0.22	0.259	0.26	0.473	0.30	0.883	0.35	1.400	0.40	2.290	0.45	4.310	0.53		22.5
25.0		0.148	0.23	0.275	0.27	0.501	0.32	0.936	0.38	1.490	0.42	2.430	0.48	4.570	0.56		25.0
27.5		0.156	0.25	0.290	0.29	0.529	0.34	0.987	0.40	1.570	0.45	2.560	0.50	4.820	0.59		27.5
30.0		0.164	0.26	0.305	0.30	0.556	0.36	1.030	0.41	1.640	0.47	2.680	0.53	5.050	0.62		30.0
32.5		0.172	0.27	0.319	0.32	0.581	0.37	1.080	0.43	1.720	0.49	2.810	0.55	5.280	0.65		32.5
35.0		0.179	0.28	0.333	0.33	0.606	0.39	1.120	0.45	1.790	0.51	2.920	0.58	5.500	0.67		35.0
37.5		0.186	0.29	0.346	0.34	0.629	0.40	1.170	0.47	1.860	0.53	3.040	0.60	5.710	0.70		37.5
40.0	0.30	0.193	0.30	0.359	0.36	0.653	0.42	1.210	0.49	1.930	0.55	3.150	0.62	5.920	0.73		40.0
42.5		0.200	0.31	0.371	0.37	0.675	0.43	1.250	0.50	2.000	0.57	3.250	0.64	6.120	0.75		42.5
45.0		0.207	0.33	0.383	0.38	0.697	0.45	1.290	0.52	2.060	0.59	3.360	0.66	6.310	0.77		45.0
47.5		0.213	0.34	0.395	0.39	0.718	0.46	1.330	0.53	2.120	0.60	3.460	0.68	6.500	0.80		47.5
50.0		0.219	0.34	0.407	0.41	0.739	0.47	1.370	0.55	2.180	0.62	3.560	0.70	6.690	0.82		50.0
52.5		0.225	0.35	0.418	0.42	0.759	0.49	1.410	0.57	2.240	0.64	3.650	0.72	6.870	0.84		52.5
55.0		0.231	0.36	0.429	0.43	0.779	0.50	1.450	0.58	2.300	0.65	3.750	0.74	7.040	0.86		55.0
57.5		0.237	0.37	0.440	0.44	0.799	0.51	1.480	0.59	2.360	0.67	3.840	0.76	7.220	0.89		57.5
60.0		0.243	0.38	0.450	0.45	0.818	0.52	1.520	0.61	2.410	0.68	3.930	0.77	7.390	0.91		60.0
62.5		0.249	0.39	0.461	0.46	0.837	0.54	1.550	0.62	2.470	0.70	4.020	0.79	7.550	0.93		62.5
65.0		0.254	0.40	0.471	0.47	0.855	0.55	1.590	0.64	2.520	0.72	4.110	0.81	7.710	0.95		65.0
67.5		0.260	0.41	0.481	0.48	0.873	0.56	1.620	0.65	2.580	0.73	4.190	0.83	7.870	0.97		67.5
70.0		0.265	0.42	0.491	0.49	0.891	0.57	1.650	0.66	2.630	0.75	4.280	0.84	8.030	0.98		70.0
72.5		0.270	0.43	0.501	0.50	0.908	0.58	1.680	0.68	2.680	0.76	4.360	0.86	8.190	1.00	1.00	72.5
75.0		0.275	0.43	0.510	0.51	0.926	0.59	1.720	0.69	2.730	0.78	4.440	0.88	8.340	1.02		75.0
77.5		0.281	0.44	0.520	0.52	0.943	0.60	1.750	0.70	2.780	0.79	4.520	0.89	8.490	1.04		77.5
80.0		0.286	0.45	0.529	0.53	0.959	0.61	1.780	0.72	2.830	0.80	4.600	0.91	8.640	1.06		80.0
82.5		0.291	0.46	0.538	0.54	0.976	0.62	1.810	0.73	2.880	0.82	4.680	0.92	8.780	1.08		82.5
85.0		0.295	0.46	0.547	0.55	0.992	0.63	1.840	0.74	2.920	0.83	4.750	0.94	8.920	1.09		85.0
87.5		0.300	0.47	0.556	0.55	1.000	0.64	1.870	0.75	2.970	0.84	4.830	0.95	9.070	1.11		87.5
90.0		0.305	0.48	0.565	0.56	1.020	0.65	1.900	0.76	3.020	0.86	4.910	0.97	9.210	1.13		90.0

q_m	= mass flow rate	kg/s
c	= velocity	m/s
$\Delta p/l$	= pressure loss per unit length	Pa/m

PVC-U PN10

WATER AT 75 °C

$\Delta p/l$	c	32 mm		40 mm		50 mm		63 mm		75 mm		90 mm		110 mm		c	$\Delta p/l$
		q_m	c	q_m	c	q_m	c	q_m	c	q_m	c	q_m	c	q_m	c		
92.5		0.310	0.49	0.573	0.57	1.030	0.66	1.930	0.78	3.060	0.87	4.980	0.98	9.340	1.15		92.5
95.0		0.314	0.49	0.582	0.58	1.050	0.67	1.960	0.79	3.110	0.88	5.050	1.00	9.480	1.16		95.0
97.5	0.50	0.319	0.50	0.590	0.59	1.070	0.68	1.980	0.80	3.150	0.89	5.120	1.01	9.610	1.18		97.5
100		0.324	0.51	0.599	0.60	1.080	0.69	2.010	0.81	3.190	0.91	5.190	1.02	9.750	1.20		100
120		0.358	0.56	0.662	0.66	1.200	0.77	2.220	0.89	3.530	1.00	5.740	1.13	10.700	1.31		120
140		0.390	0.61	0.721	0.72	1.300	0.83	2.420	0.97	3.840	1.09	6.240	1.23	11.600	1.42	1.50	140
160		0.421	0.66	0.776	0.77	1.400	0.89	2.600	1.05	4.130	1.17	6.700	1.32	12.500	1.53		160
180		0.449	0.71	0.829	0.83	1.490	0.95	2.770	1.11	4.400	1.25	7.140	1.41	13.300	1.63		180
200		0.476	0.75	0.878	0.88	1.580	1.01	2.940	1.18	4.660	1.32	7.560	1.49	14.100	1.73		200
220		0.502	0.79	0.925	0.92	1.670	1.07	3.090	1.24	4.910	1.40	7.960	1.57	14.900	1.83		220
240		0.526	0.83	0.970	0.97	1.750	1.12	3.240	1.30	5.140	1.46	8.340	1.64	15.600	1.91		240
260		0.550	0.87	1.010	1.01	1.830	1.17	3.390	1.36	5.370	1.53	8.710	1.72	16.300	2.00	2.00	260
280		0.573	0.90	1.050	1.05	1.900	1.21	3.530	1.42	5.590	1.59	9.060	1.79	16.900	2.07		280
300		0.595	0.94	1.090	1.09	1.980	1.27	3.660	1.47	5.800	1.65	9.410	1.85	17.500	2.15		300
320		0.617	0.97	1.130	1.13	2.050	1.31	3.790	1.52	6.000	1.70	9.740	1.92	18.200	2.23		320
340	1.00	0.638	1.00	1.170	1.17	2.120	1.36	3.920	1.58	6.200	1.76	10.000	1.97	18.800	2.31		340
360		0.658	1.04	1.210	1.21	2.180	1.39	4.040	1.62	6.400	1.82	10.300	2.03	19.300	2.37		360
380		0.678	1.07	1.240	1.24	2.250	1.44	4.160	1.67	6.590	1.87	10.600	2.09	19.900	2.44		380
400		0.697	1.10	1.280	1.28	2.310	1.48	4.280	1.72	6.770	1.92	10.900	2.15	20.500	2.51		400
420		0.716	1.13	1.310	1.31	2.370	1.52	4.390	1.76	6.950	1.97	11.200	2.21	21.000	2.58		420
440		0.734	1.16	1.350	1.35	2.430	1.55	4.500	1.81	7.120	2.02	11.500	2.27	21.500	2.64		440
460		0.752	1.18	1.380	1.38	2.490	1.59	4.610	1.85	7.300	2.07	11.800	2.33	22.000	2.70		460
480		0.770	1.21	1.410	1.41	2.550	1.63	4.720	1.90	7.460	2.12	12.000	2.37	22.500	2.76		480
500		0.788	1.24	1.440	1.44	2.610	1.67	4.820	1.94	7.630	2.17	12.300	2.42	23.000	2.82		500
520		0.805	1.27	1.470	1.47	2.660	1.70	4.920	1.98	7.790	2.21	12.600	2.48	23.500	2.88		520
540		0.821	1.29	1.510	1.50	2.720	1.74	5.030	2.02	7.950	2.26	12.800	2.52	24.000	2.94		540
560		0.838	1.32	1.540	1.53	2.770	1.77	5.120	2.06	8.100	2.30	13.100	2.58	24.500	3.00	3.00	560
580		0.854	1.34	1.560	1.55	2.820	1.80	5.220	2.10	8.260	2.35	13.300	2.62	24.900	3.05		580
600		0.870	1.37	1.590	1.58	2.880	1.84	5.320	2.14	8.410	2.39	13.600	2.68	25.400	3.11		600
620		0.885	1.39	1.620	1.61	2.930	1.87	5.410	2.17	8.560	2.43	13.800	2.72	25.800	3.16		620
640		0.901	1.42	1.650	1.64	2.980	1.91	5.500	2.21	8.700	2.47	14.000	2.76	26.300	3.23		640
660		0.916	1.44	1.680	1.67	3.030	1.94	5.600	2.25	8.850	2.51	14.300	2.82	26.700	3.27		660
680		0.931	1.47	1.710	1.70	3.080	1.97	5.690	2.29	8.990	2.55	14.500	2.86	27.100	3.32		680
700	1.50	0.946	1.49	1.730	1.72	3.120	1.99	5.770	2.32	9.130	2.59	14.700	2.90	27.500	3.37		700
720		0.960	1.51	1.760	1.75	3.170	2.03	5.860	2.36	9.270	2.63	15.000	2.96	27.900	3.42		720
740		0.975	1.54	1.790	1.78	3.220	2.06	5.950	2.39	9.400	2.67	15.200	3.00	28.300	3.47		740
760		0.989	1.56	1.810	1.80	3.270	2.09	6.030	2.42	9.540	2.71	15.400	3.04	28.700	3.52		760
780		1.000	1.57	1.840	1.83	3.310	2.12	6.120	2.46	9.670	2.75	15.600	3.08	29.100	3.57		780
800		1.010	1.59	1.860	1.85	3.360	2.15	6.200	2.49	9.800	2.78	15.800	3.11	29.500	3.62		800
820		1.030	1.62	1.890	1.88	3.400	2.17	6.280	2.52	9.930	2.82	16.000	3.15	29.900	3.67		820
840		1.040	1.64	1.910	1.90	3.450	2.21	6.360	2.56	10.000	2.84	16.200	3.19	30.300	3.72		840
860		1.050	1.65	1.940	1.93	3.490	2.23	6.440	2.59	10.100	2.87	16.400	3.23	30.700	3.76		860
880		1.070	1.68	1.960	1.95	3.530	2.26	6.520	2.62	10.300	2.93	16.600	3.27	31.100	3.81		880
900		1.080	1.70	1.980	1.97	3.580	2.29	6.600	2.65	10.400	2.95	16.800	3.31	31.400	3.85		900
920		1.090	1.72	2.010	2.00	3.620	2.31	6.680	2.69	10.500	2.98	17.000	3.35	31.800	3.90		920
940		1.100	1.73	2.030	2.02	3.660	2.34	6.760	2.72	10.600	3.01	17.200	3.39	32.200	3.95		940
960		1.120	1.76	2.050	2.04	3.700	2.37	6.830	2.75	10.700	3.04	17.400	3.43	32.500	3.99		960
980		1.130	1.78	2.080	2.07	3.740	2.39	6.910	2.78	10.900	3.10	17.600	3.47	32.900	4.03		980
1000		1.140	1.80	2.100	2.09	3.780	2.42	6.980	2.81	11.000	3.13	17.800	3.51	33.200	4.07		1000
1100		1.200	1.89	2.210	2.20	3.980	2.54	7.340	2.95	11.600	3.30	18.700	3.69	34.900	4.28		1100
1200	2.00	1.260	1.98	2.320	2.31	4.170	2.67	7.690	3.09	12.100	3.44	19.600	3.86	36.600	4.49		1200
1300		1.320	2.08	2.420	2.41	4.350	2.78	8.020	3.22	12.600	3.58	20.400	4.02	38.100	4.67		1300
1400		1.370	2.16	2.520	2.51	4.530	2.90	8.340	3.35	13.100	3.72	21.300	4.20	39.600	4.86		1400
1500		1.420	2.24	2.610	2.60	4.690	3.00	8.650	3.48	13.600	3.86	22.000	4.34	41.100	5.04		1500
1600		1.470	2.31	2.700	2.69	4.860	3.11	8.950	3.60	14.100	4.01	22.800	4.49	42.500	5.21		1600
1700		1.520	2.39	2.790	2.78	5.020	3.21	9.250	3.72	14.500	4.12	23.500	4.63	43.900	5.38		1700
1800		1.570	2.47	2.880	2.87	5.170	3.31	9.530	3.83	15.000	4.26	24.200	4.77	45.200	5.54		1800
1900		1.610	2.54	2.960	2.95	5.320	3.40	9.800	3.94	15.400	4.38	24.900	4.91	46.500	5.70		1900
2000		1.660	2.61	3.040	3.03	5.470	3.50	10.000	4.02	15.800	4.49	25.600	5.05	47.700	5.85		2000

q_m	= mass flow rate	kg/s		**PVC-U PN10**
c	= velocity	m/s		
$\Delta p/l$	= pressure loss per unit length	Pa/m		**WATER AT 75 °C**

$\Delta p/l$	c	125 mm		140 mm		160 mm		180 mm		200 mm		225 mm		250 mm		c	$\Delta p/l$
		q_m	c	q_m	c	q_m	c	q_m	c	q_m	c	q_m	c	q_m	c		
0.1		0.285	0.03	0.390	0.03	0.562	0.03	0.775	0.04	1.030	0.04	1.420	0.04	1.880	0.04	0.05	0.1
0.2		0.426	0.04	0.581	0.04	0.837	0.05	1.150	0.05	1.520	0.06	2.100	0.06	2.790	0.07		0.2
0.3	0.05	0.537	0.05	0.734	0.06	1.050	0.06	1.450	0.07	1.920	0.07	2.640	0.08	3.510	0.08		0.3
0.4		0.634	0.06	0.865	0.07	1.240	0.07	1.700	0.08	2.260	0.08	3.110	0.09	4.130	0.10		0.4
0.5		0.720	0.07	0.982	0.07	1.410	0.08	1.930	0.09	2.560	0.10	3.530	0.10	4.680	0.11		0.5
0.6		0.799	0.08	1.080	0.08	1.560	0.09	2.140	0.10	2.840	0.11	3.910	0.11	5.180	0.12		0.6
0.7		0.872	0.08	1.180	0.09	1.700	0.10	2.340	0.11	3.100	0.12	4.260	0.12	5.650	0.13		0.7
0.8		0.941	0.09	1.280	0.10	1.830	0.11	2.520	0.12	3.340	0.12	4.590	0.13	6.080	0.14		0.8
0.9		1.000	0.10	1.370	0.10	1.960	0.11	2.690	0.12	3.570	0.13	4.900	0.14	6.500	0.15	0.15	0.9
1.0		1.060	0.10	1.450	0.11	2.080	0.12	2.860	0.13	3.780	0.14	5.200	0.15	6.890	0.16		1.0
1.5		1.340	0.13	1.820	0.14	2.610	0.15	3.590	0.16	4.750	0.18	6.520	0.19	8.630	0.20		1.5
2.0	0.15	1.570	0.15	2.140	0.16	3.070	0.18	4.210	0.19	5.570	0.21	7.650	0.22	10.100	0.24		2.0
2.5		1.790	0.17	2.430	0.18	3.480	0.20	4.770	0.22	6.310	0.23	8.660	0.25	11.400	0.27		2.5
3.0		1.980	0.19	2.690	0.20	3.850	0.22	5.280	0.24	6.980	0.26	9.570	0.28	12.600	0.30	0.30	3.0
3.5		2.160	0.21	2.930	0.22	4.200	0.24	5.750	0.26	7.600	0.28	10.400	0.30	13.700	0.33		3.5
4.0		2.320	0.22	3.160	0.24	4.520	0.26	6.190	0.28	8.180	0.30	11.200	0.33	14.800	0.35		4.0
4.5		2.480	0.24	3.370	0.25	4.830	0.28	6.610	0.30	8.730	0.32	11.900	0.35	15.800	0.37		4.5
5.0		2.630	0.25	3.580	0.27	5.120	0.30	7.010	0.32	9.260	0.34	12.600	0.37	16.700	0.40		5.0
5.5		2.780	0.26	3.770	0.29	5.390	0.31	7.390	0.34	9.760	0.36	13.300	0.39	17.600	0.42		5.5
6.0		2.910	0.28	3.960	0.30	5.660	0.33	7.750	0.35	10.200	0.38	14.000	0.41	18.500	0.44		6.0
6.5		3.050	0.29	4.140	0.31	5.920	0.34	8.100	0.37	10.700	0.40	14.600	0.43	19.300	0.46		6.5
7.0	0.30	3.180	0.30	4.310	0.33	6.160	0.36	8.440	0.39	11.100	0.41	15.200	0.45	20.100	0.48		7.0
7.5		3.300	0.31	4.480	0.34	6.400	0.37	8.770	0.40	11.500	0.43	15.800	0.46	20.900	0.50	0.50	7.5
8.0		3.420	0.33	4.640	0.35	6.630	0.38	9.080	0.42	11.900	0.44	16.400	0.48	21.700	0.51		8.0
8.5		3.540	0.34	4.800	0.36	6.860	0.40	9.390	0.43	12.400	0.46	16.900	0.49	22.400	0.53		8.5
9.0		3.650	0.35	4.960	0.38	7.080	0.41	9.690	0.44	12.700	0.47	17.500	0.51	23.100	0.55		9.0
9.5		3.760	0.36	5.110	0.39	7.290	0.42	9.980	0.46	13.100	0.49	18.000	0.53	23.800	0.56		9.5
10.0		3.870	0.37	5.250	0.40	7.500	0.43	10.200	0.47	13.500	0.50	18.500	0.54	24.500	0.58		10.0
12.5		4.380	0.42	5.940	0.45	8.480	0.49	11.600	0.53	15.300	0.57	20.900	0.61	27.700	0.66		12.5
15.0	0.50	4.840	0.46	6.570	0.50	9.380	0.54	12.800	0.59	16.900	0.63	23.100	0.68	30.500	0.72		15.0
17.5		5.270	0.50	7.150	0.54	10.200	0.59	13.900	0.64	18.400	0.68	25.100	0.73	33.200	0.79		17.5
20.0		5.680	0.54	7.700	0.58	10.900	0.63	15.000	0.69	19.700	0.73	27.000	0.79	35.700	0.85		20.0
22.5		6.060	0.58	8.210	0.62	11.700	0.68	16.000	0.73	21.100	0.78	28.800	0.84	38.100	0.90		22.5
25.0		6.420	0.61	8.700	0.66	12.400	0.72	16.900	0.77	22.300	0.83	30.500	0.89	40.300	0.96	1.00	25.0
27.5		6.760	0.64	9.160	0.69	13.000	0.75	17.800	0.81	23.500	0.87	32.100	0.94	42.400	1.01		27.5
30.0		7.090	0.67	9.610	0.73	13.700	0.79	18.700	0.86	24.600	0.91	33.700	0.99	44.500	1.06		30.0
32.5		7.410	0.70	10.000	0.76	14.300	0.83	19.500	0.89	25.700	0.95	35.200	1.03	46.400	1.10		32.5
35.0		7.710	0.73	10.400	0.79	14.900	0.86	20.300	0.93	26.800	0.99	36.600	1.07	48.300	1.15		35.0
37.5		8.010	0.76	10.800	0.82	15.400	0.89	21.100	0.96	27.800	1.03	38.000	1.11	50.200	1.19		37.5
40.0		8.300	0.79	11.200	0.85	16.000	0.93	21.800	1.00	28.800	1.07	39.400	1.15	52.000	1.23		40.0
42.5		8.580	0.82	11.600	0.88	16.500	0.96	22.600	1.03	29.700	1.10	40.700	1.19	53.700	1.27		42.5
45.0		8.850	0.84	11.900	0.90	17.000	0.98	23.300	1.07	30.700	1.14	42.000	1.23	55.400	1.31		45.0
47.5		9.110	0.87	12.300	0.93	17.500	1.01	24.000	1.10	31.600	1.17	43.200	1.26	57.000	1.35		47.5
50.0		9.370	0.89	12.600	0.95	18.000	1.04	24.600	1.12	32.500	1.21	44.400	1.30	58.600	1.39		50.0
52.5		9.620	0.91	13.000	0.98	18.500	1.07	25.300	1.16	33.300	1.24	45.600	1.34	60.100	1.43		52.5
55.0		9.870	0.94	13.300	1.01	19.000	1.10	25.900	1.18	34.200	1.27	46.700	1.37	61.700	1.46		55.0
57.5		10.100	0.96	13.600	1.03	19.500	1.13	26.600	1.22	35.000	1.30	47.900	1.40	63.100	1.50	1.50	57.5
60.0		10.300	0.98	14.000	1.06	19.900	1.15	27.200	1.24	35.800	1.33	49.000	1.43	64.600	1.53		60.0
62.5	1.00	10.500	1.00	14.300	1.08	20.300	1.18	27.800	1.27	36.600	1.36	50.100	1.47	66.000	1.57		62.5
65.0		10.800	1.03	14.600	1.10	20.800	1.20	28.400	1.30	37.400	1.39	51.100	1.50	67.400	1.60		65.0
67.5		11.000	1.05	14.900	1.13	21.200	1.23	29.000	1.33	38.200	1.42	52.200	1.53	68.800	1.63		67.5
70.0		11.200	1.06	15.200	1.15	21.600	1.25	29.600	1.35	38.900	1.44	53.200	1.56	70.200	1.67		70.0
72.5		11.400	1.08	15.500	1.17	22.100	1.28	30.100	1.38	39.700	1.47	54.200	1.59	71.500	1.70		72.5
75.0		11.600	1.10	15.800	1.20	22.500	1.30	30.700	1.40	40.400	1.50	55.200	1.62	72.800	1.73		75.0
77.5		11.800	1.12	16.000	1.21	22.900	1.33	31.200	1.43	41.100	1.53	56.200	1.65	74.100	1.76		77.5
80.0		12.100	1.15	16.300	1.23	23.300	1.35	31.800	1.45	41.800	1.55	57.200	1.67	75.400	1.79		80.0
82.5		12.300	1.17	16.600	1.26	23.600	1.37	32.300	1.48	42.500	1.58	58.100	1.70	76.600	1.82		82.5
85.0		12.500	1.19	16.900	1.28	24.000	1.39	32.800	1.50	43.200	1.60	59.000	1.73	77.800	1.85		85.0
87.5		12.700	1.21	17.100	1.29	24.400	1.41	33.300	1.52	43.900	1.63	60.000	1.76	79.000	1.87		87.5
90.0		12.800	1.22	17.400	1.32	24.800	1.44	33.800	1.55	44.600	1.66	60.900	1.78	80.200	1.90		90.0

q_m	= mass flow rate	kg/s	
c	= velocity	m/s	
$\Delta p/l$	= pressure loss per unit length	Pa/m	

PVC-U PN10

WATER AT 75 °C

$\Delta p/l$	c	125 mm		140 mm		160 mm		180 mm		200 mm		225 mm		250 mm		c	$\Delta p/l$
		q_m	c	q_m	c	q_m	c	q_m	c	q_m	c	q_m	c	q_m	c		
92.5		13.00	1.2	17.70	1.3	25.10	1.5	34.30	1.6	45.20	1.7	61.80	1.8	81.4	1.9		92.5
95.0		13.20	1.3	17.90	1.4	25.50	1.5	34.80	1.6	45.90	1.7	62.70	1.8	82.6	2.0		95.0
97.5		13.40	1.3	18.20	1.4	25.90	1.5	35.30	1.6	46.50	1.7	63.50	1.9	83.7	2.0		97.5
100		13.60	1.3	18.40	1.4	26.20	1.5	35.80	1.6	47.10	1.7	64.40	1.9	84.9	2.0	2.0	100
120		15.00	1.4	20.30	1.5	28.90	1.7	39.50	1.8	52.00	1.9	71.00	2.1	93.5	2.2		120
140	1.5	16.30	1.5	22.10	1.7	31.40	1.8	42.90	2.0	56.40	2.1	77.00	2.3	101.0	2.4		140
160		17.50	1.7	23.70	1.8	33.70	2.0	46.00	2.1	60.60	2.2	82.70	2.4	109.0	2.6		160
180		18.70	1.8	25.30	1.9	35.90	2.1	49.00	2.2	64.50	2.4	88.00	2.6	116.0	2.8		180
200		19.80	1.9	26.70	2.0	38.00	2.2	51.80	2.4	68.20	2.5	93.10	2.7	122.0	2.9		200
220	2.0	20.80	2.0	28.10	2.1	40.00	2.3	54.50	2.5	71.70	2.7	97.90	2.9	128.0	3.0	3.0	220
240		21.80	2.1	29.50	2.2	41.90	2.4	57.10	2.6	75.10	2.8	102.00	3.0	135.0	3.2		240
260		22.70	2.2	30.70	2.3	43.70	2.5	59.60	2.7	78.40	2.9	106.00	3.1	140.0	3.3		260
280		23.70	2.3	32.00	2.4	45.50	2.6	62.00	2.8	81.50	3.0	111.00	3.3	146.0	3.5		280
300		24.50	2.3	33.20	2.5	47.20	2.7	64.30	2.9	84.50	3.1	115.00	3.4	151.0	3.6		300
320		25.40	2.4	34.30	2.6	48.80	2.8	66.50	3.0	87.50	3.2	119.00	3.5	157.0	3.7		320
340		26.20	2.5	35.50	2.7	50.40	2.9	68.70	3.1	90.30	3.4	123.00	3.6	162.0	3.8		340
360		27.00	2.6	36.50	2.8	51.90	3.0	70.80	3.2	93.10	3.5	126.00	3.7	167.0	4.0		360
380		27.80	2.6	37.60	2.8	53.40	3.1	72.80	3.3	95.70	3.6	130.00	3.8	171.0	4.1		380
400		28.60	2.7	38.60	2.9	54.90	3.2	74.80	3.4	98.40	3.7	134.00	3.9	176.0	4.2		400
420		29.40	2.8	39.70	3.0	56.30	3.3	76.80	3.5	100.00	3.7	137.00	4.0	181.0	4.3		420
440		30.10	2.9	40.60	3.1	57.70	3.3	78.70	3.6	103.00	3.8	141.00	4.1	185.0	4.4		440
460		30.80	2.9	41.60	3.1	59.10	3.4	80.50	3.7	105.00	3.9	144.00	4.2	190.0	4.5		460
480	3.0	31.50	3.0	42.60	3.2	60.50	3.5	82.40	3.8	108.00	4.0	147.00	4.3	194.0	4.6		480
500		32.20	3.1	43.50	3.3	61.80	3.6	84.10	3.8	110.00	4.1	150.00	4.4	198.0	4.7		500
520		32.90	3.1	44.40	3.4	63.10	3.7	85.90	3.9	112.00	4.2	153.00	4.5	202.0	4.8		520
540		33.50	3.2	45.30	3.4	64.30	3.7	87.60	4.0	115.00	4.3	157.00	4.6	206.0	4.9		540
560		34.20	3.3	46.20	3.5	65.60	3.8	89.30	4.1	117.00	4.3	160.00	4.7	210.0	5.0		560
580		34.80	3.3	47.00	3.6	66.80	3.9	91.00	4.2	119.00	4.4	162.00	4.7	214.0	5.1		580
600		35.50	3.4	47.90	3.6	68.00	3.9	92.60	4.2	121.00	4.5	165.00	4.8	218.0	5.2		600
620		36.10	3.4	48.70	3.7	69.20	4.0	94.20	4.3	123.00	4.6	168.00	4.9	222.0	5.3		620
640		36.70	3.5	49.50	3.7	70.30	4.1	95.80	4.4	125.00	4.6	171.00	5.0	225.0	5.3		640
660		37.30	3.5	50.30	3.8	71.50	4.1	97.30	4.4	127.00	4.7	174.00	5.1	229.0	5.4		660
680		37.90	3.6	51.10	3.9	72.60	4.2	98.90	4.5	129.00	4.8	177.00	5.2	232.0	5.5		680
700		38.50	3.7	51.90	3.9	73.70	4.3	100.00	4.6	131.00	4.9	179.00	5.2	236.0	5.6		700
720		39.00	3.7	52.70	4.0	74.80	4.3	101.00	4.6	133.00	4.9	182.00	5.3	240.0	5.7		720
740		39.60	3.8	53.50	4.0	75.90	4.4	103.00	4.7	135.00	5.0	185.00	5.4	243.0	5.8		740
760		40.20	3.8	54.20	4.1	77.00	4.5	104.00	4.8	137.00	5.1	187.00	5.5	246.0	5.8		760
780		40.70	3.9	55.00	4.2	78.00	4.5	106.00	4.8	139.00	5.2	190.00	5.6	250.0	5.9		780
800		41.30	3.9	55.70	4.2	79.00	4.6	107.00	4.9	141.00	5.2	192.00	5.6	253.0	6.0		800
820		41.80	4.0	56.40	4.3	80.10	4.6	109.00	5.0	143.00	5.3	195.00	5.7	256.0	6.1		820
840		42.30	4.0	57.10	4.3	81.10	4.7	110.00	5.0	145.00	5.4	197.00	5.8	260.0	6.2		840
860		42.90	4.1	57.80	4.4	82.10	4.8	111.00	5.1	146.00	5.4	200.00	5.9	263.0	6.2		860
880		43.40	4.1	58.50	4.4	83.10	4.8	113.00	5.2	148.00	5.5	202.00	5.9	266.0	6.3		880
900		43.90	4.2	59.20	4.5	84.10	4.9	114.00	5.2	150.00	5.6	204.00	6.0	269.0	6.4		900
920		44.40	4.2	59.90	4.5	85.00	4.9	115.00	5.3	152.00	5.6	207.00	6.1	272.0	6.5		920
940		44.90	4.3	60.60	4.6	86.00	5.0	117.00	5.4	153.00	5.7	209.00	6.1	275.0	6.5		940
960		45.40	4.3	61.30	4.6	86.90	5.0	118.00	5.4	155.00	5.8	211.00	6.2	278.0	6.6		960
980		45.90	4.4	61.90	4.7	87.90	5.1	119.00	5.4	157.00	5.8	214.00	6.3	281.0	6.7		980
1000		46.40	4.4	62.60	4.7	88.80	5.1	120.00	5.5	158.00	5.9	216.00	6.3	284.0	6.7		1000
1100		48.80	4.6	65.80	5.0	93.30	5.4	127.00	5.8	166.00	6.2	227.00	6.6	299.0	7.1		1100
1200		51.00	4.8	68.80	5.2	97.70	5.7	132.00	6.0	174.00	6.5	237.00	6.9	312.0	7.4		1200
1300		53.20	5.1	71.80	5.4	101.00	5.8	138.00	6.3	182.00	6.8	247.00	7.2	325.0	7.7		1300
1400		55.30	5.3	74.60	5.6	105.00	6.1	144.00	6.6	189.00	7.0	257.00	7.5	338.0	8.0		1400
1500		57.30	5.4	77.30	5.8	109.00	6.3	149.00	6.8	196.00	7.3	266.00	7.8	350.0	8.3		1500
1600		59.30	5.6	80.00	6.1	113.00	6.5	154.00	7.0	202.00	7.5	275.00	8.1	362.0	8.6		1600
1700		61.20	5.8	82.50	6.2	117.00	6.8	159.00	7.3	209.00	7.8	284.00	8.3	374.0	8.9		1700
1800		63.00	6.0	85.00	6.4	120.00	6.9	164.00	7.5	215.00	8.0	293.00	8.6	385.0	9.1		1800
1900		64.80	6.2	87.40	6.6	124.00	7.2	168.00	7.7	221.00	8.2	301.00	8.8	396.0	9.4		1900
2000		66.60	6.3	89.80	6.8	127.00	7.4	173.00	7.9	227.00	8.4	309.00	9.0				2000

Appendix C4.A1 : Properties of various fluids

C4.A1.1   Air and water

See Tables C4.A1.1 and C4.A1.2.

The variation of density with pressure can be obtained using a value ρ_0 from Table C4.A1.1 or the psychrometric data, and ideal gas equation, namely:

$$\rho = \rho_0 \left(\frac{p}{1.01325} \right) \qquad (4.A1.1)$$

Values of viscosity and specific thermal capacity do not vary significantly with pressure.

Although the preferred units of dynamic viscosity (η) are $kg \cdot m^{-1} \cdot s^{-1}$, the Poise still persists in some sources of data, for which the following conversion may be useful:

$$1 \text{ cP} = 0.01 \text{ Pa·s} = 10^{-2} \text{ kg·m}^{-1} \cdot s^{-1}$$

Table C4.A1.1 Some properties of water

θ / °C	ρ / kg·m^{-3}	η / 10^{-6} kg·m^{-1}·s^{-1}	ν / 10^{-6} m^2·s^{-1}	c_p / kJ·kg^{-1}·K^{-1}
0.01	999.8	1752	1.7524	4.210
4	1000.0	1551	1.5510	4.205
10	999.7	1300	1.3004	4.193
20	999.8	1002	1.0022	4.183
30	995.6	797	0.8005	4.179
40	992.2	651	0.6561	4.179
50	988.0	544	0.5506	4.182
60	983.2	463	0.4709	4.185
70	977.8	400	0.4091	4.191
80	971.8	351	0.3612	4.198
90	965.3	311	0.3222	4.201
100	958.4	279	0.2911	4.219
110	950.6	252	0.2651	4.233
120	943.4	230	0.2438	4.248
130	934.6	216	0.2258	4.27
140	925.9	195	0.2106	4.29
150	916.6	181	0.1975	4.32
160	907.4	169	0.1862	4.35
170	897.7	158	0.1760	4.38
180	886.5	149	0.1681	4.42
190	875.6	141	0.1610	4.46
200	864.3	134	0.1550	4.51

Table C4.A1.2 Some properties of air at a relative humidity of 50% and at a pressure of 1.012 bar (from Rogers and Mayhew)

θ / °C	ρ / kg·m^{-3}	η / 10^{-6} kg·m^{-1}·s^{-1}	c_p / kJ·kg^{-1}·K^{-1}
0	1.29	17.15	1.006
5	1.27	17.39	1.009
10	1.24	17.63	1.011
15	1.22	17.88	1.014
20	1.20	18.12	1.018
25	1.18	18.36	1.022
30	1.16	18.55	1.030
35	1.14	18.78	1.039
40	1.11	19.01	1.050

Similarly, although the preferred units of dynamic viscosity (ν) are m^2·s^{-1}, the Stoke still persists in some sources of data, for which the following conversion may be useful:

$$1 \text{ cSt} = 0.01 \text{ cm}^2 \cdot s^{-1} = 10^{-6} \text{ m}^2 \cdot s^{-1}$$

C4.A1.2   Water–glycol mixtures

See Tables C4.A1.3 to C4.A1.6. The primary source for this data has been provided by Shell Chemicals. For low values of temperature this is supplemented in Tables C4.A1.4 and C4.A1.5 by some sparse internet data, the original source of which is not known, and which required interpolation from Imperial values.

Table C4.A1.3 Freezing temperature of ethylene-glycol–water mixture (derived from data provided by Shell Chemicals, Rotterdam)

Freezing temperature (/ °C) for ethylene-glycol solution at stated concentration (% by mass)						
25	30	40	50	90	95	100
−10.5	−13.7	−22.5	−33.7	−29.6	−21.8	−12.8

Note: the figure in italics was obtained by extrapolation.

Table C4.A1.4 Density of ethylene-glycol–water mixture

Temp. / °C	Density, ρ (/ kg·m^{-3}), for stated concentration (% by mass)							
	0	20	30	40	50	60	80	100
60	983.2	1007.3	1019.4	1031.7	1042.3	1052.6	1071.4	1086.7
40	992.2	1017.3	1030.3	1042.5	1054.8	1065.5	1084.5	1100.0
20	999.8	1025.6	1040.4	1053.5	1066.4	1078.1	1098.6	1114.8
0	999.8	1031.8	1047.9	1063.9	1078.6	1091.1	1112.3	1129.1

	Density, ρ (/ kg·m^{-3}) for stated concentration (% by volume)							
	0	20	30	40	50	60	80	100
−20	s	s	s	*1089*	*1103*	*1116*	*1142*	s
−40	s	s	s	s	s	*1121*	*1147*	s

Note: '% by mass' values adapted from data provided by Shell. '% by volume' values derived from unreferenced data; values shown in italics are best estimates from that source.

's' denotes solid.

Table C4.A1.5 Kinematic viscosity of monoethylene-glycol–water mixture

Temp. / °C	Kinematic viscosity, ν (/ 10^{-6}·m^2·s^{-1}), for stated concentration (/ % by mass)							
	0	20	30	40	50	60	80	100
100	0.291	0.382	0.457	0.555	0.680	0.790	1.19	2.02
60	0.471	0.675	0.812	1.00	1.27	1.56	2.54	4.54
40	0.656	0.956	1.20	1.54	2.00	2.50	4.35	8.59
20	1.002	1.56	2.01	2.60	3.38	4.44	8.41	17.9

	Kinematic viscosity, ν (/ 10^{-6}·m^2·s^{-1}), for stated concentration (/ % by volume)							
	0	20	30	40	50	60	80	100
0	*1.75*	*6.0*	*8.6*	*12*	—	—		
−20	s	s	s	*16.8*	*24*	*38*	—	s

Note: '% by mass' values adapted from data provided by Shell. '% by volume' values derived from unreferenced data; values shown in italics are best estimates from that source.

's' denotes solid.

Table C4.A1.6 Specific thermal capacity of monoethylene-glycol–water mixture

Temp. / °C	Specific thermal capacity, c_p (/ kJ·kg^{-1}·K^{-1}), for stated concentration (/ % by mass)							
	0	20	30	40	50	60	80	100
20–60	4.19	3.89	3.76	3.59	3.39	3.21	2.79	2.40

	Specific thermal capacity, c_p (/ kJ·kg^{-1}·K^{-1}), for stated concentration (/ % by volume)							
	0	20	30	40	50	60	80	100
0	4.21	*3.91*	*3.72*	*3.53*	*3.32*	*3.11*	*2.72*	*2.33*

Note: '% by mass' values adapted from data provided by Shell. '% by volume' values derived from unreferenced data; values shown in italics are best estimates from that source.

C4.A1.3   Gases

See Tables C4.A1.7 to C4.A1.11

Table C4.A1.7 Some properties of oxygen gas at 1 atm. (Eckert and Drake)

θ / °C	ρ / kg·m^{-3}	η / 10^{-6} kg·m^{-1}·s^{-1}	c_p / kJ·kg^{-1}·K^{-1}
150	2.619	11.49	0.9178
200	1.956	14.85	0.9131
250	1.562	17.87	0.9157
300	1.301	20.63	0.9203
350	1.113	23.16	0.9291
400	0.975	25.54	0.9420

Table C4.A1.8 Some properties of nitrogen gas at 1 atm. (Eckert and Drake)

θ / °C	ρ / kg·m^{-3}	η / 10^{-6} kg·m^{-1}·s^{-1}	c_p / kJ·kg^{-1}·K^{-1}
100	3.481	6.862	1.0722
200	1.711	12.95	1.0429
300	1.142	17.84	1.0408
400	0.8538	21.98	1.0459

Table C4.A1.9 Some properties of carbon dioxide gas at 1 atm. (Eckert and Drake)

θ / °C	ρ / kg·m^{-3}	η / 10^{-6} kg·m^{-1}·s^{-1}	c_p / kJ·kg^{-1}·K^{-1}
220	2.4733	11.10	0.783
250	2.1667	12.59	0.804
300	1.7973	14.96	0.871
350	1.5362	17.20	0.900
400	1.3424	19.32	0.942

Table C4.A1.10 Some properties of carbon monoxide gas at 1 atm. (Eckert and Drake)

θ / °C	ρ / kg·m^{-3}	η / 10^{-6} kg·m^{-1}·s^{-1}	c_p / kJ·kg^{-1}·K^{-1}
220	2.4733	11.10	0.783
220	1.5536	13.83	1.043
250	1.3668	15.40	1.042
300	1.1387	17.84	1.042
350	0.9742	20.09	1.043
400	0.8536	22.19	1.048

Table C4.A1.11 Some properties of ammonia gas at 1 atm. (Eckert and Drake)

θ / °C	ρ / kg·m^{-3}	η / 10^{-6} kg·m^{-1}·s^{-1}	c_p / kJ·kg^{-1}·K^{-1}
220	0.3828	7.255	2.198
273	0.7929	9.353	2.177
323	0.6487	11.03	2.177
373	0.5590	12.89	2.236
423	0.4934	14.67	2.315

C4.A1.4   Fuel gases

See Table C4.A1.12.

Table C4.A1.12 Some properties of fuel gases at 1 atm. (from Eckert and Drake and HMSO)

Fuel gas	θ / K	ρ / kg·m^{-3}	η / 10^{-6} kg·m^{-1}·s^{-1}	c_p / kJ·kg^{-1}·K^{-1}
Butane	273	2.66	6.8	—
(C_4H_{10})	288	2.52	—	1.671
Methane	273	0.717	10.44	2.207
(CH_4)	288	0.680	10.80	—
	298	0.657	11.13	2.237
Propane	273	2.02	8.03	1.625
(C_3H_8)	288	1.91	—	—
	298	1.85	—	1.703

Note: values of η and c_p do not vary much with pressure; all the properties vary with temperature.

C4.A1.5   Fuel oils

See Table C4.A1.13. The viscosity of fuel oils varies considerably with temperature. Even within a single grade of oil, properties can vary within a specified band. Thus the properties of a particular oil are best obtained from the manufacturer. Some approximate values are given in Table C4.A1.13, taken from the graphs in chapter 5 of Guide C.

Table C4.A1.13 Density and kinematic viscosity of fuel oils

Fuel oil	Class	Density, ρ / kg·m^{-3} at 15 °C	Kinematic viscosity, ν (/ 10^{-6}·m^2·s^{-1}), at stated temperature (/ °C)						
			−10	0	20	40	60	80	100
Kerosene	C2	803	0.34	2.75	1.0–2.0	—	—	—	
Gas oil	D	850	11	7.8	1.5–5.5	—	—	—	
Light fuel oil	E	940	—	600	160	58	25	13.5	8.2
Medium fuel oil	F	970	—	—	850	220	75	32	20.0 max
Heavy fuel oil	G	980	—	—	3400	705	205	75	40.0 max

Appendix C4.A4 : Steam flow in pipes

C4.A4.2   Steam flow in pipes

The pressure drop due to friction in steel pipes may be calculated from:

$$\frac{Z_1 - Z_2}{l} = \frac{30.32 \, q_\mathrm{m}^{1.889}}{10^3 \, d^{5.027}} \tag{4.A4.1}$$

where Z is given by:

$$Z = p^{1.929} \tag{4.A4.2}$$

where the following units must be used: q_m (kg·s^{-1}), d (m), l (m), p (kPa (absolute)) and Z (kPa$^{1.929}$).

These equations have been developed to cover initial steam pressures of between 100 kPa and 1000 kPa and for velocities ranging from 5 m·s^{-1} to 50 m·s^{-1}. They may be used with less accuracy for conditions outside these limits.

Pre-calculated values of pressure drop are given in Guide C Appendix 4.A4, Table 4.A4.1. Values of the pressure factor Z are given in Table C4.A4.2.

The values used for density ρ and kinematic viscosity ν were obtained from the following relationships:

— $\rho = 7.83 \times 10^{-3} \, p^{0.94}$

— $\nu = 9.79 \times 10^{-4} \, p^{-0.842}$

where the following units must be used: p (kPa (absolute)), ρ (kg·m^{-3}) and ν (m^2·s^{-1}).

C4.A4.2   Flow of condensate in pipes

The pressure drop of the condensate flow may be obtained in the same way as for hot water where:

(a)   thermostatic traps, having small pressure differentials between inlet and outlet, are employed and

(b)   air and other gases are prevented from entering the condensate drain by the use of automatic vents.

If air is required to traverse the condensate main and if flash steam is produced by the pressure drops in the trap and system then the resistance is greatly increased. The pressure drop in two-phase flow is always greater than for either phase individually, the calculation for which is beyond the scope of this Guide. In the absence of definite data it is recommended that where flash steam can occur the condensate mains should be sized for three times the normal hot water discharge.

C5   Fuels and combustion

C5.5   Specification of fuels

C5.5.1   Solid fuels

C5.5.1.2   Pelletised refuse derived fuel (d-RDF)

Pelletised refuse derived fuel remains a suitable energy source for small boilers despite some problems in manufacture and market viability. Table C5.8 compares the properties of d-RDF with a typical coal used for stoker firing. The calorific value of d-RDF is about two-thirds that of coal and ash yields on combustion significantly higher. Appreciable fuel glass contents may provide low d-RDF ash fusion temperatures and possible clinker formation under adverse combustion conditions.

C5.5.1.3   Properties of wood fuels

The sustainable use of wood fuels can provide environmental benefits in terms of reduced carbon dioxide, nitrogen oxide and sulphur oxide emissions in comparison to coal. Short rotation coppice (SRC) wood fuels, based on fast growing poplar and willow species, are becoming more available in the form of dried chips.

Table C4.A4.2 Pressure factors Z for compressible flow (from equation 4.A4.2)

Pressure, p / kPa	Pressure factor, Z (/ kPa$^{1.929}$) for stated pressure, p / kPa									
	0	10	20	30	40	50	60	70	80	90
0	0	85	323	707	1230	1890	2690	3620	4690	5880
100	7210	8670	10 300	12 000	13 800	15 800	17 900	20 100	22 400	24 900
200	27 500	30 200	33 000	36 000	39 000	42 230	45 500	49 000	52 500	56 200
300	60 000	63 900	68 000	72 100	76 400	80 800	85 300	90 000	94 700	99 600
400	105 000	110 000	115 000	120 000	126 000	131 000	137 000	143 000	149 000	155 000
500	161 000	167 000	174 000	180 000	187 000	193 000	200 000	207 000	214 000	221 000
600	229 000	236 000	244 000	251 000	259 000	267 000	275 000	283 000	291 000	299 000
700	308 000	316 000	325 000	334 000	343 000	351 000	361 000	370 000	379 000	389 000
800	398 000	408 000	418 000	427 000	437 000	448 000	458 000	468 000	479 000	489 000
900	500 000	510 000	521 000	532 000	543 000	555 000	566 000	577 000	589 000	601 000
1000	612 000	—	—	—	—	—	—	—	—	—

Table C5.8 Properties of a commercial coal and d-RDF

Fuel	Moisture / %	Volatile matter / %	Ash / %	Calorific value, as fired / MJ·kg^{-1}	Bulk density / kg·m^{-3}
Coal	8.4	25.9	10.2	27.2	900
d-RDF	7.3	67.5	15.0	18.7	600

Table C5.9 Indicative composition of a chipped wood fuel

Moisture content as fired by mass / %	Ash as fired, by mass / %	Volatile matter, dry as fired, by mass / %	O_2 dry as fired, by mass / %	Gross calorific value, dry as fired / MJ·kg^{-1}
15	0.6	80	48	19.7

Wood chips are divided into grades of super, fine and coarse covering size ranges of 2 mm to 25 mm. A European classification system for wood sizes is given in CEN/TS 1496. For small boiler plant operation it is recommended that fuel moisture content does not exceed 35% (British Biogen).

Wood fuels contain high percentage volatile matter and oxygen compositions with low ash. These properties influence smoke emission and the stoichiometric air requirement respectively. Table C5.9 gives an indicative composition of a chipped wood fuel.

C5.5.2   Liquid fuels

C5.5.2.1   Petroleum oils

British Standard specifications are published for all grades of petroleum oil fuels and are accepted as the basic requirements for the UK (BS 2869). The five classes shown in Table C5.10 cover the fuels normally used in fixed appliances. Class C1 is a paraffin type fuel for use in free-standing, flueless domestic burners, and is not detailed in this section. Class C2 is a distillate fuel of the kerosene type for vapourising and small atomising burners.

Class D is a distillate grade for larger atomising burners in both domestic and industrial use, generally known as gas oil. Under the Sulphur Content of Liquid Fuels Regulations 2000 the maximum sulphur content of Class D oils should not exceed 0.1% from January 2008.

Classes E, F and G are residual or blended fuel oils for atomising burners and generally need pre-heating before combustion. These will normally require storage and handling plant with heating facilities. Under the Sulphur Content of Liquid Fuels Regulations 2000 the maximum sulphur content of Class G oils should not exceed 1% by mass unless an exemption is granted.

Commercial specifications follow the pattern shown in Table C5.11. More detailed property data and updated information may be obtained from the fuel supplier.

Viscosity

Maximum viscosities of 500×10^{-6} m^2·s^{-1} for pumping and 12 to 15×10^{-6} m^2·s^{-1} for pressure atomisation are normally used. Rotary cup atomisers employ a viscosity range of 50 to 80×10^{-6} m^2·s^{-1}.

Pour point

Pour point (Table 5.11) is a laboratory test by which the lowest temperature at which an oil will flow under carefully defined conditions is measured. In order to ensure mobility of the fuel, minimum storage temperatures are required for class E, F and G oil fuels. The distillate grades require no heating.

Heating requirements

Fuel of classes C2 and D may be stored, handled and atomised at ambient temperatures, but exposure for a long period to extreme cold should be avoided otherwise restrictions in the flow of oil from the tank may result. The appropriate temperatures for the storage and handling of fuels of classes E, F and G are given in Table C5.12.

Normally oil burners require that residual fuel oils should be presented to the burner at a viscosity between 12 and 15×10^{-6} m^2·s^{-1}. The burner manufacturer's actual requirements should be ascertained at the design stage.

Table C5.10 Properties of petroleum burner fuels (BS 2869)

Property	Class C2	Class D	Class E	Class F	Class G
Kinematic viscosity (m^2·s^{-1}) at 40 °C	1.00–2.00×10^{-6} (min–max)	1.5–5.5×10^{-6} (min–max)	—	—	—
Kinematic viscosity (m^2·s^{-1}) at 100 °C	—	—	8.2×10^{-6} (max)	20.0×10^{-6} (max)	40.0×10^{-6} (max)
Carbon residue (% mass); Ramsbottom on 10% residue	—	0.3 (max)	15.0 (max)	18.0 (max)	20.0 (max)
Minimum closed flash point (°C):					
— Abel	38	—	—	—	—
— Pensky–Martens	—	56	66	66	66
Maximum water content	—	200 mg·kg^{-1}	0.5% v/v	0.75% v/v	1.0% v/v
Maximum sediment content by mass (%)	—	0.01	0.10	0.15	0.15
Maximum ash content by mass (%)	—	0.01	0.10	0.10	0.15
Maximum sulphur content by mass (%)	0.20	0.20	3.50	3.50	3.50

Table C5.11 Properties of typical petroleum fuel oils

Property	Kerosene Class 2	Gas oil Class D	Light fuel oil Class E	Medium fuel oil Class F	Heavy fuel oil Class G
Relative density at 15 °C	0.803	0.850	0.940	0.970	0.980
Minimum closed flash point (°C)	38	60	66	66	66
Kinematic viscosity ($m^2 \cdot s^{-1}$):					
— at 40 °C	—	3.2×10^{-6}	—	—	—
— at 100 °C	—	—	8×10^{-6}	16×10^{-6}	35×10^{-6}
Freezing point (°C)	< –40	—	—	—	—
Maximum pour point (°C)	—	—	26	24	30
Maximum cloud point (°C)	—	–5 (Mar/Sep) –16 (Oct/Feb)	—	—	—
Gross calorific value ($MJ \cdot kg^{-1}$)	46.4	45.5	42.5	41.8	42.7
Net calorific value ($MJ \cdot kg^{-1}$)	43.6	42.7	40.1	39.5	40.3
Maximum sulphur content by mass (%)	0.2	0.2	3.2	3.5	3.5
Maximum water content by volume (%)	negligible	0.05	0.5	0.75	1.0
Maximum sediment content by mass (%)	—	0.01	0.10	0.15	0.15
Maximum ash content by volume (%)	—	0.01	0.05	0.07	0.10
Mean specific heat capacity, 0–100 °C ($kJ \cdot kg^{-1} \cdot K^{-1}$)	2.1	2.06	1.93	1.89	1.89

Table C5.12 Storage and handling temperatures of fuel oils (BS 799: Part 5)

Class of fuel	Minimum storage temperature / °C	Minimum handling or outflow from storage temperature / °C
E	10	10
F	25	30
G	40	50

C5.5.3 Gaseous fuels

C5.5.3.1 Liquefied petroleum gas (LPG)

Typical properties of commercial butane and commercial propane are given in Table C5.13. Limiting requirements for the properties of commercial butane and commercial propane are given in BS 4250.

Table C5.13 Typical properties of commercial butane and commercial propane

Property	Butane (C_4H_{10})	Propane (C_3H_8)
Density at 15 °C ($kg \cdot m^{-3}$)	570	500
Relative density of liquid at 15 °C	0.570–0.580	0.500–0.510
Relative density of gas compared with air at STP	1.90–2.10	1.40–1.55
Volume of gas per kg of liquid at STP (m^3)	0.41–0.43	0.53–0.54
Ratio of gas volume to liquid volume at STP	233	–274
Boiling point (°C)	0	–45
Absolute vapour pressure at stated temperature (for products of the maximum specified vapour pressure) (kPa):		
— –40.0 °C	—	140
— –17.8 °C	—	320
— 0 °C	200	560
— 37.8 °C	580	1570
— 45.0 °C	690	1810
Latent heat of vapourisation at 15 °C ($kJ \cdot kg^{-1}$)	370	357
Specific heat of liquid ($kJ \cdot kg^{-1} \cdot K^{-1}$)	2.4	2.52
Sulphur content	Negligible to 0.02% by mass	Negligible to 0.02% by mass
Limits of flammability (percentage by volume of gas in gas/air mixture)	9.0 (upper) 1.8 (lower)	10.0 (upper) 2.2 (lower)
Calorific values (dry volumetric basis) ($MJ \cdot m^{-3}$):		
— gross	122	93
— net	113	86
Calorific values (mass basis) ($MJ \cdot kg^{-1}$):		
— gross	49.5	50
— net	46	46.5
Air required for combustion (m^3 per m^3 of gas)	30	24

Note: values of density and specific volume are given at STP, being 15 °C and 101.3 kPa; similarly values of relative density are given relative to dry air at STP; the density of dry air to normalise gas density to relative density is 1.16 $m^3 \cdot kg^{-1}$.

C5.5.3.2   Natural gas

Typical analyses and properties of natural gas are given in Tables C5.14 and C5.15. Where gas volume data are given they are based on conventional reference conditions of 15 °C and 101.3 kPa.

The thermal input of an appliance (e.g. central heating boiler) for a given pressure and burner orifice is a function of the Wobbe number. This number is defined as:

$$W = \frac{h_g}{d^{0.5}} \tag{5.3}$$

where W is the Wobbe number (MJ·m^{-3}), h_g is the gross calorific value (volume basis) (MJ·m^{-3}) and d is the relative density.

Natural gases all have Wobbe numbers falling within a narrow range and all appliances are designed to operate on gas corresponding to the mean of that range.

Table C5.14 Typical volume analysis and properties of natural gas

Components and properties	Value
Components:	
— methane	92.6%
— ethane	3.6%
— propane	0.8%
— butane	0.2%
— pentane and above	0.1%
— hydrogen	—
— carbon monoxide	—
— carbon dioxide	0.1%
— nitrogen	2.6%
Properties:	
— gross calorific value (MJ·m^{-3})	38.7
— net calorific value (MJ·m^{-3})	34.9
— relative density	0.602
— Wobbe No. (dry)	49.9
— air required for combustion (m^3·per m^3 gas)	9.73

Table C5.15 Operating properties of natural gas

Property	Value
Declared calorific value	≈ 38.7 MJ·m^{-3}
Relative density	0.59–0.61
Wobbe No.	45.7–55.0 (Gas Group H)
Distribution pressure	1750–2750 Pa*

*Legal requirement: must not fall below 1250 Pa

C5.5.3.3   Landfill gas

There is significant potential for landfill gas as a fuel for direct boiler firing or in CHP applications. Gas may require cleaning and dewatering before use. The composition is approximately 60 per cent methane and 40 per cent carbon dioxide and also includes many other gases in trace concentrations. The calorific value is in the range 15–25 MJ·m^{-3} depending upon the inert gas content and the extent of raw gas conditioning.

C5.6   Combustion data

C5.6.1   Combustion air and waste gas volume

It is necessary to determine combustion air requirements and waste gas volumes for boiler plant and chimney/flue designs. Figures C5.2 to C5.6) enable the required volume under various CO_2 per cent (excess air) conditions to be read off. Percentage CO_2 values are expressed on a dry gas basis.

Note that all volumes are standardised at 15 °C, 101.3 kPa. For volumes at other temperatures the following formula may be used:

$$V_g = \frac{V(\theta_g + 273)}{288} \tag{5.4}$$

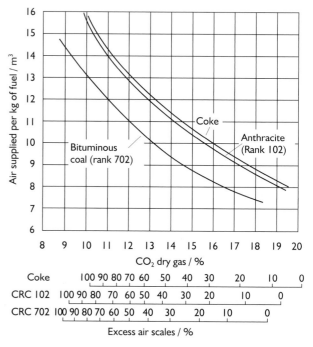

Figure C5.2 Combustion air requirements for solid fuels

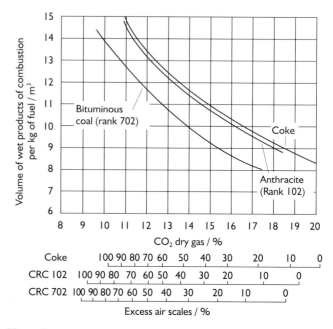

Figure C5.3 Volumes of products of combustion for solid fuels

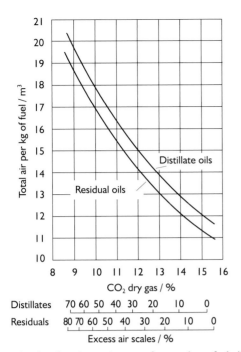

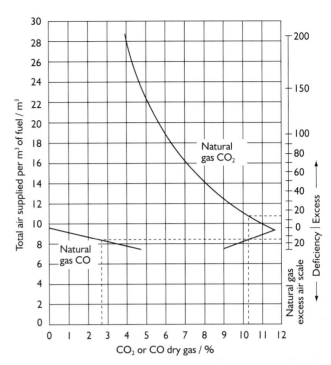

Figure C5.4 Combustion air requirements for petroleum fuel oils

Figure C5.6 Combustion air requirements for natural gas

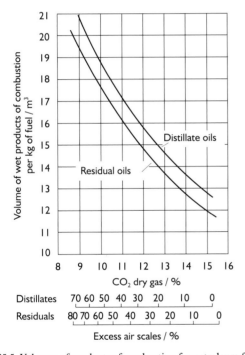

Figure C5.5 Volumes of products of combustion for petroleum fuel oils

Table C5.16 Combustion conditions

Fuel	CO_2 / %	Excess air / %	Total air volume / $m^3 \cdot kg^{-1}$	Flue gas volume / $m^3 \cdot kg^{-1}$
Solid fuels:				
— coke	13.7	50	11.7	11.9
— anthracite	12.7	50	12.3	12.7
— bituminous coal	12.3	50	10.8	11.4
Fuel oils:				
— classes C and D	11.6	30	15.4	16.3
— classes E, F and G	12.1	30	14.1	14.7

C5.6.1.2 Fuel oils

The average figures in Table C5.16 may be taken for CO_2 per cent, excess air, total air and flue gas volume requirements per kilogram of fuel with plant working under normal conditions of combustion efficiency.

Where the anticipated CO_2 per cent (excess air) varies considerably from the above averaged figures, refer to the appropriate curves on Figures C5.4 and C5.5, which are sufficiently accurate for practical design purposes.

C5.6.1.3 Gaseous fuels

With gas fired boilers the flue gas/air volumes depend on the type of boiler/burner unit installed and the design of the union between the boiler exhaust gas outlet flue and chimney.

The average figures given in Table C5.17 for natural gas have been obtained from site tests. Two types are given:

(a) boilers fitted with a naturally inspirated burner and a draught diverter

(b) boilers fitted with a forced draught burner and a direct flue connection.

where V_g is the volume at temperature θ_g (m³), θ_g is the actual air or flue gas temperature (°C) and V is the standard volume read from charts (m³).

C5.6.1.1 Solid fuels

The average figures given in Table C5.16 may be taken for CO_2 per cent, excess air, total air and gas requirements per kilogram of fuel for plant working under normal conditions of combustion efficiency.

Where the anticipated CO_2 per cent (and excess air values) varies considerably from the averaged conditions listed in Table C5.16, refer to the appropriate curves on Figures C5.2 and C5.3, which are accurate for practical design purposes.

Table C5.17 Percentage volumes of combustion products for boilers burning natural gas

Type of burner	CO_2 / %	CO / %	Flue gas temp. / °C
Natural inspirated burner and draught diverter (values measured in primary flue)	7.5–9	0.001–0.008	190–290
Forced draught burner with direct flue connection	8–11	0.001–0.006	55–320

Excess air data are given in Figure C5.6. It is important to note that it is possible to have an air deficiency when measuring CO_2 percentage alone. Since natural gas does not produce black smoke when combustion is incomplete it is necessary to measure the CO content in addition to CO_2 to determine if there is sufficient combustion air. For example, from Figure C5.6 it is seen that 10.3% CO_2 could mean either 14% excess air or 15% air deficiency; measuring the CO content will show which air value is correct.

The water dew point of natural gas exhaust gases, appropriate to typical operating conditions of forced draught condensing boilers, is approximately 55 °C.

C5.7 Stack losses

The major heat loss from combustion appliances is the heat carried away in the flue gases. Several formulae have been proposed for assessing these losses based mainly upon variations to the 'Siegert' expression. In order to simplify the assessment for practical requirements, graphs are included in this section which give the stack losses based upon the gross calorific value of the fuel. They do not include any unburned gas loss, i.e. it is assumed that there is no CO in the flue gases.

Graphs of flue gas losses for various fuels are given in Guide C section 5.7.

C6 Units, standard and mathematical data

C6.2 The International System of Units (SI)

C6.2.1 Definitions of base units

See Table C6.1.

Table C6.1 SI base units

Quantity	Name	Symbol
Length	metre	m
Mass	kilogram	kg
Time	second	s
Electric current	ampere	A
Thermodynamic temperature	kelvin	K
Luminous intensity	candela	cd
Amount of substance	mole	mol

C6.2.3 Derived units

Derived units are expressed algebraically in terms of base and/or supplementary units, see Table 6.2. Certain of these have been given special names.

Table C6.2 Examples of SI derived units expressed in terms of base units

Quantity	Name	Symbol
Area	square metre	m^2
Volume	cubic metre	m^3
Velocity	metre per second	$m·s^{-1}$
Specific volume	cubic metre per kilogram	$m^3·kg^{-1}$
Thermal conductivity	watt per metre kelvin	$W·m^{-1}·K^{-1}$
Luminance	candela per square metre	$cd·m^{-2}$

C6.2.4 Prefixes for multiples and submultiples

The magnitude of SI units may be increased or decreased by the use of named prefixes. Each prefix is allocated an internationally agreed symbol which may be added (in front) of the unit symbol. The prefixes given in Table 6.4 may be used to construct decimal multiples of units.

Table C6.4 SI prefixes

Multiplying factor	Prefix	Symbol
10^{24}	yotta	Y
10^{21}	zetta	Z
10^{18}	exa	E
10^{15}	peta	P
10^{12}	tera	T
10^{9}	giga	G
10^{6}	mega	M
10^{3}	kilo	k
10^{2}	hecto	h
$10^{1} = 10$	deca	da
$10^{-1} = 0.1$	deci	d
10^{-2}	centi	c
10^{-3}	milli	m
10^{-6}	micro	μ
10^{-9}	nano	n
10^{-12}	pico	p
10^{-15}	femto	f
10^{-18}	atto	a
10^{-21}	zepto	z

C6.5 Conversion factors

The tables of conversion factors (Table 6.8) are arranged in five columns: physical quantity, previous unit, factor, SI unit, SI symbol. To convert a quantity in previous units to the equivalent quantity in SI units, multiply by the factor. To convert a quantity in SI units to the equivalent quantity in old units, divide by the factor.

Table C6.8 Conversion factors in alphabetical subject order

Physical quantity	Previous unit	×	Factor	=	SI unit	SI symbol
Absorbed dose	rad		1×10^{-2}	E	joule/kilogram	$J \cdot kg^{-1}$
Acceleration	foot/square second		3.048×10^{-1}	E	metre/square second	$m \cdot s^{-2}$
Angle	second		4.848		microradian	μrad
	minute		2.909×10^{-1}		milliradian	mrad
	grade		1.571×10^{-2}		radian	rad
	gon		1.571×10^{-2}		radian	rad
	degree		1.745×10^{-2}		radian	rad
	right angle		1.571		radian	rad
	revolution		6.283		radian	rad
Angular velocity	revolution per minute		1.047×10^{-1}		radian/second	$rad \cdot s^{-1}$
	revolution per second		6.283		radian/second	$rad \cdot s^{-1}$
Area	square inch		6.452×10^{2}		square millimetre	mm^{2}
			6.452		square centimetre	cm^{2}
	square foot		9.290×10^{-2}		square metre	m^{2}
	square yard		8.361×10^{-1}		square metre	m^{2}
	are		1×10^{2}	E	square metre	m^{2}
	acre		4.047×10^{3}		square metre	m^{2}
	hectare		1×10^{4}	E	square metre	m^{2}
	square mile		2.590		square kilometre	km^{2}
Concentration	grain/cubic foot		2.288		gram/cubic metre	$g \cdot m^{-3}$
Conductance, electrical	mho		1	E	siemens	S
Conductance, thermal	kilocalorie/hour square metre degree Celsius		1.163	E	watt/square metre kelvin	$W \cdot m^{-2} \cdot K^{-1}$
	Btu/hour square foot degree Fahrenheit		5.678		watt/square metre kelvin	$W \cdot m^{-2} \cdot K^{-1}$
	calorie/second square centimetre degree Celsius		4.187×10^{1}		kilowatt/square metre kelvin	$kW \cdot m^{-2} \cdot K^{-1}$
Conductivity, thermal	Btu inch/hour square foot degree Fahrenheit		1.442×10^{-1}		watt/metre kelvin	$W \cdot m^{-1} \cdot K^{-1}$
	kilocalorie/hour metre degree Celsius		1.163	E	watt/metre kelvin	$W \cdot m^{-1} \cdot K^{-1}$
	Btu/hour foot degree Fahrenheit		1.731		watt/metre kelvin	$W \cdot m^{-1} \cdot K^{-1}$
	calorie/second centimetre degree Celsius		4.187×10^{2}		watt/metre kelvin	$W \cdot m^{-1} \cdot K^{-1}$
Density	pound/cubic foot		1.602×10^{1}		kilogram/cubic metre	$kg \cdot m^{-3}$
	pound/gallon		9.978×10^{1}		kilogram/cubic metre	$kg \cdot m^{-3}$
	pound/cubic inch		2.768×10^{1}		megagram/cubic metre	$Mg \cdot m^{-3}$
Diffusivity, thermal	square inch/hour		1.792×10^{-1}		square millimetre/second	$mm^{2} \cdot s^{-1}$
	square foot/hour		2.581×10^{-1}		square centimetre/second	$cm^{2} \cdot s^{-1}$
	square metre/hour		2.778		square centimetre/second	$cm^{2} \cdot s^{-1}$
Energy, work, quantity of heat	erg		1×10^{-1}	E	microjoule	μJ
	foot pound force		1.356		joule	J
	calorie★		4.187		joule	J
	metre kilogram force		9.807		joule	J
	British thermal unit		1.055		kilojoule	kJ
	frigorie†		4.186		kilojoule	kJ
	kilocalorie★		4.187		kilojoule	kJ
	horsepower hour		2.685		megajoule	MJ
	kilowatt hour		3.6	E	megajoule	MJ
	thermie†		4.186		megajoule	MJ
	therm		1.055×10^{-1}		gigajoule	GJ
Enthalpy, specific	Btu/pound		2.326	E	kilojoule/kilogram	$kJ \cdot kg^{-1}$
	kilocalorie/kilogram		4.187		kilojoule/kilogram	$kJ \cdot kg^{-1}$
Entropy	Btu/degree Rankine		1.899		kilojoule/kelvin	$kJ \cdot K^{-1}$
	kilocalorie/kelvin		4.187		kilojoule/kelvin	$kJ \cdot K^{-1}$
Entropy, specific	Btu/pound degree Rankine		4.187		kilojoule/kilogram kelvin	$kJ \cdot kg^{-1} \cdot K^{-1}$
	kilocalorie/kilogram kelvin		4.187		kilojoule/kilogram kelvin	$kJ \cdot kg^{-1} \cdot K^{-1}$
Equivalent absorbed dose	rem		1×10^{-2}	E	joule/kilogram	$J \cdot kg^{-1}$
Exposure to ionisation	roentgen		2.58×10^{-1}		millicoulomb/kilogram	$mC \cdot kg^{-1}$
Flow rate, mass	pound/hour		1.260×10^{-1}		gram/second	$g \cdot s^{-1}$
	kilogram hour		2.778×10^{-1}		gram/second	$g \cdot s^{-1}$
	pound/minute		7.560×10^{-3}		kilogram/second	$kg \cdot s^{-1}$
	kilogram/minute		1.667×10^{-2}		kilogram/second	$kg \cdot s^{-1}$

E — exact conversion factor
★ Based on the international calorie defined as 4.186 8 J
† Based on the 15°C calorie determined as 4.185 5 J

Table C6.8 Conversion factors in alphabetical subject order — *continued*

Physical quantity	Previous unit	×	Factor	=	SI unit	SI symbol
Flow rate, volume	cubic inch/minute		2.3732×10^{-4}		cubic decimetre/second	$dm^3 \cdot s^{-1}$
	litre/hour		2.778×10^{-4}		cubic decimetre/second	$dm^3 \cdot s^{-1}$
	US gallon/hour		1.052×10^{-3}		cubic decimetre/second	$dm^3 \cdot s^{-1}$
	gallon/hour		1.263×10^{-3}		cubic decimetre/second	$dm^3 \cdot s^{-1}$
	cubic foot/hour		7.866×10^{-3}		cubic decimetre/second	$dm^3 \cdot s^{-1}$
	cubic inch/second		1.639×10^{-2}		cubic decimetre/second	$dm^3 \cdot s^{-1}$
	litre/minute		1.667×10^{-2}		cubic decimetre/second	$dm^3 \cdot s^{-1}$
	US gallon/minute		6.309×10^{-2}		cubic decimetre/second	$dm^3 \cdot s^{-1}$
	gallon/minute		7.577×10^{-2}		cubic decimetre/second	$dm^3 \cdot s^{-1}$
	cubic metre/hour		2.778×10^{-1}		cubic decimetre/second	$dm^3 \cdot s^{-1}$
	cubic foot/minute		4.719×10^{-1}		cubic decimetre/second	$dm^3 \cdot s^{-1}$
	cubic metre/minute		1.667×10^{1}		cubic decimetre/second	$dm^3 \cdot s^{-1}$
	cubic foot/second		2.832×10^{-2}		cubic metre/second	$m^3 \cdot s^{-1}$
Force	dyne		1×10^{1}	E	micronewton	μN
	poundal		1.383×10^{-1}		newton	N
	pound force		4.448		newton	N
	kilogram force		9.807		newton	N
	kilopond		9.807		newton	N
Frequency	cycle/second		1	E	hertz	Hz
Heat capacity	Btu/degree Fahrenheit		1.899		kilojoule/kelvin	$kJ \cdot K^{-1}$
	kilocalorie/degree Celsius		4.187		kilojoule/kelvin	$kJ \cdot K^{-1}$
Heat capacity, specific	Btu/pound degree Fahrenheit		4.187		kilojoule/kilogram kelvin	$kJ \cdot kg^{-1} \cdot K^{-1}$
	kilocalorie/kilogram degree Celsius		4.187		kilojoule/kilogram kelvin	$kJ \cdot kg^{-1} \cdot K^{-1}$
Heat emission	Btu/hour cubic foot		1.035×10^{1}		watt/cubic metre	$W \cdot m^{-3}$
Illumination	foot candle		1.076×10^{1}		lux	lx
	lumen/square foot		1.076×10^{1}		lux	lx
Intensity of heat flow rate	kilocalorie/hour square metre		1.163	E	watt/square metre	$W \cdot m^{-2}$
	Btu/hour square foot		3.155		watt/square metre	$W \cdot m^{-2}$
	watt/square foot		1.076×10^{1}		watt/square metre	$W \cdot m^{-2}$
Latent heat	foot pound force/pound		2.989		joule/kilogram	$J \cdot kg^{-1}$
	Btu/pound		2.326	E	kilojoule/kilogram	$kJ \cdot kg^{-1}$
	kilocalorie/kilogram		4.187		kilojoule/kilogram	$kJ \cdot kg^{-1}$
Length	micron		1	E	micrometre	μm
	thou' (mil)		2.54×10^{1}	E	micrometre	μm
	inch		2.54×10^{1}	E	millimetre	mm
	foot		3.048×10^{-1}	E	metre	m
	yard		9.144×10^{-1}	E	metre	m
	mile		1.609		kilometre	km
Luminance	foot lambert		3.426		candela/square metre	$cd \cdot m^{-2}$
	candela/square inch		1.550×10^{3}		candela/square metre	$cd \cdot m^{-2}$
Luminous intensity	candle		9.810×10^{-1}		candela	cd
Magnetic field strength	oersted		7.958×10^{1}		ampere/metre	$A \cdot m^{-1}$
Magnetic flux	maxwell		1×10^{-2}	E	microweber	μWb
Magnetic flux density	gauss		1×10^{-1}	E	millitesla	mT
Mass	grain		6.480×10^{1}		milligram	mg
	ounce		2.835×10^{1}		gram	g
	pound		4.536×10^{-1}		kilogram	kg
	slug		1.459×10^{1}		kilogram	kg
	hundredweight		5.080×10^{1}		kilogram	kg
	ton (short)		9.072×10^{-1}		megagram	Mg
	tonne		1	E	megagram	Mg
	ton		1.016		megagram	Mg
Mass per unit area	pound/square foot		4.882		kilogram/square metre	$kg \cdot m^{-2}$
Mass per unit length	pound/foot		1.488		kilogram/metre	$kg \cdot m^{-1}$
	pound/inch		1.786×10^{1}		kilogram/metre	$kg \cdot m^{-1}$
Mass transfer coefficient	foot/hour		8.47×10^{-2}		millimetre/second	$mm \cdot s^{-1}$
Moisture content	grain/pound		1.428×10^{-1}		gram/kilogram	$g \cdot kg^{-1}$
	pound/pound		1	E	kilogram/kilogram	$kg.kg^{-1}$
Moisture flow rate	pound/square foot hour		1.357		gram/square metre second	$g \cdot m^{-2} \cdot s^{-1}$
	grain/square foot hour		1.94×10^{-1}		milligram/square metre second	$mg \cdot m^{-2} \cdot s^{-1}$
Moment of inertia	pound square foot		4.214×10^{-2}		kilogram square metre	$kg \cdot m^2$

E — exact conversion factor   The word 'litre' may be employed as a special name for dm^3

Table C6.8 Conversion factors in alphabetical subject order — *continued*

Physical quantity	Previous unit ×	Factor	=	SI unit	SI symbol
Moment of momentum	pound square foot/second	4.214×10^{-2}		kilogram square metre/second	$kg \cdot m^2 \cdot s^{-1}$
Momentum	pound foot/second	1.383×10^{-1}		kilogram metre/second	$kg \cdot m \cdot s^{-1}$
Permeability, vapour	grain inch/hour square foot inch of mercury (perminch)	1.45		nanogram metre/newton second	$ng \cdot m \cdot N^{-1} \cdot s^{-1}$
		1.45		nanogram/second pascal metre	$ng \cdot s^{-1} \cdot Pa^{-1} \cdot m^{-1}$
	pound foot/hour pound force	8.620		milligram metre/newton second	$mg \cdot m \cdot N^{-1} \cdot s^{-1}$
		8.620		milligram/second pascal metre	$mg \cdot s^{-1} \cdot Pa^{-1} \cdot m^{-1}$
Permeance, vapour	grain/square foot hour inch of mercury (perm)	5.72×10^1		nanogram/newton second	$ng \cdot N^{-1} \cdot s^{-1}$
	grain/square foot hour millibar	1.940		microgram/newton second	$\mu g \cdot N^{-1} \cdot s^{-1}$
	pound square inch/square foot hour pound force	1.965×10^{-1}		milligram/newton second	$mg \cdot N^{-1} \cdot s^{-1}$
	pound/hour pound force	2.834×10^1		milligram/newton second	$mg \cdot N^{-1} \cdot s^{-1}$
Power, heat flow rate	British thermal unit/hour	2.931×10^{-1}		watt	W
	kilocalorie/hour	1.163	E	watt	W
	foot pound force/second	1.356		watt	W
	calorie/second	4.187		watt	W
	metric horsepower (cheval vapeur)	7.355×10^{-1}		kilowatt	kW
	horsepower	7.457×10^{-1}		kilowatt	kW
	ton of refrigeration	3.517		kilowatt	kW
	Lloyd's ton of refrigeration	3.884		kilowatt	kW
Pressure	millimetre of water	9.807		pascal	Pa
	pound force/square foot	4.788×10^1		pascal	Pa
	millimetre of mercury	1.333×10^2		pascal	Pa
	torr	1.333×10^2		pascal	Pa
	inch of water	2.491×10^2		pascal	Pa
	foot of water	2.989		kilopascal	kPa
	inch of mercury	3.386		kilopascal	kPa
	pound force/square inch	6.895		kilopascal	kPa
	kilogram force/square centimetre	9.807×10^1		kilopascal	kPa
	bar	1×10^2	E	kilopascal	kPa
		1×10^{-1}	E	megapascal	MPa
	standard atmosphere	1.013×10^2		kilopascal	kPa
		1.013×10^{-1}		megapascal	MPa
Pressure drop per unit length	inch of water/hundred feet	8.176		pascal/metre	$Pa \cdot m^{-1}$
	foot of water/hundred feet	9.810×10^1		pascal/metre	$Pa \cdot m^{-1}$
Radioactivity	curie	3.7×10^1		nanosecond^{-1}	ns^{-1}
Resistance, thermal	square centimetre second degree Celsius/calorie	2.388×10^1		square decimetre kelvin/watt	$dm^2 \cdot K \cdot W^{-1}$
	square foot hour degree Fahrenheit/Btu	1.761×10^{-1}		square metre kelvin/watt	$m^2 \cdot K \cdot W^{-1}$
	square metre hour degree Celsius/kilocalorie	8.598×10^{-1}		square metre kelvin/watt	$m^2 \cdot K \cdot W^{-1}$
Resistivity, thermal	centimetre second degree Celsius/calorie	2.388×10^{-3}		metre kelvin/watt	$m \cdot K \cdot W^{-1}$
	foot hour degree Fahrenheit/Btu	5.778×10^{-1}		metre kelvin/watt	$m \cdot K \cdot W^{-1}$
	metre hour degree Celsius/kilocalorie	8.598×10^{-1}		metre kelvin/watt	$m \cdot K \cdot W^{-1}$
	square foot hour degree Fahrenheit/Btu inch	6.933		metre kelvin/watt	$m \cdot K \cdot W^{-1}$
Second moment of area	quartic inch	4.162×10^5		quartic decimetre	dm^4
	quartic foot	8.631×10^{-3}		quartic metre	m^4
Specific heat (volume basis)	kilocalorie/cubic metre degree Celsius	4.187		kilojoule/cubic metre kelvin	$kJ \cdot m^{-3} \cdot K^{-1}$
	Btu/cubic foot degree Fahrenheit	6.707×10^1		kilojoule/cubic metre kelvin	$kJ \cdot m^{-3} \cdot K^{-1}$
Specific volume	cubic foot/pound	6.243×10^{-2}		cubic metre/kilogram	$m^3 \cdot kg^{-1}$
Stress	pound force/square foot	4.788×10^1		pascal	Pa
	pound force/square inch	6.895		kilopascal	kPa
	ton force/square foot	1.073×10^2		kilopascal	kPa
	ton force/square inch	1.544×10^1		megapascal	MPa
Time	minute	6×10^1	E	second	s
	hour	3.6×10^3	E	second	s
	day	8.64×10^4	E	second	s

E — exact conversion factor

Table C6.8 Conversion factors in alphabetical subject order — *continued*

Physical quantity	Previous unit	×	Factor	=	SI unit	SI symbol
Torque	pound force foot		1.356		newton metre	N·m
Velocity	foot/minute		5.080×10^{-3}	E	metre/second	m·s^{-1}
	kilometre/hour		2.778×10^{-1}		metre/second	m·s^{-1}
	foot/second		3.048×10^{-1}	E	metre/second	m·s^{-1}
	mile/hour		4.470×10^{-1}		metre/second	m·s^{-1}
	knot		5.148×10^{-1}		metre/second	m·s^{-1}
Viscosity, dynamic	pound/hour foot		4.134×10^{-1}		millipascal second	mPa·s
	centipoise		1×10^{-3}	E	pascal second	Pa·s
	poise		1×10^{-1}	E	pascal second	Pa·s
	pound force second/square foot		4.788×10^{1}		pascal second	Pa·s
	pound force hour/square foot		1.724×10^{2}		kilopascal second	kPa·s
Viscosity, kinematic	stokes		1×10^{-2}	E	square decimetre/second	dm^2·s^{-1}
	square metre/hour		2.778×10^{-2}		square decimetre/second	dm^2·s^{-1}
	square inch/second		6.452		square decimetre/second	dm^2·s^{-1}
	square foot/minute		1.548×10^{-3}		square metre/second	m^2·s^{-1}
	Redwood No. 1 and No. 2 seconds		No direct conversion			
	SAE grades		No direct conversion			
Volume	cubic inch		1.639×10^{-2}		cubic decimetre	dm^3
	US pint		4.732×10^{-1}		cubic decimetre	dm^3
	pint		5.683×10^{-1}		cubic decimetre	dm^3
	litre		1	E	cubic decimetre	dm^3
	US gallon		3.785		cubic decimetre	dm^3
	gallon		4.546		cubic decimetre	dm^3
	cubic foot		2.832×10^{1}		cubic decimetre	dm^3
			2.832×10^{-2}		cubic metre	m^3
	US barrel (petroleum)		1.590×10^{-1}		cubic metre	m^3
	cubic yard		7.646×10^{-1}		cubic metre	m^3
Volumetric calorific value	kilocalorie/cubic metre		4.187		kilojoule/cubic metre	kJ·m^{-3}
	Btu/cubic foot		3.726×10^{1}		kilojoule/cubic metre	kJ·m^{-3}

E — exact conversion factor   The word 'litre' may be employed as a special name for dm^3

Table C6.9 The Beaufort scale

Beaufort number	Description of wind	Observations	Limit of wind speed / m·s^{-1}
0	Calm	Smoke rises vertically	Less than 0.5
1	Light air	Direction of wind shown by smoke drift but not by wind vanes	0.5 to 1.5
2	Light breeze	Wind felt on face; leaves rustle; ordinary vane moved by wind	1.5 to 3.0
3	Gentle breeze	Leaves and small twigs in constant motion; wind extends light flag	3 to 6
4	Moderate breeze	Raises dust and loose paper; small branches are moved	6 to 8
5	Fresh breeze	Small trees in leaf begin to sway	8 to 11
6	Strong breeze	Large branches in motion; umbrellas used with difficulty	11 to 14
7	Moderate gale	Whole trees in motion; inconvenience felt when walking into wind	14 to 17
8	Fresh gale	Twigs broken off trees; generally impedes progress	17 to 21
9	Strong gale	Slight structural damage occurs (slates and chimney pots removed from roofs)	21 to 24
10	Whole gale	Seldom experienced inland; trees uprooted; considerable structural damage occurs	24 to 28
11	Storm	Very rarely experienced; accompanied by widespread damage	28 to 32
12	Hurricane	(Yacht crews take up golf)	32 to 36

With acknowledgement to P. Heaton

Guide C: abridgements and omissions

The extracts from CIBSE Guide C included above have been abridged for reasons of space. Reference should be made to CIBSE Guide C for the complete text and tables of data. In addition, the following sections have been omitted entirely from this Handbook:

Chapter 1: Properties of humid air:
— 1.2 CIBSE psychrometric chart (–10 °C to +60 °C)
— 1.3 CIBSE psychrometric chart (10 °C to 120 °C)

Chapter 2: Properties of water and steam:
— 2.1 Introduction

Chapter 3: Heat transfer:
— 3.1 Introduction

Chapter 4: Flow of fluids in pipes and ducts:
— 4.1 Introduction
— 4.2 Notation
— Appendix 4.A2: Pipe and duct sizing
— Appendix 4.A3: Capacity (K) and complex networks
— Appendix 4.A5: Compressible flow

Chapter 5: Fuels and combustion
— 5.1 Introduction
— 5.2 Classification of fuels
— 5.3 Primary fuels
— 5.4 Secondary fuels

Chapter 6: Units, standard and mathematical data
— 6.1 Introduction
— 6.3 Quantities, units and numbers
— 6.4 Metrication in the European Union

Table C6.13 Standard values and reference values

Physical quantity	Value	Units	Physical quantity	Value	Units
Air (CIBSE reference conditions):			Planck's constant	6.626×10^{-34}	J·s
— density	1.200	kg·m^{-3}	Permeability of free space	1.257	μH·m^{-1}
— pressure	101.325	kPa			
— relative humidity	43	%	Permittivity of free space	8.854	pF·m^{-1}
— specific heat capacity	1.02	kJ·kg^{-1}·K^{-1}			
— temperature (dry bulb)	20	°C	Sound, reference level:		
			— intensity	1	pW.m^{-2}
Avogadro's number	6.02217×10^{23}	mol^{-1}	— reference power	1	pW
			— reference pressure	20	μPa
Base of natural logarithms (e)	2.71828	—			
			Sound, speed of:		
Gas constants:			— in dry air at 20 °C	343.6	m·s^{-1}
— universal	8.314	J·mol^{-1}·K^{-1}	— in water at 20 °C	1497	m·s^{-1}
— dry air	287	J·kg^{-1}·K^{-1}	— in copper	4760	m·s^{-1}
— steam	461	J·kg^{-1}·K^{-1}	— in mild steel	5960	m·s^{-1}
Gravitational acceleration	9.80665	m·s^{-2}	Stefan–Boltzmann constant	56.696	nW·m^{-2}·K^{-4}
Gravitational constant	66.7	pN·m^2·kg^{-2}	Circle, ratio of circumference to diameter (π)	3.14159	—
Light, speed of (in vacuo)	299.792	Mm·s^{-1}			

Table C6.14 Velocity pressure of wind

Velocity / m·s^{-1}	Pressure / Pa	Velocity / m·s^{-1}	Pressure / Pa
0.5	1.56×10^{-1}	10	6.25×10
1	6.25×10^{-1}	11	7.55×10
2	2.5	15	1.39×10^2
3	5.6	20	2.5×10^2
4	10	25	3.9×10^2
5	1.56×10	30	5.63×10^2
6	2.25×10	35	7.61×10^2
7	3.05×10	40	1.0×10^3
8	4.0×10	45	1.27×10^3
9	5.05×10	50	1.56×10^3

Guide F: Energy efficiency in buildings

F5 Renewables, fuels, CHP and metering

F5.2 Fuels

F5.2.1.2 Environmental emissions of fuels

Table F5.2 shows a comparison of different fuels and their relative CO_2 emissions.

F5.2.3 Gaseous fuels

The key properties of the main gaseous fuels are shown in Table F5.4.

F5.2.4 Liquid fuels

The fuels commonly used for heating are Class C2 (kerosene or burning oil), Class D (gas oil), Class E (light fuel oil), Class F (medium fuel oil) and Class G (heavy fuel oil). The key properties of these fuels are shown in Table F5.5. More detailed information can be found in section (B)1.6 (page [??]), Appendix C4.A1 (page [??]) and section C5.5 (page [??]).

Fuel oil classes E to H require heating to provide the recommended storage temperatures, which are shown in Table F5.6.

F5.4 Metering

Table F5.8 suggests input powers of plant for which it would be considered reasonable to provide sub-metering. Table F5.9 shows some of the key considerations when selecting meters.

Table F5.2 CO_2 equivalents of electricity and fuels (1998 data)

Energy source	CO_2 emission / $kg \cdot (kW \cdot h)^{-1}$
Electricity (grid):	0.43*†
Coal (typical)	0.29
Coke	0.42
Coke oven gas	0.24
Smokeless fuel	0.39
Natural gas	0.19
Petroleum (average)	0.27
Heavy fuel oil	0.26
Diesel	2.98 kg/litre
Petrol	2.54 kg/litre
Propane	1.75 kg/litre

* per kW·h delivered
† 1998 figure; this has been adopted as the official standard for carbon dioxide reporting until further notice

Table F5.4 Properties of commercial gas supplies at standard temperature and pressure

Gas	Property			
	Density relative to air	Gross calorific value / $MJ \cdot m^{-3}$	Supply/working pressure / Pa	Stoichiometric air-to-gas volume ratio
Natural gas	0.60	38.7	1750 to 2750	9.73
Commercial propane	1.45 to 1.55	93	3700	24
Commercial butane	1.9 to 2.10	122	2800	30

Table F5.5 Key properties of typical petroleum fuels

Fuel	Property				
	Density at 15 °C / $kg \cdot m^{-3}$	Kinematic viscosity at 40 °C / $mm^2 \cdot s^{-1}$	Kinematic viscosity at 100 °C / $mm^2 \cdot s^{-1}$	Gross calorific value / $MJ \cdot kg^{-1}$	Net calorific value / $MJ \cdot kg^{-1}$
Class C2	803	1.0 to 2.0	—	46.4	43.6
Class D	850	1.5 to 5.5	—	45.5	42.7
Class E	940	—	≤ 8.2	42.5	40.1
Class F	970	—	≤ 20.0	41.8	39.5
Class G	980	—	≤ 40.0	42.7	40.3

Table F5.6 Storage temperatures for fuel oils

Class	Minimum storage temperature / °C	
	Storage	Outflow
E	10	10
F	25	30
G	40	50
H	45	55

Table F5.8 Size of plant for which separate metering would be reasonable

Plant item	Rated input power / kW
Boiler installations comprising one or more boilers or CHP plant feeding a common distribution circuit	50
Chiller installations comprising one or more chiller units feeding a common distribution circuit	20
Electric humidifiers	10
Motor control centres providing power to fans and pumps	10
Final electrical distribution boards	5

Table F5.9 Key considerations when selecting meters

Service	Type of meter	Approximate installed cost	Typical accuracy	Key issues
Electricity	Single phase Three phase	£100–200 £500 upwards	±1%	Single or three phase? Will current transformers be needed?
Gas	Diaphragm Turbine	£300–700 £700–1300	±2%	Pressure drop? Will pressure and temperature compensation be needed? (May cost an extra £1000.)
Oil	—	£350–2800	±1%	Strainer needed to avoid blockages?
Water	—	£250–700	±1%	
Heat	Electromagnetic Turbine	£450–1200 £400–900	±(3 to 5)%	Electromagnetic meters are more accurate. Dirty systems can be a problem

F7 Ventilation and air conditioning

F7.2 Mechanical ventilation and air conditioning

Installing mechanical ventilation and/or air conditioning will significantly increase capital costs, running costs, environmental emissions and maintenance costs. Mechanical ventilation rates should be kept to a minimum commensurate with acceptable levels of indoor air quality. Fan capacities larger than those shown in Table F7.2 suggest over-sizing of plant.

Table F7.2 Basic fan capacity benchmarks

Building	Fan capacity / (litre·s^{-1})·m^{-3} of ventilated space)
Offices	1.4
Retail stores, halls and theatres	2.1
Restaurants	3.5

F7.2.3 Need for air conditioning

F7.2.3.2 Need for humidity control

Humidification can be a significant energy user in air conditioned offices. Typical and good practice performance indicators are shown in Table F7.4. The 'energy use indicator' (EUI) is the product of:

(*a*) the installed capacity in W·m^{-2} of treated floor area

(*b*) the annual running hours

Table F7.4 Humidification benchmarks for air conditioned offices

Parameter	Benchmark for stated office type			
	Air conditioned standard office (Type 3)		Air conditioned prestige office (Type 4)	
	Good practice	Typical	Good practice	Typical
Installed capacity (W·m^{-2})	15	20	20	25
Running hours (h/yr)	2750	3500	3000	3700
Utilisation (%)	20	25	20	25
Energy use indicator (EUI) ((kW·h)·m^{-2}/yr)	8	18	12	23

Note: factors for converting treated floor area to nett and gross are given in Table F20.2

(*c*) the average percentage utilisation of the plant expressed as a decimal fraction.

The result is then divided by 1000 to obtain the EUI in (kW·h)·m^{-2} per year.

F7.3 Efficient air conditioning systems

Table F7.5 lists the systems and indicates the capital and running costs of some options, based on gross floor area and 1992 prices.

F7.3.6 Minimising transport losses

F7.3.6.1 Fan power

Air handling is one of the largest energy users in air conditioned offices. Typical and good practice performance indicators are shown in Table F7.7.

Table F7.5 Air conditioning system costs in offices

System type	Costs			CO$_2$ emission / (kg·m^{-2}) p.a.
	Capital / (£·m^{-2})	Energy / (£·m^{-2}) p.a.	Maintenance requirement	
Centralised 'all-air' systems:				
— ventilation and heating (no air conditioning)	100	1.9	Medium	30
— constant volume (single zone)	160	3.0	Medium	50
— variable air volume (VAV)	180	2.4*	Medium to high	40†
— dual duct	210	3.4	Medium	55
Partially centralised air/water systems:				
— centralised air with reheat	200	3.1	Medium to high	50
— induction units	160	3.2	High	50
— fan coil units	170	3.2	Medium to high	50
— unitary heat pump	130	3.2	Medium to high	55
Local systems:				
— heat and local ventilation (no air conditioning)	90	1.1	Low	17
— 'through-the-wall' packages	70‡	3.5	Low	75
— split unit packages	85‡	3.5	Medium to high	75
— individual reversible heat pumps	110	3.0	Medium to high	55
— variable refrigeration flow rate	130	2.8	Medium to high	50

† System fitted with variable speed fan
‡ Excludes separate provision of heating

Note: figures are indicative only and based on gross floor area and 1992 costs; capital costs exclude related building work and cost of BMS

Table F7.7 Air handling benchmarks for air conditioned offices

Parameter	Benchmark for stated office type			
	Air conditioned standard office (Type 3)		Air conditioned prestige office (Type 4)	
	Good practice	Typical	Good practice	Typical
Air handled ((litre·s^{-1})·m^{-2})	4	4	4	4
Specific fan power (W/(litre·s^{-1}))	2	3	2	3
Running hours (h/yr)	2750	3500	3000	3700
Energy use indicator (EUI) ((kW·h)·m^{-2})/yr)	22	42	24	44

Note: factors for converting treated floor area to nett and gross are given in Table F20.2

F8   Refrigeration design

F8.2   Designing energy efficient systems

Refrigeration (including heat rejection) can be a significant energy user in air conditioned offices although it is seldom as much as that used in the pumps and fans that distribute the cooling. Typical and good practice performance indicators for conventional systems are shown in Table F8.1. The 'energy use indicator' (EUI) is defined above in section F7.2.3.2.

Oversizing refrigeration plant increases capital and running costs unnecessarily. Chiller capacities greater than those shown in Table F8.2 suggest oversizing.

F9   Lighting design

F9.1   Design objectives

F9.1.1   Illuminance and power density

F9.1.1.1   Design maintained illuminance

Table F9.1 provides some examples of standard maintained illuminance for various 'typical' tasks or interiors, a more detailed list is provided in the Society of Light and Lighting's *Code for lighting*.

F9.3   Selecting light sources

Table F9.2 provides a summary of applications, advantages and disadvantages of the main lamp types. Lamp manufacturers should be consulted for information on specific lamps.

F9.6   Energy consumption

Lighting is often the single largest end-use of electricity in buildings, accounting for over 40% of electricity costs in naturally ventilated offices. Typical and good practice performance indicators for offices are shown in Table F9.14. The energy use indicator (EUI) is defined above in section F7.2.3.2.

Table F8.1 Refrigeration (including heat rejection) benchmarks for offices

Parameter	Benchmark for stated office type					
	Naturally ventilated open plan office (Type 2)		Air conditioned standard office (Type 3)		Air conditioned prestige office (Type 4)	
	Good practice	Typical	Good practice	Typical	Good practice	Typical
Installed capacity (W·m^{-2})	5	8	90	125	100	135
Average COP	2.0	2.0	3.0	2.5	3.0	2.5
Running hours (h/yr)	1500	2000	1500	2500	2500	3000
Utilisation (%)	30	30	30	25	25	25
Energy use indicator (EUI) ((kW·h)·m^{-2})/yr)	1.1	2.4	14	31	21	41

Note: factors for converting treated floor area to nett and gross are given in Table F20.2

Table F8.2 Basic chiller plant capacity benchmarks

Building type	Chiller capacity (cooling load) / W·m^{-2}
Offices, health-care, retail stores	140
Restaurants	220
Computer suites	400

Note: Indicated capacities on equipment nameplates may not be applicable; actual cooling loads may be significantly lower than those shown in table

Table F9.1 Lighting energy targets

Application	Lamp type	CIE general colour rendering index (Ra)	Task illuminance / lux	Average installed power density / $W \cdot m^2$
Commercial and other similar applications, e.g. offices, shops and schools†	Fluorescent (triphosphor)	80–90	300 500 750	7 11 17
	Compact fluorescent	80–90	300 500 750	8 14 21
	Metal halide	60–90	300 500 750	11 18 27
Industrial and manufacturing applications	Fluorescent (triphosphor)	80–90	300 500 750 1000	6 10 14 19
	Metal halide	60–90	300 500 750 1000	7 12 17 23
	High pressure sodium	40–80	300 500 750 1000	6 11 16 21

† Values do not include energy for display lighting

Table F9.2 Energy efficient light sources

Type of source	Application	Advantages	Disadvantages
Tungsten and tungsten halogen	Display lighting only as they do not meet the requirements of Building Regulations Part L2	Cheap to buy; dimmable; instant light; excellent colour rendering	Inefficient; short life; no longer meets requirements of Building Regulations Part L2
Linear fluorescent	Can be used in ceiling mounted, surface or suspended luminaires, as part of a direct, localised or task-ambient installation	Cheap to buy; dimmable with special ballasts; instant light; energy efficient; long life (12 000–15 000 hours); good colour rendering for triphosphor types	Linear luminaires or concealed lighting must be used
Compact fluorescent	Can be used in ceiling mounted, surface or suspended luminaires, as part of a direct, localised or task-ambient installation; larger lamp wattages can be used as uplighters	Cheap to buy; instant light; energy efficient; long life (10 000 hours); good colour rendering; small sizes available	Dimming can be difficult although some dimming ballasts are now available
High pressure discharge: — metal halide	Wide range of applications, often used in an uplighter as part of a task-ambient installation. They are point sources that are very bright when viewed directly	'White' light source; energy efficient; good colour rendering; small size; relatively long life	Expensive; requires warm-up period after switch on; restrike period up to 15 mins after switch off; not dimmable; many types do not meet Ra 80 requirement; older types not colour stable
— mercury vapour	As for metal halide	Relatively cheap; long life	Poor colour rendering; average efficiency; warm-up and restrike period required
— sodium	As for metal halide	High efficiency; long life (except 'white' SON)	Poor colour rendering except 'white' SON and SON deluxe which are average; warm-up and restrike period (around 30 seconds) required

Table F9.14 Overall lighting benchmarks for offices

Parameter	Benchmark for stated office type							
	Naturally ventilated cellular office (Type 1)		Naturally ventilated open plan office (Type 2)		Air conditioned standard office (Type 3)		Air conditioned prestige office (Type 4)	
	Good practice	Typical	Good practice	Typical	Good practice	Typical	Good practice	Typical
Installed capacity (W·m^{-2})	12	15	12	18	12	20	12	20
Running hours (h/yr)	2500	2500	3000	3000	3200	3200	3500	3500
Utilisation (%)	45	60	60	70	70	85	70	85
Energy use indicator (EUI) ((kW·h)·m^{-2})/yr)	14	23	22	38	27	54	29	60

Note: factors for converting treated floor area to nett and gross are given in Guide F Table F20.2

F10 Heating and hot water design

F10.3 Controls

Figure F10.8 suggests good levels of control for wet central heating systems in small commercial and multiple residential buildings.

F10.4 Energy consumption

F10.4.1 Space heating energy consumption

Typical and good practice performance indicators for space heating in offices are shown in Table F10.10. The energy use indicator (EUI) is defined above in section F7.2.3.2.

F11 Motors and building transportation systems

F11.1 Minimising the motor load

F11.1.2 Pumps and hydraulic systems

Typical and good practice performance indicators for pumps in offices are shown in Table F11.1. The energy use indicator (EUI) is defined above in section F7.2.3.2.

GOOD < 50 kW

TIME	OPTIMUM START if intermittent occupancy AND	Controlling a single zone
	ZONES TIMED FOR OCCUPANCY (e.g. motorised valves and timeswitches)	Controlling multi-zones
TEMPERATURE	WEATHER COMPENSATOR (if constant occupancy consider night set back) AND	Controlling a single zone
	ZONE CONTROL OF SPACE TEMPERATURE (e.g. motorised valves and thermostats or TRVs)	Controlling multi-zones
BOILER	BOILER INTERLOCK to link the system controls with the boilers to ensure that they do not operate when there is no demand for heat	BOILER ENERGY CONTROL to link the system controls with the boilers to ensure that they do not operate when there is no demand for heat

GOOD > 50 kW

TIME	ZONE OPTIMUM START where appropriate, e.g. separate intermittent occupancy buildings AND	Controlling a single zone
	ZONES TIMED FOR OCCUPANCY (e.g. motorised valves and timeswitches)	Controlling multi-zones
TEMPERATURE	ZONE WEATHER COMPENSATORS e.g. separate buildings (if constant occupancy consider night set back) AND	Controlling a single zone
	ZONE CONTROL OF SPACE TEMPERATURE (e.g. motorised valves and thermostats or TRVs)	Controlling multi-zones
BOILER	BOILER INTERLOCK to link the system controls with the boilers to ensure that the boiler output matches demand, e.g. using wiring, software and/or an integrated controller AND MINIMISE STANDING LOSSES in heavyweight boilers	

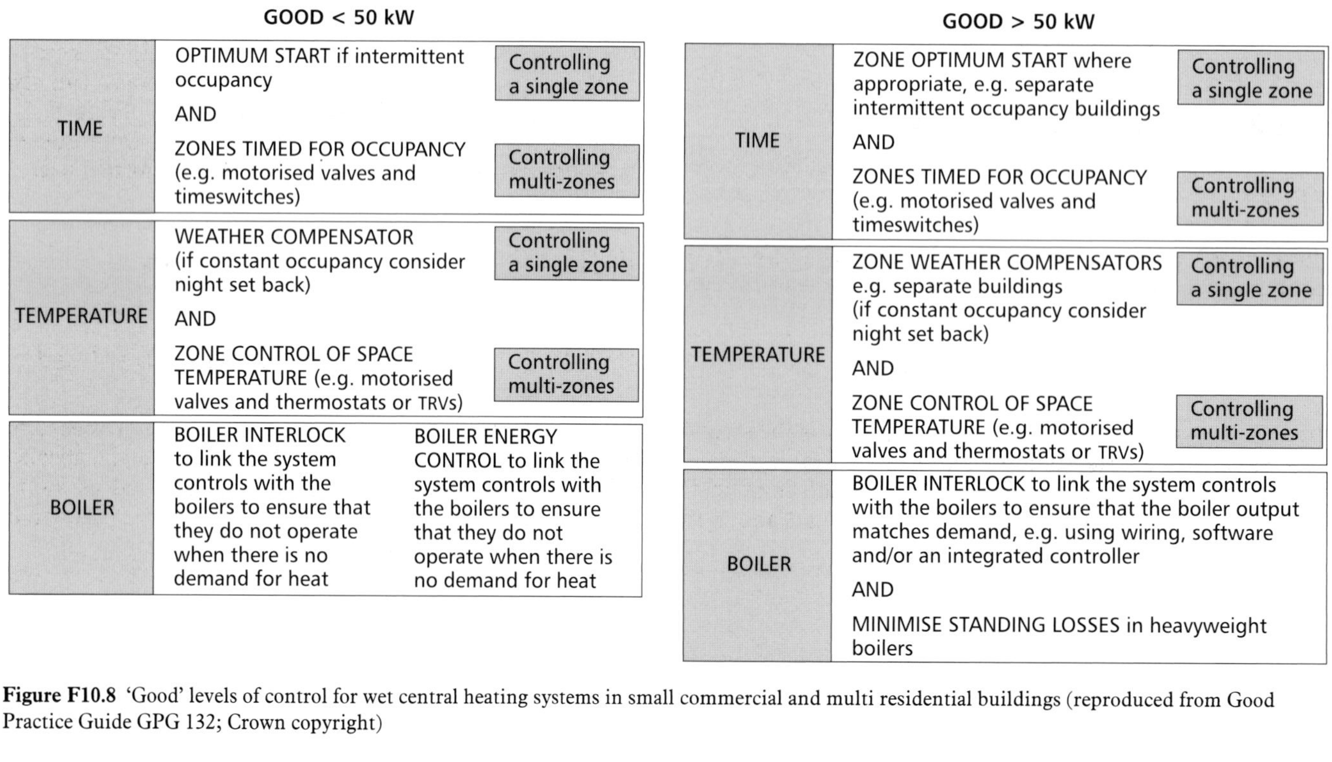

Figure F10.8 'Good' levels of control for wet central heating systems in small commercial and multi residential buildings (reproduced from Good Practice Guide GPG 132; Crown copyright)

Table F10.10 Space heating benchmarks for offices

Parameter	Benchmark for stated office type							
	Naturally ventilated cellular office (Type 1)		Naturally ventilated open plan office (Type 2)		Air conditioned standard office (Type 3)		Air conditioned prestige office (Type 4)	
	Good practice	Typical	Good practice	Typical	Good practice	Typical	Good practice	Typical
Installed capacity (W·m^{-2})	80	125	80	125	90	140	90	140
Running hours (h/yr)	2000	2500	2000	2500	2500	3000	3000	3700
Utilisation (%)	45	45	45	45	40	40	35	35
Energy use indicator (EUI) ((kW·h)·m^{-2})/yr	72	141	72	141	90	168	95	181

Note: factors for converting treated floor area to nett and gross are given in Table 20.2

Table F11.1 Energy consumption benchmarks heating and cooling pumps in offices

Parameter	Benchmark for stated office type							
	Naturally ventilated cellular office (Type 1)		Naturally ventilated open plan office (Type 2)		Air conditioned standard office (Type 3)		Air conditioned prestige office (Type 4)	
	Good practice	Typical	Good practice	Typical	Good practice	Typical	Good practice	Typical
(a) Heating pump								
Installed capacity (W·m^{-2})	0.8	1.875	1.2	2.5	1.35	2.8	1.35	2.8
Running hours (h/yr)	2000	2500	2000	2500	2500	3000	3000	3700
Energy use indicator (EUI) ((kW·h)·m^{-2})/yr	1.6	4.9	2.4	6.3	3.4	8.4	4.1	10.4
(b) Cooling pump								
Installed capacity (W·m^{-2})	—	—	—	—	1.8	3.1	2.0	3.4
Running hours (h/yr)	—	—	—	—	1500	2500	2500	3000
Energy use indicator (EUI) ((kW·h)·m^{-2})/yr	—	—	—	—	2.7	7.8	5.0	10.2

Note: factors for converting treated floor area to nett and gross are given in Table 20.2

F12 Electrical power systems and office equipment

F12.2 Office equipment

F12.2.1 Installed power loads

Table F12.1 gives typical levels of energy used by office equipment.

F12.3 Energy consumption

In naturally ventilated offices, office equipment is the second largest end use of energy after lighting. Typical and good practice performance indicators for offices are shown in Table F12.4. The energy use indicator (EUI) is defined above in section F7.2.3.2.

F12.4 Heat gains and air conditioning

Catering equipment, such as hot water boilers, kettles, refrigerators and particularly vending machines, can also contribute significantly to the heat gains. Table F12.6 indicates sensible and latent heat emissions from miscellaneous electrical cooking appliances under normal use.

F13 Checking the design

F13.1 Checking installed power loads

Rules of thumb for installed power loads that are based on gross floor area are shown in Table F13.1. In the absence of confirmed data, these figures can be used as rough indicators, but are likely to be considerably higher than those for modern, low energy designs.

Table F12.1 Typical levels of energy used by office equipment

Item	Peak rating / W	Average power consumption / W	Stand-by energy consumption obtainable / W	Typical recovery time
PC and monitor	300	120–175	30–100	Almost immediate
Personal computer	100	40	20–30	Almost immediate
Laptop computer (PIII 600 MHz)	100	20	5–10	Almost immediate
Monitors	200	80	10–15	Almost immediate
Printer: — laser — ink jet	1000 800	90–130 40–80	20–30 20–30	30 seconds 30 seconds
Modern printer/scanner/copier	50	20	8–10	30 seconds
Photocopiers	1600	120–1000	30–250	30 seconds
Fax machines	130	30–40	10	Almost immediate
Vending machines	3000	350–700	300	Can be almost immediate

Table F12.4 Office equipment benchmarks for offices

Parameter	Benchmark for stated office type							
	Naturally ventilated cellular office (Type 1)		Naturally ventilated open plan office (Type 2)		Air conditioned standard office (Type 3)		Air conditioned prestige office (Type 4)	
	Good practice	Typical	Good practice	Typical	Good practice	Typical	Good practice	Typical
Installed capacity for floor area with IT (W·m^{-2})	10	12	12	14	14	16	15	18
Running hours (h/yr)	2000	2500	2500	3000	2750	3250	3000	3500
IT area as % of treated floor area (%)	60	60	65	65	60	60	50	50
Office equipment (EUI) ((kW·h)·m^{-2}/yr)	12	18	20	27	23	31	23	32

Note: factors for converting treated floor area to nett and gross are given in Table 20.2

Table F12.6 Sensible and latent heat emissions from equipment

Item	Nameplate rating / W	In average use		
		Sensible heat gain / W	Latent heat gain / W	Total heat gain / W
Kettle	1850–2200	430–500	270–315	700–815
Hot water urn	3500	800	500	1300
Hot water urn	5000	1000	700	1700
Gas hot plate	3000–5000	1300–2300	900–1600	2200–3900
Electric hot plate	1200–1800	1200–1800	—	1200–1800
Grill (300 mm × 300 mm)	3000	600	1200	1800
Microwave	600–1400	600–1400	—	600–1400
Toaster: — two slice — four slice	2200 3000	1500 1800	400 800	1900 2600
Dishwasher	7600	1120	2460	3580
Refrigerator	125	50	—	50
Freezer	810	320	—	320

Table F13.1 Thermal and electrical installed loads

Load	Type of building (or load)	Load / W·m⁻²
Heating load	General buildings	90
	Offices	70
	Industrial	80
	Educational	100
	Retail	110
	Residential	60
Total cooling load	General office	125
	Interior zones (more than 7 m from windows)	75
	Perimeter zones (up to 6 m):	
	— 65% glazing	180
	— 60% glazing	120
	Typical buildings:	
	— retail	140
	— banks	160
	— restaurants	220
	— hotels	150–300
	— computer suites	400 (approx.)
Solar heat gains	Windows with internal blinds:	
	— south facing (June–Sept.)	250 (W·m⁻² of glass)
	— east-west facing (June–Sept.)	150 (W·m⁻² of glass)
Other heat gains (offices)	Metabolic	10
	Lighting	12
	Office machinery	15–25
Electrical services load	Lighting	10–12 (2.5 W·m⁻²/100 lux)
	Small power	15–45
	Air conditioning	60
	Passenger lifts	10
	Small computer rooms	200–400 (net area)
	Bespoke call centre	500–1000 (net area)

F19 Benchmarking, monitoring and targeting (M&T)

F19.5 M&T analysis techniques

F19.5.3 Regression analysis (degree-days)

It can be helpful to carry out an analysis to determine the relationship between energy use and the drivers that influence it. This involves developing a performance line equation (i.e. an equation of the form: $y = m\,x + c$). For example, heating consumption varies with degree-days, as shown in Figure 19.6.

Degree-day data provide a measure of the average outside temperature, which has a direct influence on heating or cooling loads. The data are normally used for analysis of monthly energy consumption. Monthly and annual figures are available from a number of sources. Tables usually show average figures for the year/month compared to an average over the last 20 years across seventeen regions in the UK. An average of the two nearest regions, or data recorded on site, may be preferred for locations remote from the central recording located in any one region. Heating degree-days are normally calculated to a base outside temperature of 15.5 °C, the base suitable for most commercial and industrial buildings.

Analysis of energy data often shows simple linear relationships, as shown in Figure 19.6. The correlation and base load data obtained from such plots can provide useful

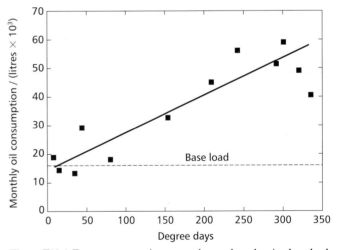

Figure F19.6 Energy consumption versus degree-days showing base load

information on energy use, particularly relating to control and standing losses. Once the performance line is established, consumption measurements can be easily compared with past results. The intersection of the sloping line and the y-axis indicates the base load consumption. This is a technique often used to identify hot water loads in buildings.

Initial attempts at producing a thermal performance line for a building sometimes reveal very poor performance or a wide scatter of points. This is invariably due either to poor adjustment, or to inadequacy or malfunction of the heating system controls. The correlation may also be poor if heating accounts for only a small proportion of the fuel requirement.

F20 Energy benchmarks

F20.1 Overall building benchmarks

Table F20.1 provides energy benchmarks for existing buildings. The figures in the shaded columns may be regarded as upper limits for new design. Conversion factors for floor areas for offices are given in Table F20.2.

Table F20.5 shows benchmarks for retail buildings. Table F20.6 shows benchmarks for various buildings based on data collected between 1992 and 1994.

The sources for benchmarks are indicated by numbers in parenthesis. A list of the sources is given at the end of this section.

Table F20.1 Fossil and electric building benchmarks (figures in shaded columns may be regarded as upper limits for new design)

Building type	Energy consumption benchmarks for existing buildings / (kW·h·m⁻²) per year (unless stated otherwise)				Basis of benchmark
	Good practice		Typical practice		
	Fossil fuels	Electricity	Fossil fuels	Electricity	
Catering:					
— fast food restaurants	480	820	670	890	Gross floor area
— public houses	1.5	0.8	3.5	1.8	(kW·h/m² per £1000 turnover)
— restaurants (with bar)	1100	650	1250	730	Gross floor area
— restaurants (in public houses)	2700	1300	3500	1500	(kW·h/cover[a])
Entertainment:					
— theatres	420	180	630	270	Gross floor area[b]
— cinemas	515	135	620	160	Gross floor area[b]
— social clubs	140	60	250	110	Gross floor area[b]
— bingo clubs	440	190	540	230	Gross floor area[b]
Education (further and higher)[c]					
— catering, bar/restaurant	182	137	257	149	Gross floor area
— catering, fast food	438	200	618	218	Gross floor area
— lecture room, arts	100	67	120	76	Gross floor area
— lecture room, science	110	113	132	129	Gross floor area
— library, air conditioned	173	292	245	404	Gross floor area
— library, naturally ventilated	115	46	161	64	Gross floor area
— residential, halls of residence	240	85	290	100	Gross floor area
— residential, self catering/flats	200	45	240	54	Gross floor area
— science laboratory	110	155	132	175	Gross floor area
Education (schools):					
— primary	113	22	164	32	Gross floor area
— secondary	108	25	144	33	Gross floor area
— secondary (with swimming pool)	142	29	187	36	Gross floor area
Hospitals:					
— teaching and specialist	339	86	411	122	Heated floor area[d]
— acute and maternity	422	74	510	108	Heated floor area[d]
— cottage	443	55	492	78	Heated floor area[d]
— long stay	401	48	518	72	Heated floor area[d]
Hotels:[e]					
— holiday	260	80	400	140	Treated floor area
— luxury	300	90	460	150	Treated floor area
— small	240	80	360	120	Treated floor area
Industrial buildings:[f][g]					
— post-1995; ≤ 5000 m²	96	—	—	—	Gross floor area
— post-1995; > 5000 m²	92	—	—	—	Gross floor area
— pre-1995; ≤ 5000 m²	107	—	—	—	Gross floor area
— pre-1995; > 5000m²	103	—	—	—	Gross floor area
Local authority buildings:					
— car park (open)	—	—	—	1	Gross parking area
— car park (enclosed)	—	—	—	15	Gross parking area
— community centres	125	22	187	33	Agent's lettable area
— day centres	203	51	349	68	Agent's lettable area
— depots	283	37	311	39	Gross internal area
— sheltered housing	314	46	432	68	Gross internal area
— residential care homes	492	59	390	75	Gross internal area
— temporary homeless units	408	48	467	71	Gross internal area
— town hall (see also offices)	138	84	205	111	Gross internal area

Table continues

Table F20.1 Fossil and electric building benchmarks — *continued*

Building type	Energy consumption benchmarks for existing buildings / $(kW \cdot h \cdot m^{-2})$ per year (unless stated otherwise)				Basis of benchmark
	Good practice		Typical practice		
	Fossil fuels	Electricity	Fossil fuels	Electricity	
Ministry of Defence (MoD) buildings:					
— aircraft hangars (heated)	220	23	—	—	Treated floor area
— junior mess	2.5	1.4	—	—	(kW·h per meal)
— motor transport facilities	317	20	—	—	Treated floor area
— multi-occupancy accommodation	225	29	—	—	Treated floor area
— officers' mess	4.4	2.5	—	—	(kW·h per meal)
— stores/warehouses (occupied)	187	34	—	—	Treated floor area
— stores/warehouses (unoccupied)	54	3	—	—	Treated floor area
— workshops	175	29	—	—	Treated floor area
Offices:[f]					
— air conditioned, standard	97	128	178	226	Treated floor area
— air conditioned, prestige	114	234	210	358	Treated floor area
— naturally ventilated, cellular	79	33	151	54	Treated floor area
— naturally ventilated, open plan	79	54	151	85	Treated floor area
Primary health care (general practitioners' surgeries and dental practices)	174?	??	270?	??	Gross floor area
Public buildings:					
— ambulance stations	350	50	460	70	Treated floor area
— churches	80	10	150	20	Treated floor area
— courts (Magistrates)[h]	125	31	194	45	Treated floor area
— courts (County)[h]	125	52	190	60	Treated floor area
— courts (Crown)[h]	139	68	182	74	Treated floor area
— courts (combined County/Crown)[h]	111	57	159	71	Treated floor area
— fire stations	385	55	540	80	Treated floor area
— libraries	113	32	210	46	Agent's lettable area
— museums and art galleries	96	57	142	70	Gross internal area
— police stations	295	45	410	60	Treated floor area
— prisons	18861	3736	22034	4460	kW·h per prisoner[i]
— prisons (high security)	18861	7071	22034	7509	kW·h per prisoner[i]
Residential and nursing homes	247	44	417	79	Gross floor area
Retail:					
— banks and building societies	63	71	98	101	Gross floor area
— banks and building societies (all electric)	—	122	—	195	Gross floor area
— book stores (all electric)	—	210	—	255	Sales floor area
— catalogue stores	37	83	69	101	Sales floor area
— catalogue stores (all electric)	—	100	—	133	Sales floor area
— clothes shops	65	234	108	287	Sales floor area
— clothes shops (all electric)	—	270	—	324	Sales floor area
— department stores	194	237	248	294	Sales floor area
— department stores (all electric)	—	209	—	259	Sales floor area
— distribution warehouses	103	53	169	67	Sales floor area
— distribution warehouses (all electric)	—	55	—	101	Sales floor area
— DIY stores	149	127	192	160	Sales floor area
— electrical goods rental	—	281	—	368	Sales floor area
— electrical goods retail	—	172	—	230	Sales floor area
— frozen food centres	—	858	—	1029	Sales floor area
— high street agencies	150	55	230	75	Sales floor area
— high street agencies (all electric)	—	90	—	160	Sales floor area
— meat butchers (all electric)	—	475	—	577	Sales floor area
— off licences (all electric)	—	475	—	562	Sales floor area
— supermarket (all electric)	—	1034	—	1155	Sales floor area
— post offices	140	45	210	70	Sales floor area
— post office (all electric)	—	80	—	140	Sales floor area
— shoe shops (all electric)	—	197	—	279	Sales floor area
— small food shops	80	400	100	500	Sales floor area

Table continues

Table F20.1 Fossil and electric building benchmarks — *continued*

Building type	Energy consumption benchmarks for existing buildings / $(kW{\cdot}h{\cdot}m^{-2})$ per year (unless stated otherwise)				Basis of benchmark
	Good practice		Typical practice		
	Fossil fuels	Electricity	Fossil fuels	Electricity	
Retail (continued):					
— supermarket	200	915	261	1026	Sales floor area
Sports and recreation:[f]					
— combined centre	264	96	598	152	Treated floor area
— dry sports centre (local)	158	64	343	105	Treated floor area
— fitness centre	201	127	449	194	Treated floor area
— ice rink	100	167	217	255	Treated floor area
— leisure pool centre	573	164	1321	258	Treated floor area
— sports ground changing facility	141	93	216	164	Treated floor area
— swimming pool (25 m) centre	573	152	1336	237	Treated floor area

Notes:

[a] 'Covers' are the number of place settings in the restaurant.

[b] Excluding balcony and circle areas.

[c] Source quotes 'low' and 'high' instead of 'Good practice' and 'Typical'.

[d] Derived from GJ/(100 m³ heated volume) assuming a floor-to-ceiling height of 2.9 m; divide by 8.06 to revert to GJ/(100 m³).

[e] For up-to-date information, see www.hospitableclimates.com

[f] Tailored benchmark is preferred; see www.actionenergy.org.uk/actionenergy/info+centre/tools for software tools.

[g] Building heating energy use only; based on building heated to 19 °C during occupied periods; 5-day, single 8-hour shift; 0.8 ACH for small buildings, 0.5 ACH for large buildings; decentralised, responsive heating system with optimised start and set-back when unoccupied; normal exposure; 2051 degree days. For any variation from these conditions, and to benchmark lighting energy, refer to www.actionenergy.org.uk for tailored benchmark.

[h] Magistrates and County courts will generally not be air conditioned and have only limited catering facilities (if any); Crown courts are more likely to be air conditioned, and to have extensive IT provision, high lighting levels, and catering facilities; combined courts are generally the largest and most modern courts and therefore relatively low specific heating use.

[i] Denominator is number of prisoners averaged over the year.

Table F20.2 Floor area conversion factors for offices

Office type	Treated % of gross	Nett % of treated	Nett % of gross
Naturally ventilated:			
— cellular	95	80	76
— open plan	95	80	76
Air conditioned:			
— standard	90	80	72
— prestige	85	80	68

F20.2 Detailed component benchmarks

F20.2.1 General component benchmarks

The component benchmarks shown in Table F20.7 are based on offices but provide useful indicators for other buildings.

F20.3 Detailed end-use benchmarks

F20.3.1 Offices

The benchmarks in Tables F20.9 and F20.10 are taken from Energy Consumption Guide ECG 19, and relate to treated floor area.

Table F20.5 Fossil and electric building benchmarks for some retail buildings

Building Type	Mixed fuel buildings					All-electric buildings			
	Electricity / kW·h·m^{-2} p.a.		Fossil fuel / kW·h·m^{-2} p.a.		Sample size	Electricity / kW·h·m^{-2} p.a.		Sample size	Floor area type
	Good	Typical	Good	Typical		Good	Typical		
Banks	71	101	63	98	1299	122	195	822	Treated
Bookstores	–	–	–	–	–	210	255	63	Sales
Butchers' shops	–	–	–	–	–	475	577	194	Sales
Catalogue stores	83	101	37	69	296	100	133	101	Sales
Clothes shops	234	287	65	108	38	270	324	1957	Sales
Department stores	237	294	194	248	221	209	259	182	Sales
Distribution warehouses	53	67	103	169	77	55	101	9	Treated
DIY stores	127	160	149	192	94	—	—	—	—
Electrical goods:									
— rental	—	—	—	—	—	281	368	577	Sales
— retail	—	—	—	—	—	172	230	298	Sales
Frozen food centres	—	—	—	—	—	858	1029	601	Sales
Off-licenses	—	—	—	—	—	475	562	131	Sales
Shoe shops	—	—	—	—	—	197	279	411	Sales
Supermarkets	915	1026	200	261	352	1034	1155	207	Sales

Note: the results from small samples, e.g. less than 50 buildings, may be unrepresentative of the whole sector

Table F20.6 Fossil and electric building benchmarks for various types of building

Building type	Mixed fuel buildings					All-electric buildings			
	Electricity / kW·h·m^{-2} p.a.		Fossil fuel / kW·h·m^{-2} p.a.		Sample size	Electricity / kW·h·m^{-2} p.a.		Sample size	Floor area type
	Good	Typical	Good	Typical		Good	Typical		
Banks	70	95	74	105	835	97	144	623	Gross
Bingo halls	117	128	203	261	29	—	—	—	Gross
Cinemas	64	81	203	261	56	—	—	—	Gross
Department stores:									
— general	238	294	199	248	221	237	371	29	Sales
— specialist	225	269	219	319	863	333	447	204	Sales
Dry cleaners	197	247	622	828	26	350	400	14	Gross
Fast food outlets	818	889	480	669	48	—	—	—	Sales
Frozen food centres	—	—	—	—	—	858	1031	602	Sales
Further education	35	49	146	216	49	—	—	—	Gross
Night clubs	106	292	50	89	13	247	297	11	Gross
Offices (multi-tenanted)	25	53	131	181	57	—	—	—	Gross
Post offices (main)	45	69	142	214	323	80	142	56	Gross
Shops/stores:									
— butchers' shops	—	—	—	—	—	475	578	195	Sales
— 'DIY' shops	128	160	151	192	94	—	—	—	Sales
— electrical goods (rental)	—	—	—	—	—	281	367	585	Sales
— electrical goods (retail)	—	—	—	—	—	172	231	299	Sales
— fashion shops	—	—	—	—	—	303	350	150	Sales
— non-food stores	224	258	82	127	59	238	307	1352	Sales
Warehouses:									
— distribution	53	67	114	175	71	—	—	—	Gross
— refrigerated	125	142	56	83	38	—	—	—	Gross

Note: the results from small samples, e.g. less than 50 buildings, may be unrepresentative of the whole sector

Table F20.7 General component benchmarks

Component	Good practice	Typical practice	Units
Fan efficiency	1.0–2.0	1.5–3.0	$W/(litre·s^{-1})$
Heating pump installed capacity	0.8–1.35	1.9–2.8	W/m^2 TFA
Cooling pump installed capacity	1.8–2.0	3.1–3.4	W/m^2 TFA
Humidification installed capacity	15–20	20–25	W/m^2 TFA
Lighting installed capacity	12	15–20	W/m^2 TFA
Lighting efficiency	3	3.75–5	(W/m^2)/100 lux
Office equipment installed capacity	10–15	12–18	W/m^2 TFA

Note: TFA = treated floor area

Table F20.9 Offices: system and building energy benchmarks

System	Delivered energy for stated office types / $(kW·h·m^{-2})$ per year							
	Type 1		Type 2		Type 3		Type 4	
	Good practice	Typical	Good practice	Typical	Good practice	Typical	Good practice	Typical
Gas/oil heating and hot water	79	151	79	151	97	178	107	201
Catering gas	0	0	0	0	0	0	7	9
Cooling	0	0	1	2	14	31	21	41
Fans, pumps and controls	2	6	4	8	30	60	36	67
Humidification	0	0	0	0	8	18	12	23
Lighting	14	23	22	38	27	54	29	60
Office equipment	12	18	20	27	23	31	23	32
Catering electricity	2	3	3	5	5	6	13	15
Other electricity	3	4	4	5	7	8	13	15
Computer room	0	0	0	0	14	18	87	105
Total gas or oil	79	151	79	151	97	178	114	210
Total electricity	33	54	54	85	128	226	234	358

Note: Type 1: cellular naturally ventilated; Type 2: open plan naturally ventilated; Type 3: 'standard' air conditioned; Type 4: 'prestige' air conditioned

Table F20.10 Offices: component benchmarks

System	Benchmark value for stated office type							
	Type 1		Type 2		Type 3		Type 4	
	Good practice	Typical	Good practice	Typical	Good practice	Typical	Good practice	Typical
Lighting:								
— installed loading ($W·m^{-2}$ floor area)	12	15	12	18	12	20	12	20
— full load hours/year (h)	1125	1500	1800	2100	2240	2720	2450	2975
— system hours/year (h)	2500	2500	3000	3000	3200	3200	3500	3500
— utilisation (%)	45	60	60	70	70	85	70	85
Fans (only):								
— consumption (kW·h per year	0	0	0	0	22	42	24	44
— full load ($W·m^{-2}$ floor area)	0	0	0	0	8	12	8	12
— full load hours/year (h)	0	0	0	0	2750	3500	3000	3700
Desk equipment:								
— load ($W·m^{-2}$ floor area (local))	10	12	12	14	14	16	15	18
— percentage floor area (%)	60	60	65	65	60	60	50	50
— load (W/m^2 floor area (building))	6.0	7.2	7.8	9.1	8.4	9.6	7.5	9.0
— operating hours/year (h)	2000	2500	2500	3000	2750	3250	3000	3500

Guide F: abridgements and omissions

The extracts from CIBSE Guide F included above have been abridged for reasons of space. Reference should be made to CIBSE Guide F for the complete text and tables of data. In addition, the following sections have been omitted entirely from this Handbook:

Guide G: Public health engineering

G2   Water services and utilities

G2.2   Water sources

G2.2.1   General

Information concerning the properties of any particular water supply may be obtained from the relevant water supply company, details of which can be obtained from *Who's who in the water industry*, published annually by Water UK (http://www.water.org.uk).

G2.3   Water supply company supplies

G2.3.1   General

Mains laid for the distribution of water from one district to another, and for the distribution of water within a district, are installed by the water supply company. Supplies must be provided by statute for domestic purposes, in both domestic and non-domestic buildings, or by agreement for industrial uses.

Ensuring compliance with the Water Supply (Water Fittings) Regulations 1999, hereafter referred to as the Water Regulations, is the responsibility of the building or premises owner or occupier.

The design of water services must be arranged to prevent the possibility of backflow (or back-siphonage) from any terminal outlet, cistern, or sanitary appliance.

G2.3.2   Mains connections

Connections to a trunk or secondary main are normally only carried out by the water supply company. It is not normal practice to allow a service pipe to be connected to a trunk main. Connections to secondary mains may be made under pressure to connect pipes of 50 mm diameter and below, whereas for larger pipes a shutdown of the main is required.

G2.3.3   Mains pressures

G2.3.3.1   *General*

Subject to the detailed requirements of the Water Act 1989, it is the responsibility of the water supply company to provide water for domestic purposes and fire hydrants 'at such a pressure as will cause the water to reach the top-most storey of every building within the undertaker's area'.

G2.3.3.2   *Mains pressure fluctuations*

Pressure fluctuations in mains will occur during periods of heavy demand, particularly in built-up areas. Night time and daytime pressures can vary considerably, this being one reason for providing storage. The water supply company can record the pressure fluctuations over a 24-hour period, for a charge.

G2.3.5.2   *Water meters*

See Figure G2.1. Surface boxes to underground meters should be readily accessible to enable the meter to be read, and the stop valves to be operated. A meter to non-domestic premises may be installed on request with a valved branch prior to the meter to enable an unmetered supply to be taken through for fire protection installations (e.g. hose reels, fire hydrants and sprinkler systems).

G2.4   Hot and cold water services

G2.4.1   Introduction

Water services should be designed and installed in accordance with the recommendations of BS 6700, the Water Regulations, relevant statutory regulations, byelaws, other relevant British Standards and manufacturers' recommendations. The Water Regulations are interpreted in the Water Regulations Advisory Scheme Water Regulations Guide which provides assistance in applying the regulations.

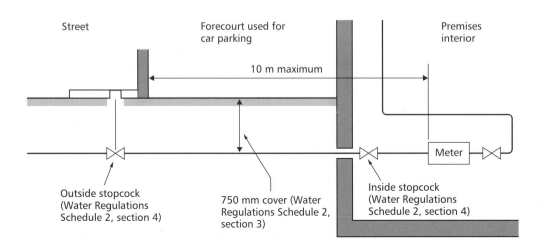

Figure G2.1 Preferred meter position inside premises

G2.4.2 Boosted water systems

Detailed guidance on boosted water systems is given in Guide G section 2.4.2.

G2.4.3 Cold water storage

G2.4.3.1 General

When designing the water storage for domestic, commercial and industrial accommodation the unit rates recommended for a number of fittings are listed in Table G2.2. Note that these figures are for congested use, and those listed in Table G2.3 are more typical.

Table G2.2 Recommended water storage rates for various fittings

Fitting	Storage / litres per 24 hours
Shower	140–230
Bath	900
WC	180
Basin	90
Sink	90–180
Urinal	110

Table G2.3 Recommended minimum storage of cold water for hot and cold water services

Type of building/occupation	Minimum storage
Hostel	90 litres/bed space
Hotel	135 litres/bed space†
Office premises: — with canteen facilities — without canteen facilities	45 litres/employee 40 litres/employee
Restaurant	7 litres/meal
Day school: — nursery — primary — secondary — technical	15 litres/pupil 15 litres/pupil 20 litres/pupil 20 litres/pupil
Boarding school	90 litres/pupil
Children's home or residential nursery	135 litres/bed space
Nurse's home	120 litres/bed space
Nursing or convalescent home	135 litres/bed space

† There will be significantly greater demand in a luxury hotel than in a budget hotel.

G2.4.5 Provision of sanitary fittings

G2.4.5.1 General

Numbers of sanitary fittings should be provided as set out in BS 6465: Part 1.

Further information on provision of sanitary fittings in healthcare premises is given in Guide G section 2.4.5, which refers to Health Technical Memorandum HTM 2027.

G2.4.6 Overflows and warning pipes

The arrangement of water storage facilities including overflows and warning pipes must comply with the Water Supply (Water Fittings) Regulations.

Every overflow and warning pipe termination should be highly visible and should not discharge to another cistern.

Every cistern below 1000 litres should be fitted with a warning pipe only, while every cistern or tank with a capacity of 1000 litres or more should be fitted with both an overflow pipe and a warning pipe or other approved device.

G2.4.7 Hot water systems

G2.4.7.1 Storage

The domestic hot water storage and heat source capacities should be calculated in accordance with BS 6700. The storage water temperature should not exceed 65 °C.

The hot water storage capacity should be related to the design consumption rate and the recovery rate. In domestic dwellings the storage capacity should normally be based on 45 litres per occupant, and 200 litres for off-peak electric installations. (Refer to BS 6700 for further guidance.)

The typical hot water system for a dwelling with a natural gas, solid fuel, or oil-fired boiler comprises a separate hot water storage vessel which is heated indirectly by a heat exchanger within the vessel. A pump or gravity feed is used to drive the primary hot water from boiler to exchanger. Often the boiler will also provide space heating and therefore the specified output greatly exceeds that required for hot water services.

G2.4.7.2 Statutory requirements and codes of practice

The Education (School Premises) Regulations 1999 require a hot water temperature not greater than 43.5 °C for baths and showers only, but in practice water is generally provided at all points of use at 43.5 °C. This can be achieved by storing the water at high temperatures and mixing it at the outlet.

Both the Factories Act 1961 and the Offices, Shops and Railway Premises Act 1963 include a requirement for hot water but no particular temperature or quantity to be stored is stated. The mandatory requirements of these Acts are monitored by the Health and Safety Executive under the Health and Safety at Work Act etc. 1974.

Table G2.10 (from the Institute of Plumbing and Heating Engineering's *Plumbing engineering services design guide*) and BS 6700 provide guidance for calculating storage quantities.

G2.4.7.3 Unvented hot water storage systems

The Water Regulations give requirements and guidance, as appropriate, for the installation of unvented hot water storage systems. Details of the design, installation, testing

Table G2.10 Daily hot water demands (adapted from Institute of Plumbing and Heating Engineering's *Plumbing engineering services design guide*)

Type of building	Daily demand / (l/person)	Storage per 24-h demand / l	Recovery period / h
Colleges and schools:			
— boarding	115	23	2.0
— day	15	4.5	2.0
Dwelling houses:			
— economic, local authority	115	115	4.0
— medium, privately owned	115	45	2.0
— luxury, privately owned	136	45	2.0
Flats:			
— economic, local authority	68	23	4.0
— medium, privately owned	115	32	2.0
— luxury, privately owned	136	32	2.0
Factories	15	4.5	2.0
Hospitals†:			
— general	136	27	1.0
— infectious	225	45	1.0
— infirmaries	68	23	1.5
— infirmaries with laundry	90	27	1.0
— maternity	225	32	2.0
— mental	90	23	2.0
— nursing staff accommodation	136	45	2.0
Hostels	115	32	2.0
Hotels:			
— 5 star rating	136	45	1.0
— 2 star rating	114	36	1.5
Offices	14	4.5	2.0
Sports pavilions	40	40	1.0
Restaurants (per meal)	—	6	2.0

Notes:

† For hospital design refer to HTM2027.

The storage capacity can be reduced by using semi-instantaneous and instantaneous hot water boilers and generators.

and maintenance of such systems are specified in BS 6700 and BS 7206.

The installation works must be carried out competent persons to comply with the Building Regulations 2000, Part G3.

See Guide G section 2.4.7.3 for further information.

G2.4.7.4   Commercial premises hot water consumption

Measured quantities of hot water consumption should not stand alone as a sizing guide. The rate at which these amounts are drawn off must also be considered. This is achieved by relating the patterns of consumption in each day to the size of plant required. Using a mathematical model the optimum size of boiler and storage can be matched to each demand pattern. See Figure G2.8 (from Institute of Plumbing and Heating Engineering's *Plumbing engineering services design guide*) for an example of a demand pattern histogram. Typical examples of daily demand are shown in Figure G2.9 and these indicate the large differences in the way hot water is used in various establishments. Guide G section 2.4.7.4 provides further information.

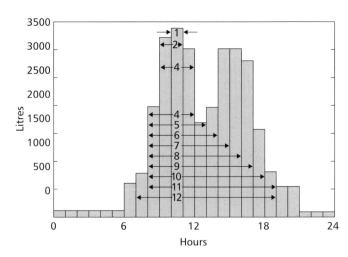

Figure G2.8 Example of demand pattern histogram (from Institute of Plumbing and Heating Engineering's *Plumbing engineering services design guide*)

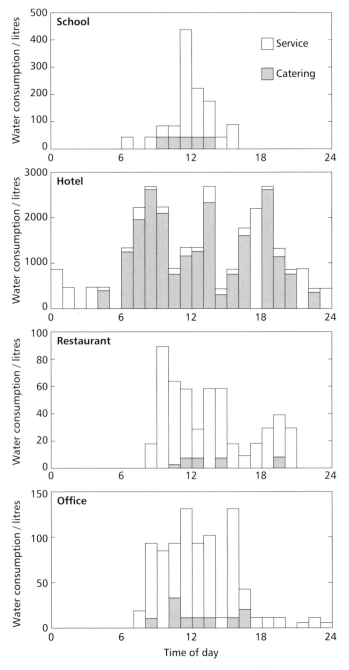

Figure G2.9 Examples of daily demand patterns for commercial premises

G2.5 Legionnaires' disease

Many types of bacteria, most of them quite harmless to people, can multiply prolifically in 'clean' water. This is neither a new observation nor should it cause any general concern. However, in recent years, hot and cold water supply systems have been implicated in outbreaks of Legionnaires' disease.

Although Legionnaires' disease can be associated with the cooling towers of air conditioning systems, evidence from the UK and overseas indicates that hot and cold water service systems can also be a source of infection. This subject is covered in detail in Guide G section 6: *Water treatment*.

The following are thought favourable to significant colonisation and should be avoided:

(*a*) dirt, scale, rust, algae, organic particulates and sludge in cisterns and calorifiers

(*b*) storage and/or distribution temperatures in the range 20–45 °C,

(*c*) large volumes of static water or small ratios of water use to system volume.

Legionella pneumophila does not survive in constant temperatures of 60 °C and above. Guidance on minimising the risk of Legionnaires' disease is given in CIBSE TM13, Health Technical Memorandum HTM 2040 and HSE Approved Code of Practice L8.

Disinfection procedures should be followed in accordance with Guide G section 6.3.5.

G2.7 Plant sizing

G2.7.1 Commercial premises

Sizing of hot water heating plant is based essentially on the load anticipated for both hot water use and system heat losses and storage recovery period. These are in turn affected by the storage and delivery temperatures.

In some systems, heat losses are small, with most of the input energy delivered at the point of use. Others may lose up to 90% of input energy in heat losses. In general, well designed systems should have low heat losses.

G2.7.2 System design

Information on the likely consumption of hot water for various purposes within different building types is given in Table G2.11.

At an early stage it must be judged whether or not the particular building is likely to have a below or above average rate of consumption in terms of both average demand and peak demand. The consequences and possible risks (e.g. legionellosis) of occasional short term failure to provide water at the required temperature must also be assessed. System recovery time must also be considered.

The most appropriate delivery temperatures for the hot water, and whether a unique temperature is suitable for all

Table G2.11 Measured daily hot water consumption in various types of commercial buildings

Building type		Total / (l/person)	Service / (l/person)	Catering	
				/ (l/meal)	Percentage of total / %
Schools and colleges	Max.	13	7	18	85
	Ave.	6	3	6	53
Hotels and hostels	Max.	464	303	62	70
	Ave.	137	80	14	28
Restaurants	Max.	17	10	73	95
	Ave.	7	3	8 (4)†	60
Offices	Max.	26	10	33	87
	Ave.	8	3	10	48
Large shops	Max.	25	6	45	91
	Ave.	10	4	8	57

† 4 l/meal is the average consumption in restaurants without large bar facilities.

Note: normalised assuming 65 °C storage and 10 °C cold feed temps.

delivery points should be taken into account. Energy efficiency (including consideration of system losses) and health and safety aspects are also relevant.

Following selection of several system designs from those available, the designer should calculate, for each option, both the capital and likely running costs. For each option the following points should be clarified:

(*a*) the recovery time

(*b*) the capital cost

(*c*) the total likely running costs and how sensitive these are to actual hot water demand

(*d*) the likelihood of failure to provide service owing to abnormal loading

(*e*) implications for siting of plant, wash rooms etc., and any savings that could be made by alterations in building layout.

Annex C of BS 6700 gives details on the calculation of storage capacity.

G2.7.3 Plant sizing curves

For smaller installations the methods given in Annex C of BS 6700 should be adopted but for larger systems the plant sizing curves given in Guide G section 2.7.3 may be more appropriate. Figure G2.16 for offices (services) is included here as an example.

G2.8 Hospital hot water storage and consumption

For detailed information on hospital hot water storage and consumption, and water supply system design, see Guide G section 2.8.

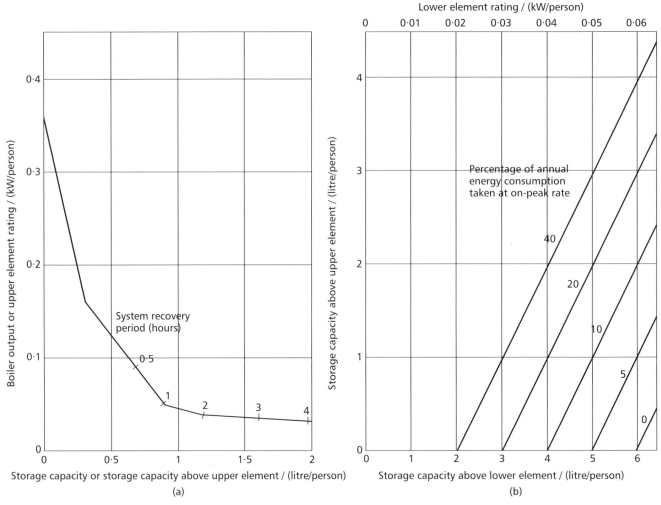

Figure G2.16 Plant sizing guide for offices — service; use for offices with between 110 and 660 persons/day

G2.9   Water supply system design

G2.9.2   Simultaneous demands

It is common today to use a computer simulation program for estimating pipe sizes.

Where manual calculations are to be carried out it is recommended that the method set out in Annex D of BS 6700 should be followed.

G3   Sanitary accommodation, pipework and drainage

G3.3   Assessment of sanitary accommodation

3.3.1   General

BS 6465: Part 1: 1994: *Code of practice for the scale of provision, selection and installation of sanitary appliances*, covers the provision of sanitary accommodation in various building types for England and Wales. Note that the Workplace Regulations also contain requirements for sanitary accommodation.

Note that provision should be made for use by disabled persons. The Building Regulations also require relevant premises to be reasonably provided with sanitary accommodation suitable for people with disabilities. It is normally necessary to consult the relevant local disabled access group to satisfy the requirements of the local building control officer.

Tables 3.1–3.8 in Guide G list the minimum recommendations for the number of water closets (WCs), urinals and baths for dwellings; offices and shops; factories; concert halls, theatres and public entertainment buildings; cinemas; restaurants and canteens; public houses; swimming pools. The tables for dwellings, and offices/shops are included here as Tables G3.1 and G3.2.

G3.4   Foul water drainage

Foul water is the waste from sanitary conveniences and other sanitary appliances, and also water which has been used for cooking or washing.

G3.4.3   Assessment of flows

The assessment of rates of discharge to waste systems and drains is a function of the appliances connected to the system, the distribution system into which the appliances connected, and the frequency of use. The rate of flow and duration of discharge from each appliance are measurable.

Table G3.1 Recommended number of water closets (wcs), urinals and baths for dwellings

Type of dwelling	Number of people	Recommended number of wcs, urinals and baths
Bungalows and flats	1–5	1 wc and 1 bath
	>5	2 wcs and 1 bath
Houses and maisonettes	1–4	1 wc and 1 bath
	>4	2 wcs and 1 bath
Small flats for the elderly	1–2	1 wc and 1 bath
Residential homes for the elderly	For every 4 people	1 wc and 2 wcs for all non-residential staff
	For every 15 people	1 bath

Table G3.2 Recommended number of water closets (wcs), urinals and baths for offices and shops

Gender	Number of people	Recommended number of wcs and urinals
Males (where no urinals provided)	1–15	1 wc
	16–30	2 wcs
	31–50	3 wcs
	51–75	4 wcs
	76–100	5 wcs
	>100	5 wcs and 1 wc for every additional 25 people or fewer
Males (where urinals provided)	1–20	1 wc
	21–45	2 wcs
	46–75	3 wcs
	76–100	4 wcs
	>100	4 wcs and 1 wc for every additional 25 people or fewer (1 in 4 of the additional appliances may be urinals)
	1–15	1 urinal stall or 600 mm space
	16–30	2 urinal stalls
	31–50	3 urinal stalls
	51–75	4 urinal stalls
	76–100	5 urinal stalls
	>100	5 urinal stalls and 1 stall for every additional 25 people or fewer
Females	1–15	1 wc
	16–30	2 wcs
	31–50	3 wcs
	51–75	4 wcs
	76–100	5 wcs
	>100	5 wcs and 1 wc for every additional 25 people or fewer

However, the simultaneous discharge of appliances can only be predicted by statistical means, based upon the likely usage pattern and level of occupation.

Designers should note that although the principle of the theory of probability is the same for both filling and emptying sanitary appliances, the rates of filling and discharge differ. The demand units used in the calculation for simultaneous demand and the demand units used in the design of water services and drainage are not interchangeable.

The calculation process and tables of discharge data are given in Guide G section 3.4.3.

G3.5 Surface water drainage

Surface water is the water that affects a building or its surround as a result of rainfall.

G3.5.1 Above-ground drainage

The drainage system should comprise the minimum pipework necessary to carry surface water away from a building and its surround quickly, quietly and with no risk to health.

Discharge from a surface water system must not be connected to a foul water system unless the sewerage system outside the site has been specifically designed to accept surface as well as foul water. Where this is the case, it is important to keep the surface and foul water systems separate up to the point of connection to the public sewer.

The design for the provision of storm water drainage depends on an assessment of the likely worst case condition for the intensity of rainfall on the site and buildings.

BS EN 752 provides the basis for assessment criteria for the design of surface water drainage based upon the likely frequency of flooding using historical data for worst case scenarios. However, climate change has resulted in wetter winters and periods of drought interspersed with very high intensity precipitation. It is therefore recommended that the practice of using the 20-year worst case be increased to the 50-year worse case. Local meteorological data should be used but for the UK the rate of 75 mm·h^{-1} can be used as a general rule for areas up to 200 hectares and storms of not more than 15 minutes at that intensity. These data should be used for external drainage systems only. Roof areas must always be drained in accordance with the appropriate data in BS EN 12056-3.

G3.5.5 Rainwater downpipes

The discharge from a rainwater outlet is normally accommodated in a vertical downpipe. The capacity of a vertical discharge pipe is very much greater than that for the inlet from the gutter, and as a general rule, the downpipe can be two-thirds of the diameter of the inlet. For half-round gutters, the sizes can be as set out in Table E3 from BRE Digest 107.

G3.6 Below-ground drainage systems

G3.6.3 Drainage calculations

Before commencing the calculations for the below-ground system it is advisable to prepare a standard form for recording the calculations. This enables the designer to check the calculations and provide the necessary data submission record for Building Regulations approval. A standard layout is given in Table E3 in BRE Digest 107.

To simplify the procedure for drainage calculations, Hydraulics Research (Wallingford) Limited has prepared a series of charts and tables based on the Colebrook-White formula. Values are recommended for the discharge rate, hydraulic gradient, pipe diameter and mean velocity for different values of the roughness coefficient, k. Graphs for 60% and full bore flow for two different surface roughness coefficients are shown in Figures G3.2 and G3.4.

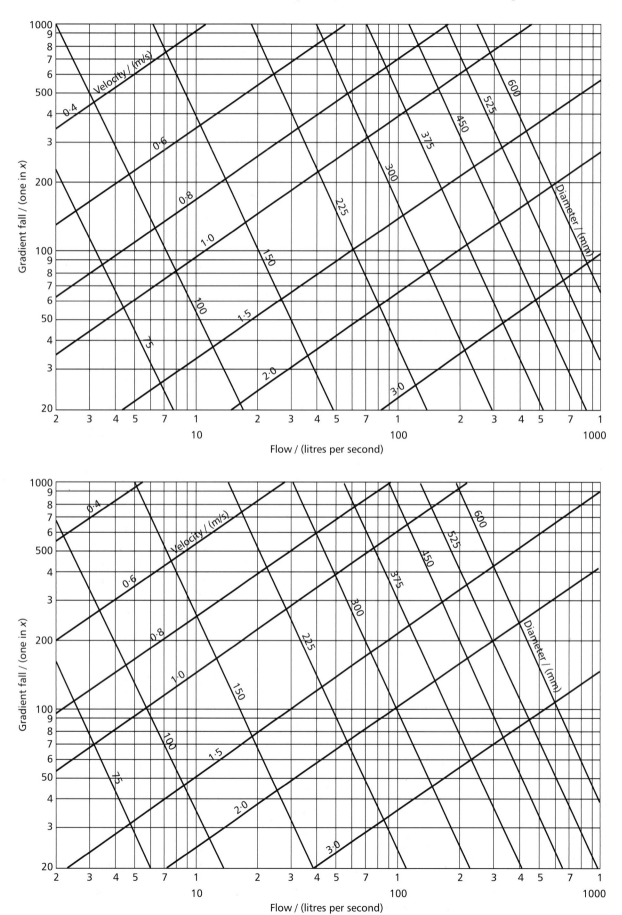

Figure G3.2 Sewage flow in pipes ($k_s = 0.15$ mm) (top: 60% flow; bottom: full bore flow)

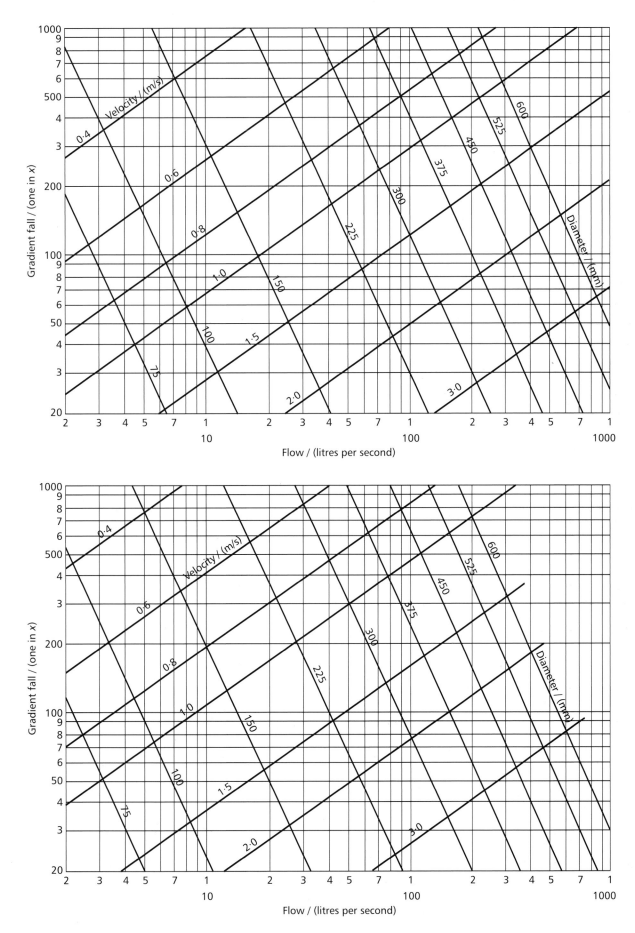

Figure G3.4 Sewage flow in pipes (k_s = 0.60 mm) (top: 60% flow; bottom: full bore flow)

G4   Waste management systems

G4.2   Solid waste disposal

G4.2.1   Introduction

Where refuse is to be collected by a local authority or independent contractor then these organisations should be contacted prior to commencing any design for storage and collection facilities etc.

The key steps in the design process are:

(a)   assessment of quantities and composition of the waste

(b)   consideration of appropriate legislation

(c)   consultation with the relevant authorities

(d)   undertake detailed design.

Important issues to consider in the design are as follows:

(a)   access

(b)   storage, collection and separation

(c)   transport

(d)   equipment:

—   containers

—   chutes

—   pneumatic systems

—   waterborne systems

(e)   incineration

(f)   volume reduction:

—   compactors

—   shredders

—   crushers

—   balers

(g)   hazardous and liquid wastes

(h)   health, safety and environmental considerations

(i)   capital and running costs.

G4.2.3   Assessing quantities and composition of solid waste

G4.2.3.1   General

Estimates for quantities of solid waste generated from various types of buildings can be obtained by reference to BS 5906 which gives 12 ± 1.2 kg per week at a bulk density of 133 ± 13.3 kg/m^3 per domestic dwelling. Tables G4.1 to G4.4 provide estimates for quantities and compositions of differing types of commercial waste.

Further information including street cleaning and grass cutting is provided in Guide G section 4.2.3.

G4.2.4   Regulations

The four principal regulations relating to solid waste in buildings are as follows:

—   Public Health Act 1936: this sets out the powers and duties of the local authorities for carrying out this function, and also enables the local authority to make bye-laws relating to collection of waste

—   Building Regulations 2000: Part H4: Solid Waste Storage (for Scotland see Building Standards (Scotland) Regulations 1990 (as amended), for Northern Ireland see Building Regulations (Northern Ireland) 2000)

—   Control of Pollution Act 1974 Section 13, sub-section 7

—   Health and Safety at Work etc. Act 1974.

Table G4.1 Typical bulk and composition of commercial waste

	Typical bulk density / kg·m^{-3}	Composition of waste / (% by mass)				
		Multiple retail outlets	Depart-ment stores	Super-markets	Hotels	Offices
Folded newspaper, packed or baled cardboard; loosely crumpled paper, office stationery; wastepaper (loose in sacks)	500	81	65	50	8	80
Mixed general refuse, similar to domestic (no solid fuel residues)	150	13	31	40	55	16
Separated food waste, uncompacted vegetable waste or well compacted, moist pig swill	200	4	2	—	33	4
Salvaged bones and fat	600	2	2	10	—	—
Empty bottles	300	—	—	—	4	—

Table G4.2 Typical waste output per week

Type of building	Waste output per week / kg
Multiple stores (per m^2 of sales area for a six-day week)	1.0
Departmental stores (per m^2 of sales area for a six-day week)	0.54
Supermarkets† (per m^2 of sales area for a six-day week)	
— small	1.8
— large	5.8
Hotels (per head (staff and residents) for a seven-day week)	3.0
Offices (per employee for a five-day week)	1.68

† Supermarkets can be placed in one of two categories, depending on their output of refuse: small stores with a small output and large stores in prime shopping areas.

Table G4.3 Typical waste output per dwelling

Waste output	1969	1979	1980	1981*
Output (kg/week)	12.8	11.1	11.2	11.0
Density (kg·m^{-3})	143.0	141.02	146.7	141.0
Volume (m^3/week)	0.09	0.08	0.08	0.08

* Estimated

Table G4.4 Typical waste volumes for various types of commercial premises

Building type	Assessed density† / kg·m^{-3}	Volume of waste produced in stated period
Multiple store	110	0.009 m^3/m^2 of sales area (6-day week)
Department store	115	0.005 m^3/m^2 of sales area (6-day week)
Supermarkets:		
— small	128	0.014 m^3/m^2 of sales area (6-day week)
— large	128	0.0455 m^3/m^2 of sales area (6-day week)
Hotels	175	0.017 m^3/head (7-day week)
Offices	58.5	0.0285 m^3/employee (5-day week)

† If a sample analysis indicates any considerable variation from the density assessed above, then volumetric output will vary accordingly

G4.2.7 Equipment

G4.2.7.1 General

Table G4.13 summarises equipment for a range of applications.

Further information on chute, pneumatic and waterborne systems, incineration and compaction is given in Guide G sections 4.2.7–4.2.9.

Table G4.13 General recommendations for solid waste disposal

Application	Recommendation
Housing	If using Palladin containers allow one Palladin per 10 housing units
	If using 1100-litre containers allow one 1100-litre container per 10 housing units
	Or use a static compactor and containers
Offices	Use a static compactor and containers
Hotels	For main guest waste use static compactor and containers
	For kitchen and restaurant waste use catering compactors
Shopping centres	Use multiple located static compactor and containers plus wheeled 1100-litre containers
Supermarkets	Use static compactor and containers
Department stores	Use static compactor and containers
Restaurants	Use catering compactors
Industrial units	Use closed skips or compactor and containers

G5 Corrosion and corrosion protection

G5.1 Introduction

G5.1.1 General

A wide variety of materials, both metallic and non-metallic are used for building services. All these materials, under certain environmental conditions, can break down prematurely impairing the function of a component or system.

To select the most appropriate material, it is necessary to understand the likely conditions, both environmental and functional, which have to be accommodated. In addition to the operational conditions, account must also be taken of manufacturing, installation, idle and vandal situations.

System performance must also be protected. Deterioration of a system can result from the internal build-up of corrosion products blocking flow paths or deposition causing further attack elsewhere in the system. In an inadequately protected system, scale can also change heat transfer characteristics eventually resulting in, for example, the fracture of boiler sections due to overheating. Micro-biological growths need to be controlled as they also lead to blockages and can result in corrosive attack on some metals.

Chapter 5 of Guide G provides detailed information on corrosion and corrosion protection, including:

— factors affecting corrosion

— bimetallic effects

— contact with other materials

— gases

— assessment of corrosive environment

— prevention of corrosion

— chemical cleaning and passivation

— 'mothballed' protection

Figure G5.1 and Tables G5.1, G5.2 and G5.3 provide relevant information.

G6 Water treatment

G6.1 Introduction

G6.1.1 General

Water treatments are designed to remove, reduce or inactivate specific impurities in order to provide a product suitable for a particular purpose. Water for public supply is treated to a standard which ensures that it is suitable and safe for drinking and other domestic purposes; it is not necessarily suitable for specialist or industrial processes. Where the water quality for any given purpose has to meet specific requirements to ensure optimum process operation or performance, it must be re-treated on-site.

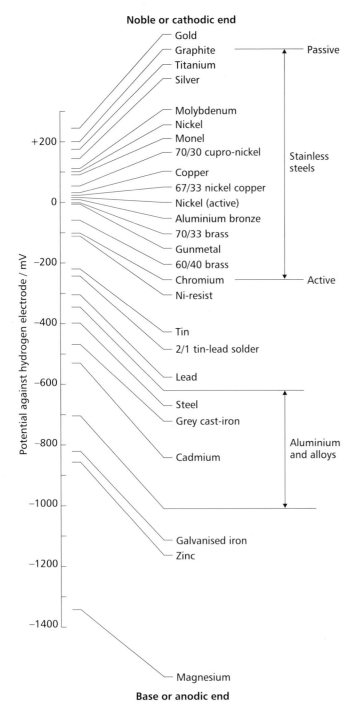

Figure G5.1 Galvanic series for common metals and alloys when in contact with natural waters

The choice of treatment will depend on the quality of the water available and the requirements of the particular application for which it is required. Adequate monitoring, both manual and automatic, is essential to ensure the continued effectiveness of the water treatment process.

Further information on the water cycle and sources, water quality and general principles of potable water treatment is provided in Guide G chapter 6.

G6.3.4 Inorganics removal or reduction

G6.3.4.1 Water hardness and softening

Water hardness is caused by the presence of dissolved calcium and magnesium salts. It is generally classified as 'temporary' or 'permanent' according to whether or not the hardness salts can be removed by boiling. In most natural waters a proportion of the 'total hardness' will be temporary and will be precipitated as calcium carbonate, slowly on heating above 60 °C, and rapidly on boiling.

Table G6.1 shows the generally accepted classification of waters according to their total hardness.

Table G6.1 Water hardness classification (taken from *The examination of water and water supplies*)

Hardness	A	B	C
Very soft	<5	<50	<3.5
Moderately soft	5–10	50–100	3.5–7
Slightly hard	10–15	100–150	7–10.5
Moderately hard	15–20	150–200	10.5–14
Hard	20–30	200–300	14–21
Very hard	>30	>300	>21

Key:
A = parts per 100 000 as $CaCO_3$ or French degrees
B = parts per million as $CaCO_3$ or mg·litre^{-1}
C = degrees Clark or English degrees

G6.3.5 Disinfection

G6.3.5.1 General

Disinfection is the process by which pathogenic micro-organisms are inactivated and the water rendered safe for human consumption and industrial processes. Disinfection does not sterilise the water; indeed acceptable numbers of harmless bacteria, indicated by the colony counts incubated at 22 and 37 °C, are allowed to remain. The production and distribution of a completely sterile public water supply is not feasible, nor is it necessary.

Each stage of the water treatment process usually contributes towards an improvement in microbiological quality. Thus there may be instances (particularly if the raw water source is good, e.g. underground), where the final water, prior to disinfection, is sometimes of sufficiently good microbiological quality to make the final disinfection stage appear unnecessary. In practice however, very few waters are of guaranteed acceptable microbiological safety at this stage. Continuous and 'instantaneous' microbiological monitoring is not yet feasible and until such systems are developed and proven, final disinfection must always be regarded as the ultimate safeguard. The process must never be omitted or allowed to fail.

G6.6 Contamination of water

Water is readily contaminated unless suitable precautions are taken to prevent it. Even relatively insoluble materials will leach from pipes, tanks and fittings producing contamination in themselves, and often providing nutrients to support the growth and multiplication of micro-organisms.

Microbiological contamination of water can be derived from the regrowth of the harmless bacteria surviving the disinfection process or more serious infections by bacteria, viruses or parasites entering the system at vulnerable points. Back-siphonage, cross connections, broken mains

Table G5.1 Methods of corrosion monitoring and their characteristics

Technique	Time for individual measurement	Type of information	Speed of response to change	Relation to plant	Possible environments	Type of corrosion measured	Ease of interpretation
Electrical resistance	Instantaneous	Integrated	Fast	Probe	Electrolyte	General	Normally easy
Polarisation resistance	Instantaneous	Corrosion state and indirect indication of rate	Fast	Probe or plant in general	Electrolyte	General or localised	Normally relatively easy but needs knowledge of corrosion. May need expert
Galvanic measurements (zero-resistance ammeter)	Instantaneous	Corrosion state and indication of galvanic effects	Fast	Probe or occasionally plant in general	Electrolyte	General or in favourable conditions localised	Normally relatively easy but needs knowledge of corrosion
Analytical methods	Normally fairly fast	Corrosion state, total corrosion in system, item corroding	Normally fairly fast	Plant in general	Any	General	Relatively easy but needs knowledge of plant
Acoustic emission	Instantaneous	Crack propagation, cavitation and leak detection	Fast	Plant in general	Any	Cracking, cavitation and penetrated components	Normally easy
Thermography	Relatively fast	Distribution of attack	Poor	Localised on plant	Any; must be warm or sub-ambient	Localised	Easy
Optical aids (closed circuit TV, light tubes etc.)	Fast when access is available, otherwise slow	Distribution of attack	Poor	Localised on plant	Any	Localised	Easy
Visual, with aid of gauges	Slow; requires entry on shutdown	Distribution of attack, indication of rate	Poor	Accessible surfaces	Any	General or localised	Easy
Corrosion coupons	Long duration of exposure	Average corrosion rate and form	Poor	Probe	Any	General or localised	Easy
Ultrasonics	Fairly fast	Remaining thickness or presence of cracks	Fairly poor	Localised on plant	Any	General or localised	Easy; detection of cracks or pits requires experienced operator
Hydrogen probe	Fast or instantaneous	Total corrosion	Fairly poor	Localised on plant or probe	Non oxidising electrolyte or hot gases	General	Easy
Sentinel holes	Slow	'Go/no go' on remaining thickness	Poor	Localised on plant	Any; gas or vapour preferred	General	Easy
Radiography	Relatively slow	Distribution of corrosion	Poor	Localised on plant	Any	Pitting, possibly cracking	Easy

and open tanks are the most common causes of serious microbiological contamination.

The use of inappropriate materials, often exacerbated by poor design and/or maintenance is the major cause of excessive microbial regrowth and corrosion. Corrosion products contaminate the water with soluble and particulate metal salts, giving rise to discoloration, staining and blockages. Failures of pipes, tanks and fittings will eventually occur if the process is allowed to continue unchecked.

Table G5.2 Recommended maximum water velocities at different temperatures for copper pipes

Type of pipe	Maximum velocity (/ m·s⁻¹) at stated water temperature (/ °C)			
	10	50	70	90
Pipe that can be replaced	4.0	3.0	2.5	2.0
Pipe that cannot be replaced	2.0	1.5	1.3	1.0
Short connections (e.g. to taps)	16.0	12.0	10.0	8.0

Table G5.3 Guide to solvent applicability and compatibility with construction materials

Material	Solvent											
	Hydrochloric acid	Hydrochloric acid + ammonium bifluoride	Acetic acid	Formic acid	Phosphoric acid	Sulphamic acid	Sulphuric acid	Nitric acid	Ammoniated citric acid pH 3.5	Trisodium phosphate	Organic solvents	Caustic solutions
Inorganic deposits:												
— calcium carbonate and magnesium hydroxide	●	●	●	●		●		●				
— calcium and magnesium phosphates	●	●	●	●		●		●				
— calcium sulphate										●		●
— silica and silicates		●										
— iron oxides	●	●		●	●	●	●	●	●	●		●
— copper oxides	●	●		●			●	●	●			
— zinc oxides and salts	●	●		●			●	●				
— sulphides	●	●					●					
Deposits containing organics and organic deposits:												
— light greases and mineral oils										●	●	●
— mineral oils										●	●	
— animal and vegetable oils											●	
— carbonaceous deposits										●	●	
Construction materials:												
— mild steel	○	○	○	○	○	○	○		○	○	○	○
— cast iron	49 °C†	49 °C†	49 °C†	49 °C†	49 °C†	49 °C†	49 °C†		○	○	○	○
— low alloy steel	○	○	○	○	○	○	○		○	○	○	○
— stainless steel, martensitic	60 °C†	60 °C†	60 °C†	60 °C†	60 °C†	60 °C†	60 °C†	○	○		○	
— stainless steel, austenitic			○	○	○	○	○	○	○		○	
— copper	○	○	○	○	○	○	○	¶	○	○	○	○
— copper alloys	○	○	○	○	○	○	○	¶	○	○	○	○
— cupro-nickels	○	○	○	○	○	○	○	¶	○	○	○	○
— nickel alloys	○	○	○	○	○	○	○		○	○	○	○
— zinc (galvanising)			‡							○	○	
— aluminium			66 °C†			66 °C†				○	○	
Other materials												
— enamels												
— glass												
— silica ware												
— some plastics												

Key:
● Solvent may be used on indicated deposit
○ Solvent may be used on indicated material at all temperatures
† Maximum cleaning temperature
‡ Limited attack
¶ Rapid dip only

Excessive microbial growth within a system can lead to complete de-oxygenation of the water, resulting in foul odours and eventual blockage with microbiological slimes. The colonisation of water cooling towers by the bacterium *Legionella pneumophila* is a classic example of regrowth in a recirculating system.

Further information on the general principles of water distribution, point-of-use treatments, contamination and industrial uses is provided in Guide G chapter 6.

G7 Swimming pools

G7.1 Introduction

The main source of information is the Pool Water Treatment Advisory Group (PWTAG) publication *Swimming Pool Water Treatment and Quality Standards*. In addition, moves to develop a common European standard are progressing.

The PWTAG publication provides improved data and information in respect of the requirements for leisure pool complexes, more compact equipment designs, available options for disinfection and an increase in the intensity of use of facilities. In 1999 the Health and Safety Commission and Sport England published updated guidance as HSG 179: *Managing Health and Safety in Swimming Pools*. The requirements of the Construction (Design and Management) Regulations also mean that options which minimise the hazards associated with the handling and use of chemicals need to be a primary consideration.

There is public concern as to the personal health risks that can be associated with the use of pools, the sea and rivers for bathing. The public are now much more informed and have a greater perception as to what constitutes acceptable water quality. The design and performance of the water treatment system is therefore fundamental to the financial viability of a facility.

G7.2 Objectives

G7.2.1 Design considerations

Swimming and bathing pools vary considerably in size, shape and in the intensity and pattern of use. The design and operational management brief should be considered by all the relevant professionals and no aspect should be determined in isolation. The choice of water treatment system is dependent on a variety of factors, including:

(*a*) the nature of the incoming water supply

(*b*) the size and shape of the pool and variety of features to be incorporated in the scheme

(*c*) the anticipated bathing loads and pattern of use

(*d*) the finances available.

The type of system selected also has implications for the design of pool hall air handling and heat recovery equipment and on operating costs.

7.2.2 Water treatment system

The objective of a pool water treatment system is to provide a hygienic, safe, comfortable and aesthetically pleasing environment for bathing. This needs to be achieved irrespective of the loading within the pre-determined parameters.

The water treatment system should be capable of:

(*a*) providing clear, colourless and bright water by removing suspended and colloidal matter

(*b*) removing organic matter, which may provide a source of food for bacteria and cause a cloudy, dull appearance to the water

(*c*) destroying and removing bacteria and ensuring that the water is bactericidal

(*d*) maintaining the pH of the water at an optimum for disinfection and bather comfort

(*e*) maintaining the water at a comfortable temperature for bathers.

The primary functions of the system are to filter, disinfect, and heat the recirculating pool water so as to achieve these objectives.

G7.3 Filtration design

G7.3.1 System volume flow (turnover times)

The accepted method of establishing system volume flow has been to estimate the turnover time required for the particular pool arrangement under consideration. The pool water volume in m^3 divided by the turnover time in hours equates to the system flow in $m^3 \cdot h^{-1}$.

Typical turnover times are shown in Table G7.1 and they are based on the assumption that the greater the intensity of use and/or proportion of shallow water then the faster the turnover time required.

Table G7.1 Recommended pool water turnover times

Pool type	Turnover time / h
Leisure water bubble	<0.33
Flume splash	0.5
Leisure waters <0.5 m deep	0.5
Leisure waters 0.5–1.0 m deep	0.5–1.0
Leisure waters 1.0–1.5 m deep	1.0–2.0
Leisure waters >1.5 m deep	2.0–2.5
Teaching/learner	0.5–1.5
Leisure (overall)	1.0–1.5
Conventional pool up to 25 m long with >1.0 at shallow end:	
— municipal	2.5–3.0
— school	2.5–3.0
— hotel	2.5–3.0
— club/private (heavy use)	2.5–3.0
— club/private (light use)	4.0
Training/competition	3.0–4.5
Diving (>2.0 m deep)	4.0–8.0
Paddling	0.33–0.5
Residential (domestic use)	6.0–7.0
Spa:	
— heavy use	0.1
— light use	0.125
— residential	0.25

G7.3.2 Bathing loads

The filtration system should be capable of supporting an approximate bather load of one person for each $2\ m^3$ of treated water returned to the pool in a 24-hour period, i.e:

Total bathers per day = system volume flow ($m^3 \cdot h^{-1}$) × 12

The filtration plant hourly average capability can be expressed as the total bathers per day divided by the number of hours the facility is open.

The maximum number of bathers that the pool can physically accommodate at any time without compromising safety or comfort depends on the depth of water and the activity taking place.

Table G7.2 Recommended minimum pool water surface area per person for comfort and safety

Depth range / m	Surface area per person / m^2
<1.0	2.2
1.0–1.5	2.7
1.5–2.0	4.0
Diving pools	4.5
Spa pools†	0.37

† Spa pool shells should also provide a minimum of 0.25 m^3 of water per bather.

Table G7.2 shows the minimum acceptable pool water surface area per person applicable for a variety of water depth ranges. In circumstances where a pool covers more than one depth range the total should be established on a zonal basis.

G7.4   Water distribution design

G7.4.6   Heating

The recommended water temperature mainly depends on the activity taking place and in some circumstances on the age and/or disposition of the bathers. The operating temperature for hydrotherapy pools will usually be decided by the physiotherapist in charge of the treatment.

In many cases pools need to cater for a variety of activities over a relatively short timespan and the selected operating temperature will be a compromise but the design should be capable of achieving the maximum in accordance with Table G7.6. The operating temperature range for the pool should also be compatible with the design of the shell structure and tiling if damage is to be avoided.

Table G7.6 Maximum recommended pool water temperatures

Pool type	Water temperature / °C
Conventional	28
Leisure	29
Teaching	29
Training/competition	25–27
Diving	28
Hydrotherapy	32–40
Spa	40

G7.8   Plant space and location

Water treatment plant should ideally be located as close as practicable to the pool with suction and delivery pipe runs and chemical dosing lines as short as possible. There should be sufficient external access to the plant room to allow for initial installation and for possible replacement and refurbishment.

Table G7.9 Guide to water treatment plant space requirements

Pool type	Disinfection system	Space allocation as percentage of pool area
Conventional	Hypochlorite	20%
	Hypochlorite (electrolytic generation)	25%
	Ozone and hypochlorite	30%
Leisure	Hypochlorite	30%†
	Hypochlorite (electrolytic generation)	35%†
	Ozone and hypochlorite	40%†
Spa	Depends on the complexity of the selected disinfection and filtration plant	up to 200%

Note: add up to a further 10% to the allocation shown for a conventional pool in each case depending on number and type of features provided in leisure pools

There are many factors which determine the extent of the space required for water treatment plant, but Table G7.9 may be used as a guide when employing vertical sand pressure filters.

For information on filter types, water distribution design, pool heating, features, chemical water treatment and chemical dosing plant, see Guide G section 7.

G10   External drainage, local storage and treatment of waste water

G10.1   Introduction

G10.1.1   Legislation and codes of practice

Sewage and sewerage are controlled by many Acts of Parliament and Regulations. In addition to these, many codes of practice cover aspects of acceptable design and workmanship, satisfactory materials and correct testing and maintenance procedures.

The engineer must also consult the requirements of the local authorities when considering the design of any system. Some authorities have taken over control of the management of the sewers and will need to be approached for information. Local authorities may not only have special requirements and bye laws, but their local knowledge and records could provide vital design criteria.

G10.2   Surface water drainage

G10.2.1   Assessing contributing flows

In designing a surface water sewer or drain, the engineer is primarily concerned with determining the peak rate of flow that the proposed system will be expected to carry. However, if storage of the flow is anticipated or required, the engineer must determine the expected volumes.

G10.2.4 Rainfall and storm return periods

As indicated above, and in order for the engineer to determine flow in the system, a suitable rate of rainfall (intensity) must be selected. Rainfall intensities selected for carrying out flow calculations depend on a number of factors, the main three being:

(a) an assessment of acceptable risk to life and property

(b) statutory requirements imposed

(c) an assessment of economic viability.

The storm return periods listed in Table 10.2 were suggested by the Water Authorities Association in the fifth edition of *Sewers for adoption* as being appropriate for all smaller schemes in the absence of any other requirement.

Table G10.2 Storm return periods

Location	Return period / years
Sites with average surface gradient greater than 1%	1
Sites with average surface gradient of 1% or less	2
Sites where consequences of flooding are severe, e.g. existing basement properties adjacent to new developments	5

G10.2.5 Ground water drainage

G10.2.5.1 Applications

Ground water drainage should be considered when the soil is, or is likely to become, saturated and will present a problem to the works either during or after construction. The saturation of the soil can be attributed to, for example, poorly draining cohesive soils, trapped ground water (as a result of perched water tables), or the presence of an underground water course. It may also be simply the case that the natural water table is high and is at or close to the ground level. In cases where it is necessary to permanently lower the water table to enable a development to proceed, specialist advice should be sought.

Typical circumstances where ground water drainage should be considered are as follows:

— when poor draining soils are encountered and surface ponding will be undesirable

— to improve the ground conditions and increase stability, typically beneath playing fields and sports facilities

— to relieve water pressure behind retaining walls and other earth retaining structures and provide protection to foundations

— to protect road sub-bases during construction when materials not resistant to frost heave are used.

G10.2.9 Surface water storage

G10.2.9.1 General

Historically, most urban development has occurred along the routes of rivers, to take advantage of natural sources of irrigation, transportation and water supply. The types of development have changed over the years, resulting in a much greater proportion of impervious run-off. The effects of this are two-fold:

(a) higher volumes of surface run-off due to the increased population and impervious surfaces

(b) reduced times of entry into the system, giving rise to surcharging and flooding conditions.

Because of the increase in the peak flows brought about by the lack of natural attenuation, local storage is frequently required within the development and often imposed by the Environment Agency and/or water company.

Storage can be provided by a number of means:

(a) within the drainage pipe system

(b) by permitting dedicated areas to flood

(c) by constructing tanks

(d) in open reservoirs.

G10.3 Foul and combined drainage

G10.3.1 Assessing flows

In general, for building drainage, flows occur within the drains in the form of waves, each wave having a peak varying with the type, number and frequency of the fittings discharging. Building drainage flows are largely intermittent, with this effect decreasing with larger drains and as the volume of flows increase.

In the absence of any known or empirical data, such as data from a similar development, the engineer should use 220 litres per head per day (includes 10% infiltration). This figure gives the average flow, or dry weather flow. (Information taken from BS 8005: Part 1.)

G10.3.2 Methods of disposal

Almost without exception, the use of a public gravity sewer to discharge the sewage to the treatment works is the most frequently preferred option, assuming levels and underground obstructions permit, and should always be considered first.

Other methods that the engineer may have to consider include:

(a) requisitioning a public sewer under the Water Act 1973

(b) constructing a private sewer and offering it for adoption

(c) constructing a vacuum drainage system

(d) disposal to on-site treatment plant

(e) disposal to a cesspool or septic tank.

Cesspools do not provide any treatment and merely receive and store the raw sewage. They should only be considered where satisfactory arrangements for emptying are available. Cesspools are not permitted in Scotland.

Before considering any of these options, the engineer should seek the advice of the local authority and, in the case of cesspools and septic tanks, consider the costs of emptying the tank.

G10.4   Sewage treatment

G10.4.1   Principles of sewage treatment

There are a number of stages required in the treatment of raw sewage to an acceptable standard. The number of these stages, and the degree of sophistication, used will depend upon the standard of effluent required and to some degree the nature of the effluent being treated, i.e. whether the treatment is for an isolated dwelling with occasional use, or a larger development with a high potential impact on the environment.

The ambient temperature affects the type of treatment necessary. The objective of sewage treatment is to obtain a final effluent capable of being discharged to the water course or to soakaway in an efficient manner. Treatment plant should provide and maintain the conditions for this largely natural process to occur.

The most basic standard quoted in the UK is that laid down by the Royal Commission in 1912, which gives the minimum criteria (assuming a dilution ratio in the receiving water of 8 parts water to 1 part sewage):

—   30 mg·litre^{-1} suspended solids (SS)

—   20 mg·litre^{-1} biochemical oxygen demand (BOD)

and is abbreviated to 30:20.

G10.4.5   Population equivalent (PE)

In the UK, a single domestic resident is assumed to produce 60 grams of BOD per day or 120 litres per day. Where premises are occupied part-time, or sewage emanates from a non-residential establishment (such as restaurants or hotels), it is often convenient to express the total organic load per day in terms of population equivalents (PE):

$$PE = \frac{\text{Total organic load per day (g/day)}}{55 \text{ ((g/head)/day)}}$$

G10.4.10   Design loads

Loading data showing typical organic and hydraulic loadings are given in Table G10.11. The figures should only be considered in the absence of actual site measured data which provide a more accurate basis for design.

Table G10.11 Typical loading data

Sources of sewage	Allowance per head per day (24 h)		Notes
	Hydraulic loading / (litre/head per day)	Organic loading BOD / (g/head per day)	
Domestic dwellings†	130–250	50–75	
Normal residential buildings (average)	180	55	
Normal hotel guests (not non-resident bar and restaurant)	250	75	
Prestigious hotel	300	85	
Nursing home/home for the elderly	250	75	
Hospitals	450	120	
Hospital day staff accommodation	45	18	
Day schools (not including canteen)	45	18	per pupil
Bars	12	12	
Fast food-type cafe	12	10	per client
Restaurants and canteen with WDU‡	18	25	
Restaurants and canteen without WDU‡	12	14	per meal
Sports centres	50	15	
Public toilets at parks/picnic sites	10	10	per use
Holiday camps not including non-residents bar and restaurant	227	75	
Road cafe:			
— meal (cover)	10	10	
— staff	80	30	
Petrol station (visitor toilet)	8	5	
Lodge guests (already eating)	80	40	
Camping sites§:			
— residential caravans	150	50	
— non-residential static van/chalet with individual service	150	49	
— non-residential static van/chalet with central toilet block	100	28	
— touring vans with site toilet block facilities	100	25	
— tenting with site toilet block	100	25	

† In the absence of information to the contrary assume 3.5 persons per domestic dwelling or 1 person per bedroom (0.5 persons per dwelling)
‡ Waste disposal unit
§ In the absence of information to the contrary, assume 3 persons per van, chalet or tent. Chemical toilet waste is not included in these figures and must be dealt with separately.

G11 Miscellaneous piped services

G11.1 Gas fuels

G11.1.1 Statutory and non-statutory guidance

Applicable regulations and legislation are listed in Guide G section 11.1.1.

Most of the regulations are aimed at the installers of gas supply systems. There are no present regulations for designers or specifiers of gas systems. It is the installer's responsibility not to complete the installation if the design does not comply with the appropriate gas regulations. However, the designer should ensure that the design complies with the regulations.

G11.1.2 Design principles

For all gas installations, excluding domestic installations, reference should be made to the Institution of Gas Engineers publication IGE/UP/2.

G11.1.3 Gas pipework sizing

The flow of gas in pipes is given by Poles' formula:

$$Q = 0.001978 \, d^2 \sqrt{\frac{H \, d}{S \, L}} \qquad (11.1)$$

where Q is the volume flowrate (litre·s^{-1}), d is the pipe diameter (mm), H is the pressure drop (mbar), S is the specific gravity (0.58–0.59), L is the length of pipe (m).

Pipe diameters are evaluated by calculating a proportional pressure drop for each pipe section, based upon the total allowable pressure drop between the primary meter and the point of use isolating valve.

Low-pressure gas supplies are normally metered at 21 mbar, with a total allowable pressure drop of 1 mbar. For supplies where the pressure at the meter is above 21 mbar, the total allowable pressure drop should not exceed 10% of the pressure at the meter.

Where gas is supplied from a booster or compressor at above 21 mbar, the total allowable pressure drop should not exceed 10% of the pressure drop at the booster outlet.

The total allowable pressure loss in the system may be increased by considering the increase in pressure caused by rises in the system. A pressure gain of 0.5 mbar per 10 m increase in height can be applied, although this will only produce a significant effect in high-rise applications.

When calculating pressure losses, allowances for pressure losses through fittings should be made. These will vary with the materials used. The equivalent lengths of fittings (in metres) can be found in Table G11.1

Normal maximum flow pipe velocity should not exceed 45 m·s^{-1} on supplies filtered down to 250 mm. The maximum velocity for unfiltered supplies should not exceed 20 m·s^{-1}. Maximum velocities may range up to 75 m·s^{-1}, but only on a basis of engineering judgement and experience.

Useful conversion figures and data are provided in Table G11.2.

Working pressures for pipes, fittings and valves of various materials are listed in Table G11.3, and relevant standards or specifications for certain types of pipe are provided in Table G11.4. Table G11.5 lists appropriate steel pipe jointing methods for various pipe bores and pressures.

Table G11.1 Equivalent lengths of fittings (m) for various materials and types of fitting

Material and type of fitting	Equivalent lengths of fittings / m			
Cast iron/mild steel:	≤ 25 mm	32–40 mm	50 mm	80 mm
Stainless steel/copper:	≤ 28 mm	35–42 mm	54 mm	76 mm
Elbows	0.5	1.0	1.5	2.5
Tees	0.5	1.0	1.5	2.5
90° bends	0.3	0.3	0.5	1.0

Table G11.2 Useful conversion figures and data

Unit	Equivalent	Equivalent
1 ft^3	28.32 litres	0.02832 m^3
1 ft^3/h	0.007866 litre·s^{-1}	
1 in WG	249.1 Pa	2.491 mbar
1 btu	1055 J	
1 btu/h	0.2931 W	
Specific gravity of natural gas	0.57–0.58	

Table G11.3 Working pressures for pipes, fittings and valves of various materials

Material	Pipe	Fittings	Valves
Steel	5 bar	5 bar	5 bar
Ductile iron	2 bar	2 bar	5 bar
Polyethylene	2 bar	2 bar	2 bar
Malleable iron	Not to be used	5 bar	5 bar
Grey cast iron	Not to be used	2 bar	5 bar
Copper	75 mbar	75 mbar	—

Table G11.4 Specifications for pipe

Pipe details	Relevant standard
Steel ≤ 150 mm	BS 1387
Steel >150 mm	BS 3601
Ductile iron	BS EN 969
Polyethylene (PE)	BS 7281
Polyethylene (PE) fittings	BS 7281

Table G11.5 Appropriate steel pipe jointing methods for various pipe bores and pressures

Pipe bore	Pressure		
	0–75 mbar	76 mbar–2 bar	>2 bar
≤ 25 mm	Screwed or welded	Screwed or welded	Screwed or welded
32–50 mm	Screwed or welded	Screwed or welded	Welded
65–80 mm	Screwed or welded	Welded	Welded
≥ 100 mm	Welded	Welded	Welded

G11.1.7   Approximate connected loads

Before a gas supply network can be sized, the gas consumption and pressure requirements of the equipment to be served must be known. Typical gas consumption figures of some appliances are given in Table G11.7.

Table G11.7 Typical gas consumption figures of various appliances

Appliance	Gas consumption		
	$m^3 \cdot h^{-1}$	$ft^3 \cdot h^{-1}$	litre·s^{-1}
Boiling pan:			
— 45 litre	2.5	90	0.7
— 90 litre	3.4	120	0.95
— 135 litre	4.3	150	1.2
— 180 litre	5.0	175	1.4
Hot cupboard	1.0	35	0.275
— 1200 mm	2.7	95	0.75
— 1800 mm	3.0	110	0.85
Oven:			
— steaming	2.1–2.9	80–100	0.6–0.8
— double steaming	5.75	200	1.6
— two-tier roasting	2.9	100	0.8
— double range	10.0–12.0	350–400	2.75–3.2
— roasting	1.7	60	0.47
Gas cooker	4.3	150	1.2
Drying cupboard	0.3	10	0.08
Gas iron heater	0.3	10	0.08
Washing machine	1.1	40	0.31
Wash boiler	1.7–2.9	60–100	0.47–0.8
Bunsen burner	0.15	5	0.04
— full on	0.6	20	0.16
Glue kettle	0.6	20	0.16
Forge	0.85	30	0.23
Brazing hearth	1.7	60	0.47
Incinerator	0.36–1.2	12–40	0.1–0.32

Note: these values are approximate; manufacturers' literature should be referred to for full design calculations

G11.2   Non-medical compressed air

G11.2.1   Relevant codes of practice and statutory regulations

Non-medical compressed air is primarily used as a source of power to drive, for example, items of machinery or equipment, or controls. Under no circumstances should medical and non-medical gasses be interconnected.

Statutory regulations applicable to compressed air systems exist to protect employees and the general public and are enforced by the Health and Safety Executive. A code of practice for the installation of compressed air is published by the British Compressed Air Society (BCAS).

G11.2.2   Design loadings

G11.2.2.2   Maximum and average loadings

For factory or workshop environments guidance should be sought from the owner or users. In the absence of specific data reference should be made to the BCGA's *Compressed air guide for consumption rates*, examples of the most

common items are given in Table G11.8 as maxima. For average loadings, usage factors vary from 10 to 50% dependent upon operational use. The BCGA publication gives indications in the absence of client requirements.

Table G11.8 Compressed air requirements for non-medical equipment

Unit type	Maximum consumption / litre·s^{-1}	Average pressure requirement / bar (gauge)
Workshops:		
— air hoists 0.5 tonne	33	5.5
— air hoists 5 tonne	97	5.5
— air motors (per kW)	16–22	5.5
— drills (heavy)	33	3.5–5.0
— drills (medium)	8	3.5–5.0
— grinders (medium)	23	5.5
— screw drivers	8	3.5–5.0
— spray guns	5	0.5–10
Controls (typical)	0.005–0.01	1.0
Laboratories:		
— bench outlet (HP)	15	5.5
— bench outlet (LP)	5	1.5
Laboratory/pathology equipment:		
— de-ionising plant	1.0	0.4
— flame photometer	0.4	1.4
— glass drying machine	3.0	2.8
— stirrers	1.5	1.5

G11.2.3   Plant selection

G11.2.3.1   Compressors

Principle compressor types are reciprocating, rotary, centrifugal and axial the ultimate selection depends on power source (electricity, combustion engine, or turbine) and system characteristics. Figure G11.10 gives general guidance on approximate capacity and pressure limitations of the above compressor types. Consideration should be given to the use of multiple units to give flexibility of use, stand-by facilities and cascade controls to give economic running costs.

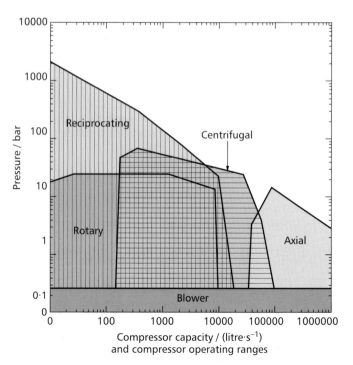

Figure G11.10 Compressor type ranges

G11.2.3.2 Air receivers

The air receiver serves two principle functions:

— to eliminate pulses from the compressor

— to provide a reservoir to cope with temporary demands in excess of the compressor's capacity.

The receiver also acts as a cooling device with the resultant effect of precipitating water from the air. Air receivers are covered by BS 5169 and BS 6244. For initial sizing the vessel should have a capacity between 6 and 10 times the compressor volume output. The use of duplicate units should be considered for continuity of supply.

Fur further information on system distribution, materials, testing and commissioning, medical and non-medical vacuum, see Guide G chapter 11.

G11.5 Medical gases

G11.5.1 Introduction

The size of facility, demand and risks should be evaluated before any system is installed. In many cases portable point-of-use cylinders may be most appropriate but, in large facilities, it may be preferable to install a medical gas pipeline system.

Typically the following medical gases are found in medical pipelines:

— oxygen

— nitrous oxide

— medical air

— oxygen/nitrous oxide mixture (50:50 (by volume))

— surgical air

— nitrogen.

Vacuum systems are also included and guidance can be found in Guide G section 11.3.

Air is a mixture of mainly oxygen and nitrogen (approximately 21% and 79% respectively). 'Medical air' is this mixture delivered at 400 kPa, whereas 'surgical air' is delivered at 700 kPa .

G11.5.3 Design principles

In order to design the system the designer must be aware of the following:

— the number and location of outlets

— the flow and pressure required at each of the outlets

— the likely simultaneous usage of the outlets (diversity)

— the requirements for safety.

Necessary supplies of each of the gases can be found in Table 2 of NHS Estates' Health Technical Memorandum HTM 2022. However, consultation with the health care facility managers is necessary to establish the requirements for specific projects.

Table G11.11 Gas flow: flows required at terminal units

Service	Location	Nominal pressure / kPa★	Flow rate / litre·min⁻¹	
			Design	Typical
Oxygen	Theatres	400	100[(a)]	20
	All other areas	400	10[(c)]	6
Nitrous oxide	All areas	400	15	6
Nitrous oxide/oxygen mixture	Delivery rooms	310[(b)] (min.)	275	20
	All other areas	400	20	15
Medical air	Theatres	400	40[(c)]	40
	Intensive treatment unit (ITU); neonatal	400	80[(c)]	80
	Coronary care unit (CCU)	400	80[(c)]	80
	Other	400	20	10[(c)]
Surgical air/nitrogen	Theatres	700	350[(d)]	350
Vacuum	Theatres	40	40	40
	Recovery rooms	40	40	40
	Coronary care unit (CCU)	40	40	40
	Ward areas	40	40	40
Nitric oxide	Intensive treatment, unit (ITU); neonatal; theatres	400	15	6
Oxygen/carbon dioxide mixture	Cardio-thoracic theatres, oncology	400	100	40

★ Pressure required at terminal unit, not in pipeline

Notes: (a) during oxygen flush in operating and anaesthetic rooms; (b) minimum pressure at 275 litre·min⁻¹; (c) these flows are for certain types of gas-driven ventilators under specific operating conditions, and nebulisers etc; (d) surgical tools/tourniquets.

G11.5.3.1 Design loadings

Flows must be considered as a triumvirate:

— flow at each point of use

— flow within the area / branch

— total flow.

The level of diversity applied should be agreed with the health care facility management.

HTM 2022 provides relevant guidance for different departments, see Table G11.11.

Pressures for compressed medical gases at point of delivery should not vary by more than 10% from nominal pressure, typically 400 kPa. Surgical air can vary by as much as 15% from the requisite 700 kPa. The ranges of nominal distribution pressures are given in BS EN 737.

Guide G: abridgements and omissions

The extracts from CIBSE Guide G included above have been abridged for reasons of space. Reference should be made to CIBSE Guide G for the complete text and tables of data. In addition, the following sections have been omitted entirely from this Handbook:

Chapter 1: Introduction and scope:
1.1	General
1.2	Purpose of the Guide
1.3	Contents and scope
1.4	Other sources of information

Chapter 2: Water services and utilities:
2.1	Introduction
2.6	Energy efficiency
2.8	Hospital hot water storage and consumption
2.9	Water supply system design
2.10	Water Fittings and Materials Directory
2.11	Frost protection
2.12	Maintenance procedures

Chapter 3: Sanitary accommodation, pipework and drainage
3.1	Introduction
3.2	Drainage design procedure
3.7	Connections to sewage systems

Chapter 4: Waste management systems
4.1	Introduction
4.4	Health, safety and environmental considerations
4.5	Capital and running costs

Chapter 5: Corrosion and corrosion protection
5.2	Factors affecting corrosion
5.3	Assessment of corrosive environment
5.4	Prevention of corrosion
5.5	Chemical cleaning and passivation
5.6	'Mothballed' protection

Chapter 6: Water treatment
6.2	Water quality
6.4	General principles of water distribution
6.5	Point-of-use treatments
6.7	Industrial uses

Chapter 7: Swimming pools
7.5	Chemical water treatment
7.6	Chemical dosing plant
7.7	Swimming pool electrical requirements
7.9	Pool hall conditioning
7.10	Operation and maintenance

Chapter 8: Water features and fountains

Chapter 9: Irrigation

Chapter 10: External drainage, local storage and treatment of waste water
10.5	Structural design of pipes
10.6	Pipe renovation and surveys
10.7	Pipe and sewerage materials
10.8	Connection to sewers
10.9	Access to sewers
10.10	Inspection and testing
10.11	Adoption of sewers
10.12	Water companies and drainage authorities

Chapter 11: Miscellaneous piped services
11.3	Medical vacuum
11.4	Non-medical vacuum
11.5	Medical gases

Chapter 12: Glossary of terms

Code for lighting

Since 2002, the Society of Light and Lighting's *Code for lighting* has been published on CD-ROM together with a printed version containing the three principle parts of the *Code*:

— Part 1: Visual effects of lighting

— Part 2: Recommendations

— Part 3: Lighting design.

Extracts from these parts are included here. The CD-ROM version was updated in 2004 and 2006. The printed version has not changed since the 2002 edition except for the publication of an addendum in 2004 to reinstate information on areas omitted from the General Schedule. Full technical data are available in the printed *Code* (plus addendum) and CD-ROM.

L1   Visual effects of lighting

L1.1   Introduction

The lighting of an interior should fulfil three functions. It should:

(*a*)   ensure the safety of people in the interior

(*b*)   facilitate the performance of the visual tasks

(*c*)   aid the creation of the appropriate visual environment

Safety is always important, but the emphasis given to task performance and the appearance of the interior will depend on the nature of the interior. For example, lighting considered suitable for a factory tool room will place much more emphasis on lighting the task than the appearance of the room. In a hotel lounge these priorities would be reversed. The variation in emphasis should not be taken to imply that either task lighting or visual appearance can be completely neglected. In most situations the designer should give consideration to both aspects of lighting.

Lighting affects safety, task performance and the visual environment by changing the extent and the manner in which different elements of the interior are revealed. Safety is ensured by making hazards visible. Task performance is facilitated by making the relevant details of the task easy to see. Different visual environments can be created by changing the relative emphasis given to the various objects and surfaces in an interior. Different aspects of lighting influence the appearance of the elements in an interior in different ways.

L1.2 Daylight and electric light

People prefer a room with daylight to one that is windowless, unless the function of the room makes this impractical. Few buildings are in fact windowless, but it is true that in the majority of present day buildings some of the electric lighting is in continuous use during daylight hours. Electric lighting and daylighting should always be complimentary.

The use of daylight with good electric lighting controls can lead to a significant saving in the primary energy used by a building, to national advantage and the benefit of the environment and building users.

L1.2.2 Increasing general room brightness

A user's perception of the character of a room is related to the brightness and colour of all visible surfaces, inside and outside. The general lighting in a room is a separate consideration from the task lighting but it is as important. It can be achieved by using daylight or electric light, or both, but the natural variation of daylight is valuable. The light from a side window in particular enhances the architectural modelling of a room and its variation with time gives information about the weather and the time of day.

The character of a naturally lit room is often considered valuable by the users. A room can appear daylit even though the principal illumination in the working plane is from electric sources. Contrast between inside and outside is reduced when there is a high level of diffuse daylight internally and when light from luminaires falls on the walls and ceilings. The detailed design of the window frames or surrounds is also important.

L1.3 Lighting levels

The human eye can only perceive surfaces, objects and people through light which is emitted from them. Surface characteristics, reflection factors and the quantity and quality of light determine the appearance of the environment.

These variables create unlimited permutations between the physical elements and the light which strikes them. Nevertheless, when dealing with an interior, it is useful to quantify the luminous flux received per unit of area (i.e. the illuminance measured in lumens per square metre or lux). The commonly used planar illuminance relates to

tasks which lie in a horizontal, inclined or vertical plane. The plane within which the task is seen is called the reference plain.

L1.3.1 Task performance

The ability to see degrees of detail is substantially determined by size, contrast and the viewer's vision. Improvement to lighting quantity and quality makes an important contribution to improved visual performance. The effect of lighting on task performance depends on the size of the critical details of the task and on the contrast with their background. Three important points are:

— increasing illuminance on the task produces an increase in performance following a law of diminishing returns

— the illuminance at which performance levels off is dependent on the visual difficulty of the task

— although increasing illuminance can increase task performance, it is not possible to bring a difficult visual task to the same level of performance as an easy task by simply increasing illuminance

L1.4 Variation in lighting

When applied to lighting, 'variation' can be either time or space and can have at least three meanings:

(a) short term variation occurs either naturally with daylight or with controlled lighting equipment which may change automatically, prompted by changes in daylighting in response to various signals, or user manual control

(b) Long term variation which occurs as a result of light loss as lamps age and dirt accumulates over a period of months. Some modern lighting control equipment can counteract this effect.

(c) Spatial variation means the uniformity or diversity of illuminance over the task and room surfaces throughout an interior space. This can include the gradation of light revealing texture or form of objects.

L1.5 Glare

Glare occurs whenever one part of an interior is much brighter than the general brightness in the interior. The most common sources of excessive brightness are luminaires and windows, seen directly or by reflection. Glare can have two effects. It can impair vision (disability glare), and it can cause discomfort, (discomfort glare). These can occur together or separately.

L1.6 Directional qualities and modelling

The direction and distribution of light within a space substantially influence the perception of the space as well as objects or persons within it. Decisions which determine such perception relate partly to the provision of desirable illuminance values and partly to the subjective issues of architectural interpretation, style and visual emphasis. Good lighting design results both from an appreciation of the nature and qualities of the surfaces upon which light falls and the methods of providing such light. The visual characteristics of surfaces and sources of light are interrelated and interdependent. The appearance of a surface or object will depend on:

(a)   Its colour and reflectance and whether it is specular or diffuse, smooth or textured, flat or curved. All surfaces reflect some portion of the light falling on them and so become sources of light. Depending on their degree of specularity, texture and shape, their appearance will also vary with the direction of view.

(b)   The layout and orientation of luminaries and sources of reflected light. Single sources of relatively small size will produce harsh modelling, the effect becoming softer as the number and size of the sources increase. The predominant direction of light has a fundamental effect on appearance; lighting from above provides a distinct character that is totally different to that achieved by lighting from the side or lower angles. In addition, colour differences between sources of light of various distributions and orientation strongly influence the lit appearance of spaces, surfaces and objects. With so many variables, luminance patterns become too complex to predict in detail.

This element of unpredictability is generally acceptable, or even desirable, providing that the basic rules of good lighting practice are observed, such as the limitation of extremes of glare, contrast and veiling reflection. The importance of modelling is obvious for retail display, exhibition work and the creation of mood. However, any lighting installation which fails to create appropriate degrees of modelling will provide visual results which are perceived as bland and monotonous. Virtually all environments can benefit from a lighting approach which considers the question of direction and the resulting revelation of modelling form, texture and facial modelling. Further information is provided in the *Code for lighting*, section 1.6.

L1.7   Surfaces

The effect a lighting installation creates in an interior is strongly influenced by the properties of the major room surfaces. For this reason, the lighting designer should always attempt to identify the proposed surface finishes and their reflectance and colour early in the design process. The main properties of the room surfaces that are relevant to the appearance of the space are their reflectance and their colour.

L1.8   Light source radiation

The *Code* is primarily concerned with light source radiation from 400 nm to 780 nm of the electromagnetic spectrum which stimulates the sense of sight and colour. However, all light sources radiate energy at shorter wavelengths and in the ultraviolet as well as longer wavelengths and in the infra-red parts of the spectrum. This radiation can promote physiological effects which are either a benefit or a hazard. The basic function of luminaries is to control the visible radiation (light) but they can also concentrate, diffuse or attenuate the non-visible radiation from lamps. The lighting designer needs to be aware of the effects of all radiation that is being emitted.

Light has two colour properties; the apparent colour of the light that the source emits and the effect that the light has on the colours of surfaces. The latter effect is called colour rendering.

L1.8.1   Apparent colour of emitted light

The colour of light emitted from a near-white source can be indicated by its correlated colour temperature. Each lamp type has a specific correlated colour temperature, but for practical use they have been grouped into three classes by the Commission Internationale de l' Eclairage (CIE), see Table L1.2.

The choice of an appropriate colour appearance of a light source for a room is determined by its function. This may involve such psychological aspects of colour as warmth, relaxation, clarity etc. and more mundane considerations such as compatibility with daylight whilst providing 'white' colour at night.

Table L1.2 Colour appearance and colour temperature

Colour appearance	Correlated colour temperature / K
Warm	< 3300
Intermediate	3300–5300
Cool	> 5300

L1.8.2   Colour rendering

The ability of a light source to render colours of surfaces accurately can be conveniently quantified by the CIE general colour rendering index. This index is based on the accuracy with which a set of test colours is reproduced by the lamp of interest relative to how these are reproduced by an appropriate standard light source, perfect agreement being given a value of 100. The CIE general colour rendering index has some limitations but it is the most widely accepted measure of the colour rendering properties of a light source. Lamps with a colour rendering index below 80 should not be used where people stay for long periods. Recommendations are given in the lighting schedules in the *Code*.

L1.9   Light modulation

All electric lamps operated on an AC supply (50 Hz in Europe) have an inherent modulation in light output at twice the supply frequency. With most discharge lamps there is also a small component at the supply frequency itself, which can increase as the lamp ages. The 100 Hz modulation is not perceptible to most people.

If lights with a large modulation are used to light rotating machinery, co-incidence between the modulation frequency and the frequency of rotation may cause moving parts to appear stationary. This is called the stroboscopic effect and can be dangerous. Light modulation at lower frequencies is called flicker and is visible to most people. This is a source of discomfort and distraction.

L2   Recommendations

L2.2   Recommendations for daylighting

L2.2.1   Daylight for general room lighting

In most types of buildings, users prefer rooms to have a daylit appearance during daytime hours. This appearance can be achieved, even though there is a significant amount of daytime electric lighting, by ensuring that the changing brightness of daylight is clearly noticeable on walls and other interior surfaces. It is also necessary to achieve sufficient bright interior surfaces to avoid glare from contrast with the sky. The following values should be adopted where a daylit appearance is required:

L2.2.1.1   *Interiors without supplementary electric lighting during daytime*

If electric lighting is not normally used during daytime hours, the average daylight factor should not be less than 5%.

The internal reflectances and positions of windows should be such that inter-reflected lighting in the space is strong and even. When the shape of the room causes the distribution of daylight to be very uneven (such as when a large area lies behind the no-sky line) supplementary electric lighting may still be necessary.

L2.2.1.2   *Interiors with supplementary electric lighting during daytime*

If electric lighting is to be used during daytime hours, the average daylight factor should not be less than 2%.

In a room where the average daylight factor is significantly less than 2%, the general appearance is of an electrically lit interior. Daylight will be noticeable only on room surfaces immediately adjacent to the windows, although the windows may still provide adequate views out for the occupants throughout the room.

For information on daylight for task illumination, supplementary electric lighting design and colour in relation to daylight, see section 2.2.2 of the *Code*.

L2.3   Recommendations for electric lighting with daylighting

The two distinct functions of electric lighting used in connection with daylight are to enhance the general room brightness and to supplement the daylight illuminance on visual tasks.

Where there is a significant amount of daylight (an average daylight factor of 2% or more) electric lighting may be required to reduce the contrast between internal surfaces and the external view. It needs to fall on walls and other surroundings of the window opening. The brighter the view, the higher the luminance required of the surfaces surrounding the window. Electric lighting may also be required to increase the general illumination of parts of the room distant from the window. If this is the case, the average working pane illuminance from electric lighting in the poorly daylit areas should not be less than 300 lux. If a lower luminance is used, in circulation areas for example, there may be noticeable contrast between areas near windows and other parts of the room, with a corresponding impression of harshness and gloominess.

L2.3.4   Luminance and illuminance ratios

Luminance distribution in the field of view controls the adaptation level of the eyes, which affects the task visibility.

Luminance differences may be specified or measured in terms of the ratio between one luminance and another. Suggested targets are:

—   3:1 for task-to-immediate surround

—   10:1 for task-to-immediate background.

Ranges of useful reflectances and relative illuminance for the major interior surfaces are given in Table L2.2.

Table L2.2 Ranges of useful reflectances

Room surface	Reflectance range	Relative illuminance
Ceiling	0.6 – 0.9	0.3 – 0.9
Walls	9.3 – 0.8	0.5 – 0.6
Working planes	0.2 – 0.6	1.00
Floor	0.1 – 0.5	—

L2.4   Energy efficiency recommendations

The environmental impact of lamps is discussed in the LIF *Lamp Guide* (see *Code for lighting* CD-ROM).

Building Regulations Part L (2002) contains requirements for maximum energy use in lighting installations. These apply to England and Wales. In Scotland Part J of the Building Standards (Scotland) Regulations include similar requirements.

L2.4.1   Power and time

The energy (kW/h) used by a lighting installation depends on both the power (kW) and time (h). Energy efficiency can be achieved by:

—   using the most efficient lighting equipment to obtain the desired solution, i.e. the electrical load is kept to a minimum whilst achieving the lighting design objectives

—   using effective controls so that the lighting is not operating when not needed

The lighting designer can limit the electrical power loading and use of electricity, but it is the operator who will ultimately be responsible for achieving high energy efficiency

L2.4.2   Energy efficient equipment

Information is provided in the *Code for lighting* CD-ROM.

L2.4.3 Lighting energy targets

Table L2.5 provides targets of power density, averaged over the space, for general lighting for a range of applications. These are based on current good practice, however improvements should be possible. The targets are for average sized space (room index 2.5) with high room surface reflectances and a high degree of installation maintenance.

Table L2.5 Lighting energy targets

Lamp type	CIE general colour- rendering index (R_a)	Task illuminance (lux)	Average installed power density (W/m²)
Commercial and other similar applications (e.g. offices, shops and schools*):			
— Fluorescent triphosphor	80 – 90	300	7
		500	11
		750	17
— Compact fluorescent	80 – 90	300	8
		500	14
		750	21
— Metal halide	60 – 90	300	11
		500	18
		750	27
Industrial and manufacturing applications:			
— Fluorescent triphosphor	80 – 90	300	6
		500	10
		750	14
		1000	19
— Metal halide	60 – 90	300	7
		500	12
		750	17
		1000	23
— High pressure sodium	60 – 90	300	6
		500	11
		750	16
		1000	21

*Values do not include energy for display lighting

L2.5 Lighting schedules

The *Code* (plus addendum) provides recommendations for lighting for 65 different applications of lighting. Examples for offices, educational buildings, hotels/restaurants and health care buildings are shown as Tables L2.A to L2.D.

L3 Lighting design

Figure L3.1 is a flow diagram summarising a design approach. The design process is described in detail in the *Code*, including financial evaluation, switching, luminaire maintenance, space to height ratios, discomfort glare and emergency lighting.

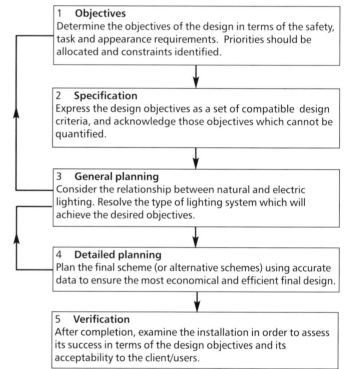

1   Objectives
Determine the objectives of the design in terms of the safety, task and appearance requirements. Priorities should be allocated and constraints identified.

2   Specification
Express the design objectives as a set of compatible design criteria, and acknowledge those objectives which cannot be quantified.

3   General planning
Consider the relationship between natural and electric lighting. Resolve the type of lighting system which will achieve the desired objectives.

4   Detailed planning
Plan the final scheme (or alternative schemes) using accurate data to ensure the most economical and efficient final design.

5   Verification
After completion, examine the installation in order to assess its success in terms of the design objectives and its acceptability to the client/users.

Figure L3.1 The design process

Table L2.A Extract from lighting schedule: offices

Activity	Maintained illuminance* (lux)	Limiting glare rating	Minimum colour rendering (Ra)	Notes
Filing, copying, etc.	300	19	80	1
Writing, typing, reading, data processing	500	19	80	2
Technical drawing	750	16	80	
CAD work stations	500	19	80	2
Conference and meeting rooms	500	19	80	3
Reception desk	300	22	80	
Archives	200	25	80	1

* Illuminance values may be varied to suit circumstances

Notes: (1) For filing the vertical surfaces are especially important; (2) See *Code for Lighting* section 2.3.10; (3) The lighting should be controllable

Table L2.B Extract from lighting schedule: educational buildings

Activity	Maintained illuminance* (lux)	Limiting glare rating	Minimum colour rendering (Ra)	Notes
Classrooms, tutorial rooms	300	19	80	1
Classroom for evening classes and adult education	500	19	80	1
Lecture hall	500	19	80	1
Black board	500	19	80	2
Demonstration table	500	19	80	3
Art rooms	500	19	80	
Art rooms in art schools	750	19	90	4
Technical drawing rooms	750	16	80	
Practical rooms and laboratories	500	19	80	
Handicraft rooms	500	19	80	
Teaching workshops	500	19	80	
Music practice rooms	300	19	80	
Computer practice rooms	300	19	80	5
Language laboratory	300	19	80	
Preparation rooms and workshops	500	22	80	
Entrance halls	200	22	80	
Circulation areas, corridors	100	25	80	
Stairs	150	25	80	
Student common rooms and assembly halls	200	22	80	
Teachers' rooms	300	19	80	
Stock rooms for teaching materials	100	25	80	
Sports halls, gymnasiums, swimming pools	300	22	80	6
School canteens	200	22	80	
Kitchen	500	22	80	

* Illuminance values may be varied to suit circumstances

Notes: (1) Lighting should be controllable; (2) Prevent specular reflections; (3) 750 lux in lecture halls; (4) Colour temperature of the light should be greater than 5000 K; (5) *Code for lighting* section 2.3.10; (6) See CIBSE Lighting Guide LG4: *Sports*

Table L2.C Extract from lighting schedule: healthcare premises — general rooms

Activity	Maintained illuminance* (lux)	Limiting glare rating	Minimum colour rendering (Ra)	Notes
Waiting rooms	200	22	80	1
Corridors: during the day	200	22	80	1
Corridors: at night	50	22	80	1
Day rooms	200	22	80	1
Staff office	500	19	80	
Staff rooms	300	19	80	

* Illuminance values may be varied to suit circumstances

Notes: (1) Illuminance at floor level

Table L2.D Extract from lighting schedule: hotels and restaurants

Activity	Maintained illuminance* (lux)	Limiting glare rating	Minimum colour rendering (Ra)	Notes
Reception/cashier desk, porters desk	300	22	80	1
Kitchen	500	22	80	2
Restaurant, dining room, function room	—	—	80	3
Self-service restaurant	200	22	80	
Buffet	300	22	80	
Conference rooms	500	19	80	4
Corridors	100	25	80	5

* Illuminance values may be varied to suit circumstances

Notes: (1) Localised lighting may be appropriate; (2) There should be a transition zone between kitchen and restaurant; (3) The lighting should be designed to create the appropriate atmosphere; (4) Lighting should be controllable; (5) During night-time lower levels may be acceptable. Late night low-level lighting may be used with manual over ride or presence detection

Table L3.A Summary of the choice of electric lighting system

Type	Summary	Advantages	Disadvantages
General	Approximate uniform illumination over whole working plane. Luminaires normally in uniform layout. No co-ordination with task location	Allows flexibility of task location	Ceiling void may not allow uniform layout. Energy may be wasted illuminating whole area to level of most crucial task
Localised	Arrangement of luminaires provides required illuminance at work areas with lower illuminance for other areas	Less energy than general lighting	System can be inflexible. Changes to work area may be difficult.
Local	Illumination only over small area occupied by the task. General lighting must be provided for ambient illumination.	Very efficient way of providing adequate task illumination	Lamps inefficient and luminaires more expensive

L3.5   Choice of electric lighting system

Table L3.A is a brief summary of the information on selecting an appropriate electric lighting system contained in section 3 of the *Code for lighting*. This table does not appear in the *Code*.

Code for lighting: abridgements and omissions

The extracts from the printed version of the *Code for lighting* included above have been abridged for reasons of space. Reference should be made to the *Code* for the complete text and tables of data. In addition, the following sections have been omitted entirely from this Handbook:

—	2	Recommendations
	2.1	Introduction
—	3	Lighting design
	3.1	Objectives
	3.2	Specification
	3.3	General planning
	3.4	Daylight
	3.6	Choice of lamp and luminaire
	3.7	Energy management
	3.8	Detailed planning
	3.9	Design checklist
	3.10	Statement of assumptions
—	4	Glossary

Index